STATES AGAINST M̶̶̶̶̶̶̶̶̶̶̶̶̶

Everywhere countries are looking for ways to compete and increase their share of exports. For the most part, this has led to the lowering of national borders and greater co-dependence. At the same time, the recent attacks by financial dealers on national currencies provide evidence of the way the international market can influence national policy. To many, this climate of globalization signals the end of the nation-state as an effective manager of national economic policy.

In *States Against Markets: The limits of globalization* the authors challenge this perceived threat to the nation-state. They examine the fundamental issues of competitiveness and market power. This involves:

- a discussion of whether or not globalization is really such a novel development;
- assessment of the success of globalization as a means of convergence and uniformity across nations;
- an update of the Hayek vs. Keynes debate within this context; analysis of how all those involved can maximize the benefits from globalization;
- strategic options open to the state to protect itself from the global business sector;
- an appraisal of the future of the nation-state.

The authors are drawn from both market-driven and social-democratic societies. Throughout the work, the arguments and analysis are clearly presented and discussed while the volume also has a strong empirical dimension and includes much useful comparative data. The lack of jargon and minimal mathematical formulae make the book accessible to those with limited prior knowledge of economics.

Robert Boyer is Directeur de Recherche CNRS and CEPREMAP, Directeur d'Études EHESS, Paris. **Daniel Drache** is Director of the Robarts Center for Canadian Studies and Professor of Political Economy at York University, Toronto. He has published widely on trade blocs, industrial policy and workplace organization.

INNIS CENTENARY SERIES
Daniel Drache
Series Editor

Harold Innis, one of Canada's most distinguished economists, described the Canadian experience as no one else ever has. His visionary works in economic geography, political economy, and communications theory have endured for over fifty years and have had tremendous influence on scholarship, the media, and the business community.

The volumes in the Innis Centenary Series illustrate and expand Innis's legacy. Each volume is written and edited by distinguished members of the fields Innis touched. Each addressed provocative and challenging issues that have profound implications not only for Canada but for the 'new world order' including the impact of globalization on national decision-making; interactions among the state, social movements, and the environment; the nature of the 'market' in the future; the effect of new communications technology on economic restructuring; and the role of the individual in effecting positive social change.

The complete series will provide a unique guide to many of the major challenges we face as we enter the twenty-first century.

The Innis Centenary Celebration was made possible by the generous support of Innis College, the University of Toronto, York University, and through private donations.

STATES AGAINST MARKETS

The limits of globalization

*Edited by Robert Boyer
and Daniel Drache*

London and New York

First published 1996
by Routledge
11 New Fetter Lane, London EC4P 4EE
Simultaneously published in the USA and Canada
by Routledge
29 West 35th Street, New York, NY 10001

Routledge is an Independent Thomson Publishing Company.

© 1996 Robert Boyer and Daniel Drache

Typeset in Garamond by
Ponting–Green Publishing Services, Chesham, Bucks
Printed and bound in Great Britain by
TJ Press (Padstow) Ltd, Padstow, Cornwall

British Library Cataloguing in Publication Data
A catalogue record for this book is available from the
British Library

Library of Congress Cataloging in Publication Data
A catalogue record for this book has been requested

ISBN 0–415–13725–x (hbk)
ISBN 0–415–13726–8 (pbk)

CONTENTS

CONTENTS

CONTENTS

Part VI New politics in an uncertain world

FIGURES

TABLES

CONTRIBUTORS

Tetsuo Abo is Professor of International Economics and Business at the Institute of Social Sciences, University of Tokyo, Tokyo, and the Director of the Japanese Multinational Study Group. He is a leading authority on Japanese automobile production.

Paul Bairoch is a Professor of Economics at the Center of International Economic History, University of Geneva, Geneva. He is an authority on trade and economic development issues.

Isabella Bakker is a Professor of Political Science, York University, Toronto, and has written extensively on the impact of globalization, women, labour markets and state policy.

Gordon Betcherman is a leading labour market economist in Canada and specialist in work and employment service economy and employment issues, Ottawa.

Manfred Bienefeld is a Professor of Political Economy, School of Public Administration, Carleton University, Ottawa, and is an authority on development questions and global finance.

Paul Bowles is a Professor of Economics, University of Northern British Columbia, Prince George. He is a specialist on development issues and has published extensively on East Asia and China.

Robert Boyer is a Directeur de Recherche, CNRS at CEPREMAP, Paris, and one of the founders of the Régulation School. He is a macro-economist who specializes in national and international comparisons of labour market, state macroeconomic policy and technology.

Janine Brodie is a Professor of Political Economy in the Department of Political Science, York University, Toronto. She has published extensively on issues of regionalism, democratic theory, feminism and new social movements.

Harold Chorney is an Associate Professor of Economics and teaches at the

School of Community and Public Affairs, Concordia University, Montreal. He has published extensively on public finance, Keynesian economics and monetary theory.

Marjorie Griffin Cohen is an Economist in the Department of Political Science, Simon Fraser University, British Columbia. She is a recognized authority on women and trade as well as economic adjustment under NAFTA.

Daniel Drache is Director of the Robarts Center for Canadian Studies and Professor of Political Economy, York University, Toronto. He has published widely on globalization, trade blocs, and jobs and investment strategies.

Gerald Epstein is a Professor of Economics, University of Massachusetts, Amherst. He has published on the economic impact of globalization on US macroeconomic policy, international finance and central bank policy.

Eric Helleiner is a Political Economist in the Department of Political Science, York University, Toronto. He has published extensively on global finance and international political economy.

Fred Lazar is an Associate Professor of Economics in the Faculty of Business Administration, York University, Toronto. He has published extensively on monetary questions, public finance and corporate strategy.

Brian MacLean is an Associate Professor of Economics, Laurentian University, Sudbury, and specializes in Japanese monetary questions.

Charles McMillan is a Professor of Business Administration, Faculty of Administrative Studies, York University, Toronto. He is a recognized authority on Japan and has published numerous books and articles on Japan's industrial systems.

Riel Miller is a macroeconomist, formerly with the Ministry of Finance, Government of Ontario, and now working with the OECD in Paris. He is a specialist on local economic development and the information economy.

Ramesh Mishra is a Professor of Social Work in the School of Social Work, York University, Toronto. He is a noted authority on the welfare state and has written and published widely on the topic.

Riccardo Petrella is Professor of Political Economy and Director-General of the Forecasting and Assessment in Science and Technology (FAST), Commission of the European Communities, Belgium.

Wolfgang Streeck is Director of the Max Planck Institut, Köln and a leading authority on European integration, work and employment in modern industrial settings and state–market relations.

INTRODUCTION
Robert Boyer and Daniel Drache

During the four decades following the Great Depression, governments had little difficulty in demonstrating their capacity to tame markets, promote growth and keep social inequality within strict limits. Nowadays, markets have taken their revenge. Financial institutions decide which state policies are acceptable and which are not. In these new circumstances, governments are beholden to market forces in a way few could have predicted. Markets now define the limits of politics; the dismal economic science is back and economists now exert unprecedented influence in shaping public policy. Everywhere countries are looking for ways to compete and increase their global share of exports. Strikingly, most advanced economies have ceased to consider their home market crucial to a strong performance even though innovation seems to be happening everywhere; the new industrialized countries now openly challenge the technical leadership of the mature countries. If all this intense activity could be reduced to a single concept, it would be that of globalization. Globalization is redefining the role of the nation-state as an effective manager of the national economy. The question is why is this happening and how can nations everywhere maximize their leverage despite highly volatile conditions in price and demand?

Four issues in particular stand out. Does the internationalization of state policy call for institutional innovation and brand new objectives and instruments for governments everywhere? Can markets be the key mechanism governing modern society? Is global free-trade-for-all the best means to promote international co-operation and a strong economic performance? And what future, if any, is there for the nation-state? These four penetrating questions form the theoretical core of this book in which scholars from various disciplines and persuasions examine just how globalized the nation-state system has become. The common thread linking all the different perspectives presented in this volume is the contention that nations everywhere need to make a democratic assessment of the burden and benefits of the new competitive conditions in responding to these challenges. If countries expect to prosper from the new international environment, they need to take stock of changes in production relations, corporate practices, investment

1

patterns and the export potential of their industries. Sophisticated co-ordination of their economies is also required. But, first of all, countries have to address three pivotal issues.

THREE PIVOTAL ISSUES

Is globalization as new as it appears? For many, globalization appears to define a new stage in the international economy. The critical issue here is the speed and direction of this process. Will it happen in one or two decades or is it a century-long affair? Is it realistic to expect a broad convergence of productivity and standard of living at the world level? Evidence suggests that globalization is limited to the core of industrialized countries – Europe, North America and Japan. For instance, 85 per cent of foreign investment flow is between the members of the triad. Thus, intense 'triadization' of financial markets is more apparent and likely than full-scale globalization. Here, too, casual observation should not replace deeper analysis. For instance, the law of a single price everywhere for the same good is far from a reality. Big Macs are available all over the world, but the price differs according to local conditions. Clearly, transnational corporations do exploit national differences for their own profit-making ends without, however, totally eroding them. Once again, this is further evidence that nation-states still matter.

Does globalization bring convergence and uniformity across nations? Here, too, there are counter-tendencies within the scheme of global competition. The spread of global markets has a direct bearing on the future of democracy. Some governments might be tempted to use free trade agreements in order to control and limit rights, especially for minority groups wherever they are. Recent experience in Western and Eastern Europe reveals the dangers of such a strategy. Xenophobic and right-wing nationalist movements have reacted against the international pressure of supranational bodies to reassert national values. Thus, globalization generates powerful cross-currents at the national and international levels. These are all channelled into the political arena first, but it is doubtful that markets can handle such demands. The 1994 New Year's Day uprising of the Mayan Indians of Chiapas, Mexico exhibits the close links between international trade agreements and grass-roots political movements. Once again, the nation-state is the crucible for political movements the world over.

Is there any room for national governments to manoeuvre? Governments used to manage their economies with Keynesian policies aimed at full employment. They were able to do so by controlling capital markets, but this is no longer the case. High interest rates, new kinds of financial instruments and electronic networking globally have changed the strategy of firms and governments. During the recession of the 1990s, public deficits soared and have subsequently proved almost impossible to get under control. Powerful financial markets now monitor many, if not all, aspects of state spending and, therefore, are able to set broad policy goals with respect to employment, social welfare policy, taxation and the like. These developments raise the immediate question about the desirability and irreversibility of having such a high degree of financial overhang: speculators relish this era, but industrialists do not. They need sufficiently stable expectations and moderate real interest rates if there is to be a recovery and long-term growth. In this respect, the state is back again. It needs to reduce uncertainty, set new rules of the game as well as negotiate them at the international level. For instance, the state could reconsider the merits of past financial deregulation and then decide to promote a new environment. It would not be absurd to contemplate imposing limits on short-term capital, even if this is quite difficult to do politically. What has been done during a decade of deregulation can be undone or reversed. After all, markets are organized by public intervention and not the reverse.

And yet, even if markets are not always efficient in promoting growth, alternatives are anything but self-evident. Markets require organization to function; the market as a social institution and economic force is more fragile and complex than is assumed by its enthusiastic supporters. Nevertheless, the scope and objectives of markets and states cannot be confused. Markets are efficient in allocating scarce resources in the short-run. By contrast, the nation is the conduit for investing in the future. Moreover, the state organizes the market by ensuring transparency, fairness and access. Thus, whatever the future scenario is, state and market will co-exist. But the question remains: how good is the argument that Hayek is back and Keynes dead?

WHAT IS A MARKET?

Basically, a market is the co-ordinating mechanism where the forces of supply and demand in an economy determine prices, output and methods of production via the automatic adjustment of price movements. At the point of market equilibrium, supply and demand balance and no agent can get a better result than the outcome derived from the equilibrium price. Thus, it is quite possible to see the great attraction of a theory of pure competition. Under pure and perfect competition there are many sellers and buyers and, if the nature of the good is well-defined, the outcome delivered by the market is among the best which can be realized. Two famous theorems in microeconomic theory define the conditions under which an equilibrium is an optimum. Conversely, any desired Pareto optimum can be reached by the interplay of markets and transfers via subsidies and taxation. But these results are quite abstract and do not play a major role in debates about the kinds of interventions states make.

The reality is that in sharp contrast to what conventional neo-classical theory teaches, markets do not rule everything. More important is how states

3

adapt to new market pressures. This is the real test for any country. Does it have the institutional means to transform a static comparative advantage into a dynamic one? If not, how does it acquire the leverage to operate in a world increasingly without borders? Consider the case of contemporary Japan, a country that used its technological power to transform a war-battered economy after the Second World War. Popular media describe Japan as a 'miracle', but this characterization is simplistic. It was never a foregone conclusion that Japan would overtake the US, its principal industrial rival. But eventually Japan did move into the fast lane for a very specific reason. It used state intervention, strategic targeting, superior technology and financing to transform the market. But, above all, the Japanese state, private sector and labour were forced to find ways to develop a new production model in the workplace in terms of public policy. As McMillan shows in his detailed analysis of Japanese power, institutional forms and practices made the critical difference.

The Japanese lean production model is now presented as the new standard for all countries. In fact, the Japanese system has clear strengths, but also many weaknesses, as evidenced by the present turmoil it is undergoing. Here then is another paradox to consider. At the very moment when Western countries believe that they must adopt Japan's leading edge practices, the country's system is in crisis. Thus, the challenge is not to copy the Japanese production techniques holus-bolus, but to find a localized equivalent or alternative systems. These must correspond with national needs, institutional arrangements and domestic economic specialization. Evidently, nations and their particular cultures matter.

COPING WITH GLOBAL CHANGE: DO STATES NEED NEW POLICY INSTRUMENTS?

Western companies have not grasped the essential lesson behind Japan's economic transformation, namely that technological change occurs with novelty. The social capability to innovate matters more than ever when countries appropriate the leading technologies of others. In this context, human resources and public infrastructures are equally important to the successful transfer of technologies; they are the basic ingredients for a superior national economic performance. The nation-state, as mediating structure, makes the strategic difference between winning and losing in a highly volatile international economy. It is thus a fallacy to reduce state intervention to Keynesian fine-tuning. Modern government has to provide all the basic ingredients for competitiveness. At the top of the list are education, health, job training, research and development policies, infrastructure support, competition policy and so on, hardly a minor role for government at the end of the millennium. Yet, on both the right and the left, state policy is going in exactly the opposite direction.

All governments are under pressure to cut spending. Acute conditions of intense international competition are eroding the underpinnings of the welfare state as we know it. After the Second World War, all industrialized countries aspired to become modern welfare states. This was generally achieved through high productivity growth, a stable international order and strong workers' movements. If, on the contrary, conditions are such that productivity and growth lag and the international order deteriorates, welfare is perceived by business as an obstacle to demand and product innovation. With workers and unions weakened by industrial restructuring and rising unemployment, the state cannot easily protect social rights. Throughout the Western world, governments are cutting welfare nets. But, despite the appearance of a common trend, there is as much diversity as similarity between nations.

At one extreme are the market-driven societies of Canada, the US, Great Britain, Australia and New Zealand that have experienced mediocre economic performances along with deepening social inequality. At the other end are the more social democratic countries such as Germany, France and Sweden that have faced equally severe adjustment problems and rising unemployment levels without sacrificing, to the same extent, their social entitlements. What accounts for these fundamental differences in approach? This is the critical issue.

THE POST-SECOND WORLD WAR FORDIST GROWTH REGIME REVISITED

The Paris-based Régulation School of Political Economy has developed its own response to these very different examples of national welfare and industrial growth by reference to concepts of Fordism, state forms and institutional arrangements. What it has demonstrated in its comparative studies of capitalist societies is that each national welfare state is the outcome of deeply embedded compromises and that these compromises were the result of past struggles that shaped social stratification, politics and economic specialization. The school's adherents maintain that the novelty of the post-Second World War Fordist growth regime is directly linked to the way liberal democratic society was forced to assert itself against the destructive forces of the market. Growth-centred Fordism created an institutional setting that proved extremely efficient in enhancing innovation, productivity and continuous increases in standards of living. The success of the system was in its impressive synchronization between mass production and mass consumption. What does this reveal about the markets' claim to be the ultimate instrument of efficiency? It underlies the fact that markets work best when the state is a strong regulator (see Chapter 3 for a detailed discussion). Analysis indicates that, despite claims to the contrary, nation-states are unlikely to go the way of the plough horse. The reasons for this are many.

First of all, to be efficient, markets have to be socially constructed via a set of agreed on or imposed rules of the game; there is no 'natural' or 'spontaneous' implementation of market mechanisms. If specific markets give the impression of being self-equilibrating mechanisms, this is the result of their adherence to sophisticated regulations concerning the quality of the goods exchanged, the inner organization of transactions, the legal penalty for non-compliance, etc. In the absence of such surveillance mechanisms, private sector opportunism and corporate self-interest would severely distort the alleged smooth adjustment process of supply and demand.

The last two decades have been times of structural crisis; the market has made an impressive comeback. But régulation theory contends that the overriding presence of markets is fundamentally destructive. Wherever governments have been unable to reform tax and credit systems and social partners are unwilling to renegotiate a social accord to take account of stiffening of international competition, market mechanisms have intervened in channelling institutional restructuring. In this, the ideology of the market must not be confused with the reality of its power and limits. Free market-oriented nations such as the US, the UK and Canada have not been successful in coping with innovation and market variability, i.e. structural competitiveness. Conversely, where market forces have been kept under control as in Japan, Germany and Austria, their individual economic performances have been far superior in terms of growth, unemployment and innovation.

And finally, from a theoretical point of view, régulation theory underscores the importance of the market as just one institutional device among others co-ordinating the governance of society. In this, it challenges the conventional notion that there is a single and unique method of organizing capitalist economies. Historical investigations of the US, France and other European countries show that 'regulation' modes have been changing significantly over a century-long period: revolutions, world wars and major crises such as the 1929 Stock Market crash play a significant role in effective structural change, mainly by promoting and legitimizing new political social and economic institutions. At any given period of time, a range of institutional configurations may characterize societies at equivalent stages of development. Thus, it is very hard to imagine any viable economy organized in accordance with pure market logic. There are simply too many other institutional factors which shape markets even if money is the primary social institution which makes possible all other transactions. The most obvious is labour itself. It is not produced as a commodity since demographic reproduction is not governed at all by profit mechanisms. Furthermore, a state's administrative efficiency is closely related to its compatibility with the existing monetary regime, competition, the nature and degree of openness to the international system as well as its style of economic regulation. Seen in this perspective, the state's role is to organize political power for the purposes of governance and cannot be reduced to being a pro-market, pro-capitalism institution. Thus, in the régulation perspective, the welfare state is of fundamental importance in maintaining social solidarity. It provides the institutional glue without which the preservation of national identity is impossible. Finally, social policy – including welfare, health and education entitlements as well as employment security – is an exclusively national (as well as regional) responsibility, not a supranational one.

THE MARKET OR THE SUPRANATIONAL STATE? DO COUNTRIES HAVE TO CHOOSE?

Faced with a new global order in the making, states are unlikely to stand still and remain indifferent to the greater possibilities for co-operation at the international level. Nations, no less than individuals, have to change and adapt to new circumstances. For the vast majority of nation-states, this is perceived as a fundamental shift in orientation. State intervention no longer means using public power to organize the private sector, but is now equated with the unleashing of market forces. There is, however, another interpretation. The dominant position of markets may be due to the fact that no supranational authority has the power to discipline transnational markets which increasingly threaten the sovereignty of nations. The reluctance of nation-states to negotiate a transfer of power to supranational bodies to guide and direct the current restructuring process is easy to explain. But, by default, market forces are in command, intent on disciplining national governments who want to hold onto the instruments of national power.

With governments politically unable to rise above the national interest, the market wins. This expression of inertia, seemingly due to the so-called vested interests of 'old state forms', is not convincing evidence that the nation-state is about to vanish. The European Community is a case in point. It is unable to organize economic, social and political integration that merits the name. Instead, the vacuum created by the attempt at economic integration is now filled by market forces. Transnational firms are moving from one country to another looking to compete on labour costs; they seek national jurisdictions where employment standards are lowest. Under NAFTA, corporations have greater latitude to invest and divest and locate in new production sites in Mexico, Canada or the US. Thus, the modern multi-national corporation is in a good position to benefit from the Agreement's inability to define common social standards. Moreover, transnational corporate and business interests now successfully lobby for sectoral agreements in Brussels and are able to win new trade concessions directly from Washington. This has created a proliferation of private interest governance mechanisms at the international level. Corporations alone have the resources to be global players. The UN World Investment Report reveals that there were more than 35,000 transnational corporations with over 200,000 subsidiaries in 1992 and that this number is expected to rise dramatically by the end of the century. Such a form of governance suffers from a lack of democratic accountability. Furthermore, these kinds of corporate-enhancing agreements are far too partial to be an effective basis for the promotion of growth with stability. The present instability of financial markets is a good example of the limits of governance without state intervention. The prospects of economic recovery remain more uncertain than ever and the internationalization of markets has not delivered its most important promise: national autonomy and fast growth.

Thus, the idea that global markets will totally erode the legitimacy, indeed, *necessity* of the nation-state does not stand up to scrutiny. Even if the effectiveness of the post-Second World War state is in question, new state intervention is not automatically doomed to fail. On the contrary, a market is only viable in the context of the larger social and political order. The intellectual and analytical challenge is to discover whether there is a theory that can analyse the subtle balance between markets and economic arrangements in today's highly complex economies?

KEYNES, POLANYI AND INNIS: THE VOLATILITY OF MARKETS

The present period has many striking parallels with the interwar period. Then, as today, finance and competition set the agenda for national economic policies. During both periods, unemployment reached record levels and national economies were subject to unprecedented swings in international demand and interest rates. In the 1980s and 1990s, economists believed that governments had to return to 'basics'. The intimation was that state policy and trade unions prevented pure competition from delivering full employment. In both periods, the ideal seems to be to transform labour and financial markets into pure commodities that would obey the iron law of supply and demand. During the 1930s, few dissented. John Maynard Keynes, Karl Polanyi and Harold Innis were exceptions. They maintained that markets were not only incapable of being self-organizing, but do not move from equilibrium point to equilibrium point. They saw instead the instability and uncertainty that results when state policy is unnecessarily internationalized. The present volume takes its point of departure from the highly original work of these theorists as they explored the question of national and international markets in internationalized settings.

Keynes's *General Theory* (1936) stands out as a seminal text in the transformation of the role of the state in economic life in the early twentieth century. But modern theoreticians remember him only for his advice to government to 'fine-tune' the economy by means of a counter-cyclical fiscal and monetary policy. Keynes's lasting contribution, however, is contained in his statements outlining the fact that in a world governed by radical uncertainty, the search for liquidity may inhibit investment decisions, thereby creating insufficient demand. Thus, an unemployment/investment disequilibrium may persist, however irrational it might seem to workers on

8

the dole and bankrupt firms. Keynes's great insight was to understand that no one individual can overcome such barriers to recovery. Only direct or indirect state intervention can end a recession and put the economy back on track towards full employment. Injecting more money into the private economy, investing in public infrastructures and, more generally, restoring the confidence of investors and consumers are some of the various means available to governments to correct the malfunctioning of a market economy.

Keynes's concept of state intervention went even further. He believed, for example, that the state was the only institution that could operate as a countervailing force in a world where financial markets had become extremely sophisticated. Similarly, the state had to cope with the organization of workers, probably imposing a given level for nominal wage. Keynes provided a general framework which described how stagnation and unemployment could be defeated by introducing highly original kinds of state policies to counteract the inherent instability of pure market mechanisms.

During the last two decades, neo-classical economists have been fond of pointing out the lack of a micro-foundation for the Keynesian concept of involuntary unemployment. But, in the *General Theory*, there are several starting points which illuminate why markets and especially labour markets will not clear, forcing governments to intervene. By contrast, most, if not all, neo-classical contemporary theories are unable to explain the persistence of high levels of involuntary unemployment even when governments have adopted pro-market strategies. It is, therefore, still worthwhile to begin with Keynes in order to understand certain aspects of the new global order that run parallel with his own time: the rapid expansion of financial markets worldwide, the competitive struggle of nations for exports, the radical uncertainty of future investment opportunities and the failure of existing government strategies to address the worldwide economic crisis. Not surprisingly, several authors of this book argue that Keynes might be dead, but that his illuminating framework continues to provide valuable insights (see in particular Chapters 1, 8, 9, 16 and 19).

Even more than Keynes, Polanyi addressed the question: can societies be ruled exclusively by markets organizing activity along the principle of supply and demand? He was the first to give a persuasive explanation of why markets rapidly encounter limits for such strategic and unconventional commodities as money, labour, culture and nature. No one has better described the inner paradox of market economies. For Polanyi, the core truth is that markets can deliver good outcomes when they are restricted to typical products but collapse when their influence is extended to more basic elements of economic life, labour, land and money – that is, when markets are no longer an 'accessory feature of an institutional setting controlled and regulated . . . by social authority'. Polanyi powerfully outlines the destructive impact of markets on monetary stability, social justice and the environment in his *The Great Transformation*:

A market economy must comprise all elements of industry, including labour, land and money . . . But labour and land are no other than the human beings themselves of which every society consists and the natural surroundings in which it exists. To include them in the market mechanism means to subordinate the substance of society itself to the laws of the market . . . But labour, land and money are obviously *not* commodities; the postulate that anything that is bought and sold must have been produced for sale, is emphatically untrue in regard to them . . . Labour is only another name for human activity, which goes with life itself . . .; land is another name for nature, which is not produced by man . . .; actual money, finally, is merely a token of purchasing power which, as a rule, is not produced at all, but comes into being through the mechanisms of banking or state finance . . . The commodity description of labour, land and money is entirely fictitious. Nevertheless it is with the help of this fiction that the actual markets for labour, land and money are organized.

(Polanyi 1957: 71–2)

During the 1980s and 1990s, the deregulation of financial markets, the strategies of labour market flexibility and recurring discussions concerning environmental degradation give special importance to Karl Polanyi's warning about the destructive impact of markets. If Polanyi's analysis of the finite nature of markets retains any credibility, we are probably on the edge of the second great transformation. The *laissez-faire* credo that pushed industrial countries to embrace extreme forms of monetarism in the 1980s will have to be reassessed. Even if many countries are far from this goal, it is likely to happen. This is an important theme in many of the chapters in this volume.

Harold Innis, Canada's most brilliant political economist whose work spanned the interwar period, is a third source of inspiration. Innis's pioneering research on economic settlement, national development and world markets from the sixteenth to the twentieth centuries established his preeminence as a scholar without equal among his contemporaries. His most important achievement remains his exhaustive archival research on Canada's place in the global economy. Innis's method was simple and effective: he set out to study the actual economic life of a frontier economy, not a model of *laissez-faire* 'frictionless' development.

What was particular about the frontier economy was that it required constant in-flows of foreign capital to pay for the infrastructure of resource-dependent development. This meant that its development would be burdened by high debt charges that capital would off-load onto labour. Incomes would be highly variable as producer groups were subject inevitably to a shifting global business cycle. Thus, a country dependent on major staples would find itself subject to pressures from the structure of capital, technological rigidities due to the rapid exploitation of new resources, the price structure

10

of transportation costs and the constraints of highly regionalized labour markets.

Using a straightforward analytical framework, Innis did something original. As an economic historian, he attempted to chart the underlying economic currents whose larger significance only emerges over a great span of time. Starting with furs and cod, working his way through the staple trades of the nineteenth century – square timber, agricultural products and wheat to the present-day energy staples of oil and gas – Innis discovered the extent to which the power of commerce left its mark on each phase in the evolution of Canada's social structure. In the process, he ascertained much about the inner workings of capitalist economies and the formation of markets. His *problématique* gave him a work space stretching over more than 400 years. Innis's grasp of the *longue durée* remains absolutely compelling and refreshing despite the passage of time.

Innis's account of events is of crucial significance for an understanding of the way a frontier country or any country overspecialized in a narrow band of economic activity is battered by events and forces it cannot control. He was a strong internationalist who believed in having world order that was stable and equitable. Narrowly based competitive strategies pushed countries to adopt beggar-thy-neighbour policies and, without adequate institutional protection, frontier economies would become 'storm centres to the modern international economy'.

Far from accepting the 'market' as an abstract entity, Innis preferred to study the dynamics and interactivity of markets as real entities in time that produced unpredictable outcomes under the best conditions and were not subject to invariable universal laws of supply and demand in the worst of times. The idea that markets have multiple, continuous and contradictory effects, and hence are unstable structures and subject to the constant need for organization and reorganization, is due to the fact that they emerge out of social relationships. Innis's principal insight was that markets are like open-ended social spaces constantly subject to spontaneous countermovements by producers, consumers, owners, workers and government threatened by the price system's rapacious excesses. When the price system does not work *ex mirabulis*, society must rely on the state to find ways to stabilize it and the larger economy.

That Innis turned to the language and concepts of political economy to compose his ideas may have had much to do with the fact that, in Canada, economic life has always had a strong institutional dimension. For political economists of his persuasion, material prosperity could not be taken for granted. Business activity had only one objective: to make a quick profit – the quicker the better. By contrast, the aim of contemporary statecraft was to make society better off materially while also enhancing its social values. As a political economist, Innis subscribed to the belief that development had a higher goal than the accumulation of individual wealth. Instead, his main preoccupation was to explain the way the institutional side of economic life is used to counter the highly erratic nature of market outcomes. For example, small-scale individual commodity production will always be competitive, fluid and driven by price considerations in contrast to large-scale industrial production where a handful of dominant firms, vertically integrated, will support monopoly pricing practices, restrict competition, engage in predatory market strategies and seek protection from the state.

Innis realized that the general dynamics of exchange relations and the process of accumulation take different forms depending upon the stage of development and the balance of forces between the internal and external markets. Thus, commerce assumed a central role in Innis's concept of market formation. Trade is a mega-force because it can be conducted on liberal principles of openness or, alternatively, organized on a closed basis such as mercantilism. An economy without any tariff protection risks sacrificing its industries on the altar of competition, but a developmental process dominated by a set of narrowly protectionist policies without strong governmental oversight is a burden on consumers. National policies, too, must become critical from his perspective because, without strong and effective national measures, domestic markets cannot be integrated to serve national needs but must remain local and fragmented.

The three approaches outlined above nicely complement each other. Keynes subscribed to a belief in the legitimacy of state intervention because such intervention removes the structural weaknesses of pure market mechanisms. Karl Polanyi perceived the dangers of treating the most important ingredients of society – that is, money, labour and the environment – as mere commodities. And Innis warned against the highly volatile nature of international markets and the danger that international markets presented to countries with over-specialized economies. Having said this, it would be wrong to say that the contemporary crisis is but a repetition of conditions in the 1930s. Not so.

The very real limits of Fordist economic institutions are now clear. Such systems were designed to prevent stagnation and under-consumption in the immediate post-war period when tariff walls were high and there were many other barriers to trade. It makes little sense today to call for a programme of Keynesian reforms based on the same set of concerns. Contemporary capitalism has entered a turbulent period of trial and error; there are now new institutional forms and practices emerging for labour markets, financial and external trade. But once the current restructuring comes to an end, what will happen then? Will the market be the exclusive and unique co-ordinating mechanism for society? Which institutions of the Fordist nation-state have proved adequate in responding both to the competitiveness of global markets and to the new demands from citizens for a different kind of society? Finally, what lies beyond the Fordist nation-state?

FROM THE 1990s TO THE TWENTY-FIRST CENTURY: SIX PARADOXES

The authors of this volume reject the contention that the nation-state is *passé* or, worse still, an accident of history. Their starting point begins from a different assessment of the power and limits of markets. For the contributors, the embeddedness of economic institutions is essential for a strong economic performance. Hence the nation-state cannot be easily replaced by the market for any significant period since it is the only institution society has to organize itself, protect the social solidarity of its citizens and safeguard its social values which cannot be 'traded' like commodities. Yet its future is not guaranteed by any means. There are at least six counter-tendencies deciding its fate.

Globalization is important, but not totally new or overwhelming

The first counter-tendency is that we do not live in a totally integrated global world. The quantitative evidence demonstrates that globalization is not a totally new phenomenon if measured by such national indicators as the share of exports as percentage of GDP or the share of foreign investment in total investment flows. The internationalization of economic activity has not changed dramatically from the time when Great Britain was the leading global power (see Chapter 7). Many features of our contemporary world were already present then. In fact, the internationalization of trade, production and finance fluctuates dramatically over time, collapsing at the end of the 1930s and only recovering in the 1950s. Even so, today's globalization is qualitatively and quantitatively different from that of previous periods. State activity has been internationalized to an unprecedented degree in all industrial countries. Even Japan, Sweden and France, countries which were not initially advocates of *laissez-faire* practices, have accepted the need to open their markets in spite of the cost and regardless of the consequences. Furthermore, despite recurring financial crises and a worldwide slowdown in economic growth, governments have not changed their basic policy frameworks. They continue to support the belief that external markets must be kept open. This is quite unlike state behaviour in the 1930s when countries faced with a global crisis closed their economies to international trade and built high tariff walls to keep the competition at bay. Thus, financial markets have totally new features which could never have been incorporated into the highly regulated national systems of the 1960s. It would, however, be erroneous to conclude that capitalism has become global, since production methods, industrial relations, taxation and economic policy styles remain very specific to each national state.

Hence, the first paradox: the Fordist era opened the door to globalization, but a fully integrated world economy remains a distant reality and will not happen even during the next century. International forces will continue to influence national decisions more than ever, but they will not form a fully fledged alternative system. The absence of a strong recovery is a powerful reminder that a global order based on the principles of free trade and trade liberalization is for the time being creating more problems than solutions. The opening of the domestic economy to the gale-force winds of international competition has not led to either stronger growth or enhanced employment opportunities for most countries. Moreover, history teaches that internationalization is not at an irreversible process, especially when countries are faced with the anonymous and often destructive forces of the market. At that point, they see much to be gained by asserting the primacy of their own interests. This alone will preserve the nation-state.

Japanese transplants travel better than national systems of innovation

There is a second paradox to consider: Japan's rise to a world power is behind the internationalization of the production of cars, consumer electronics and related equipment (see in particular Chapters 4–6). During the 1980s, the surge in foreign investment from Japan convinced many experts that new sources of competitiveness are generally linked to the research and development of large Japanese-based multinationals. The triumph of Japanese management practices is supposed to have led to the Japanization of US, European and Asian multinationals.

This book provides a wider view. The surge of Japanese transplants all over the world is responsible for changing corporate practices in the Triad (see Chapter 2 in particular). Nevertheless, the diffusion and process of corporate adaptation is very uneven and many firms are not able to adopt the human resources strategy currently operating in Japan. On the other hand, few countries are in the race to acquire leading-edge Research and Development. Despite this, there are significant differences between US and Japanese multinationals as well as between European 'best' practices and there is no evidence that the differences are narrowing significantly. What explains the absence of convergence?

The very process of internationalization reveals the persistence of national systems of innovations which are deeply embedded in a web of interrelated political, educational and financial institutions which cannot easily be copied or adapted. During the last two decades, these differences among national systems of innovations have been reinforced by increased capital mobility. Poor regions do less research than previously whereas richer and better educated societies are more highly specialized than ever in the technologically intensive sectors of the economy: car and consumer electronics in Japan; chemical and intermediate equipment goods in Germany; pharmaceutical and finance in the UK; computers, leisure, health and finance in the US; high-speed trains, nuclear plants, telecommunications in France; agricultural products in Denmark; resource-based industries in Canada and in the

14

Scandinavian countries. Thus, globalization does not mean that technology will diffuse equally to all regions of the globe. On the contrary, globalization and localization are occurring simultaneously and it is too early to tell whether globalization will lead to an upgrading of industrial capacity for most countries or whether trade liberalization is making it more difficult for most countries to restructure their industrial sectors shattered by the economic crisis. What is not in doubt is that this new division of labour now includes many newly industrialized countries which are gaining increasing market shares in typically Fordist goods at the expense of the developed world.

The domination of financial markets can and must be reversed

With finance markets operating 24 hours a day, every major event is immediately converted into asset prices, currency exchange rates, in-flows or out-flows of capital. Not surprisingly, governments have to watch carefully these signals and pursue an economic policy which does as little harm to the national interest as possible. In fact, during the last two decades, the economic policy of every country seems to have lost most of its individual autonomy as public spending, monetary and tax policy are constantly under scrutiny by international financial lenders.

Is such a state of affairs desirable and/or irreversible? Many authors in this book argue that this conventional wisdom has to be challenged. First of all, it is simply not true that the national investment rate is exclusively determined by the investment flows and searching for the highest profit rate operating at the world level. Chapter 9 shows that, by contrast, there is a large discrepancy between profit rates across nations that is not sufficient to trigger huge in-flows and out-flows of capital. What matters to international lenders is the level of risk. They want to put their money where they, as creditors, can protect their investment. This practice is widespread. Consider, for example, why foreign capital is not currently investing in Russia; even if the return on capital is extremely profitable, the risk is too high so long as the political order is unreliable.

Thus, the third paradox. The way national financial systems are organized still matters for economic performance. In spite of a common trend towards financial deregulation, the banking system and corporate financing in Germany, Japan and partially in France significantly differ from the Anglo-Saxon financial systems largely dominated by their stock markets. But there is a second and still stronger argument to consider. The expected benefits from financial globalization have not materialized. The real interest rates have not declined, but remains at unacceptably high levels which feed the deflationary expectations of international investors. Even floating exchange rates do not exhibit the smooth pattern of adjustment that neo-classical economists promised gullible politicians when fixed exchange rates were abandoned. Evidently, external commercial disequilibria are not at all cured by the volatile currency fluctuations of the dollar, the yen and the Deutschmark. Further-more, many governments fear going against financial markets and, as a result, have not developed policies to fight unemployment; instead, they passively accept globalization. Clearly, the opposition of interests between national governments and international capital markets is a key feature of this decade (see Chapters 8, 13, 16 and 19).

Unfortunately, if politicians have undone *national* financial regulations, they have been unable to agree upon a new regulatory system at the *international* level. None the less, there is now a general feeling that financial markets have been given excessive power. Not only do they determine the direction of foreign investment flows, but they have more control over governments than even democratically elected bodies. The most powerful countries in the world today – the US, Japan and Germany – are unable unilaterally to dampen the speculative fever of international bankers. Financial markets have won by default given the inability of nations to define and create a positive role for supranational institutions.

The weakening of labour in the absence of institutionalized co-operation

The current wave of internationalization of labour markets provides a fourth paradox. The stiff competition by leading firms to enhance their market share by any means possible, coupled with the drastic effects of monetary policies, have significantly weakened the collective bargaining position of labour in all industrial countries. Thus, firms have adopted tough-minded defensive strategies: lowering wages, cutting social benefits, using short-term labour contracts at the very moment when competitiveness calls for higher skills, a continuous upgrading of skill levels and new rules of the game in order to enable workers to share the benefits from working smarter.

The drive to compete globally has had adverse consequences for workers and unions. First, workers have had generally fewer opportunities than firms to move from one country to another in order to exploit skills scarcities. Only professionals and low-skilled workers are free to migrate from one country to another; the vast majority of the population is tied to the national territory by language, family ties, the rigidities of the housing market and the absence of portable welfare entitlements, particularly retirement pensions. Second, social deregulation has encouraged the growth of low-wage, but high-skill, economies. The progressive standardization of know-how in assembly-type manufacturing industries has transformed the productivity levels in these sectors, but the growing numbers of unemployed have kept wage gains to a minimum. Many firms want to relocate in low-wage areas where there is a plentiful supply of skilled and semi-skilled labour. Thousands of manu-facturing companies based in Canada and the US have closed their doors only to reopen south of the Rio Grande. The exodus of manufacturers from Michigan and Ontario to Mexico suggests that this is not a transient phenomenon but a large-scale permanent trend. In Europe, the absence of the social charter has provoked a limited number of firms to move from France to the UK. So far, European firms are less footloose than their US counterparts, but this may change as the former countries of the Eastern bloc aggressively seek Western companies to locate in their territories.

Overall, the painful restructuring of Fordist industries has left a void which the rapid growth of the service sector has not been able to fill. There are more jobs in the sunrise service sectors, but far fewer than expected and generally with lower-than-average skill levels. So far, the hi-tech future promised by business gurus has not materialized. Wages remain depressed, companies are not investing in their employees and job security is unknown. In North America, the toppling of the wage pyramid is already evident. There are more working poor than ever before. In Europe, by contrast, wage inequalities have been kept within existing limits and welfare entitlements have been only marginally reduced. But this has been at the cost of more unemployment. The threat of losing jobs is now so acute and widespread that European firms have had little difficulty in wresting concessions from their workers and their unions with respect to working hours, hiring and firing, speed-up and, of course, wages.

With the private sector more powerful than ever, the 1990s may appear as an unparalleled time for business to invest in new plants and equipment. The irony is that wage austerity in the context of high unemployment is likely to encourage firms to opt for labour-intensive techniques instead of developing new organizations and new products capable of sustaining a high-wage economy. The US is a good example of what is wrong with this strategy. Even if many American firms are at the technological edge of innovation, most new jobs are not being created at the high-wage end of industry, but in the low- or medium-tech sectors that pay poorly. This is because flexible labour market strategies encourage firms to bid-down wages rather than see the benefits of high-skill, high-wage strategies. Conversely, when unions are able to maintain solidarity among wage earners and only negotiate limited wage concessions in a few sectors, leading firms have a strong incentive to improve production methods, customer service and local productivity by investing in new equipment, upgrading the skill training of their employees and increasing R&D expenditures on new products and production methods. The latter investment strategy is critical for any country that expects to have a rising standard of living in the long run. The paradox is that a much weakened labour movement pushes business in the wrong direction even if the lowering wage costs might be more efficient for the individual firm in the short run.

The difficult but necessary reform of the Keynesian and the Beveridgian states

A similar fallacy permeates most of the debates about the so-called impotence of the nation-state and the impossibility of a retooled Keynesian policy aimed at restoring full employment. The crisis of the Fordist welfare state is often interpreted as evidence that the *laissez-faire* strategy à la Hayek has triumphed over its Keynesian rival. If Hayek is right, then the nation-state should restrict its activities largely to property rights enforcement, implementing pro-market reforms, enhancing private sector competitiveness and attracting foreign capital. But he is not. In this decade and the next, countries everywhere will not experience a structural decline in government intervention. Rather, the modern nation-state has entered a difficult transition period where its institutional forms have to be drastically altered in order to sustain the emergence of a new growth regime (see Chapters 14 and 15 which address the issue of the future of the welfare state). This is the fifth paradox.

Nevertheless, it would be erroneous to maintain conventional Keynesian economic policies as they are: Keynes's *General Theory* is at best an inspiration to encourage new and pragmatic policies. It must be remembered that Keynes's counter-cyclical policies were designed for the post-Second World War growth engine, typically built upon an unprecedented linking of mass production and mass consumption at the micro and macro levels of society. The brake and accelerator are not to be confused with the engine (i.e. Fordism), fuel (fast technical change) and oil (permissive monetary policies). Second, the very success of this regime has created adverse tendencies which have finally halted this golden era and legitimized the conservative backlash of monetarism, supply-side economics, social deregulation and the opening of national economies to world competition. Finally, from the mid-1960s onwards, external trade has grown faster than domestic production. Since the 1980s, foreign investment flows have significantly encouraged firms to organize mass production wherever costs are cheapest. National borders matter less to business than ever before. These three structural changes force a reconsideration of many of the specific ideas in Keynes's *General Theory*, but they do not challenge the most durable part of his larger vision that markets are not self-organizing and require adequate levels of state intervention in order to function optimally.

In order to prevent monetarism from becoming a worldwide orthodoxy (a requirement of the Maastricht Treaty), political economists must argue that price stability is not the final aim of economic policy. Unemployment has been used by conservative governments as a disciplinary device. Post-Keynesian theorists must propose *new income policies* in order to induce social partners to keep wages and profits in line with competitiveness without jeopardizing job creation. Furthermore, it is simply not true that any market outcome is fair; the concern for social justice may call for wide-scale redistributive measures. After all, the nation has value and meaning for people and social stability is important for any community's sense of well-being. It must be remembered that Japan and Germany have less income inequality and regularly achieve a better macroeconomic performance than the US,

Canada and the UK, all of which rely more heavily on the market mechanism to drive their economies. Again, the Japanese national system of innovation shows how essential it is to combine public intervention with market mechanisms. With this in place, impressive performances can result. In the 1990s, and in the next century, the new growth regime will be built upon a large provision by the state for essential public goods requiring long-term investment in scientific policy, telecommunications and transportation as well as education and healthcare. States also need a high-trust industrial relations system to foster co-operation and innovation in the industries and firms. Thus, state institutions will have to be redeployed and strengthened so that they can address both the allocative and redistributive impacts of markets.

Economic internationalization calls for a renewed democratic national polity

There is a final paradox to confront. With the collapse of the Soviet regime, the major crisis of the Swedish model (which used to be considered as a third way between capitalism and communism), and the worldwide triumph of the market over the state, it appears that the end of ideology has arrived. The pretext is that the world has become so complex that no single government can control the social and economic processes taking place within its jurisdiction. The reality is that, for more than a decade, governments have been off-loading their responsibilities onto business. Public intervention is seen as having less and less utility even though in the past it was compatible with (and stimulated) fast-growing economies and kept in check rising social inequality. In the 1990s, governments on both the right and left approach policy-making as a spectacular casino where everybody is trying to guess the next move of the Bundesbank, the results of the next election in Canada, Germany, the UK or France or the forthcoming statement by President Clinton on interest rates. Economic activity is presented as obeying universal and timeless laws and any interference from politicians or interest groups is assumed to be detrimental and self-defeating. In other words, a powerful transnational financial community is exerting more and more political control over governments that used to have exclusive responsibility for their democratic institutions.

The final part of this book argues against the *de facto* political choices implicit in this kind of anonymous, abstract and apolitical determinism (see Chapters 17–19). If people are to understand the dynamics of globalization, they have to see that NAFTA or the Maastricht Treaty are no longer about trade principally, but are more investment and production agreements. There is nothing deterministic in the way they have been designed. The move towards a single European currency and the institution of a North American free trade zone are designed to override the national political process. Both agreements contain explicit clauses making all participating members accept free competition, capital mobility and minimal state intervention as the only options on offer. The take-it or leave-it determinism embodied in these agreements is not an innocent or innocuous move. During the 1960s, national compromises concerning agriculture, capital/labour relations, the environment and the organization of competition were the cornerstones of social and economic activity and not directly subject to international competitive pressures. They were 'off the table'. These measures were defended by an adequate foreign policy. Now policy-makers present complex arguments requiring the deregulation of public policy as a goal in itself and promote the internationalization of their firms as inescapable even when many countries need to deepen their home market and restructure their industries.

France, Italy and Sweden are good examples of these processes at work. When the French government decided in 1983 to support European integration, it justified its decision to follow a policy of deflationary competitiveness as one of the constraints imposed by Brussels. Similarly, the Maastricht Treaty puts severe constraints on public deficit and debt during the intermediate phase towards adopting a single currency: the Italian political crisis is the direct outcome of such a supranational constraint. Finally, when the Swedish government decided to adhere to European union, the argument did not relate only to the issue of the access of Swedish firms to the large European market. Rather, it was also convenient to present the unprecedented surge in unemployment and the drastic reform of welfare, the tax system and industrial relations as the unescapable consequences of adherence to Europe.

But this process cannot be sustained in the long run. Markets are not an illusion, but societies everywhere need direction and orientation. There is no social order on offer which aims at an efficiency so narrowly defined that it is no longer linked to job creation. Even the idea of a better economic performance is problematic for most companies. The majority of firms sell in local or regional markets, not internationally. The deeper question is: can a wage-based system of capitalism overcome the disorientation of its labour-saving efficient technologies creating more wealth with less and less labour? With no end in sight to the economic crisis, the ever-growing number of social outcasts provides a ready source of recruits for the current revival of ethnically based nationalist movements. Xenophobic social movements are a direct reaction to the global bulldozer. On the left side of the spectrum, women's organizations, environmental activists and popular sector organizations are examples of the kinds of social groups which have been battered by highly volatile markets. They will not accept their fate passively. They are thus putting forward the idea that markets should be controlled by democracy, not the other way around. A new ideology must be elaborated in order to deliver a deeper understanding of the present, provide a method for different groups to develop unifying strategies and, finally, propose new ways to socially control economic activity. This will not be easy, but it will happen because the instability of markets requires society to find innovative ways to stabilize their economies in order to safeguard their future.

SOME CONCLUDING COMMENTS

Demanding fundamental change in state policy is one of the most difficult challenges facing people everywhere. Governments want to look good and promise prosperity by opening the economy to powerful market pressures. This kind of pump-priming requires more than stop-gap measures to address the larger issues at stake. Decision-makers will have to make tough choices in many different areas of public policy. This includes looking again at the sustainability of trade blocs on both sides of the Atlantic. Canadian policy-makers will have to decide whether there are enough benefits in the Canada–US Free Trade Agreement (FTA) and the North American Free Trade Agreement (NAFTA) to justify Canada's long-term participation. As well, governments will have to learn to say 'no' to corporate interests who want to log, fish, mine and produce goods and services without regard for the future well-being of the environment. With labour-saving technologies being relied on to boost productivity in all sectors of the economy, the work revolution requires governments with vision to develop a commitment to a different kind of job creation. Industrial societies need full-time jobs that are well-paying, permanent and secure which the private sector, with its limited resources, cannot possibly create. But more is needed as well. People need governments that will make social-policy and welfare concerns a top priority. Many new initiatives are needed if the demands of women for equity and affirmative action are to be satisfied. How is this change in perception and political choice to occur?

It is often said that everyone needs a local view of global issues and a global view of local concerns. There is a caveat however. Developing this perspective does not happen automatically. Tools are needed to link all kinds of community-based needs to global-oriented issues. Political economy is a powerful analytical discourse that offers a window on the complexities of the international economy in a number of areas. It lets one see how economic concerns are linked to political change. By focusing on the macro-conditions of state policy – production relations, distribution norms, investment practices, consumption patterns and social regulation – it helps identify the key factors that drive the public agenda. Even this is not enough. Everywhere electorates are looking to government to be a counterweight to footloose corporations. It is this intuitive perception to rein-in markets that will increasingly occupy centre stage and be the real frontier between the Left and Right for the rest of the decade. For social movements, the nation-state continues to be the chosen instrument for the organization of society. However much social institutions will have to evolve and adapt to new global pressures, what is not in doubt is that the nation-state remains the crucible for equality seeking movements the world over. Efficiency, profitability and competitiveness have not won the hearts and minds of people worldwide. There are larger and more compelling horizons which define the global agenda in the closing years of the millenium.

STRUCTURE OF THE VOLUME

With countries everywhere looking for ways to compete and increase their global share of exports, what is distinct about the global economy in the 1990s is the magnitude and pace of globalization. No corner of economic and social life is exempt from market pressures. And yet, when public policy-makers exhort society to be more competitive it is far from clear what exactly is expected. Are there different ways to compete? If so, which is the optimal choice? What should the role of governments be? What range of alternatives are there? Should they intervene less or more? Is free trade the most efficient way to organize the international economy? Is trade liberalization essentially job-positive or is it a major source of job loss? Is the nation-state as we have known it *passé*? What are the counter-tendencies to the era of global competition? These and other fundamental questions are examined in the following six sections.

1 *Globalization: Unleashing the Market.* This section addresses what is different about globalization at a time of increased capital mobility and the internationalization of production. Drache's chapter explores the new state structures of the 1990s. He shows that if Keynes, Beveridge and Fordist industrial relations practices were once the pillars of state policy, they no longer are. The emergence of the 'lean and mean' K-mart state dedicated to providing a much lower level of services is emblematic of the new order. Yet, the shift from Keynes to K-mart remains highly problematic. It is question-able whether complex societies can afford the luxury of privatizing the essential functions of government particularly when dynamic efficiency gains require governments to invest and spend money on people, infrastructure and communities. For countries grappling with the new competitive pressures many have forgotten that in an age of trade blocs, the home market remains where the best jobs are, where investment needs to occur and where local firms make the difference between success and failure. Petrella examines the principles, dynamics, actors and structures of the new global economy and provides a road map to the world of globalized markets. His contribution stresses that globalization is partial, unstable and creates deep cleavages not only between the social classes in advanced industrial countries but, just as importantly, between the north and the south. If there is to be a stable global order, countries need to find ways to make the multinational enterprise accountable but even this important initiative may not be sufficient to stabilize a highly volatile international order. State/market relations are the subject of the final chapter. Markets are often seen as the most efficient way to organize economic life. Boyer's broad theoretical analysis shows how inadequate this proposition is in fact. The market is a complex institution that is not self-organizing in the way conventional economic theory assumes, nor does it respond to universal laws of supply and demand as is frequently believed. To be efficient, markets have to be embedded in national institutions

governing money, labour and the environment. His principal point is that in the next decade states will likely turn away from their pro-market conservative strategies.

2 *The Limits of Japanese Power.* The rise of Japan to the status of a world power constitutes a watershed of the twentieth century. It is now not only a technological leader, but also one of the leading countries in science and research policy. McMillan examines the different perspectives on Japan's post-war metamorphosis as a key player in the new multipolar world of the next century. None the less, Japan's technological creativity has identifiable limits. While Japan is the undisputed leader in many fields, its techno-nationalism has not begun to grapple with the economic fall-out from globalization both at home or on the developing countries of the world. Tetsuo Abo's empirical study of Japanese transnationals in Europe and Asia focuses on their attempts to transfer technology and their labour market practices. His article presents a wealth of information about Japanese corporate practice in a comparative setting. Bowles and MacLean question the ability of Japan to lead an East Asian regional bloc. They point out that politics matter. A country's industrial strategy is, in the final analysis, the determining factor in doing well in the global economy rather than the so-called 'market forces' operating out of control.

3 *Finance and Trade: The Erosion of National Sovereignty.* Financial deregulation and computerized networks for the trading of money are the defining characteristics of globalization in this era. Yet, all three contributors in this section warn against the widely accepted idea that financial markets rule everything. Bairoch's contribution is particularly important because it serves as a corrective to the idea that globalization is a totally new phenomenon. Indeed, throughout the twentieth century all countries have had to grapple with foreign direct investment flows and the costs of adjustment resulting from having a very large share of a country's GDP development rely on export markets. The more fundamental issue is not the degree of international expansion but the issue of social dumping – the way countries with positions of international power artificially lower their prices to obtain a greater market share. Eric Helleiner addresses the question of whether there will be a backlash against financial deregulation. His analysis leaves little room for doubt that financial liberalization has promoted the growth of speculative non-productive international financial activity. The challenge all countries face is whether they can afford these policies any longer, particularly when there is no end in sight to the deep-seated economic crisis of the 1990s. Helleiner's article suggests that it is not inconceivable that there will be re-regulation of the world's financial markets. He makes the persuasive case that countries everywhere will have to re-examine the regulatory rules of the game. Epstein picks up on this theme and in his contribution demonstrates that international financial markets are based on asymmetrical power relations. Thus, it is not a question of whether financial markets need to be

regulated but, rather, when. The originality of this chapter is to argue that the nation-state and capital mobility are not opposites but go hand in hand.

4 *Globalization and Labour.* The current recession is sharper, longer and more debilitating than the last. Unprecedented job-shedding in mass production industries, a record high number of business failures, falling family incomes and an unparalleled growth in food banks are the most visible signs of the human costs of technological change. From an institutional perspective, labour markets, work practices and corporate strategies are at the eye of this hurricane. Drache examines the work world of lean production in three Japanese auto transplants situated in southern Ontario. What he demonstrates is that while lean production in some aspects represents an advance over earlier production systems, the claim that it empowers workers is false. The new model of production expands management's rights without developing an equivalent concept of industrial citizenship. For workers in the industrial side of the economy, they need a modern system of collective bargaining to protect workers' rights from arbitrary management behaviour. Gordon Betcherman's contribution on globalization, labour markets and public policy broadens the debate. Globalization has changed the way labour markets operate and he demonstrates that countries need to adopt policies that link their external trade strategy to their labour market adjustment priorities. If they do not, Betcherman maintains that globalization will bid-down labour entitlements and lead to a two-tier labour market. If this deterioration of employment opportunities is to be avoided, a country such as Canada has to spend more on education and training. Even this may not be enough. Countries need to strengthen international standards and working conditions. Lazar's study on global corporate strategy concludes this section. He addresses the question: is there a 'smart' way to compete which does not sacrifice either the home market or labour standards? His argument is that highly competitive forces are requiring governments and business to spend more not less money. Competition requires firms to act strategically and invest on a long-term basis. Increased prosperity requires governments to spend and not simply cut. Lazar makes the essential point that not all global strategies enhance the competitiveness of a firm. Canadian policy-makers have to support those that enhance the position of Canadian firms in the domestic market and enable them to gain access to international markets.

5 *Are Keynes and Beveridge Really Dead? The Strategic Dilemma For Policy-Makers.* All states live increasingly in an interdependent world where they have markedly less power to direct their own economic future. The day of the nation-state as we have known it appears to be over. European union is the most advanced attempt to build an alternative system of international economic governance. In a closely argued chapter, Streeck contends that the idea of supranational authority is not on the cards. Rather, a new kind of state is emerging. The paradox is that public power is more fragmented at the same time that economic integration has created more international obliga-

tions that many countries may not be able to fulfil. The internationalization of state policy is the subject of the second contribution by Ramesh Mishra. In it, he contends that social welfare policy is far from being a thing of the past even though all industrial countries have cut back their spending. Why is social policy such a 'staple' of modern society for so many industrial countries? There is no functionalist logic that can justify retrenching social expenditure. Rather, he shows that politics, culture and ideology are just as important as globalization in determining a country's welfare policy. Specifically, he proposes that industrial countries will move from some version of social citizenship towards 'welfare pluralism' where the non-state sector will play a larger role in the provision of welfare. Next, Bakker and Miller explore the new state forms of administrative services. They examine the option presented by the liberal alternative state vs. the democratic alternative state. Since all countries have had to experiment with ways to deliver state services on a decentralized and flexible basis, Bakker and Miller contend that shifting power away from the state is a prerequisite for effective state action. The disintegration of Fordism makes this not only possible but goes far beyond existing practice. Community economic development and the delivery of health services in Ontario are two areas where deep-seated changes in public sector output are already occurring. It becomes clear that financing state activity holds the key to a renewed polity in all industrial countries and that debt levels and deficit-spending are major concerns for all governments. Chorney provides a non-ideological examination of this key issue, arguing that there is no a priori way to establish how much debt is too much or whether deficits are out of control. He argues that there is a perverse logic at work and that deficit-cutting will not provide the stimulus needed for getting people back to work.

6 *New Politics in an Uncertain World.* In the 1990s despite the focus on market-centred policies, politics are back with a vengeance and social movements have re-emerged at the local and regional level in all countries. What is the potential of these new movements to tame markets and redefine public power? Brodie argues that boundary-shifting between the public and private is likely to be seismic for most societies. Not only are market forces unleashed but the breakdown of the post-war compromise has reinvigorated oppositional movements. Anti-poverty groups, the women's movement and labour have as yet to find a common discourse. Brodie blames the current focus on competitiveness and globalization for driving a wedge between groups. If there is a light at the end of the tunnel, social movements have to build a social consensus about the boundaries between the public and private. Marjorie Cohen addresses the way the nation-state is being challenged and changed by new international trade agreements. She presents a powerful case that the future of nations will depend on how much each can retain of its own self-determination. She concludes that free trade agreements will negatively affect equality seeking groups such as women. Her contention is that these

agreements disenfranchise disadvantaged groups by excluding them from the locus of power. With fewer avenues open to groups seeking fundamental societal change, many social movements will try to change the political order through new kinds of activism. The final question addressed is whether a strong national economy is a Utopian goal at the end of the twentieth century? Bienefeld contends that it is not. The heart of the matter is that the nation-state is a necessary and feasible response to the increasing pressures driven by global disorder. In theoretical terms, he demonstrates that the nation-state is the only entity capable of restoring a degree of congruence between the social, economic and political dimensions of reality.

BIBLIOGRAPHY

Aglietta, Michel. 1982. *Regulation and Crisis of Capitalism*. New York: Monthly Review Press.

Aglietta, Michel, Anton Brender and Virginie Coudert. 1990. *Globalisation Financière: l'aventure obligée*. Paris: Economica.

Akerlof, Georges A. 1984. *An Economic Theorist's Book of Tales*. Cambridge, Mass.: Cambridge University Press.

Boyer, Robert. 1988. *The Search for Labour Market Flexibility*. Oxford: Clarendon Press.

Boyer, Robert. 1990. *The Regulation School. A Critical Introduction*. New York: Columbia University Press.

Boyer, Robert and Yves Saillard. 1995. *Handbook on Regulation of Economics*. Armonk: Sharpe.

Braudel, Fernand. 1979. *Civilisation materielle, economie et capitalisme XV–XVIIIe siècles*, 3 vols. Paris: Armand Colin.

Campbell, John L., J. Rogers Campbell and Leon N. Lindberg. 1991. *Governance of the American Economy*. Cambridge, New York, Melbourne: Cambridge University Press.

Chandler, Alfred D. 1977. *The Visible Hand. The Managerial Revolution in American Business*. Cambridge, Mass.: The Belknap Press of Harvard University Press.

Drache, Daniel. 1994. *Canada and the Global Economy*. Athabasca: Athabasca University Press.

Drache, Daniel and Meric Gertler (eds). 1991. *The New Era of Global Competition*. Montreal: McGill–Queen's University Press.

Freeman, Chris and Luc Soete. 1994. *Work for All or Mass Unemployment Computerised Technical Change into the 21st Century*. London: Pinter.

Freeman, J.R. 1989. *Democracy and Markets. The Politics of Mixed Economies*. Ithaca: Cornell University Press.

Freidman, Milton. 1962. *Capitalism and Freedom*. Chicago: University of Chicago Press.

Friedman, Milton. 1980. *Free to Choose: A Personal Statement*. New York: Harcourt Brace Jovanovich.

Gorz, André. 1994. *Capitalism, Socialism, Ecology*. London: Verso.

Hayek, Fredrich von. 1973–1981. *Law, Legislation and Liberty*, 3 vols. Chicago: University of Chicago Press.

Hayek, Fredrich von. 1980. *Individualism and Economic Order*. Chicago and London: University of Chicago Press.

Hollingsworth, Rogers J., Philippe Schmitter and Wolfgang Streeck (eds). 1993. *Governing Capitalist Economies: Performance and Control of Economic Sectors.* New York: Oxford University Press.

Ingrao, B. and G. Israel. 1990. *The Invisible Hand. Economic Equilibrium in the History of Science.* Cambridge, Mass.: The MIT Press.

Innis, Harold. 1994. *Staple Markets and Cultural Change: Essays in Economic History* (Daniel Drache, ed.). Montreal: McGill–Queen's University Press.

Keynes, John Maynard. 1936. *The General Theory of Employment, Interest and Money.* London: St Martin's Press; Macmillan.

Kuttner, Robert. 1991. *The End of Laissez-Faire.* New York: Alfred A. Knopf.

Ledyard, J.O. 1987. 'Market Failure', pp. 326–8 in J. Eatwell, M. Milgate and P. Newman (eds), *The New Palgrave. A Dictionary of Economics*, vol. 3. London: Macmillan.

Polanyi, Karl. 1957. *The Great Transformation*, Boston: Beacon Hill.

Wolf, Charles, Jr. 1990. *Markets or Governments: Choosing Between Imperfect Alternatives.* Cambridge, Mass. and London: The MIT Press.

Part I

GLOBALIZATION: UNLEASHING THE MARKET

1

FROM KEYNES TO K-MART
Competitiveness in a corporate age
Daniel Drache

INTRODUCTION

The unprecedented expansion of markets worldwide is unlike anything seen in this century. With national economies more open than ever, countries have less ability to pursue independent economic policies as firms operate increasingly without regard to domestic borders (Small 1993). Nations now seem to have lost control of a large part of their economic destiny to the global 'bulldozer' that is intent on building a new world order on the ruins of once-powerful national economies.

The globalization-of-everything syndrome does not mean that national boundaries are disappearing. Far from it. There are more nation-states in the world today than any other time previously[1] (Latouche 1993). Yet, what is also different about the 1990s, compared to even a decade ago, is that a new kind of state is emerging with its own institutional forms. Some call it a post-national regional state (Ohmae 1993). Others refer to it as the post-sovereign state (Clarkson 1993). Still others see, in this age of diminished expectations, a restatement of economic liberalism (Brittan 1988). The common thread is that the basic precepts of public finance, work organization, trade policy, wealth creation and citizen rights are being rethought. For Kenichi Ohmae, the catalyst is the nation-state itself. '[It] has become an unnatural, even dysfunctional unit for organizing human activity and managing economic endeavor in a borderless world' (Ohmae 1993: 78). National institutions have lost their principal importance of representing a genuine shared community of economic interests for national ends. Ohmae is of the view that 'it defines no meaningful flows of economic activity' any longer. The claim that economic activity is no longer bounded by national economies may turn out to be without foundation. None the less, the dramatic change to the way the world economy is organized brings us to the heart of the matter.

Efficiency has become the universal belief of all major corporations and most leading industrial powers. In their view, capital has to be free to move across national boundaries if the world economy is to recover its past *élan* (OECD 1993a). Firms have to learn to reorganize their production to take

31

advantage of the new opportunities. People are expected to adapt and accept new employment conditions to accommodate a world where business is no longer bound by national borders.

The relentless pursuit of export markets is part of the new circumstances. The emergence of trade blocs committed to a radically expanded version of free trade and a vast overall re-ordering of the world's trading system are two of the most far-reaching developments of our times. If the building of a world order on the principle of global free trade for all comes to pass, it will make all national economies more subject than ever to cost-cutting strategies that depend on firms having smaller workforces and countries less state regulation. What accounts for these dramatic changes to the social fabric of nations? What kinds of policy instruments are needed to protect governments from the global business cycle? How is the sovereignty of nations being redefined by this drive to compete?

A NEW STATE STRUCTURE/NEW MARKET FORCES

The answers to these central questions are anything but simple. What is irrefutable is that the structure of local, national and international markets has always shaped state policy and civil society in modern times. In no era is this more apparent than the present. As capital becomes increasingly mobile, the investment characteristics of capital flows reflect increasingly the pressures of the global market over local markets. The aggressive pursuit of these heightened investment and trade opportunities by business and government is changing the structure of the modern state.

For the last forty years, the state's Keynesian-inspired set of policies supported a seemingly inexhaustible virtuous growth cycle (Table 1.1) for all industrial nations (Polanyi 1957; Boyer 1991; Cox 1991). All Western democratic governments accepted responsibility for employment creation and the maintenance of high levels of consumer demand in the economy. This was achieved through a variety of measures. Unions were given a new status through Wagner Act kinds of legislation everywhere and this reform, more than any other, forged an institutional link through modern collective bargaining between consumption norms, real wage growth and increased productivity (Drache and Glasbeek 1992). From their wartime experience, governments learned a great deal about the practical problems of macro-economic management and, once the hostilities were concluded, countries took advantage of the situation to expand even further the state's role in the administration of the economy. Planning was seen as positive for the well-being of business and society and, as well, the proper role of governments. Virtually all industrial countries adopted Keynesian-inspired policies to make full employment, if not a reality, at least a primary goal for public policy-making.

Table 1.1 The three-in-one virtuous growth model: a comparison of state interventionist strategies

	Beveridge-inspired social policy	A Fordist capital/labour compromise	Keynesian macroeconomic management
Canada	Low to medium social net coverage but universal health system and unemployment insurance	Decentralized collective bargaining; fragmented labour markets; 25,000 individual collective bargaining agreements in force	Export-led growth made rather than Keynesian policies; uncompetitive manufacturing sector that competes on wages; over 70% of exports for US market
United States	Poor UIC benefits for only 25% of workforce. Health benefits mostly private but with public funds for low-income earners	Decentralized collective bargaining; weak capital/labour accord and becoming weaker; less than 15% private sector unionized; less than 30% of public sector workers unionized	Weak commitment to Keynesian redistributive and stabilizing principles; military R&D expenditures crucial to US industrial might
Western Europe	Universal social programmes and coverage; high levels of skill training; training compulsory and paid for by employers and public funds	Sector and centralized collective bargaining; strong national labour movements external to individual workplace; initially high levels of industrial unionism	Initially a strong Keynesian commitment to full employment with incomes policy and deepening domestic demand in many countries; gradual trade liberalization measure that do not imperil industrial policy or strategies

In time, all kinds of universal programmes became embedded in the culture of all Western industrialized countries. They were good for people and good for business. Governments of every stripe saw their utility. Social policy became a bi-partisan issue in every major industrial country. There were few exceptions to this general rule and the consensus arrived at guaranteed social peace. The promise to defend social welfare entitlements helped governments of the right to hold on to power and get themselves re-elected. For the socialist left, welfare rights were also a code word for an expanded concept of citizenship which ensured that people had work, that they could not be dismissed arbitrarily and that social inequality remained static rather than dynamic (Esping-Andersen 1990; Mazier *et al.* 1993).

For four decades, no political party on the right nor the left dared question the need for market-correcting social programmes to protect their citizens against unregulated markets. Today, that is no longer the case. Social democratic, liberal reform and centre governments are all intent on cutting benefits despite their electoral promises not to do so. Now even the strongest economies have succumbed to slow-growth monetarist practices. Governments want to cut their spending to the bone. Taxes on business have to be reduced in order to make the private sector more ready to invest in restructuring industries. Consumers are promised cheaper goods while the unemployed are guaranteed new jobs once a recovery begins. So far, the promises have remained just that – only promises. Some have called this policy betrayal, the 'social Munich' of our times (Julien 1993b). In a world where the rules of the global economy are being redefined and state policy transformed, governments have to decide whether the new state forms constitute an optimal choice with respect to two critical challenges.

TWO POLICY CHALLENGES

The first challenge comes from trade-led development itself. In a world where the rules of international trade are being redefined, countries have to look carefully at the design of their commercial policy. It is not good enough for a government to subscribe uncritically to the dictates of free trade that require it to open its markets regardless of costs and consequences. Rather, it should not give more than it is getting from the globally driven system. It has to have the option to protect itself when the negative effects of trade-led development threaten its national interest. In the past, countries often resorted to beggar-thy-neighbour policies when things went wrong and the international economy failed to live up to its promise to provide jobs through exports. Today, a return to traditional protectionism is not on the cards for any country. Thus, all states require an alternative. They need to have strong policy instruments that will let them plan and finance their strategic goals including job creation, science and technology policy, R&D, environmental policy, affirmative action programmes and the like. This re-tooling of state regulatory policy does not require governments to choose between free trade or protectionism, but between the diminishing prospects for free trade and expanding the conditions for managed trade. In the words of Robert Kuttner, protection-like industrial policies can be either 'a refuge to shelter losers' or the most effective way to incubate new industries (Kuttner 1984: 93). Countries can react to globalization in its most extreme form by joining a trade bloc or by reducing their exposure to global forces by strengthening the instruments of state policy.

The advantage of the second option is that if a country is intent on competing smarter, it has to strengthen the link between investment, jobs and productivity, growth. This is the only avenue that leads to higher levels of welfare. With firms being less state-bound than ever, countries have to find ways to ensure that the best business practice of leading firms benefit their respective national economies. They have to take measures that require that firms invest in new production facilities, skill-training of their employees and critical kinds of science and technology initiatives. The question is what kinds of policy instruments do governments need so that this option does not become a missed opportunity. This is the crucial challenge now facing all countries.

The second challenge is that a world order posited on trade liberalization has no proactive role for the nation-state in shaping its economic future. Rather, the new rules of the game are premised on a single-minded belief in comparative advantage – that is, specializing in those activities which give a country a leg-up on the competition. The way this is supposed to happen is that the home country's environment creates a pattern of country-based advantages or disadvantages that, independent of any industrial strategy, shape its trade outcomes in global markets. Over time, a country may face higher costs or a profit squeeze when markets contract. When this happens, it has to shift gears and develop a new expertise thanks to a competitive selection process determined largely by market forces rather than state policy.

Where this theory is flawed is that countries respond differently to these competitive pressures. Distinct national systems are able to redefine the rules of the game by responding to, in Laura Tyson's words, 'different incentive environments' (Tyson 1992). The evidence is overwhelming that divergence in regulatory institutions, antitrust laws and their enforcement, in patent procedures and in industrial relations practices play an important role in shaping national markets. Research suggests that those who do best in the global arena are ones which manage change and use their institutional arrangements to protect their national economies from international disorder. The strategic issue is what kind of measures do countries need to transform a state comparative advantage into a dynamic one?

This chapter will explore the new neo-liberal state forms and practices to address both these challenges. The inspiration for many of the changes now restructuring the welfare state comes from Margaret Thatcher's view of social policy, the monetarist ideas of the Nobel-winning economist Milton Fried-man and the industrial relations practices of the US giant retailer K-Mart. These are 'ideal' types and have to be understood as such. The individual response of countries to the emerging global order has to be examined on a case-by-case basis since the political culture, institutions and the resulting capital–labour entente differs markedly in each national setting. What is not in doubt is that a new state order is in the offing with its own dynamic and a completely different conception of markets and social relations. In the post-war world, the state structure of government rested on three identifiable principles: a Beveridge-inspired social policy, a Keynesian-based macro-economic management approach and a Fordist model of employment rela-tions (Boyer 1991; Drache and Gertler 1991). As we will see, the new pillars of the modern state are strikingly different from its Keynesian antecedents. For purposes of simplicity and brevity, I prefer to use the term 'the K-Mart' state, emblematic of the new work world of the casual, part-time low-wage, non-unionized service sectors of the economy. Analysing the policy founda-tion of the emerging K-Mart state is the principal focus of the first part of the chapter. Alternative kinds of institutional strategies are examined in the final section.

GLOBALIZATION: THE EYE OF THE HURRICANE

The growth of the global trading system is redefining state norms and practices everywhere and represents a threat to the way national economies are constructed. With the internationalization of production and increased capital mobility, states face a double challenge. Traditional economics holds that a country's ability to do well in international markets is determined by its comparative advantage. The idea is that through specialization, industries develop expertise in mass producing a select number of products. This enables them to gain a price and market advantage in those industries that make the most intensive use of the productive factors they have in abundance. So, if a country has a significant amount of low-cost labour it would export labour-intensive products; if it has a rich endowment of natural resources it would export resource-intensive products.

This traditional explanation to define a country's national competitive advantage makes less and less sense when a country's leading firms are able to source raw materials in one country, buy their equipment and machinery in another, arrange their financing wherever interest rates are lowest and sell their finished products in a fourth. Thus, firms are less dependent than ever on the endowment factors in their home nation. If the home market seems less important than ever for many corporations, it is. Business sees new value in the importance of regions, industrial districts and world cities as the nodal point for major investment and production decisions. Even so, countries still matter because the region or the world city is an integral part of the national economy. If these sub-national levels of economic life are expected to flourish, then countries have to find ways to transform a static comparative advantage into a dynamic performance.

In the past, governments believed that upgrading trade opportunities occurred through the proactive measures of the state and in response to market pressures. States regarded the pursuit of export opportunities as a way to increase the strength of their domestic economies and to support higher wage levels. A well-managed economy stood a fair chance in making gains in foreign markets provided that it had a core group of national champions. This is no longer so. With so many plant closings and layoffs across North America and throughout Europe, the industrial landscape of every country looks more and more like a war zone. Since 1990, Europe has experienced five years of rising unemployment. In North America, the picture is equally grim with no end in sight to the jobless crisis. It is estimated that there are more than 35 million people either unemployed or underemployed in the industrial world (OECD 1993a). The OECD forecasts that the European jobless rate will rise to 11.5 per cent in 1995, when more than 22 million will be officially out of work (OECD 1993b). The employment outlook is bleak compared to 1991 when more than 16.5 million Europeans were unemployed.[2]

The frenetic restructuring of industry is the principal reason behind these figures and, not surprisingly, the social costs are enormous. More and more, firms close down their production centres without regard to consequences. The justification given is that these corporate downsizings have some planned rationale. But they do not. According to the latest survey of 400 top US executives conducted by the Gallup Organization most firms do not plan for the future.[3] Only 1 per cent of the firms surveyed had created a special team or department responsible for charting the company's way in the future. The most revealing finding from the interviews of these top executives is that they cut jobs even when costs were not their main problem.

If this survey is to be believed, certainly the corporate world is not prepared for the global economy. Only 27 per cent said that the new competitiveness caused them to alter their business practices and plan for the future. Another 12 per cent cited changing markets as a reason to adopt new business practices. The most revealing finding was that new technology was the least important incentive to modify corporate practice.

Even though many firms extol the virtues of globalization, the same survey found that 82 per cent of management said that it had a vested interest in the status quo. What they feared more than anything was economic change. It had to be resisted because in many corporations executives feared it meant loss of managerial control. In the words of one of the consulting companies that is in the business of helping companies adapt to the new global circumstances, the bottom line is that most corporations 'don't know what the hell they're doing about managing change'.[4] They do not understand the way the world economy functions.

Despite this, world trade negotiations continue to be premised (Figure 1.1) on the idea that global free trade for all will be a milestone for international commerce. In practice, the system of global trade bears little resemblance to this often believed ideal. The neo-liberal vision is significantly at odds with the way companies do business:

- Approximately 25 per cent takes place inside global companies. This is called intra-company trade and not subject to arm's-length market transactions.
- Another 25 per cent is bilateral trade organized by preferential trade agreements such as found in the European Community and the North American Free Trade Agreement.
- Yet another 25 per cent is barter trade where goods and services are exchanged against other goods and services rather than money. A country rich in resources but poor in manufacturing will sell a fixed amount of wheat or zinc, for example, for a turn-key factory or major machinery and equipment.
- Finally, at most only 25 per cent can be considered free trade governed by GATT-rules. Even here, there are many exceptions. Services, textiles and agriculture are not subject to GATT, but are regulated by special side agreements or not at all.

(Ruigrok 1991)

The recently concluded Uruguay Round is an attempt to enlarge GATT's control over the world economy. Even so, after more than forty years of liberalized trade, experts agree that only one-quarter of global trade is considered to conform to the precepts of trade liberalization. With so little of the international economy marching to the precepts and principles of the free-trade drummer, what is left of the theory of free trade that supposedly provided the theoretical foundation of the post-war expansion of international trade? Since the logic of efficiency is only present in part of the trading order, there is much more space nationally and internationally for countries to respond to the new global pressures. How then should countries respond to global markets that take an ever-increasing share of their goods and services?

A NEW SYSTEM OF GOVERNANCE?

Faced with an increasingly dysfunctional global economy and the continued existence of hard-to-dismantle barriers to trade and commerce, the system of national governance needs renewal and reform. So far, this has not happened. Governments need new policy instruments to address the structural changes in the international economy. Any country which wants to have a higher standard of living has to enhance its productivity performance. It has to find ways to reorganize all the different parts comprising its production system:

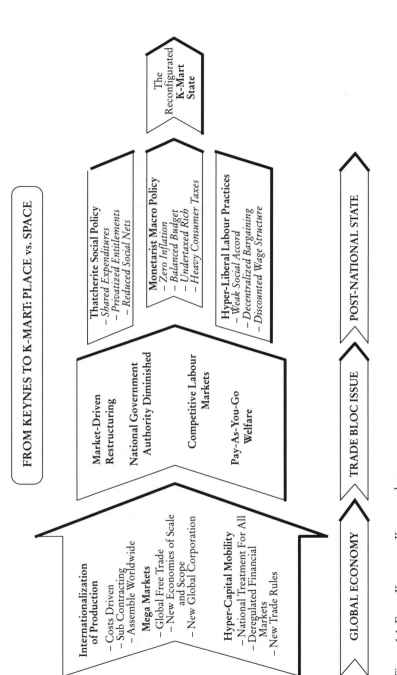

FROM KEYNES TO K-MART: PLACE vs. SPACE

Internationalization of Production
– Costs Driven
– Sub Contracting
– Assemble Worldwide

Mega Markets
– Global Free Trade
– New Economies of Scale and Scope
– New Global Corporation

Hyper-Capital Mobility
– National Treatment For All
– Deregulated Financial Markets
– New Trade Rules

Market-Driven Restructuring

National Government Authority Diminished

Competitive Labour Markets

Pay-As-You-Go Welfare

Thatcherite Social Policy
– *Shared Expenditures*
– *Privatized Entitlements*
– *Reduced Social Nets*

Monetarist Macro Policy
– *Zero Inflation*
– *Balanced Budget*
– *Undertaxed Rich*
– *Heavy Consumer Taxes*

Hyper-Liberal Labour Practices
– *Weak Social Accord*
– *Decentralized Bargaining*
– *Discounted Wage Structure*

The Reconfigurated **K-Mart State**

GLOBAL ECONOMY   TRADE BLOC ISSUE   POST-NATIONAL STATE

Figure 1.1 From Keynes to K-mart: place vs. space

the organizations, the plants, the management culture, the equipment and the people on the shop floor to the chief executive that produce the goods and deliver them to the customer (Dertouzos *et al.* 1989: 3).

All of this is a tall order because a country's productive performance cannot be solved without change in the macro-environment that is largely determined by the level of private and public investment. Interest rates, exchange rates and tax laws are critical to a better performance, but these key factors are never enough. Some firms will always do well but the key question is to find the most effective way to cure the organizational deficiencies that prevent all of a country's industries from doing better. Many economists believe that the central issue is to find ways to change existing investment practices. If these change, then firms stand a chance to take advantage of new opportunities and redeploy human and capital resources. If they do not, they are likely to be burned at the stake of international competition.

Already the new international order has had marked consequences on people and governments (Drucker 1986). First, the post-industrial corporation is producing more goods than ever with fewer people on its payroll. Countries, too, are producing more goods than ever with fewer workers employed in industry. What is radically different is that the number of jobs in the industrial side of the economy is shrinking in absolute terms. The number of unemployed continues to grow because private enterprise everywhere is cutting its workforce and producing more goods with fewer people. Since 1989, unemployment figures for the European Community have risen persistently. If discouraged workers are included, there are more than 50 million men and women belonging to an ever-increasing army of unemployed labour in the advanced industrial economies. The situation has become so grave that Jacques Delors, the former head of the European Community, has called upon the Commission to reduce mass unemployment which is now 'paralysing European societies'. The Commission has set a target of creating 20 million new jobs by the end of the decade (*Financial Times* (London), 27 October 1993).

Second, the nature of trade has changed. Total world trade in commodities and services totalled $3 trillion in the mid-1980s. By contrast, foreign exchange transactions, capital movements and credit flows dwarf the conventional forms of commerce. Foreign exchange transactions in which one currency is traded against another run at about $1 trillion a day. No wonder that the real economy comprised of goods and resources of all kinds and the symbol economy composed of investment flows and currency speculation seem to be operating independently of each other. The explosion of international financial markets invites currency speculation and other kinds of speculative activities on a scale never before possible.[5]

With corporations more footloose than ever, states have less power to manage their own economic affairs. With the accumulation process no longer state-centred, the global economy leads more and more and the national

Table 1.2 The 'social' redefined

Defining norm	Trade competitive welfare	Post-Fordist welfare	Keynesian social democratic welfare
Degree of universal coverage	Targeted and means-tested programmes	Eroding; no new initiatives	Targeted and universal programmes; asymmetrical needs recognized
Financial instrument	Individual and employer. Tied to labour market participation	Increasingly individual. Employer contributions reduced	Employer and state. Goal mobility-enhancing
Social wage	Diminishing. Individual pays larger share of health and retirement benefits; education; users' fees. Welfare linked to export performance	Smaller. High employment society. Individuals to work longer and at a variety of jobs	Stable. Guaranteed annual income; social wage linked to industrial policy. Welfare tied to productivity growth regime
Redistributive norm	Minimal. Taxation base predominantly personal. Guaranteed annual income for bottom 20%	Moderate. Growing inequality; rising unemployment offset by multiple family income	Redistributive tax system
Trade Union coverage	Low to medium	Low to medium	Medium to high; broad-based
Skill training	Largely private sector; extensive state subsidies to employers; multi-tasking	Low to medium national priority. Flexibility-driven agenda	Multi-skilling; income security while retraining

economy follows. The results, however, are far from what the rhetoric of unleashing the market promises (Table 1.2).

Employment prospects: the old and new orders compared

In the past, trade was perceived as an employment-enhancing activity (Boyer 1994). The very essence and rationale of the Fordist system of mass production was to generate new employment possibilities through enhanced exports. All governments recognized the potential that resulted from expanded production runs and increased output provided by these export opportunities. Critically, this strategy was seen by workers and unions to be employment-friendly so long as regularized collective bargaining in core industries effectively took wages out of competition. Wages were thus to be

41

set by the bargaining cycle and not by competitive labour markets (Mazier *et al.* 1993).

This system gained widespread acceptance because employers in the strategically important smokestack industries understood the rules of the game: competitiveness was compatible with higher wage levels provided that productivity kept pace with wage pressures. From the 1950s to the mid-1970s in almost every industrial country, real wages rose as exports grew. This is no longer the case.

Now the drive for flexibility requires smaller workforces, fewer workplace rules, weaker unions and wages that are tied to the global business cycle (OECD 1993a). Wages which were once 'sticky' upwards are being put back into competition. Governments want to make labour markets more competitive and, as well, remove hard-won collective bargaining rights. These measures have already had an impact on wage levels and collective bargaining outcomes. For a decade, wage growth has been on hold or negative throughout the industrialized world (Boyer 1994).

Industrial strategy: major changes here also

On the commercial front, the drive behind Cold War trade liberalization did not require countries to give up national power to participate internationally. All it demanded was that countries gradually open their economies and slowly dismantle their tariff barriers. Since the process was slow, countries could adapt gradually to the new rules of the game. And, since there was no airtight legal definition of a subsidy, Western countries discerned no inconsistency between their state-ordered industrial policy and their market-driven trade policy (Schott 1991). This compromise allowed nation-states everywhere to flourish, flex their muscles when they had to and protect their citizens from the global business cycle. The genius of this policy mix was that nations could safeguard their economic integrity without fear of losing control of the economic levers of power.

Now these old rules of the game have been discarded. Instead the pressure is to pit one nation's industries against another's in head-to-head confrontation. The fall-out from this practice has undermined existing living standards. Inequality is on the rise as the better paying full-time jobs are being lost in record numbers as the organization of work and the terms and conditions of employment are being radically redefined (Betcherman 1992). Labour standards and the existing wage levels, once tied to a collective bargaining mechanism in the mass production industries, are now set more and more by competitive global pressures. The result is that there are far fewer people in the middle income ranks; many more at the bottom end with smaller incomes than ever; and far fewer at the top end of the wage pyramid (Betcherman 1992). The deterioration in family incomes as well as the decline in the pay packet of the average wage earner has forced the European

Community to increase dramatically its aid to industrially depressed regions. In the past, the bulk of these funds went to Spain, Portugal, Italy and Greece. Now the UK and France are bidding for a very large slice of the assistance fund. The UK wants funding to cover 40 per cent of the British population, while France wants coverage for one-third of its inhabitants (*Financial Times* (London), 17 December 1993).[6]

Social policy on the table

Faced with a growing distributional crisis, governments everywhere do not see any way to reconcile the demands by footloose business to put the economy on a competitive footing with the need to preserve their existing social programmes such as health, education and retirement – as well as income-protection schemes – without means testing. The Beveridge kind of universally based social policy ensured social stability in countries with large industrial working classes. The extension of economic citizenship went hand in hand with the belief that the primary task of government was to deepen domestic demand by supporting a high wage economy in core industries, creating corporate champions in leading sectors and relying on an industrial strategy to do well in foreign markets. Now these basic assumptions of public policy are being challenged by commercially inspired arrangements such as trade blocs. A radically down-sized nation-state structure is the hope of business everywhere. These new market forces require other far-reaching changes in the instruments of governance (Albert 1991). If present trends continue, what are those founding principles?

A THATCHERITE POLICY FOR ALL

The old policy commitment to full employment inspired by Keynes and Beveridge has been abandoned and a totally new concept of 'high employment' is now the accepted norm of the political élites throughout advanced industrial economies (Emerson 1988). What the concept means, in effect, is that people will have to work longer and harder without the protection of existing social security nets, pension and retirement benefits.

The push to dismantle existing social programmes comes from business which believes that it must change its cost structure to compete internationally. The message of the manager of Phillips International labour relations in a recent seminar put the case with brutal frankness, arguing that Europeans 'have lived above our means too long. High wage and non-wage costs ... drive European industry to relocate in areas such as eastern Europe and China where costs were around a tenth or lower.' What business wants, she said, was 'a very high amount of flexibility' on jobs, employer contributions, social security premiums and the like. The bottom line is that business can no longer afford to pay its current share of social programmes (*Financial Times*, 10 September

1993). Universal social programmes are increasingly stigmatized as being outdated and obsolete in the fast-changing world of the 1990s.[7]

In this Thatcherite world, the wealthy will be given the choice of opting out of welfare benefits. By relinquishing their entitlements to certain publically provided services, they will receive a tax rebate. The state will benefit because the public costs of providing pensions, education and health benefits will fall as many middle-class professionals choose to opt-out. It is unlikely that many states will accept such a radical dismantling of welfare programmes. But the driving principle behind this proposal is one which many governments now openly entertain. Wherever possible, social benefits will become increasingly individually secured rather than universally guaranteed.[8]

Welfare reform is now a priority for most governments. The goal behind the reform is not in doubt. People who are on welfare have to get off it. Conservatives favour the concept of a strict time limit for welfare support. If benefits are not to be paid indefinitely, the argument goes, the individual will be forced to free him or herself from the vicious cycle of welfare dependency. By removing the social net, individuals will be forced to take responsibility for themselves. Many find this kind of social policy thrust unacceptable. Instead, much more stress is put on the idea of making people 'employable'. People who can work will have to do so. The alternative to the outright ending of social welfare is to require those on welfare to take jobs at the minimum wage or just below it. The welfare state will be replaced by the 'work ethic state'. The Clinton Administration has already set targets for the gradual introduction of workfare. States will only receive federal assistance if at least 15 per cent of the 'employable' welfare case load is working. By 1995, the required ratio rose to 20 per cent (Prowse, *Financial Times* (London), 31 August 1993).

The working premise of these and other reform-minded proposals is that all individuals will have to look after their own welfare as much as possible. For those with regular employment prospects, access to education, medical services, job training, unemployment benefits, all of which were once protected with the status of an entitlement, will no longer have that standing that put them beyond the reach of the market and greedy employers. Now business wants to provide a vast array of these services to the public at a profit. Homecare, healthcare, day care, care for the disabled, skill-training, reskilling, technical training are perceived not only as a business opportunity for the burgeoning service economy, but something very different indeed. More and more governments now accept the idea that the delivery of these services is a business right and entitlement.[9]

In this dramatic sea change, what is being lost is any viable notion of social responsibility – the institutional capacity for the achievement of a more equitable society. Those who want training have to pay for it. Those who want a better education will have to finance it. Those who want daycare will have to ante up. Those who receive welfare will have to accept workfare. What else is different is that society will no longer pay for these entitlements through taxes. As governments tax the corporations less, governments have less money to spend overall and on social policy. Should this trend continue, it is the end of social welfare programmes as we have known them.

A NEW CAPITAL–LABOUR ACCORD

Work and employment norms are also at the eye of this storm. The feminization of the labour market is the most dramatic visible evidence of the gender revolution that has marked this new work world. Throughout much of the economy, firms now rely on non-standard female workers. Work without job security has become the norm for the young and the old. Jobs are no longer full-time, but part-time, casual and contractual (Drache 1992). With working time reorganized, the pay structure is being revised downward. The better-paying good jobs have disappeared in record numbers as companies have downsized and laid off workers in the hundreds of thousands in North America and Europe. The new jobs are for the most part at the low-end of the pay scale (Economic Council of Canada 1990).

Union representation has also suffered a dramatic reversal of fortune everywhere. The shift from goods production to the service industries has encouraged employers to de-unionize the workplace whenever the opportunity presents itself. The unionized workplace of the Fordist variety has been overtaken by the aggressively non-unionized work world of K-Mart, named appropriately after the large US discount consumer outlet chain. Its practices are emblematic of the new capital–labour accord now taking shape. Management's rights have been strengthened, work rules tightened, job security reduced and wages hover as close as possible to the minimum set by law. In such an environment unions are not welcome. With the huge resources of business and employer-friendly governments, the changes of any successful unionization drive are slight even when protected by law. In addition, the most dramatic change is in the way working time has been reorganized, particularly for those in the service sector where the majority of jobs are to be found. Working time is becoming more skewed as part-time work becomes the norm. Part-time employment in Canada, for instance, is three times more common in this sector than in the goods economy (Economic Council of Canada 1990). The Canadian situation is by no means unique. Throughout Western economies, more people are working longer hours than ever and for less pay (Julien 1993a).

In terms of the future of industrial relations practices, much else has also changed. To ensure highly competitive labour markets, governments are finding ways to remove much of the institutional protection accorded to unions in the past. On both sides of the Atlantic, organized labour in the public sector is being required to enter into social contracts with the express aim of reducing pension, retirement, vacation and other pay-related benefits.

A shorter working week is seen as a principal way to offer work to the unemployed, but it is also being used by employers to reduce wages. Measures like these will weaken further industrial unions already battered by declining memberships. The long-term goal behind these kinds of ad hoc measures is to reduce state reliance on collective bargaining as the principal wage-setting mechanism for the economy (Standing 1992). Wages which were once protected from international competitive pressures by regularized collective bargaining agreements now are to fluctuate with the business cycle and more closely reflect international price movements. In particular, the upward pressure on wages much in evidence for the Cold War era has been reversed. There is now an equally strong, downward pressure on the wage structure in most countries as governments open their borders to new competitive pressures, regardless of the immediate consequences that these measures have on dampening consumers' spending patterns.

In many employment settings, the long-run consequences of the return to a competitive wage-setting mechanism for society are already evident. Wage growth has remained stagnant for the better part of a decade in most industrial countries, but the real measure of the way real labour income has been affected can be seen in one statistic. Income inequality is on the rise as the middle-class income pyramid has toppled. The figures of the increase in income disparity for the greater metropolitan Toronto area are not unique by any means but are typical of the kind of reordering which is now underway throughout the industrial world (Yalnizyan 1993).

For Toronto, the average income of families in the top 10 per cent grew throughout the 1980s. In 1991 it was $124,000 and the richest saw a 7 per cent increase in their market income in the second half of the 1980s. The contrast with the bottom 10 per cent was marked. They saw a 47 per cent decline in their share of market income. The average *market* income for these families was $3,422 a year and, despite living in the heartland of Canada, it is harder than ever for them to stay afloat through their own efforts. By 1993, one family in five had been forced to rely on some form of income support in metropolitan Toronto. The deterioration of living standards has been harsh for many. Just how sharp the decline has been is captured by a single statistic. In 1973, only 8.5 per cent were similiarly dependent compared with recent times. Yalnizyan concludes that the 'proliferation of precarious jobs [is] creating a colony of the excluded, a society of insiders and outsiders' (Yalnizyan 1993: 3).

The finding that the decline in full-time work has triggered a dramatic income shift in its wake is tied to equally far-reaching practices that are redefining the terms of employment for many new entrants into the labour market. Just how major a change can be seen from the fact that the recession has accelerated the trend to create mainly part-time work as the principal kind of new employment opportunity. Business is looking to hire fewer full-time people than ever. In the second half of 1993, Statistics Canada found that there had been no new full-time jobs created in the past five and a half years. Over the same period, the number of part-time jobs has grown by 320,000 to 2.15 million, or an increase of more than 17 per cent (*Globe & Mail*, 19 July 1993). Following the 1982 recession, full-time and part-time jobs continued to grow at an equal rate. This is unlikely to be the case in the 1990s. Banks and governments, the last two havens of full-time employment, are trimming their workforces and cutting back their full-time positions. If present trends hold, full-time work will be scarcer than ever for the rest of the 1990s. The flow-through effects are already visible. The income structure of society is being downgraded to fit the new work and employment conditions.

A MONETARIST STATE?

Finally, what of state macroeconomic strategy itself? Here the surgery is most pronounced. Governments weaned on Keynesian principles must radically redefine the first principles of responsible macroeconomic management. For monetarists, with capital free to roam the world, a new orthodoxy is in the making. Full employment is no longer the basic goal of government, but creating an environment for inflation-free money is the task that imposes itself on all industrial nations.

The compelling logic behind monetarism is real enough. The real value of goods, services and income needs to be permanently aligned and protected against the discretionary effects of Keynesian debt borrowing practices. If inflation declines, output and the economy can recover provided that monetary targets hold. The problem is that high interest rates necessary to achieve zero-inflation targets hinder growth and, for governments who are committed to a recovery, this new orthodoxy is fraught with risk. For public policy-makers, the principal difficulty is that it is next to impossible to decide what is a sustainable debt level when unemployment is so high. There is no objective criteria to decide whether a 3 per cent deficit measured against GDP is excessive, too low or about right for any given country. Setting an artificially arrived at target to reduce debt levels has proved next to impossible to achieve. So, in a world where national economies are linked increasingly through financial markets, the framing of policy has had to be broadened.

For industrial countries, the main innovation in the 1990s has been to establish formal or informal currency and interest rate targets with the monetary authority of a country's principal trading partner. This is the principal purpose of a trade bloc – namely, to impose cross-border discipline on participating governments. The 'soft' currency of the smaller country has to be pegged to the 'hard' money of the major trading power. This explains why the European Union increasingly functions as a Deutschmark bloc under the control of the Bundesbank and the US dollar is the reserve currency of NAFTA managed by the US Federal Board of Reserve.

These and other developments underscore a basic point: the new financial order is highly structured and asymmetrically organized requiring a rigid set of controls if deflationary goals are to be met. In practice, making good on the promise of inflation-free money has meant that every government not only has to win the approval of the international money markets but keep it. In practical terms, governments are pushed to cut spending because when deficits come down, they borrow at lower interest rates. This is the principal incentive to bring spending under control. What the money brokers want to see is a 'subdued' inflation rate. If not, governments will face new pressures from the moneylenders to get their house in order. In the real world, the politics of monetary convergence has immense consequences for governments shaped in the Keynesian mould.

Under Keynesian macro-management, wealth creation was shared between the public and private with the state taking the long-term responsibility through public spending. The monetarist preoccupation with deficit reduction stems from a very special set of beliefs. Wealth creation is now regarded as the principal responsibility of the private sector. The drive to be competitive is a critical part of this process because it is firm or sector specific. The way these two aspects of macro-policy are linked is through the state. Taxes need to be cut so that business will be encouraged to invest and generate a recovery. For many corporations, the actual tax burden is not the issue. Rather, what counts much more is the signal sent to the private sector that lower taxes are in the offing. Price stability is made the number one goal because it provides the largest incentive to unleash the 'animal spirits' of private investors.

In the monetarist vision, the government's revenue structure also has to be re-examined. Traditionally, taxation revenues come from a blending of taxes on firms, businesses, corporations and individuals. What matters in this instance is the mix. Fair taxation is based on the principle of ability to pay. This meant that private corporations and wealthy individuals paid higher rates than those who had less taxable income.

In the new scheme of things, individuals have to pay more and corporations less. This has already happened in most industrialized countries. Governments have resorted to consumer taxes to fill their coffers. The predicament is that consumer-based taxes are not income-neutral but fall disproportionately on low- and middle-income earners. At the same time, governments have created new tax expenditures such as retired savings plans, registered pension plans, lifetime capital gains shelters, all of which are used by the wealthy as a means of tax avoidance. Because these measures reduce the effective rate of taxation on the well-off, the rich receive a privileged tax position compared to others. The upshot is that not only has there been a dramatic fall in tax rates for corporations as a percentage of government revenues (Brooks 1991; UN 1991) but also, in many jurisdictions, government revenues are falling faster than most public authorities can cut expenditures. The current crisis in Canada is perhaps typical of the broader picture. In the first seven months of 1993, government spending declined by 1.3

per cent, but revenues fell even faster, dropping by over 5.7 per cent
(*Globe & Mail*, 4 December 1993). In cases like this, governments find
themselves under even more pressure to downsize and cut their spending
even further.

The idea that deficits make countries internationally uncompetitive is a
radical departure from past practice. Running deficits created few problems
for governments when the real interest rates were 3 per cent. But, with money
now free to move across national boundaries, current real interest rates for
long-term government debt remain two and three times higher than their
average over the last decade (Wood Gundy 1993). Even though government
spending has been dramatically reduced in most countries, revenues from
taxes continue to fall faster than spending cuts. Spending restraint is not
enough. Debt charges continue to balloon even when governments are
committed to austerity. They are unable to make an appreciable dent into the
mountain of debt on the books. Faced with these conditions, it comes as no
surprise that the cost of borrowing and financing public debt continues to be
the single largest factor responsible for the huge deficits burdening the public
purse today. What is stymieing governments is their struggle to cope with the
rising tide of debt charges, falling tax revenues, high real rates of interest and
economies that have stopped growing.

With the rules governing global free trade being rewritten, the great trade
reformation has curbed the power of governments to manage their domestic
economies. Every sector and every aspect of society is now to be open to
competition. Governments are no longer committed to results-driven policies
that ensured a high degree of equity for people. Now they are rule-driven.
This means that once the rules are established market processes are supposed
to dominate. The new role for the state is to maintain a trade-friendly
environment and accept its obligations to open national markets regardless
of the adjustment costs. This is the underlying essence of free trade. In
Bhagwati's words, it is a covenant between governments and markets that
'the logic of efficiency has to determine the allocation of activity among all
trading nations' (Bhagwati 1988: 33).

REBUILDING THE LINK BETWEEN INVESTMENT AND PRODUCTION: SURVIVING THE GLOBAL ECONOMY IN THE 1990s

So far, no country has been able to adapt to the new competitive pressures
easily. The new world economy may or may not be as real as business claims
but the intense drive to globalize has changed the nature of competition and
rendered the sovereignty of nations more fragile than ever. National
economies were never closed systems. They were always permeable, and yet
they were able to control much of the economic activity within their
boundaries. By contrast, the new global order exposes more countries than

ever to the global business cycle with fewer policy buffers. Without these policy instruments, too many businesses are left to their own resources; workers lose their jobs without any hope of economic recovery; communities have no way to build sustainable industries.

If a country's industries are to survive, they need a better macroeconomic environment and matching investment practices to strengthen their industrial effectiveness. Firms that focus exclusively on wage costs have lost sight of the essential. The concept of 'investment' includes much more than business spending for plant and equipment however important that component is. In the words of the influential MIT study, 'investment is any use of current resources for the purpose of achieving a future return' (Dertouzos et al. 1989: 33). Investment not only includes new plant and better machinery but, also, the use of public resources to improve roads, harbours, schools, healthcare and the like. Expenditures on training are an investment in the future as are public day-care centres. So also is all spending connected with research and development whether carried out in universities, business or government laboratories. Basic research which is clearly future-oriented is one of the best investments that any country can make.

But a top-down perspective on the economy is hardly sufficient to understand how firms interact with customers, develop a new relationship with their employees or uncover new opportunities. There are many non-economic factors which have a more pervasive impact on determining whether or not a firm is able to do better economically and address its organizational and attitudinal deficiencies. For this to happen a purely macroeconomic approach is inadequate. Different outcomes are only possible when deeply rooted organizational structures of the corporation and its social attitudes adapt to new conditions. Only then, when the institutional fabric of society evolves, are new outcomes possible. How then can the link between investment and productivity be strengthened?

All states have to choose a global strategy; they have to look at the full range of choices, then they have to decide what is in their best interest. In the new era of global competition, trade liberalization via the market remains the most dangerous choice of all. It demands that trade barriers of all kinds be dismantled. In particular, governments have to let international competitive pressures restructure industries without recourse to state aids or other protectionist measures. This requires countries to open their borders regardless of the costs and consequences on industries and vulnerable workers. Markets are seen to be a self-organizing social and economic space responding to universal price and demand signals.

For countries everywhere who accept this liberal view of the world economy, state power to make policy independent of a country's major trading partner is being progressively eroded as countries find themselves trapped in a seamless web of interdependency. Larger markets do not come without a cost. When money, technology, factories, and equipment move, in

Robert Reich's evocative words, 'effortlessly across borders', the idea of a Canadian economy, a Canadian product or a Canadian corporation becomes meaningless. When companies become so disconnected from their home base, what happens to the national economy? How can it be expected to perform well when the profitability of its corporations no longer depends on the national economy for the best investment opportunities. In what sense will Canada be a society when it no longer has a national economy? The separation of economics from politics when globalization is such a pervasive force presents stark challenges for people everywhere.

Further, in the drive to be competitive, consumers face an impossible choice. They are being forced to choose between wanting cheaper goods and their social identity as producers and job-holders. For many people in different sectors of the economy, export-led growth now has become job-destructive rather than employment-positive.

Finally, the major issue confronting businesses is that they have to make strategic investment and production decisions that affect not only themselves but the community in which they operate. Companies have to decide what part of their 'home base' should remain domestically based, where they should conduct their research and development and where their strategic interests ultimately lie. With firms looking to produce where wages are lowest and government regulation minimal, companies are less and less bound by national considerations.

THE POST-NATIONAL STATE DEFINED

Countries which accept a neo-liberal commitment to all-out privatization and full regional integration will have fewer instruments to shape markets. This prospect raises the question: to what extent can a nation continue to be a society when it no longer has a strong national economy (Reich 1991)?

It used to be taken for granted that nations should be considered as communities of people which share responsibility for their mutual well-being. Yet, this is becoming less and less so. What defines the post-national nation-state are two characteristics: first, a weak national economy since the country's well-being is *externally* determined by its export and trade bloc performance; second, a substantial reduction in the ability of the state to engage in day-to-day *internal* economic management.

The more countries open their borders, the more their economies come to rely on global price movements to set social standards. This is the primary mechanism of market-driven integration. Since the 1960s, the percentage share of exports and imports of total GNP has increased in each succeeding decade for all industrialized countries (Sbragia 1992). If there is one measure of globalization which identifies the essential reason for the decline in nation-state power, none speaks more directly to this condition of interdependence than the growth of trade dependency.

For political economists, *trade dependency* can be defined as an ever-larger share of a country's economic prosperity that is determined by its export performance (see Table 1.3). It is usually measured as the percentage of exports in its gross domestic product. *Trade openness* is a more comprehensive measure of the kind of production and employment adjustments that a country faces when it opens its borders to global pressures (see Table 1.4). It is defined as the combined weight of tradables – imports and exports – in a country's economy. Both these measures are the transmission belt tying the national economy to the global, and cause the power and influence of nation-states to wane everywhere.

Over 50 per cent of GNP of most industrial countries is now directly affected by international movements of price and demand. Only the US is the exception to this general rule. It is better protected from the downswings of interdependency than any other industrial country and can more easily afford a new dosage of free trade. A third measure yields an even broader picture of the magnitude of adjustment a country encounters from the further internationalization of production and commerce. Trade dependence can be estimated as the amount of products now made at home but which could be imported in the future (Mellis 1992). A purely competitive economy with no restrictions and no protection could conceivably be the target goal for all countries. In a recent study of Japan, McKinsey Consultants found that only 13 per cent of Japan's economy was competitive. If all protectionist measures were removed and the consumer could choose to buy products from wherever, it calculated that Japan's rate of unemployment would soar from 2.5 per cent to over 40 per cent.[10] From a policy perspective, no government can embrace this hyper-liberal nineteenth-century view of markets. There are strict social limits to trade-led growth which even the most ardent supporters of the new competitive circumstances cannot publicly advocate.

None the less, guaranteeing such 'openness' is the root idea behind such instruments as NAFTA or the EEC. These new framework agreements go far beyond the provisions found in the GATT codes on the Liberalization of

Table 1.3 Trade dependence of core industrial economies (exports as a percentage of GDP)

Country	1960	1972	1985	1990
Canada	17.2	22.0	28.4	29.2
United States	5.2	5.8	7.1	10.5
Japan	10.7	10.6	14.6	18.1
West Germany	19.0	20.9	32.4	39.7
France	14.5	16.7	23.9	25.2
Italy	13.0	17.7	22.8	23.8
United Kingdom	20.9	21.8	29.1	29.4
Spain	10.2	14.6	20.1	19.6
Portugal	17.3	27.2	37.3	47.3

Source: OECD National Accounts, vol. 1: main aggregates 1960–88, Paris, 1990

Table 1.4 Trade openness of core industrial economies (exports plus imports as a percentage of GDP)

Country	1960	1972	1985	1990
Canada	33.0	44.4	52.3	60.4
United States	8.5	11.9	17.8	22.0
Japan	14.7	21.2	28.7	36.5
West Germany	28.1	43.1	66.2	76.3
France	22.6	36.3	45.1	52.6
Italy	22.5	42.1	43.6	51.0
United Kingdom	42.9	53.0	56.3	62.6
Spain	14.7	29.9	36.1	45.1
Portugal	41.5	60.9	78.7	112.1

Source: OECD National Accounts, vol. 2: detailed table, Paris, 1979 and 1992

Capital Movements. The OECD code was basically a standstill agreement containing only a commitment to gradual liberalization measures (UN 1992: 38). The stated aim of NAFTA is to provide for the complete elimination of restrictions by all signatories. Governments will not be allowed to discriminate between national and foreign interests as was once the accepted practice. For middle-power countries such as Canada and Mexico, the new rules will diminish control over the management of their national economies in a variety of ways. Because many of the traditional levers of government will be subject to the external norms imposed by the trade agreement, these countries will not be able to subsidize regions or industries or mount strong national policies in the future (Hufbauer and Schott 1992). With policy being made more and more by bureaucratic fiat of one sort or another, the days of the nation-state do in fact seem numbered even if its sovereignty remains formally intact.

THE K-MART STATE RECONSIDERED:
SOME ALTERNATIVES

Trade blocs have become the primary means to redefine nations and states throughout the industrialized world. New supranational structures are emerging as modern societies adapt to the powerful competitive pressures unleashed by the new global economy. What, then, remains of national sovereignty?

Interdependency has long been a fact of life for all countries. Nations have little to fear from it. In the new era of global competition the threatening dimension is the growth in corporate power. The sovereignty of nations is in peril not on account of the international economy but because of the power of corporations to invest with less restriction, to reshape public policy in support of private wealth generation and, most of all, to appropriate the political culture of nations for corporate ends. The message is as clear as it is simple: national 'place' has to give way to commercial 'space'.

Despite this, an essential fact remains. The corporate age has failed to win public support to its cause. In a fundamental way, people and communities everywhere distrust corporate power. This was why Clinton had such difficulty in persuading the US Congress that NAFTA was a popular measure with the public. In Canada, public support for NAFTA, for instance, has fallen persistently. Close to 60 per cent of the Canadian public remain opposed to it even if it has just scraped through the US Congress. NAFTA remains a political millstone for the new Liberal government despite the fact that Chrétien was forced to bow to US pressures and sign the deal.

In Europe, popular backing for economic integration is also at an all-time low. The decline in support is tied to the deterioration in economic conditions within the Community. More and more countries find themselves on notice that national structures need reinforcing rather than weakening. This is why more and more states on both sides of the Atlantic have no alternative but to rely on national strategies to restructure their industries. The strategic issue is, can national power be somehow protected from world markets' incessant demand for freer movement of money, fewer barriers to information flows and easier access to goods?

Countries who think that powerful trends of internationalization and interdependence have eroded the basis of national sovereignty *tout court* are mistaken. Despite all the claims to the contrary, it is premature to announce the death of the nation-state. Countries still remain in charge of the essential part of their national sovereignty: law-making and jurisprudence; macro-economic policy, including money, finance and taxation. National governments are as much responsible today as ever for the environment, education, training, labour-market policy, industrial relations and economic restructuring; pensions, family law and well-being, health and safety; police and security; social policy, science and technology; transportation and communication; forestry, agriculture, fishing, mining and water. No supranational authority has yet been designed to replace a highly efficient system of national government. Today, more than ever, the tide of history is running against the emergence of any supranational authority. The collapse of the Soviet Union and the inability of the European Community to move forward with its far more modest goal of pooling sovereignty for a limited number of ends testify to this.

At this time, to construct a powerful supranational authority on the basis of the federal model is not realistic. Governments instinctively understand that this kind of governance can only produce policy incoherence rather than encouraging strong effective policies nationally or regionally. States know full well that a divided jurisdiction between state and national government is a perennial breeding ground for all kinds of jurisdictional conflicts. In a corporate age, this is also why business has such a vested interest in weakening national governments. Multinational business has long understood that the nation-state is the only counterweight to its global reach. The question for states everywhere is can they find a way to reinforce the sovereignty of nations and stop the global bulldozer in its tracks?

BUILDING COUNTERWEIGHTS: STRATEGIC GOALS FOR STATES AND NATIONS

In a post-national world, countries need to have *four* immediate priorities in order to promote a different basis for international activity.

First, governments have to regain control of their economies. There is no single way to achieve this critical goal, but without it hemispheric co-operation will remain little more than an empty rhetorical flourish. The first step is to find ways to transform NAFTA and the EU into viable instruments of development. As presently defined, they are not simply about trade but about wide-ranging economic integration on an unprecedented scale. Far from encouraging countries to co-operate, they force countries to compete even when it is not in their best interests. The first step to remedy this deficiency is to limit these giant market projects by taking critical policy areas such as the environment, health services, education, subsidies and regional programmes off the table (Julien 1993b). By making them more about trade and less about integration, countries will be able to broaden market access by realistic means rather than relying on artificial measures. If trade blocs cannot be transformed, they will have to be abandoned. Abrogation is an option that will make possible more viable and realistic forms of multilateral co-operation.

Second, the most important initiative any country can take is to put its own house in order. Economic globalization cannot succeed when national economic management is in disorder everywhere. A stable international regime requires strong national economies. If this *sine qua non* condition does not exist, countries have no option but to export their economic misery to their neighbours. This creates an international environment which is subject to further chaos and beggar-thy-neighbour policies (Strange 1988). Seen from this perspective, the narrow focus on export markets has become a destabilizing force for most advanced industrial countries and for the developing world as well. This has occurred for a critical reason.

Trade liberalization is a euphemism for waging economic warfare by the most powerful private actors in the world seeking increased market share. Success means knocking out the competition by any and all means possible, legal and illegal. The stakes are high because the transnationals with their deep pockets are better positioned to see their profits enhanced while smaller national and regional firms, more often than not, face bankruptcy and failure.

Foreign multinationals now control a larger part of the domestic market in every industrial country than at any time previously (United Nations 1992). This unbridled pursuit of export markets divides the local business community, drives a wedge between governments and peoples, and pits the competitive sectors of the economy against domestic and regional producers (Petrella 1989).

In a global economy where goods can be produced anywhere, supranational management demands much more planning, much more foresight and much more innovation to succeed. The de-industrialization of the workforce is a new development that has accelerated during the 1980s. Now, more than ever, countries need to rethink fundamentally the limits to new employment growth imposed by export-led growth strategies.

The challenge is to find effective measures that put employment creation rather than the restless pursuit of export markets at the centre of the public agenda. Governments everywhere want to promote a high-wage, high-quality and high-value-added economy. This requires harnessing trade to ensure that when industries restructure, good jobs are the result. Wages and employment structure have to be tied to productivity growth. This involves discouraging companies from competing on wages and low employment standards.

For most governments, a strategic trade policy rather than global free trade for all is the optimal choice. A strong trade performance depends on government investment in infrastructure, in skill-training and in economic restructuring. For these important reasons, state subsidies remain a dominant part of US economic policy despite all the talk to the contrary. The challenge is to find ways to promote transparency in the way subsidies are employed, but not at the expense of employment-creating possibilities or by hobbling governments from restructuring their economies.

Third, in an era of global competition, markets need the steadying hand of governments. Markets are complex structures that have to be shaped, moulded and regulated by national governments if they are to function in an efficient and effective manner. Countries that are committed to protecting their institutional networks and national practices against the volatility of the global business cycle will do well in the new global economy. They will safeguard the well-being of their people, their industries and their markets from the predatory pricing policies of footloose capital (Daly and Goodland 1992). By contrast, countries which go with the flow and adopt ideological responses to complex market conditions will have no capacity to counter the short-term needs of business interests. In the area of job creation they will be seriously handicapped because many industries cannot restructure on their own without government providing funds and/or retraining and reorganization. Germany, Japan and Sweden fall into the first category. Each of the forementioned has policies, programmes and the institutional muscle to shape markets and adapt to global pressures gradually with much less human cost. At the other end of the spectrum, Canada, the US, Britain, Australia and New

Zealand are mired in a cycle of industrial decline and crisis for the foreseeable future. They are handicapped because they have no means to redistribute the benefits from open markets nor have they the necessary programmes to restructure their industries strategically.

Finally, countries need to sit up and recognize that first-wave globalization is an essentially financially driven phenomenon that has changed forever the state-bounded accumulation process. Money is on the move as never before. Each day billions of dollars change hands. Financial markets span the globe in ways that few could have imagined even ten years ago. The IMF boasts that there are more than 100 stockmarkets in operation on all continents. The amount of investment capital in any one market may not be all that significant, but the principle is that finance capital is the new 'sun god', the new 'Versailles'. The separation of the money economy from the goods-producing economy has created a deep hiatus between the local and the global for an essential reason. Money is free to roam the globe looking for the brightest investment opportunities.

Yet, countries cannot afford to plan their future around the speculative needs of global capital. Strikingly, the organization of goods production in most smokestack industries remains largely local and regional. Companies can outsource; they can decentralize operations; they can relocate. But when all is said and done, even multinational giants have to put down roots and build strong ties with communities if they expect to excel (Ohmae 1990). On this simple point all experts agree: the home market is where the best jobs are, where the skilled workers have to be found and where quality production occurs.

For the moment, the cutting edge of globalization is largely economic due to two of its principal characteristics. New technologies of every description are enabling devices for business to produce where they want and with a cost structure that suits their corporate strategy. The internationalization of financial markets has given capital a licence to roam the world looking for investment havens (Spero 1988–9). It should not be forgotten that this era of interdependency has many other features. Dramatic advances in communications technologies support global information networks that enhance the right of people to knowledge and information. These new technologies have revolutionized the distribution of information and production of knowledge. The intense competition between multidirectional and one-way communications technologies will make possible other kinds of cultural change on an unprecedented scale. This too makes possible further political change (Postman 1992).

The compression of time and space has forced countries to rethink many of their national policies and to look for new ways to further international co-operation at the community level.[11] Global civil society is not a myth but an emerging reality. The rules of the game are not well-established but the demand to rein in global business creates a political dynamic of a different kind. These and other demands for equity and identity politics have other unintended consequences that will eventually establish limits on the movement of capital. Countries want both greater contact with each other and a more open world, but not at the price of losing control over their culture, their language and, above all, their future. Risk-reduction has become the name of the game as the only way to shore up the sovereignty of peoples. In this corporate age, even some of the giants of the business world are beginning to understand the dangers of being burned at the stake of unrestrained international competition. This may be a sign that the pendulum is beginning to swing back from right to left, but there are still too many storm clouds on the horizon to be naïvely optimistic that the worst is over.

NOTES

1 Another key feature of the 1990s is that the major international organizations responsible for world order such as GATT and the World Bank aggressively support the reorganization of transnational corporations worldwide.

2 At the time of economic union, the employment crisis in the Community was much worse than most realized. In November 1994, 15.2 per cent of people under 25 were out of work, with 28 per cent in Ireland, 30 per cent in Italy and 37 per cent in Spain. There is a very real risk of a 'social explosion' according to senior officials in Brussels. This danger is reflected in Delors' recent White Paper in which he recognizes that 40 million people are living in poverty in Europe. He wants the right to permanent re-training and education to be universal though he is equally adamant that the managerial right to hire and fire without restriction be strengthened.

3 The results were published in the *Toronto Star*, 13 September 1993.

4 Ibid.

5 In the past, when commodity prices were aligned to the price of industrial goods, developing countries were able to pay for manufactured goods with the revenues derived from the export of raw materials. This is no longer the case and the implications are far-reaching. What it means is that the developing countries lack hard currency to buy machinery, machine parts and essential consumer goods. Without hard currency their development slows to a snail's pace. The collapse of commodity prices has forced countries like Mexico, Brazil and Argentina to raise funds by selling off state enterprises to repay the loans they borrowed from Western banks in the 1980s. As their hard currency revenue base has contracted, governments have looked to foreign investment flows to be the locomotive of their economic development.

6 The deterioration of living standards forced the EU to revise its structural aid to industries in industrially depressed regions. Eligibility for Objective 2 aid requires an unemployment rate higher than the EU average, a higher percentage of industrial employment than the EC and a decline specifically in industrial employment.

7 Typical of this genre is the new study from the National Forum on Family Security, *Family Security in Insecure Times*; the National Forum is a Canadian-based group of social activists. Even though many of the group are not against universal social programmes, it made front-page headlines by charging Canada's social programmes as being out of date (*Globe & Mail*, 17 November 1993).

8 See Dennis J. Snower's commentary, 'Opting Out From the Welfare State', *Financial Times*, London, 20 October 1993.
9 The privatization of services has proceeded furthest in the US compared to Western European countries. One of the effects of the Uruguay GATT-round talks will be to 'liberalize' the delivery of social services by private corporations. This will make it easier than ever for governments to let business provide these critical social services.
10 Kenichi Ohmae, address to the Japan Society, Toronto, 2 December 1993.
11 The work on global markets and the impact of communications systems of Canada's pioneering political economist Harold Innis is particularly relevant in this regard. The centenary of his birth occurred in 1994 and this afforded the occasion to examine his contribution to a theory of the global order and disorder. See the new edition of his collected essays, Daniel Drache (ed.), *Staples, Markets and Cultural Change*, Montreal: McGill–Queen's University Press, 1995.

BIBLIOGRAPHY

Albert, M. 1991. *Capitalisme Contre Capitalisme*. Paris: Seuil.
Armstrong, P., Andrew Glwyn and John Harrison. 1991. *Capitalism Since 1945*. London: Blackwell.
Betcherman, G. 1992. 'The Disappearing Middle', in D. Drache (ed.), *Getting on Track*. Montreal: McGill–Queen's University Press.
Bhagwati, J. 1988. *Protectionism*. Boston: MIT Press.
Bhagwati, J. and Hugh T. Patrick. 1990. *Aggressive Unilateralism: America's 301 Trade Policy and the World Trading System*. Ann Arbor: University of Michigan Press.
Bowles, S., David Gordon and Tom Weisskopf. 1983. *Beyond the Waste Land*. New York: Pantheon.
Boyer, R. 1987. 'Labour Flexibilities: Many Forms, Uncertain Effects.' *Labour and Society* 12: 1.
Boyer, R. 1991. *Markets Within Alternative Co-ordinating Mechanisms: History, Theory and Policy in the Light of the Nineties*. The Comparative Governance of Sectors Project, Bigorio, Switzerland.
Boyer, R. 1994. 'New Directions in Management Practices and Work Organisation: General Principles and National Trajectories', Working Paper CEPREMAP 9130, August, Paris.
Brittan, Samuel. 1988. *A Restatement of Economic Liberalism*. Atlantic Highlands, N.J.: Humanities Press International.
Brooks, Neil. 1991. 'The Changing Structure of the Canadian Tax System: Accommodating the Rich', Unpublished paper, presented at Toward the 21st Century: Canadian/Australian Legal Perspectives, Osgoode Hall Law School, York University, North York, Canada, June.
Cappelletti, M., M. Secombe and J. Weiler. 1986. *Integration Through Law: Europe and the American Federal Experience*. Berlin/New York: Walter de Gruyter.
Clarkson, S. 1993. 'Constitutionalizing the Canadian–American relationship', in D. Cameron and M. Watkins (eds), *Canada Under Free Trade*. Toronto: Lorimer.
Commission of the European Communities. 1993. *Report on United States Trade and Investment Barriers and Problems of Doing Business with the US*. Brussels: CEE.
Cox, R. 1991. 'The Global Political Economy and Social Choice', in D. Drache and M. Gertler (eds), *The New Era of Global Competition*. Montreal: McGill–Queen's University Press
Daly, H. and Robert Goodland. 1992. *An Ecological Assessment of Deregulation of International Commerce under GATT*. Washington, DC: World Bank.

Dehousse, R. 1989/91. '1992 and Beyond: The Institutional Design of the Internal Market Programme.' *Legal Issues of European Integration*, no. 1, 109–36.
Dehousse, R. (ed.). 1994. *Europe After Maastricht: An Ever Closer Union*. Munich: Law Books in Europe.
Dertouzos, Michael, Richard K. Lester and Robert Solow. 1989. *Made In America. Regaining the Productive Edge*. Cambridge, Mass.: MIT Press.
Drache, Daniel (ed.). 1992. *Getting on Track: Social Democratic Strategies for Ontario*. Montreal: McGill–Queen's University Press.
Drache, D. 1993. 'Trade Blocs and Free Trade in the Post-Modern Era: Are NAFTA and the EEC Converging?' Unpublished manuscript.
Drache, D. and M. Gertler (eds). 1991. *The New Era of Global Competition, State Policy and Market Power*. Montreal: McGill–Queen's University Press.
Drache, Daniel and Harry Glasbeek. 1992. *The Changing Workplace: Reshaping Canada's Industrial Relations System*. Toronto: Lorimer.
Drucker, P. 1986. 'The Changed World Economy.' *Foreign Affairs* 64: 4.
Economic Council of Canada. 1990. *Good Jobs, Bad Jobs: Employment in the Service Economy*. Ottawa: Ministry of Supply and Services.
Emerson, Michael. 1988. *What Model for Europe?* Boston: MIT Press.
Esping-Andersen, G. 1990. *The Three Worlds of Welfare Capitalism*. Princeton: Princeton University Press.
Grinspun, Ricardo and Maxwell Cameron (eds). 1993. *The Political Economy of North American Free Trade*. Montreal: McGill–Queen's University Press.
Hufbauer, G. 1990. *Europe 1992: An American Perspective*. Washington, DC: The Brookings Institution.
Hufbauer, Gary and J. J. Schott. 1992. *North American Free Trade Issues and Recommendations*. Washington, DC: Institute for International Economics.
Jackson, A. 1993. 'A Social Democratic Economic Agenda for the 1990s: A View from the NDP.' *Canadian Business Economics* 1: 2 (winter).
Jacquemin, A. 1990. 'Competition and Competition Policy in Market Economies', in W. Comanor (ed.), *Competition Policy in Europe and North America: Economic Issues and Institutions*. Chur, Switzerland: Harwood.
Julien, Claude. 1993a. 'Ces élites qui rènent sur des masses des chomeurs.' *Le monde diplomatique*, April.
Julien, Claude. 1993b. 'Le libéralisme contre la société.' *Le monde diplomatique*, December.
Krugman, P.R. 1987. 'Economic Integration in Europe: Some Conceptual Issues', reprinted from 'Efficiency, Stability, and Equity' in Tommasco Padoa-Schioppa (ed.), *The European Internal Market Trade and Competition*. London: Oxford University Press.
Kuttner, Robert. 1984. *The Economic Illusion*. Boston: Houghton Mifflin.
Latouche, D. 1993. *Quebec in the North American Emerging Configuration*. North American Institute Conference on Identity, Culture and North American Society. Sante Fe: New Mexico.
Mazier, Jacques, Maurice Basle and Jean-François Vidal. 1993. *Quand Les Crises Durent . . .* (2nd edn). Paris: Economica.
Mellis, C. 1992. 'Tradeable and Non-Tradeable Prices in the UK and the European Community.' *Bank of England Bulletin*, February.
OECD. 1993a. *Employment Outlook*, July. Paris: OECD Publications.
OECD. 1993b. *Economic Outlook No. 54*, December. Paris: OECD Publications.
Ohmae, K. 1990. *The Borderless World. Power and Strategy in the Interlinked Economy*. New York: Harper Business.
Ohmae, K. 1993. 'The rise of the Regional State.' *Foreign Affairs* 72: 2 (Spring).

Petrella, R. 1989. 'Globalization of Technological Innovation.' *Technology Analysis and Strategic Management* 1: 4.

Petrella, R. 1990. 'Technology and the Firm.' *Technology Analysis and Strategic Management* 2: 2.

Piore, M. and Charles Sabel. 1984. *The Second Industrial Divide*. New York: Basic Books.

Polanyi, Karl. 1957. *The Great Transformation*. Boston: Beacon Press.

Porter, M. 1990. 'Competitive Advantage of Nations'. *Harvard Business Review* 90: 2.

Postman, Neil. 1992. *Technopoly: The Surrender of Culture to Technology*. New York: Knopf.

Reich, R. 1991. *The Work of Nations*. New York: Knopf.

Ruigrok, Winifried. 1991. 'Paradigm Crisis in International Trade Theory.' A paper prepared for the Forum on Applied Science and Technology (FAST), Commission of European Community, Brussels.

Sbragia, A.M. 1992. *Euro-Politics Institutions and Policymaking in the 'New' European Community*. Washington, DC: The Brookings Institution.

Schott, J.J. 1989. *More Free Trade Areas? Policy Analyses in International Economics*. Washington, DC: Institute for International Economics.

Schott, J. 1991. 'Trading Blocs and the World Trading System.' *The World Economy* 14: 1 (March).

Small, Cornelia. 1993. 'A Kaleidoscopic View of the 21st Century.' New York: Scudder Equities.

Spero, J. 1988–9. 'Guiding Global Finance.' *Foreign Policy* 73 (Winter).

Standing, G. 1992. 'Fragmented Flexibility: Labour and the Social Dividend', in Daniel Drache (ed.), *Getting On Track: Social Democratic Strategies For Ontario*. Montreal: McGill–Queen's University Press.

Strange, S. 1988. *States and Markets*. New York: Blackwell.

Streeck, W. 1991. 'On the Institutional Conditions of Diversified Quality Production', in E. Matzner and W. Streeck (eds), *Beyond Keynesianism*. Aldershot: Edward Elgar.

Tyson, L.D. 1992. *Who's Bashing Whom? Trade Conflict in High-Technology Industries*. Washington, DC: Institute for International Economics.

United Nations. 1991. *Economic Growth in the Market Economies 1950–2000*. New York: United Nations Economic Commission for Europe.

United Nations. 1992. *World Investment Report 1992: Transnational Corporations as Engines of Growth*. New York.

Weiler, J. 1991. 'The Transformation of Europe.' *The Yale Law Journal* 100.

Wood Gundy Economics. 1993. 'The Deficit. How Big?' *Economic Indicators*, April.

Yalnizyan, A. 1993. *Market Madness: The Distribution of Money and Time Over the Last 20 Years*. Toronto: The Social Planning Council of Metropolitan Toronto, *Social Infopac* 12: 1.

Yoffie, David and Helen V. Milner. 1989. 'An Alternative to Free Trade or Protectionism: Why Corporations Seek Strategic Trade Policy.' *California Management Review* 31: 4 (Summer), pp. 111–31.

2

GLOBALIZATION AND INTERNATIONALIZATION

The dynamics of the emerging world order

Riccardo Petrella

GLOBALIZATION IS A NEW PHENOMENON

A new 'competitive era' has emerged in the last twenty years, especially in connection with the globalization of economic processes. Competition no longer describes a mode of functioning of a particular market configuration such as a competitive market as distinct from oligopolistic and monopolistic markets. To be competitive has ceased to be a means. Competition has acquired the status of a universal credo, an ideology.

For industrialists and bankers, competitiveness has become the short- and middle-term primary goal, whilst profitability remains the long-term goal and the *raison d'être* of the firm. For government, the competitiveness of the nation is now the primary concern, with a view to attracting and retaining capital within its territory, in order to secure a maximum level of employment, access for local capital to global technology, and revenue needed to maintain a minimum of social peace.

Yet the globalization of the economy is only one dimension in the emerging reconfiguration of the world and the globalization of human affairs. In a larger perspective, the 'global world' is the result of a profound reorganization of the economy and society in what used to be called the 'first world' (the Western capitalist developed countries), the 'second world' (the communist, state command economies) and the 'third world' (the underdeveloped and poor countries of Latin America, Africa, Asia). This division of the world into these three economic regions is less and less valid. Another configuration now characterizes the geo-economy of the planet. The countries of Asia form a powerful growth pole. This has other effects as well. Global markets are putting an end to the *national* economy and national capitalism as the most pertinent and effective basis for the organization and management of the production and distribution of wealth. How is globalization a different process from internationalization and multinationalization?[1]

Globalization, internationalization and multinationalization

The internationalization of economy and society refers to the ensemble of flows of exchanges of raw materials, semi-finished and finished products and services, money, ideas and people between two or more nation-states. Trade (exports/imports) and population movement statistics are the most visible instruments to measure and monitor the nature, scope and direction of internationalization.

For centuries, people have traded goods and services across nations and have moved from one country to another, with or without force. In modern capitalism, internationalization took shape through the conquest of colonies and the rise of mercantilism. In 1972, George Modelski used the term 'globalization' to refer explicitly to European-led expansion to gain control over other communities in the world and integrate these into one global trading system.[2] The same interpretation was behind the French expression 'economie-monde' used by the historian Fernand Braudel[3] in his great *fresque* on the emergence of capitalism. Over the centuries, the pattern and degree of internationalization has changed as old powers have declined and new ones have emerged with different interests and strategies. Figure 2.1 indicates the steady growth of internationalization of the economy since the 1950s.

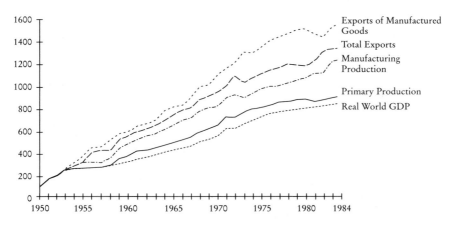

Figure 2.1 World exports and production
Source: GATT, *International Trade 1986*, Geneva, 1987

By contrast, the multinationalization of economy and society is characterized fundamentally by the transfer of resources, especially capital and, to a lesser extent, labour, from one national economy to another. A typical form of multinationalization in the economy is the creation of production capacities of a firm in another country via direct subsidiaries, acquisitions, or various types of co-operation (commercial, financial, technological and industrial). A multinational firm is a corporation whose activities have been gradually extended to other countries (see Figure 2.2).

Because corporations are seen as powerful and influential economic actors from a foreign country, they often acquire the capacity to control the host country's economy and even their future. This is why, contrary to internationalization processes, multinationalization provokes a strong cultural and political nationalistic reaction to the presence of 'foreign-owned enterprises' and 'foreign investments'. Economic protectionism has been often used against the strategic presence of multinational firms, particularly of US origin. Today, it is the turn of the Japanese to be the target of this phobia. The United States and many European and Asian countries are troubled by the rapid penetration of Japanese firms in an increasing number of important sectors of their economies (see Chapter 5).

By comparison, the globalization of societies is a much more recent phenomenon and, therefore, the forms and processes occurring are more difficult to capture in a single sentence.[4] Some of the most obvious aspects may disappear in ten or fifteen years or lose their relevance all together. None the less, the principal characteristics of globalization consist of the following:[5]

- the globalization of financial markets;
- the internationalization of corporate strategies, in particular their commitment to competition as a source of wealth creation;
- the diffusion of technology and related R&D and knowledge worldwide;
- the transformation of consumption patterns into cultural products with worldwide consumer markets;
- the internationalization of the regulatory capabilities of national societies into a global political economic system;
- the diminished role of national governments in designing the rules for global governance.

A summary of the concepts and actual processes of globalization is presented in Table 2.1.

The acceptance of the concept of globalization by an increasing number of people is not due to fashion alone. It expresses the need for understanding processes that have lost meaning in terms of the more traditional concepts. In fact, our definition is closer to the one proposed by McGrew and his colleagues:

> Globalisation refers to the multiplicity of linkages and interconnections between the states and societies which make up the present world system. It describes the process by which events, decisions, and activities in one part of the world come to have significant consequences for individuals and communities in quite distant parts of the globe. Globalisation has two distinct phenomena: scope (or stretching) and intensity (or deepening). On the one hand, it defines a set of processes

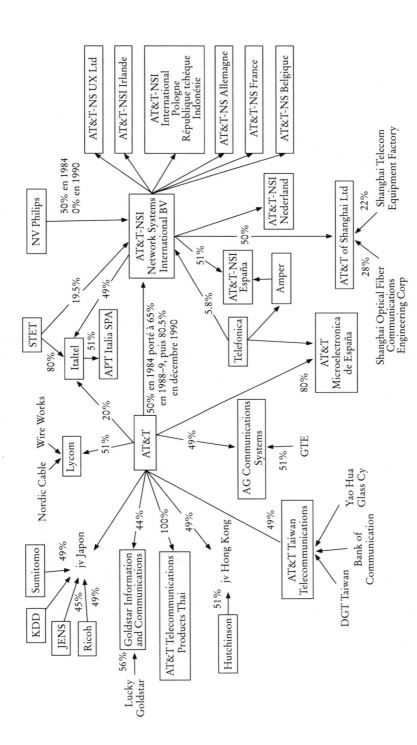

Figure 2.2 AT&T in the world: an example of economic multinationalization
Source: Groupe de Lisbonne 1995

Table 2.1 Concepts of globalization

Category	Main elements/processes
1 Globalization of finances and capital ownership	Deregulation of financial markets, international mobility of capital, rise of mergers and acquisitions. The globalization of shareholding is at its initial stage.
2 Globalization of markets and strategies, in particular competition	Integration of business activities on a worldwide scale, establishment of integrated operations abroad (including R&D and financing), global searching of components, strategic alliances.
3 Globalization of technology and linked R&D and knowledge	Technology is the primary catalyst: the rise of information technology and telecom enables the rise of global networks within the same firm, and between different firms. Globalization as the process of universalization of Toyotism/lean production.
4 Globalization of modes of life and consumption patterns; globalization of culture	Transfer and transplantation of predominant modes of life. Equalization of consumption patterns. The role of the media. Transformation of culture in 'cultural food', 'cultural products'. GATT rules applied to cultural flows.
5 Globalization of regulatory capabilities and governance	The diminished role of national governments and parliaments. Attempts to design a new generation of rules and institutions for global governance.
6 Globalization as the political unification of the world	State-centred analysis of the integration of world societies into a global political and economic system led by a core power.
7 Globalization of perception and consciousness	Socio-cultural processes as centred on 'One Earth'. The 'globalist' movement. Planetary citizens.

Source: A broadened and revised table based upon W. Ruigrok and R. van Tulder, 'The Ideology of Interdependence'. Doctoral dissertation, University of Amsterdam, June 1993

which embrace most of the globe or which operate worldwide; the concept therefore has a spatial connotation. On the other hand, it also implies an intensification in the levels of interaction, interconnectedness or interdependence between the states and societies which constitute the world community. Accordingly, alongside the stretching goes a deepening of global processes. Far from being an abstract concept, globalisation articulates one of the more familiar features of modern existence. Of course, globalisation does not mean that the world is becoming more politically united, economically interdependent or culturally homogeneous. Both its scope and intensity is highly differentiated in its consequences.[6]

Most of the features of contemporary globalization raise serious concerns for the present and the future. It is already creating undesirable consequences that will become magnified even further if current forms of globalization remain unchallenged by governments and peoples.

Nation-states have played a crucial role in the development of capitalism and are not about to disappear. Far from it. Their numbers have increased as a result of decolonization and recently following the collapse of the Soviet Union. However, it is an over-simplification to say that the nation-state is a form of political organization of society that has become too small to respond to a growing number of global challenges and, at the same time, too big to cope with local issues and solutions. And yet, the notion of national sovereignty, however important it may still be, is increasingly challenged by events beyond its reach and perception. Environmental protection is only one such area. The Chernobyl explosions highlighted the growing distortion between the theoretical and political model of state sovereignty and the technological and environmental reality of the biosphere.[7]

Equally, national languages and cultures have not lost their importance but they are no longer considered to be *the* exclusive and ultimate form of individual and collective cultural ingenuity and expression. Multi-linguism and multi-culturalism are seen as assets for all societies and require positive encouragement and support.

It is not just the economic changes wrought by globalization that are changing our perception of ourselves and the world we live in; we are also witnessing the beginning of the end of the 'national' as the starting and finishing point of strategic relevance for scientific, economic, social and cultural actors. The 'national' continues to be one of the levels of significant relevance, but it is no longer the *main* strategic level for the key actors in the areas of scientific development, technological innovation and socioeconomic growth.[8]

Put differently, the growing globalization of the economy is eroding one of the basic foundations of the nation-state, i.e. the national market. The national space is being replaced as the most relevant strategic *economic* space by the nascent global space. This does not mean that the power of the nation-state, in military and security matters, is declining absolutely, nor that the role and power of nation-states has been replaced in the economic sphere by transnational firms as some observers wrongly predict.[9] In many instances, the national economy remains as important for any country as it once did. This is especially so with regard to the less-developed economies of recently created nation-states.[10] The economic fight for global leadership amongst the most developed 'national economies' of the world such as Germany, USA, Japan, France, Italy, and the United Kingdom also underlines just how important the national economy is to each industrial power. But despite all of this counter-evidence, what is different today from thirty years ago is that the national economy is no longer the name of the game. If this is so, what explains this remarkable shift?

The one factor that has changed more than any other is that the production of wealth in Germany, France, Japan, Finland or Costa Rica is no longer dependent upon the performance of their 'local' firms in local technology, capital and labour markets but on those firms which are increasingly part of global networks of financial and industrial corporations.[11] And they respond to strategic interests that are not bound to the German, French, Japanese, Finnish or Costa Rican national needs. They are even more dependent on technology designed, produced and transformed everywhere in the world, on capital made available at the global and world level (as confirmed by the fast-growing globalization of financial and capital markets) and, increasingly, on highly skilled labour, not necessarily trained in their country.[12]

Since the Industrial Revolution, the drive to modernize has been essentially the history of a national industry. The rise and growth of national capitalism has expressed the sense and direction of the historical processes. Though one would be wrong to declare the death of national capitalism, it is correct to say that national capitalism has ceased to be the *only* coherent form of organization of capital, and that its predominance will rapidly disappear in the coming decades. The history of capitalism has ceased to be defined by and limited to national boundaries. It would be wrong to draw the conclusion that the world has entered a post-capitalist era. The ownership of capital still matters and it still remains the dominant factor of economic and socio-political power in the world. The great change that is occurring is not between a capitalist and a post-capitalist society, nor between a 'good' capitalism (the social market economy) and a 'bad' capitalism (the jungle, the 'casino' market economy).[13] Rather, it is between a weakening of all aspects of a society founded on national capitalism and the growing power and dynamic of global capitalism.

The one event that signalled the arrival of the new era was Richard Nixon's 1971 declaration of the non-convertibility of the US dollar. In taking this historic step, his decision accelerated the shift towards global capitalism and the wealth of the world. This shift, stark and monumental in its consequences, has produced epoch-making changes with respect to capital flows. The result is that the world is slowly starting to move from the era of the *wealth of nations* to the era of the *wealth of the world*.

CAPITAL FLOWS: THE PRIMARY CATALYSTS OF GLOBAL CAPITALISM

The global movement of capital has become the nerve centre for the globalization of the international economy.[14] Capital flows fall into three main categories:

- monetary and financial flows, linked to the trade of goods and services (for example import/export transactions, tourism expenditures);

- foreign direct investment that not only implies financial capital transfers but also transfers of physical, human and technological capital;
- portfolio investments and various types of financial transactions (including speculative operations).

While capital flows at the world level exhibited a relative atrophy from the end of the Second World War until the end of the 1960s, the 1970s witnessed a rapid acceleration and intensification of the globalization of financial markets. In Aglietta's and his colleagues view, the tremendous growth of foreign direct investment was characterized by the transfer of surplus capital from OPEC countries to many Third World nations by First World banks.[15] During this period, the northern countries became richer by using the petro-dollars to finance the development of poorer southern countries. What happened was that the developing world found themselves trapped in a vicious circle of debt and dependency while the oil-rich countries of the South financed the economic development of the rich North.

Other changes followed in the 1980s (Figures 2.3 and 2.4). Increasingly, capital flows became more concentrated within the Triad between the three richest regions of the North: Japan and the 'four dragons', Western Europe, and the United States. By the end of the decade, more than 80 per cent of world's foreign direct investment originated from and went to the three regions of the Triad. By contrast, the share of the world's capital stock going to poor countries had been reduced from about 14 per cent in 1982 to zero in 1989 (Figure 2.3). Even the mild recovery in 1989 did not alter this basic financial division of labour of the world's financial resources.[16]

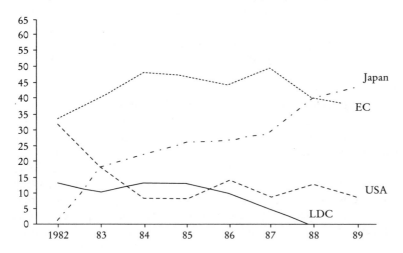

Figure 2.3 International capital flows according to their origin*
Source: Data from the IMF balance of payment's)
* Not including the reserves and operations of international organizations

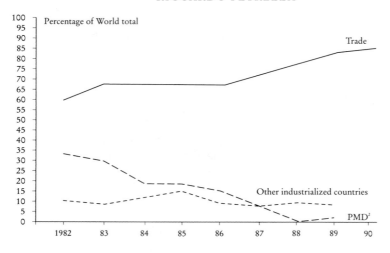

Figure 2.4 International capital flows according to their destination*
Source: Data from the IMF balance of payments)
* Not including the reserves and operations of international organizations

However, there was one new development. While the 1970s were centred on the recycling of OPEC surpluses, the 1980s have been centred on the recycling of Japanese surpluses. Of course, the process took place almost exclusively in the OECD countries, and Japan's capacity to steer the process has proved to be more than adequate. The result was that during the years 1986–9, on average, Japan represented 26.93 per cent of total world capital flows, a figure far above the funds coming from the United States (16.41 per cent). But 64 per cent of Japanese trade loans, 70 per cent of direct investments abroad and 86 per cent of portfolio investments (95.5 per cent in 1988) went to the two other regions of the Triad between 1984 and 1988.[17]

Less-developed countries have been abandoned as sites for investment. In 1980, all LDCs attracted about 55 per cent of world capital flows and together accounted for 14 per cent of the outgoing flows. Ten years later both percentages had almost vanished, declining to 2 per cent. If one excludes those LDCs that have become major offshore financial centres (Panama, Hong Kong, the Cayman Islands and the Dutch Caribbean) and the capital flows from international organizations and public donations, the result is that the total investment flows and loans both from the public and private sectors that went to the less-developed and poor countries of the world represented less than 3 per cent of the world flows between 1986 and 1991. The gradual exclusion of the large majority of LDCs from receiving badly needed investments is staggering by any standard. Starting in 1982, there has been a brutal halt to the growth of international bank loans destined for the LDCs. Again, if countries such as Hong Kong, South Korea, Taiwan, Singapore,

Thailand, China and Turkey are excluded, the very 'south' of the LDCs no longer attracts any capital outside of public donations and multilateral aid, due more to humanitarian considerations than to any economic logic.

This financial delinking of much of the world from the new economic order raises a crucial question. How will the global world evolve in the future? Will a new economic logic influence the process of globalization in such a way that 'the wealth of the world' will be shared between all countries, the result of their creativity and individual contributions?[18]

GLOBALIZATION: THE NOVELTY OF OUR TIMES?

The potential is there. The new phenomenon of globalization makes possible the design, development, production, distribution and consumption of processes, products and services on a world scale, using instruments such as patents, databases, new information, communication and transport techno-logies and infrastructures. Many of the new products are geared to satisfy increasingly diversified and customized global markets regulated by 'quasi-universal' norms and standards. As well, the modern corporation has changed its organizational structure dramatically. More than ever, successful firms are looking to form networks with other private-sector actors capable of operating on a world basis. Finally, capital too is increasingly owned by a multiplicity of shareholders from different countries; business culture is said to obey a world strategy even if it is difficult to identify the specific territorial and legal basis of these organizations.

Here are a few examples of the kinds of intensive forms of inter-relationships and integration that lead to the production, distribution and consumption of global kinds of goods and services.

Credit cards are a typical illustration of a global service 'devised' for a specialized, high-value-added world market, based on the integration of whole clusters of new technologies (data processing, materials, telecommun-ications, etc.), and managed by globalized organizations with a growing world expertise.

The car is also a typical example of a global product. The car is no longer 'Made in the USA', 'Made in France', 'Made in Japan', but is more and more 'Made in the world'. This applies not only to the production side, but, more importantly, to the whole system which facilitates the production of about 30 million cars per year. The globalization of the car industry is at its initial stage. Many European markets are still closed to Japanese exports. None the less, the Japanese car complex is heavily dependent upon the world market for its exports but hardly at all for its imports. Simply on the basis of this data, it is easy to understand the Japanese government's trade policy strategy: promote a liberal international trade regime, yet ensure that such a regime will not lead to a dramatic rise of imports. Notwithstanding these phenomena, the globalization of the car sector and players at the organizational, behavioural and strategic levels is growing in importance.

Of even greater significance is the explosion of interfirm strategic alliances (see Table 2.3 and Figure 2.5), that have, in the last fifteen years, deeply modified the internal structures of the car sector and, even more, other sectors of the economy.[19] The main reasons motivating firms to co-operate with each other are:

- to reduce the costs for R&D;
- to ensure access to complementary technology;
- to capture a partner's tacit knowledge and technology (often called technological leap-frogging);
- to shorten the product life cycle;
- to share costs in product development;
- to gain greater access to foreign markets;
- to obtain access to highly qualified people;
- to broaden access to financial resources.

In this manner, an increasing number of products are jointly designed by several firms requiring their engineers to work together on the same idea over a long period of time. Similarly, the complexity of the elements in the

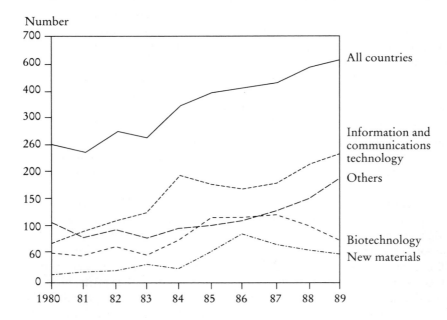

Figure 2.5 Growth of newly established strategic technology alliances in core technologies and other fields, 1980–9
Source: MERIT-CATI

production process requires firms from different countries to collaborate. Different firms have to share their strategies with others, even if, as is the case for the majority of the alliances, there is the hidden hope or, indeed, the intention of absorbing the partner. In its present form, the phenomenon of interfirm strategic alliances is quite new. It 'exploded' in the 1980s and although it has been most strongly developed in technology-based computer industries and telecommunications, strategic alliances are destined to expand further in the future. One may easily anticipate that in ten or fifteen years' time it will be difficult to identify who does what and which part of the network is related to that segment or that production centre of a given firm.[20]

This is not a futuristic statement. Already a new phenomenon has emerged, i.e. the virtual corporation. 'Virtual corporations' are ephemeral corporations created to finance very costly research or the development of a product only to be dissolved once they have achieved their goal.[21]

An even stronger component of globalization is foreign direct investment (FDI). For example, between 1983 and 1989 world exports increased by 9.4 per cent a year and the average annual growth of world gross domestic product was 7.8 per cent, but during the same period foreign direct investment grew by 28.9 per cent a year! According to a report by the former United Nations Centre on Transnational Corporations on FDI, 'international transactions are increasingly dominated by transnational corporations. . . One implication of such a development is that the global patterns of trade, technology transfers and private financial flows could tend to converge on the foreign direct investment patterns, making the latter a principal force in the structuring of the world economy.'[22]

Foreign direct investment is by no means a new phenomenon. It has been present since the last century and has been a force behind much of the growth of the international economy in this century as well. The intensive liberalization of trade and capital has been a mixed blessing. For instance, when a European firm buys an American one, the result is an increase in the concentration of production activity in Europe and the USA under the ownership or control of the European firm. If present forecasts are correct, the number of global players in the telecommunications area will be reduced in 2010 to 6–7 from 14–15 companies in 1991–2 through mergers and acquisitions. This trend will not lead to a higher level of globalization in the telecom industry, but rather to a drastic increase in the degree of concentration of financial and industrial structures at a world level.

THE FIRM: GLOBAL ACTOR NO. 1

Table 2.2 shows why the large multinational firm has emerged as the key global actor. 'Going global' has been far easier for firms than for governments, parliaments, trade unions or universities, which are not sufficiently flexible institutions ready to adapt easily or quickly to changing conditions. Without this strategic capability multinationals have found themselves as the only real global players at the world level. Another reason is linked to the fact that advanced industrial societies have given greater importance over the last forty years to the production of more and more goods. With the leading industrial nations gripped by the remarkable progress made by mass production technology, it is no wonder that the dominant global culture is determined and shaped by these very same giant economic entities. As producers of the technology infrastructure and services for the world economy they claim that 'what is good for them is good for the world'.

Table 2.2 Why the firm is No. 1

1 It is the only organization that has transformed itself to become a 'global' player. It operates at the real decision-making level.

2 Our society has given top priority to technology and to the growth of tools. Firms are the producers of tools.

3 Firms are considered to be key actors that produce wealth, ensure employment and, therefore, individual and collective well-being.

Today's global corporate leviathans decide which regions and countries of the world will receive new flows of investment for job creation and where the new production facilities will be built. A handful of global companies such as Olivetti, Alcatel, IBM, Mitsubishi, Nestlé, Thomson, Siemens, BP, BASF, Monsanto, Ericsson, Northern Telecom, Nissan, Société Générale have the power to fashion the world as they deem fit. So extensive is this power that it is also extended to domains such as universities which have previously escaped the direct influence of business in their internal affairs.

To a large degree, states everywhere seem to be playing a pale, secondary, and even in extreme cases, a receding role compared to the new-found aggressive confidence of global business. States seem to react rather than anticipate, and follow rather than lead. In these circumstances, the globally oriented enterprise is in the process of becoming the main organization 'governing' the world economy, with the support of 'the national' state which may be as small as Denmark or as large as the USA. With business in line to be the principal beneficiary, it is not difficult to see why multinational enterprise has promoted competitiveness as the universal discourse of our times.

Large businesses need a long-term perspective to justify the risk involved in large-scale technological investments. If they are to be profitable, they require large open markets, rapidly growing demand and large-scale public projects to help defray the costs. This is why global enterprises are building corporate networks of co-operation and forming alliances around easily definable clusters of technologies, products and markets. Despite their ideological commitment to competitiveness at all costs, they are far from this ideal themselves. Instead they are forming a network of oligopolistic market structures. For example, in 1980, thirteen companies shared 80 per cent of world turnover in the tyre industry. In 1990, no more than six companies produced 85 per cent of the total output, and many experts and industrialists feel that between now and the year 2000 there may be only three or four large firms monopolizing the world tyre industry, perhaps in the form of a cartel.[23]

Despite the general rhetoric calling for 'less state and more market', enterprises expect more from their governments if they are to secure markets for their products. In fact, the private sector requires four principle kinds of support and services from governments:

- covering the costs of basic 'infrastructures' (funding of basic and high-risk research; funding of universities and vocational training systems; promotion and funding of mechanisms for dissemination of scientific and technical information and technology transfers);
- providing the tax incentives needed for investment in industrial R&D and technological innovations;
- guaranteeing that 'national' enterprises from the given country have a sufficiently stable home base by privileged access to the internal market via public contracts (defence, telecommunications, health, transport, education, social services). Industrial policy, particularly for those in the high-technology strategic sector (defence, telecommunications, data processing), also guarantee a certain degree of basic scientific and technical competence, as well as protecting designated sectors of the internal market on which 'local' enterprises may depend;
- providing the necessary support and assistance (regulatory, commercial, diplomatic and political) to local enterprises in their activities and in their fight to better survive in international markets.

Enterprises are also pressing the state to introduce policies favourable to their freedom of action in the field of labour market regulation. They want lower labour standards in the name of competitiveness.

The global proliferation of sophisticated production technologies forces the state to adopt new methods of protecting and expanding local innovation and technological adoption. National economic well-being will depend more than ever on the mastery and marketing of advanced basic technologies such as semiconductors, composite materials, robotics, highly sophisticated instrumentation, microcomputing, supercomputers, cognitive sciences and biological technology. The state's political and social legitimacy, based on its capacity to secure the country's continuous socioeconomic development, is at risk. It has an interest to intervene and support its 'own', 'national'

RICCARDO PETRELLA

enterprises by pursuing technological, industrial and commercial policies shaped to fit its needs.

Thus, most states are adopting a combination of strategies of national R&D programmes and participation in public international programmes, manipulating public markets, by tax breaks and commercial measures. In the process, they are carrying out a massive transfer of collective public resources to private enterprises, mostly multinational corporations, in order to enable them to remain competitive in the so-called 'fight for survival' at the world level.

In so doing, all states hope to ensure the conditions needed for the economic development of the country and thus to protect the basis of their legitimacy. In other words, states tend to maintain their own social role by *de facto* delegating to the enterprises the task of ensuring the socioeconomic development of the country.

Such is the nature of the new alliance: enterprises need 'local' (national) states in order to cope with globalization and to globalize themselves. The states need global enterprises to ensure the continuity of their legitimacy and perpetuation as 'local' political and social entities. Accordingly, the enterprises gradually acquire historical legitimacy and a social role which in many respects approximates the legitimacy and role appropriate to the state. As a result, there is an increasing separation of economic and political power on a world scale.

The more a company becomes globalized, the more it is likely to lose its own identity within a tangle of companies, alliances and markets. In this process, the aim of maintaining and expanding its own decision-making power and its ability to control the allocation of the planet's material and non-material resources to which the enterprise may, and hopes, to have access, becomes its sole true, realistic, and attainable aim. However, an enterprise knows that if it restricted itself to that aim, it would sooner or later be swept off the economic map by stronger enterprises allied with stronger states. It, therefore, needs to acquire a 'historical' social legitimacy in the eyes of both local society (the country) and world society. The alliance with the state enables it to find the new legitimacy it needs. Through the alliance it may claim that the state has assigned it the task of defending and promoting the economic and social well-being of the 'local' society by ensuring its own industrial and commercial success on the world scene – a claim the state cannot deny.

As far as 'global' society is concerned, the enterprise lays claim to a kind of historical legitimacy based on the fact that it has become globalized. It makes this claim implicitly in that it presents itself as the only organization able to assure the optimal worldwide management of available material and non-material resources.

In practice, therefore, the enterprise privatizes (and internationalizes for its own purposes) the role of the state. It does so repeatedly in all the countries where it is active and where it can claim to form an integral part of the local country and to be a determining factor in the economic and social well-being of this country. Similarly, in the absence of a world public governance, it privatizes more and more the function of organizing and governing the world economy.

TRIADIZATION

The privatization of the function of organizing and governing the world economy is not inconsistent with another key characteristic of present globalization processes.

Today's globalization is a truncated globalization: 'triadization' is a more correct definition of the current situation. By 'triadization' is meant the fact that the process of technological, economic and socio-cultural integration amongst the three most developed regions of the world (Japan plus the NICs from South-East Asia, Western Europe and North America) is more diffused, intensive and significant than 'integration' between these three regions and the less-developed countries, or between the less-developed themselves.

'Triadization' exists also in people's minds. According to the Japanese, North Americans and Western Europeans, the world that counts is their world in which is located the scientific power, technological potentials and supremacy, military hegemony, economic wealth, cultural power and, therefore, mastery of conditions and ability to govern the world economy and society into the future.

The phenomenon of 'triadization' is demonstrated in the geographical patterns of interfirm alliances.

Out of the 4,200 interfirm strategic co-operation agreements that were signed by enterprises in the world in the period 1980–9, 92 per cent were between enterprises from Japan, Western Europe and North America (see Table 2.3, column 3).

Available statistics on foreign direct investments also reveal that, in the last ten years, Japan, the USA and Western Europe have increasingly invested more and more amongst themselves.

The 'triadization' of FDI is the result of investment flows which have created a fundamentally different international economic situation than that of the 1960s and 1970s. Until the beginning of the 1980s, the developing countries had a role to play, though limited, as countries of origin and of destination. During the 1980s, the Triad accounted for around four-fifths of all international capital flows! The developing countries share fell from 25 per cent in the 1970s to 19 per cent despite a 30 per cent rate of growth per year of FDI and a near doubling of average annual flows to the developing countries between 1980–4 and 1985–9.

Though the flow of foreign direct investments destined for Latin America, Asia (NICs excluded) or even Africa may increase again in the future, the

Table 2.3 Distribution of interfirm strategic technology alliances, by field and group of countries, 1980–9

Fields of technology	Number of alliances (1)	% for developed economies (2)	% for Triad (3)	% for Triad-NIC (4)	% for Triad-LDC (5)	Other (6)
Biotech.	846	99.1	94.1	0.4	0.1	0.5
New materials	430	96.5	93.5	2.3	1.2	–
Computer	199	98.0	96.0	1.5	0.5	–
Industrial automation	281	96.1	95.0	2.1	1.8	–
Microel.	387	95.9	95.1	3.6	–	0.5
Software	346	99.1	96.2	0.6	0.3	–
Telecom.	368	97.5	92.1	1.6	0.3	0.5
Misc. IT	148	93.3	92.6	5.4	0.7	0.7
Automot.	205	84.9	82.9	9.8	5.4	–
Aviation	228	96.9	94.3	0.9	1.3	0.9
Chemical	410	87.6	80.0	3.9	7.1	1.5
Food and beverages	42	90.5	76.2	9.5	–	–
Heavy electr.	141	96.5	92.2	1.4	2.1	–
MT/Instr.	95	100.0	100.0	–	–	–
Others	66	90.9	77.3	1.5	4.5	3.0
Total	4,192	95.7	91.9	2.3	1.5	0.5

Source: Chris Freeman and John Hagedorn, *Globalisation of Technology*, Report for the FAST Programme, Commission of the European Communities, June 1992, p. 41

tendency will remain in the foreseeable future as one of preference directed towards the regions of the Triad.

The same trend applies to the other two components of capital flows, together with foreign direct investments – namely, monetary and financial flows (we have shown the triadization process in Figures 2.3 and 2.4) and portfolio investments and other types of financial transactions. The 'triadic' countries are increasingly interacting and integrating with each other.

DE-LINKING

If the target is to win, only a few will be winners. The losers will be excluded and abandoned to their situation. The winners will continue to remain together, and increasingly integrate with one other. The need for maintaining or re-establishing linkages between the excluded and the integrated declines in importance. Thus, a new divide in the world appears, coinciding with the emergence of globalization. De-linking is the process through which some countries and regions are gradually losing their connections with the most economically developed and growing countries and regions of the world. Rather than participating in the processes of increasing interconnections and integration that are constructing the new 'global world', they are moving in the opposite direction. De-linking concerns almost all countries of Africa, most parts of Latin America and Asia (with the exception of countries from South-East Asia) as well as parts of the former Soviet Union and Eastern Europe.

Available data are self-explanatory. In 1980, as is shown in Table 2.4, the share of world trade of manufactured goods of the 102 poorest countries of the world was 7.9 per cent of world exports and 9 per cent of imports. Just ten years later, these shares fell to 1.4 per cent and 4.9 per cent respectively. Conversely, the share of the three regions of the Triad increased from 54.8 to 64.0 per cent of world exports and from 59.5 to 63.8 per cent of world imports.

Table 2.4 Relative share of the world market for manufactured goods

	Exports		Imports	
	1980	*1990*	*1980*	*1990*
Industrialized world (24 countries)	62.9	72.4	67.9	72.1
of which G7 (USA, CND, J, D, F, UK, I)	45.2	51.8	48.2	51.9
– the Triad	54.8	64.0	59.5	63.8
– other industrialized countries	8.1	8.5	8.4	8.3
Developing world (148 countries)	37.1	27.6	32.1	27.9
of which, group 'stars' (11 countries)	7.3	14.6	8.8	13.5
– group 4: 20 countries	7.8			
– group 3: 7 countries				
– group 2: 8 countries				
– group 1: the poorest (102 countries)	7.9	1.4	9.0	4.9
Total	100	100	100	100

Source: U. Muldur, FAST, 1993

Further evidence demonstrates that in 1970 intracontinental exchanges within each of the three regions of North America, Western Europe and Pacific/Asia represented 21.4 per cent of the world trade of goods. If one adds intercontinental exchanges between them (39.4 per cent), these regions represented 60.8 per cent of world trade in 1970 (see Figure 2.6).

In 1990, cumulative intracontinental exchanges within each region were 48.7 per cent and the intercontinental exchanges between the three regions rose to 24.9 per cent. Altogether, the exchanges of the three regions made up 73.6 per cent of world trade, the remaining 26.4 per cent being shared between Russia and Central Europe, the Middle East, Africa and Latin America.

It is worth underlining the high rate of growth of intracontinental exchanges concerning Pacific/Asia and Western Europe which moved from 6.3 to 10.2 per cent and from 27.1 to 33.4 per cent respectively. In contrast, the intracontinental share of Africa and the Middle East fell from 14.1 per cent in 1970 to 9.9 per cent in 1990, that of Latin America from 7.8 to 6.1 per cent and the countries from the ex-communist bloc from 7.3 to 4.1 per cent.

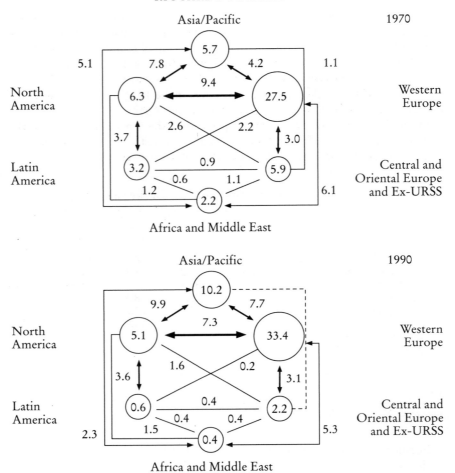

Figure 2.6 Share of regional trade flows of world trade of manufactured goods (as percentage of total world trade), 1970 and 1990
Source: Ugar Muldur, *Les formes et les indicateurs de la globalisation*, FAST, Commission of the European Communities, Brussels, 1993

In other words, the world economy has been characterized in the last twenty years at least by a gradual *reduction* of the exchanges between the richest and fast-growing countries of North America, Western Europe and Pacific/Asia and the rest of the world – Africa in particular. If this tendency were to be extended for the next twenty years, the share of Africa, the Middle East, Latin America, Russia and Central/Eastern Europe (39.2 per cent of world trade in 1970 and 26.4 per cent in 1990) would be reduced to 5 per cent in 2020.

That is de-linking. That is the new division of the world between the increasingly *integrated* 'global' world and the increasingly *excluded* fragments outside of the Triad. Only time will tell whether such an unequal world is viable before political conflicts, either domestic or international, will require that drastic changes be made to the now seemingly irreversible pattern of globalization.

NOTES

1 A first attempt to distinguish the three phenomena was made by Michel Beaud in *L'Economie Mondiale dans les annees '80*, La Decouverte, Paris, 1989. See also Riccardo Petrella, 'La mondialisation de l'économie, une hypothèse prospective', in *Futuribles*, Paris, September 1989.
2 George Modelski, *Principles of World Politics*, Free Press, New York, 1972.
3 Fernand Braudel, *Civilisation nationale, economie et capitalisme-XI–XVIII*, 3 volumes, Armand Colin, Paris, 1979.
4 A well-documented and in-depth analysis and discussion of globalization is contained in Winfried Ruigrok and Rob van Tulder's doctoral dissertation, 'The Ideology of Interdependence', University of Amsterdam, June 1993, 497 pages. One member of the 'Group of Lisbon', Riccardo Petrella, was a member of the 'opposition committee' at the dissertation defence.
5 Winfried Ruigrok and Rob van Tulder, op. cit., p. 26. These authors consider that Ohmae's *Ideology of Globalisation* has both a domestic and foreign target. Japanese people are advised to behave as 'good world citizens' and to foster good relationships with the local communities where they choose to set up establishments. The term *glocalization*, invented by the Japanese, responds to such a need. The Japanese government is urged to reduce its role in the domestic economy (cf. our previous analysis on the process of weakening the welfare state) and to dismantle remaining trade and investment barriers to foreign companies, in conformity with GATT regulations. The message to Western business people and government people and government representatives, in Ruigrok's and van Tulder's opinion, is to welcome rather than oppose Japanese internationalization.
6 Anthony G. McGrew and Paul Lewis *et al. Globalisation and the Nation States*, Polity Press, Cambridge, 1992, p. 22. We are aware of the fact that this proposition is not shared by other people in research, politics and business. Many people consider that the importance and novelty attributed to globalization is simply overstatement. See for instance P. Patel and K. Pavitt, 'Large Firms in the Production of the World's Technology: An Important Case of Non-globalisation', *Journal of International Business Studies*, First Quarter, 1991, pp. 1–21. Generally speaking, they believe that the most significant track of contemporary societies remains the 'national system'. In this view, the *national system of innovation* is of far greater importance and plays a much more decisive role than all the global processes we have described. See in particular the thesis by Michel E. Porter, *The Competitive Advantage of Nations*, Macmillan Press, London, 1990.
7 Jeremy Howell and Michelle Wood, *The Globalisation of Production and Technology*, Belhaven Press, London & New York, 1993.
8 See Jeffrey Henderson Jeffrey and Manuel Castells (eds), *Global Restructuring and Territorial Development*, Sage Publications, London, 1987.
9 According to formula used by Daniel Bell (the author of *The Coming of Post Industrial Societies*) in *Towards the year 2000*, Houghton, Boston, 1968.

10 See *The Earth Summit's Agenda for a Change*, a plain language version of Agenda 21 and the other Rio Agreements, Centre for Our Common Future, Geneva, 1993.

11 See Riccardo Petrella, 'Technology and Firm', *Technology Analysis and Strategic Management*, vol. 1, no. 4, 1989.

12 A strong criticism of the perverse effects associated with the maintenance of a multitude of nation-states defending their absolute sovereignty has been developed since the 1950s by, amongst others, Pugwash, the association of scientists created by Albert Einstein and Bertrand Russell after Hiroshima. See Joseph Rotblat, President of Pugwash, 'Removing Incentives to Waging War', *Pugwash Newsletter*, October 1991.

13 The debate between the pros and cons regarding the shift from national towards global capitalism has been enriched recently by the debate on 'communitarian' (acceptable – good) and 'wild' (rejectable – bad) capitalism. Lester Thurow and Robert Reich in the USA, for instance, are supporters of 'communitarian' capitalism. They are closer to the line of reasoning of most German leaders who believe in the 'sozialmarket Kapitalism'.

14 See the rather ill-founded proposition of Henry Wendt, *Global Embrace: Corporate Challenge in Transnational World*, Harper, New York, 1993.

15 See in particular Michael Aglietta, Anton Brender and Virginia Coudery, '*La Globalisation Financiere' aventure oblige*, CEPII, Euronomica, Paris, 1990.

16 All data flows are taken from Ugur Muldur, *Les formes et les indicateurs de la globalisation*, FAST, Research Document, Commission of the European Communities, June 1993, 216 pp.

17 Charles Albert Michalet and Michel Beaud are amongst the strong supporters of this thesis. In Michalet's view, globalization is *the deregulation of national financial markets and the subsequent internationalization of capital flows*. In the early 1980s, as production investments were lagging in large parts of the industrialized world, a surplus of capital circulated on a national and global scale, searching for short-term, lucrative investments. Hence, the 1980s became the period of 'casino capitalism' in Susan Strange's definition (*Casino Capitalism*, Blackwell, Oxford, 1986) or the 'raider era' in Michalet's terms (*Globalisation, Competitiveness and its Implications for Firms*, OECD, Paris, 1989).

18 The thesis in favour of the shift towards a post-capitalist society has been developed by Peter Drucker, *Post-Capitalist Society*, Harper, New York, 1993. The opposition between good and bad capitalism is defended by Michel Albert in *Capitalisme contre Capitalisme*, Le Seuil, Paris, 1991.

19 A state-of-the-art study concerning the growth of interfirm strategic alliances up to 1985 including a review of major studies available at the time is François Chesnais, *Technical Cooperation Agreements between Firms. Some Initial Data and Analysis*, OECD, Paris, 1986, and Riccardo Petrella, *Cooperations technologiques, européennes*, Dossier FAST, Bruxelles, 1987.

20 John Hagedoorn and Jan Schakenraad, *The Role of Interfirm Cooperation Agreements in the Globalisation of Economy and Technology*, FAST Commission of the European Community, Brussels, November 1991

21 William H. Davidow and Michael Malone, 'The Virtual Corporation', *Business Week*, 8 February 1993. This corporation has no similarity at all with the 'virtual corporation' ('Enterprise virtuelle') described by Devi Etthoffer, *L'enterprise virtuelle ou les nouveaux modes de travail*, Editions Odile Jacob, Paris, 1992 and based on new forms of organizations of production made possible by the new information and communication technology.

22 See the overview of foreign direct investment in the 1980s by United Nations Centre on Transnational Corporations (UNCTC), *World Investment Report*

1991. The Triad in Foreign Direct Investment, United Nations, New York, 1991, p. 82.
23 Cf. Jacques Delcourt, *Les Fondements des transferts sociaux dans une économie globale*, Report to the Euro-American Conference on 'Globalisation of Industrial Economy. A challenge to the social contract', 28–30 May, FAST, Commission of the European Communities, Brussels.

3

STATE AND MARKET

A new engagement for the twenty-first century?

Robert Boyer

CAN THE MARKET RULE ANYTHING?
AN OLD DEBATE REVISITED

The last decade has seen an impressive challenge by *laissez-faire* and pro-market strategists to the pro-state theories advanced by post-Second World War economists. The debate is not at all new since the discussion of the relative merits of market and state has been the cornerstone of political economy from the beginning. A short retrospective analysis is, therefore, useful in order to assess what is actually new in the 1990s. Conceptions concerning the self-regulating mechanism of markets have come full circle. During the Great Depression, the majority of economists criticized all institutional impediments to free functioning of markets. Too many regulations and state interventions were assumed to be the direct cause of unemployment, stagnation and financial instability. Only a minority of social scientists argued that it was the very nature of 'pure' and 'perfect' markets to trigger large instabilities and/or stagnation.

After the Second World War, Keynesian heterodoxy became the core of a significant revolution in the conception of the respective roles which state and market should have in the long-run social and economic reproduction of capitalism. Even the most conservative governments subscribed to the views of Richard Nixon who in 1971 declared, 'Now we are all Keynesians.' Adequate public regulations and fine tuning of monetary and fiscal policies were believed to promote full employment and a fast and steady growth path. Market mechanisms had to be tamed by legislation, regulations, collective agreements, built-in stabilizers in the tax system and the reactive functions of the Central Bank. As Joan Robinson has pointed out, markets are probably efficient mechanisms in the allocation of scarce resources and the setting of prices, but they are generally unable to provide full employment and prevent major macroeconomic instabilities. Thus, governments had to control markets and intervene.

In the 1970s and 1980s, with a radical move away from the Keynesian model, markets came to be seen as the most efficient means of organizing modern societies. In this view, public intervention is thought to do more harm than good. Such a change is supported by a great deal of empirical evidence. The Keynesian compromise has in recent years not delivered the same results as during the 1950s. Most national reflations – at least outside the United States – have been subject to inflation, external deficit and capital flight and have ended up with austerity policies. The French experience of Keynesian reflation is a good example of this phenomenon (Boyer 1987). Current trends seem closely related to a deepening in the internationalization process regarding trade, investment, finance and, of course, money. Firms, regions, nations can no longer depend upon the stable oligopolistic national markets which used to rule during the 1950s and 1960s. The competition in world markets is perceived as a strong constraint upon national compromises and forms of organization. In extreme cases, the financial troubles of certain nations clearly exhibit the leading role given to market mechanisms which are currently selecting the more efficient firms and productive organizations. Most governments have deregulated their financial and labour markets precisely in order to respond more efficiently to the changing patterns and recurrent disturbances associated with the globalization of economic activities. The final factor in the revival of the market is the adoption of free market ideology and economic recipes by governments and policy-makers. The dynamism of financial innovations (Aglietta 1991) and the progressive transition from one productive regime to another (Coriat 1991) have contributed to a resurgence of interest in pure market mechanisms: regulators who have lost many of their objectives and instruments have embraced the most extremist *laissez-faire* strategies.

Moreover, two major structural changes have strengthened the pervasiveness of market mechanisms. European integration implemented in 1992, as well as NAFTA, have clearly made competition in the product and financial markets cornerstones in continental integration. Again, each firm, region or even nation has to compete over a larger economic space than previously and in such a way that markets seem to lead political and institutional transformations. This is decidedly at odds with what was observed in the Bretton Woods system, during the Keynesian era (Kuttner 1991). The market is seemingly triumphant in all developed capitalist economies. Such largely unexpected success would have been partial, had not the Eastern bloc economies totally collapsed at the end of the 1980s. In conventional terms, market economies correspond to complex institutional settings. Here, markets are the leading force, contrary to what was observed in the so-called socialist or controlled economies. The eagerness of the new democratic governments of the former Eastern bloc countries to embrace the project of a fast transition to free market economies has made the triumph of free marketers overwhelming in the early 1990s. Consequently, the market is now considered by a majority of businessmen and politicians as the co-ordinating mechanism *par excellence*. Some economists, more cautious, might recognize minor or significant limits to markets, but still consider that it is, along with democracy, the least imperfect co-ordinating mechanism for economic activity in complex, decentralized societies.

This chapter recognizes the impressive record of market capitalism for its achievements in terms of allocative and static efficiency (this is generally admitted), but still more in terms of dynamic efficiency (and this is often neglected). In fact, the major achievement of markets is not so much due to the 'invisible hand' process advanced by Adam Smith and then formalized by modern general equilibrium theory, but the markets' ability to stimulate innovation, technological and institutional change. In such a system, even radical or potentially disturbing social struggles can finally exert a positive role by channelling the restructuring of basic institutions and organizations. Eastern European economies have collapsed, not so much due to cumulative imbalances between supply and demand, but due to their inability to deliver mass consumption to the whole population (Boyer 1993). This problem is related, in turn, to the inhibition by planning and political institutions of major innovations in the mass production of consumer durables and agricultural efficiency. Thus, market economies have to be assessed in accordance with their ability to promote a cumulative increase in the standard of living.

The basic aim of this chapter is to challenge the omnipotency of the market as a co-ordinating mechanism within contemporary societies. Markets only become truly efficient when they are embedded into systems developed by the state or private corporations which then play the role of government. In any case, collective agreement and implementation are clearly necessary in order to set up market mechanisms. Any hesitancy in the return to the free market is said to derive from misperceptions or erroneous interpretations of the structural changes which have taken place in recent decades. It is my contention that the prognosis is quite different: market mechanisms will find a significant, but not exclusive role within emerging 'regulation' modes.

The twenty-first century will probably experience a genuine social and political engagement of markets with networks, associations and local communities along with renewed state intervention. It is the task of governments to set political priorities; they cannot simply be replaced by any other mechanisms, especially not markets which usually are quite myopic and generally unable to deal with strategic complementarities which are so crucial in modern economies. The domain for state intervention is, therefore, large indeed, and comprises education and training, the access and financing of healthcare and last, but not least, the production of knowledge, i.e. innovations which are at the core of economic growth. It is, therefore, an illusion to think that during the next century markets will rule. Polanyi's and Keynes's ideas have a promising future, provided they are updated in the context of a new wave of internationalization which defines new constraints and new opportunities for the nation-state.

THE PRO-MARKET STRATEGIES: METHODS FOR ERODING OR DESTROYING THE POST-SECOND WORLD WAR INSTITUTIONAL LEGACY

Post-war stability was not based on the extension of unfettered markets; it was made possible by institutional reforms that constrained the ill effects of markets on society. On the one hand, final and intermediate product markets were organized according to oligopolistic competition, cartel formation at the national or international levels, as well as in accordance with sophisticated public regulations. Consequently, price wars were replaced by gentlemen's agreements between large firms which adopted mark-up price formation and cosmetic product differentiation. On the other hand, two fictitious commodities were protected from competition coming from market pressures. First, money and credit had too important a role in macroeconomic equilibrium to be left to the influence of myopic expectations or the free banking principle. The Keynesian revolution taught that a stable monetary regime was a public good to be provided by a central bank along with complex regulations imposed on commercial banks and financial institutions (Aglietta *et al.* 1990). Second, wage formation was too serious an issue to be left to the vagaries of pure market forces. Implicit in the post-Second World War order was a genuine capital–labour compromise that codified the respective benefits drawn from the implementation of Fordism. Managers were free to organize production and labour processes, whereas workers benefited from an implicit (or explicit) indexation of nominal wages with respect to consumer prices along with productivity sharing schemes (Boyer 1990b).

This entire set of co-ordinating mechanisms has been severely challenged during the last two decades. Such a 'counter-revolution' with respect to the Keynesian breakthrough is so general and universal that it must have strong underlying reasons linked to the economic crisis, but with ideological and political roots.

The 1970s and the 1980s: a general thrust towards market-driven adjustments

First, let us examine how the core Fordist institutional forms have been transforming themselves in response to two oil shocks, fiercer international competition, financial instability and globalization. The following analyses briefly summarize the major findings of the 'regulation' approach (Aglietta 1982; Boyer 1990a) and concern only the larger OECD countries. In sum, virtually all the organizational forms which formed the basis of the un-precedented growth of the 1950s, 1960s and 1970s have been challenged (Table 3.1).

Price competition has become a conventional method for solving com-petitive struggles between large multinational firms, as well as between small

Table 3.1 The pervasiveness of market forces in most of the basic Fordist institutional forms during the 1980s

Institutional forms	Interwar period	The Golden Age 1945–67(73)	Uncertain restructuring of the 1970s and 1980s
1 Wage labour nexus			
• Industrial relations	• Low institutionalization, weak unions' bargaining power	• Rather large institutionalized unions and collective bargaining	• Decentralization of bargaining, decline of most unions
• Wage formation	• Highly decentralized and rather competitive	• More administered than market determined	• More competitive pressures and market-driven wages
• Welfare payment	• Embryonic	• A significant part of indirect wage is institutionalized	• Rationalization or scaling down; some trends towards private insurance
2 Competition among firms			
• On product market	• Strong, price wars during the Great Depression	• Rather weak, competition by the perceived quality	• Fiercer due to international competition and technical change
• On financial market	• Large concentration, but prices are still rather competitive	• Large concentration at the national level, prices are oligopolistic	• Large restructuring at the world level, price wars are back again
3 Monetary regime			
• Credit versus securities	• Incomplete pure credit system, major role of stock market and speculation	• Institutionalization of pure credit systems, little speculation	• Globalization of finance speculation
• Financial regulations	• Emerging but very partial	• Highly regulated and protected banks	• Significant financial deregulations
4 State interventions			
• Public services	• Except for defence, quite limited	• Developed for health, education, transportation	• Austerity and rationalization policies
• State-owned firms	• Very few, except after the crisis of 1929	• Rather significant in some European countries	• Important privatization in some countries
• Welfare	• Emerging but generally not institutionalized	• Institutionalized to varying degrees across countries	• Some reorganization and slimming down, more insurance, less welfare
5 International regime			
• Trade	• Rather open and then protectionism and currency wars	• Progressive liberalization of trade	• In spite of protectionist temptations, ongoing internationalization
• Finance	• Highly active financial flows	• Rather limited *private* financial flows	• Explosion of short-run private capital flows, financial globalization
• Capital	• Limited extent of foreign direct investment	• Significant, mainly American, direct investment	• Important surge of foreign investment

Source: Synthetic table derived from a series of historical studies in terms of 'regulation'

and medium-sized companies. Due to recurring excess capacities, most businesses have tried to sell abroad all the production which could not be absorbed by the home market due to austerity policies in public spending and wage moderation. Given the huge fixed costs associated with most process and hi-tech industries, some sectors (e.g. electronic components, air transportation, telecommunications) have experienced the equivalent of the price wars of the 1930s. A renewal of market competition seems to have destabilized powerful, but sleepy monopolies. At a more theoretical level, modern analyses of contested markets tend to suggest that pure competition should and will prevail as soon as free entry is possible without experiencing too high sunk costs. The ideal of pure and perfect competition has replaced that of a gentle and organized system.

The labour flexibility debate has put a strong emphasis upon the need for more competition in the labour market, especially concerning wage formation. Many reports from international organizations such as the IMF, World Bank and OECD have urged unions, managers and policy-makers to design much more flexible pay systems and labour contracts with variable hours or easy termination (OECD 1985). According to this interpretation, if labour markets are not self-equilibrating – and this was clearly the case in the mid-1980s since unemployment had been rising permanently in highly unionized European countries (Lindbeck and Snower 1986) – then complex public regulations and high unemployment benefits were clearly responsible for what was perceived as an inefficient state. Were the labour market truly competitive, this line of reasoning goes, full employment would be obtained at each moment in time. For example, M. L. Weitzman (1982, 1985) has suggested that profit-sharing schemes would promote a fast return to full employment by reducing labour marginal costs, thus inducing firms to hire more workers. Even if these diagnoses have been challenged, they have been very influential in the design of social deregulation policies, not only within conservative strategies but for some social democratic governments as well (Boyer 1988). The ideal of many firms is now to grant only short-run labour contracts, with flexible wages and easily varied hours worked, in order to make labour markets function as conventional commodity markets do.

Numerous financial innovations have similarly transformed national and international regimes. The banking system inherited from the New Deal and post-Second World War legislation used to apply highly administered interest rates and credit rationing in such a manner that the money market was more a convenient metaphor for presenting the IS-LM model, elaborated by John Hicks to interpret *The General Theory*, than an actual market co-ordinating money supply and demand. The major imbalances generated by the surge of inflation during the 1960s and early 1970s, the financial shocks associated with the rise of oil prices and the emerging competition between banks to capture deposits and grant credits, have promoted the invention of genuine and sophisticated financial instruments. Consequently, the competition over money and financial markets has become more effective and structured than the strategies of the firms and even the households searching for the best returns for their liquidities. Central bankers have been losing a large part of their control over credit which manifests itself via the rapid obsolescence of most of the monetary aggregates designed to monitor monetary supply. Again, competition on the financial market is back and recalls some of the episodes of the interwar period, even if most of the New Deal regulations have not been removed. This explains why the December 1987 Wall Street crash did not trigger any cumulative depression (Boyer 1988). Nevertheless, the ideal of financial authorities is still to debalkanize the previously fragmented credit institutions and organize a global market implementing more competition if not a pure and perfect one. Some advocates of free banking consider that a central bank is no longer necessary and should be replaced by the removal of any barrier to entry, whatever the danger of systemic imbalance (Aglietta 1991). In the terminology of Karl Polanyi this expresses the belief in the possibility of 'One big self-regulating market' for products, labour and money.

Governments have pursued significant deregulation policies just to curb or interrupt the apparent adverse trends associated with larger and larger income transfers by the state. A major conservative counter-revolution has taken place during the last two decades. Whereas the post-Second World War state was allowed to be interventionist in order to promote the emergence of Fordism, to enhance the implementation of welfare systems and to control the level of economic activity by fine tuning, rising difficulties have resulted in a drastic shift towards more *laissez-faire* strategies. According to this approach, nationalized firms in the productive sector should be privatized (and actually have been in the United Kingdom and in France), under the view that, by nature, private managers are more competent than any bureaucrat. Second, the public welfare system has been seen by a vocal fraction of businessmen as an incentive to laziness, inefficiency and low saving rates. From a conceptual point of view, the principle of solidarity has been challenged and replaced by the objective of private insurance. Let free individuals choose the type of income security they can afford. Third, the argument goes that the state should remove most of the regulations which prevent firms, workers and bankers from concluding mutually beneficial arrangements. Here, any limitation to price formation is seen as detrimental to the welfare of society. Finally, according to the neo-Austrian school (Hayek 1976–82) and the rational expectation theorists (Lucas 1988), individual economic agents are assumed to be better informed than distant and probably not-so-competent bureaucrats. Any attempt to influence the level of macroeconomic activity will be circumvented by clever agents who know that in the future the government will have to raise taxes in order to pay for present public deficit spending or that any excess in money supply results in inflation, without any long-term impact upon unemployment. As far as ideology and theory are concerned, Keynes is dead and Doctor Pangloss has been revived! Let the market guide and co-ordinate the difficult choices that nobody is able to outline, let alone explain.

The current international regime is a strange mix of a decaying Bretton Woods system with more and more market adjustments upon currency markets. The same reversal has taken place in the international area as for domestic affairs (Kuttner 1991). Following the interwar distrust of the ability of markets to make compatible contradictory national monetary and economic policies, the Bretton Woods agreement implemented a largely institutional process of adjustment, with a limited scope for market logic. The exchange rates were fixed and set by national authorities in accordance with principles shared by the international community. The progressive demise of this international regime (for a general analysis see Krasner 1983; Keohane 1984; Campbell and Dougan 1986; Rosenan and Czempiel 1992) has brought back competitive mechanisms in interest rate and exchange rate formation. Consequently, the floating exchange rates which were supposed to deliver smooth adjustments and high predictability have generated totally opposite outcomes; large swings in the relative position of the dollar, the yen and the Deutschmark have repeatedly surprised even the most sophistic-ated analysts. Since speculation is now the leading motive for buying or selling a currency, financial markets have lost their previous built-in stability (Kaldor 1939; Orléan 1990). Nevertheless, in the absence of any alternative and more coherent international financial regime, the market mechanism is still assumed to be the only co-ordinating device available to make various and contrasted national policies more or less congruent. Surprisingly, the poor macroeconomic and financial outcomes observed since 1971 have not seriously affected the optimism of most advocates of pure market mechan-isms.

Clearly, the invisible hand of Adam Smith is affecting all the institutional forms generated by the Fordist growth regime. Of course, the previous analysis is quite general and mainly applies to conservative governments such as those of Reagan, Thatcher and Mulroney. One could find societies in which such moves towards the market have been more a tribute to the orthodoxy of the 1980s than an actual strategy. Japan and Germany have scarcely deregulated their financial, labour and product markets. By contrast, France and Sweden, with socialist or social democratic governments, have been engaged in significant revisions of their financial institutions as well as of their labour markets. Such an acceptance of the belief in market mechanisms as well as their actual implementation deserves an explanation.

'Facing these mysteries we do not understand, let us pretend that we invented them . . .'

Several converging reasons can serve to explain the current paradigmatic change concerning core co-ordinating economic mechanisms. First, there has been a turn from collective actions and public interventions to a reliance on the invisible hand, i.e. a purely anonymous market adjustment. In addition, an argument relying upon cognitive maps can be added. The whole set of political compromises, productive organization, collective representations, economic theory and policies has been progressively eroded and has lost its credibility in explaining the rather surprising events of the 1980s (Figure 3.1).

At the same time, alternative models have collapsed or lost attractiveness. On one hand, the emerging crisis of the Eastern European bloc was perceived long before the collapse of the Berlin Wall and the exceptionally rapid and surprising transition towards markets and political democracy. In other words, the old model of a command or planned economy was raising as many imbalances, frustrations and inequalities as the capitalist 'anarchy of the market', according to the conventional Marxist view. Clearly, in the Western world, even the most orthodox communist parties did not dare to express their adherence to the Soviet economic model. In the actually existing socialist economies, the defects and limits of this model had been perceived very early on by the persons in the street and by politicians and economists who had been desperately pursuing one economic reform after another (in the Soviet Union, Hungary and Poland).

To a much lesser extent, a similar reappraisal has taken place for the social democratic model as implemented in Scandinavian countries and in Austria. Even when this model was still believed to deliver full employment and equal income distribution, it was more admired abroad than at home. Especially in Sweden, the new generations were attracted by individualistic values, whereas firms and businesses complained about reduced wage differentials and an excessive tax burden. In actuality, a drastic reduction in the share of public spending and welfare has been observed in Sweden since the mid-1980s. Most politicians and even many unionists admit that more market flexibility has to be brought into the Scandinavian model. The globalization of competition, the surge of Swedish investment abroad and the prospect of joining the European Community reinforce the erosion of this quite original model, even if it remains largely unique. To recast a well-known Marxist formula: is not the market the inescapable future for modern societies?

After all, markets could veil our ignorance of complex and largely unintended contemporary structural transformations. If fully fledged alternatives to the Fordist regime could be designed and implemented according to a clear process, then the market could be used as a tool in guiding this transition. But, on the contrary, the belief in the omnipotence of the market is frequently adopted just to hide a poor understanding of the ongoing processes. On a closer look, the justifications for adopting basic market mechanisms belong to four broad categories:

1 The invisible hand argument is again fashionable, in the very sense Adam Smith meant it in the eighteenth century. Markets are the only known mechanisms for making compatible initially independent and possibly

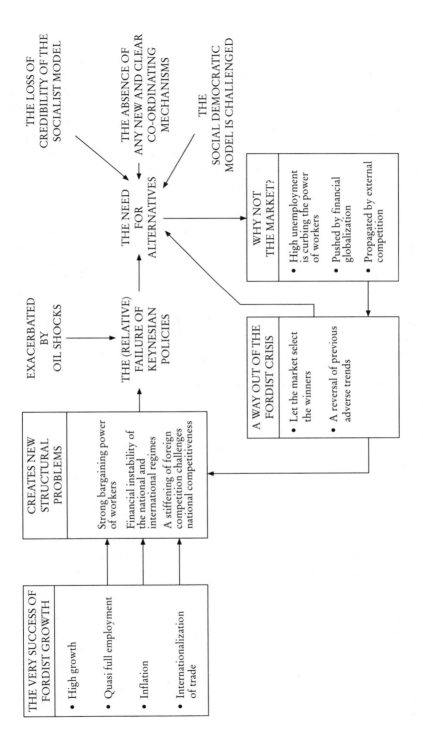

Figure 3.1 How to explain the return to the belief of self-regulating markets

conflicting strategies of a large number of individual agents pursuing their own self-interests. This process unintentionally delivers an efficient use of the existing resources and talents, i.e. a *Pareto optimum*; the satisfaction of one agent cannot be improved without impairing that of another. By contrast, even the more sophisticated central planning routines would be less efficient, more costly in information management and statistics (Heal 1971) and less alert in responding to changing consumers' needs or desires. This argument has been recurrently used in interpreting the structural crisis of the Soviet model and its subsequent collapse (Bourguignon 1990). Demonstration of the possibility of general equilibrium is fairly complex, but policy debates need not dwell on technicalities.

2 Socializing and combining scattered and partial information is a second and major attribute of market economies. In the Austrian case, which follows the ideas of von Mises and F. von Hayek, the main task of markets is not only to organize transactions and set prices and incomes, but to take into account the scattered and specific knowledge owned by each household or firm and transmit it to the rest of society via supply and demand and ultimately price formation. Contrary to the hopes of socialist market economists (Brus 1987), no central planner will ever be able to collect the relevant information about consumers' tastes and firms' production functions. In really existing socialist economies, the managers have vested interests in hiding their true productive capabilities, whereas the planners do not have any method to reveal the changing preference of consumers nor to enhance organizational and techno-logical innovations.

3 Stimulating technical change and innovations precisely defines a third feature for economic systems ruled by strong competition associated with the diffusion of markets as the main co-ordinating mechanism. The *Wealth of Nations* opens with four rather neglected, if frequently quoted chapters. The argument does not relate to the role of the market in converging towards the so-called 'natural prices', i.e. the only legacy taken into account by the Marshallian or Walrasian theories. In the case of the Soviet Union, the model has not only collapsed due to its static inefficiency (how to make an equal number of right and left shoes), but even more on account of its failure to deliver the possibility of raising living standards. The socialist system has not caught up with the capitalist world, due to its inhibition of technical change and innovation. Consequently, one of the best arguments for market capital-ism is that competition enhances the division of labour, invention of machinery, learning by doing and thus a cumulative decline in some relative prices and the opening of new markets in a cumulative causation model. In other words, markets might be somehow inefficient in the short run (in-ducing, for example, oversupply, unemployment and possibly some transit-ory instabilities). Nevertheless, they are the necessary ingredients for reaping the dynamic increasing returns of scale associated with competition and its stimulus of innovation.

4 Selecting among alternative organizations and institutions might be another task quite well fulfilled by markets. If the model of development is clear, the role of the market will be simply to co-ordinate decentralized behaviours along this growth path. Unfortunately, the visible hand implemented by the large firm and conglomerates (Chandler 1977) or the invisible handshake between capital and labour (Okun 1981) have somehow vanished into contrasted and competing models for firm internal organization, subcontracting and the wage–labour nexus (Boyer 1988, 1990b). Therefore, how can choices be made among alternatives given that most economic agents do not have the relevant information for deciding on purely rational criteria (i.e. maximizing the flow of actualized profits over an infinite period with perfect knowledge)? It is very tempting to consider that the markets are indeed a Darwinian mechanism for selecting among numerous and complex strategies. Here, one recognizes the evolutionary process put forward by Joseph Schumpeter and his modern followers: let the market decide among options that individuals are unable to screen out and discriminate between. For example, if in the Golden years, some successful and innovative industrial policies could be implemented, the 1980s have undergone a drastic revision of the possibility that governments or public agencies could influence efficiently strategic choices. 'Pick the winners!' has been the only motto put forward by these very passive industrial policy-makers. They should eventually speed up the process of diffusion of new technologies and organizations once the market forces have selected the good ones.

LOOSE AND CONTRADICTORY DEFINITIONS OF THE MARKET HELP THE DIFFUSION OF MARKET IDEOLOGY

The Keynesian 'Paradox of saving' is not easy to understand by the person in the street: during depressions, the more people save in order to restore investment, the lower the employment level, the less optimistic views of the future and the lower the investment level. By contrast, the notion of market equilibrium is so straightforward, practised and widely observed in everyday transactions, that most of the arguments of free marketers find immediate support in public opinion. (For instance, in order to induce a recovery in investment, is it not sufficient to save more?) Similarly, most economists would recognize that in many instances the replacement of administrative or bureaucratic organization by a free market would improve the welfare of both suppliers and demanders. These two observations call for closer investigation.

From the middle-age market-place to market economies: a clarification

As Monsieur Jourdain in Molière's *Comedies* states without being conscious of being so literate, everybody knows about markets and by his (her)

95

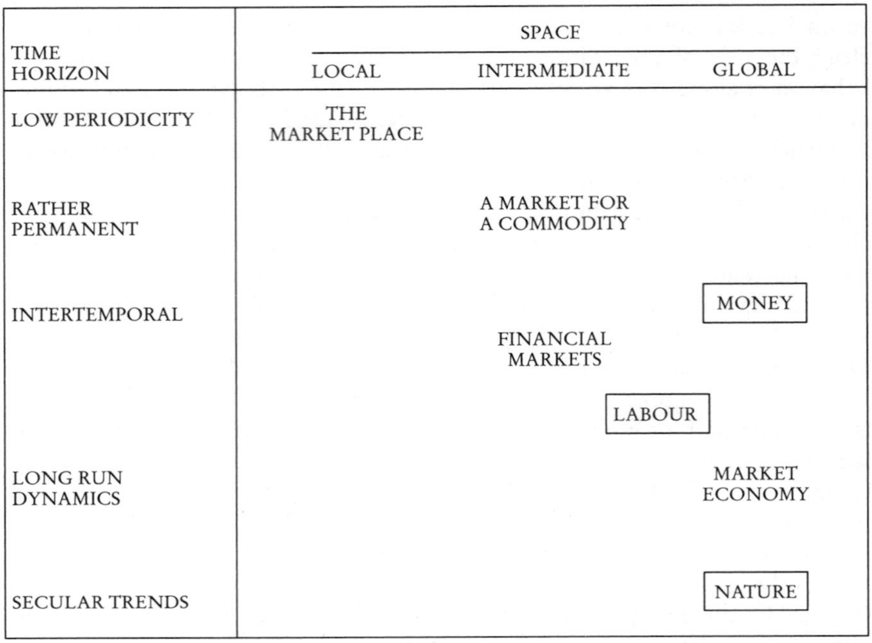

TIME HORIZON	SPACE		
	LOCAL	INTERMEDIATE	GLOBAL
LOW PERIODICITY	THE MARKET PLACE		
RATHER PERMANENT		A MARKET FOR A COMMODITY	
INTERTEMPORAL		FINANCIAL MARKETS	MONEY
		LABOUR	
LONG RUN DYNAMICS			MARKET ECONOMY
SECULAR TRENDS			NATURE

Figure 3.2 From a micro-adjustment process to a complete economic system: too many meanings for the single word 'market'
Note: The rectangles are used to label fictitious commodities in the sense of Karl Polanyi

everyday experience and behaviour has a seemingly clear definition or view. Unfortunately, the word 'market' has taken on so many meanings that the success of any reference to it might be attributed to very loose and partially contradictory definitions which inevitably vary from one culture and language to another. Newspapers, financial articles, applied research and economic theories suggest at least six different meanings (Figure 3.2):

1 In French, the term 'marché', which is usually translated as market, very often defines the equivalent of a contract, i.e. a bilateral agreement for delivering at some date a given quantity of a specified good for a fixed price eventually revised according to some explicit formula. For example, building companies have been competing for getting the contract of the Paris la Défense Arch new tower. The bid and the related and sophisticated public legislation and private routines for organizing this competition are named 'un marché'. In English, public or private procurement would be the approximate equivalent to this selection device. In this case, the market does not coordinate independent strategies, but organizes the screening of the various offers and helps in selecting the best (i.e. generally the least costly) bid.

Significantly, the final contract, as negotiated, is bilateral and is enforced by the general legal system provided by the commercial laws prevailing in the area considered. This scenario is at odds with the conventional definition of the market as the locus where anonymous supplies and demands interact, with weak or no legal involvement. Nevertheless, this conception is less marginal than it might seem, as it is commonplace in capitalist economies, if not in formally socialist countries. In the latter case, this absence contributes to blocking the transition towards market mechanisms, commercial contracts being an elementary but basic ingredient of markets.

2 In the emergence of modern capitalist economies, the market is clearly associated with a precise locale and time schedule. A market-place is 'an authorized public concourse of buyers and sellers of commodities, meeting at a place more or less strictly delimited or defined, at an appointed time'. This is the definition provided by the British Royal Commission on Market Rights and Tolls in 1891 (Hill 1987). In contemporary economies, however, only few markets are organized accordingly, with the exception of itinerant and periodic markets for food, agricultural products, flowers, antiques (i.e. a very limited scope in the whole set of transactions). Nevertheless, Karl Polanyi (1946) and Fernand Braudel (1979) have carefully investigated how market mechanisms have emerged from a highly regulated and institutionalized economic life. Contemporary global markets are the last followers of this embryonic form of market, which has been conquering a larger and larger fraction of commodities, and ultimately some factor markets such as labour (Rothenberg 1992).

3 Classical and neo-classical economists have given an even wider definition of markets: 'In the literal sense, [a market is] a place in which things are bought and sold. In the modern industrial system it has expanded to include the whole geographical area in which sellers compete with each other for consumers' (Marshall 1890). One can, for example, read in the financial press that in 1990 the market for tyres had undergone a severe recession in the United States due to the decline of car sales in Detroit, or alternatively that the price of apartments in New York has declined since the latest recession began in 1990. This third concept posits a kind of aggregation over a given geographical area and/or for one product or close substitutes. Note that here the market is losing its concrete nature – it is no more the market-*place* – but is gaining in its increasing abstraction increased analytical relevance, at least for economists or people engaged in marketing. In some extreme cases, the market could mean the demand addressed to a given sector, or even the economy at large, implying the equivalent of effective aggregate demand. This second definition is not at all equivalent to the first one.

4 According to a fourth conception, the market is basically a mechanism for making compatible a series of individual supplies and demands. Consequently, some theoreticians insist upon the fact that the market is stable when the equilibrium price is obtained. This notion goes back to Adam Smith and has resurfaced in neo-classical economics. To quote Alfred Marshall

(1890), 'Economists understand by the term of market, not only particular marketplaces in which things are bought and sold, but the whole of any region in which buyers and sellers are in such a free intercourse with one another that the price of the same goods tends to equality, easily and quickly.' A new and rather abstract property is, therefore, added to the definition of a market; it should adjust and converge towards a unique price. Thus, the concreteness of the market-place is contrasted with the theoretical and abstract properties of a self-equilibrating mechanism. The shift from a positive conception to another one, much more normative, is very clear in Marshall: 'The more nearly perfect the market is the stronger is the tendency for the same price to be paid for the same thing at the same time in all parts of the market.' Here is the ideal type of pure and perfect market mechanism.

5 A fifth conception recognizes a whole set of interdependent markets. When, for example, economists and politicians consider the transition of socialist economies towards markets, they characterize an economic system in which market competition is dominant or exclusive. For example, intermediate products can be distributed according to large-scale planning (consider the surprising success of early French planning after the Second World War), but markets still prevail for consumer durables and final goods – land, labour and capital. Therefore, there exists a complete spectrum of so-called market economies. Implicitly, or explicitly for some authors (Braudel 1979), market economy is an alternative labelling for capitalism, private property and competition – i.e. terms which are not logically equivalent. As far as economic theory is concerned, the conception of L. Walras is extended in modern equilibrium theory (Arrow and Hahn 1971). On this view, all economic agents are interacting via the equilibration of a complete system of interdependent demands expressed in every commodity market, but also for capital goods and the services of labour. Only money is not supplied and offered since it is the simple *numéraire* in which all nominal prices are expressed. Here, any kind of macroeconomic mechanism is abolished. Again, one is struck by the large discrepancy between the empirical definition of a market economy and its more sophisticated formalization. Truly existing institutions are implicitly compared with the ideal of a society co-ordinated by a series of pure and perfect markets upon which no single individual has any influence but is free to choose (Friedman 1962, 1981).

6 In a metaphoric view, a market is assumed to exist when and where social actors compete with each other in order to get scarce resources or some restricted positions or status. When individuals with conflicting objectives interact and finally converge towards an agreement or transaction, some economists or sociologists might conclude the existence of a 'market'. For example, the Chicago School has extended the concepts of rationality, equilibrium and market to a large diversity of social issues: the market for marriage, the economics of crime, the supply and demand of justice, the market for donations to churches and or beliefs in eternal life (Becker 1964,

1981). Such an extensive, perhaps imperialist use of the concept of market is not without interest and simultaneously exhibits very severe limits. On one side, Karl Marx and his followers – including the American Institutionalist School à la Veblen – have quite rightly pointed out that under capitalism everything (e.g. social respect, love, the promise of eternal life, political influence) becomes a commodity. In a sense, the Chicago theoreticians have taken the Marxist prognosis seriously. But, on the other side, the use of the concept of market becomes so loose that it is more mystifying than enlightening. For instance, even if some private firms specialize in matching offers and demands for marriage, is it reasonable to assume that the market is the distributing mechanism between husbands and brides? Similarly, a market of political ideas and programmes probably exists, but does not provide any deep insight into the underlying issues of political debates. In fact, the interactions between markets and politics are far more complex (Hibbs 1987; Alesina and Carliner 1991). At this point, the market becomes so wide in its scope that it does not mean anything any more.

Undoubtedly, however, the polyvalency of the notion of 'market' has played some role in the impressive comeback of free market ideas. Everybody has encountered one form or another of a market and intuitively applies some meaning to the concept, at the possible cost of major misunderstandings. Is there any relation between the market-place for antiques and the call for a transition of Eastern European economies towards a market system?; between a contract or public procurement and the enchanted world of the Marshallian partial equilibrium or Walrasian general equilibrium? Probably little or none, and in troubled times political programmes and ideologies benefit from such ambiguity.

What is a market economy? A variety of configurations

For the purposes of this chapter it is important to propose a clear definition of 'market', however imperfect and provisional, in order to bring some clarity to the following analyses. Four different levels of definition have to be disentangled and recombined in a second step.

At the level of a single commodity, a market is an institution which co-ordinates *ex post* the strategies of multiple competing traders, initially independent, but finally interacting via price formation. Moreover, a full-fledged market supposes a well-defined commodity, as respects quality and quantity; it presumes repetitive transactions, regularly organized and somehow centralized, or at least made compatible by joint adjustments. In really existing economies, any single market is inserted into a whole set of other markets, organizations and institutions. For example, the existence of a monetary system is a prerequisite in the functioning of any commodity market: in what unit are nominal prices expressed? How are transactions

99

paid? What are the methods for balancing the agents with deficit and surplus, i.e. how is the credit market structured? Similarly, a minimum legal environment is needed in order to guarantee economic agents buying and selling parity which necessitates either the existence of a business association in charge of the functioning of the market, or a public authority enforcing private contracts. In the absence of these two institutions enforcing the rules of the game, any market will collapse due to the spreading of opportunistic behaviour among traders. For instance, insider trading upon the stock market can destroy the confidence of outsiders and stop or reduce transactions. Even if pure and perfect markets can be self-equilibrating they are not self-enforcing, for they need an external foundation in the legal system, business ethics or agreed rules of the game (Shand 1990).

There is not just one, but rather a multiplicity of functioning regimes for various markets. Contrary to the ideal of markets of pure and perfect competition, characterized by Adam Smith, elaborated by Alfred Marshall and generalized by Leon Walras, the interactions between a limited number of traders, with unequal wealth and market power, might deliver contrasting market structures. For example, a market may emerge as a structure of roles with a differentiated niche for each firm (White 1981). Joint competition over quality and price does not necessarily lead to a sustainable market configuration since at least three market failures are theoretically observed. Thus, a large variety of markets (White 1988) are structurally embedded into a series of constraints (Leifer and White 1988). Further, the very precise institutionalization of the market may have important consequences on its functioning and the overall macroeconomic outcome (Lesourne 1991). Modern industrial economics, as well as micro-formalizations about technical change and innovation, exhibits a complete spectrum of market configurations: complete or partial monopoly, cartel and collusion, oligopoly, contestable market, perfectly contestable market, pure and perfect competition, complete or partial monopsony, etc. And this is only a partial list of forms of competition (Stiglitz and Mathewson 1986; Tirole, 1988). As far as the efficiency and welfare aspects of a market are concerned, they cannot be assessed independently from such phenomena. Such considerations should inform any decision taken concerning deregulation and privatization. If, for example, Eastern European firms as monopolies or oligopolies are privatized in the absence of any foreign competition, then few of the expected benefits of a pure and perfect competition will be reaped. The same remark could be addressed to the privatization programme launched by the British and French governments in the mid-1980s; changing the forms of property does not automatically imply any strengthening of competition.

The extent and the scope of the market can itself vary from a totally marginal role (for instance the long-distance trade in the Middle Ages) to an overwhelming mechanism percolating within the whole of society and transforming even subtle social relations into mere commodities transacted in specific kinds of (pseudo-)markets. Thus, the notion of a market economy as one unique configuration is misleading and largely contradicted by international comparisons between North and South, East and West (Freeman 1989; Esping-Andersen 1990) as well as by long-run historical studies showing the very slow process of market emergence (Polanyi 1946; Lindblom 1971 Braudel 1979; Galenson 1989). It is important to investigate if market mechanisms are limited to the exchange of intermediate products between firms, or concern final goods directed to the domestic or international markets. Similarly, the property itself can be priced on specific markets such as the stock exchange, whereas the various financial assets may or may not be traded upon specific markets. After the wave of financial innovations of the last two decades, even more sophisticated markets have been implemented in which traders are exchanging forecasts about the evolution of key macroeconomic variables, i.e. the so-called market for futures. This kind of market, based upon the photography game imagined by John Maynard Keynes, consists in finding the equivalent of the prettier face as seen by the *majority*, not oneself. This bears little relation to the market place for antiques in Foire Saint Germain which takes place each year near Paris! Ultimately, the market might become a big co-ordinating mechanism for fictitious commodities traded in very specific markets: labour, if a social relation could be regulated by pure supply and demand mechanisms; money, if various banks can issue their own currency, the value of which would be assessed upon an interbank currency market; polluting rights, when they can be exchanged between firms. Remember that in this case it is not an exchange between economic agents and nature, but between individuals buying and selling rights granted by a local or national public authority. In fact, it is not a private good but a public good, with strong externalities and consequently possible failures of pure market adjustments.

Thus, an economic system with a leading role given to market competition should be characterized by cross-definition between several factors (Figure 3.3):

1 The list of institutions, organizations, legislation or associations which are organizing the functioning of the various markets, with a detailed description of their responsibilities, objectives, tools and enforcement tools or incentives.
2 The series of commodities, the supply and demand of which is regulated by market institutions, with their possible interactions with alternative co-ordinating mechanisms (hierarchies, networks, state regulation).
3 A characterization of the forms of competition, according to the number of traders, the distribution of ownership, the distribution of market power and the possible explicit or implicit co-ordinating mechanisms in order, for example, to solve over-capacity problems or to respond to uncertainty and/ or structural changes.

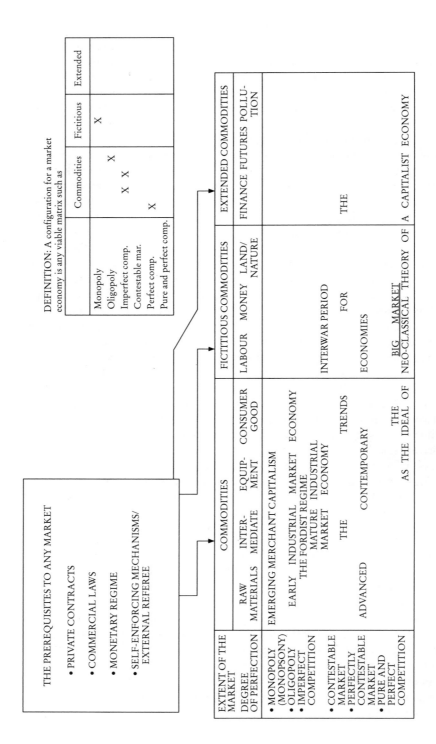

Figure 3.3 What is a market economy? A quasi-continuum of configurations

Such a three-dimensional system could define as many market economic systems as there are combinations of cells in the original matrix. The relative proportion of markets employing alternative mechanisms could constitute a measure for a pure, perfect and complete market economy. For instance, it has been argued that, in modern economies, the co-ordination between the large firms is as important as market adjustments (Coase 1937, 1988) and that planned co-ordination has largely replaced market co-ordination (Lazonick 1991). Then, the most interesting problem for the social sciences, especially political economy and economic analysis, would be to assess the viability of these various configurations and compare them with respect to their welfare properties.

Generally, each form of market is completed by or embedded within a series of other co-ordinating mechanisms which are based either on obligation (and not only self-interest) and/or vertical co-ordination, alliances, hierarchies, communities, networks, public authorities (Coleman 1990; Schmitter 1990; Campbell *et al.* 1991). The task for social scientists would then be to assess the viability – and not so much the efficiency – of such a complex hierarchy of constitutional principles, institutions, incentive schemes and organizations (North 1990). Thus, the product, labour and credit markets might organize a competition between alternative organizations (Favereau 1989) and not only between old and new technologies (Nelson and Winter 1982). This is the huge but stimulating agenda which is proposed by recent analyses (Hollingsworth *et al.* 1993).

MODERN ECONOMIC THEORY AGAINST DR PANGLOSS'S OPTIMISM

The idea that markets are self-regulating has traditionally been criticized by economic historians, anthropologists and sociologists. Clearly, the emergence of markets has been a very long and contradictory process associated with structural crises and instabilities. And, at the micro level, the few examples of markets implementing a pure and perfect competition suggest that their viability depends on a complex and tricky nexus of public regulations and collective organizations (commodity markets, Wall Street, the markets for futures, etc.). In each case, the market is the end-product of a social and political construction.

Surprisingly, the most critical reassessment of the power of markets comes from within economic theory itself. Recurrently, the idea of the invisible hand has proved to be far more problematic than envisioned by Adam Smith and, more recently, *laissez-faire* economists. A careful reading of the theory of markets shows how numerous and precise are the hypotheses necessary to ensure the optimum state of market equilibrium. This optimum will be challenged or the market may totally collapse under the weight of the following conditions: if the quality of the good is uncertain and information

103

asymmetric; if the technology derives from a learning by doing and using process or from network externalities; if the auctioneer is replaced by a complete decentralization of transactions in a monetary economy; if only few contingent markets or insurance mechanisms can be implemented; and when the commitment of workers is related to the fulfilment of fairness criteria, i.e. if the equity principle partially explains static and dynamic efficiency (Wolf 1990). There might be no equilibrium or too many or unstable ones, and more generally the market can be Pareto inferior to alternative organizations provided by networks, associations or even vertically integrated firms. Modern theoreticians therefore strongly disagree with the rather optimistic views propagated by the more vocal advocates of free markets; when the economy becomes complex, the reliance on pure market mechanisms raises as many problems as it solves.

Markets are unable to deal with collective goods such as education and the environment

Even if one supposes that quality is well defined and that a large number of economic agents are pushing towards a competitive equilibrium, the result might be far away from a Pareto optimum if the services derived from the use of a product cannot be totally appropriated by the buyer. A well-known example relates to public goods such as security, law enforcement, defence or clean air; the benefits from such goods cannot be appropriated privately and, conversely, it is difficult to rely on pure market mechanisms in order to organize the equilibrium between supply and demand (Coase 1960). Everybody would like such collective goods to be available, but nobody is ready to pay for them. When asked if they should be implemented by a public agency, people refuse to reveal their private utility. One recognizes the free-rider problem inherent to public goods (Schotter 1990) and collective action (Olson 1965; Sandler 1992). Consequently, the market mechanism has to be replaced by another co-ordination device, which might be, for example, regulations, compulsory requirements, delegation to an agency or provision of a typical public good by the state. A special field of economic theory has been built in order to facilitate public choices. It consistently shows that it is quite difficult to design optimal devices which would be as efficient as markets for purely private goods. Consequently, the market failure related to their inability to deal with public goods finally leads to state or associations interventions which might nevertheless be plagued by many other kinds of failures (Wolf 1979, 1990).

But the existence of externalities is far more general than the diffusion of pure public goods; some can be partially appropriated but, nevertheless, have either positive or negative external effects. For instance, it has been shown that education enhances innovation, health, growth and productivity at a society-wide level. If individuals freely decide to both consume and invest in education, the level of aggregate investment will be inferior to the optimal level for the whole economy. Again, the pure market mechanism has to be mitigated or complemented by collective intervention in order to restore more efficient results: through subsidies to schools or students, public funding of the educational system and the participation of associations in delivering the adequate level of education. *Mutatis mutandis*, the same arguments could be put forward for healthcare: in the absence of adequate insurance or welfare, individuals will tend to under-invest in prevention and health maintenance, since the general level of health is the equivalent of a public good.

The same inefficiency of markets prevails when these externalities are negative. If clean air and water are considered as free goods, then firms and individuals will prefer to save costly resources instead of preserving the environment. Again, some public intervention is needed: either standards limiting pollution levels or implementation of laws governing polluting rights. This seems to mimic a market mechanism, but is not at all the equivalent of a conventional supply and demand adjustment since Nature does not react in accordance with economic objectives. Nor is its behaviour easy to forecast given the basic uncertainty about the underlying physical and chemical mechanisms (weather warming, ozone layer, urban pollution, etc.). In all cases, a pure market economy would under-invest in health, education and infrastructure. Given the importance of these issues in contemporary societies, there is clearly a limit to the omnipotence of markets.

Markets against innovation, dynamic efficiency and growth

A special configuration for positive externalities relates to the increasing returns of scale associated with the division of labour. This idea may be traced back to Adam Smith, who put forward the basic hypothesis that labour division allows specialization and consequently large productivity increases, which are positively related to the size of the product market. The *Wealth of Nations* delivers a paradox: the stability of a monetary order induces the diffusion of markets which in turn allows labour division and increasing returns of scale. But this hypothesis is quite disruptive for General Equilibrium Theory: if the returns to scale are superior to one, then no pure and perfect competition equilibrium can be sustained (Debreu 1959). In really existing economies, one large monopoly firm would capture the whole market and then would charge an oligopolistic price. This would deplete the level of demand and the output below the optimum level of the society. In old-fashioned terms, in the presence of increasing returns of scale, competition leads to oligopolistic or even monopolistic configurations which are nowhere near the optimum towards which market mechanisms were supposed to converge according to the two welfare theorems.

This argument has been rejuvenated in recent research on the sources of capitalist growth. It has been shown that in the absence of increasing returns of scale or positive externalities, the growth of any national economy will exhaust itself (Romer 1986; Amable and Guellec 1992). This was precisely the Schumpeterian argument concerning the viability of capitalism; the competitive process induces the search for innovation, that in turn delivers monopoly rents which can be invested. But followers usually copy the path-breaking innovation, and the diffusion process progressively erodes profit, ultimately putting an end to the long boom triggered by the initial innovation. Endogenous innovation and technical change are the two basic features of capitalism, both development (i.e. a long-term trend towards rising productivity and standard of living) and the unescapable recurrence of booms and depressions. This reality is far different from the smooth process postulated by conventional economic theory.

Another paradox of contemporary economic theory emerges. If the emphasis is shifted from a static adjustment process to the sources of innovation and endogenous growth, then increasing returns of scale have to be taken into account as a prerequisite for any cumulative and sustained growth. Provided that the firms take for granted the external effects exerted by their own decisions, a series of static equilibria can be obtained by a totally decentralized market economy (Lucas 1988; Romer 1990). But the related equilibria will no more correspond to Pareto optima since everybody will generally under-invest in research development which exhibits positive external effects. Thus, alternative co-ordinating mechanisms have to be designed in order to fight market failures: subsidies to innovative firms, public laboratories, credit incentives. In some extreme cases, the rivalry in innovations may induce a duplication of R&D expenditures and consequently too quick an innovation rate leading to possible structural unemployment; more old jobs are destroyed by innovation than created by its implementation (Aghion and Howitt 1993).

Therefore, markets may be good for triggering innovation, but bad in monitoring the optimum pace for technical change. In short, market mechanisms may stunt economic growth, i.e. the inner mechanisms for capitalism's dynamism and survival. Modern economic theories have definitely discarded the Panglossian optimism of old conventional neo-classical theory: there exists an *optimum* degree for market competition which is not necessarily the maximum one.

Markets may destroy basic social values

For conventional economic theory, distributional equity issues are totally separable from efficiency. Economic theory has only to consider efficiency; the philosopher and political scientist will take into account the equity issue. If, for example, the distribution of income and wealth is not accepted by the public, an optimal redistribution scheme can be implemented in order to shift the economy from one Pareto equilibrium to another more satisfactory from a social justice point of view (Wolf 1990). From this standpoint, the market would be neutral with respect to social justice.

This vision has been challenged by many analysts; for societies, social justice is as essential as truth for scientific theories – efficiency follows. Thus, inefficient economic configurations can be accepted provided they fit with prevailing conceptions concerning fairness and social justice. Really existing democratic regimes and market economies are now facing a dilemma between economic efficiency and social justice. The conventional answer is to let the economist depict the related trade-off and give the politician the task of selecting the optimal mix between efficiency and equity (Samuelson and Nordhaus 1992).

More recent research challenges this clear-cut distinction, but implements contrasted strategies. On one side, some economists suggest that initially, even if the outcome of market mechanisms is perceived as unfair, when the game is played again and again, agents finally consider the outcome just (Kahneman *et al*. 1986). Here, economic efficiency shapes prevailing conceptions of social justice. On the other hand, some theoreticians argue that law and juris-prudence are finally aimed at increasing the surplus or welfare of the economy (Posner 1981); the institutions devoted to the implementation of justice, therefore, enhance efficiency.

It is clear that some extreme inequalities which result from the strengthen-ing of market allocation might finally hurt the acceptance of the principles of a market economy, especially if citizens can vote and express their dissent with the prevailing configuration of income and wealth distribution. Accord-ing to this vision, extreme inequalities finally do more harm than good *vis-à-vis* market efficiency; they foster poor commitment and loyalty, insecurity, threats to private property and personal security. All these negative factors call for more public intervention and spending which induces the allocation of scarce resources to unproductive uses. These ideas especially apply to the contemporary labour market. If unfairly treated, wage-earners will reply with poor productivity, low quality, high absenteeism and a growth in social conflict. By contrast, a more equitable income distribution can enhance private and global efficiency (Akerlof 1984). Similarly, labour markets are not self-adjusting as typical good markets because workers have definite feelings about the unfairness of wage cuts which would destroy group solidarity (Solow 1990).

Historical analyses suggest that market failure is related precisely to the inability of this mechanism to cope with prevailing conceptions of social justice. For example, the widening of inequalities during the early stages of the Industrial Revolution was responsible for political and social flux, which finally hurt economic efficiency. *Mutatis mutandis*, the current transition of Eastern European countries towards a market economy has put forward the possible contradiction between the implementation of the market and the preservation of a minimum degree of solidarity and equity. Evidently, social acceptance of markets is not automatic but supposes a voluntary adhesion to their values and consequences, i.e. a definite social fabric (Douglas 1986).

The advances of research in microeconomic theory have weakened most of the conventional reasons for believing in the absolute efficiency of markets. They are self-equilibrating and deliver Pareto optima only under very restricted conditions (Fleurbaey 1990): it is a question of empirical analysis of each issue, not of a grand totalizing theory. This leads to a much more modest approach. Markets may be the least unsatisfactory way to deal with private information, given the inability of agents to draw a complete picture of a myriad of interdependent decisions in a quite uncertain environment. This is the argument first expressed by Hayek in his 1945 essay, 'The Use of Knowledge in Society' (Hayek 1980), and has been recently rediscovered by the economic profession outside the neo-Austrian school (Lavoie 1986).

Quite paradoxically in the 1990s, the reliance on markets has become more a question of informed (or naïve) opinion than the outcome of mathematical demonstration. In this respect, Eastern European governments may rightfully prefer the dynamism (and possible disorder) of markets to the stagnation of centralized planning (Kornai 1980, 1992). It is only by adequate institutional design that markets deliver an acceptable mix between short-run efficiency, long-run innovation and a minimal degree of social justice (Kregel *et al.* 1992). The need for Eastern Europe to invent new rules of the game and institutions along with markets is more and more recognized by experts (Clague and Rausser 1992).

STILL THE EPOCH OF THE NATION-STATE

The present analysis leads to an impressive paradox. At the very moment when post-Second World War institutions are being reassessed and partially reformed under the pressures of deregulation, foreign competition and anti-Keynesian political programmes, the sophistication of modern economic theory warns about the numerous market failures which would affect societies devoid of any complementary or alternative co-ordinating mechanisms. The state remains the most powerful institution to channel and tame the power of markets. In the absence of countervailing regulation, economic analysis shows that persisting unemployment, recurring financial crises, rising inequalities, under-investment in productive activities such as education and research, cumulative asymmetry of information and power, are some possible outcomes of a complete reliance on pure market functioning.

The events of the 1980s and early 1990s warn us that these evils do not belong to the realm of theory but are clearly experienced by major advanced countries. A second and important argument in favour of renewed state intervention is precisely that the free marketers have simply not delivered the

Table 3.2 The promises and outcomes of the free marketers

	Promise	*Outcome*
1 Capital–labour relation	• Deregulation will allow full employment	• No clear impact
2 Forms of competition	• Deregulation will erode oligopolistic market power and restore free competition	• Re-regulation, less producers: from one oligopolistic form of competition to another
3 Monetary regime	• Control of monetary base is possible	• Monetary innovation prevents this control
4 State	• Minimal state will enhance growth and productivity	• Lack of public investment • Poor private productivity due to the lack of education infrastructures
5 International regime	• Smooth currency adjustments	• Large up and down of exchange rates
	• Vanishing external disequilibria	• Unprecedented and stable polarization of deficit and surplus countries
	• Complete autonomy of national economic policies	• Stronger constraints upon national room for manoeuvre

goods. A greater reliance on markets has not had the positive expected returns (Table 3.2).

The deregulation of the labour market and the slimming down of the welfare state have not succeeded in promoting a return to full employment. At the same time, inequalities have become a major issue for future social stability. The removal of price controls and product market deregulations should have restored free competition among numerous firms. The result is just the opposite, since in many cases one national oligopolistic configuration has been replaced by another one in which economic power is still more concentrated; the airline business is a good example of this. After all, competition is evolving towards oligopoly or monopoly, as Karl Marx pointed out a century ago! Similarly, the obsessive search for price stability was supposed to benefit economic growth and job creation. Again, the outcome of the monetarist principles is just the opposite. Given financial deregulation and the multiplication of innovations, central banks have lost most of their power. And high real interest rates have had a negative impact upon investment, growth and employment, at least in Europe. Inflation has been defeated, but the social cost is huge, indeed: mass and long-lasting unemployment in Europe and rising inequalities in North America.

The same story accompanies the reduction in state intervention. The supply-siders sold the idea that a shrinking of public spending would mean higher private investment, more innovation and productivity. On the contrary, however, the more market-oriented economies, such as the US, Canada and the UK have suffered from a lack of public investment in education, training and infrastructures, i.e. the very sources of growth in the new emerging model. Last, but not least, the international regime has not been put in order by letting financial markets decide where to invest and what should be the adequate exchange rate. At the world level, the system has become quite unpredictable as market forces permeate more and more domains. John Maynard Keynes reminds us that an international regime is the outcome of the bargaining among national governments and never the result of a series of myopic financial market adjustments.

Of course, the motto 'let us return to free market economies' has played some role in disciplining and restructuring most of the institutional forms inherited from the Fordist era. Similarly, in most Eastern European countries the market has been used as a dissolving device for communist political organizations and centrally planned mechanisms. But it is now realized that the market *per se* cannot create the requisites which would warrant its long-term efficiency: clear rules, a stable monetary regime, adequate property rights, minimal security via a welfare state, the emergence of Schumpeterian innovators as well as lucky speculators. It took nearly two centuries for capitalist countries to make familiar and acceptable the harsh logic of typical market mechanisms. Clearly, the great transformation which is currently taking place in Eastern Europe is not a matter of years, but of decades (Boyer 1993).

Even Western financial markets, in order to be efficient, have to be constantly reformed and adequately regulated by a large number of institutional or technological devices. For example, the Wall Street crash in October of 1987 has not instituted a repetition of the Great Depression since many equilibrating mechanisms have been implemented by institutional design, thus preventing the recurrence of such a catastrophic episode. Similarly, the reforms undertaken after October 1987 have so far excluded a dramatic collapse of stock markets of the 1929–32 type. It is evident that markets have to be constantly redesigned in order to be self-equilibrating. This basic lesson from economic history is too frequently neglected.

Thus, at odds with conservative and pro-market ideologies, markets will never replace governments in making strategic choices, organizing solidarity over a given territory and still more in institutionalizing markets. Conceptually, state interventions are superior to market mechanisms, since public authorities may both create and monitor markets. Our epoch needs more political interventions and fewer naïve beliefs that markets will overcome our ignorance and make the strategic choices that governments have been unable, until now, to make and implement.

This decade will probably experience a major turning point, from pro-market and conservative strategies towards more solidaristic policies oriented by rejuvenated state intervention in the domains of taxation, welfare, innovation and education. To be efficient, market mechanisms would have to be embedded in adequate national institutions governing money, labour and relations with nature. We probably live in the epoch of the second great transformation as Karl Polanyi would say. But alternative rules of the game will have to be defined at the international level. This is a matter of political will and bargaining, not the spontaneous outcome of the *homo oeconomicus*'s rational calculus nor the miraculous outcome of an enlightenment of large multinational corporations. The next century will still be the era of nation-states in charge of disciplining and taming the markets, but the contours of this involvement are still largely unknown. To explore possible configurations is a promising, but difficult, task for social scientists.

BIBLIOGRAPHY

Aghion, Philippe and Peter Howitt. 1993. 'A Model of Growth through Creative Destruction', in Dominique Foray and Christopher Freeman, *Technology and the Wealth of Nations*. London and New York: Pinter Publishers, pp.145–72.

Aglietta, Michel. 1982. *Regulation and Crisis of Capitalism*. New York: Monthly Review Press.

Aglietta, Michel. 1991. 'Ordre monétaire et banques centrales', Colloque *L'Economie des conventions*, Paris, 27–28 March.

Aglietta, Michel, Anton Brender and Virginie Coudert. 1990. *Globalisation financière: l'aventure obligée*. Paris: Economica.

Akerlof, Georges A. 1984. *Economic Theorist's Book of Tales*. Cambridge, Mass.: Cambridge University Press.

Alesina, Alberto and Geoffrey Carliner (eds). 1991. *Politics and Economies in the Eighties*. Chicago and London: The University of Chicago Press.

Amable, Bruno and Dominique Guellec. 1992. 'Les Théories de la croissance endogène.' *Revue d'Economie Politique* 102: 313–78.

Arrow, Kenneth and Frank Hahn. 1971. *General Competitive Analysis*. San Francisco: Holden Day.

Becker, Garry S. 1964. *Human Capital*. New York: Columbia University Press.

Becker, Garry S. 1981. *A Treatise on the Family*. Cambridge, Mass.: Harvard University Press.

Bourguignon, François. 1990. 'L'après communisme: une troisième voie?' *Le Débat* 59: 11–14 (March–April).

Boyer, Robert. 1987. 'Labour flexibilities: many forms, uncertain effects.' *Labour and Society* 12: 1, pp. 107–29.

Boyer, Robert. 1988. *The Search for Labour Market Flexibility*. Oxford: Clarendon Press.

Boyer, Robert. 1990a. *The Regulation School. A Critical Introduction*. New York: Columbia University Press.

Boyer, Robert. 1990b. 'The Capital Labor Relations in OECD Countries: From the "Golden Age" to the Uncertain Nineties.' *Couverture Orange CEPREMAP* 9020 (September).

Boyer, Robert. 1991a. 'Capital Labor Relation and Wage Formation: Continuities and Changes of National Trajectories among OECD Countries', in Toshiyuki Mizogushi (ed.), *Making Economies more Efficient and Equitable: Factors Determining Income Distribution*. Tokyo: Kinokuniya Company Ltd, and Oxford: Oxford University Press, pp. 297–340.

Boyer, Robert. 1991b. 'Justice Sociale et performances économiques: De l'alliance cachée au conflit ouvert?' *Couverture Orange CEPREMAP* 9135 (August).

Boyer, Robert. 1993. 'La grande transformation de l'Europe de l'Est: Une lecture régulationniste.' *Couverture Orange CEPREMAP* 9319 (March).

Boyer, Robert and Genevieve Schmeder, 1990. 'Un retour à Adam Smith.' *Revue Française d'Economie* 5: 1 (Winter), pp. 125–94.

Braudel, Fernand. 1979. *Civilisation matérielle, économie et capitalisme XV–XVIIIe siècles*. 3 vols, Paris: Armand Colin.

Brus, W. 1987. 'Market socialism', in J. Eatwell, M. Milgate and P. Newman (eds), *The New Palgrave. A Dictionary of Economics*. London: Macmillan, Vol. III, pp. 337–42.

Campbell, Colin D. and William R. Dougan. 1986. *Alternative Monetary Regimes*. Baltimore and London: The Johns Hopkins University Press.

Campbell, John L., J. Rogers Hollingsworth and Leon N. Lindberg. 1991. *Governance of the American Economy*. Cambridge, New York, Melbourne: Cambridge University Press.

Chandler, Alfred D. 1977. *The Visible Hand. The Managerial Revolution in American Business*. Cambridge, Mass.: The Belknap Press of Harvard University Press.

Clague, C. and G. C. Rausser. 1992. *The Emergence of Market Economies in Eastern Europe*. Oxford: Blackwell.

Coase, Ronald. 1937. 'The Nature of the Firm.' *Economica*, n.s., 4 (November). Reprinted in Ronald Coase. 1988. *The Firm, The Market and the Law*. Chicago and London: The University of Chicago Press.

Coase, Ronald. 1960. 'The problem of social cost.' *Journal of Law and Economics*, vol. 3, pp. 1–44.

Coase, Ronald. 1988. *The Firm, The Market and the Law*. Chicago and London: The University of Chicago Press.

Coleman, William D. 1990. 'State Traditions and Comprehensive Business Associations: A Comparative Structural Analysis.' *Political Studies* 38: 2, 231–52

Coriat, Benjamin. 1991. *Penser à l'envers. Travail et organisation dans l'entreprise japonaise*. Paris: C. Bourgois, Editeur.

Debreu, Gérard. 1959. *Theory and Value: An Axiomatic Analysis of Economic Equilibrium*. Cowles Foundation, Monograph no. 17. New York: John Wiley.

Douglas, M. 1986. *Les institutions parlent*. Paris: Editions de Minuit.

Dumenil, Gérard and Dominique Lévy. 1989. 'Micro Adjustment Behavior and Macro Stability.' *Seoul Journal of Economics* 2: 1, 1–37.

Eggertsson, T. 1990. *Economic Behavior and Institutions*. Cambridge, Mass.: Cambridge University Press.

Esping-Andersen, G. 1990. *The Three Worlds of Welfare Capitalism*. Princeton, N.J.: Princeton University Press.

Favereau, Olivier. 1989. 'Marchés internes, marchés externes.' *Revue Economique* 40: 2 (March), 273–328.

Fleurbaey, Marc. 1990. 'Le marché: Horizon indepassable?' Mimeograph INSEE. Paris (June).

Freeman, J.R. 1989. *Democracy and Markets. The Politics of Mixed Economies*. Ithaca, N.Y.: Cornell University Press.

Friedman, Milton. 1962. *Capitalism and Freedom*. Chicago, Ill.: University of Chicago Press.

Friedman, Milton and Rose. 1981. *Free to Choose*. New York: Aron.

Galenson, D.W. (ed.). 1989. *Markets in History. Economic Studies of the Past*. New York: Cambridge University Press.

Hayek, Fredrich. 1976–82. *Law, Legislation and Liberty* (3 vols). Chicago, Ill.: University of Chicago Press, London: Routledge and Kegan Paul.

Hayek, Fredrich. 1980. *Individualism and Economic Order*. Chicago and London: University of Chicago Press.

Heal, G.M. 1971. 'Planning, Prices and Increasing Returns.' *Review of Economic Studies* 38; 281–94.

Hibbs, Douglas A. 1987. *The Political Economy of Industrial Democracies.* Cambridge, Mass., and London: Harvard University Press.

Hill, P. 1987. 'Market Places', in J. Eatwell, M. Milgate and P. Newman (eds), *The New Palgrave. A Dictionary of Economics.* London: The Macmillan Press, Vol. II, pp. 332–4.

Hollingsworth, Rogers J., Philippe Schmitter and Wolfgang Streeck (eds). 1993. *Governing Capitalist Economies: Performance and Control of Economic Sectors.* New York: Oxford University Press.

Kahneman, Daniel, Jack L. Knetsch and Richard H. Thaler. 1986. 'Fairness as a Constraint on Profit Seeking: Entitlements in the Market.' *American Economic Review* 76: 4, 728–41. Reprinted in Richard H. Thaler. 1991. *Quasi Rational Economics.* New York: Russell Sage Foundation, pp. 199–219.

Kaldor, Nicholas. 1939. 'Speculation and Economic Stability.' *Review of Economic Studies* (October). Reprinted in *Essays on Economic Stability and Growth.* 1960 London: Duckworth.

Keohane, Robert. 1984. *After Hegemony: Cooperation and Discord in the World Political Economy.* Princeton, N.J.: Princeton University Press.

Kornai, Janos. 1980. *The Economics of Shortage.* Amsterdam: North Holland.

Kornai, Janos. 1992. *The Socialist System. The Political Economy of Communism.* Oxford: Clarendon Press.

Krasner, Stephen D. (ed.). 1983. *International Regime.* Ithaca, N.Y.: Cornell University Press.

Kregel, Jan, Egon Matzner and G. Grabher (eds). 1992. *The Market Shock, An Agenda for the Economic and Social Reconstruction of Central and Eastern Europe.* Ann Arbor, Mich.: The Austrian Academy of Sciences and University of Michigan Press.

Kuttner, Robert. 1991. *The End of Laissez-Faire.* New York: Alfred A. Knopf.

Lavoie, D. 1986. 'The Market as a Procedure for Discovery and Conveyance of Inarticulate Knowledge.' *Comparative Economic Studies* 28: 1.

Lazonick, William. 1991. *Business Organization and the MYTH of the Market Economy.* Cambridge, New York, Melbourne: Cambridge University Press.

Leifer, Eric M. and Harrison C. White. 1988. 'A Structural Approach to Markets', in Mark Mizruchi and Michael Schwartz (eds). *Intercorporate Relations.* Cambridge, New York, Melbourne: Cambridge University Press, pp. 85–108.

Lesourne, Jacques. 1991. *L'économie de l'ordre et du désordre.* Paris: Economica.

Lindbeck, A. and D. J. Snower. 1986. 'Wage Setting, Unemployment, and Insider–Outsider Relations.' *American Economic Review*, vol. 76, pp. 235–9.

Lindblom, C. 1971. *Politics and Markets. The World's Political Economic Systems.* New York: Basic Books (re-edition 1977).

Lucas, Robert E. 1984. *Studies in Business Cycle Theory.* Cambridge, Mass.: MIT Press.

Lucas, Robert, E. 1988. 'On the Mechanisms of Economic Development.' *Journal of Monetary Economics* 72 (July), 3–42.

Marshall, Alfred. (1890). *Principles of Economics.* Reprinted. London: Macmillan.

Nelson, Richard R. and Sidney Winter. 1982. *An Evolutionary Theory of Economic Change.* Cambridge, Mass.: Harvard University Press.

North, Douglass. 1990. *Institutions, Institutional Change and Economic Performance.* Cambridge and New York: Cambridge University Press.

OECD (1985). *Perspectives de l'Emploi*, September.

Okun, Arthur M. 1981. *Price and Quantities: A Macroeconomic Analysis.* Washington, DC: Brookings Institution.

Olson, Mancur. 1965. *The Logic of Collective Action.* New Haven: Yale University Press.

Orléan, André. 1990. 'Le rôle des influences interpersonnelles dans la détermination des cours boursiers.' *Revue Economique* 41: 5 (September), 839–68.

Polanyi, Karl. 1946. *The Great Transformation.* Traduction française. Paris: Gallimard. 1983.

Posner, R. A. 1981. *The Economics of Justice.* Cambridge, Mass.: Harvard University Press.

Romer, Paul. 1986. 'Increasing Returns and Long-run Growth.' *Journal of Political Economy* 94 (October), pp. 1002–38.

Romer, Paul. 1990. 'Endogenous Technological Change.' *Journal of Political Economy* 98: 5, 71–102 (2nd part).

Rosenan, James N. and Ernst-Otto Czempiel (eds). 1992. *Governance without Government: Order and Change in World Politics.* Cambridge, New York, Melbourne: Cambridge University Press.

Rothenberg, Winifred B. 1992. *From Market-Places to a Market Economy: The Transformation of Rural Massachusetts 1750–1850.* Chicago and London: The University of Chicago Press.

Samuelson, Paul A. and William D. Nordhaus. 1992. *Economics.* New York: McGraw-Hill, pp. 35–47.

Sandler, Todd. 1992. *Collective Action. Theory and Applications.* Ann Arbor, Mich.: The University of Michigan Press.

Schmitter, Philippe C. 1990. 'Sectors in Modern Capitalism: Models of Governance and Variations in Performance', in Renato Brunetta and Carlo Dell'Aringa (eds), *Labour Relations and Economic Performance.* London: Macmillan and International Economic Association.

Schotter, A. 1990. *Free Market Economics.* Cambridge, Mass.: Basil Blackwell, 2nd edition.

Shand, Alexander D. 1990. *Free Market Morality: The Political Economy of the Austrian School.* London and New York: Routledge.

Smith, Adam. 1776. 'An Inquiry into the Nature and Causes of the Wealth of Nations', R. H. Campbell, A. S. Skinner and W. B. Todd (eds). 1976. London: Croom Helm.

Solow, Robert M. 1990. *The Labor Market as a Social Institution.* Cambridge, Mass.: Basil Blackwell.

Stiglitz, Joseph E. and Frank G. Mathewson (eds). 1986. *New Developments in the Analysis of Market Structure.* Cambridge, Mass.: The MIT Press.

Tirole, Jean. 1988. *The Theory of Industrial Organization.* Cambridge, Mass.: The MIT Press.

Weitzman, Martin L. 1982. 'Increasing Returns and the Foundations of Unemployment Theory.' *Economic Journal* 92 (December), 787–804.

Weitzman, Martin L. 1985. 'Steady State Unemployment Under Profit Sharing.' *Working Paper 399*, Department of Economics MIT, Cambridge, Mass.

White, Harrison C. 1981. 'Where Do Markets Come From?' *American Journal of Sociology* 87: 3, 517–47.

White, Harrison C. 1988. 'Varieties of Markets', in B. Wellman and S. D. Berkowitz (eds), *Social Structures: A Network Approach.* Cambridge, New York, Melbourne: Cambridge University Press, pp. 226–60.

Wolf, Charles, Jr. 1979. 'A Theory of Nonmarket Failure.' *Journal of Law and Economics,* no. 22.

Wolf, Charles, Jr. 1990. *Markets or Governments: Choosing Between Imperfect Alternatives.* Cambridge, Mass. and London, UK: The MIT Press.

Part II

THE LIMITS OF JAPANESE POWER

4

SHIFTING TECHNOLOGICAL PARADIGMS
From the US to Japan
Charles McMillan

INTRODUCTION

The demise of the Soviet Union as an integrated economic entity with the Comecon countries of the Warsaw Pact, and the emergence of three triad economic and industrial blocs in the capitalist industrialized world, have raised many questions about the shape and form of the New World Order. Rarely in the past two centuries have the changes to the international geopolitical organization of peoples been so profound. The post-Napoleonic era starting in 1814, the post-First World War European and colonial carve-up, and the post-Second World War era beginning with the 1945 Yalta Conference stand as truly dramatic impositions of defining boundaries, allocating spheres of influence, developing balances of power and alliances, and establishing the rules of the world order.

But what has been common in all the four great 'new world orders' – beginning respectively in 1814, 1919, 1945, 1989 – have been dramatic changes in economic rivalry. The defeat of Napoleon led to the century-old, un-questioned economic supremacy of Britain, its imperial extensions, and the first true application of domestic *free trade* – the export of manufactured goods, and the import of raw materials and food. The 1919 order introduced a new era of financial capitalism through the domination of London and then New York as *exporters of capital* to finance imperial manufacturing and its extension through transportation and infrastructure.

And the post-war expansion of the 1945 settlement ushered in a funda-mentally new era of *investment capital* to the developed world, starting in North America, as it had in the 1920s, but accelerating with the rebuilding of Europe in the 1950s. This expansion of investment capital was led by US multinationals and followed by European corporations in the 1970s and the Japanese with a vengeance in the 1980s and 1990s.

In the 1980s, these patterns began to shift, and so too did the underlying analysis. For one thing, not all growth countries had raw materials, immigra-tion or surplus capital. For another, not all countries could calibrate their political muscles via military power to their economic needs, such as access to raw materials in South America or the Middle East. Clearly, any country which could build a superpower base on lack of raw materials, lack of immigration, lack of military strength, and lack of leverage over markets had something going of commanding interest. The new case study was Japan.

Clearly, the old equations were incomplete. Japan in the 1980s added a new equation to the international policy mix. Colonies, raw materials, military alliances, and all the old currency did not mean much – witness Britain's pathetic decline in the generation from Suez to the Falklands. Japan, in fact, added a new dimension, mainly in finance and technology. Finance has always been central to the imperial power of nations – for military adventures to be sure, but also for economic goals, art and culture and various forms of patronage. But the technology dimension is new and newer still is the 'finance–technology nexus'. Why is this so important?

Table 4.1 Profile of the world's largest banks (31 December 1992)

	Top 25	Top 50	Top 100
Japan	15	19	29
Germany	1	8	12
France	4	6	11
UK	2	3	6
China	2	4	4
The Netherlands	1	3	3
Iran	–	1	1
Switzerland	–	2	3
Italy	–	1	8
USA	–	3	7
Sweden	–	–	2
Australia	–	–	2
Belgium	–	–	4
Canada	–	–	4
Spain	–	–	3
Brazil	–	–	1

Source: *Wall Street Journal*, 29 September 1993

Technology, defined as the packaging of knowledge for commercial markets, promises to be the battleground of international business in the 1990s, the era of 'techno-nationalism'. Inexorably, the world economy is making a steady but fundamental shift, from an economy based on physical units of production to knowledge-based units, from a corporate-based system of national economies to a technology-centred form of production, requiring global markets (McMillan 1993; also Drucker 1992).

Technology is the new tool of dynamic, competitive economies, the foundation on which countries and firms will expand jobs or lose markets, build enterprises to attack global competitors or retreat and seek domestic protection around local governments. The longer-term prognosis is as inexorable as it is predictable. A century ago, first in political and economic thinking, and then in *de facto* government policy, there arose the central view that physical control of technology and its outcomes was the key to industrial policy and economic expansion. Empires arose, prosperity expanded, and the key technologies of the eighteenth and nineteenth centuries flourished – steam and iron, rail transport, ocean-going vessels, chemical technology and early forms of telecommunications. Physical assets are important but diminishing in importance; brainpower, technology and skilful management of assets are everything. The new empires are based on brain power and information technology and the means to organize them. Few countries outside Japan and the US are at the forefront of these trends (Derian 1990).

This chapter has three goals. It reviews Japan's science and technology strategies in the 1990s and into the next century, including the setting of key priorities. Second, it highlights some key Japanese differences with the only other technology superpower, the USA. And third, the chapter draws on some key findings to examine some major trends into the next century.

JAPAN THE SUPERPOWER: INVESTING IN TECHNOLOGY

The world holds two views of Japan, and so too do the Japanese. They are conflicting perspectives about Japan's post-war development and metamorphosis as a key player in the new global, multipolar environment of the next century. What the Japanese have achieved in technology, finance, manufacturing, exports and now power in the Pacific has no historical precedent in world history. The Japanese have begun to create a twenty-first century vision of their own country and their own values which gives shape and form to their industrial structure of the future (Abegglen and Stalk 1985; McMillan 1994). With a clarity not readily seen in any other era, the Japanese are telling the world in what direction they are headed and what this means for their economy. In all of this, the Japanese are simply doing what they have done best among all industrial economies since 1945; they have shaped their domestic economy according to the changing trends and configurations of the world economy. They have not fought off global trends; they have embraced them. The following trends based on a study of the US Council on Competitiveness tells the basic story:

- The US accounted for 27.5 per cent of technology-intensive products in 1965, 22.9 per cent in 1980 and 25.2 per cent in 1984.
- Japan's world market share of semiconductors exceeds the US by more than 2 : 1, 65 per cent versus 30 per cent.
- American shares of vital industry sectors are declining precipitously: from 100 per cent of consumer electronics in 1970 to 5 per cent in 1988; from

99 per cent in phonographs to 1 per cent; from 90 per cent in colour TVs to 10 per cent; from 100 per cent in machine tools to 35 per cent.

- From 1976 to 1980, Americans introduced twice as many new drugs as Japan; in the past five years, Japan introduced 60 new drugs to America's 58.
- The US faces a need for 300,000 additional maths and science teachers; about 60,000 secondary teachers are not fully qualified.
- Japan's emphasis on technology results in 16,000 Japanese patents received in the US, more than double the 6,350 patents received in 1965. Moreover, the three companies registering the most patents in the US were all Japanese.
- Federal funding of US university research facilities has decreased about 95 per cent in two decades; less than 10 per cent of federal R&D funding is relevant to commercial applications of US industry.
- The US faces dramatic shortages in the engineering faculties in US universities; about 57 per cent of faculty are non-US citizens; 1,300–1,800 positions remain vacant.

These kinds of statistics have been high-profile news items in recent years, raising the spectre of America's economic decline and the rise of new competitive forces to challenge American economic and technological supremacy.

Of course, Japan was not always a superpower. In the immediate post-war period, Japanese productivity in comparison to the USA was incredibly low: 5 per cent in coal mining and chemicals for example, 10 per cent in rubber and 20 per cent in rayon. Within decades, this position has been reversed. Japan rivals the US in integrated circuits, mainframe computers, and leads both Europe and the United States in high-technology trade. How has Japan been able to make these phenomenal leaps in technology, especially in contrast to a country like Britain? Have Japan's government and corporate strategies been the key? Are there other factors at play, such as the unwitting role of American corporations?

Consider the case of US sales of technology to Japan in the 1950s and 1960s. Japan imported an enormous amount of US technology, which is often credited with the 'catch up' hypothesis of Japanese economic growth. Foreign technology was a tool to close the gap with the West and importing it was a major policy of the Japanese government ever since Meiji. In point of fact, the central role placed on technology by Japan persists even today, when Japanese non-defence technology is on a par with Western countries. Japan is innovating technology in many new sectors. Despite the persistence of factors favouring strategies of imitation, there remains an insatiable thirst for buying technology from Western countries. As a result, technology trade deficits are sizeable with, for example, the US and France. For instance, Abegglen and Hout (1978) note that the cumulative cost to Japan of technology purchases from abroad – more than 25,000 contracts covering essentially all the technology the West had to offer, most of it from the United States – has been about six billion dollars. This is the equivalent of a little more than 10 per cent of the annual R&D expenditure of the United States. More to the point, the same authors found that technology has nurtured competitors who now enter or threaten US markets. The final irony is that US technology which might have been a lever to enter the Japanese market has been surrendered to Japanese firms.

TRADE IN TECHNOLOGY

This picture of Japan's trade in technology illustrates some of the basic themes of Japan's industrial system and corrects many mistaken ideas about Japan's technological policy. Too often Western analysts emphasize Japan's technology strategy in terms of imports (particularly from the US) and the imitation tactics of applying foreign technology. Yet technological policies and practices go hand in hand with many micro and macro strategies at the level of the firm, industry and society. For example, Japan's R&D policies help explain the strong emphasis on and skill at process development as well as its enviable record in manufacturing productivity and quality control.

In addition, the special kinds of technology policies help explain Japan's export development and evolving industrial structure around knowledge-intensive industries. Whereas in the 1960s, Japan's exports were heavily concentrated in industries with low R&D (e.g. textiles, iron and steel, cars), the exports in the 1990s are in high R&D sectors, with electronics, machinery and biotechnology at the forefront. Nor is this technology plan one of imitating or buying foreign technology. Japan now registers more than two and a half times the number of patents as the US, eight times as many as Britain. Japan's 147 per capita, resident patents, compares with 28.8 in the US, 35 in Britain, and 64 in Switzerland. The seeds of Japan's technology future lie in these investments. Technology is a central element of Japan's general approach to industrial planning and highlights the priorities for new products, materials and production systems. Six of the top ten R&D investors in the world's private sector are Japanese corporations.

TECHNOLOGY AND ECONOMY

For years, policy-makers have accepted the dictum that an economy evolves from manufacturing to services much like the evolution a century ago from agriculture to manufacturing. Indeed, President Reagan's 1985 statement on trade to the Congress actually celebrated the transformation of the US economy (Toffler 1990; Drucker 1992).

> The move from an industrial society to a post-industrial service economy has been one of the greatest changes to effect the developed

world since The Industrial Revolution. The progression of an economy such as America from agriculture to manufacturing to services is a natural change.

But, beneath these mega-changes, are more ominous trends. Many of the growth areas in the service sector simply reflect changing consumption patterns of leisure and household spending. Some of the growth is in sectors such as fast-food outlets and the retail trade. They have hourly earnings less than manufacturing and low productivity growth. Other fast-growing service sectors in advanced countries are based on the strength and productivity of manufacturing. Indeed in computer services, transportation and investment banking, the increase in the service sector may reflect basic changes in the manufacturing process itself: this can occur through the contracting out of particular functions to suppliers and sub-contractors or through the realigning of production tasks across more complex 'systems' or linkages. Further, many service categories arise from the global mobility of capital, information, and technology, such as banking, communications, telecommunications, transportation and insurance, where domestic markets, not global markets, were once key. In short, manufacturing demand for goods is not only growing, but that demand exceeds the sale of exported services by a factor of twenty (McMillan 1991). Service exports simply will not pay for the potential impact of manufacturing from abroad.

Japan's emphasis on technology has been a central factor in its catching up to the West. While the government has played a leading role, the success of individual entrepreneurs, various research institutes, and the universities should not be underestimated. For example, businessmen such as S. Ishibashi, founder of Bridgestone Tire, innovated in *jika-tabi* or rubber sole socks in the tyre industry independently of Michelin in France. Sakichi Toyoda, founder of Toyota, pioneered many innovations in automatic weaving machines and even sold his equipment abroad. As far back as 1918, The Nitrogen Research Institute carried out basic research based on German patents in such areas as ammonia synthesis, production of nitric acid and hydrogen, and methanol. In the development of the imperial universities, the government created chairs for research in applied chemistry and these have become the forerunners of chairs in industrial chemistry and several new fields today. For example, Tokyo Imperial University had chairs in such areas as acid, alkali and fertilizer, dyestuff and coal chemistry, fibre and cellulose chemistry, plastic and petroleum chemistry, and electric and photochemistry (McMillan 1994).

A theme far more prominent in Japan's post-Meiji technological development than in other industrial countries such as Britain, the US and Germany was a remarkable 'information awareness', partly as a result of inviting foreign technologists to Tokyo (Uchida 1980). Japan's institutional conditions and managerial attitudes were positive historic influences for technological diffusion and development and indicate a pattern which exists even today.

Moreover, Japan's service sector is in the vanguard of the information revolution, exemplified by credit cards, debit cards and other forms of new software. In microelectronics, the information revolution is at its most dramatic, transforming separate industries and national boundaries and making nonsense of the old belief that so-called 'software' and 'hardware' are comfortably separate. Charles Ferguson (1990), a prescient student of these trends, observes as follows:

> We are witnessing the digitization of everything. Previously unrelated industries – camera, computers, stereos, photocopiers, typewriters – are converging to form a huge, unified information technology sector, itself based on common digital components and standard interfaces. Increasingly, competition in all kinds of hardware is driven by the same new logic governing competition in computers – growing commoditization of product markets and growing advantage for companies with superior components technologies, manufacturing systems and strategic leverage.
>
> (Ferguson 1990: 57)

This sector illustrates well the changes now underway across the entire service sector, from technology to new organizational forms, from the impact of government regulation to the entire question of international trade in financial services.

THE ORGANIZATION OF SCIENCE IN JAPAN

It is no accident that the Japanese have traditionally placed education and science at the top of the national agenda. The Meiji era was a period devoted to catching up to the West, which in today's terms was a bid to make the playing field level. Japan's government machinery reflects this historical feature and national obsession. Unlike any Western industrialized country, the Japanese government gave technology pride of place in public policy. The Japanese Prime Minister chairs the key advisory body, the Council for Science and Technology. The major co-ordinating body for public policy in S & T, the Science and Technology Agency, resides in the Prime Minister's Office. The entire scientific apparatus of the state, acting as a mixture of centralized direction and decentralized activity, promotes the policy agenda in the areas of science and technology policy.

The Western stereotype of Japanese science and technology is based on two quite false premises:

- that government is the primary engine of technological development;
- that MITI is the basic vehicle for science promotion.

Science and technology are a national priority in Japan, led at the centre, but pervasive in all elements of an extremely well-educated society. Know-

123

ledge creation and diffusion are given the same priority as international relations, trade and industry, and social and welfare policy.

Science policy is implemented by an enormous apparatus of overlapping consultative committees, typically representative of élite individuals and groups representing academe, industry, research centres, labour and bureaucratic agencies. The focus is not just national but international; not just public sector but private sector. Okimoto (1986) describes the networking in Japan as follows:

> Informal intermediate organizations – those not requiring special legal dispensation – include industrial associations, business federations, MITI advisory councils, Diet member caucuses, and countless study groups, linking MITI officials with leaders from industry, banking, the legislative branch, the mass media, labour and academics – the core centres of power in Japan . . .
>
> (Okimoto 1986: 41–2)

Who are the actors and key players in Japanese science policy? What are the implications? The starting point is the Prime Minister's Office and the two major instruments, the Council on Science and Technology and the Science Council of Japan. In particular, the Prime Minister's Office also houses a number of advisory committees and agencies such as the Science Council of Japan, Council for Science and Technology, Atomic Energy Commission, Space Activities Commission, Council for Ocean Development, Science and Technology Agency, six National Research Institutes for Aerospace, Metals, Electronics, Inorganic Materials, and Radiological Science and Disaster Prevention.

The way the system works is that the major science departments of government in Japan each have their own extensive network of research establishments, science priorities, international contacts and affiliations, and separate budgets. What needs to be recognized in Japan's research efforts is that each line department has a consultative body of outside experts to help advise on priorities and directions. Additionally, each science department has its own panel of experts, drawn from a cross-section of the private sector, to advise on internal operations and future directions and research priorities.

Special emphasis is placed on forward planning in order to determine where Japanese science will be in the year 2000. Departments recognize that the vast bulk of science effort is directed to current priorities but their administration keeps the focus on forward agendas, meaning that dead-wood activity gets dropped.

Further, research is co-ordinated across departments by having overlapping departmental committees, bureaus and agencies work from different departments on common problems. To cite just one example, Japan's Ministry of Health and Welfare undertakes research in the field of electronics, engaging the departments of MITI, Education and the Science and Technology Agency to work on diagnostic care equipment. This is an almost impossible situation to visualize as standard practice in most Western research departments.

Finally, each department produces an annual report, available in Japanese and English, on its organization, research priorities, financial outlays, research successes, facilities and personnel. Each document is complete with organization charts, brief histories, international highlights and a mission statement.

By contrast, the American research system is divided in three – government agencies, such as the National Institute of Health, the Department of Defense and the Atomic Energy Commission; the universities and The National Science Foundation; and private corporations operating largely alone. It is a vast arena of well-funded scientists, many of them immigrants from Europe. For most of the post-war period, US industry had relative supremacy not only in the level of scientific production, but in the advanced state of manufacturing after the Second World War and the management skills and processes developed over decades. Even in defence research, which roughly matched the level of R&D spending in the post-war environment, much of the actual research was carried out in private companies, especially in such fields as aerospace, computers, engines, and semiconductors and advanced communications.

Japan's approach to research co-ordination stems from the country's former status as a technological follower. This 'follower role' has resulted in a university system that is underdeveloped in basic research. There is an almost total absence of military research as an instrument of government funding and incubation of commercial products. Equally important, however, are two less tangible considerations. First, Japan was and is a resource-poor country, a factor which instils in the population and key decision-makers a desire and, indeed, an obligation to husband resources and use them efficiently. Second, since the Meiji era, the Japanese have adopted a national ethic to learn from abroad. Where does Japan's deeply rooted interest in science and technology come from?

Japan's interaction with the West has always had a scientific bent in comparing their own weapons (bamboo swords, wooden ships), cooking habits (raw fish, open-fire cooking) and artistry (printing, calligraphy, paper-making), to name some obvious examples to their Western counterparts. The phrase 'Wakon Yosai' – Western Technology, Japanese Essence – illustrates this historic obsession with science and technology issues (Okimoto 1986; McMillan 1994). Japan's vast network of industry associations, industrial groups, banking relationships, manufacturer–supplier linkages and business federations provides an enormous infrastructure of sophisticated understanding of the role of technology in growth, in technological trends in Japan and elsewhere, and in the public awareness of the technological imperative at large.

125

The paradox between the US and Japan is this: the US system of pluralistic research development diminishes competition because the technological threat is not seen as external; in Japan, where the technological threat is external, co-operative mechanisms for analysing technological trends lead to fierce competition in the domestic market. Ironically, in recent years, US companies have understood this change, especially in such areas as semiconductors, consumer electronics and high-definition television.

GETTING A 'LEG-UP' ON THE COMPETITION: TECHNOLOGICAL DIFFUSION

None the less, the competition between the US and Japan in the field of technology innovation is likely to increase. This is because Japan's primary research emphasis is not in government or the universities and so the pattern of rewards and psychic incomes are quite different. In the US, for example, it is common practice for scientists working in the commercial sector to publish, to participate in academic gatherings, and to aspire to scientific reputation. In Japan, where there is an equivalent number of researchers per capita as the US (about double the number in France and Germany), the thrust of rewards and career incentives is for economic and corporate success, as well as for short-run commercial payoff. This pattern is fostered by close consultation and research support for university faculty. In the field of robotics, it is not unusual to have university faculty provided 'on permanent loan' as well as experimental equipment for testing and trials. Some companies in chemicals and pharmaceuticals publish research undertaken by faculty members.

A second consideration in Japan's diffusion of technology is the country's very high level of literacy and knowledge of mathematics, economics and basic engineering. On balance, Japanese managers and workers are among the most educated in the world, and this formal training combines with a strong motivation to succeed and a value system emphasizing learning and curiosity. While the US focuses its public R&D funding on capital-intensive sectors such as aerospace, electronics and nuclear energy, the Japanese focus theirs on low-intensive industries. In particular, this research effort usually takes the form of three or four research centres in each of Japan's forty-seven prefectures (provinces) which are oriented to technical issues affecting small and medium-sized companies. The centres generally concentrate on specific problems or sectors such as ceramics, textiles, metals, machinery or paper, and the emphasis is on adapting new techniques or technologies.

Despite the high foreign regard for many of Japan's more centralized technology schemes such as mainframe computers, telecommunications, high-speed railways and aerospace, the most dramatic of the new initiatives in strategic alliances is a nationwide system of technopolis centres to link private capital, research consortia and universities to long-term research goals.

126

Table 4.2 Top R&D spenders around the world

	Latest spending ($m)	Change (%)	As percentage of Sales	As percentage of Profits	Number of companies
Japan	35,035	9	5	109	75
Germany	14,402	7	5	149	19
France	9,103	8	4	66	22
Britain	8,098	10	3	33	29
Switzerland	5,206	10	6	90	11
Italy	3,781	5	4	558	8
Sweden	3,500	15	6	283	10
The Netherlands	3,104	−8	6	187	6
Canada	2,474	3	5	74	7
Australia	466	0	2	23	3
Belgium	445	1	5	100	2
Finland	384	99	4	NA	3
Norway	96	29	11	48	1
South Africa	95	17	NA	33	1
Austria	65	0	4	310	1
World composite	87,951	8	4	81	200
US composite	79,439	7	4	67	900

Source: Global Vantage (Standard & Poor's Compustat Services)

The government's role in technology planning is particularly crucial in developing a competitive focus in Japanese industry. In this respect, many foreign perceptions of Japanese technology policy, especially in such areas as licensing restrictions and foreign investment regulations, hark back to programmes in existence before trade liberalization under the GATT tariff reductions. The government has consistently favoured the presence of many firms in all leading sectors. As Peck and Goto noted: 'We also regard the competitive character of Japanese industry as a factor that promoted technical change. While there is a stereotype of Japan as the home of cartels and government limitations on competition, the extent of competition appears significantly high for the industrialized oligopolistic economy that is found in all major market economies' (1981: 238).

CREATIVE TECHNOLOGY POLICIES

Japan's efforts to catch up with the West in economic development and technological prowess were concentrated, initially, on such core industries as natural resource consuming sectors (e.g. iron and steel and petrochemicals), their engineering off-shoots (cars, shipbuilding, fibres, plastics) and in pollution industries allied to chemical processes. Aside from the social costs of this rapid development there has been a fairly clear recognition that other basic technologies had to be mastered, such as the electronic and computer revolution with its implications for work, production processes, and spin-off industries. Research by MITI officials argued for a shift in focus to overcoming energy constraints, improving quality of life and developing knowledge-intensive industries. The key to these developments were new-materials technology, biotechnology and new functional technology. As Japan reorders its industrial priorities and undertakes another major re-structuring, the aim is to spend up to 4 per cent of GNP on research and development by 1995.

This planning framework illustrates the new strength of Japanese cor-porations with respect to:

- long-term basic research in fundamental technologies;
- capability to apply science to commercial opportunities.

Most Japanese major corporations have adapted to the appreciation of the yen by introducing new technologies, adding value to products and constant workforce retraining. This approach explains why Japanese plants located in overseas markets can apply equally adaptive approaches to export from overseas markets. An illustrative example is the case of environmental technology. In the 1970s, Japan was universally recognized as a polluted

Table 4.3 Examples of high-value-added products

Iron and steel	High-tension plates
	Surface-processed plates
Non-alloy steel	Shape-memory alloys
Automobiles	Over 2000 cc cars
	Leisure vehicles
Personal computers	Notebook-type personal computers
	Personal computers with high-speed CPU
Computer peripherals	Page printer
	Optical magnetic disk drives
Cameras	Auto-focus SLR cameras
	Compact cameras with zoom lens
Copy equipment	Colour copy equipment
Electronic calculators	Electronic notebooks
Film	Disposable cameras
Televisions	High-definition TV
	Large-screen TV, Projection TV
VCRs	High-quality VCRs
	Hi-Fi VCRs, Camcorders
Metalworking machinery	Numerical-control metalworking machinery
	Metalworking machinery for fine processing
Air conditioners	Inverter air conditioner
Household appliances	Household appliances with full-logic control

Source: White Paper on International Trade (1992)

industrial country, demonstrating the very worst of industrial contamination, absence of regulatory controls and unchecked economic growth at the expense of the natural environment. Yet, only a decade later thanks to basic changes in laws, societal values, political pressures and corporate initiatives, Japan is a potential world leader in the application of technology to environmental problems. It is developing exportable products and services as a result.

The pervasiveness of the cultural valorization of technology, including the ideas and research infrastructure, has raised the profile of intellectual property to unprecedented levels, not only in international trade talks but also as an issue in trade disputes. Clearly this is the new conflict zone in international commerce, and the area where populist sentiment may be most provoked. Nor are the stakes small. The US International Trade Commission estimated in 1988 that American firms lost a potential sale of $24 billion owing to inadequate patent, copyright and trademark protection – the centrepiece of intellectual property. US perceptions of unfair trade practices by the Japanese have led to some headline-producing disputes and a new move towards techno-nationalism:

- US blockage of Japan's takeover of American-owned producer of semi-conductors, the Fairchild Corporation;
- successful lawsuits by IBM against Hitachi and Fujitsu for computer software infringements;
- the FSX fighter dispute, involving the licensing of US technology to a Japanese military consortia, led by Mitsubishi Heavy Industries.

International trade talks have raised both the prominence and the immediacy for initiatives in intellectual property, particularly in such areas as trademarks, copyright for computer software and book publishing and patent policy. While government policy has attempted to prevent individual firms from gaining a temporary monopoly through foreign technology licences (and at times actively interceded to make sure a competing Japanese firm will have equal access to one already obtaining foreign licences), the shift to superior domestic technology makes this role less important. This point is still not a view widely appreciated in North America and Europe. Fierce domestic competition provides the impetus to greater technology diffusion and productivity, far better than government edict or bureaucratic mandates. This, in large measure, explains the growing productivity gap between Japan and other industrial countries.

TECHNOLOGY POLICY IN COMPARATIVE PERSPECTIVE

In Japan technology and science planning are viewed as central to industrial strategy, economic development and competitive advantage. In virtually every European country, this issue has taken on a level of national prestige

129

and sovereignty. One author has raised the fear that European countries will get caught in the competitive squeeze between the high-technology products of the US and Japan and the low-wage products of the Third World (Stoffaes 1979; Derian 1990). Even in the United States, where a co-ordinated approach to technology and industrial development is the least developed, there has been a major concentration of government R&D expenditure in three areas – namely, space, defence and atomic energy (Mansfield, 1968). France, West Germany and Britain have likewise concentrated government resources on high-technology sectors such as computers, nuclear power and aerospace. Even small countries like Holland, Belgium and Sweden have attempted to specialize in particular technologies to win export markets and gain national prestige.

The contrasts between government policies in most Western countries and in Japan rest in two basic areas: those that deal with commercial applications for global markets and those that might be termed technology-pull government programmes. The contrasts are really matters of degree, but they reflect a basic understanding on the part of Japanese corporations, academics and science bureaucrats of international market and technology trends of knowledge intensification. There is widespread understanding in Japan of the difference between pre-competitive generic research, where government, business and university alliances are critical, and competitive research, where technology is proprietary and private sector alliances are pivotal.

Technology-pull refers to the range of incentives and inducements which promote technological innovation. These processes contrast with technology-push, the processes of direct support for new technology development or modification of existing technology. Research consortia are neither novel nor confined to Japan. Denmark uses the approach for export sectors such as furniture, where there is a pooling of resources for export and technology studies, translation, industry fairs and overseas export promotion. In Britain, ICL has launched a parallel processing initiative called 'Goldrush' to build competitive computer networks for such sectors as airlines and bank groups. In Germany the textile machinery association develops collective strategies for advertising, overseas markets, links to trade schools and research with technical institutes.

Despite the efforts of the European governments to 'plan' technology on a national basis, success has been minimal. In defence and aerospace, two areas where European technology has been as good as or superior to the US, Japanese technology and competition have been weak or non-existent. In the basic technologies that are likely to have the most significance in years ahead, such as information technology, biotechnology and energy, European technology trails both the USA and Japan, despite costly consortia initiatives such as Esprit and Alvey.

The most fundamental area is in information technology, which covers the full range of basic technology (microcircuits, microprocessors and semiconductors) through to computers, office technology, telecommunications and data transmission devices. So significant is this development that it has been likened to a second industrial revolution. Information technology and information technology industries have become such a ubiquitous and pervasive presence in the Japanese economy that a simple definition is very difficult. Traditional industry boundaries, such as telecommunications, computers, consumer electronics, cable TV and office equipment have become all but meaningless as companies became vertically integrated and diversified. American companies remain the sales leaders in information technology (see Table 4.4), but the international trend is clearly towards complex global integration and sales outside the home market. Moreover, because the electronics revolution has pervaded Japanese industry to such an extent, Japan is rapidly becoming a truly information economy, no less so because finance and automobiles, two of the most formidable industries, have become so reliant on the sophisticated production, application and use of information technology.

Table 4.4 Japan–US comparisons in information technology

	Japan	US
Personal computers (per 100 workers)	9.9	41.7
Internet use	39,000	1.18m
Cellular phones (per 100 population)	1.4	4.4
Local area networks (per 100 PCs in business)	13.4	55.7
Cable subscribers (% of households with TV)	2.7	60.0
Commercial databases	900	3,900

Source: *New York Times*, 21 November 1993, B1

Perhaps no sector illustrates the dramatic changes taking place in Japanese industry more than telecommunications. Since Japan's telephone monopoly was deregulated in 1984 and fully privatized in 1987, new entrants have come into the market bringing together corporate networks of companies with quite diverse skills. The deregulation and privatization initiative invited fierce political debate within Japan's corporate groups and government departments (in particular MITI and the Ministry of Posts and Telegraphs). MITI was especially dissatisfied with both MPT and NTT, seeing the bureaucratic inertia as an obstacle to new media developments such as cable television, teletext, value-added networks and new integrated information networks for Japanese industry.

In Japan, the NTT network remains intact. The four major long distance NCCs (new common carriers) have concentrated on the heavy-use traffic area between Tokyo and Osaka, employing different technologies based on the strengths of the consortia members. There were two immediate results. First, and predictably, NTT has improved its cost performance. Second, the NCCs have spurred growth in the telecommunications sector, from about 6.5 per cent from 1983–5 to 9.7 per cent in the period 1987–8, and price discounts on long-distance calls have averaged about 25 per cent, although the price gap between NTT and NCCs will decrease to only 8–13 per cent.

JAPAN'S TECHNOLOGICAL EDGE

As in most areas, foreign stereotypes of Japanese technology abound. First, while Japan has been an importer of foreign technology, so have most other Western countries at one point or another. Indeed, the cost of developing new technologies in many fields may well be beyond the resources of even the richest countries, including the United States. More than any other country, Japan has recognized the economic calculus of buying technology in global markets rather than making it because of a desire for technological sovereignty. At the other extreme, France and Britain have gone the other route and have devoted enormous sums to basic research in a wide spectrum of fields. The underlying cost advantage to Japan of this technology division of labour has been to provide domestic industry with opportunities for more widespread diffusion of existing technology than any Western country. In the 1990s, international strategic alliances across a broad spectrum of sectors will accelerate this trend.

The second and related issue involves the managerial and organizational skills needed to absorb new technology via 'gatekeepers' and scanning techniques. That encompasses organizational decision-making and co-ordination across production, marketing and research and development departments to mobilize technology for commercial applications. In this view, technology is market-driven. The key is a management system which can transform complex ideas and techniques into a simplified stream of processes, components and end-products for volume production with perfect quality and high price elasticities.

Among industrialized countries, Japan is particularly well placed to apply technology to the needs of everyday life. As a resource-poor country, it has the most to gain. Moreover, as a rapidly ageing society, where longevity among males and females is among the highest in the world, Japan can apply its enormous commercial strengths to develop products and processes for the new demographics typical of most advanced industrial societies. In fact, Japanese technological developments and science policy are at a watershed for a very specific reason. Japan has almost no room to continue its century-old policy of learning from abroad. In almost all major areas, Japanese science has caught up to the West; in the mechanisms for commercialization, Japan may be the leader. The consequence is that science itself may no longer advance in many fields on the basis of continuity, incremental improvements and progressive refinements, an approach which thus far has given Japan the wherewithal to close the technology gap with the US. As the entire technology frontier is changing, this opens up new opportunities for other countries to challenge Japan's technology leadership. Yet, Japan's efforts to become a science pioneer require not only new commitments of financial and human resources but also new methods to organize science, including the need to move beyond such traditional areas as nuclear energy, computers and space. Japan's role as a science pioneer needs fundamental new approaches to the role of the universities, especially in the role of scientists pursuing basic research independently of potential commercial outcomes.

SUMMARY AND CONCLUSION

The economic and technological discontinuities in an era of globalization and the information revolution, and the collapse of the communist system, suggest profound changes in the world economy.

Economic rivalry among industrialized countries is shifting from one based on control of raw materials and products to competition around key enabling technologies. From aerospace to entertainment, telecommunications to pharmaceuticals, the triad blocs of Europe, North America and Japan–Asia are positioning resources – corporations, banking, government, universities – to plan this new game of techno-nationalism.

Japan is the new centre of focus, as a new superpower in finance and technology. Japan's efforts are different. The primary engine behind the country's technological progress is not government, or defence, or the universities. Japan's technology engine is private sector corporations – immensely competitive in global markets. Moreover, Japan has the weight of Asia – the huge growth markets of South-East Asia (the so-called Asian Dragons) and the looming world colossus – China. As the world's economic centre of gravity moves unequivocally to Asia, Japan is in the dominant position – for technology, for investment capital, for management and ideas.

But Japan's successes are not without problems. Japan's political system is immature and too tied to the old ways – towards the rural voter at the expense of the urban, the landowner over the potential home buyer, the senior citizen over the baby boomer (Japan's consumer spending is about 10 per cent of GNP below America's or Europe's). Japan's regulatory system on land and real estate, on taxation, and banking still imposes a rigidity and conformity that stifles growth and innovation. The yen's rise against foreign currencies, especially the dollar, will halt the growth of cost-sensitive exports, but yen revaluation will actually strengthen Japan's economy over the long term by shifting resources towards more competitive sectors.

Changes in Japan's technology 'vision' signal a shift: in sectoral priorities and in the role of government. More fundamentally, it inaugurates a new era where Japan becomes a pioneer in new and creative technologies. As it happens, the reports emphasized abroad have concentrated on such high-glamour items as computers and memory chips and the competition with the best and brightest of US industry. In the long run, some of Japan's major technological creativity may come in other fields, in such areas as food technology, housing, lifestyle and the environment. It has been said that in the twenty-first century, the world's three largest industries will be leisure, entertainment and education: that is an optimistic perspective. In a world where a million people a year die of malnutrition, substandard living and sanitary conditions, and poor medicine, Japan's role in world welfare development could be more profound than even MITI planners have thought so far.

Table 4.5 Comparative financial systems

	USA	*Japan*	*Germany*
Central characteristic	Separate banking and securities	Bank-centred groups	Universal banking
Main priority	Return on equity	Capital appreciation	Capital appreciation
Risk/reward	Short term	Long term	Medium term
Corporate governance	Shareholders	Management	Bankers
Information	Pluralistic, driven by equity markets	High group communications	Mixed, bank centred
Investment discipline	Quarterly returns	New technologies	Sales growth
Social effects	Encourages conglomerate acquisitions	Encourages technology diversification	Encourages existing investments

BIBLIOGRAPHY

Abegglen, James. 1970. *Business Strategies For Japan*. Tokyo: Sophia University.
Abegglen, James and Thomas Hout. 1978. 'Facing Up To The Trade Gap With Japan.' *Foreign Affairs* (Fall), 146–68.
Abegglen, James and George Stalk, Jr. 1985. *Kaisha, The Japanese Corporation*. New York: Basic Books.
Council on Competitiveness. *Competitiveness Index*. Washington, DC.
Derian, Jean-Claude. 1990. *America's Struggle for Leadership in Technology*. Cambridge, Mass.: MIT Press, ch. 8.
Drucker, Peter F. 1992. *Post-Industrial Society*. New York: Dutton.
Ferguson, Charles. 1990. 'Computers and the Coming of the U.S. Keiretsu.' *Harvard Business Review* (July–August), 55–70.

Kennedy, Paul. 1987. *The Rise and Fall of the Great Powers*. New York: Random House.

McMillan, Charles. 1991. 'Going Global: Japanese Science-Based Strategies in the 1990s.' *Managerial and Decision Economics* 12 (April), 171–82.

McMillan, Charles. 1993. *Building Blocks or Trade Blocs: NAFTA, Japan and The New World Order*. Ottawa: Canada–Japan Trade Council.

McMillan, Charles. 1994. *The Japanese Industrial System* (revised edition). New York: De Gruyter.

Mansfield, Edwin. 1968. *The Economics of Technological Change*. New York: W. W. Norton.

Okimoto, Daniel I. 1986. 'Regime Characteristics of Japanese Industrial Policy', in Hugh Patrick and Larry Meissner (eds), *Japan's High Technology Industries*. Seattle: University of Washington Press, pp. 41–2.

Okoci, Akio and Hoshimi Uchida (eds). 1980. *Development and Diffusion of Technology*. Tokyo: University of Tokyo Press.

Peck, Merton J. and S. Tamura. 1976. 'Technology', In H. Patrick and H. Rosovsky (eds), *Asia's New Giant: How the Japanese Economy Works*. Washington, DC: Brookings Institution.

Peck, Merton J. and Akiro Goto. 1981. 'Technology and Economic Growth: The Case of Japan.' *Research Policy* 10, 222–43.

Peterson, Peter. 1987. 'The Morning After.' *The Atlantic* (October), p. 49.

Stoffaes, Christian. 1979. *La Grande Menace Industrielle*. Paris: Calman-Levy.

Tapscott, Don and Art Caston. 1993. *Paradigm Shift: The New Promise of Information Technology*. Toronto: McGraw-Hill.

Toffler, Alvin. 1990. *Powershift: Knowledge, Wealth and Violence at the Edge of the 21st Century*. New York: Bantam Books.

Uchida, Hoshimi. 1980. 'Summary of Concluding Discussion', in Akio Okochi and Hoshimi Uchida (eds), *Development and Diffusion of Technology*. Tokyo: University of Tokyo Press.

5

THE JAPANESE PRODUCTION SYSTEM

The process of adaptation to national settings

Tetsuo Abo

INTRODUCTION

Since the early 1980s, Japanese management and production systems have attracted worldwide attention because they offer techniques and methods of production that outperform existing US or European engineering technologies.[1] The so-called Japanese transplants, while not very large, have spread with surprising speed into almost every nook and corner of the world. The decision to establish a worldwide network of local production factories has only been taken reluctantly.[2] This is because the Japanese production model draws its strength from the human-related dimension of engineering technologies, workplace practices and a corporate culture that is deeply rooted in Japanese society and culture. Even Japanese manufacturing firms with considerable overseas market commitments have for this reason often delayed starting foreign production.

But once the decision is taken to locate new manufacturing operations in foreign markets for whatever reason, it is important to understand the dynamics of the transfer process. Is the entire Japanese production system being transferred, including the labour and management practices that the Japanese are so famous for? How have leading Japanese corporations been handling the human relations features of their production systems? Even if the overseas factories look very similar to their parent factories, is it so easy for Japanese companies to bring the parent systems into the day-to-day operations of their subsidiary plants? Are the transplants equal to the parent corporation in the two critical dimensions of efficiency and quality that provide the competitive edge of the Japanese production system?

Along with the above questions, it is critical to establish whether the Japanese transplants are a powerful factor in diffusing the new productive methods in all countries equally? Can we expect a convergence of the Japanese production systems towards the same efficiency and quality levels for the same sectors? What components of a country's industrial culture assist the application–adaptation of the Japanese engineering model to new conditions and local needs? Finally, will all countries eventually be required to adopt the Japanese model rather than develop distinct national trajectories?

These critical questions are the starting point for this chapter and draw upon the main results and data of the Japanese Multinational Enterprise Study Group (JMNESG).[3] JMNESG has been undertaking research on the range of issues associated with the transferability problem of Japanese-style production systems in subsidiary plants and joint venture and technology co-operation agreements, not only in the US[4] but, more recently, in the South-East Asian countries[5] and in Europe.[6]

THE WORLDWIDE EXPANSION OF JAPANESE MANUFACTURING PLANTS

Globally, Japanese corporations have more than 14,000 subsidiaries employing over 2.4 million people on their payrolls in 127 countries (see Table 5.1). Manufacturing industries count for a third of the total and close to 2 million people in 91 countries. When looked at closely it can be seen that Japanese transplants exhibit a number of characteristics.

While the largest number of plants are concentrated in Asia, North America and Europe, there are also considerable numbers of plants in mid-South America, Oceania, and even in Africa and the Middle East. Judging from the average number of employees per plant (326.5), they are relatively small or medium-sized operations. The diffusion of Japanese transplants has occurred mainly since the early 1960s. The fact that they are of such recent vintage compared to American or European multinationals that were established more than fifty or even a hundred years ago suggests that in the coming two decades Japanese transplants will continue to expand their operations in the major markets of the world.

The largest concentration of transplants is in Asia. This region has the highest number of transplants (55 per cent of total manufacturing subsidiaries). In each of the nine Asian countries from the Philippines to Taiwan, there are between 100 and 500 Japanese plants; all of these are relatively large in terms of total employees per plant, but operate with a much smaller number of Japanese expatriates. There are 561 Japanese transplants in Korea, 305 in Taiwan, and 366 in Thailand. On the other hand, only four non-Asian countries have more than 100 plants and, by comparison, these plants are smaller and are operated with a far higher number of Japanese expatriates. The US has 280 transplants, the UK 224 and Germany 268. The reasons for this can be partly explained by the fact that in Asian countries Japanese corporations rely more heavily on joint ventures which work with local entrepreneurs and managers, including operations where the Japanese have a minority share in locally owned plants (more than 10 per cent). With the majority of cases, this has had important implications for the adaptation of the Japanese production system to national settings.

Table 5.1 Number of Japanese companies and their employees, by country to end of 1992

	All industry				Manufacturing			
	Country	Company	Employee	Expatriate	Country	Company	Employee	Expatriate
Asia	21	5,482	1,212,181	15,720	17	2,842	1,012,059	9,084
Korea		385	203,484	461		315	176,582	391
China		444	82,708	855		289	68,433	617
Taiwan		767	168,154	2,032		501	152,711	1,381
Hong Kong		856	74,164	2,738		165	47,921	746
Thailand		870	211,286	3,026		494	180,915	1,928
Singapore		858	92,360	2,854		267	68,024	1,196
Malaysia		592	150,716	1,814		371	130,564	1,431
Philippines		204	66,014	395		104	44,564	293
Indonesia		378	120,136	1,399		204	101,307	998
India	11	66	32,435	73		61	32,016	65
Others		47	10,724	73	7	34	9,022	38
Middle East	10	80	9,568	301	10	22	5,363	50
Europe	29	3,087	265,880	9,483	22	622	141,419	2,156
UK		871	82,519	3,349		180	40,355	765
The Netherlands		370	16,235	883		39	10,000	99
Belgium		147	21,466	644		34	7,415	142
Luxemburg		55	1,460	111		4	1,130	51
France		333	28,254	757		89	13,929	231
Germany		598	53,837	2,438		105	28,179	381
Switzerland		107	5,141	248		5	42	1
Spain		128	21,395	366		45	18,338	217
Italy		164	11,877	296		46	6,194	68
Others	20	296	23,696	391	13	75	15,837	201

	All industry				Manufacturing			
	Country	Company	Employee	Expatriate	Country	Company	Employee	Expatriate
North America	2	3,890	580,735	18,142	2	1,234	342,531	6,548
Canada		332	39,490	866		93	23,367	275
USA		3,558	541,245	17,276		1,141	319,164	6,273
Mid-S. America	27	858	255,778	1,799	20	300	127,577	847
Mexico		113	39,178	377		68	36,318	247
Panama		123	964	66		1	3	1
Brazil		322	188,798	841		160	72,162	497
Others	24	284	26,838	555	16	71	19,094	102
Africa	25	142	21,470	211	16	34	17,726	61
Liberia		78	–	–		–	–	–
Others	24	64	–	–	15	34	–	–
Oceania	13	672	70,297	1,656	6	105	37,580	223
Australia		481	54,804	1,147		81	31,827	183
New Zealand		87	5,889	112		18	4,123	21
Guam		55	4,319	196		2	379	3
Others	10	48	5,285	201	3	4	1,251	16
Total	127	14,211	2,415,909	47,312	93	5,159	1,684,255	18,969

Source: Toyo Keizai Inc., *Kaigai Shinshutsu Kigyo Souran by Country*, 1993

Distribution of automobile manufacturers by country (best reading of symbol matrix):

Company	USA	Canada	UK	W. Germany	France	Italy	The Netherlands	Belgium	Ireland	Greece	Spain	Portugal	Switzerland	Austria	Brazil	Argentina	Mexico	Venezuela	Peru	Chile	Uruguay	Colombia	Puerto Rico	Ecuador	Panama	Bolivia	Costa Rica	T. & Tobago	Turkey	Iran	Iraq	U.A. Emirates	Saudi Arabia
A Nissan Motor Co.	◎		◎							◎	◁	◁					◎	◎	◎					◁			◁	◎		◎			
Nissan Diesel	◎	◁	◁								◁																	◁					
Fuji Heavy Industries	◎																																
B Toyota Motor Corp.	◎	◎	◎					◁				◁			◀			◎		◁	◎			◁	◁	◁	◎	◎					
Hino Motors	◁	◁	◁				◁		◁										◎					◁			◁	○					
Daihatsu Motor Co.								◁	◁			◁												◁	◁	◁				◁			
C Mazda Motor Corp.	◎		◎									◁							◁			◎		◁				◎					
Mitsubishi Motor Corp.	◎	◎	◁					◁				◁							◁		◎	◎		◎	◁			○	◁				
Honda Motor Corp.	◎	◎	◁								◀									◎		◁		◎			◁		◀				
Isuzu Motors	◎		◁				◀					◁						◎				○		○									
Suzuki Motor Co.		◎	◁																														
D GM (1991)	◎	◎	◎	◎							◎	○				◎	◎	◎	○	○		◀	○	○					○	◀			
Ford (1980)	◎	◎	◎	◎							◎	○				◎	◀	◀	○			○	○	○					◁	○			

Figure 5.1 Distribution of overseas production plants of Japanese and American motor firms, by country and company, 1989 and 1980

Sources: Nissan Motor Co. (ed.), *Jidosha Sangyo Handobukko* (Automobile Industry Handbook): *Kinokuniya shoten*, 1988 (in Japanese). GM: *Information Handbook 1991–92*; Ford: *Moody's Industrial Manual*, 1980

Notes:
1. Planned plants are partially included.
2. A: Nissan Group; B: Toyota Group; C: Others; D: American firms.
3. ◎ Passenger car manufacturing; ○ Passenger car KD; ▲ Truck manufacturing; △ Truck KD.

In the overseas countries, Toyota and Nissan had 25 and 21 manufacturing plants respectively (including licensing production agreements) and employed 45,774 and 32,328 people in the period 1990–2 (mostly production people). Their presence is small compared to GM's with 21 plants (including 4 plants in Canada) and Ford with 14 plants (3 plants in Canada). GM had 517,000 people on its payroll while Ford had 256,167 employees during their peak years 1979–80, but since then these numbers have been cut in half. The average number of employees per overseas plant for Toyota is 1,830; 1,539 for Nissan; 24,619 for GM and 18,298 for Ford.[7] Generally speaking, the overseas plants of Japanese auto companies have been located everywhere in the world, but with major emphasis on the US, Europe and Asia. By comparison, US branch plant companies are concentrated mainly in Canada and Europe and, more recently, in Mexico and other Latin American countries. They employ more than ten times as many people as do their Japanese counterparts.

A similar comparison can be made in terms of the consumer electronics industry with product makers such as Matsushita, Sanyo[8] and Sony[9] on one hand, and GE and Westinghouse on the other. Furthermore, a comparison may be drawn between semi-conductor makers such as NEC and Fujitsu and Motorola, TI and National Semiconductor Corporation. It is likely that the results follow much the same pattern but, unfortunately, not all the data have been assembled.

A COMPARISON OF THE HYBRID NATURE OF JAPANESE AUTO AND ELECTRONICS PLANTS IN THE US AND KOREA/TAIWAN AND EUROPE: SOME EMPIRICAL FINDINGS

Japanese transplants have been transferring their production systems to local industrial settings for more than three decades. The hybrid model is a research tool designed to determine the extent to which Japanese-style engineering systems are introduced and applied in their foreign subsidiaries.[10] This model emphasizes those aspects of Japan's production system that are vital for achieving high product quality and efficient production throughout the entire range of operations. This includes building a strong sense of employee identity with the company and by flexible work practices at all aspects of the production cycle. Its focal point stresses the human factor of Japanese production methods which is the backbone of the Japanese production system. This latter factor is intimately related to the historical and cultural background of Japanese society but also is derived from the commitment of Japanese business to a great deal of continuous in-house education and training. It is our hypothesis that when Japanese firms 'apply' their sophisticated technological system to foreign countries, they will face problems in 'adapting' to the local environment. This poses a dilemma for the Japanese production model in the sense that it has to make trade-offs with local customs and ways of doing things if it is to succeed. The result of the twin dynamic of application and adaptation at the local level is, of course, a 'hybrid' of the principal elements of the Japanese production system.

With this explanation in mind, it is possible to discover just how much of Japanese technology, employment and organizational practices are being followed in the overseas plants of Japanese firms. In our system of rating, a score of 5 indicates the highest possible degree of application and transfer of the Japanese system with the lowest level of adaptation to local conditions. This transplant would be most like a Japanese plant operating in Japan. Conversely, a score of 1 represents the highest degree of adaptation of a Japanese plant operating in a non-domestic setting and would depart the most from established Japanese practice and custom.

The Japanese production model can be divided into 23 essential elements and 6 core groups of operations (see Table 5.2). This methodology enables us to determine the degree of hybridization from the viewpoint of the operating system of the parent company in Japan. The second perspective entails combining the extent to which the production methods and the elements of the Japanese model and technology are transferred from the viewpoint of the local economy and society.

Table 5.2 evaluates 34 US plants (1989) and 25 plants in Korea and Taiwan (1992). The figures shown in this table are the average scores for each of the four chosen industries. The findings were obtained by analysing company records mainly based on information collected during plant visits. The four industries are automobile assembly, auto parts, consumer electronics and semiconductors. Each plant was awarded a score rating from '1' to '5' based on evaluating each of 23 component elements of the Japanese production model.[11]

The overall average score of Japanese transplants in the US and Korea/Taiwan is 3.3 (see Table 5.2). This indicates that Japanese and local elements are mixed in nearly equal portions with a slight tendency towards the Japanese application side of the scale. It is particularly interesting that scores from 3.0 to 3.3 are very common in many other regions where Japanese transplants operate, except for non-Asian developing countries. We could even say this is a 'standard score' for many Japanese transplants, reflecting the practice of Japanese transplants to mix local elements with the ideal model.

None the less, there are some significant differences between Japanese transplants in North America compared with Korea and Taiwan. In the higher groups, labour relations (3.5) is one of the most important supporting conditions for the Japanese system; production control (3.4) is another critical element for any Japanese transplant as it represents the hardware-related core of Japanese production technologies. In the middle range, although the scores for work organization (3.3) and team sense (3.3) are the same, the level of human-related activities is more important than team sense. The first is the

Table 5.2 The 'hybrid ratios' of the Japanese production system in the USA and Korea–Taiwan

	USA (A)	Korean–Taiwan (B)	Av.	A–B
G1. Work org./Adm. av.	**2.9**	**3.7**	**3.3**	**−0.8**
1 Job classific.	3.7	4.9	4.3	−1.2
2 Job rotation	2.6	2.9	2.8	−0.3
3 Training	2.9	3.4	3.2	−0.5
4 Supervisor	2.9	3.4	3.2	−0.5
5 Wage	2.4	3.9	3.2	−1.5
6 Promotion	3.1	3.7	3.4	−0.6
G2. Prod. control	**3.3**	**3.5**	**3.4**	**−0.2**
7 Equipment	4.3	3.5	3.9	0.8
8 Quality cont.	3.4	3.6	3.5	−0.2
9 Maintenance	2.6	3.3	3.0	−0.7
10 Oper. cont.	3.0	3.5	3.3	−0.5
G3. Parts procure.	**3.0**	**3.2**	**3.1**	**−0.2**
11 Local cont.	2.7	2.9	2.8	−0.2
12 Suppliers	3.9	3.5	3.7	0.4
13 Methods	2.5	3.2	2.9	−0.7
G4. Team sense	**3.2**	**3.4**	**3.3**	**−0.2**
14 Small group	2.5	3.2	2.9	−0.7
15 Information	3.6	3.5	3.6	0.1
16 Unity	3.5	3.6	3.6	−0.1
G5. Labour relat.	**3.6**	**3.4**	**3.5**	**0.2**
17 Employ. policy	3.4	3.0	3.2	0.4
18 Employ. securi.	3.4	3.3	3.4	0.1
19 Union	4.4	4.0	4.2	0.4
20 Grievance	3.3	3.2	3.3	0.1
G6. Parent/subsi.	**3.6**	**2.3**	**3.0**	**1.3**
21 JPN ratio	3.7	1.5	2.6	2.2
22 Power delega.	3.6	2.7	3.2	0.9
23 Local managers	3.6	2.7	3.2	0.9
Total av. (23 items)	3.3	3.3	3.3	0.0

(A) 34 Japanese transplants in the US (1989)
(B) 25 Japanese transplants in Korea/Taiwan (1992)

core of the whole system; the second is only at the sub-system level. The lower levels of parts procurement practices (3.1) and parent/subsidiary relations (3.0) look good in terms of local sourcing needs. But if a low application score is hardware-related, this could result in poor managerial control with low efficiency and poor quality control as the result.

When we turn from looking at average scores, there are significant differences between the dynamics of adaptation and the transfer process in the case of branch plant operations in the US and Korea/Taiwan (see Figure 5.2). The sharp contrast between work organization and parent subsidiary relations by region is obvious, while the results in the other four groups are

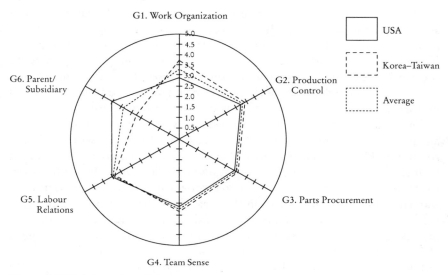

G1. Work Organization

G6. Parent/
Subsidiary

G2. Production
Control

G5. Labour
Relations

G3. Parts Procurement

G4. Team Sense

USA

Korea–Taiwan

Average

Figure 5.2 Hybrid ratios of six groups

all very close to each other. This reveals the single most important difference between Japanese plants in the US and Korea/Taiwan: at the US work sites, there are more Japanese expatriates with managerial authority but fewer Japanese elements of the production model overall; at the Korea/Taiwan work sites there is much less Japanese managerial authority on site but considerably more of the Japanese production model in total. Needless to say, the Korean/Taiwan shape of the hexagram is more desirable as an ideal pattern than the US one. As well, further evidence collected suggests that the Japanese plants in the US depend more on the local business environment for support than on the formal corporate system itself compared with those transplants in Korea/Taiwan.

HOW HYBRID ARE JAPANESE TRANSPLANTS?

Table 5.2 focuses on variations in the way the Japanese production model is transferred to its US and Korean/Taiwan operations. It shows that even though there are significant differences in the way critical elements of the Japanese production model are transferred in the two countries, these may not be all that significant. What matters is that a transplant receives other aspects of the Japanese system that compensates for the missing components. Among the higher score items for both Korean/Taiwan and US operations are job classification (4.3), equipment purchase (3.9), and parts and component suppliers (3.7), all of which are the key elements in the Japanese production model compared with union representation (4.2) that is only seen as a supporting condition. By contrast, job classification is the critical precondition for flexible work organization and for training a multi-functional skilled workforce. Equipment acquisition and parts suppliers are the hardware-related core areas of the Japanese production model that directly determine the levels of efficiency and quality of a transplant's overall performance. Union representation is one of the most sensitive areas that seriously affects the essential human side of work organization, teamwork and production quality. On the other hand, among the lower-score items, job rotation (2.8) is obviously an item that is more than compensated for by a high score in the area of job classification (4.3). The low score with respect to job rotation means that the potential provided by the full application of standard Japanese work norms in the area of job classification is not being sufficiently utilized. Local content purchasing practices (2.8) and production methods (2.9) are also items that potentially could be offset by parts suppliers (3.7). The results show the slowness in Japanese corporate practice in relying heavily on local parts and material. Small group work practices on the production floor (2.9) is one of the most difficult Japanese production methods to transfer because it is based on the corporate-orientation of Japanese firms and is an important element in the formation of Japanese work practices. The lowest score of the ratio of Japanese managers to local talent (2.6) occurred simply because in Korean/Taiwanese Japanese transplants, Japanese companies have a low ratio of Japanese managers compared to their practice in the US where the reverse is true (3.7).

What, then, are some of the key differences of the findings between Japanese transplants in the US and those in Korea/Taiwan? US plants scored highest in maintaining the efficiency and quality levels in the application of Japanese production methods in quality of equipment (4.3), part suppliers (3.9) and Japanese/US manager ratio (3.7). By contrast, they did less well in terms of the core work-based elements of the Japanese system even though US-based Japanese transplants did much better in the area of labour relations including union representation. In particular, the lower scores of training-related elements such as job rotation (2.6), training and supervision (2.9) and incentive-related elements such as wages (2.4) and promotion (3.1) suggest that US-based transplants are weaker with respect to the transfer of this kind of human-related Japanese systems compared with their counterparts in Korea/Taiwan. The low score registered for small group work (2.5) is representative of the sorts of problems encountered by these kinds of voluntary and self-motivating activities that do not fit the work habits and industrial culture of the American people.

These differences become even sharper when US transplants are compared with those of Korea/Taiwan and can be easily seen in columns A and B of Table 5.2 and in the shift between the two shapes in Figure 5.3.

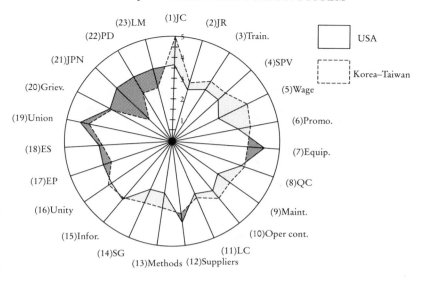

Figure 5.3 Hybrid ratios of twenty-three items

The most remarkable difference between Korean/Taiwanese firms and their American counterparts is that in the Korea/Taiwan operations of Japanese transplants there is a much higher job classification (4.9: difference −1.2) and wages (3.9: −1.5) as well as many other elements in work organization that occurred despite the fact that these operations have a low Japanese-to-local manpower ratio (1.5 : 2.2). The single one exception is job rotation (2.9: −0.3), which is the key item in implementing a very active multi-skilling programme of the workforce. In addition to what has already been described, there are several additional important points to be made.

First, the almost complete transfer of the job classification system in the case of Korea/Taiwan manufacturing operations is not easy to explain. It may be due to a shared cultural affinity in the sense that it is easier to implant this aspect of the Japanese work model in many South-East Asian countries in comparison with Western countries because the former have such limited industrial traditions of their own.

Second, the large gap in the way wage systems are organized reflects two different approaches to salary. Wages are job-related in the US operations but are based on an individual evaluation system as in Korea and Taiwan.

Finally, the distinctive differences in equipment, maintenance and administrative methods are all closely related to significant variations in the ways in which local managers deal with the technological aspects of machine parts and components. Since the interaction between technology and human resource management is such a large part of the Japanese production model, this area needs to be looked at in greater depth. Tables 5.3, 5.4 and Figure 5.4

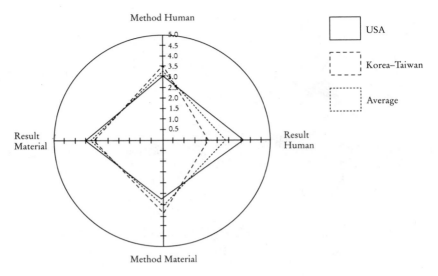

Figure 5.4 Four-perspective evaluation

reveal the critical findings (by 4-P-E). Note that method refers to the transfer of invisible techniques and know-how necessary for organization-building and personnel administration. This requires transplanting a large amount of Japanese-style skills and technologies locally. On the other hand, 'result' refers to the transfer of visible elements of 'ready-made' hardware such as machines, parts, and even Japanese people, which may not leave any local traces when they are repatriated.

What is significant is the degree of convergence in comparing the successful introduction of 'methods' with 'results' in two sharply different contexts.

Table 5.3 Four-aspect evaluation of 'hybrid' model

Mode of transfer element	Human elements	Material elements
Method	• G1 (Work organ. & admin.) – All elements: (1)–(6) • G4 (Team sense) – All elements: (14)–(16) • G5 (Labour relations) – All elements: (17)–(20)	• G2 (Production control) – (8) Quality control – (9) Maintenance • G3 (Parts procurement) – (13) Methods
Result ('ready-made')	• G6 (Parent–subsid. relations) – (21) JPN expatriate ratio – (23) Local manager	• G2 (production control) – (7) Equipment • G3 (Parts procurement) – (11) Local content – (12) Suppliers

But, there is also strong divergence between Japanese transplants in the US and Korea and Taiwan with respect to human resource management and the technological system of Japanese production. This is mainly due to the extremely low score of human resource management outcomes 'result-human', (2.1) in Korea/Taiwan compared with the strong performance of its US counterpart (3.7). Despite the apparent convergence in the overall score, this should not be allowed to hide the fact that there are important points of convergence. In two critical areas the successful introduction of Japanese methods are lower in the US than in Korea/Taiwan. (On the other hand, the 'result' score is higher in the US than in Korea/Taiwan.) Thus, we have two widely differing management/result ratios of 81.1 per cent for the US and 129.6 per cent for Korea/Taiwan. Two important implications follow from this. Bringing in 'ready-made' elements such as equipment, parts and component suppliers is a common practice in both regions and supports both high levels of efficiency and production quality in the transplants. A qualification, however, is in order. This is not necessarily the type of technology transfer that can substantially be rooted in the local soil. On the other hand, relatively high scores of 3.1 and 3.5 in human resource management methods in both regions means that the Japanese production system has been transplanted and adapted to local conditions.

Table 5.4 Four-aspect evaluation of Japanese car and electronics plants in the USA and Korea–Taiwan

	USA (A)	Korean–Taiwan (B)	Regional average	[A–B]
Human	3.1	3.5	3.3	−0.4
Method material	2.8	3.4	3.1	−0.6
Av.	3.0	3.5	3.2	−0.5
Human	3.7	2.1	2.9	1.6
Result material	3.6	3.3	3.5	0.3
Av.	3.7	2.7	3.2	1.0
Method (av.) (%) / Result (av.)	81.1	129.6	100.0	

Yet here also there are some notable differences. US Japanese transplants did less well in such areas as quality control, maintenance, and procurement methods where the accumulated skills of finding the right balance between machines and humans is critical. The above results can be explained by the fact there is such a large number of Japanese expatriates in US operations. But the case of Korean/Taiwan branch plant operations, with a far lower ratio of Japanese managers to local talent and a much higher adherence to Japanese production methods, is the more ideal combination.

IS THERE A TYPICAL JAPANESE HYBRID?

A typical Japanese overseas plant is a 'hybrid' system of Japanese production methods and adaptation to local conditions. It is important to note that such half-and-half 'factories' are none the less able to compete in local markets and to some extent even in international ones. This is due to the fact that they have locational and cost advantages in areas such as wages, materials, transportation benefits as well as human skills. What is striking is that the efficiency and quality of Japanese transplants in any region depend largely on a set of key factors: production control, the use of Japanese equipment, close relations with parts suppliers and proper evaluation methods and quality control over machines and people. On the other hand, it is important to stress that using the 'ready-made' Japanese machines and parts provided by parent plants does not mean that the transplant receives the core of the system – namely, the 'methods' part of the Japanese production model.

This finding alerts us to the fact that the human aspect of the transfer process is the most critical test in the final analysis. In this respect the different scores of plants in the US and in Korea/Taiwan are striking. The US operations had far higher scores in human management and lower scores in the area of system production methods and materials while Japanese operations in Korea/Taiwan recorded a much lower score with respect to the human side of the Japanese management system but did much better on the materials management end of things. Also, we find the following similar combinations: lower work organization and higher parent/subsidiary relations in the US transplants with the reverse being the case in Korea/Taiwan. The key point is the way power is delegated from Japanese expatriates to local managers. Needless to say, the situation in the Korea/Taiwan transplants is more desirable. These operations get more of the production system with smaller numbers of Japanese people in positions of control than do Japanese transplants in the US. The key role of local managers in implementing Japanese-style management in Asian countries is remarkable.

If the human element is the essential factor in Japanese transplants, one would expect heavy emphasis on education and training which is, in fact, the case. For this reason, the most impressive achievement of Japanese multinationals is at the grass-roots level where they train the workforce. Therefore, in the coming decades, we will see these and other 'hybrid' effects of Japanese-style production systems in the main regions and countries of the world. This commitment to training and education has a lasting impact on local people that is likely to spark other socio-cultural changes in local populations.

We cannot forget another important issue regarding international technology transfer by the Japanese transplants. Transplants have a 'demonstration effect' on local managerial practice which leads to better-managed local companies. Many experts point to such effects and this study corroborates these findings.[12]

JAPAN: THE NEXT WORLD POWER?

In terms of the larger picture, what is the relationship between the future of the nation-state and the process of adaptation? What kinds of national policies matter for the Japanese production system? In a word, the fundamental issue is that of authority and responsibility. Who has the responsibility for the organization and adaptation of the production system to local circumstances?

There are a clear set of choices to be made between a 'job-centred' model of work in Western societies and a 'personal-skills centred' system in Japan and, to a certain extent, in Korea/Taiwan. The distinguishing feature is that the former is individually oriented and the latter group-directed. There are other aspects to be considered as well with respect to education and training. Should the state provide all the skill training programmes or should it be left to the private sector? Here the difference between the formal and informal is important. For a 'job-centred' labour training market, a formal education system establishes a standard set of qualifications that an individual requires in order to get into the labour market. For a 'person-centred' system, an on-the-job method of in-house training develops a firm-specific, multi-skilled workforce.

In terms of industrial relations, the critical problem is the extent to which a 'them and us' consciousness exists in the workplace. For Western kinds of industrial trade unions principally organized in 'job-centred' labour markets, it is more essential to keep a horizontal relationship with their rank-and-file members and this tends to create an 'us' feeling. On the other hand, for Japanese-type company unions, the more important issue is the vertical relationship between the union and the company where a 'them and us' consciousness is blurred. Trust building is another area where institutional arrangements matter a great deal. It is difficult to say which comes first – the industrial relations system which creates a high level of trust between workers and employers, or the process of trust building through workplace participation which leads to an industrial relations system reinforcing this goal. In Japan, the so-called 'my company' consciousness supports an 'us' sentiment among all employees in a company. This sharing of a common concern is an important basis for developing multi-skill training programmes which need a broad perspective and flexible framework of industrial relations.

Generally speaking, however, a 'my company' consciousness for Japanese-style management is the more essential goal if we take the example of a well-organized firm with a combination of co-operation and competition among its employees. The common understanding among company people is that even very severe competition can be allowed within limits defined by an individual merit system that evaluates all the employees. Slight differences in salary from year to year are allowed even over a ten-year period. This kind

151

of fine-tuning of the pay schedule would be difficult to sustain in most industrial countries.

For the majority of Japanese top managers, the ultimate purpose is not necessarily to take strong leadership on the basis of their own individual ideas. But, as 'employees', their responsibility is to co-ordinate the ideas and opinions of their 'colleagues' at various levels of the company organization and to motivate all of the employees to be as hard working as a 'top manager' is supposed to be. Therefore, the notorious 'long hours of work' are not simply compelled by the company's order, but are partly a 'voluntary' response. Japanese-style entrepreneurship has, of course, both merits and demerits. In any case, this kind of intense pressure on individual employees would not be popular in many nations.

Two other issues need to be considered. In the above, I have emphasized the remarkable spread of Japanese systems everywhere in the world. However, as the influence of Japanese production methods penetrates the consciousness and customs of people that are firmly connected to their own institutions, the way the Japanese model adapts and the extent of the transfer of its labour-saving technologies must differ from region to region throughout the world. Some of the elements of the Japanese production system can be absorbed without much resistance from a society, but others come with many costs. Since the levels of efficiency vary between these 'hybrid systems' it is not always relevant to introduce the entire production model to every industry in a given country. For example, a chemical industry would be very costly to re-organize along Japanese lines because it is not assembly-type machine industry. This is one of the main reasons why I do not see the possibility of a strong convergence in Japanese-type production technologies with the same productivity performance and quality levels all over the world.

For a similar reason, I believe that the idea of national hegemony is a useful approach as a theoretical framework to better understand the historical changes in the world economic system. Such changes explain the loss of power of a once powerful 'centre nation' or region whose influence was based on the competitive strength of its dominant industries. Their technological superiority is largely influenced by the socio-cultural environment of the region. This means that convergence theory so narrowly focused on economic factors is far too limited a perspective to explain adequately the long-run trends of world history. The fact is that it is still too premature to talk about the time when Japan's hegemony as a nation-state is unchallenged. This is because the diffusion of the Japanese model of production throughout the world is not the same thing as Japan becoming the leading power in the world. Japan, just like a top manager at a Japanese company, is not able to plan its place in the new world order as the United States tried to do after the First World War. Therefore, what we can reasonably anticipate in the near future is the 'hybridization' of its management practices and production systems worldwide. Japan will be the leader in both. For Japan to be the dominant world power, more is needed. Its management and social systems will also have to be transformed. It needs a new policy-making environment, although the extent and direction of these reforms should not be exaggerated. Japan has not entered the 'post-Toyotism' era.

None the less, Japan faces many challenges across a broad front. First of all, it has to deal with the international pressures from Japanese–US trade negotiations. It is under strain to accommodate the new waves of a rising yen, the most effective political pressure on Japan's power as a 'nation' to move its production bases abroad. There are also signs that its political and social frameworks will have to be reformed, beginning with the end of the one-party domination by the Liberal Democratic Party and the introduction of an 'equal opportunity law' for women, the ageing population, and so on.

And last, but not least, after all the above problems, two far greater technology problems should be pointed out: the energy-resource change from oil and the earth-environment which are closely interrelated. Both have been succeeded from American-type mass production to a Japanese-type 'flexible production system', but have not yet been resolved. A new production system that could overcome this problem would be the 'post-Toyotism'.

NOTES

1 Representative books regarding this include: Dertouzos, M.L., R. K. Lester and R. M. Solow, *Made in America*, Cambridge, Mass.: MIT Press, 1989; Womack, J.P., D. T. Jones and D. Roos, *The Machine That Changed the World*, New York: Macmillan Publishing Co., 1990; and Kenney, M. and M. Florida, *Beyond Mass Production*, New York: Oxford University Press, 1993.

2 See Yoshino, M., *Japan's Multinational Enterprises*, Cambridge, Mass.: Harvard University Press; and Trevor, M., *Japan's Reluctant Multinationals*, London: Frances Pinter, 1983.

3 The Japanese Multinational Enterprise Study Group (JMNESG), directed by Professor T. Abo, University of Tokyo, has been awarded grants from the Toyota Foundation in 1985 and 1987–8 for research under the title of 'Local Production by Japanese Manufacturing Firms in the United States'. We undertook field studies in the summer–fall of 1986 and 1989 in the USA and published two Japanese books, along with an English version of one of them (The Institute of Social Science, University of Tokyo, Research Report, No. 23 (ed. by T. Abo), *Local Production of Japanese Automobile and Electronics Firms in the United States; The 'Application' and 'Adaptation' of Japanese Style Management*, 1990). The second English version, which is the final report for the comprehensive research undertaken in 1989, has been published under the title *Hybrid Factory: Japanese Production System in the United States*, T. Abo (ed.), New York: Oxford University Press, 1994.

4 See Abo, *Hybrid Factory*, referred to in note 3.

5 JMNESG conducted the same kind of research in Asian countries in 1992–3 (directed by Professor H. Itagaki). See Abo, T., 'Overseas Production Activities of Nissan Motor Co.', in S.-J. Park. (ed.), *Managerial Efficiency in Competition and Cooperation*, Frankfurt and New York: Campus Verlag, 1992; and Abo, T., 'Sanyo's Overseas Production Activities', in *The Global Competitiveness of the Asian Firm*, H. Schutte (ed.), London: Macmillan, 1994.

6 See Abo, *Hybrid Factory*, op. cit.
7 Sources for the above are annual reports, '10 Ks', and directories of these companies, and *Moody's Industrial Manuals*.
8 See Abo, 'Sanyo's . . .', op. cit.
9 See Abo, 'A Report of On-the-Spot Observation of Sony's Four Major Color TV Plants in the US, the UK, West Germany and Japan', *Annals of the Institute of Social Science* (University of Tokyo), No. 29, 1987.
10 See *Hybrid Factory*, op. cit., chs. 1 and 2.
11 For evaluation criteria, see Abo, *Hybrid Factory*, op. cit.
12 In so far as the information derived from my own plant visits, such foreign companies are as follows: Motorola, IBM, Samsung, Gold Stars, Chrysler, GM, Ford, Volkswagen, Rover, three Korean auto firms, and so on.

6

REGIONAL BLOCS
Can Japan be the leader?
Paul Bowles and Brian MacLean

INTRODUCTION

The world economy is currently witnessing two distinct trends: globalization and regionalization. To some these are competing trends and we are offered the choice between the benefits of a liberalized multilateral trading order and the costs of balkanized, bloc-dominated, global disorder. This dichotomy is, however, a false one and the emerging global economy is considerably more complex. What is clear is that states and firms are pursuing a variety of different strategies as they seek to manufacture competitive and political advantage. This is especially clear in the case of the US which has adopted a strategy based on the 'triple play': support for GATT, a key role in APEC and leadership of an expanding NAFTA. In this chapter, we consider whether Japan might wish to assume leadership of an East Asian bloc, or 'yen bloc', not as part of a 'Fortress East Asia' de-linked from the rest of the global economy, but as one element of a wider strategy.[1]

While the existing literature on the 'yen bloc' question features solid empirical work and occasional flashes of analytical brilliance, it typically is burdened by an orthodox economic approach. The most serious weakness of the literature, however, has been an over-reliance on the examination of market-level trends in East Asian trade and in the use of the yen as an intra-regional currency.

We argue that examination of capital flows (both official and private) is also necessary to make evident the strategies which states and firms have pursued. The analysis of capital flows provides an essential part of the background necessary to evaluate whether formal trading arrangements are likely to emerge in the East Asian region.[2] Moreover, for investigating the possibility of formal currency arrangements in the region, it is necessary to go beyond examination of market-level trends to consider the structural forces impacting on states in the region, particularly Japan. We attempt to demonstrate, then, the strength of a political economy approach to analysing the pressures on East Asian states which could lead to the formation of a Japan-centred bloc.

155

BLOCS: VARIOUS MIXES FOR TRADE AND CURRENCY INTEGRATION

We shall say that a bloc is formed when states in a particular region agree to implement trade policies which lower (or eliminate) tariffs between member countries and/or currency policies which (at least partially) harmonize exchange rate regimes in the member countries. This still leaves a wide variety of possible bloc formations and several are observed in practice.

In the Asian Free Trade Association (AFTA) and NAFTA, for example, member countries have agreed to lower tariff barriers on selected goods and services traded between them, reduce barriers to capital mobility, but retain their own individual tariff structures against imports from non-member countries. In the EC before 1992, member countries not only negotiated lower tariffs among themselves but also common tariffs against non-members, this form of bloc being known as a *customs union*. With the further integration of the EC associated with 'EC 1992', the customs union has evolved further with the formation of a single market in which capital, goods and labour have become increasingly free to move between member countries.

A bloc need not involve any currency harmonization, as with AFTA and NAFTA. Alternatively, currency harmonization may take the form of mutual currency management with exchange rates kept in fixed relationship to each other, as in the European Monetary System, or may involve the further step to a common currency as envisaged in the Maastricht Treaty.

To clarify the combinations of trade and currency integration which have been associated with the term 'yen bloc' we will refer to the matrix depicted in Figure 6.1.

Japan and East Asia today do not form a yen bloc but they nevertheless exhibit a substantial degree of economic integration. They could be said to form both a *geographic trade zone* and a *currency zone* (as indicated by the

Increasing currency integration ↓	Increasing trade integration →		
	Geographic trade zone	Preferential trading arrangements	Single market
Currency zone	Japan and East Asia 1994	US and Canada 1994	
Mutual currency management		Europe 1994	
Single currency			Europe 2000?

Figure 6.1 Trade and currency integration
Source: Adapted from Crockett (1991: 114)

156

'Japan and East Asia 1994' cell of the matrix), where a geographic trade zone comprises a region 'within which trading links are closer and more important than they are with the outside world' (Crockett 1991: 113). A currency zone consists of a set of economies which tend towards a common intra-regional currency in (1) invoicing trade within the region; (2) denominating the instruments of intra-regional capital flows, and (3) in their choice of a key currency for official reserves and exchange rate considerations.

The mere strengthening of a Japan-centred geographic trade and currency zone in the sense of the 'Japan and East Asia 1994' cell of the matrix is a development which would not in itself have major implications for the world economy. The critical and meaningful question about a yen bloc, then, is whether one will emerge involving either (1) preferential trading arrangements and a strengthened currency zone, or (2) preferential trading arrangements and mutual currency management. We start by considering the contribution of economists to the evaluation of this question.

TRADE PATTERNS ARE IMPORTANT, BUT NOT SUFFICIENT

When bloc formation is explicitly considered, economists often analyse the issue by estimating the importance of intra-regional trade flows. The idea is that the (static) welfare gains for countries joining a preferential trading area are likely to be greater the higher the percentage of intra-regional trade (because welfare-enhancing, trade-creating effects are more likely to outweigh welfare-reducing, trade-diverting effects). Thus, 'economic logic' suggests that if intra-regional trade flows are high and/or increasing, a basis exists for rational states to consider forming a trading bloc. Frankel (1991) utilizes this approach in examining East Asian trade and decomposes the time series changes in the ratio of intra-regional trade of a bloc to two components of world trade: one captures the impact of changes in the propensity (or bias) to trade with other economies of the bloc, and the other captures the impact of changes in the share of intra- and inter-regional trade involving the bloc to total world trade (Table 6.1). Changes in the share component are more than sufficient to explain the growing importance of intra-regional East Asian trade in world trade. Frankel argues, therefore, that rising intra-regional trade in East Asia is seen because economies in that region are growing faster than in the rest of the world, rather than because of a growing bias to intra-regional trade in East Asia.

Although a knowledge of aggregate trade flows is without doubt useful for understanding the issue there are at least three serious weaknesses in using such summary statistics as the primary (or sole) basis on which to make an assessment of potential bloc formation.

First, the aggregate trade data for the 1980s may not be a sound basis on which to discern long-term trends because of the influence of 'special' factors.

PAUL BOWLES AND BRIAN MACLEAN

Table 6.1 Intra-regional vs. inter-regional trade in three blocs

	Billions of dollars			Fraction of total		
	1980	1986	1989	1980	1986	1989
East Asia						
Total trade	577.6	723.3	1,199.6	1.0	1.0	1.0
Of which: intrareg. trade	189.2	234.3	448.1	0.328	0.328	0.374
X+M from ROW	388.5	489.0	751.5	0.673	0.676	0.626
X+M from N. America	127.7	223.2	330.6	0.221	0.308	0.275
+M from EC12	70.8	98.9	177.1	0.122	0.137	0.148
European Community 12						
Total trade	1,517.7	1,577.9	2,299.9	1.0	1.0	1.0
Of which: interareg. trade	768.6	896.7	1,355.0	0.506	0.568	0.589
X+M from ROW	749.2	681.2	954.5	0.494	0.432	0.415
X+M from E. Asia	74.8	99.9	170.7	0.049	0.063	0.074
X+M from N. America	132.6	150.9	205.0	0.087	0.096	0.089
North America						
Total trade	639.8	805.5	1,145.1	1.0	1.0	1.0
Of which: intrareg. trade	207.0	279.5	415.7	0.323	0.347	0.363
X+M from ROW	432.8	526.0	729.4	0.676	0.653	0.637
X+M from E. Asia	116.3	218.3	317.8	0.182	0.271	0.277
X+M from EC12	117.5	149.1	206.1	0.186	0.185	0.180

Source: Frankel (1991: 7)

In particular, the increase in East Asian exports to the US between 1980 and 1985 reflected an unsustainable surge in US imports associated with Reaganomics.

Second, capital flows are also important in driving economic integration. This is particularly true for the 1980s when world FDI grew at nearly three times the rate of exports and nearly four times the rate of world GDP during the period 1983–9.[3] Furthermore, analysis of trade flows is often taken to imply that economic integration is a purely market-driven phenomenon. By looking at private and official capital flows, it is clear that states as well as private capital have been important in forging new patterns of integration.

Third, blocs are formed by states responding to internal and external pressures and this cannot necessarily be predicted by patterns of intra-regional trade. Especially interesting for this study, the AFTA was signed in 1992 even though the share of intra-ASEAN exports in total ASEAN exports was only 17.7 per cent in 1990 and had in fact *fallen* from 19.7 per cent in 1985.[4] Clearly, factors other than intra-regional trade flows were important in explaining the formation of AFTA.

CAPITAL FLOWS MATTER FOR REGIONAL BLOC FORMATION

Japan's role in East Asia has expanded considerably during the past two decades and its use of East Asia as a production site has increased since the appreciation of the yen which followed the 1985 Plaza Accord. Japan's FDI grew at an annual average rate of 62 per cent over the 1985–9 period, driven in large part by the yen's appreciation and by the fear (realized or not) of growing protectionism in US and European markets. Japan's share of world FDI rose rapidly from 8.9 per cent in the period 1980–4 to 18.8 per cent in the period 1985–9.

The rapid growth in Japanese FDI in response to changing international economic conditions cannot be understood solely by looking at the actions of the Japanese private sector. The rise in FDI has been encouraged by the Japanese government for about a decade. Japan discouraged FDI in the 1950s before moving to a more neutral policy in the 1960s and 1970s and towards one of positive encouragement in the 1980s (see Hill 1990; Guisinger 1991). Thus, the rise in FDI must be explained not simply as a response to market signals but also from the perspective of the evolving state responses to international restructuring.

The US and Europe have been the major destinations of Japanese FDI. Asia's share of Japanese FDI has declined over the past two decades, which might be interpreted to indicate Japanese indifference towards a regional East Asian economy. However, there are a number of reasons why this conclusion does not follow.

First, Japan's total FDI has grown substantially, so a declining share to East Asia still represents a considerable absolute increase.

Second, the share of FDI going to developing countries has significantly declined over the past decade but Asia has managed to attract a growing proportion of this declining share. East Asia's increasing share of developing country FDI and its near constant share of total world FDI is due in large measure to the redirection of Japanese FDI to the region. In the 1975–9 period, East Asia accounted for about 50 per cent of Japanese FDI in developing countries, but by 1985–8 this had risen to about 80 per cent (Riedel 1991: 144).

Table 6.2 Japanese FDI as a percentage of total FDI flows to selected East Asian countries, 1985–8

Country	Percentage Japanese FDI	Rank of Japan in Triad members' FDI*
South Korea	51.8	1
Thailand	46.1	1
Hong Kong	31.9	1
Taiwan	30.9	1 (US 27.9)
Singapore	39.2	1 (US 38.6)
Indonesia	24.4	1 (EC 22.1)

Source: Adapted from UNCTC (1991: 55)
* Figures for other Triad members' FDI are given if they are within 10 per cent of the Japanese figure

Third, the volume of Japan's FDI flowing to Asia has increased to the point where Japan is the major source of FDI for most East Asian developing countries, indicating the dominant role played by Japan in the region and its importance as a source of FDI relative to the US and the EEC. The importance of Japanese FDI in total FDI inflows for countries in the region is shown in Table 6.2.

Fourth, and most importantly, differences exist between Japanese FDI in Western Europe and North America and Japanese FDI in the developing countries of Asia, reflecting the different strategies which Japanese trans-nationals employ in these regions.

The strategy of regional core networks being pursued by Japanese trans-nationals suggests that Japanese FDI in the US and the European Community is *trade-replacing*. Japanese firms operating in the US and in the EEC sell over 95 per cent of their output to the respective domestic markets and are increasingly being supplied by other Japanese transnationals in the host country. They are thus becoming 'insiders' in the two existing trading blocs of North America and Europe, and the motivation for Japanese transnationals investing heavily in North America and Europe during the past decade has been defensive export substitution.[5]

Within East Asia, investment by Japanese transnationals has been directed much more towards lowering costs and ensuring access to natural resources. Some Japanese FDI has been aimed at the rapidly expanding local markets in East Asia, but it is ambiguous in its trade effects depending on the relative sizes of the market expansion and the inward FDI flows.

Cost-reducing FDI in East Asia by Japanese transnationals has fostered a distinct regional division of labour. Typically, the highest value-added products are manufactured in the NICs, with the lower value-added in the ASEAN countries where low wages, rather than a skilled labour force, are the main attraction. The regional division of labour goes beyond product division and also involves an intra-process division of labour. For example, 'the "ASEAN car", a product of Mitsubishi Motor company, belongs to this category: the car radio is manufactured in Singapore, the doors in Malaysia, transmission in the Philippines, wheels in Australia, engine in Japan, chassis and assembly in Japan' (Ishigami 1991: 25).

Thus, Japanese FDI in the East Asian region is largely *trade-enhancing* while Japanese FDI outside of the East Asian region is best described as *trade-replacing*. The strategy of regional core networks implies that 'intra-regional trade is likely to grow (that is, within North America, the EC and Asia), while inter-regional trade (primarily from Asia to the EC and the US) would decline' (UNCTC 1991: 47). The strategy of regional core networks suggests that Japanese transnationals have already implicitly divided the global economy into three distinct production and consumption regions, a strategy which is also evident from the activities of US transnationals.

The foregoing discussion has highlighted the extent to which economic integration has taken place in East Asia as a result of FDI flows. We now turn to official capital flows.

A TARGETED PUBLIC POLICY: JAPANESE OFFICIAL DEVELOPMENT ASSISTANCE

The largest recipients of Japan's ODA are located in the East Asian region, as is shown for the 1985–9 period in Table 6.3. Note that the ten largest recipients of Japanese aid are located in Asia and that the four leading recipients, accounting for over 39 per cent of total ODA, are in the East Asian region.

Table 6.3 Major recipients of Japanese bilateral aid, total 1985–9 (US $ millions, net disbursements)

Country	Amount	Shares (%)
Indonesia	3,159	12.7
China	2,943	11.9
Philippines	1,995	8.0
Thailand	1,676	6.8
Bangladesh	1,416	5.7
India	967	3.9
Pakistan	851	3.4
Myanmor (Burma)	829	3.3
Sri Lanka	895	2.4
Malaysia	401	1.6
Total		59.7

Source: Japan's ODA 1990, p. 44

It is notable that the grant share of Japan's ODA is the lowest of all eighteen Development Assistance Committee (DAC) members.[6] The low proportion of grant aid in total aid, and hence the high proportion of loan aid, has two important implications. First, recipient countries are obliged to make repayments in yen at a later date and this will increase the demand for yen and the use of the yen in international transactions. Second, recipients need to increase exports to acquire the funds for repayment. This boosts trade and is likely to boost exports to Japan. Given Japan's heavy reliance on imported raw materials, provision of ODA in loan form can be seen as one element in Japan's strategy to secure needed imports from its major aid recipients, a strategy also confirmed by an analysis of the sectoral composition of Japanese ODA.

The sectoral allocation of aid reveals some important priorities for Japan and illustrates the complementarity of its aid expenditures with the structure of its own economy (Table 6.4). The 31.7 per cent share of aid in the economic infrastructure and services sector is double the DAC average; the figure was

Table 6.4 Sectoral distribution of Japanese bilateral ODA commitments, 1989 (US$m)

Sector	Grants	Percentage of total	Loans	Percentage of total loans	Total	Percentage of total ODA
Social infrastructure and services	1,024	34.4	355	7.0	1,379	17.5
Economic infrastructure and services of which:	364	12.0	2,131	43.6	2,495	31.7
Transport	196	6.5	908	18.6	1,104	14.0
Energy	25	0.8	471	9.6	495	6.3
Production sectors, of which:	764	25.6	563	11.5	1,328	16.9
Agriculture	572	19.2	213	4.3	785	10.0
Industry mining and construction	165	5.5	350	7.1	525	6.6
Programme assistance			1,650	3.1	1,620	20.6
Other	828	27.8	220	4.5	1,047	13.3
Total	2,980	100.0	4,889	100.0	7,869	100.0

Source: Japan's ODA 1990, p. 47

previously 39.4 per cent in 1988 and a remarkable 49.2 per cent in 1987.[7] Within this sector, the major categories of expenditure are transport and energy. The transportation sub-sector, involving road building as well as marine facilities, is important for opening up markets as well as the more obvious creation of demand for Japanese vehicle manufacturers. The relatively high levels of aid to economic infrastructure have undoubtedly been of benefit to Japanese transnationals investing in the region and have led to greater regional economic integration (see also Unger and Blackburn 1993). By bringing FDI and ODA into the discussion, we get a much clearer picture of the strengthening economic ties between Japan and her East Asian neighbours. For an even more complete picture, we must bring the intra-regional use of the yen into the discussion.

A JAPAN-CENTRED EAST ASIAN CURRENCY SYSTEM?

Orthodox economic analyses of currency bloc formation have tended to focus narrowly on market-driven trends in the use of the yen as an intra-regional currency (Melvin and Peiers, 1993). A proper analysis of currency bloc formation, like a proper analysis of trade bloc formation, must grapple with corporate and state strategies. It will be useful to begin with a discussion of the uses of an intra-regional currency.

First, a currency may be widely used in invoicing foreign trade (Table 6.5). Thus, trade tends to be denominated in the currency of the exporting country (especially for the OECD countries), but because the US dollar has been the

Table 6.5 The uses of an intra-regional currency

| Function | Sector | |
	Private	Official
Unit of account	1 Currency used in invoicing trade	2 Currency used in defining parities
Means of payment	3 Vehicle currency in foreign exchange markets	4 Intervention currency
Store of value	5 Currency in which deposits, loans and bonds are denominated	6 Currency in which reserves are held

Source: Kenen (1983: 16)

leading international currency, exports to the US tend to be denominated in US dollars (Krugman 1984: 271).

Compared with other advanced capitalist countries, a relatively small share of Japanese trade is invoiced in the domestic currency. It is notable, however, that the share of yen-invoiced Japanese trade with South-East Asia is considerably higher than yen-invoiced Japanese trade with the rest of the world. According to Tavlas and Ozeki (1991: 39), in 1989 approximately 35 per cent of all Japanese exports were denominated in yen, but 44 per cent of Japanese exports to South-East Asia were so denominated. Similarly, about 14 per cent of all Japanese imports were denominated in yen, but almost 29 per cent of Japanese imports from South-East Asia were so denominated.

The second possible use of an intra-regional currency is to define parities or serve as a unit of account for pegging exchange rates. The number of countries which peg their exchange rate to the US dollar has, of course, declined drastically since the early 1970s, but no countries have started to peg their exchange rates to the yen. As Melvin and Peiers (1993: 318) note, however, a number of East Asian countries 'do follow a de facto basket peg that potentially involves the yen'.

Third, an intra-regional currency may function as a vehicle currency in foreign exchange markets, as a currency used to facilitate foreign-exchange trading by banks.

Fourth, an intra-regional currency can function as one which central banks use to intervene in the foreign exchange markets, for example, to keep their currency from appreciating. To the best of our knowledge, statistics are not available on the use of the yen as a vehicle and an intervention currency. The US dollar dominates worldwide as a vehicle currency and, apparently, as an intervention currency as well.

The fifth use of an intra-regional currency is as a store of value in international financial markets. This role increased dramatically in the 1980s. The yen appears to be particularly important as a store of value for financial assets issued in East Asia. For example, the yen share of the external debt of five East Asian countries totalled almost 38 per cent in 1988.

163

The sixth use of an intra-regional currency is as a store of value for central banks. The underlying principle of the Bretton Woods system was that the US would hold gold and other countries would (mainly) hold dollars. Since the breakdown of the Bretton Woods system, there has been a diversification of central bank reserve assets into international currencies other than the dollar, a diversification which has been most pronounced for the developing countries. Recent statistics indicate that on a global basis the yen is now the third most important national currency in official holdings of foreign exchange. The yen share of official reserve holdings, however, has tended to be far larger in Asian countries than in non-Asian countries.

We see, then, that for particular functions the yen is important as an intra-regional currency in East Asia; for others, it is not. The evidence may best be summarized with the following quotation from Tavlas and Ozeki:

> The availability of data on the yen's regional use is limited, but suggestive of a somewhat larger use of the yen. In particular, there have been marked increases among Asian countries in the yen's use as a reserve currency and as a currency used to denominate and hold foreign debt. However, the yen's use as a numeraire and means of payment in Japanese trade with other Asian countries is still relatively small, and the vehicle use of the yen within Asia appears to be very limited.
>
> (Tavlas and Ozeki 1991: 49)

Mere evidence on the use of the yen as an intra-regional currency is obviously not sufficient to make predictions about the potential for a yen-centred East Asian exchange rate system. Evidence must be related to a set of hypotheses or a theory.

For neo-classical economists, it is convenient to reduce the issue of the management system to the issue of the propensity of central banks in East Asia to peg their exchange rates to the yen (Melvin and Peiers 1993). A central bank's propensity to peg its exchange rate to the yen is further assumed to depend upon the central bank's demand for the yen as a reserve currency. Demand for the yen as a reserve currency will in turn depend upon a transactions motive and a portfolio motive. While Japan is a major trading partner for East Asian countries, it does not possess the degree of dominance which Germany exerts relative to other European countries in the US. Furthermore, transactions demand for yen is overstated by actual trade flows because most of Japan's trade is not yen-denominated. Melvin and Peiers (1993) conclude that the East Asian central banks are unlikely to peg their currencies to the yen and hence that a yen currency bloc will not emerge in East Asia. This prognosis contains some critical flaws.

First, the evidence relating to the transactions motive is unconvincing. The use of the yen as an invoicing currency has lagged behind the growth of Japanese trade but the factors determining the use of a currency for invoicing (such as the existence of deep short-term financial markets) must be considered if one is to analyse future trends in the use of the yen for trade invoicing.

Second, if optimal holdings of reserve currency are determined by the two forms of demand, it seems quite conceivable that a currency with short-comings from a portfolio perspective could still be the best overall choice because of its attractiveness in terms of transactions demand considerations.

Third, unlike firms, most central banks have some responsibility for trying to reduce the output variability of the domestic economy. If pegging to a particular currency (or to a basket with a large weight for the particular currency) offers the prospect of reducing domestic output stability relative to other exchange rate alternatives, then the propensity of the central bank to peg to that currency will be increased. Research by Kwan (1992) indicates that although ASEAN countries like Indonesia, Thailand and Malaysia are more heavily dependent upon trade with Japan than NICs (newly indus-trializing countries) like South Korea and Taiwan, it is the NICs that would gain the most in terms of reduction in output variability as a consequence of pegging to the yen.

Fourth if a yen currency bloc were to be formed, central bankers would no doubt play an important role in the process, but national governments would be the key decision-makers. Moreover, a yen currency bloc could only operate with the active support of the Japanese government and the Bank of Japan and their propensities to support a yen currency bloc can obviously not be reduced to transactions and portfolio motives. It is notable that Yoshio Suzuki (1989: 173), perhaps the most influential economist in Japan (formerly with the Bank of Japan and now with Nomura Securities), has argued that if Japan's neighbours desire yen-centred currency management, then 'Japan should be prepared to offer the yen and its financial market as international public goods for them, and to become an anchor for the stability of neighbouring economies who could then stabilise their own currencies' exchange rates vis-a-vis the yen.'

POLITICAL STRATEGY COUNTS MORE THAN MARKET FORCES

Market-level trends only loosely determine bloc formation. Growing economic integration in East Asia does increase the likelihood that a trading bloc could be formed. Here we wish to emphasize the central political-economic con-sideration for 'yen bloc' formation: that the US is in conflict with key East Asian states, especially Japan, over the trade deficits which the US runs with them, and this conflict constitutes the most likely trigger for 'yen bloc' formation.

The US has run trade deficits with several East Asian countries for many years. With the continuation of negative US total current account balances throughout the 1980s and the fading of the Cold War in the late 1980s, trade deficits with East Asia have become a central concern in US foreign policy. In this context, the US has initiated bilateral talks with the leaders of economies such as Japan, South Korea and Taiwan. The talks have been aimed at reducing US trade deficits, with the US pushing East Asian countries for currency appreciation and measures to increase imports of US goods and services.

The US practice of 'aggressive unilateralism' towards key East Asian states shows no signs of abating. US demands for market-opening measures in an East Asian country have typically been backed by appeals to free-trade ideology. Indeed, Suzuki (1991) has also argued that a key ideological division developing in the world economy of the 1990s appears to be between the free-trade ideology of the advanced capitalist economies and the interventionist-development ideology of most newly industrializing economies. Others have provided evidence that the Japanese élite is much more sympathetic than, say, the American élite to the interventionist-development ideology of the newly industrializing economies, and that this bodes well for Japan's ties with her East Asian neighbours. Most East Asian countries wish to continue pursuing interventionist industrial policies and by grouping together they could potentially offer more resistance to US pressure to remodel themselves along the lines of Anglo-American capitalism.

To round out this sketch of our evaluation of 'yen bloc' prospects, however, we must deal briefly with three common arguments about the political infeasibility of a 'yen bloc'.

The arguments to be considered are that: (1) other East Asian countries would never join a bloc with Japan because of historical experience with the notorious 'East Asian Co-prosperity Sphere'; (2) the other countries prefer Pacific Basin-type arrangements in which the power of Japan is offset by that of the US; and (3) Japan and the NICs would never join an East Asian bloc for fear of antagonizing the US, their major trading partner.

First, while animosity towards Japan persists in parts of East Asia, it is naturally fading with the passing of the generations who experienced Japanese imperialism during and prior to the Second World War. Indeed, that animosity has already died out in many East Asian countries and persists mainly in China and South Korea, where it has been artificially prolonged by official anti-Japanese state ideology (designed to enhance domestic support for the ruling élites). Most importantly, the formation of a coalition government following the Japanese election of 1993 marked the rise to power of a new generation of leaders in Japan, a generation willing to admit the historical wrongs committed by Japanese forces and able to build stronger ties with the rest of East Asia.

Second, while Japan remains the technological superpower of East Asia, the possibility of Japanese domination of East Asia is less of a concern in the region than it was in the 1970s. The 1970s and 1980s witnessed the rise of the so-called East Asian NICs, countries which have become major suppliers of outward FDI to neighbouring countries over the past several years. Indeed, combined NIC FDI in each of the ASEAN countries has recently been greater than that of Japan. As Lincoln has stated:

the recent emergence of South Korea, Taiwan, and Singapore as investors throughout the region, as well as the regional trade ties outside of Japan . . ., provide an alternative countervailing power [to the US]. That is, as ties within the region other than those with Japan strengthen, these nations should become more tolerant of strengthening ties with Japan as well.

(Lincoln 1992: 37)

Third, the argument that Japan and the NICs would never join an East Asian bloc for fear of antagonizing the US is often set up as an argument that in considering their long-term interest these countries would never elect to put all of their eggs in the East Asian basket. But the appropriate image is not one of independent investors deciding upon an optimal trade basket. As noted in the preceding section, the most likely motive for these countries joining an East Asian bloc would be to group together as allies to counter ever more aggressive US demands for market-opening measures.

A PROCESS OF INTEGRATION IS TAKING PLACE

A process of regional economic integration is firmly established and the prospects for a further deepening of that integration over the medium term in the form of an East Asian bloc are considerably higher than suggested by orthodox economists. Persistent trade conflict between the US and several East Asian states provides the likely trigger mechanism for the formation of an East Asian grouping.

Our judgement is that an East Asian grouping involving preferential trading arrangements but without mutual currency management is the most likely outcome. If mutual currency management were to arise, it would most likely do so years after the establishment of preferential trading arrangements.

The reader can no doubt imagine many of the implications which a 'yen bloc' would have for the global economy, such as a reduction in US political power. We would like to point out that whereas EC integration is interesting for thinking about bloc formation with common minimum social standards and NAFTA has raised the issue of bloc formation integration with common minimum environmental standards, an East Asian economic grouping may be significant for showing how bloc formation might proceed while allowing states the necessary degree of leeway for industrial and macroeconomic strategies.

NOTES

We would like to acknowledge funding from Pacific 2000 (External Affairs and International Trade Canada) and the Canada-ASEAN Centre. Helpful comments were provided by participants in the 'Global Markets: Do Nation-States Have a

Future?' conference. The authors are, of course, solely responsible for the views expressed herein.

1 The terms 'East Asia', 'Asia', 'Asia Pacific' are used somewhat flexibly in the existing literature. In this paper, by East Asia we mean countries which include Japan, South Korea, Hong Kong, Taiwan, Singapore, Malaysia, the Philippines, Indonesia and Thailand. Other countries, notably China, are also included where appropriate to the discussion.
2 A discussion of all the states in the region is beyond the scope of this chapter and we focus specifically on Japan, the East Asian NICs (Taiwan, South Korea, Singapore and Hong Kong) and the ASEAN-4 (Indonesia, the Philippines, Thailand and Malaysia) without which an East Asian bloc is unlikely to form. We discuss both the trade and currency dimensions of such a bloc.
3 See UNCTC (1991). World FDI outflows reached nearly US $200 billion in 1989.
4 Calculated from IMF, *Direction of Trade Statistics*, 1991.
5 This reflects the relative immaturity of Japanese FDI. US transnationals undertook defensive export-substituting investment in Europe several decades ago. For more on this, and on the different motives for FDI and their effects on trade within and between economically integrated regions, see UNCTC (1990).
6 The grant share is defined as being equal to the percentage of aid that consists of grant aid plus contributions to international organizations plus other forms of assistance that do not require repayment. Members of the DAC are Australia, New Zealand, Ireland, Sweden, Switzerland, Canada, Norway, Denmark, the UK, Finland, the USA, The Netherlands, Belgium, Italy, France, West Germany, Austria and Japan.
7 The figure fell as programme assistance loans increased towards the end of the 1980s.

BIBLIOGRAPHY

Crockett, A. 1991. *Financial Market Implications of Trade and Currency Zones.* Federal Reserve Bank of Kansas City, Policy Implications of Trade and Currency Zones.

DAC Chairman's Report, various. Paris: OECD.

Frankel, J. 1991. 'Is a Yen Bloc Forming in Pacific Asia?', in R. O'Brien (ed.), *Finance and the International Economy: 5 (The AMEX Bank Review Prize Essays).* Oxford: Oxford University Press.

Guisinger, S. 1991. 'Foreign Direct Investment Flows in East and Southeast Asia.' *ASEAN Economic Bulletin* 8: 1 (July), 29–46.

Hill, H. 1990. 'Foreign Investment and East Asian Economic Development.' *Asian-Pacific Economic Literature* 4: 2 (September), 21–58.

Ishigami, E. 1991. 'Japanese Business in ASEAN Countries: New-industrialisation or Japanisation?' *IDS Bulletin* 22: 2, 18–21.

Kenen, Peter B. 1983. *The Role of the Dollar as an International Currency.* Occasional Papers No. 13. New York: Group of Thirty.

Krugman, P. 1984. 'The International Role of the Dollar: Theory and Prospect', in J. Bilson and R. Marston (eds), *Exchange Rate Theory and Practice.* Chicago: University of Chicago Press.

Kwan, C.H. 1992. 'An Optimal Peg for the Asian Currencies and an Asian Perspective of a Yen Bloc.' *Nomura Asian Perspectives* 9: 2 (April), 1–40.

Lincoln, E. 1992. 'Japan's Rapidly Emerging Strategy Toward Asia.' *OECD Development Centre Technical Papers*, No. 58.

Melvin, M. and B. Peiers. 1993. 'On the Possibility of a Yen Currency Bloc for Pacific-Basin Countries.' *Pacific-Basin Finance Journal* 1: 309–33.

Ministry of Foreign Affairs – Japan. 1990. *Annual Report of Japan's ODA 1990*. Tokyo: Ministry of Foreign Affairs.

Riedel, J. 1991. 'Intra-Asian Trade and Foreign Direct Investment.' *Asian Development Review* 8: 1, 111–46.

Suzuki, Y. 1989. 'Policy Targets and Operating Procedures in the 1990s', in *Monetary Policy Issues in the 1990s*. Kansas City: Federal Reserve Bank of Kansas City.

Suzuki, Y. 1991. *Nihon Keizai no Yakushin* [The Rapid Advance of the Japanese Economy]. Tokyo: NTT.

Tavlas, G. and Y. Ozeki. 1991. 'The Japanese Yen as an International Currency.' *IMF Working Paper* WP/91/2.

United Nations Centre on Transnational Corporations (UNCTC). 1990. *Regional Economic Integration and Transnational Corporations in the 1990s: Europe 1992, North America and Developing Countries*, Series A, No. 15. New York: United Nations.

United Nations Centre on Transnational Corporations (UNCTC). 1991. *World Investment Report 1991: The Triad in Foreign Direct Investment*. New York: United Nations.

Unger, D. and P. Blackburn. 1993. 'Japanese ODA and the Creation of an East Asian Economy.' *Japan's Emerging Global Role*. Boulder, Colo.: Lynne Reinner Publishers.

Part III

FINANCE AND TRADE: THE EROSION OF NATIONAL SOVEREIGNTY

7

GLOBALIZATION MYTHS AND REALITIES

One century of external trade and foreign investment[1]

Paul Bairoch

Contemporary scholars and policy-makers have come to consider that the world economy has entered into a totally new phase and that globalization will have unprecedented effects on trade, technology, finance and even economic policies. Interdependence is rapidly becoming the norm of the new order. The evidence to support this view is derived from the erosion and transformation of the national and international system inherited from the Second World War. But the Annales School and the *longue durée* approach suggest that what many regard as a new phenomenon is not necessarily so.

For an economic historian, these complex issues have to be approached cautiously and posed as a series of precise questions: is it really true that the contemporary proportion of external trade as a share of a country's GDP is unprecedented? Is it the case that foreign investment is a totally new phenomenon? Or does the British example give some precious insight about the contemporary erosion of US domination in the world system? Whereas economists generally view free trade and internationalization positively, does economic evidence support this assumption? Under some circumstances, could not international trade be the arena for generalized dumping where nations artificially lower their prices on manufactured goods in order to obtain greater market share?

This chapter provides various economic indicators in order to capture these complex issues even if they are not complete and definitive in all respects. Further, the contemporary conventional wisdom about the novelty of globalization is challenged: international trade has been a long-term phenomenon. Extending our view backwards to the 1920s and 1930s puts more recent changes since the 1960s in context. This earlier period contained different power relations and so a comparative quantitative approach will be complemented here by an institutional perspective.

INTERNATIONAL TRADE

The continuous growth in imports and exports is seen as evidence that countries are becoming more dependent on global markets.[2] If we include the trade of services, the picture is somewhat modified. The following analysis will first focus on the trade of goods since it is four times more important than the trade of services.

Figure 7.1 shows the evolution of exports as a percentage of the GDP between 1950 and 1993 (both aggregates expressed in current values). It reveals that since 1968 – and even more so since 1973 – the rate of exports has represented an increasingly significant part of the economy of Western developed countries.[3] That rate only rose from 8.4 per cent to 8.8 per cent in 1950 to 9.0 per cent in 1964/5, but reached 15.9 per cent in 1980 and stabilized at 14.5 per cent from 1974 to 1993. The rate of exports in the economy of Western developed countries has risen by two-thirds since the early 1970s. This increase surely reveals a trend to globalization rather than a minor structural change in international trade.

When looking at this trend to globalization, we need to take into account three important factors (which will exclude the obvious consequences of both oil crises): (1) American international performance follows a pattern dissimilar to other industrialized countries; (2) export prices and local prices show a different pattern of evolution; and (3) a historical perspective must undergird this analysis.

The regional differentiation

Before focusing on the regional growth of the still-dominant trade of merchandise, I will briefly analyse the exports of services[4] since 1970.[5] In 1970/2, the exports of services (referred to as 'credits' in the statistics of the balance of payments) represented 28.8 per cent of the exports of goods in Western developed countries. This rate dropped to 24.0 per cent for 1979/81 then rose to 27.4 per cent for 1990/2. This growth converts into a modest increase in terms of percentage of GDP (3.0 per cent for 1970/2 to 4.0 per cent for 1990/2). In comparison to the exports of goods which increased by two-thirds, the exports of services only rose by one-third. This increase results, to a significant extent, from the fact that the exports of services in the United States grew more rapidly (1.3 per cent to 2.7 per cent of the GDP between 1970/2 and 1990/2). It is worth noting that since 1986 the United States has enjoyed a growing surplus in the balance of payments for services (about 21 per cent in 1991), despite its important deficit in the export of merchandise. Table 7.1, which uses the same data as Figure 7.1, clearly shows the difference in the rates of exports. It also shows that the latter evolve according to divergent patterns.

The reason for divergent export rates is already well known and can be

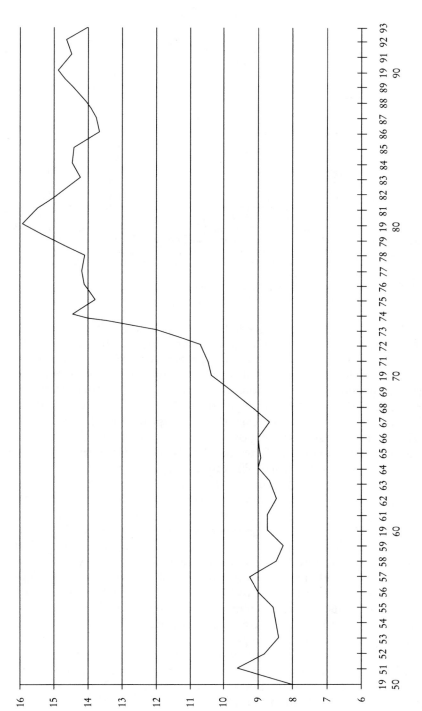

Figure 7.1 Exports as percentage of GDP of Western developed countries (in current values)

Table 7.1 Exports of merchandise as percentage of GDP

	Western developed countries	United States	Western Europe	EEC (12 members)	Japan
1950	7.8	3.8	13.4	13.0	6.8
1953	8.4	4.3	13.4	13.2	7.5
1959/61	8.6	3.8	14.8	14.3	8.9
1969/71	10.2	4.0	17.4	16.7	9.7
1974/6	14.1	6.6	21.3	20.9	11.0
1979/81	15.5	7.7	22.7	22.0	11.8
1989/91	14.6	7.2	23.0	22.2	9.6
1991/3	14.3	7.5	21.7	21.1	8.8

Sources: Author's calculation based on the following sources:
Exports: United Nations, *Yearbook of International Trade Statistics*, New York, various issues; United Nations, *UNCTAD, Handbook of International Trade and Development Statistics*, New York, various issues; and for 1993 data communicated by the Secretariat of the GATT.
GDP after 1959: OECD, *National Accounts, Main Aggregates*, vol. 1: 1960–1992, Paris, 1993; OECD, *Main Economic Indicators*, March Paris, 1994.
GDP before 1960: author's estimates on basis of national data
Note: For the geographical definitions see note 3 on p. 190

stated briefly. It results from a general – and widely accepted – 'law':[6] *ceteris paribus*, the larger a country is, the lower its rate of exports. It is worth noting, nevertheless, that the American rate of exports rose by 90 per cent from the early 1970s to the early 1990s while in Western Europe it rose by one-third despite the phenomenon of economic integration. Japan experienced an even more modest increase of less than one-fifth. A comparison of the 1959/61 period with the 1989/91 period even shows a stagnation for Japan. The rate of exports of the Western developed countries (excluding the United States) has risen by less than one-sixth for the 1969/71 period (15.9 per cent) to the 1989/91 period (18.4 per cent).[7] The rate of exports of the EEC (excluding the intercommunity trade) from 1959/61 to 1989/91 rose from 7.1 per cent to 8.7 per cent which converts into an increase of one-fourth while the total exports increased by one-third.

The United States had the biggest increase in their trade deficit. This trend is more obvious if we measure the rate of imports as a percentage of GDP. Indeed, the latter rose from 3.9 per cent in the period 1969/71 to 9.4 per cent in the period 1989/91. This means that the rate of imports increased 140 per cent while the rate of exports rose by 90 per cent. Moreover, between the early 1950s and early 1960s, the rate of imports increased more rapidly than the rate of exports. If we rely on the most recent statistics available for the United States,[8] it appears that the total imports of goods and services represented 5.9 per cent of the GDP in the period 1969/71 and 13.9 per cent in 1989/91. The increasing globalization of export trade appears more pronounced in the United States than in Europe. But, in the early 1990s, the United States just reached the level that Western Europe was at in the early 1970s.

Exports: generalized dumping?

Let us examine the divergent evolution of the volume of exports and the volume of GDP in other developed countries.

In all countries since the Second World War, the volume of exports has grown more rapidly than the volume of GDP (see Table 7.2). As far as all the Western developed countries are concerned, this discrepancy has been more significant in the last two decades than in the preceding two. In the 1950 to 1970 period, the gap was very significant, although the rate of exports of the economy was rather stable. Calculating the 'quantitative rate of exports' brings these issues into sharper focus. It is done simply by applying to the rate of exports the growth indexes of the volumes of the GDP and of the exports starting from a specific year. The year 1950 shall serve as a starting value (see Table 7.3).

Table 7.2 Yearly growth rate of the volume of total GNP and of exports (three years' annual average)

	1950–60	1960–70	1970–80	1980–90
Western developed countries GDP	4.2	4.7	3.3	2.5
Exports	6.3	8.7	6.3	4.3
Exp. on basis GDP = 100	150	185	190	170
United States GDP	3.2	3.7	2.7	2.5
Exports	–	5.9	7.0	4.0
Exp. on basis GDP = 100	–	160	260	160
Western Europe GDP	4.9	4.5	2.4	2.8
Exports	7.9	8.9	5.6	5.1
Exp. on basis GDP = 100	160	195	235	180
Japan GDP	8.2	10.2	4.7	4.1
Exports	14.8	16.8	9.4	5.1
Exp. on basis GDP = 100	180	165	200	125

Sources: See Table 7.1
Note: For the geographical definitions see note 3 on p. 190

In quantitative terms, the rate of exports of the Western economy has tripled from 1950 to 1990 (7.8 per cent to 23.7 per cent). In terms of value, it has only doubled (7.8 per cent to 14.8 per cent). The 1970 to 1990 period is thus not characterized by an acceleration of the phenomenon. On the contrary, from 1970 to 1990, the quantitative rate of exports has increased annually by 2.5 per cent compared to 3.1 per cent for the 1950 to 1990 period.

Table 7.3 Exports of merchandise as percentage of GDP of Western developed countries

	A	B	Yearly increase A	Yearly increase B
1950	7.8	7.8	–	–
1959/61	8.7	10.0	1.1	2.5
1969/71	10.2	14.4	1.6	3.7
1979/81	15.5	19.5	4.3	3.1
1989/91	14.8	23.7	−0.5	2.0

A: rate of exports in terms of current values
B: rate of exports in terms of volume
Sources: See Table 7.1 and the text
Note: For the geographical definitions see note 3 on p. 190

The analysis of Table 7.1 reveals an intriguing fact. Although Japan has been reputed to be a very successful exporter, the Japanese rate of exports appears to be almost stagnating. This is an extreme example of the impact which the divergence in the evolution of local vs. export prices can have on the interpretation of the rate of exports if the analysis relies on the volume of GDP and of exports rather than on the current value of those two aggregates. Between 1969/71 and 1989/91, the rate of Japanese exports decreased by 0.1 per cent while the GDP volume and the volume of exports rose respectively by 195 per cent and 305 per cent. If one accepts the hypothesis that exports and local prices are evolving in a similar way, the analysis should demonstrate an increase of 36.3 per cent of the Japanese rate of exports rather than a decrease of 0.1 per cent.

This paradoxical evolution can, indeed, be explained by the fact that the productivity growth of the export sectors does not evolve at the same rhythm as the general economy.

A simple calculation based on data available for Japan (see above) shows that such an evolution is likely to require the productivity in exports sectors to increase more than the productivity in the general economy by 1.6 per cent every year. Since the productivity by hours of work of the Japanese economy has risen annually by 4.1 per cent between 1969/71 and 1989/91, the evolution has to imply an increase of 5.7 per cent of the export sectors. The productivity by hours of work of the Japanese manufacturing industry (manufactured goods count for 97 per cent of total exports) increased by 4.5 per cent between 1969/71 and 1989/91. These figures indicate a difference of 0.4, not 1.6 percentage. But this discrepancy may result from an uneven rhythm of growth between the productivity in export and non-export sectors of the manufacturing industry.

This divergent pattern could be due to 'generalized dumping', a concept which began to be apparent to me about thirty years ago when I conducted a study of about fifty enterprises in three industrial sectors (shoes, furniture and plastic moulding) for the European Community. When these enterprises wanted to maintain their production at an optimum level, they would export their products at a price often below the average production cost. Comparative studies of European exports prices[9] revealed that this dumping process was likely to be more pronounced than traditional analyses suggested. This illustration must suffice, but the process of 'generalized dumping' is worth mentioning for two reasons. First, the increase of the rate of exports and of imports appears more obvious if it is expressed in quantitative terms. Second, an imbalance of this dumping strategy can have negative effects – especially if divergences in trade policies occur concurrently. I have illustrated this idea by showing the imbalance between Japan and the rest of the Western World.[10]

Export rate growth: the long-run term

As Table 7.4 shows, the rate of exports in Western economies reached its highest point almost everywhere just before the First World War. For all the Western developed countries, exports represented about 12.9 per cent of GDP in 1913. The same level was not reached again until 1974 when the high increase of oil prices provoked a rapid progression of the international trade value. In 1974, the rate of exports was 12.1 per cent against 10.6 per cent in 1972 and 9.2 per cent in 1967/9.

Table 7.4 Exports of merchandise as percentage of GDP (three-year average, except for 1950)

	Western developed countries	United States	Western Europe	EEC (12 members)	Japan
1890	11.7	6.7	14.9	–	5.1
1913	12.9	6.4	18.3	–	12.6
1929	9.8	5.0	14.5	–	13.6
1938	6.2	3.7	7.1	–	13.0
1950	7.8	3.8	13.4	12.9	6.8
1970	10.2	4.0	17.4	16.7	9.7
1992	14.3	7.5	21.7	21.1	8.8

Sources: For the 1950–93 period, see Table 7.1
For the 1890–1938 period, see P. Bairoch, 'European Foreign Trade in the XIXth Century: the Development of the Value and Volume of Exports (Preliminary Results)', *The Journal of European Economic History*, vol. 2, no. 1, Rome, Spring 1973, pp. 5–36; P. Bairoch, 'Europe's Gross National Product, 1800–1975', *The Journal of European Economic History*, vol. 5, no. 2, Rome, Fall 1976, pp. 273–340; and national data for the non-European countries
Note: For the geographical definitions see note 3 on p. 190

Despite the creation of a 'common market' (now EC) in the 1960s, Western Europe did not hit the 'historical' peak until 1972 – not much earlier than any other region. For 1991/3, Western Europe's export rate was only 34 percentage points or 18 per cent higher than the 1913 rate. Japan reached its highest rate of exports (13.6 per cent) in 1929. From 1987 to 1993, Japan's average rate of exports was 9.3 per cent. Despite a peak of 13.4 per cent in 1984, it appears that Japan's average rate of exports has maintained itself at one-third below the 1929 rate, which it has never managed to equal since.

The United States reached its highest rate of exports before 1913. For 1898/1900, the American rate of exports was 7.6 per cent against 6.7 per cent in the period 1889/91 and 6.4 per cent in 1913. It is not until the 1980s that the 1898/1900 level was surpassed. As Table 7.4 shows, this occurred only in 1989/91 and 1992/3. Between 1950 and 1980, the American rate of exports was at about half of the 1898/1900 level.

Thus, even for the country where the process of globalization seems the most obvious, the process is not a new one. Furthermore, differences in a product composition may exist. At the turn of this century, manufactured goods represented only 25 per cent of American exports. In early 1995, this proportion rose to 75 per cent. On the other hand, the share of imported manufactured goods rose from 35 per cent to 75 per cent. Although the rate of exports of all the Western developed countries is only one-third above the 1913 level, the volume of exports grew 20 times, which means that even the volume per inhabitant is eight times higher.

One also needs to compare all the Western developed countries from the point of view of the intra-regional trade. As a percentage of GDP, the intra-regional exchanges rose from 6.6 per cent in the period 1959/61 to 7.7 per cent in the period 1969/71 and 11.4 per cent in the period 1989/91. A comparison with the rates in 1913 and 1928 can only be made approximately because of a lack of detailed studies and of differences in country borders. Relying on data collected for one of my studies,[11] as well as on other data, I came up with 9.1 per cent to 9.3 per cent. A more accurate figure can be provided for 1928 thanks to a study done by the League of Nations[12] and to the fact that the political map is more similar to the contemporary one. This figure is 6.5 per cent. Despite the process of integration, it was not until 1973 that the 1913 rate of intra-regional trade was surpassed. The 1991/2 rate is only 2.2 percentage points higher than it was in 1913. The increase is less important in comparison to the total exports since it represents an increase of less than a quarter.

INTERNATIONAL INVESTMENTS[13]

The following analysis focuses on direct investment. Although most studies deal with direct international investment, other flows of long-term capital (as well as stocks) were – and still are – of more importance. If one looks for instance at the Western developed countries' annual average for 1988 to 1991 (the last three-year period before the recession), the flows of direct investment represented $206 billion while the portfolio investments equalled $250 billion and the long-term capital $65 billion. Thus, direct investments accounted for only 40 per cent of the total flows of long-term capital.[14] The interest in direct capital draws from the fact that it has a bigger impact on the international economy. As far as capital stocks are concerned, the situation appears to be slightly different. The present repartition between direct investments and portfolio investments is very different now from what it used to be in the nineteenth century or even at the beginning of the twentieth century.

It is difficult to trace the long-term evolution of international investments since no relevant data on direct investments are available for the pre-Second World War period. Moreover, the data relating to long-term capital stocks other than those relating to direct investments are incomplete for the period following the Second World War. I shall examine first the data regarding the flows before turning to stocks. This division is, of course, artificial and their relation must be kept in mind.

Flows of international investments

Data on direct investment flows are routinely problematic. The fact that such data exist does not necessarily imply that the statistics are very reliable. It is interesting to note that despite the fact that statistics about the United States have always been among the most accurate, statistics given for that topic in the *Statistical Yearbook* are preceded by the following note: 'Estimates . . . subject to considerable error due to nature of basic data.'[15] It was not until 1970 that strictly comparable yearly data on flows of direct investments became available. Figure 7.2 shows the evolution of investment outflows in the Western developed countries between 1970 and 1993. Data are given as percentages of GDP in current prices.[16]

The evolution of direct investment outflows has been very sensitive to economic fluctuations. It has been especially sensitive to the 1982 and 1991/2 recessions, while it was less affected by the 1974/5 recession. The important drop that occurred in 1982 (more than 50 per cent in volume) mainly resulted from a very important drop in American investment flows (around 90 per cent). If one does not take the conjuncture into account, one can say that the volume of direct investment outflows of the Western developed countries which had started to increase in the 1960s rose more rapidly in the early 1970s. The increase was extremely abrupt in the second half of the 1980s. A more sophisticated statistical analysis based on a precise chronology would reveal that this 'pattern of trend and cycles is consistent with the picture that emerges from a casual observation of the year-to-year movements in FDI (Foreign Direct Investment) outflows. What is not apparent from observing FDI flows is that the bulge in the second half of the 1980s is similar to that in the late 1970s. Instead, it is the drop in these outflows in the early 1980s that appears to be an aberration in the underlying pattern.'[17]

In terms of relative importance in relationship to the GDP, the direct investment outflows rise from 0.4 per cent to 0.5 per cent in the 1960s to

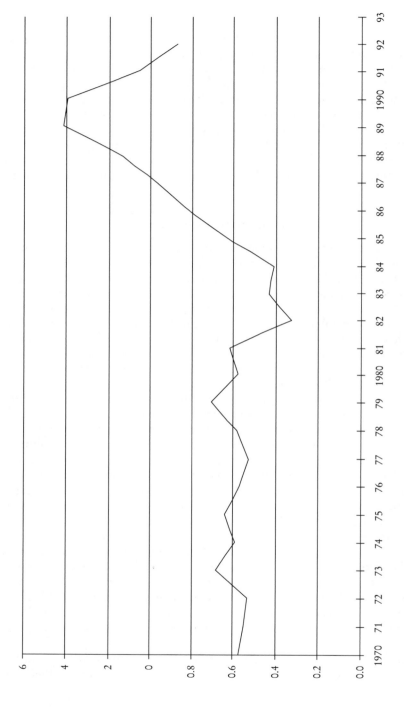

Figure 7.2 Outflows of foreign direct investment of Western developed countries (as percentage of GDP in current prices)

0.7 per cent in the early 1980s and 1.4 per cent in 1989/90. The rate of outflows of direct international investments have tripled while the rate of exports has increased by only two-thirds. Moreover, Western developed countries play a more important role in direct investment than in trade. They account for 97 per cent of all the international foreign investment, although they are responsible for 72 per cent of exports. The outflows of direct investments are more intra-regionally marked than trade. For instance, 85 per cent of the 1990 direct investment flows of the Western developed countries were directed to other countries of the Western world in comparison to only 77 per cent of exports. This factor reinforces the globalization of the Western economies.

Table 7.5 Country distribution of outflows of direct investments abroad

	In billion of $ (yearly average)			As percentage of total		
	1970/2	1978/80	1988/90	1970/2	1978/80	1988/90
Belgium	0.16	0.70	6.62	1.2	1.5	2.8
Canada	0.31	2.99	5.09	2.4	6.6	2.5
France	0.45	2.32	22.92	3.4	5.1	11.5
Germany	1.16	4.07	18.78	8.8	9.0	9.9
Italy	0.24	0.48	12.30	1.8	1.1	6.2
Japan	0.48	2.55	42.14	3.6	5.6	21.1
The Netherlands	0.56	3.45	12.30	4.2	7.6	6.2
Sweden	0.22	1.34	10.32	1.6	3.0	5.2
Switzerland	–	–	7.64	–	–	3.8
United Kingdom	1.60	6.62	30.23	12.1	14.6	15.1
United States	7.64	19.56	25.71	57.9	43.2	12.9
Total Western developed countries	13.20	45.30	199.70	100.0	100.0	100.0

Source: Derived from IMF, *Balance of Payments Statistics Yearbook*, Washington, DC, various issues
Note: For the geographical definitions see note 3 on p. 190

Table 7.5 shows how direct investment outflows are divided among countries. The eleven countries considered in the table are responsible for 98 per cent of all the outflows of Western developed countries (and 95 per cent of the world flows). The most striking case is Japan. In the early 1970s Japan was a very marginal exporter of capital: exports of capital only represented 3 per cent of those of the Western countries. Japan moved into second place in the early 1980s and became the leader in 1989 (21 per cent for 1989/90). The Japanese direct investment flows have begun to represent an increasingly significant share of the movements of the developed countries since 1972. In 1971, Japan accounted for 2.9 per cent of international capital flows and 5 per cent by 1972. The United States shows a different pattern: its share in the total of the Western developed countries was 63 per cent in the period 1970/1 against 14 per cent in the period 1989/90. The United States is hardly higher than the United Kingdom, France and Germany which are the three other important exporters of capital; these countries are only exporting twice as much capital as small countries like Sweden and The Netherlands. In short, the table shows that capital movements and trade evolve in opposite directions. The American economy has become more extroverted while Japan's export rate has remained stable.

In terms of relative importance, direct investment outflows have reached their highest historical point in the last few years. Despite gaps in statistical data, changes in the historical pattern can be demonstrated. The inter-war period is an appropriate point of departure for analysis. The most complete study covering that period was realized by the United Nations.[18] Unfortunately, it only looks at net movements. We know the capital movements seriously slowed down after the 1929 crisis and during the 1930 depression, but question marks remain for the late 1920s. Relying on incomplete information, one can nevertheless estimate that in 1929 the net capital movements represented some 1.7 to 1.8 billions of dollars for all developed countries which exported capital. But one needs to decide on the relative order of the level of the total capital flows. For 1989/91, the long-term capital flows represented $521 billion or 3.3 per cent of GDP. In 1984, they represented $168 billion or 2 per cent of GDP. In the early 1960s, they represented $7 to $10 billion or 0.6 per cent to 1.1 per cent of GDP. If we estimate that the total flows surpassed the net flows by 30 to 50 per cent (including the net imports of capital), the above figures for 1929 come to $2.3 to $2.6 billions. This amount represents $20 to $22 billions in 1990 prices and equals 1 per cent of GDP. This is lower than current levels, but the highest rate was not in 1929.

Relatively more data are available for 1913. The total gross outflows of long-term capital were estimated at $2.2 to $2.8 billion.[19] In 1990 prices, that amount would translate into $32 to $40 billions and it represents 2.3 to 2.9 per cent of GDP of the time. This figure (as those of the inter-war period) is more of an underestimation than an overestimation. The 1913 figure is likely to be 3 per cent of GDP or even more. This percentage was not reached until the final years of the 1980s. Even the recent figure, which is a historic peak, is only 0.3 of a percentage point or less than 10 per cent higher than 1913. Although the data are too incomplete to allow us to make any credible calculation regarding the direct investment flows in 1929 or 1913, it is difficult to talk about globalization as something new.

The foreign direct investment stocks

The analysis focuses on direct investment stocks mainly because direct investment played a more important role than portfolio investments or other long-term capital.

Data for this analysis are shown in Figure 7.3. It shows the annual evolution of the volume of foreign direct investment stocks from 1970 to 1993. Three countries are taken into account: the United States, the United Kingdom and Japan which together make up two-thirds of those investments.

The annual evolution of the stocks of direct investment is more stable than the evolution of capital flows even if the declines are rarer and less deep. This evolution is none the less influenced by the economic conjuncture. Figure 7.3 clearly shows the impact of the 1981 recession. But in 1991, 1992, and even 1993, the investment stocks of all the Western developed countries have continued to increase. The increase between 1990 and 1993 converts to 8 per cent when expressed in 1990 prices. Figure 7.3 does not show data for the total of the Western developed countries since the annual series regarding the stock of direct investments are not available. ▪

The figure shows another striking fact – namely, Japan's fast rise and the relatively important decline of the United States. As Table 6.7 will show, Japan was only responsible for 1 per cent of all the foreign direct investments made in the late 1960s. This figure rose to 2.9 per cent in the early 1970s and to 6.5 per cent in 1985. From 1986 to 1991, Japan's share in investment rose even more rapidly – 6.6 per cent to 12.3 per cent. The data available for 1992 and 1993 are still provisional. This would explain why despite the sharp increase in the flows, the stocks stagnated.

In 1980, the United States started being less predominant among all the Western developed countries although it still commanded 43 per cent of the total foreign direct investments stocks. In 1990, this share declined to 25 per cent. In fact, the decline of the United States started at the end of the 1960s. In the mid-1960s, the United States owned about 60 per cent of the total foreign direct investments against 47 per cent in the early 1970s. If the data are given in terms of relative importance to GDP, this decline is less important although it is still real. In 1960/2, it represented about 6.4 per cent. After that the evolution goes up and down: 7.7 per cent in the periods 1974/6 and 1978/80; 6 per cent in the mid-1980s; 8 per cent at the end of the 1980s and in the early 1990s. The historical peak (8.1 per cent) reached after the Second World War was equalled again in the period 1991/3.

The data used in this chapter, which are provided by the OECD and by the UNCTAD, may differ sometimes from the data released by the countries themselves. This is mainly the case of the United States where, for instance, the series of figures published by the American Statistical Services are significantly higher since the mid-1970s than the figures given here. The OECD and the UNCTAD do not take into account, among others, the following items: finance, real estate and insurance. If we rely on the official data regarding the American foreign direct investments stocks at current cost, we may retrieve annual data as far back as 1945. In terms of proportion of the GDP, the figure rose from 4.4 per cent in the period 1949/51 to 6.4 per cent in the period 1960/2. The highest level (13.7 per cent) was reached in the 1979/81 period. The figure is 9.7 per cent in the 1984/6 period and 11.4 per cent in the period 1990/2.[20] Thus, as far as foreign direct investments are

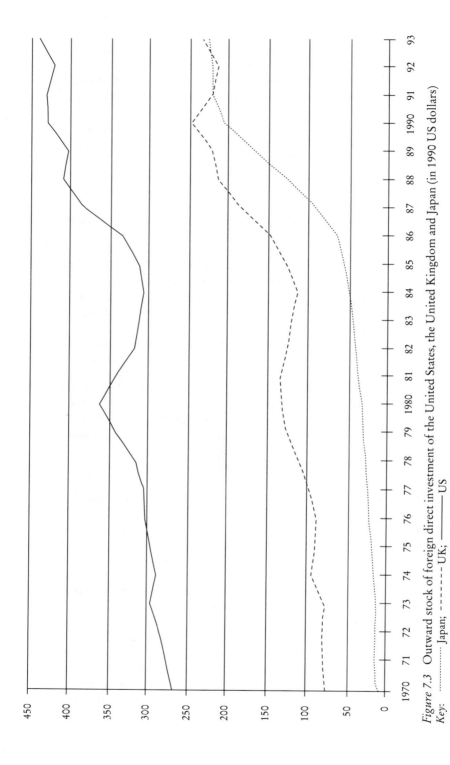

Figure 7.3 Outward stock of foreign direct investment of the United States, the United Kingdom and Japan (in 1990 US dollars)
Key: ·········· Japan; - - - - - UK; ———— US

Figure 7.3 Outward stock of foreign direct investment of the United States, the United Kingdom and Japan (in 1990 US dollars)

Table 7.6 Outward foreign direct investments stocks

	1960	1971	1980	1985	1990	1993*
In millions of current dollars						
Belgium	1.0	2.4	6.0	4.3	22.0	–
Canada	2.6	6.5	21.6	38.7	73.1	–
France	4.1	7.5	12.2	20.3	110.0	161.0
Germany	0.8	7.3	43.1	59.9	151.6	187.0
Italy	1.1	3.0	7.1	16.4	57.1	–
Japan	0.5	4.4	19.6	44.0	202.4	264.0
The Netherlands	7.0	4.0	42.1	47.7	107.0	–
Sweden	4.0	2.4	8.0	13.9	24.9	–
Switzerland	2.3	9.5	21.5	25.3	65.7	–
United Kingdom	12.4	23.7	80.7	101.2	244.8	252.0
United States	31.9	82.8	220.2	251.0	423.2	489.0
Western dev. countries	68.0	156.0	508.0	678.0	1,594.0	2,100.0
As percentage of total GDP:						
Belgium	1.5	1.5	1.2	0.6	1.4	–
Canada	3.7	4.2	4.3	5.7	4.6	–
France	6.0	4.8	2.4	3.0	6.9	7.6
Germany	1.2	4.7	8.5	8.8	9.5	8.8
Italy	1.6	1.9	1.4	2.4	3.6	–
Japan	0.7	2.8	3.9	6.5	12.7	12.6
The Netherlands	10.3	2.6	8.3	7.0	6.8	–
Sweden	5.9	1.5	1.6	2.1	1.6	–
Switzerland	3.4	6.1	4.2	3.7	4.1	–
United Kingdom	18.2	15.2	15.9	14.9	15.4	11.9
United States	46.9	53.1	43.3	37.0	26.5	23.1

* Preliminary figures

Sources: Derived from OECD, *International Direct Investment Statistics Yearbook, 1993*, Paris, 1993 (and data communicated by the Sercretariat of OECD); United Nations, *Transnational Corporations in World Development: Trends and Prospects*, New York, 1988; United Nations, *World Investment Directory*, vol. III: *Developed Countries*, New York, 1993; United Nations, *World Investment Report*, New York, various issues

Note: For the geographical definitions see note 3 on p. 190

concerned, one may not speak of a growing globalization of the American economy.

Nevertheless, and this is very important, the foreign direct investments in the United States have been growing very rapidly since 1973. From the early 1960s to the early 1970s, they only represented 1.3 per cent of the GDP of the United States. They started to rise in 1973. They represented 2 per cent in 1979, 4.1 per cent in 1985 and 7.4 per cent in 1990. The stocks of foreign direct investments in the US almost reached the level of the stocks of American direct investments abroad. One of the reasons for the rise of direct – and other – investments in the US is the devaluation of the dollar that started in 1971 and was very serious in 1974. Although the trend may be a new one for the last half century, throughout the nineteenth century to the beginning of the First World War, the US attracted foreign investment. This was the case of other European offshore settlements. In June 1914, the United States had invested $3.5 billion in foreign countries while it enjoyed $6.7 billion of foreign investments. It is true that most of the foreign investments were portfolio investments. The stock of foreign direct investments in the United States represented $1.3 billion in 1914 which would equal $19 billion in 1990 prices: this figure was reached in 1949. In terms of proportion of the GDP $1.3 billion represents 3 per cent of the 1914 GDP: this proportion was equalled again in 1978 according to the American statistics and in 1981 according to the revised figures provided by the international organizations. Around 1913 the stocks of all the foreign investments in the United States represented 17 per cent of the US GDP. One has to wait until the end of the 1970s for the stocks of foreign investments to reach the same level. This figure then reached 28 per cent in 1985 and almost 43 per cent in 1992.

Let us now end this long discussion of the United States and look at the rest of the developed world where the stocks of investments made abroad have risen since the early 1970s. The reason given above to justify the massive flow of foreign capital into the United States is *ipso facto* relevant to explain the growth of the stocks of investments owned abroad by most of the other Western developed countries. In 1990, 62 per cent of Japanese investments were in the United States. The dollar devaluation explains well the increase of investments made abroad by Japan but also by European countries like Germany and France (as shown in Table 7.6). Since the mid-1970s, instead of two leading countries (the US and the UK), six countries have been leading in the area of investments: United States, United Kingdom, Germany, France, Japan, and The Netherlands.

This multi-polarization of international investments provokes a significant increase of the relative importance at the level of investments of all the Western developed countries. International investments represent 6.5 per cent to 7 per cent of the GDP until 1980. This proportion rose to 7.8 per cent in 1985, 9.9 per cent in 1990 and almost 11 per cent in 1993. These figures show an increase of about 60 per cent of the relative importance of these international investments, an important indicator of globalization. But is anything new happening from a longer-term perspective? The answer to that question is uncertain considering that the data available for 1913 are in-complete in the area of stocks of direct investments.

The estimates for that period are mainly related to the total stocks of investments and they give very little information on the relative importance of the direct investments. Moreover, the data available for the more recent years focus on stocks of direct investments. Our estimates, which rely on very incomplete data, allow us to conclude that for the whole of the Western developed countries the total stocks of international investments must have represented 46 per cent to 53 per cent of the GDP in 1913. Relying on the incomplete data on the proportion of direct investments of both the

Table 7.7 Outward stocks of foreign direct investments as percentage of GDP

	Western developed countries	United States	Western Europe	Japan
1950	–	4.2	–	–
1960	7.1	6.2	10.4	1.1
1971	6.6	7.5	6.9	1.9
1980	6.6	8.1	6.4	1.9
1985	7.7	6.2	10.3	3.3
1990	9.8	7.8	12.1	6.9
1993*	11.4	8.2	15.2	6.3

* Preliminary figures
Source: See Table 7.1 and Table 7.6. For 1993, the missing data for countries were estimated by the author on the basis for 1990 or 1991 data for stocks, and data for outflows for the missing years
Note: For the geographical definitions see note 3 on p. 190

capital exporting and importing countries,[21] we may conclude that direct investments must have represented about 15 per cent to 20 per cent of the total investments in 1913. If this proportion is to be accepted, the direct investments would represent 8 per cent to 10 per cent of the GDP. This is likely to be an underestimation.

Another source of data on foreign direct investment is provided in H. Dunning's study of the changing level and structure of international production.[22] He provides figures concerning the stock of foreign direct investment both for 1914 and 1938. For obvious reasons, I shall concentrate on 1914. For that year, he arrives at a total of $14.3 billion in the stock of foreign direct investment in developed countries in current dollars, which can be reduced to a little below $14 billion if we restrict ourselves to the Western developed countries as we do for the later periods. This is sensibly higher than our estimate of some $8.5 to 10 billion, which I felt was probably an overestimate. It is, therefore, likely that the reality lies somewhere between $10 and 14 billion or 11 to 14 per cent.

As Table 7.7 shows, the relative importance of the stocks of direct international investments of the Western developed countries was still lower in 1985 than in 1913. In the early 1990s, it was the same or almost the same especially if one takes into account the probability that the 1913 figure is an underestimation. According to any probability, for all the Western developed countries, the 1913 level may have been hardly surpassed if indeed it has been. On the other hand, Japan, a late industrializer, had a very low level in 1960 which was still by far higher than the 1913 level or the level in any other year before 1960. Western Europe, which had a rate twice higher than Japan's in 1993 (15.2 per cent against 6.3 per cent), probably had a higher rate eighty years before.

PAUL BAIROCH

CONCLUSION

The preceding analysis is both too global and too limited. The absolute and relative importance of the direct investments represent only one aspect of a possible globalization. The impact of a similar proportion of direct investments may obviously change according to the nature of the enterprises. One may argue the same thing about trade where the nature of the traded items has various influences on the economy. The analysis would be less global if it put more emphasis on international differences. It would also be less limited if it looked at other factors of globalization even though trade and investments are two of the most important factors.

A purely quantitative analysis does not reveal so obviously the fact that contemporary economies are extraverted and interdependent through direct investment in an unprecedented manner. Not until recently did they indeed surpass the rate of exports they had reached at the beginning of the First World War. As a consequence of that, the trends revealed by the analysis of the pre-Second World War become relative. One may also wonder about the reason why exports and internal markets show different price patterns. Is this a sign of the well-being of international trade or is it a consequence of the phenomenon of generalized dumping? According to the first assumption, the lowering of tariffs would be justified. On the other hand, international economic relations would be rich in conflicts and instabilities.

The changing levels of direct investments demonstrate the decline of the US share and Japan's rise as a major investor. It is true that foreign investment flows are more important than previously and represent a slightly bigger share of the GDP. But is the concept 'globalization' appropriate? Here again the historical approach contradicts the vision of most economists and politicians who draw their conclusions from the study of shorter periods of time.

International trade has a history of fast internationalization alternating with drawback. This fact gives a different perspective on the thesis of globalization as an irreversible movement. The most significant changes might very well be institutional. In that case, they would not be clearly revealed by statistical analysis on which economic history relies. The other chapters of this book deal precisely with that point.

NOTES

1 Translated from French by Marilyn Lambert-Drache.
2 This basic argument of economics relies on the fact that since the early 1970s international trade of goods in Western developed countries has been growing more rapidly than the whole economy.
3 The term 'Western developed countries' refers here to the following regions and countries: Western Europe (excluding Yugoslavia), United States, Canada, Australia, New Zealand and Japan. Apart from Turkey, all of these countries are now members of the OECD. They are qualified as 'industrialized countries' by the World Bank and the IMF.

4 The OECD defines 'Services' as 'Travel', 'Transportation', 'Government services', 'Other private services' which include processing and repair, insurance, advertising, films and television, etc.

5 Rather homogeneous data regarding the flow of services were not available until 1970, *Services: Statistics on International Transactions, 1970/1991* (OECD, Paris, 1993).

6 Without giving the history of this law, we shall quote our colleague and friend Herbert Glejser's article: 'An Explanation of Differences in Trade-Product Ratios Among Countries' (*Cahiers économiques de Bruxelles*, no. 37, 1st term, 1968, pp. 47–58).

7 Please note that although most tables feature data regarding the 1991 to 1993 period (because of the more specific conjuncture of that period), the analysis focuses more on the 1989 to 1991 period.

8 *Survey of Current Business*, June 1993. Note that the definition given by American statisticians is broader than the OECD one.

9 See P. Bairoch, *Commerce extérieur et développement économique de l'Europe au XIXe siècle* (Paris and La Haye, Mouton, 1976).

10 P. Bairoch, *Economics and World History. Myths and Paradoxes* (New York and London, Harvester, Wheatsheaf, 1993), pp. 168–70.

11 P. Bairoch, 'Geographical Structure and Trade Balance of European Foreign Trade from 1800 to 1970', *The Journal of European Economic History*, vol. 3, no. 3 (Rome, Winter 1974), pp. 557–608.

12 League of Nations, *The Network of World Trade* (Geneva, 1942).

13 Many thanks to my young colleague, David Thomas, who helped me to collect some data on this aspect of my research. Many thanks also to my colleague and friend Fred Pryor of Swarthmore College who generously and spontaneously let me use an important and exhaustive set of data he had collected thirty years ago on this topic.

14 All the figures used in this section refer to private capital and they exclude short-term flows. Therefore, flows of public investments are not studied here. The latter investments are still marginal compared to the private investments although they have increased since the 1960s as a consequence of the increasing aid to the Third World. In 1989 to 1991, for instance, there were 521 billions of dollars in annual flows of private investments against 70 billions of dollars in annual flows of public investments. As far as direct investments are concerned, public flows and stocks are almost insignificant with the exception of industrialized state enterprises.

15 See J. O. Martins, 'L'incertitude des statistiques internationales. Le cas des balances des payements', *Revue d'économie financière*, no. 14 (Autumn 1990), pp. 201–19.

16 Whenever series have been deflated, the implicit GDP deflator of all the OECD countries has been used.

17 UNCTAD, *World Investment Report 1993* (New York, 1993), p. 93.

18 United Nations, *International Capital Movements During the Inter-War Period* (New York, 1949).

19 Refer to the data and sources used in chapter V, section A of P. Bairoch, *Commerce extérieur et développement économique de l'Europe au XIXe siècle* (Mouton, Paris and La Haye, 1976), pp. 98–111.

20 For the series on investments, refer to US Bureau of the Census, *Historical Statistics of the United States. Colonial Times to 1970* (Washington, 1975, vol. 2), pp. 868–9. See also US Bureau of the Census, *Survey of Current Business*, June 1993.

21 For sources, refer to note 19.

22 H. Dunning, 'Changes in the Level and Structure of International Production: The Last One Hundred Years', in M. Casson (ed.), *The Growth of International Business*

(London, Allen & Unwin, 1983). I would like to thank Richard Kozul-Wright, Transnational Corporation Affairs Officer, Division on Transnational Corporations and Investment, UNCTAD, Geneva, for bringing this source to my attention.

8

POST-GLOBALIZATION
Is the financial liberalization trend likely to be reversed?[1]

Eric Helleiner

At the forefront of the economic globalization trend in recent years has been a rapid expansion of international financial activity. The daily volume of trading in the world's major foreign exchange markets, for example, reached almost $1 trillion by the early 1990s, a figure close to forty times the daily value of international trade.[2] It is often assumed that the globalization of financial markets is irreversible because the process is said to have been caused primarily by technological developments which cannot easily be turned back. In this chapter, I challenge this assumption by drawing on a growing body of literature in the field of international political economy (IPE) that tells a different historical story. While not discounting technological pressures, this IPE literature demonstrates that financial globalization has also been heavily dependent on state support and encouragement.[3] I focus on one of the key aspects of this support: the decisions by advanced industrial states to abolish their capital controls over the last two decades.

The importance of these decisions was that they removed significant barriers to the cross-border movement of financial assets that had been in place in most countries for nearly a half century. Indeed, by the early 1990s, an almost fully liberal regime of international financial movements had emerged within the OECD region, granting financial operators more freedom to act internationally than they had experienced since before the First World War. Although many believe that the liberal pattern of financial relations within the OECD region is here to stay, I argue that a closer look at the causes of the financial liberalization trend may point to a different conclusion. Drawing on the recent IPE scholarship, I divide these causes into developments at the domestic, regional, and systemic levels. They include: domestic support from neo-liberal advocates and internationally oriented businesses; inter-state bargains and regional objectives within the European Community; and an international competitive dynamic encouraged by US and British actions. After outlining these developments, I suggest that they may each be increasingly challenged in significant ways in the near future. This leads to the conclusion that a reversal of the liberalization trend is more likely than is often assumed. While such a reversal would not bring an end to global financial activity, it is likely to reduce the degree of capital mobility somewhat, thus perhaps marking the beginnings of what Robert Cox has called a 'post-globalization' movement in the international political economy.[4]

A DOMESTIC BACKLASH AGAINST FINANCIAL LIBERALISM?

The financial liberalization trend across the advanced industrial world in the last two decades has been partly propelled by domestic developments. One of these has been the increased political prominence of supporters of market-oriented or 'neo-liberal' thought.[5] Neo-liberal advocates have favoured the elimination of capital controls partly on efficiency grounds; capital would be able to move across borders to find its most productive employment. They have also argued that financial liberalization would allow private international financial markets to discipline government policy effectively. In addition, the abolition of capital controls has also been seen as desirable in that it gives individuals the freedom to diversify their financial portfolios and thus reduce their risks and vulnerability to financial upheavals.

A second domestic development encouraging financial liberalization has been the growing demand for it from large financial firms and multinational businesses in recent years.[6] In almost every one of the episodes in which advanced industrial states have abolished their capital controls over the last two decades, these business groups have been a key domestic constituent pressing for the move. With the rapid internationalization of corporate activities in Europe, North America and Japan in the 1970s and 1980s, capital controls have increasingly come to be seen as a cumbersome interference by these firms.

Interestingly, in most countries, this domestic coalition of neo-liberal enthusiasts and internationally oriented business groups encountered very little resistance when they called for the abolition of capital controls. The highly technical and seemingly complex nature of international financial issues appeared to give these groups a high degree of autonomy to influence state behaviour in this area.[7] Indeed, it is striking that in none of the liberalization decisions in the 1970s and 1980s was the kind of controversy generated among the general public that regularly emerges concerning liberalization decisions in the trade sector. The relative conservatism of the one group in government that usually dominates international financial policy-making – specialists in finance ministries and central banks – also ensured that they were often sympathetic to the free-market orientation of neo-liberal ideas. Indeed, they were often the most enthusiastic advocates of financial liberalization in this period.

If supporters of financial liberalization met little resistance in promoting their goals, why should we expect a move away from financial liberalism in the near future? One reason is that there has been a growing backlash in the last few years against neo-liberal financial thinking in light of some of the consequences of the financial liberalization trend. Two broad areas of concern have been highlighted by the critics. First, some argue that, instead of producing a more efficient use of resources, financial liberalization has tended to encourage the growth of speculative, non-productive international financial activity. In foreign exchange markets, for example, increased capital mobility is said to have resulted in large currency misalignments which in turn have disrupted international trading patterns and encouraged protectionist tendencies.[8] Critics, such as Susan Strange, have suggested that the current global financial order resembles nothing more than a casino in which assets are traded almost entirely for speculative profit rather than for the benefit of the 'real' economy. Moreover, because this trading affects the value of currencies, interest rates and other economic prices, it is said to be a casino from which no one in the world can escape and which is causing considerable social dislocation around the world. Indeed, Strange warns of a growing political backlash if the global financial 'casino' is not 'cooled' and brought under political control.[9] The large volume of flight capital that moved from South to North in the 1980s has also been highlighted by critics to support their argument that the emerging open international financial order has encouraged harmful speculative movements of capital instead of beneficial productive flows.[10]

The second principal area that concerns many critics is the loss of policy autonomy. While neo-liberals praise the ability of international financial markets to discipline domestic policy, many critics see the loss of policy autonomy in a more negative light. As one prominent critic argues: 'the mobility of financial capital limits viable differences among national interest rates and thus severely restricts the ability of central banks and governments to pursue monetary and fiscal policies appropriate to their internal economies'.[11] This loss of macroeconomic policy autonomy has been particularly worrisome to many during a period of high unemployment when they would have preferred governments to have pursued more expansionary policies than international financial markets sometimes permitted. In addition to concerns about macroeconomic autonomy, others have worried that the new liberal international financial environment has imposed new constraints on government's tax and regulatory policies by increasing the opportunities for powerful market actors to 'exit' the domestic financial system when they disapproved of such policies.[12] In broader political terms, there have also been concerns that states are being forced to become increasingly 'internationalized', responding to the judgements of those who move internationally mobile funds rather than to the opinions of their domestic citizenry.[13]

How do these critics propose to reverse the liberalization trend? While some advocate the reimposition of tight capital controls,[14] most support milder measures aimed at reducing international capital mobility. In the latter category, the most prominent proposal comes from economist James Tobin who suggests that governments impose a small transaction tax on all spot foreign exchange transactions. Without seriously interfering with productive long-term capital flows or payments related to trade transactions, such a tax would be designed to reduce undesirable speculative financial movements by increasing 'the weight that market participants give to long-range funda-mentals relative to immediate speculative opportunities'. As Tobin puts it, the objective would be to 'throw some sand into the wheels' of international finance.[15]

Despite their support for the Tobin tax, many critics of financial liberal-ization are sceptical that it will ever be introduced. In addition to resistance from conservative financial officials who tend to dominate policy in this area, they anticipate enormous opposition to any initiative that attempts to reduce the mobility of international financial capital from banks and multinational firms who favour the current liberal pattern of financial relations.[16] To overcome this opposition, supporters of the Tobin tax would clearly need to generate considerable interest in the issue among the general public, a development that seems unlikely given the low domestic political visibility of international financial issues. Some critics point out that the latter is related not only to the complexity of the issues, but also to the fact that the costs of financial liberalism outlined by the critics are ones that tend not to impinge very visibly and directly on societal groups. In this respect, the domestic political dynamics surrounding financial liberalization are seen to be as the exact reverse of those in the trade field. As a recent UNCTAD report argued:

> (the) costs of financial openness (loss of policy autonomy, increased financial instability, etc.) being collective are anonymous in their incidence, whereas the benefits accrue to particular economic agents (especially international financial and non-financial enterprises, and rentiers). Political pressure by the latter therefore does not meet significant resistance. By contrast, in the field of trade, it is the costs of restrictiveness that are borne collectively, and the benefits accrue to particular groups.[17]

Although these domestic political dynamics may suggest that financial liberalization cannot in fact be easily reversed, there is one event which can alter such dynamics considerably: a major international financial crisis. Such a crisis may, for example, lead governments to ignore the opposition of domestic actors and reimpose capital controls as a way of defending the balance of payments. More broadly, international financial crises may also, in Bryant's words, 'catalyze a widespread awareness of the underlying trends' in the otherwise obscure international financial sector.[18] Both of these developments were well demonstrated during the European currency crisis of 1992/3.

With their currencies under attack, three European governments – Spain, Portugal and Ireland – were prompted to temporarily impose or tighten capital controls in the autumn of 1992. At the same time, by highlighting the speculative nature of the foreign exchange market, the crisis also attracted considerable public attention to the arguments of the growing number of critics of financial liberalization. Tobin's views and his proposal for a transaction tax on currency trading, for example, were widely discussed in this period.[19] Even traditional supporters of financial liberalization acknowledged that authorities might be tempted to begin to reverse the liberalization trend of the previous decade. As one financial reporter noted: 'The danger is that central banks might harness the angry public mood to try and regulate the [foreign exchange] market.'[20] Indeed, the French Economic Minister Michel Sapin indicated the depth of the anger held in some quarters towards international financial speculators with his warning: 'During the [French] revolution, such people were known as agiteurs, and they were beheaded!'[21]

The European currency crisis was important not just in giving strength to critics of financial liberalization and in demonstrating the degree to which a major crisis could alter the domestic political dynamics surrounding financial liberalization. It also highlighted the vulnerability of the new liberal international financial order to future currency crises. What surprised both government officials and market operators was the enormous volume of international financial activity in foreign exchange markets during the crisis. Indeed, studies published soon after showed that between 1986 and 1992, daily activity in the world's major foreign exchange markets had grown threefold to almost $1 trillion. As US Treasury Secretary Nicholas Brady noted: 'This is roughly double the total reserves of the major industrial countries and well beyond the resources governments can bring to bear in the markets.'[22] Not surprisingly, the liberalization of capital controls itself was a key cause of this dramatic growth in foreign exchange activity. In particular, it encouraged large cross-border investing by non-bank institutional investors who had much larger resources at their disposal than banks who had traditionally dominated foreign exchange markets.[23] If their cross-border investments continue to grow, as most analysts predict, it will become increasingly difficult for governments to prevent crises such as that in Europe from recurring. In this way, the liberalization trend may in fact be creating conditions which will lead to its reversal. For if the 1992/3 crisis is any guide, such crises will likely give further political strength to critics of the emerging liberal pattern of financial relations.

CHANGING REGIONAL DYNAMICS IN EUROPE?

Although the European currency crisis highlighted the possibility of a reversal of the liberalization trend, it also revealed an important barrier on this road: the commitment undertaken by European Community (EC) members in 1988 to liberalize their capital controls. In the wake of the autumn 1992 currency upheavals, the three governments that had introduced or tightened capital controls were reminded by many of this commitment. As the IMF Managing Director, Michel Camdessus, put it: 'They know full well that they will not be able to maintain these [controls] because the community law, that of the single market, prohibits it.'[24] Indeed, despite continued uncertainty in foreign exchange markets, these countries did abolish their controls by the end of the year, the deadline set for them in the 1988 financial liberalization directive.[25]

What brought about the European decision to liberalize financial movements? In addition to the domestic factors already outlined and some systemic pressures (to be elaborated below), the decision also reflected two regional developments, both of which have been called into question in the aftermath of the European currency crisis. First, financial liberalization was strongly promoted by the European Commission after the mid-1980s in the hope that it might increase pressure on Community governments to move towards Economic and Monetary Union (EMU). This hope rested on a point made in 1987 by a group of EC experts that it would be impossible for financial freedom, stable exchange rates and national monetary independence to coexist within Europe.[26] With the removal of capital controls, Commission President Jacques Delors predicted that governments would thus recognize the need to abandon their commitment to national monetary independence and move towards EMU if they wanted to preserve stable exchange rates within the European Monetary System (EMS).[27] The decision to establish the so-called Delors Committee to study the EMU process immediately after the financial liberalization agreement appeared initially to confirm his hopes.

The European currency crisis of 1992/3, however, exposed the risky nature of the European Commission's plans. When faced with increased speculative financial pressures unleashed by the removal of capital controls, European countries chose to abandon stable exchange rates instead of moving more rapidly to EMU. Not only did Britain and Italy withdraw from the exchange rate mechanism (ERM) of the EMS altogether in the autumn of 1992, but the governments of those countries that remained in the ERM decided in August 1993 to widen dramatically the bands within which currencies could move to 15 per cent. The possibility of this result had in fact been raised by a number of observers during the late 1980s.[28] But in the atmosphere of Euro-enthusiasm of that period, it had seemed a relatively improbable scenario. The Danish and French referenda on the Maastricht Treaty in June and September 1992, however, revealed the extent to which this mood had faded by the early 1990s. This in turn both reduced the likelihood of states following the Commission's plans and provided the trigger for aggressive speculative activity by international market operators. The enormity and persistence of these speculative pressures also increased the chance that some governments would choose the option of abandoning exchange rate stability at this point. In a crisis when even governments that were pursuing 'appropriate' policies (such as France) found their currencies to be targets, it appeared to many that only an immediate move to a common currency would assuage the markets. At such an early stage in the transition phase to EMU, however, this was an unlikely prospect for all but a few countries.

If financial liberalization has had the effect of disrupting European monetary co-operation in the transition phase to EMU rather than strengthening it, might not European governments conclude that it is desirable to reimpose controls for the duration of these transition years? The reimposition of controls (perhaps in the form of a regional Tobin-style tax) has been increasingly discussed as a means of restoring exchange rate stability in Europe. Even Delors raised the idea publicly in September 1993 as an alternative to the option of moving to more flexible exchange rates.[29] Given the costs of exchange rate fluctuations for the small, open European economies as well as the disruptive impact such fluctuations will have on the project to integrate the European market for goods and services, it seems likely that support for the option of reimposing capital controls will continue to grow, particularly in the event of further currency instability in Europe.

The second reason why some European governments may choose to reimpose capital controls is that the currency crisis exposed the weakness of two inter-state bargains made in the late 1980s between countries which strongly favoured financial liberalization and those which were more wary of it. In the former camp were West Germany and Britain, each perceiving that their financial institutions and markets would benefit from the freeing up of European capital flows.[30] Most of the other Community members were more wary of financial liberalization because their capital controls either were helpful in defending a weak balance of payments position or were a key element in national credit allocation strategies. To go along with West German and British goals, the other Community members demanded two concessions. First, they extracted a commitment from West Germany in the 1987 Basle–Nyborg Agreement that it would intervene more generously to defend weaker currencies with the EMS.[31] Second, France, Italy and some of the smaller members of the European Community linked their support for financial liberalization to Germany's and Britain's commitment to discuss the EMU project. If they were to give up monetary independence in a financial and monetary context that would be increasingly dominated by West Germany and Britain, these less powerful countries wanted this context to be made more accountable to them through the EMU plan.[32]

The currency crisis has called both of these inter-state bargains into question, a development that in turn may undermine the region-wide commitment to financial liberalism. To begin with, in the wake of the currency turmoil in the autumn of 1992, Germany insisted that limits be placed on the financial obligations it had accepted in the Basle–Nyborg Agreement in order that it not be required to intervene with as large funds as it had been forced to during the autumn.[33] This development has deprived weaker currency countries of the financial support they had counted on to defend their currencies in the new more liberal financial environment created by their decisions to abandon capital controls. Without this support, these countries might be tempted to renege on their commitments to maintain financial liberalism in the face of future speculative attacks.

The events surrounding the crisis of 1992/3 also demonstrated the weak nature of both Germany's and Britain's support for the EMU project. The Bundesbank's refusal to cut interest rates substantially just before the crisis, for example, was widely criticized abroad as demonstrating the German central bank's limited commitment to European monetary co-operation. The Bundesbank was indeed deeply uneasy about the EMU project largely because the project would result in it being absorbed in a broader European central bank. In committing to EMU, the German government had over-ridden the Bundesbank's opposition to the project primarily because it saw EMU as a concession to other European countries in return for their support of German reunification.[34] In the wake of Maastricht, however, the German government was unable to dictate the Bundesbank's actions. Moreover, the Bundesbank's position was bolstered by rising popular opposition in Germany to the idea of giving up the German currency.

Britain's weak defence of the pound during the crisis was also extensively criticized abroad and it too reflected the country's ambivalence concerning the EMU project. Britain's doubts had been made apparent the previous December in its demand for an opt-out from the final third stage of the project at Maastricht. They had also been evident in its October 1990 decision to enter the ERM, a decision motivated primarily by the goal of lowering inflation in the short term rather than by the broader objective of encouraging EMU.[35] Britain's wariness towards EMU stemmed not only from broad concerns about losing sovereignty, but also from fears about London's future as an international financial centre in a united Europe. While London might benefit if the future European central bank (or at least its principle operating arm) were located in London, this was far from likely and there were important potential costs to London from closer European integration. There was, for example, the possibility of the European Commission introducing financial regulations which interfered with London's liberal financial environment, a possibility which had already been raised by Brussels' proposals in 1989 for a Europe-wide withholding tax and a reciprocity provision in the second banking directive.[36] There were also fears that a future European central bank might impose German-style reserve requirements across Europe, a move that would seriously harm London's position as a financial centre.[37] Dangers such as these led important financial figures in Britain to believe that Britain would be better served outside of a European monetary union.[38]

The weak nature of the German and British commitment to the EMU project may further encourage some European countries to reconsider their decisions to liberalize capital controls. Without the prospect of regaining some degree of influence over monetary policy in a common European central bank, for example, weaker currency governments may decide that the cost of giving up monetary independence through financial liberalization is too high. They may also resent the fact that Germany and Britain are able to benefit from the abolition of capital controls across Europe without paying the 'cost' of agreeing to EMU. Furthermore, if it is not clear that EMU will ever materialize given German and British reticence, many countries may prefer to sacrifice financial freedom now to restore more stable exchange rates rather than put up with volatile exchange rates for the purpose of securing an uncertain EMU sometime in the distant future.

OVERCOMING INTERNATIONAL COMPETITIVE PRESSURES?

Even if the domestic and regional factors that promoted the liberalization trend in finance are being undermined, there is a final reason to question whether the trend can be reversed: the prominence of an international competitive dynamic in the financial sector. This dynamic represents the third broad factor that IPE scholars have pointed to in explaining the financial liberalization trend. Given the responsiveness of financial operators and investors to regulatory differentials between countries, governments across the advanced industrial world have been tempted in recent years to liberalize external capital controls and deregulate domestic financial systems in an effort to lure footloose international capital and financial business to their own country. Once one major state began to pursue this 'mercantilist' strategy of competitive liberalization and deregulation, others have been forced to follow if they hoped to secure capital and financial business in the emerging international financial order.[39]

Britain and the United States played the key role in initiating this competitive dynamic.[40] Britain's role began with its support for the regulation-free Euromarket in London as far back as the 1960s and then became even more important when the British government abolished its exchange controls in 1979 and encouraged the extensive liberalization and deregulation of British securities markets in 1986. The US decision to remove its capital controls in 1974 was also important in unleashing competitive pressures, pressures that were only reinforced by the deregulatory trend in its domestic financial system during the 1970s and 1980s. The need to respond to competition from British and US financial markets was then a key factor behind the decisions by other states across the advanced industrial world – from Japan to Sweden – to launch financial liberalization and deregulation programmes in the 1980s. Without copying the British and American moves, they risked losing financial capital and business to these two countries.

This competitive dynamic ensures that any effort to reverse financial liberalization must be co-operative. Tobin, for example, argues that his tax on foreign exchange dealings must be imposed uniformly in every financial centre in the world. Without such co-operation, governments will likely be wary of unilaterally imposing a tax that would damage their country's ability to attract capital and financial business relative to countries that do not impose it.[41] Governments will also be aware that their unilateral move may not be very helpful in diminishing the overall level of international capital mobility as long as financial centres elsewhere in the world are willing to remain open for international business. The obvious difficulty with such co-operative proposals, however, is that they will encounter collective action problems. There will always be one state that is tempted to 'free ride' on the benefits of a more regulated international financial order (e.g. greater exchange rate stability and policy autonomy), while refusing to implement regulations itself in order to attract capital and financial business to its markets. Indeed, the difficulties involved in overcoming such collective action problems have led many to discount the feasibility of co-operative proposals such as that proposed by Tobin.[42]

While these difficulties are substantial, they should not be overstated. Indeed, the fact that they may be able to be overcome has been demonstrated by two recent international regulatory initiatives. The first was the effort to impose common capital adequacy standards on all international banks from G-10 countries. This effort was led not by figures seeking to reduce international capital mobility, but rather by US and British central bankers who hoped to minimize the risk of an international banking crisis. Although it was thus a 'pro-market' form of international financial regulation, the initiative faced similar competitive pressures that a more 'anti-market' regulatory initiative would. If the US and Britain were to impose capital standards unilaterally on their own banks, these banks would be put at a competitive disadvantage in international banking markets. To overcome this problem, US and British officials used their central position in the international financial system to pressure other states to join their initiative. After reaching a bilateral agreement in January 1987, they raised the prospect of foreign banks being excluded from New York and London financial markets unless these banks and their governments went along with the deal. Because no major foreign bank could expect to be successful internationally without operating in New York and London, this threat was significant enough to encourage other G-10 governments to reach an agreement within the next year.[43]

A similar threat was used by the US to overcome collective action problems involved in its effort in the late 1980s to curtail drug money laundering in international financial markets. Recognizing that unilateral US reporting requirements and regulations would hurt the international competitive position of US banks and US financial markets, US regulators sought to secure the co-operation of foreign authorities. The key measure which encouraged such co-operation was the Kerry amendment to the 1988 Anti-Drug Abuse Act which empowered the US President to restrict foreign access to the US financial system and US-based dollar-clearing mechanisms if foreign banks did not go along with new regulations and reporting requirements.[44] This threat was very effective in pressuring foreign banks and governments to agree to the US initiative because of the importance of US financial markets and the dollar in international finance. Within a short period of time, the US had negotiated agreements with fourteen other countries (including Switzerland) to impose various reporting requirements on their own banks.[45]

Although neither of these initiatives represented a reversal of the liberalization trend, they demonstrated that it is possible to overcome the collective action problems that threaten to obstruct proposals for co-operatively reregulating international financial markets. As Susan Strange has long argued, this result can be achieved by dominant financial powers using their central position in the international financial system to encourage compliance abroad. Just as Britain and the US led the liberalization and deregulation trend, the above initiatives indicate that they are the key states for leading a reregulatory movement, both because of the centrality of their financial markets and, in the US case, because of the international prominence of its currency.[46] What, then, is the likelihood of these two states leading initiatives to reverse the liberalization trend?

To answer this question, it is necessary to investigate why these two states were so keen on promoting financial liberalization in previous years. In addition to the domestic pressures outlined in the first section, the enthusiasm of both Britain and the US for financial liberalization stemmed from an awareness that they would derive special benefits from a more open international financial order. British officials predicted, correctly, that London's long history as a dominant financial centre in the world economy would enable it to be particularly successful at attracting international financial business in such an order. US policy-makers were also aware that their financial markets would be very competitive in an international context because of their unique depth and liquidity as well as because of the dollar's position as the key global currency. They anticipated – once again, correctly – that US financial markets would attract not only international financial business to US territory but also private capital that could help finance American current account and fiscal deficits in the 1970s and 1980s.[47]

Although Britain and the US have obtained special benefits from the financial liberalization trend, it is no longer clear that these benefits will continue. By highlighting the competitive advantage of British and US financial markets, the liberalization trend has increasingly prompted foreign financial authorities to deregulate and reform their domestic financial markets in an effort to try to compete more effectively with those in Britain and the US. This has led prominent bodies such as the OECD and Bank for International Settlements to predict that the liberalization trend is in fact increasingly threatening to undermine the dominant financial position of Britain and the US. Moreover, they note that financial reforms abroad – particularly in Japan and Germany – are also likely to reduce the prominence of the dollar as the leading currency in international finance.[48] In the face of these challenges, it is possible that British and US officials will begin to see financial liberalization in a less favourable light. Indeed, such sentiments have already become prominent within British financial circles in the face of growing competitive pressures from Europe.[49] Some form of co-operative reregulation may begin to be perceived by Britain and the US as a way to lessen the competitive pressures on foreign financial authorities that are encouraging them to undermine British and American financial pre-eminence.

There are also two further developments that might lead the US to support such action in the coming years that are associated in part with its changing position in the world economy. First, the growing vulnerability of the US to global financial markets as the world's largest debtor may encourage American policy-makers to look more favourably on a Tobin-style tax which promises to reduce destabilizing speculation against the dollar (but which does not tamper with long-term capital inflows). A dollar crisis of a similar magnitude as that in the late 1970s, for example, might produce the catalyst for such support to emerge.[50] Second, several observers have noted that there is a growing scepticism within the US towards 'free market finance', a mood that is said to have been encouraged partly by a reaction against the financial excesses of the 1980s but also by a perception in some circles that free market traditions in US financial markets may be contributing to America's economic decline. Indeed, the Clinton administration has brought into office a number of prominent critics of neo-liberal arguments in finance who might be attracted to proposals such as the Tobin tax.[51]

CONCLUSION

In this chapter, I have attempted to challenge the argument that the globalization of financial markets is irreversible. To do this, I have drawn on a growing body of IPE literature which has shown that the globalization trend has been dependent on state support and encouragement from its beginnings in the 1960s. A particularly important form of support involved the decisions of states across the OECD region to remove their capital controls over the last two decades. Although many assume that the new freedom which states have given to financial market operators to move funds across borders without restrictions will not be taken away, I have called this assumption into question. My reasons can be briefly summarized.

The financial liberalization trend was propelled by a distinct set of factors at the domestic, regional and systemic levels, each of which is increasingly being undermined. At the domestic level, as some of the negative consequences of the new liberal international financial order have become apparent in recent years, a growing number of critics of financial liberalization have emerged to challenge the neo-liberal advocates and internationally oriented firms that supported the trend. Although the critics worry that the low domestic political visibility of international financial issues will make it difficult for them to mobilize broad support for their reregulatory proposals, the recent European currency crisis demonstrated that support may increase considerably during and after such crisis. With the liberalization trend having encouraged a large increase in speculative activity in international financial markets, it will prove increasingly difficult for governments to prevent such crises and their accompanying political fall-out in the coming years.

At the regional level, the plans of the European Commission and the specific inter-state bargains which encouraged the 1988 European Community decision to liberalize capital controls look somewhat tattered after the currency crisis. The crisis demonstrated, for example, the risky nature of the Commission's plan of using financial liberalization to encourage close monetary co-operation. By contributing to the onset of a major crisis in the EMS instead, financial liberalization may increasingly become a target of those seeking to restore exchange rate stability. The bargains between states that favoured liberalization and those that were more wary of it also look increasingly fragile after the crisis. In particular, the latter may come to resent their commitment to financial liberalization in light of both the weakening of Germany's obligations to the Basle–Nyborg Agreement and the indications that neither Germany nor Britain are strongly committed to EMU.

Finally, at the systemic level, several recent initiatives have demonstrated that it is possible for states to overcome the international competitive dynamic which helped encourage the liberalization trend. These initiatives have been led by the US and Britain who have used their dominant international financial position to encourage other states to join in co-operative reregulatory projects. Although no initiative has yet been launched to reverse the liberalization trend, these two states may become more attracted to such an idea as the new liberal international financial order threatens to undermine their financial pre-eminence by prompting foreign competition. The US may also become more inclined to support such an initiative because of its new debtor status and changing domestic perceptions of the benefits of 'free market finance'.

In sum, there are important reasons to believe that the enthusiasm of OECD governments for financial liberalization may soon wane, a development which would pose a considerable challenge to the financial globalization trend. It would be foolish, of course, to assert anything more definitive than this. Given the enormity of the upheavals in world politics in recent years, it is clearly hazardous to attempt to predict political developments even in the short term. This, however, highlights one of the key points that I have tried to emphasize in this chapter. The pattern and degree of financial integration between states has been and will continue to be influenced not just by technological developments but also by those in the political realm.

This point can be reinforced in one final way. It is worth noting that even if states choose not to reintroduce capital controls, the open global financial order could still be threatened by a second development: a major global financial crisis that shatters the confidence of market actors who operate at international level. It was, for example, the international financial crisis of 1931 that brought down the last open global financial order within the international political economy. Once again, the behaviour of states will be important in determining the likelihood of such a scenario given that they can play a key role in preventing such crises through lender-of-last-resort activities, prudential supervision and regulation of international financial markets, and the co-ordination of macroeconomic policies.[52] Although there is not room in this article to discuss the politics surrounding state behaviour in these areas, suffice it to say that it is by no means certain that states will successfully prevent such crises. There are, for example, important domestic political constraints and collective action problems which might hinder their efforts. These difficulties are also compounded by the rapid rate of growth and innovation in international financial markets which can quickly render existing co-operative strategies for handling crises ineffective. The inadequacy of existing crisis-prevention strategies is also often not apparent to policy-makers until it is too late; that is, until it is revealed by a crisis of some kind.

This was demonstrated most recently by the European currency crisis which showed the leading economic powers that their limited co-operative efforts since the mid-1980s to reduce currency turmoil were no longer sufficient to counter the growing volume of activity in international financial markets and the new market actors operating therein. As Spanish finance minister Carlos Solchaga told the annual meeting of the Board of Governors of the IMF at the height of the crisis in the fall of 1992: 'These events serve to show that the mechanics for multilateral coordination of economic policy are partially incapable of dealing with the globalized, decontrolled and liberalized economy that has emerged since the end of the 1980s . . . '[53] At the same meeting, Nicholas Brady echoed this view: 'The world has changed significantly since the coordination process was developed. Capital markets have grown dramatically in size and complexity . . . New ways of cooperating must be developed to fit the changed circumstances of this new world.'[54] Whether the major powers are successful in developing such 'new ways of co-operating' to prevent currency turmoil and other international financial crises will have an equally important bearing on the future of the open global financial order as the developments discussed in this chapter.

NOTES

1 Acknowledgements: For their helpful comments on an earlier version of this Chapter, I would like to thank David Andrews, David Felix, Charles MacMillan, Susan Strange and Michael Webb. I am also grateful to the Social Sciences and Humanities Research Council for helping to finance part of the research.
2 Morris Goldstein, David Folkerts-Landau, Peter Garber, Liliana Rojas-Suarez and Michael Spencer, *International Capital Markets: Part 1. Exchange Rate Management and International Capital Flows* (Washington: International Monetary Fund, 1993), p. 1.
3 I have summarized and built upon this work in E. Helleiner, *States and the Reemergence of Global Finance: From Bretton Woods to the 1990s* (Ithaca: Cornell University Press, 1994). Much of the historical discussion that follows draws from this work.
4 Robert Cox, 'Structural Issues of Global Governance: Implications for Europe', in Stephen Gill (ed.), *Gramsci, Historical Materialism and International Relations* (Cambridge: Cambridge University Press, 1993).
5 Helleiner, *States and the Reemergence*, chs 5, 7. A recent example of neo-liberal thinking in the international financial realm is Richard McKenzie and Dwight Lee, *Quicksilver Capital: How the Rapid Movement of Wealth Has Changed the World* (New York: Free Press, 1991).
6 See Jeffry Frieden, 'Invested Interests: The Politics of National Economic Policies in a World of Global Finance', *International Organization* 45 (1991), pp. 440–2; J. Goodman and L. Pauly, 'The Obsolescence of Capital Controls? Economic Management in an Age of Global Markets', *World Politics* 46 (1993), pp. 50–82; Helleiner, *States and the Reemergence*, chs, 5, 7; Michael Moran, *The Politics of the Financial Services Revolution: The USA, UK and Japan* (London: Macmillan, 1991), pp. 12, 130–1.
7 Helleiner, *States and the Reemergence*, pp. 203–5
8 These critiques generally stem from Tobin's early writing: James Tobin, 'A Proposal for International Monetary Reform', *The Eastern Economic Journal* 4 (1978), pp. 153–9. Even some who are traditionally sympathetic to neo-liberal ideas acknowledge the validity of this criticism. See, for example, Philip Turner, *Capital Flows in the 1980s* (Basle: Bank for International Settlements, 1991), pp. 102–3; Rimmer De Vries, 'Adam Smith: Managing the Global Capital of Nations', *World Financial Markets* (23 July 1990), p. 9; and the comments of the Bank of England director in Adrian Hamilton, *The Financial Revolution* (New York: Free Press, 1986), p. 237.
9 Susan Strange, *Casino Capitalism* (Oxford: Blackwell, 1986). Others have also predicted a political backlash; see, for example, Michael Loriaux, *France After Hegemony: International Change and Financial Reform* (Ithaca: Cornell University Press, 1991), p. 307; Antony Sampson, *The Midas Touch* (Dunton Green, Kent: Coronet Books, 1990), pp. 275–6.
10 For a good overview of this critique, see David Felix, 'Suggestions for International Collaboration to Reduce Destabilizing Effects of International Capital Mobility on the LDCs', Working Paper No. 173, Department of Economics, Washington University, pp. 19–28.
11 Tobin, 'A Proposal', p. 154.

12 See, for example, UNCTAD, *Trade and Development Report, 1990* (Geneva: UNCTAD, 1990); Juliet Schor and Tariq Banuri (eds), *Financial Openness and National Autonomy* (Oxford: Clarendon, 1992); Herman Daly and John Cobb, *For the Common Good* (Boston: Beacon Press, 1989), ch. 11.

13 See, for example, Robert Cox, 'Global Perestroika', in Ralph Miliband and Leo Panitch (eds), *New World Order?* (London: Merlin Press, 1992); Stephen Gill and David Law, 'Global Hegemony and the Structural Power of Capital', *International Studies Quarterly* 33 (1989), pp. 475–99.

14 Andrew Glyn, 'Capital Flight and Exchange Controls', *New Left Review* 155 (1986), pp. 37–49.

15 Quotations from James Tobin, 'Tax the Speculators', *Financial Times*, 22 December 1992; Tobin, 'A Proposal', p. 154. Some recent supporters have included UNCTAD, *Trade and Development*, pp. 132–3; Felix, 'Suggestions' (his paper is an advisory paper to the G-24); Stephany Griffith-Jones (with Vassilis Papgeorgiou), 'Globalisation of Financial Markets and Impact on Flows to LDCs: New Challenges For Regulation', June 1993, Mimeo, pp. 31–2; Rudiger Dornbusch, 'World Economic Problems for the Summit: Co-ordination, Debt and the Exchange Rate System', Mimeo, April 1988; William Grieder, 'The Money Question', *World Policy Journal* 5 (1988), p. 604. See further references in note 19.

16 See, for example, Strange, *Casino*, p. 190; Griffith-Jones, 'Globalisation', p. 32; Dornbusch, 'World Economic Problems', p. 18; Felix, 'Suggestions', p. 35. The lack of support in international financial circles for capital controls or even some kind of Tobin tax is noted in a recent report produced by the IMF that surveyed opinions after the European currency crisis: Goldstein *et al.*, *International Capital Markets*, p. 21.

17 UNCTAD, *Trade and Development*, p. 112.

18 Ralph Bryant, *International Financial Intermediation* (Washington: Brookings, 1987), p. 153.

19 The arguments he outlined in his well-known 1978 article were, for example, discussed prominently in *The Economist* on 3 October 1992 ('The Way We Were'). Its article concluded: 'Lately, one imagines, a good many government economists have been dusting down their copies of that article.' The *Financial Times* also published an article of his entitled 'Tax the Speculators' on 22 December 1992. In the US, Robert Kuttner also endorsed the Tobin tax idea in his column in *Business Week* on 30 May 1993.

20 James Blitz, 'New Anxieties for the Banks', *Financial Times*, 26 May 1993. *The Economist* also noted: 'Increasingly, the case for a return to (explicit or implicit) restrictions on capital flows is likely to be put, and on both sides of the Atlantic' (3 October 1992, 'The Way We Were').

21 Quoted in *The Economist*, 10 October 1992, 'Splendid Speculators'. In response, IMF Managing Director Michel Camdessus noted: 'Mr Spain was quite right . . . The difference is that during the French Revolution the law prohibited speculation with currencies. Now, the law allows it, allows all forms of speculation. And so far, the world has seen itself as being well served by the absolute freedom of the movement of capital.' *IMF Survey*, 12 October 1992, p. 304.

22 International Monetary Fund, *Summary Proceedings of the Forty-Seventh Annual Meeting of the Board of Governors* (Washington: International Monetary Fund, 1992), p. 103. Statistics from Goldstein *et al.*, *International Capital Markets*, p. 4. For the surprise of even market operators to the growing size of the markets see, for example, Saul Hansell, 'Taming the Trillion Dollar Monster', *Institutional Investor* (December 1992), pp. 33–9.

23 See especially Goldstein *et al.*, *International Capital Markets*.

24 *IMF Survey*, 12 October 1992, p. 304.

25 Spain lifted its controls on 22 November 1992, Portugal on 16 December 1992 and Ireland on 1 January 1993.

26 See, for example, John Goodman, *Monetary Sovereignty: The Politics of Central Banking In Western Europe* (Ithaca: Cornell University Press, 1992), p. 202.

27 Tomasso Padoa-Schioppa, 'Milan, Hanover, 1992', *Review of Economic Conditions in Italy* 3 (1988), pp. 437–40.

28 See, for example, Padoa-Schioppa, 'Milan, Hanover', pp. 440–1.

29 Eric Helleiner, 'Reevaluating the Prospects for a Tripolar Financial Order', *Behind the Headlines* 51 (1993). *The Economist* ('Storming the Bastile', 17 July 1993) noted that many European governments were being urged to reintroduce capital controls. Barry Eichengreen and Charles Wyplosz (in 'Mending Europe's Currency System', *The Economist*, 5 June 1993) recommended that an implicit tax be placed on speculation in Europe in the form of deposit requirements on institutions that take open positions in the foreign exchange markets. Following Tobin, they argued: 'The idea is to throw sand, not concrete, in the wheels of international finance.'

30 Jonathan Story and Marcello De Cecco, 'The Politics and Diplomacy of Monetary Union: 1985–1991', in J. Story (ed.), *The New Europe* (Oxford: Blackwell, 1993), pp. 334–5.

31 For the link between this commitment and the 1988 financial liberalization decision, see Delors' comments in the *Financial Times*, 13 May 1989.

32 See, for example, Story and De Cecco, 'The Politics and Diplomacy', p. 344; David Andrews, 'Germany, Maastricht and EMU: The Limits of Integration Theory', paper prepared for delivery at the annual convention of the International Studies Association, 1–4 April 1992, Atlanta, pp. 8–11.

33 Lionel Barber, 'Currency Crisis Study Spreads Blame', *Financial Times*, 24 May 1993.

34 Andrews, 'Germany, Maastricht', pp. 8–11.

35 Wayne Sandholtz, 'Choosing Union: Monetary Politics and Maastricht', *International Organization* 47 (1993), p. 9.

36 For these fears, see David Lascelles, 'Discreet Charm of the Bank', *Financial Times*, 5 March 1990; Robert Preston, 'EC Seen as Threat to City Success', *Financial Times*, 23 March 1992.

37 See, for example, Garry Evans, 'Bundesbank Clings to Power', *Euromoney*, April 1992, p. 56. In December 1992, the Bundesbank President also suggested that the European central bank should refrain from active lender-of-last-resort actions, again a pattern of behaviour that would hurt London's status as a major financial centre. Peter Norman, 'Time to Discuss a Europe-wide Monetary Policy', *Financial Times*, 4 January 1993.

38 See, for example, the views of Eddie George, now Governor of the Bank of England: 'London "To Remain City of Finance"', *Financial Times*, 3 October 1991; Charles Leadbeater, 'Bank Says ERM Exit Will Not Hurt London', *Financial Times* 3 March 1993; Peter Norman and Richard Lambert, 'A Steady Hand at the Helm', *Financial Times*, 1 July 1993.

39 Quotation from John Plender 'London's Big Bang in International Context', *International Affairs* 63 (1986/7), p. 41.

40 See Susan Strange, 'Finance, Information and Power', *Review of International Studies* 16 (1990); Moran, *The Politics;* Yoichi Enkyo, 'Financial Innovation and International Safeguards: Causes and Consequences of "Structural Innovation" in the US and Global Financial System: 1973–86', Ph.D. Dissertation, London School of Economics, 1989.

41 After its decision to reimpose controls during the European currency crisis, the Spanish government made it clear that it hoped to remove them as quickly as

possible in part because of such competitive considerations. P. Bruce and A. Gowers, 'A Testing Time of Spanish Mettle', *Financial Times*, 5 October 1992.

42 See, for example, Bryant, *International Financial*, p. 157.
43 See Ethan Kapstein, 'Between Power and Purpose: Central Bankers and the Politics of Regulatory Convergence', *International Organization* 46 (1992), pp. 265–87. The threat of denying market access has also been used relatively successfully by the G-10 countries as a whole to ensure that small offshore financial centres co-operate with their efforts to supervise and regulate international banking activities (Helleiner, *States and the Reemergence*, p. 188).
44 See, for example, 'A Torrent of Dirt Dollars', *Time*, December 1989, pp. 44–50.
45 Karin Lissakers, *Banks, Borrowers and the Establishment: A Revisionist Account of the International Debt Crisis* (New York: Basic Books, 1991), pp. 157–8.
46 Strange, *Casino*, argues that the US alone could lead a reregulatory initiative. The experience of the capital adequacy negotiations, however, suggests that it may be important for the US to work in tandem with Britain on issues where London's financial markets are significant. This would be particularly true for an initiative such as that proposed by Tobin given the importance of London's foreign exchange market.
47 For a detailed discussion of British and US goals, see Helleiner, *States and the Reemergence*, chs 4–5, 7.
48 The OECD and the BIS predicted these developments in separate reports in 1989 ('Another Happy New Year?', *The Economist*, 23 December 1989; Stephen Fidler, 'Dollar Share of Cross-Border Lending Falls', *Financial Times*, 9 May 1989). See also the conclusion of a more recent BIS economic paper: Turner, *Capital Flows*, p. 105.
49 The *Financial Times* of London, for example, has begun in its editorials to criticize the British government strongly for encouraging financial liberalization on these grounds. See, for example, its editorials on 9 December 1989 and 17 September 1991. The Bank of England has also concluded that the financial liberalization trend is threatening London's financial pre-eminence (Richard Lambert, 'The City Finds Its Head Start Under Attack', *Financial Times*, 1 June 1989).
50 *The Economist* also suggests this possibility, 'The Way We Were', 3 October 1992.
51 Robert Teitelman, 'The Revolt Against Free Market Finance', *Institutional Investor* (June 1992); 'Wall Street and the New Economic Correctness', *Institutional Investor* (February 1993), pp. 36–44. The new under-secretary for international affairs in the US Treasury, Larry Summers, for example, has shown considerable interest in the past in the idea of transaction taxes over financial market activity. See, for example, Peter Lee, 'Forceful Academic Steps into Mulford's Shoes', *Euromoney* (March 1993), p. 29.
52 See Kapstein, 'Between Power and Purpose'; E. Helleiner, 'States and the Future of Global Finance', *Review of International Studies* 18 (1992), pp. 31–49.
53 IMF, *Summary Proceedings*, p. 85.
54 IMF, *Summary Proceedings*, p. 103. See also comments of the IMF Managing Director on pp. 238–9, as well as the conclusions of Goldstein *et al.*, *International Capital Markets*, p. 2 and those of the B15 as reported in 'Warning for Central Banks', *Financial Times*, 15 June 1993.

9

INTERNATIONAL CAPITAL MOBILITY AND THE SCOPE FOR NATIONAL ECONOMIC MANAGEMENT[1]

Gerald Epstein

INTRODUCTION

A revolution in communications technology has facilitated a worldwide counter-revolution in public policy. At the push of a button, financial capital moves around the globe at such an amazing speed that national governments seem helpless in its wake. Legislatures and citizens who want to buck the trend and achieve goals of high employment, egalitarian development and sustainable growth are paralysed by the threat that any policy which lowers the rate of profit will cause capital to be moved to more profitable environs, thereby reducing investment and lowering the community's standard of living.

As a reaction, mainstream economists have developed a theory of perfect 'global' markets in trade and finance that provide the lens through which governments and labour unions view their prospects. The old Keynesian view which saw national governments as having sufficient autonomy to pursue national goals is now seen as hopelessly *passé*. The new global view eschews any government interference in this global financial market as unrealistic and unproductive given the new reality. Instead, it calls for tight money, financial deregulation, balanced budgets and 'responsible' wage demands.

Despite the widespread acceptance of mainstream economic thought on global financial markets, different measures of international capital mobility give a startlingly different picture of how footloose international capital really is. While, as we will see, some data indicate unprecedented quantities of international financial activity, Robert Zevin (1992), on the other hand, has recently shown that the correlation among short-term interest rates in major financial centres is no higher now than in the late nineteenth century, when satellite technology was hardly a twinkle in the inventors' eyes. Perhaps not much has changed after all.

Yet, at a deep level, we know we are no longer in the 1960s. We know that countries do borrow and lend large amounts over a long period of time. We

211

know that the sheer quantity of short-term finance moving around the globe has become startlingly large. We know that the common perception of policy-makers in many parts of the industrialized world is that they are boxed in by international financial constraints (Crotty 1993). Evidently, then, neither the global view nor the old closed Keynesian model is correct. What theory can make sense of these apparently contradictory trends?

The best chance of understanding these trends and prospects is to examine the data on international capital mobility and the real dynamics between lenders and borrowers in international financial markets. The basic argument of this chapter is that international capital can only be mobile to the extent that there is political and governmental intervention into financial markets. Financial markets in general, and *international* financial markets especially, require asymmetric power relations and institutional structures of enforcement to operate at all (Epstein and Gintis 1992). Hence, the important issue is not whether there can and ought to be state intervention in international financial relations but, rather, what type of intervention is desirable. Thus, the nation-state and capital mobility are not opposites; they go hand in hand.

The second main message, however, is that if groups within nations want to have certain types of capital mobility, then that implies serious constraints on the institutional structures and economic policies that they can pursue. Countries that want to attract a great deal of foreign capital are constrained to play by one set of rules of the game; countries which want to attract less capital, but perhaps of a different type, are constrained to follow a different set of rules. Given the high degree of short-term capital mobility that currently exists, however, all countries are constrained to try to maintain the confidence of short-term investors, or they must interfere with short-term capital mobility if they are to pursue independent policies.

The final point is that current trends towards free trade blocs are likely to herald a higher degree of long-term and real capital mobility.[2] Progressive forces should continue to fight for more democratic control over these free trade and investment agreements because they are the harbingers of a new enforcement structure for facilitating international capital mobility.

HOW MOBILE IS INTERNATIONAL CAPITAL?

Trying to answer the question, 'How mobile is international capital?' is enormously puzzling primarily because different measures appear to give very different answers (Zevin 1992; Frankel 1993; Obstfeld 1995). Economists have two kinds of yardsticks by which to measure this mobility: quantities and prices. High levels of international capital mobility imply large amounts of international financial transaction in foreign exchange, stocks and bonds, businesses and factories. And, indeed, virtually all measures of international capital mobility making use of these types of data show a dramatic increase over the post-Second World War period, when measured in absolute terms and in relation to the size of national and world economies (Bosworth 1993).

This is by no means the whole story. Data on the net mobility of capital measuring the in- minus the outflow of capital in a given period of time (flows), or on an accumulated basis over time (stocks), give a very different picture. Data on net asset positions in the nineteenth and twentieth centuries (relative to GDP or their capital stock), which represent how much capital has been transferred from one country to others on a net basis over a long period of time, clearly show that there was much more capital mobility on a net basis in the late nineteenth century than there is in the late twentieth century.

Despite the high degree of international capital mobility encouraging wealthy households and institutional investors in one country to invest a substantial share of their wealth in stock and bonds in other countries, the degree of international diversification of investments is surprisingly low. For example, in December 1989, US investors held 94 per cent of their stock-market wealth in their home country stocks, Japanese investors 98 per cent in home stocks, and UK investors 82 per cent (Obstfeld 1995: 35). This lack of diversification exists despite a huge volume of transactions in foreign securities: for example, in 1989 over 500 billion dollars in US stocks and bonds were bought and sold by foreigners; in the same year, over 200 billion dollars (Canadian) in Canadian stocks and bonds were bought and sold by foreigners (Tesar and Werner 1992). Indeed, the rate of buying and selling domestic stocks (the so-called turnover rate) is substantially lower than that for foreign stocks – seven times lower in the case of the Canadian stock market (Tesar and Werner 1992, Table 12)!

Most damaging to the global case are the famous results of Martin Feldstein and Charles Horioka (1980). Feldstein and Horioka reasoned that if there was as great a degree of international capital mobility, then domestic investment would not bear any necessary relation to domestic saving. A country could have a high profit rate and a high rate of investment and, yet, a low rate of savings because it could simply borrow from abroad to come up with the funds it needed. If this were true, a country's level of investment would no longer be determined by its savings. Conversely, a country that had a high savings rate and a low domestic rate of profit, could simply invest abroad. Thus, over the long term, savings would be uncoupled from national investment.

In contrast to these predictions of the 'global' view, Feldstein and Horioka (and dozens of studies since) found that countries that want to invest more, must save more. They cannot borrow from abroad as the global view implies. Conversely, a country that increases its savings invests at home, not abroad. This view implies a high degree of international independence and a low degree of international capital mobility on a net basis – that is, very little capital is transferred either into or out of economies, on average. While some studies indicate that there has been a loosening of the relationship between saving and investment in the 1980s, with the United States borrowing large amounts from abroad and the Japanese lending large amounts on a net basis, the correlations between domestic saving and investment, even among the advanced capitalist economies, remain high (Obstfeld 1995; for a dissenting view, see Bosworth 1993).

What these data point to is a startling trend. The virtual explosion in the quantity of cross-border financial transactions compared to the amount of production, consumption and trade of goods and services has not led to the long-term transfer of financial resources from one economy to another as might have been expected. With the dramatic decline in formal governmental barriers to international capital movements in the last several decades, there is much less movement of equity investment from one economy to another although there has been an enormous increase in the gross mobility of short-term financial capital.

The second common way of measuring the degree of international capital mobility is to look at rates of return to financial assets in different countries. If capital is highly mobile, then, the rates of return on financial assets, properly adjusted for risk, should be equal in different countries. Once again, the picture is mixed. It holds relatively well for certain kinds of short-term financial assets, but not for longer-term equity assets nor for foreign direct investment (Zevin 1992; Frankel 1993; Obstfeld 1995)[3] This suggests a high degree of short-term international capital mobility. The result is that in order to attract funds, interest rates on dollar deposits in the Eurodollar markets in London have to be virtually equal to rates on dollar deposits in the markets in Tokyo.

But here, too, financial markets are not always co-operative. During the turbulent European currency crises of the summer and autumn of 1992, for example, large deviations in interest rates between offshore and onshore deposits opened up (Obstfeld 1995). Even in periods of tranquility, Zevin (1992) has shown that the degree of integration of short-term capital markets is no greater today than it was at the turn of the century. So the tremendous advances in technology cannot account for the integration of these markets, as a great deal of commentary erroneously claims.[4]

Similarly, much of the evidence with respect to foreign direct investment flows raises further questions about the new global system of financial markets. For instance, Epstein studied the rate of profit on US foreign direct investment abroad, looking at the profit rate on US foreign direct investment in twenty-one countries countries from 1951 to 1986. If declining transaction costs and reduced political barriers over that period had resulted in a higher degree of capital mobility, then one would expect to find less variation in rates of profit across countries as the post-war period wore on. However, variation in the rate of profit across countries in each year did not decline for two out of the three measures used; in other words, there is virtually no evidence of an increased tendency towards profit rate equalization over the post-war period.[5]

In the same paper, Epstein also looked at the sensitivity of US foreign direct investment to differentials in profit rates across countries. According to the same logic described above, a reduction in barriers to direct foreign investment ought to have made foreign direct investment more sensitive to profit rate differentials over time. However, he found no tendency for increased sensitivity. Finally, Koechlin studied the sensitivity of domestic investment by US firms to foreign profitability. He found that US domestic investment does not fall when its profitability declines relative to the profitability of investment abroad.

Empirical results like these call into question the degree to which multinational corporations are able to shift investments internationally in line with the global view of financial markets. Evidently, the globalized economy, if it exists at all, does not reflect the mainstream global Walrasian vision. Yet, with close to a billion dollars being traded daily on markets, the world of independent Keynesian welfare states is receding as well. Is there a theory of the way international financial markets work to explain these puzzling findings? And what does that theory imply about the ability of the nation-state to make policies to foster full employment, and egalitarian and sustainable growth?

THE ENFORCEMENT APPROACH TO UNDERSTANDING INTERNATIONAL CAPITAL MOBILITY

Much of the push towards deregulation and financial integration has been political, rather than technological (see Chapter 8, this volume). Because of this, all financial markets, even completely deregulated financial markets, require a political structure of power relations between creditors and debtors if they are to operate. This is particularly true of international financial markets.

The standard economic view of financial markets assumes erroneously that both lenders and borrowers have perfect information about each other's intentions, that both will do what they promise, that power relations are irrelevant to their behaviour, and that, apart from government regulations, the institutional environment within which lending takes place is irrelevant. In this situation, the prime determinants of the amount of lending are the opportunity for profitable trade (namely, a discrepancy between rates of return in one market relative to another), and transactions costs (that is, the costs of actually making the loan, or investment). It is only a small step from this analysis to the argument that, in the presence of very low transactions costs, rates of return on all assets will be the same, because if they were not, financial investment would flow from where returns were lower to where they were higher until all returns were the same.[6]

And from here comes the vision that characterizes the new conventional wisdom about international financial markets: low transaction costs and technological advances have led to the massive capital flows subjecting governments and citizens to strict interest rate and profit rate constraints.

However, in the last ten to fifteen years analysts of financial markets have grown increasingly sceptical of this view and have formulated alternative theories of the way such markets work (Stiglitz and Weiss 1981; Gintis 1986). This work stresses that financial markets are fundamentally different from goods markets.[7] In goods markets, money is exchanged today for goods today. By contrast, in financial markets a lender (investor) gives money today in the hope that he or she will be repaid (earn a return on) that investment tomorrow. In financial markets, then, the lender's information about future intentions of the borrower, the degree of trustworthiness and the power of the lender to get the borrower to live up to his/her commitments are crucial. In short, this perspective stresses that financial markets are characterized by imperfect information, that lenders and borrowers are opportunistic (they do not always do what they say), and that the power relations between lenders and borrowers are asymmetric and crucial for financial market outcomes. As a result, governmental and private institutions are used to gather information about the intentions of borrowers, and to try to enforce repayment to lenders. For lenders, what is critical is that these enforcement structures give them *confidence* that they will be repaid.

Until recently these insights have not been utilized to understand international capital mobility in general and the implications for national economic policies in particular (Eaton *et al.*, 1986). In a recent paper, Epstein and Gintis (1992) show that theories of finance which stress the problem of enforcement can help us to understand the nature of international capital mobility in today's world and the constraints and possibilities facing the nation-state.[8] The theory starts from the simple idea that lenders want to be repaid and borrowers would rather not repay. Thus, lenders need some type of enforcement of loan contracts if they are going to be willing to lend. In domestic lending there are various legal remedies which a lender can bring to bear to improve the chances of being repaid. In other words, there is a provision for the external enforcement of contracts such as a legal system.

The lack of such enforcement mechanisms poses the principal obstacle in international capital markets. Credit contracts must be executed through some other means such as credit rationing, threatened economic sanctions or military sabotage. In such markets, it is obvious that the mainstream ideal in which powerless individuals face a given interest or profit rate that will clear the market for lending or investment is incorrect. Instead, the enforcement model implies that power relations more than ever are central to the proper functioning of international credit markets despite the computer and satellite revolution. This is so for a very specific reason. With the decline of US economic hegemony over other nations, enforcement costs for international credit markets are now at least as high if not higher than in the nineteenth century. The fact is that the *transactions costs* have dramatically decreased with the removal of financial barriers but, by contrast, the *enforcement costs* have not.

The result is that in the 1990s major lenders are reluctant to lend enough on international money markets to equalize profit rates; some countries face credit rationing. Similarly, still other countries are not able to borrow as much as they want because they are worried that in the future their credit will be abruptly cut off. Thus, according to the enforcement model, the world is increasingly filled with *reluctant borrowers* and *reluctant lenders* due to a surplus of funds that, paradoxically, is the result of widespread credit rationing in both the industrialized and non-industrialized world.

What this model tells us is that rich industrialized creditor countries with large net foreign assets are likely to be few and far between. To qualify, these few economies must have the international economic, political and military power to enforce their international loans and investments. Great Britain and the US had such power in their heyday but have it no longer. By contrast, the oil-producing countries have not had anywhere near the power and so their influence quickly faltered.

The position of debtor countries, by contrast, is very different. They must attract loans and foreign direct investments. For example, they must orient a large part of their economies towards exporting and make themselves dependent on imports; in this way, debtor countries expose themselves to potential creditor sanctions and thereby reduce the likelihood that they will renege on their loan commitments.

The 'enforcement' model is thus consistent with the idea that countries can export and import huge amounts of capital over a limited period of time. But then, eventually, their ability to export or import capital will be limited by their economic growth and the enforcement capacities of creditors.

The offer of a collateral guarantee is the most effective means of enforcement, both in domestic and in international capital markets. In international capital markets, since national power limits the degree to which securities residing in one country can be seized by force from another, foreign lending or investment is the best hedge against uncertainty. The theory is that when country A lends or invests in country B it is the collateral guarantee for country B to lend or invest in country A. The two-way flows of financial investment are the best guarantee that debts will be paid; without this enforcement mechanism there would be very little capital movement from one country to the next.[9]

217

THE INTERNATIONAL CREDIT REGIME

These rules of the game and enforcement practices are embodied in what we call the International Credit Regime (Lipson 1985). The International Credit Regime consists of: (1) an Enforcement Structure which creditors institute in order to improve the likelihood that their debts will be paid back in full; and (2) a Repayment Structure that ensures that lenders will repay their debts and attract further investment inflows.

The enforcement structure of the post-Second World War period included the International Monetary Fund and World Bank (Broad 1988; Payer 1991), which offered credit and the stamp of approval to 'good' borrowers and attempted to discipline 'bad' ones by refusing to extend credit. This policy of identifying 'good' and 'bad' borrowers enabled private lenders to pick and choose between competing investment opportunities (Lipson 1985). Another aspect of the post-Second World War enforcement structure was the US government's commitment to free trade (Block 1977). This policy rewarded economies that played by the rules of the game, but imposed penalties on those that did not. Finally, despite the decline of the use of force in enforcing international credit relations since the nineteenth century, in the late twentieth century the US Marines, the Central Intelligence Agency and the massive programmes of military assistance all were employed to help the economic élites maintain their internal structures that were conducive to repayment.[10] All of the foregoing have been used both as the carrot as well as the stick to ensure that creditors honoured their debts.

The repayment structure allows creditors to more easily punish recalcitrant debtors. Military dependence on creditor nations also increases dependence and helps create a repayment structure. Making an economy dependent on foreign credit itself serves to reduce incentives for non-repayment and expedites repayment. Finally, institutions which limit the power of groups in society that threaten foreign property rights, or have an incentive to reallocate foreign debt payments toward domestic uses, enhance repayment. These institutions also constitute an important component of the repayment structure.

International credit relations thus impose strict curbs on the behaviour of countries which are involved in international financial markets. However, as the enforcement approach indicates, power relations in international credit markets are likely to be inherently asymmetrical with creditor nations having the power to enforce their investments on less-powerful debtor nations.

From the above it is possible to see why the International Credit Regime is the object of significant political struggle in both creditor and debtor nations. In creditor nations, for example, there may be political battles between industry and finance over the desirability of policies to increase large net creditor positions; domestic industry may oppose low tariffs which bankers support because the revenues generated by tariffs ensure that their loans will be quickly repaid. In debtor countries, workers and farmers may oppose dependence on foreign direct investment on the grounds that it makes it more difficult to exert their power over wages and work conditions. These fights over the enforcement structures and repayment structures are essentially political battles over a country's integration into the international economy and the limits imposed on its sovereignty.

Seen from this perspective, the relationship between nation-states and international capital flows is strikingly different than in the conventional wisdom that globalized financial markets largely crowd out the role of the state. In the enforcement view, state power provides the foundation stone for the smooth functioning of international financial markets.

But how much autonomy do states have in light of the current nature of international financial markets? How does the current International Credit Regime affect the ability of nation-states worldwide to mount policies that go against the tide? Finally, what can nations do to increase their autonomy *vis-à-vis* the international capital markets?

NATIONAL AUTONOMY AND INTERNATIONAL CAPITAL MOBILITY

Understanding the possibilities for alternatives to the neo-liberal policies of austerity and deregulation requires that the structure of these international capital flows and their accompanying political and economic institutions of enforcement be examined.

The essential problem posed by international capital mobility is that short-term capital mobility undermines a country's ability to undertake policies that threaten investor confidence in its economy. Countries which undertake macroeconomic policies, such as expansionary monetary or fiscal policy, or dramatic changes in tax or welfare policy, might find that investors react strongly by moving finance out of the country to invest in short-term assets abroad. When this occurs, this short-term capital flight can cause a precipitous decline in the exchange rate as well as a sharp rise in short-term interest rates as the central bank raises interest rates to try to prevent the depreciation of the currency.

Countries which experience abrupt outflows of capital as a result of a decline in confidence brought about by changes in policies will find it difficult to attract replacement finance simply by raising interest rates. This contrasts with the global position, which implies that increasing interest rates would suffice to keep the capital at home. Where international moneylenders doubt a country's capacity to repay, increases in interest rates will not be of much help. Indeed, jacking up interest rates may reduce its confidence even more by signalling that the country is such a high credit risk that the new indebtedness undermines its ability to service its debt.[11]

Hence, the combination of a high gross mobility of short-term capital plus

219

a low net mobility of long-term capital which is based on confidence in repayment structures, makes the constraints on short-term capital outflows potentially a serious constraint on economic policy.

However, it is important to note that these constraints are of a different kind than those implied by the conventional wisdom of globalization. According to this wisdom, countries are constrained by short-term rates of return and cannot deviate from those without bringing about possibly unwanted changes in exchange rates. The enforcement approach stresses, however, that what is at issue is confidence in the enforcement of financial contracts. Hence, if countries can undertake policies which enhance confidence then they may have more autonomy to undertake expansionary policies than the standard view implies (Epstein 1992; Rose 1994).[12] Hence, declines in interest rates or profit rates below world levels do not automatically engender capital outflows and exchange rate depreciations, assuming the level of confidence in repayment is increased accordingly.

To maintain enforcement confidence while pursuing policies which reduce rates of return at home below those abroad, institutional changes are required to win the support of the international moneylenders. A current example is the creation of independent central banks to convince investors that political groups supporting higher levels of indebtedness and inflation will not be able to influence decision-makers (Eichengreen 1992; Prem 1995).

The challenge facing progressives is how to create institutional structures that will reduce the capital flight that runs away as enforcement confidence is reduced, without at the same time abdicating goals of high levels of employment, an equitable distribution of resources, sustainable development and democratic control over the economy. Creating independent central banks is not likely to be the institutional choice best designed to reach these goals.

Currently there are three forces of change. Like the move towards independent central banks, they may enhance enforcement confidence and, therefore, the mobility of capital, but are unlikely to do so in such a way as to facilitate progessive economic goals. The first force of change are the so-called 'free trade' agreements such as NAFTA. They ought to be called 'free trade and investment agreements' because so much of the actual texts of the agreements guarantee foreign direct investment and international portfolio investment rights. Governments are required to extend the right of national treatment to foreign investors which prohibits governments from discriminating against foreign capital. As well, these free trade and investment agreements double as enforcement mechanisms to ensure prompt repayment of loans and debts. In the case of NAFTA, with new investments going to countries having a higher than average expected rate of profitability, there ought to be an increase in the flow of direct foreign and equity investment out of the US and Canada to Mexico (Koechlin and Larudee 1992).

The second trend now in evidence is the political programme of financial deregulation, particularly in the banking and financial sector. This should raise the already high levels of capital mobility and make the problems of macroeconomic management more acute than they already are.

Finally, countries have less democratic control over the formation of their national economic policies. Decisions that used to be determined by democratically elected legislatures will now be forced by non-elected commissions set up under the terms of these kinds of free-trade agreements. As well, the power of central banks to operate independently of elected popular bodies effectively places the control of money, credit and interest rates outside of democratic accountability. These kinds of policies in Western Europe, Eastern Europe and other parts of the globe reduce the possibility to enhance the power of groups who oppose international economic integration, driven by the market, to challenge these agreements. Is there an alternative set of policy responses to a world increasingly dominated by financial markets? Can the rules of the game be reformed to include more accountability than presently exists?

CONCLUSION

The control of capital mobility only makes sense by changing the rules of the game of the new international credit regime. The point of view developed here is that technology is not the only or even the major factor that creates capital mobility. Power and politics, established by the nation-state, establish the context for international capital mobility.

Countries need to decide what they want their position to be within the international economic system. But it is critically important to understand that the choice is not between free trade in financial assets vs. protection. Rather, the whole point of the enforcement approach to capital mobility is to show that so-called perfect mobility of capital only occurs where creditor and debtor countries undertake specific domestic and international structures and develop clearly enunciated rules of the game to facilitate this mobility. International credit markets do not enforce themselves except by severely limiting the amount of international credit and investment that flow across borders.

Élites who want to optimize international capital mobility need to have the upper hand in the political process. They in turn will want to construct political and economic institutions that enhance their dependency on international financial markets. However, this is not the only possibility facing countries. If broad-based popular groups are influential enough, an investment strategy can be devised to attract capital inflows which benefit the economy without having to incur most of the disruptive aspects of short-term capital mobility. But to do so, democratic groups must continue to fight over the content of the so-called free trade agreements; for these represent the enforcement regimes of the future. Setting a norm of democratic and

221

economic rights for the majority in all the major capital importing countries will be the set of constraints that international capital will learn to live with; because, as the enforcement approach suggests, it is ultimately political power that calls the tune in the arena of international investment.

NOTES

1 This chapter grew out of a joint research project with Herbert Gintis. I am indebted to him for many critical discussions of these issues.
2 By real capital mobility I mean foreign direct investment, that is, investment in equities abroad in a company in such a way as to give a measure of operating control over the company.
3 The short-term interest rate comparison which is thought to best measure the idea of international capital mobility is the comparison of interest rates on short-term deposits denominated in the same currency but in different financial centres – for example, a US dollar three-month deposit in the Eurodollar market vs. a US dollar three-month deposit at a New York bank. This comparison controls for exchange rate risk and other risks that might be differentially associated with different types of assets. Comparing interest rates on so-called covered investments, where investors have eliminated exchange rate risk by locking in a future exchange rate, is comparable and gives similar results (Frankel 1993).
4 The evidence of a high degree of capital mobility is much less promising with respect to rates of return to equity and to the profitability of foreign direct investment. Much of the recent research on equity diversification suggests that, even among the most advanced capitalist economies, risk-adjusted rates of return are not equalized among countries on stocks (Obstfeld 1995; Frankel 1993; Tesar and Werner 1992).
5 The three measures differ in the way the stock of foreign direct investment is measured: book value, market value and replacement value. In the first two, the variation in the rate of profit does not decline; whereas in the third it did. One possible reason for the failure of profit equalization to increase despite the decline in transaction costs is that the later period was characterized by increased instability in the world economy. If different countries were faced with different 'shocks' then their profit rates may vary. However, adjusting for the variation in shocks across countries did not change the basic results.
6 There can be risk differences between borrowers or investments. The standard theory argues that rates of return will be equalized except for a risk premium that will vary according to the riskiness of the investment. Hence, risk-adjusted rates of return will be equalized.
7 Though, as stressed by Gintis (1986) and Bowles and Gintis (1988), they share important characteristics with labour markets.
8 There is related important work by political scientists. For some most closely related to the work here see Lipson (1985) and Frieden (1989).
9 The enforcement approach has proved to be useful theoretically and empirically in explaining a number of important phenomena and historical periods in international financial relations: repayment experiences of debtor countries in the nineteenth century (Kelly 1992), the nature and determinants of key currency status (Frank 1994; Prem 1995), as well as the determination of net asset positions (Epstein and Gintis 1992).
10 Of course, there were much broader goals of US foreign policy implemented with the use of these carrots and sticks.

11 See Rose (1994) and Frank (1994) for models which illustrate these difficulties of attracting finance where credit rationing and concerns over confidence are at issue.
12 This belies the conventional wisdom that what Rose calls 'the Holy Trinity' cannot go together: high capital mobility, fixed exchange rates and an independent monetary policy. Rose finds, for example, that in the European Monetary System countries had a surprising degree of monetary independence despite having high levels of capital mobility and fixed exchange rates. He argues that a more important determinant of the degree of exchange rate stability is the ability of the government to convince investors that the band of exchange rate fluctuation will remain fixed.

BIBLIOGRAPHY

Banuri, T. and J. Schor (eds). 1992. *Financial Openness and National Autonomy.* Oxford: Oxford University Press.

Block, Fred. 1977. *The International Economic Disorder.* Berkeley: University of California Press.

Bosworth, Barry P. 1993. *Saving and Investment in the Global Economy.* Washington, DC: Brookings Institution.

Bowles, Samuel and Herbert Gintis. 1988. 'Contested Exchange: Political Economy and Modern Economic Theory.' *American Economics Association Papers and Proceedings* 78: 2 (May), 145–50.

Broad, Robin. 1988. *Unequal Alliance: The World Bank, The International Monetary Fund, and the Philippines.* Berkeley: University of California Press.

Crotty, James. 1993. 'The Rise and Fall of the Keynesian Revolution in the Age of the Global Marketplace', in Gerald Epstein, Julie Graham, Jessica Nembhard (eds), *Creating a New World Economy: Forces of Change and Plans for Action.* Philadelphia: Temple University Press, pp. 163–83.

Eaton, Jonathan, Mark Gersovitz, and Joseph E. Stiglitz. 1986. 'The Pure Theory of Country Risk.' *European Economic Review* 30, 481–513.

Eichengreen, Barry. 1992. *Golden Fetters.* Oxford: Oxford University Press.

Epstein, Gerald. 1992. 'Monetary Policy in the 1990s: Overcoming the Barriers to Equity and Growth', in Gary Dymski, Gerald Epstein and Robert Pollin (eds), *Transforming the US Financial System.* Armonk, N.Y.: M. E. Sharpe, ch.4.

Epstein, Gerald and Herbert Gintis. 1992. 'International Capital Markets and the Limits of National Economic Policy', in Tariq Banuri and Juliet B. Schor, *Financial Openness and National Autonomy.* Oxford: Oxford University Press.

Feldstein, Martin and Charles Horioka. 1980. 'Domestic Saving and International Capital Flows.' *Economic Journal* 90 (June), 314–29.

Frank, Ellen Tierney. 1994. 'Three Essays on Key Currencies and Currency Blocs.' Unpublished Dissertation, University of Massachusetts, Amherst.

Frankel, Jeffrey A. 1993. 'Quantifying International Capital Mobility in the 1980s', in Jeffrey Frankel, *On Exchange Rates.* Cambridge, Mass.: MIT Press.

Frankel, Jeffrey A. 1994. 'The Internationlization of Equity Markets', *NBER Working Paper No. 4590*, December. In Jeffrey A. Frankel, *The Internationalization of Equity Markets.* Chicago: University of Chicago Press.

Frieden, Jeffry A. 1989. 'The Economics of Intervention: American Overseas Investments and Relations with Underdeveloped Areas, 1890–1950.' *Comparative Studies in Society and History* 31, 55–80.

Gintis, Herbert. 1986. 'International Capital Markets and the Validity of National Macroeconomic Models.' Mimeo, University of Massachusetts, June.

Gordon, David M. 1988. 'The Global Economy: New Edifice or Crumbling Foundations?' *New Left Review* 168, 24–64.

Kelly, Patricia 1992. 'Ability and Willingness to Pay in the Age of Pax Britannia, 1890–1914.' Mimeo. University of Massachusetts.

Koechlin, Timothy. 1992. 'The Responsiveness of Domestic Investment to Foreign Economic Conditions: An Analysis of Seven OECD Countries.' *International Review of Applied Economics* 6: 2, 203–16.

Koechlin, Timothy and Mehrene Larudee. 1992. 'The High Cost of Nafta.' *Challenge Magazine*, September–October, pp. 19–26.

Lipson, Charles. 1985. *Standing Guard: Protecting Foreign Capital in the Nineteenth and Twentieth Centuries*. Berkeley: University of California Press.

Obstfeld, Maurice. 1995. 'International Capital Mobility in the 1990s', *NBER Working Paper No. 4534*. In Peter Kenen (ed.), *Understanding Interdependence: The Macroeconomics of the Open Economy*. Princeton, N.J.: Princeton University Press.

Payer, Cheryl. 1991. *Lent and Lost*. London: Zed Books.

Prem, Roohi. 1995. 'International Currencies and Endogenous Enforcement: An Empirical Analysis.' Mimeo, International Monetary Fund.

Rose, Andrew K. 1994. 'Exchange Rate Volatility, Monetary Policy and Capital Mobility: Empirical Evidence on the Holy Trinity', *NBER Working Paper No. 4630*, January.

Stiglitz, Joseph and Andrew Weiss. 1981. 'Credit Rationing in Markets with Imperfect Information.' *American Economic Review* 71, 393–410.

Tesar, Linda and Ingrid M. Werner. 1992. 'Home Bias and the Globalization of Securities Markets', *NBER Working Paper No. 4218*, November.

Zevin, Robert B. 1992. 'Are World Financial Markets More Open? If So, Why and With What Effects?', in Tariq Banuri and Juliet B. Schor, *Financial Openness and National Autonomy*. Oxford: Oxford University Press.

Part IV

GLOBALIZATION AND LABOUR

10

NEW WORK AND EMPLOYMENT RELATIONS
Lean production in Japanese auto transplants in Canada

Daniel Drache

INTRODUCTION

In all industrial countries, collective bargaining arrangements and trade unions are under fierce pressure to change and adapt to new competitive pressures. Governments are trying to negotiate social pacts with organized labour that offer workers little in return for concessions on labour reforms and wage rollbacks.[1] They are using their power to push through sweeping labour law reforms. The question is will the decline in union organization and bargaining power now in evidence in all industrialized countries be reversed? Or will the marginalization of organized labour on both sides of the Atlantic continue well into the twenty-first century?

The answers to these questions are anything but simple. Since the early 1980s, the North American automobile industry has been cutting production costs and economizing production time. All firms now need less inputs to produce a greater variety of products of higher quality at lower unit prices. Product cycles are shorter, design breakthroughs more frequent and effective and the workforce is smaller than ever (Womack 1991; Dankbaar 1993). The influence of Japanese-inspired lean production has given all companies regardless of national origin substantial savings with respect to the quality, design, workforce complement and the engineering aspects of the production process.

This chapter looks at the achievements and limitations of the lean production experience in the three Japanese auto transplants in Canada. In particular, this chapter attempts to capture the essential dynamics of the employment relationship under lean production.[2]

The thesis developed here is the following. With markets more in command than ever, if employers want a strong economic performance, they need to rely on their workforce, their most valuable asset. Reducing wages and entitlements and attacking the workplace representation is not going to help Canadian employers in a tough competitive world. A union-free workplace is highly problematic because Canadian employers need co-operation from their workforce. No matter how important the new technologies are, far more critical is the role of the productive worker in any enterprise. The workforce is the most valuable asset on the production site. In the words of the former president of Toshiba Corporation, 'no production machine can hope to match their flexibility or ability to respond to change'.[3] While lean production in certain respects may represent an advance over earlier production systems, the claim that it empowers workers is false. In reality, lean production expands management rights without developing a correlative concept of industrial citizenship where the interests of workers are genuinely balanced with those of employers.[4] Some claim (Womack *et al.* 1990) that Japanese production management or lean production represents a system of production where employers and workers can share a common destiny through the joint elaboration of new workplace norms and participatory employment relationships. This is not true. Indeed, if new technologies are to be used to transform the existing workplace, for their optimal deployment they require a modern system of collective bargaining to protect workers' rights from arbitrary management behaviour.

This chapter is divided into three sections. The first discusses the concept of lean production, with particular emphasis on how this production system deals with issues such as workplace representation, workplace participation and employment norms. The second reports on the experience of the three Japanese auto transplants in Canada (CAMI, Toyota Canada and Honda Canada), which represent the best examples of the application of the lean production model in this country. The third examines the critical features of the lean production model in the Canadian context that emerge from the experiences of the three transplants.

This chapter has used a variety of research techniques to explore the complex world of Japanese-style work relations. The principal information is derived from twelve in-depth interviews conducted by the author between June 1992 and July 1993 with representatives from the three Japanese transplants in Canada. At the CAMI plant, only union officials were interviewed. At the Honda and Toyota plants lack of union representation meant that only company officials were interviewed.[5]

LEAN PRODUCTION AND THE MODERN EMPLOYMENT RELATIONSHIP

Lean production as an ideal type

The term 'lean production' was popularized by James Womack *et al.* in the book *The Machine that Changed the World*, published in 1990 as the final report of the MIT International Motor Vehicle Program.[6] Lean production developed in Japan, with Japanese auto companies, particularly Toyota, the standard-bearers of the model. According to Womack *et al.*

(1990), the hallmarks of lean production are teamwork, communication and efficient use of resources, while the results are products with fewer defects produced with less factory space and labour input. Lean production represents a major advance over the mass production model which has characterized North American manufacturing since its development in the auto industry by Henry Ford early this century.

Table 10.1 Lean production as an ideal type

System of production	Model of productivity	Product design
Continuous improvement (*kaizen*)	Time management	Top-of-line engineering
Work teams	Sub-contracting	Short design cycle
Zero down time	Multi-skilling	Highly consumer sensitive
Zero defects	Savings by task simplification	Emphasis on quality and cost control
Continuous innovation	Small workforce	
Just-in-time production	Worker flexibility	
Union free	High stress levels	
Employment security	High productivity levels	

Source: Daniel Drache

A summary of the features of lean production as an ideal type developed by the author is found in Table 10.1. While no plant probably meets this ideal type, it is nevertheless useful for gaining an understanding of the nature of lean production. Key characteristics of the system of production are *kaizen* or continuous improvement, continuous innovation, work teams, just-in-time production, an emphasis on product quality as evidenced by zero defects, zero down time, a relatively high degree of employment security and a union-free environment. Key features of the model of productivity are time management, worker flexibility, high stress levels, high productivity levels, multi-skilling, a small workforce and savings by task simplification. Key characteristics of product design under lean production include top-of-the-line engineering, a short design cycle, highly consumer-sensitive products and emphasis on quality and cost control in product design.

A comparison with Fordism

Employment relationships in lean production differ significantly from those that developed under mass production or Fordism (Drache and Glasbeek 1992: 224–7). Under the old regime, work organization was a rules-based system that assigned a powerful role for unions in supervising and enforcing the collective bargaining agreement. Workers could not be fired without cause; layoffs were regulated by the collective agreement and shop floor conflict was settled by an arm's-length grievance system. The principle of delimiting managerial rights also extended to the shop floor. Work in mass-production settings relied on rigid job ladders, narrow job descriptions, a confrontational management–labour system, buffers at every step to avoid disruptions, low-quality production norms and multi-layered management hierarchies. Fordism's great strength was that it provided employers with a way to stabilize their workforce and yet achieve high levels of output.

The Fordist model of industrial relations struck a balance between management's prerogative to exercise total control over all aspects of production and the right of individual mass production workers to enter into a collective bargaining relationship. At first, employers fought tooth and nail against any delimitation of their authority. But eventually they saw that modern collective bargaining was an efficient institutional innovation in a mass employment setting (Sabel 1982). Their power remained intact but their authority was limited by the liberal tenets of due process and just cause (Arthurs 1967). Collective bargaining was conceived as a counterweight to the employer's untrammelled exercise of authority derived from property rights.

The innovative part of the Fordist employment contract was that wages were no longer subject to the universal market mechanism. By entering into a collective bargaining relationship, supply and demand were socialized because the parties had to negotiate the terms and conditions of work without employers simply turning around and sacking their workforce to keep wages low and the terms of work minimal. To this end, unions were given a new status in return for limitation of their strike rights. Companies were obliged to recognize the legally certified unions and bargain with them in good faith.

In addition to the differences, lean production shares some common features with its Fordist antecedent: fewer workers have to produce more cars, more quickly and in less time. Ford invented the rule; lean production rediscovered its importance and took it one step further by combining quality with volume. This is why the lean production model stresses the importance of workplace participation and worker motivation. Group work becomes the linchpin between a flexible production system and quality work.

Workplace representation

Non-unionized transplants like Toyota Canada and Honda Canada are intent on creating a functional alternative to unions through new management practices. They aim to minimize the number of work rules and introduce flexible work practices. These objectives are difficult to accomplish. Large plants are rife with problems. For workers, these problems can assume a huge importance because they concern fundamental issues such as working conditions (e.g. the number and accessibility of water coolers), discipline and, frequently, the ultimate employer weapon, dismissal.

A Japanese firm driven by productivity and efficiency concerns is in a difficult position. Its production methods are organized to reinforce a results-driven system. It may say that it respects its employees' rights, but the incessant drive to cut costs and boost productivity is likely to put aside employee rights when these rights conflict with the material interests of the company. In such a situation, a key issue is whether workers are likely to turn towards unions to fill the 'representation gap'.

Lack of worker representation in many lean production plants (other than the Human Resources Office of the company) raises serious questions about the long-term viability of such a highly sophisticated production system. Such a system relies on the most advanced labour-saving technology yet employs paternalistic forms of industrial citizenship.

Workplace participation

Second, the lean production model is designed to involve workers as 'self-directed participants' in the production process. However, this commitment by workers to a different kind of workplace is questionable because it entails such an enlargement of managerial rights. Basically, workers in these trans-plants have to rely on the goodwill of management to live up to their promises. Management has created a high-trust system where it is the self-appointed guardian of the system and it alone makes the rules. Without a third party to administer and enforce these rules there is no counterweight to the way management exercises its rights.

Does lean production mark a return to traditional concepts of authority despite the widespread use of work teams and other forms of on-the-job participation? Just how tenable are these Japanese workplace practices in a Canadian setting?[7]

Employment norms

If lean production did in fact offer a new employment relationship for workers, it would represent an improvement over existing employment norms and practices. There must be potential for this new employment relationship to emerge gradually over time with respect to extensive on-the-job training for production line employees, fewer repetitive strain injuries, a continuous technological upgrading of the assembly line, a gender-neutral distribution of work, higher wages and benefits to match the higher productivity levels and an autonomous management capable of taking decisions independently of the Japanese parent company.

As firms adopting lean production search for new ways to cut costs, it is far from clear whether their employment principles and practices constitute the basis for a modern concept of industrial citizenship (Boxes 10.1 and 10.2). Without clearly defined rules and norms to delimit the rights of management

> **Box 10.1 Employment Principles Under Lean Production**
>
> * self-direction but not self-management
> * work teams
> * work without supervision
> * *kaizen* or continuous improvement
> * employment security
> * company workplace representation
> * work simplification but also work intensification
> * greatly expanded management rights

> **Box 10.2 Checklist for a New Employment Relationship in Auto Transplants**
>
> * on-the-job continuous generic skills training
> * fewer repetitive strain injuries
> * technological upgrading of the production process
> * simplification of assembly line work
> * gender-neutral work assignment
> * productivity-sharing wage agreements
> * independent workplace representation
> * third party conflict resolution
> * an autonomous management structure with respect to technological and investment decisions

and an organizational hierarchy to permit workplace participation, what kind of workplace is envisaged? Is it significantly different from the work environment at Ford or GM? Yet, without proper workplace representation, will the transplants abandon their pledge of secure employment to their employees?

JAPANESE AUTO TRANSPLANTS IN CANADA

Overview

In the 1980s, because of the appreciation of the yen, trade barriers and political pressure, Japanese auto producers established production facilities in North America. Three Japanese firms located in Canada. Honda was the first to arrive, beginning production in 1986 in Alliston, Ontario. Toyota was second, establishing operations in Cambridge, Ontario in 1988. The third plant was a joint venture between Suzuki and General Motors called CAMI, which started production in 1989 in Ingersoll, Ontario.

In 1991, Japanese transplants accounted for 17 per cent of Canadian car production and a little more than 25 per cent of total market sales. Total investment by Japanese automakers now exceeds $1.4 billion (JAMAC 1992). Despite their relatively small weight in the Canadian auto industry,[8] the Japanese transplants have played a very important role in redefining employment norms for the entire industry (O'Grady 1993).

Table 10.2 Production profile of Japanese auto transplants in Canada

	CAMI	Toyota	Honda
Date of production start	1989	1988	1986
Number of production	2,000	1,000	1,200
Type of car	Suzuki Sidekick Geo Metro Chef	Corolla 4-door	Civic Hatchback
Parts supplier	High-end parts from Japan; low-end parts from Canada/US; maximum 50 per cent Canadian	High-end from Japan; only 30–40 per cent Canadian	High-end from Japan; only 30–40 per cent Canadian
Destination	85 per cent or more exported to United States	Same	Same
Technology	Above average; Japanese equipment	High-end super-automated	Leading edge machinery
Production time per vehicle	20 hours	18 hours	Not available
Number of problems per 100 cars, 1993	129 per 100 cars	71 per 100 cars	82 per 100 cars
J. D. Power	Plant ranked 37th out of 80 assembly plants	Ranked 1st	Ranked 4th
Number of minutes per die	12 minutes	8 minutes	Not available

Source: Daniel Drache

The three Japanese auto transplants operating in Canada have many common features as well as a number of important differences. (Tables 10.2, 10.3 and 10.4). Like the Big Three in general, all the transplants are located in Southern Ontario, export the bulk of their production to the United States, provide workers with above-average compensation, and employ sophisticated technology. Unlike the Big Three, all transplants rely on Japan for their high-end parts, are located in small town/rural settings, and, most importantly, use the lean production model of *kaizen* or continuous improvement based on work teams.

There are a number of differences between CAMI and the two other transplants that should be highlighted. In contrast to the operations of Honda Canada and Toyota Canada, the CAMI plant is unionized, employs a larger workforce, produces for the lower end of the market, has a lower ranking for product quality, and has been more successful in integrating women into the production line. Similarities and differences between the Big Three and the transplants and among the transplants will be elaborated in the next sections of the chapter.

Table 10.3 A synoptic view of employment practices of Japanese auto transplants in Canada

	CAMI	Toyota	Honda
Authority	GM style – confrontational	Corporatist – seeking to create an organic link between company and workforce	Paternalistic – motivating workers through company identity
Organizational hierarchy	Flat	Super flat	Flat
Wage levels	Slightly below Big Three	On par	On par
Gender mix	Workforce 20 per cent women; high level of integration of women on production line	15 per cent women; women poorly integrated on production line	15 per cent women; women poorly integrated on production line
Dispute resolution	Formal grievance system; very active	Informal; company-organized; some review powers in event of discharge	Informal; company-organized; low-level review procedures; effectiveness unclear
Workplace representation	Canadian Autoworkers Union (CAW) exclusive bargaining agency	Vigorously non-unionized	Deliberately non-unionized

Source: Daniel Drache

CAMI: high hopes for the GM–Suzuki partnership

CAMI, a General Motors and Suzuki joint venture or partnership, is a particularly interesting case study of new employment practices because it is the only unionized transplant in Canada. It is the largest Japanese transplant in Canada, with an annual capacity for building 200,000 cars and light trucks. In many ways, CAMI is unique among Japanese auto producers in North America. It brings together a Canadian union, Japanese production technology, American and Japanese ownership and produces a popularly priced car (Robertson *et al.*, 1992; CAW-Canada 1993b). This differentiates it from most other Japanese transplants in North America, which are largely non-unionized, are not joint ventures, and produce a product for the higher end of the market.

From the outset, CAMI has tried to elicit superior performance from its workforce by attempting to blend the lean production model with

234

Table 10.4 A comparison of human resources practices of Japanese auto transplants in Canada

	CAMI	*Toyota*	*Honda*
Organization of production	8–14 person production teams; *kaizen* and quality circles; company rewards innovation with points system to buy CAMI products	6–8 person production teams; *kaizen* and quality circles; cash incentives for money-saving suggestions to cut production costs	Variable sized production teams; quality circles and *kaizen*; innovation compensated by company
'Hard-skill' or technical training	Minimal for production	Minimal for production	Minimal for production
Appointment of team leader	Elected by co-workers	Chosen by company	Chosen by company
Overtime policy	Compulsory, up to 2 hours a shift	Compulsory; up to 1.5 hours a shift	Compulsory; 1 hour or more a shift
Repetitive strain injury	Permanent problem; unions see little evidence of improvement	Diminishing according to Toyota; below industry average	Not available
Quit rate, 1993	1–2 per cent per year	1–2 per cent per year	1–2 per cent per year
Age of workforce	85 per cent of workforce between 22 and 40 years old	Slightly older	Slightly older

Source: Daniel Drache

GM-trained industrial relations managers in a Canadian setting (Boyer 1992). A visitor cannot help but notice the large sign over the reception desk explaining CAMI's principal values: *kaizen* (continuous improvement), empowerment and employee responsibility, open communications and team spirit.

Workplace organization – the heart of the system

Management is looking to improve efficiency and lower costs from the synergy resulting from employee co-operation. The system is designed to enable CAMI to benefit from increasing productivity through labour-saving changes to the production process. All employees participate in work teams, ranging in size from six to ten members depending on responsibilities. Each team elects one of its members leader. Within the team, work tasks are rotated so that no production worker will do one assembly-line job for more than two hours. Gone from the production line is the foreman and most work is done without direct supervision.

Area managers are available when problems arise, but the workplace environment is very different from the closely supervised, highly structured, Fordist auto factory.

Production is organized around the principles of the lean production model. It is a highly automated process of continuous production. Just-in-time supply, quality circles, *kaizen* and zero defects are central features of the organization. It is a technologically driven system designed to support constantly higher productivity levels. In the car plant, the essential problem is to assure quality production from the moment that assembly work commences.

The company and the union – a living contract?

The desire to do things differently also extends to CAMI's relationship with the union. The company wanted a living contract; that is, an employment relationship which can evolve and develop. Hence, the idea that the rules and work procedures should not be specified in detail. In theory, union and management have joint responsibility to solve problems efficiently and quickly as soon as they arise. Area supervisors are given the authority to settle problems on the spot without recourse to the grievance system. It was hoped that few, if any, disputes would go to arbitration. The contract is very explicit on this point. CAMI did not want to be bound by inflexible precedent-setting arbitration decisions. Instead, CAMI proposed procedures that were to be innovative in finding 'realistic' solutions to settle workplace problems without a highly expensive legal procedure.

The company's philosophy of relying on informal problem-solving permeates the collective agreement. The language of co-operation and trust are omnipresent in the legal text. The contract stresses how it has to be 'administered in the spirit of mutual trust and in support of CAMI's values'. In the purpose clause, these values are again stressed calling on company and union to 'work productively, avoiding confrontation' (CAW-Canada 1993a). In the standard management rights clause, the union acknowledges the right of management to a flexible system. It states that 'the union recognizes the right of CAMI to formulate, revise and publish personnel policies, which shall be administered in a fair, impartial and consistent manner to all members of the bargaining unit'.

Work methods are also protected by the collective agreement. Again, the norms are clear. The team leader and the team have a responsibility to carry out their responsibilities in exemplary fashion and are required to promote the spirit of 'teamwork and co-operation'.

For the union, the most difficult problem has been the lack of clearly articulated rules and the arbitrariness of company decisions. Without written rules, management has wide discretionary authority. This can result in inconsistent disciplinary actions which are perceived as unjust.

For a minor work code infraction, one worker may receive only a warning from a friendly supervisor, while another worker may be disciplined for the same infraction by another supervisor. For example, CAMI has formally forbidden employees to read material on the job, yet does not object to employees reading company material. So, what is the rule? Some material? No material? The issue is fundamental to both the company and the union. If there are to be rules, they have to be applied in an even-handed fashion.

Recently, the company installed a television camera on the walkway between the cafeteria and the production facilities despite union objections. The intention was to monitor workers leaving their workstations during production time. Such actions raise questions about the company's commitment to treating workers with 'dignity and respect'. While it pays lip service to problem-solving, trust and communication, CAMI's actions can at times fall short of its stated ideals.

Despite good intentions, it has been very difficult for CAMI to forge a conflict-free relationship with its workforce. In the first year of operations, there were few grievances. Basically, the union adopted the attitude that it would try to solve problems as they arose. But, by the second year, the number of grievances multiplied. Inability to settle many of these issues was a major factor, along with monetary demands, leading to the 1992 strike. At that time, there were over ninety outstanding disputes, most relating to the company's exercise of its discipline rights.

Given vague or non-existent clauses in the collective agreement, many crucial work rules were not properly defined. For instance, if a worker is injured on the job and sent to the hospital, who decides whether the injury entitles the worker to collect salary benefits as stipulated in the contract? The worker's doctor? The company doctor? The absence of clearly specified procedures to handle such routine issues has been an obstacle in the way of building a high-trust system of co-operation.[9] As a result, many company workers now perceive CAMI's management as being arbitrary and inconsistent. The failure to deliver on its promises of making CAMI into a better workplace has made workers highly suspicious of many of the company's practices to increase participation.

Since the signing of the 1992 contract, there have been over forty new grievances, most involving minor work infractions. According to the union, the problem again was 'a company that wants to control everything'. This has led to a power struggle that now colours every aspect of company–union relations. In theory, CAMI is committed to joint problem-solving. But with respect to key issues such as time-off, scheduling of work, overtime, relief work, workforce size, and even the use of parking lot exits, the union feels CAMI management wants to minimize their input even when 'joint-decision-making and open communication' is provided for by the collective agreement and by CAMI's own philosophy.

The fact that the company has not itself been open with its workforce has created an atmosphere of distrust. Top management is perceived to manipulate its own rules in its own interests.[10] Not unexpectedly, many of its workers have become disillusioned with what they perceive as CAMI's record of broken promises.

Training is considered an essential element of the lean production model. Plant officials constantly emphasize how much time and energy is spent on continuous skill training. Yet, the picture at CAMI is far from the ideal model of lean production. It is true that skilled tradespersons receive considerable training. This is not surprising. Skilled workers who repair machinery must maintain high skill levels. But these workers represent only a small minority of the workforce. The majority of production employees have received no additional 'hard skills' or technical training since being hired. Instead they receive considerable low-cost 'soft skill' workplace orientation (Premier's Council of Ontario 1990).

After more than four years of production, much of the training at CAMI is largely in-house, at low cost to management and designed to promote the human resource side of the work-team philosophy. The union has emphasized training in contract negotiation and in 1992 won support for upgrading the educational qualifications of the workforce. The employer now pays tuition costs for workers who take courses at a nearby university.

The failure to upgrade the hard skills of the workforce is related to the fact that there have been only incremental changes to its production technology since the plant was opened. While CAMI constantly stresses the need for implementing *kaizen* principles throughout its assembly process, much of the technical innovation is carried out elsewhere. Management makes no secret of the fact that all of the engineering decisions are taken as a matter of company policy in Japan.[11] By Japanese standards, Suzuki is not a leading edge firm. It lets others innovate and then refines the new technological breakthroughs to fit its production needs. In this fundamental sense, CAMI is run like an American branch plant. Research and development remains tightly controlled by its head office, while Canada is regarded as a production site mainly for assembly work (Porter 1992).

Joint problem-solving

At CAMI, the low level of skill training for most of the production workers reflects a deeper problem – namely, the low level of joint problem-solving. To the untrained eye, the plant looks like a factory out of the twenty-first century. It is an open-plan operation with many windows, good air-circulation, brightly painted and very clean. Yet, many of the production methods are not as advanced as those in operation at Toyota Canada and Honda Canada. Certainly, CAMI is not at the cutting edge of car production technology.

Many workers are not convinced that CAMI is as automated as it could be, and point to the poor ergonomics record as proof of a failure to automate. For instance, at the Chrysler Bramalea plant the underside of the vehicle is built on a pallet. The pallet may be as radical an innovation in the auto assembly as the moving assembly line was in Ford's time. The pallet turns the vehicle so that the operator does not have to bend to put parts in the interior. Nothing like this exists at CAMI. The high number of repetitive strain injuries because of limited automation is a source of constant tension between CAMI and its workforce. Many problems arise from the failure of management to be continuously innovative in its production methods. The union charges that it is cheaper to stay with standard practices than commit resources to upgrade the line. The unwillingness of CAMI to invest in new production practices has become a contentious issue. So far the company has shown little enthusiasm for settling these matters. Its GM-trained managers have refused to use the problem-solving mechanisms in the collective agreement creatively in order to reduce this source of worker discontent. In 1992, union officials reported that there were over 150 work refusals which resulted in 106 hours of lost production for the plant. This figure corresponds to two full weeks of production.

A key indication of the effectiveness of the lean production model is the degree of downtime. The existence of considerable downtime at CAMI shows that the model is not being successfully applied. This is because many of the key elements of lean production are missing, including training, joint problem-solving, constant upgrading of the production process and the development of a viable concept of industrial citizenship premised on transparent rules and procedures. Far from being a pure model of a very dynamic system of production, CAMI is a static adaptation of lean production's management practices. Its early promise of new and better employment relationships has not been realized.

Toyota's productivity paradox – a mixture of old and new

In comparison to CAMI, Toyota Canada has developed a highly innovative system of production while following a more traditional employment relationship with its workforce. It combines a sophisticated model of lean production with an expanded belief in management rights. Management has attempted to create a functional equivalent of union representation. This more traditional model of workplace organization has not been put to the test by its workers. In the early 1990s, high levels of local unemployment mollified the workforce; many workers feel lucky to have a well-paid job. Turnover is consequently very low – less than 2 per cent annually. In these conditions, the Canadian Auto Workers (CAW) have found it difficult to gain a foothold. But there are, none the less, real limitations to this form of corporate organization.

Toyota's Cambridge facilities were designed for a workforce of 1,000 production workers, yet it functions with a much smaller complement. Even though the company is looking to expand its production capacity, it is not hiring more people even when they are needed to balance the line.

In 1993, the Toyota Canada Cambridge plant ranked third out of eighty auto assembly plants in North America in terms of product quality according to the J. D. Power and Associates (1993) product quality survey. In 1992, it was second.[12] The secret behind this impressive performance lies in the plant's productivity record. In the car industry, improved productivity comes from a variety of factors, including introduction of more advanced technology, simplification of manual operations, skill-upgrading, outsourcing of difficult operations, and work intensification. Toyota Canada likes to think that it is their management system which has resulted in top performance. The workers argue that it is their commitment and skills that has made the critical difference. In fact, there is no single answer.

According to management experts, roughly 40 per cent of any manufacturing-based advantage comes from the layout, design and structure of its operations (Skinner 1989). Another 40 per cent comes from changes to equipment and process technology. A final 20 per cent arises from conventional cost-cutting. Most firms assume that their competitive position is best strengthened by running cost-reduction programmes alongside their goal of boosting production by taking a long-term view. Any or all of these factors will boost productivity. What is key is the mix of the company's strategy and the motivation and skill of the workforce.

With a young workforce, Toyota Canada has reintroduced the basic principle of car production used by every car producer since Henry Ford invented the moving assembly line: simplification of jobs for each operator, but intensification of the amount of work performed by everyone on the line. Lean production does not permit speed-up in the traditional way. This is because if the line moves too quickly, the number of defects increases. Therefore, the company has to rely on a different tack. It uses a more scientific approach to squeeze time out of motion. In this regard, *kaizen* has made a significant difference.

Neo-Taylorism: a lesson from the past used in the present

The *kaizen* style of organization is the essential means to socialize the workers into the company's system. The drive to create a loyal corporate employee is the chief source of the company's quest for productivity and is the central reason why 'Toyotaism' remains a hard sell as an ideology.

Despite the existence of work teams and quality circles, Toyota does not have effective procedures to settle disputes that arise in the mass production setting concerning job assignment, and attendance and leave procedures. Without these safeguards, the participatory rights of workers to delimit managerial authority are limited.

Toyota's Cambridge plant is a classic instance of mixing the 'old' ways of squeezing a better efficiency performance out of the workforce by tighter discipline on a department by department basis. Work teams are the linchpin in this strategy. Workers have to become involved to ensure that the production norms based on Taylorist time and motion studies and high standards set by the company are, in fact, met. Each team has to find ways to squeeze 'waste' out of the system. While this goal does not immediately threaten individual jobs, life on the line does not get any easier for the individual operator. The stress levels are high even if the work becomes simpler to execute. The main beneficiary of 'cutting time out of motion' is the company. It is able to cut direct labour costs and be as innovative as possible by shortening lead times, improving customer service, by adopting flexible production schedules and contracting outwork to low-cost suppliers.

One reason why Toyota Canada does so well is that it continues to rely on contracting-out to cut costs. While it pays its workers an hourly rate of roughly $19, it holds down manufacturing costs by relying on US and Mexican sub-contractors for as much as 40 per cent of component parts and sub-assembly units. No more than 40 per cent of the components come from high-cost Canadian suppliers while almost all the high value-added components like the engine and drive train come from the Japanese parent corporation. Management makes no secret of the fact that many of its suppliers are located in the American 'sun belt' where the hourly rates are no higher than $8–10 (US) and in Mexico where workers are only paid roughly the equivalent of $2.25 Canadian an hour for sub-assembly work.[13]

In addition to cutting costs by sub-contracting, Toyota Canada pushes its workforce very hard. It schedules considerable compulsory overtime when required. Toyota has a young workforce capable of putting in long hours. With young families, they are eager to take the extra work when available. Again, Toyota is no different from the Big Three auto producers. But where it has an advantage over the competition is that it has constantly employed a small workforce. This is probably its most effective cost-cutting weapon in its drive for efficiency and productivity.

Honda's corporate structure: branch plant or transplant?

In many respects, Honda Canada is like the other transplants in believing that its work teams and other innovative employment practices entitle it to a union-free workplace. It subscribes to a results-driven system that broadens its managerial prerogative to reward, discipline and discharge its employees. If a collective agreement were in force, Honda would undoubtedly insist on a limited role for union participation, not only at the shop-floor level but throughout the production chain (Womack 1991). This is why its senior management is overtly anti-union.[14] They expect to exercise their authority without restrictions over the workforce.

Management is relying on *kaizen* practices to boost productivity levels to their optimal levels as quickly as possible. From this point of view, it is not readily apparent how different this workplace is from any of its Big Three counterparts such as at the best Ford and GM assembly plants in North America. Auto work at Honda remains a high-stress vocation that is physically demanding. Workers are able to stop the line only when they see that there is a production problem, but this does not happen frequently. What is much in evidence is that there is less need for constant supervision because the responsibility for overall production surveillance is now shared by all employees. Each employee is expected to be an assembly-line watchdog.

Managerial rights: still the core issue

In terms of the way management at Honda Canada exercises its supervisory prerogative, there is no evidence to suggest that it is a more enlightened employer than auto companies adopting Fordist management principles. As a producer of a quality car, it has had to find ways to increase the pace of the assembly line to meet its production target. Its answer to this challenge has been anything but innovative. It uses traditional practices to motivate its employees: compulsory overtime, a bonus system for rewarding employees whose suggestions result in cost savings and, most important of all, a great deal of management paternalism.

At Honda Canada, senior management wants the employee to identify with the firm. It believes that this sense of belonging to a corporate entity, if properly nurtured, is the best guarantee to keep unions out of the plant and employees satisfied. Within Honda

Canada's concept of a modern employment relationship, there is no system of life-long employment of the kind that is found in Japan. But there is a clear company objective to concern itself with maintaining and developing the morale and abilities of employees. This is why a feeling of belonging may develop (Matusomoto 1991).

It is necessary to qualify this outlook. The worker is put in this position by being forced to share responsibility with management that each car produced meets the high production norms. However, compared to the way Japanese companies operate at home, the level of worker participation is very low. For instance, there is no fully fledged labour–management consultation system.

The company has no obligation to consult its employees on important matters such as the modification of production lines, the establishment of new plants, worker health and safety and worker benefits. It is only natural that a certain degree of conflict will arise between the interests of management and workers. Employees who are excluded from management decision-making will see issues in a very different light. There is no mechanism that solicits the views of workers and regularly incorporates them into management practices.

Two further uncertainties

With such an entrenched traditional management structure, it is doubtful that Honda Canada can be an innovative employer in dealing with its employees. On the basis of the company's internal structures, its workers are workers first and corporate employees a distant second. Because they are marginal to the company's decision-making structure, it is hard to see how a new employment relationship is possible. Without an effective mechanism of workplace representation, joint problem-solving is not possible. Decision-making in Honda Canada is concentrated at the top and relies heavily on a traditional American style of management.

The bigger quandary facing Honda Canada is that, despite having a streamlined production system, it has a very bureaucratic management structure with the parent company in Japan. It is run like a traditional branch plant with little autonomy over investment and technology decisions. Honda Canada must seek the approval of its parent company for all major decisions regarding new investment. This includes not only the purchase of equipment but any substantial modification of production methods and procedures. The key, long-term management decisions are made in Japan even though management is committed to building a strong Canadian operation.[15] The question is whether the parent company will allow its Canadian managers to take control (Walmsely 1992). Until now, Honda Canada has been run like an American branch plant.[16]

CRITICAL FEATURES OF THE LEAN
PRODUCTION IN CANADA

The three case studies shed important light on work practices inspired by the lean production model of workplace organization. Despite differences in management and market strategies, CAMI, Toyota Canada and Honda Canada share much in common, relying on a highly skilled and stable workforce from a rural/small-town-based labour market. All three transplants are seen as success stories that rely on sophisticated production techniques. What they share in common is that in a global economy subject to competitive pressures, efficiency driven corporations want as much power as possible to organize every production detail (Drache and Gertler 1991). From the point of view of the development of a balanced employment relationship between management and labour, the experiences of the three Canadian transplants are not reassuring.

First, instead of being delimited, managerial authority has been expanded beyond existing norms. The Japanese manufacturers have seriously underestimated the need for effective arm's-length conflict resolution procedures. It is clear that workers need independent representation with regard to issues such as discipline, scheduling, pay, and promotion.

Second, the workplace is not gender neutral. Women can now be integrated into almost all aspects of line production thanks to new labour-saving technologies but, for the moment, in two of the transplants, this has not been the case. Only at the unionized CAMI plant, have women been integrated into the production line. This may come later at the other two plants, but, without independent workplace representation, it seems unlikely.

Third, there are doubts about the ability of the Japanese transplants in Canada to offer long-term employment security, a key element of the lean production model, to their workers. Canadian firms have preferred to lay off their workforce in the downturn of the volatility of the business cycle in this country. Moreover, the existence of unemployment insurance as an adjustment mechanism encourages layoffs. Consequently, the long-term employment security promise implicit in the lean production model may only be applicable in countries like Japan where swings of the business cycle were less pronounced. The volatility of the Canadian business cycle suggests that even with relatively small workforces, the three Japanese transplants may well have difficulty in avoiding layoffs if there is a prolonged slump in the auto market.[17]

Fourth, the lean production model still remains strongly Fordist in the assembly operations despite the different types of workplace participation schemes, with the result that the work effort has intensified. The drive to cut costs through *kaizen* has meant that the transplants have perfected many Fordist techniques. The Japanese concept of work simplification is essentially a labour-saving philosophy for taking fewer steps in order to find ways to exert less effort. *Kaizen* has a decidedly neo-Taylorist dimension to it despite the fact that its operative principle is that workers themselves, not engineers, solve production bottlenecks.

In these conditions, productivity means doing more assembly line work faster. The great attraction for management is that if an entire work team is finding more efficient ways to produce, productivity improves sharply. For the lean production employer, work simplification becomes a permanent way of life, a means of increasing efficiency without sacrificing quality. So, unlike a Fordist-style factory where productivity meant 'speed-up' and poorer workmanship, in the lean production system group intensification of production holds one of the keys to a shorter product cycle and lower unit labour costs. For the workforce, however, the daily effect of the lean production system creates a demanding factory environment because of the constant pressure to intensify work effort.[18]

Fifth, the recent Canadian experience with lean production has taken place in a high unemployment environment. When the unemployment rate nears 12 per cent, any model may be said to work. What will happen when regional unemployment levels fall and employees have better employment alternatives? Will the auto workers at Honda Canada and Toyota Canada continue to support management's desire for a non-union workplace? Compared to other industrial settings, the transplants pay well. On the other hand, with such high levels of productivity their wages should be higher than in many of the Big Three plants. This, however, is not the case. Job enrichment and job enlargement does not mean more take-home pay. Should unemployment levels decline, all these employment practices will be put to the test. Workers will be able to march with their feet or decide to bargain with their employer for new and more favourable terms and conditions of work and employment.

CONCLUSION

The ultimate aim of lean production is to cut costs. To achieve this, lean production has developed employment practices (e.g. work teams, long-term employment security guarantees) which give the worker more independence of action and greater employment stability than was the case in rules-based, layoff-prone Fordist workplaces. But the experience of the Japanese auto transplants in Canada shows that this

245

experience can be a double-edged sword for workers. Instead of resulting in the development of an industrial citizenship where the interests of workers are genuinely balanced with those of employers, lean production can result in expanded managerial rights (particularly in non-unionized workplaces) and in the intensification of work to meet the higher production norms. Unless Japanese transplants address the inadequacy of many of their new work practices, they will remain an insufficient basis to build a lasting system of industrial relations. This is the uncertain future confronting lean production in the 1990s.

NOTES

The author would like acknowledged the assistance of all individuals who agreed to be interviewed for this research project. He would also like to thank Robert Boyer, Arthur Donner, H. J. Glasbeek, Andrew Sharpe and John Holmes for useful comments.

1 The Ontario NDPs social contract embodies the shift in government policy to reduce the collective bargaining rights of public sector and (by implication) private sector unions. It is but one example of this disquieting trend. For a more general discussion, see Daniel Drache and Harry Glasbeek, *The Changing Workplace* (Toronto: Lorimer, 1994).

2 An earlier version of this chapter appeared in *Canadian Business Economics*, Spring 1994, pp. 45–59.

3 *Globe and Mail*, 7 June 1994.

4 The concept of industrial citizenship includes a minimum *six principal components*: a number of agreed-upon rules and norms to delimit the rights of management; an organizational hierarchy to permit workplace participation; a broad-based pay structure to enable workers to share productivity gains; a gender-neutral pay and employment setting that promotes access and equity for women; an independent dispute resolution mechanism free of management interference; and the guarantee of autonomous workplace representation by a bona fide union or its equivalent. These six aspects of industrial citizenship are protected by a number of minimum standards, human rights-type statutes and contract of employment and collective bargaining provisions (Arthurs 1967; Sabel 1982; Drache and Glasbeek 1992).

5 Field interviews bring much empirical information to light. However, the researcher should be aware of the limitations of this approach. First, since researchers must choose a sample of persons to interview out of a larger universe, those selected may not be representative and bias may emerge. Second, interviews capture opinions and views at a particular point in time and responses may change over time. To believe otherwise is to forget that research interviews function like a thermometer which helps identify the major trends and changes in the social climate. In factories, the dynamics between workers, team leaders, union personnel and supervisory and engineering personnel constantly fluctuate.

6 For additional discussion of lean production, see Berggren (1992), Adler (1993) and International Labour Office (1993). See Fucini and Fucini (1990) for an excellent study of the experience of the lean production model in a Mazda auto assembly plant in Detroit, Michigan.

7 The auto industry has a long tradition of spontaneous rank-and-file work protest. In the transplants it could take a number of yet-to-be-determined forms,

including a successful unionization drive of non-unionized plants, high labour turnover, a fall-off in product quality, increased absenteeism, wildcat strikes, etc.

8 By any standard set of economic indicators, the Big Three auto companies, and not the Japanese transplants, continue to be the heart of Canada's auto industry. One out of every five cars produced in North America originates from an Ontario-based North American car assembler. Canada's car industry turned out over 2 million cars in 1993 with a workforce of over 60,000 production workers. If the auto parts industry is included the figure totals close to 140,000 production jobs (Donner and Lazar 1993). Chrysler is the smallest car assembler in Canada yet produces more cars than all the transplants combined.

9 From interview May 1993.

10 From interviews with union executive.

11 CAMI is by no means unique. In my interviews with the plant managers at Toyota and Honda, I was told much the same story: engineering decisions are the preserve of head office in Japan.

12 Other Canadian auto assembly plants also ranked highly. Both Ford, St Thomas and Honda, Alliston, were in the top five. The Volvo Dartmouth plant ranked fourteenth.

13 The labour rights of Mexican workers are not protected from aggressive multinational employers. Recently, under the terms of the NAFTA side deal, three complaints have been filed by the AFL-CIO with the National Administrative Office of the US Department of Labor against Sony, General Electric and Honeywell for firing workers for seeking to organize. NAO can only issue a non-binding report which will do little to force these multinationals to change their ways. *Financial Times* of London, 11 May 1994.

14 From interviews with plant and human resources managers.

15 From an interview with the Canadian plant manager, July, 1992.

16 To make matters worse, Honda Canada's future ability to expand is extremely uncertain in the light of the signing of the North American Free Trade Agreement (NAFTA) and growing American protectionism. Under the Canada–United States Free Trade Agreement (FTA), Honda is exempt from paying customs duties on parts and is able to ship assembled cars duty-free into the US market. American customs officials allege that Honda Canada has not met the 50 per cent North American content rule. As a result, it has been slapped with customs duties (*Business Week*, 1991). If this penalty stands, Honda Canada will be forced to reconsider its production strategy of using Canada as an export platform to ship Canadian-made cars to the United States. If Japanese transplants in Canada are discriminated against under the NAFTA, they will not have the same access to the US market as the Canadian Big Three. The consequence of this 'trade barrier' will be a major blow for any expansion plans. In these conditions, it will be difficult for Honda Canada to offer its employees life-time security when it does not have secure access to its principle market.

17 The fact that consumers are keeping their cars longer will have a negative impact on future sales and make the adjustment process ever more difficult to manage. Certainly, the one-time dominance of the Japanese in the North American market will come under increasing pressure. Consumers are less ready to pay a premium price for Japanese cars. Since 1985, the Big Three have invested heavily in Japanese-inspired engineering practices. This has led to a closing of the quality gap between Japanese producers and the North American assemblers. Faced with these new competitive pressures, the Japanese transplants face an uncertain future in the North American market.

18 Unionized workers through collective bargaining tend to have greater ability to

capture productivity gains than non-unionized workers. Without a union, productivity growth is likely to exceed any real wage increases unless there are offsetting factors.

BIBLIOGRAPHY

Adler, Paul. 1993. 'Time-and-Motion Regained.' *Harvard Business Review*, January–February, pp. 97–108.

Arthurs, H.W. 1967. 'Developing Industrial Citzenship: A Challenge for Canada's Second Century.' *Canadian Bar Review* 45.

Berggren, C. 1992. *Alternatives to Lean Production: Work Organization in the Swedish Auto Industry*. Cornell International Industrial and Labour Relations Report No. 22. Ithaca, N.Y.: ILR Press.

Boyer, Robert. 1992. *La Suprenante Capacité D'Hybridation Du Modèle Japonais: L'exemple de la CAMI (Suzuki-General Motors, Ingersoll, Ontario)* Paris: Gerpisa.

Business Week. 1991. 'Honda: Is It An American Car?' 18 November.

Business Week. 1992. 'Detroit South Mexico's Auto Boom: Who Wins, Who Loses.' 16 March.

CAW-Canada. 1993a. *Agreement Between CAMI Automotive and CAW Local 88*. Toronto: CAW.

CAW-Canada Research Group on CAMI. 1993b. *The CAMI Report: Lean Production in a Unionized Auto Plant*. September. Toronto: CAW.

Dankbaar, Ben. 1993. *Economic Crisis and Institutional Change: The Crisis of Fordism from the Perspective of the Automobile Industry*. Maastricht: Maastricht Economic Research Institute.

Donner, Arthur and Fred Lazar. 1993. 'The Outlook for the North American Auto Sales and Implications For Ontario.' Ontario Ministry of Industry, Trade and Technology Special Adviser on Economic Adjustment for the Province of Ontario, Toronto, Ontario.

Drache, Daniel and Meric Gertler (eds). 1991. *The New Era of Global Competition, State Policy and Market Power*. Montreal: McGill–Queen's University Press.

Drache, Daniel and H. J. Glasbeek. 1992. *The Changing Workplace: Reshaping Canada's Industrial Relations System*. Toronto: James Lorimer.

Fraser, Damian. 1993. 'Sony in Mexico; Labour Complaints.' *Financial Times*, 14 May.

Fucini, Joseph J. and Suzy Fucini. 1990. *Working for the Japanese: Inside Mazda's American Auto Plant*. New York: Free Press.

International Labour Office. 1993. *Lean Production and Beyond: Labour Aspects of a New Production Concept*. Geneva: International Institute for Labour Studies.

Japan Automobile Manufacturers Association of Canada (JAMAC). 1992. *JAM Canada Annual Report*. Toronto.

Matusomoto, Koji. 1991. *The Rise of the Japanese Corporate System*. London: Kegan Paul International.

O'Grady, John. 1993. 'Direct and Indirect Evidence on the Extent of Changes in Work Organization in Canada.' Toronto: Premier's Council on Economic Renewal.

Porter, Michael. 1992. *Canada at the Crossroads: The Reality of a New Competitive Environment*. A Study Prepared for the Business Council on National Issues and the Government of Canada. Ottawa.

Power, J.D. and Associates. 1992. *The Harbour Report 1989–92*. Los Angeles.

Power, J.D. and Associates. 1993. *1993 New Car Initial Quality Study.* Los Angeles.

Premier's Council of Ontario. 1990. *People and Skills in the New Global Economy.* Toronto.

Robertson, David, James Rinehart, Christopher Huxley and the CAW Research Group on CAMI. 1992. 'Team Concept and Kaizen: Japanese Production Management in a Unionized Auto Plant.' *Studies in Political Economy* 39, Autumn.

Sabel, Charles. 1982. *Work and Politics.* Cambridge: Cambridge University Press.

Skinner, Wickham. 1989. 'The Productivity Paradox.' *Harvard Business Review,* July–August.

Toyota Canada. 1993. *Toyota Today.* Toronto.

Walmsely, Ann. 1992. 'Trading Places.' *Globe and Mail Report on Business,* March.

Womack, James. 1991. 'The Lean Difference: An International Productivity Comparison and the Implications for U.S. Industry.' *Viewpoint* 17, March.

Womack, James P., Daniel T. Jones and Daniel Roos. 1990. *The Machine That Changed the World: The Story of Lean Production.* New York: Rawson Associates.

11

GLOBALIZATION, LABOUR MARKETS AND PUBLIC POLICY[1]

Gordon Betcherman

For labour in a rich country like Canada, globalization is a 'two-edged' sword. On the one hand, international trade and investment historically have brought workers job opportunities, higher wages, and gains as consumers. On the other hand, the growing competitiveness and the increasing sophistication of international capitalism have raised threats of downward pressures on wages, working conditions, and protective standards. As the North American free trade debates in recent years have underlined, workers are deeply concerned about the ability of existing national institutions to meet their needs in a global economy.

This chapter examines the implications of closer economic integration for Canadian workers and for Canadian labour policy. How real is globalization and what are its labour market impacts? What are the resulting challenges facing policy-makers? To what extent does globalization call for a reconsideration of the traditional split between domestic and international policy?

The discussion is organized into three sections. The first briefly reviews recent labour market trends in Canada. The rising unemployment rate and lack of real wage gains over the past two decades provide an important context for appreciating labour's anxiety about further economic upheavals, including those stemming from globalization. Although it would be a mistake to attribute all of the growing labour market problems to freer international trade and investment, the reality for many workers is that the deterioration of employment opportunities has occurred precisely during the period when economic integration has accelerated.

While there are strong views – not only pessimistic but optimistic as well – on the employment and wage implications of globalization, there is actually very little empirical analysis on the subject. In the second section of the chapter, after describing the nature and magnitude of the 'globalization' phenomenon, I review the evidence that is available. This review suggests that both the optimistic and pessimistic viewpoints overstate the impacts of economic integration on the Canadian labour market, at least to this point in time. However, this assessment is accompanied by two important qualifications. First, the effects are very uneven, with the benefits of integration going disproportionately to highly skilled workers and the costs to those without much human capital. Second, analysis based on past data is probably not a good guide to the future because the nature of globalization is rapidly changing in ways that are likely to magnify and fundamentally alter its effects.

The third section is concerned with policy issues, and the kinds of responses that are necessary to deal with the impacts of globalization. Paradoxically, as openness increases, domestic labour policies become more and more important. More competitive global markets place a premium on human resource development, particularly in the case of high-cost countries like Canada. In fact, education and training is increasingly seen as one of the most important, if not *the* most important, sources of national competitive advantage in the global economy. As well, economic liberalization creates winners and losers, and therefore the need for adjustment and redistribution initiatives to support the latter group.

While domestic responses are important in shaping the labour impacts of globalization, I argue that, in the long run, new policy initiatives on the international front will be necessary. As markets expand beyond borders, national governments find it increasingly difficult to deal with certain traditionally internal concerns. Some (but by no means all) meaningful 'public' policy goals will be achievable only through supranational jurisdictions. Unfortunately, the historical record of international co-ordination in the social and labour areas offers little reason for optimism. If globalization is to unfold as a democratic process benefiting labour as well as capital, however, workable approaches enforcing minimum standards and encouraging improvements in the well-being of workers will be critical.

RECENT TRENDS IN THE CANADIAN LABOUR MARKET

The issue of globalization needs to be viewed in light of trends in the Canadian labour market. As is the case in virtually all of the OECD countries, the overall employment situation has worsened in Canada since the mid-1970s. For much of this period, the Canadian labour market has been troubled by European-style unemployment levels and American-style polarization.[2] Problems of unemployment, wage stagnation and inequality, and increasing insecurity have become more acute. Against this backdrop, workers have become especially concerned, and less than sanguine, about further upheavals stemming from economic restructuring.

Unemployment

Figure 11.1 documents the upward trend in the national unemployment rate over the post-war period. The horizontal lines indicate average unemployment rates by decade; note the inching up of these decade averages and then

251

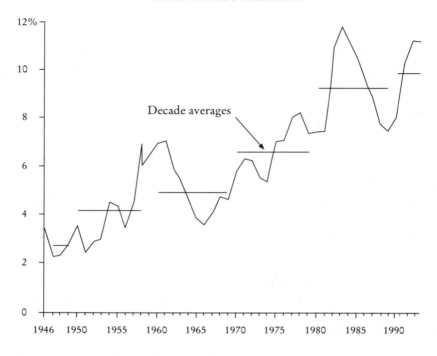

Figure 11.1 Unemployment rate, Canada, 1946–93
Source: Based on data from Statistics Canada

the substantial increase for the post-1980 period. It is striking to realize that, prior to 1975 (at least in the post-war period), the unemployment rate was never above 7.5 per cent; since then, it has never been below it.

Furthermore, an increasing proportion of unemployment is 'structural' – i.e. it does not go away when macroeconomic conditions improve. By definition, this type of unemployment is long-term in nature and, as Figure 11.2 shows, the proportion of unemployment that lasts at least six or twelve months has grown substantially over the past two decades. This has become a particular problem for workers 45 years and over losing jobs in declining sectors of the economy.

Job quality

Unemployment statistics ignore the fact that job creation has been substantial in Canada over the past two decades – over 3 million net new jobs since 1975. However, the types of jobs that have been created must be considered. Recent analysis by Statistics Canada has documented the significant declines in real earnings of workers in the lower part of the wage distribution since the 1970s.[3]

Per cent of unemployed

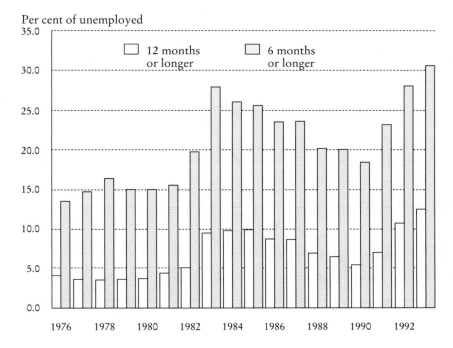

Figure 11.2 Incidence of long-term unemployment, Canada, 1976–93

An important part of this has been the proliferation of 'non-standard' employment which has accounted for much of the net increase in total employment, at least since 1980. Non-standard workforms, which include part-time, short-term, and temporary-help work, and own-account self-employment, now represent 30 per cent of total employment, and their share continues to increase (Figure 11.3). Workers in these jobs tend to have lower wages, fewer benefits, and less security than employees in 'standard' jobs. While some individuals choose this type of employment, there has clearly been a growing preference among employers for these jobs because of the flexibility and cost savings they offer.[4]

Wages and the distribution of earnings

After substantial gains in the first thirty years of the post-war period, earnings have stagnated in Canada since the mid-1970s. As Table 11.1 indicates, real wages increased 42.5 and 36.8 per cent during the 1950s and 1960s and then slowed to 8.5 per cent in the 1970s and to just 2 per cent in the 1980s. Over the long run, real wages inevitably move in tandem with labour productivity

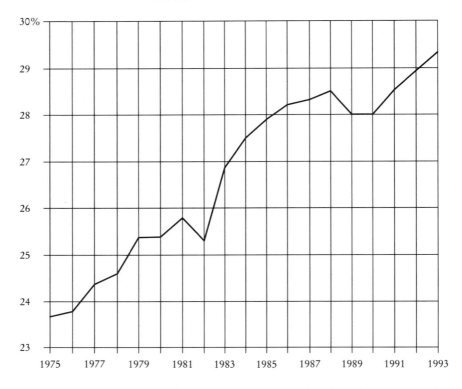

Figure 11.3 Non-standard employment as a proportion of total employment, Canada, 1975–93

Source: Estimates by the authors, based on data from Statistics Canada

Note: Non-standard employment, as defined here, consists of part-time employment, short-tenure (full-time) employment and independent contracting (full-time, long-term)

trends and the wage stagnation reflects the productivity slowdown experienced since the mid-1970s.

At the same time, the distribution of wages has become more unequal and 'polarized' at the high and low ends as opposed to the middle.[5] As Table 11.2 indicates, the Gini coefficient, measuring the degree of inequality, rose throughout the 1980s and early 1990s. The measure of polarization used in Table 11.2 is the proportion of workers earning between 75 and 150 per cent of the median: by 1991, this proportion was lower than it had been ten years earlier and substantially lower than it had been in the 1960s.

Explaining the trends

Many observers believe that these trends are indicative of a fundamental shift in the labour market and the economy more broadly. While the 1945–75

Table 11.1 Average annual real wages and decade wage growth rates, Canada, 1920–90

Year	Av. annual wage ($1990)	Period	Decade wage growth rate (%)
1920	6,773	1920–30	12.1
1930	7,590	1930–40	10.3
1940	8,370	1940–50	34.4
1950	11,249	1950–60	42.5
1960	16,031	1960–70	36.8
1970	21,928	1970–80	8.5
1980	23,791	1980–90	2.0
1990	24,259		

Source: Abdul Rashid. 1993. 'Seven Decades of Wage Change.' *Perspectives on Labour and Income* 5: 2, 9–21

Table 11.2 Earnings inequality and polarization, Canada, 1967–91*

	Gini coefficient	Proportion of workers earning between 75 and 150% of median
1967	0.363	0.42
1973	0.379	0.37
1981	0.378	0.36
1986	0.396	0.32
1988	0.396	0.32
1990	0.398	0.34
1991	0.403	0.32

Source: Data from Statistics Canada
Note: Based on annual earnings of workers aged 18–64 earning at least 5 per cent of national annual average

period was the 'golden age' for workers in Canada (and much of the OECD region), the experience since then suggests that we are now in a different, and less favourable, long-term cycle.

There is no firm consensus about why the trends described above (or similar ones in other OECD countries) have occurred. Nevertheless, the pervasive restructuring of the past two decades has clearly been the product of the complex interplay of a number of different forces. Rapid technological change spurred by the microelectronic and telecommunication revolutions has altered products and services, the production process, and the organization of economic activity. These changes have been intertwined with, and reinforced by, the national and international deregulation of markets.

Not unexpectedly, individuals and institutions have responded to the shifting environment. Business has typically adjusted to the increasing market pressures and the new technological opportunities by adopting management strategies emphasizing flexibility and cost control.[6] This has led to downward pressure on wages, the substitution of non-standard workforms and contracting out for full-time, permanent jobs, and attempts to replace long-standing organizational methods with more fluid work practices. The result has been a shift in the traditional set of trade-offs in the workplace, away from labour's concern for security and towards management's interest in operational flexibility and efficiency.

Historically, workers have looked to governments and unions to protect their interests and to redress any power imbalances between labour and capital. However, the role of governments in social and labour policy areas – a role that had been increasingly activist in the 1960s and 1970s – was reversed after the early 1980s with changing voter preferences and the growing fiscal crisis.

With respect to unions, management's strategic initiatives, coupled with the move towards a small-firm, service-based industrial structure and the protracted macroeconomic slowdown, have tended to weaken the collective bargaining system. This is true to varying degrees throughout the OECD region.[7] It is obviously most applicable to the US experience where only 15 per cent of the labour force is now unionized. In Canada, the union movement has been much more resilient. However, the challenges facing Canadian organized labour should not be minimized. Traditional strongholds like mining, manufacturing and construction have experienced declines in unionization in the order of 10–15 per cent since the late 1970s. And, in the growth industries, now exclusively in the commercial service sector, unions have never established a foothold.[8]

GLOBALIZATION AND ITS IMPACTS

'Globalization', as it is used here, refers to the increasing flow of goods, services, technology and capital across national borders. 'Regionalization' is a variant on the globalization theme, focusing on the organization of investment, production and trade within three multi-country blocs known collectively as the 'Triad' – Western Europe, North America and East Asia. Regionalization has gathered steam in the 1980s and early 1990s with the ongoing integration of the European Union, the passage of the FTA/NAFTA, and strengthening economic linkages between Japan and its neighbours.[9]

The extent of global economic integration

How strong are these forms of economic integration? The most direct indicators are international trade and foreign direct investment. Between 1970 and 1991, a period when world real GDP just about doubled, global exports nearly tripled in real terms. Foreign direct investment flows quadrupled over these years. Growth in FDI was particularly strong in the second half of the 1980s, with real annual increases over 25 per cent.

As well, the operations of many multinational corporations seem to be becoming more global. Historically, MNCs have been clearly identified with a particular home country. They have tended to locate the co-ordination, research, and other strategic activities there, with branch plants, or replica production and distribution operations, in foreign host countries. For growing numbers of MNCs, this model is being replaced by a more integrated model that organizes operations on a worldwide basis. According to the United Nations, this evolution will profoundly change investment decision-making, sourcing patterns, and even the form of MNCs.[10] It will also increase the capacity of multinationals to exploit different types of comparative advantage, including those that are cost-based.

While economic integration across borders is increasing, it is important to note that, to this point in time, there have been limitations on the extent of the process. First, globalization has been largely concentrated within the industrialized countries: it is between these nations that the bulk of trade and investment flows. Second, much of the integration thus far has been on a regional rather than a truly global basis. Third, despite the emerging trend noted above, the ultimate symbol of the global economy – the transnational corporation operating worldwide without national identity – is still more image than reality; most MNCs still concentrate their assets, decision-making and most creative activities in their home country.[11]

Implications of economic integration for jobs and incomes

The expected impacts of global economic integration depend on one's theoretical perspective. Two very different views dominate, one coming out of neo-classical economics and the other having roots in a more critical political economy tradition. Each leads to a unique set of policy conclusions.

Relative comparative advantage

This perspective flows from neo-classical trade theory and is based on the proposition that relative comparative advantage dictates what a nation produces in an open global regime. In this view, the resulting international specialization maximizes aggregate efficiency, productivity and income. The comparative-advantage perspective has provided the intellectual grounding for the liberalization of the global economy.

This theory leads to domestic policies targeted at increasing productivity and the competitiveness of individual producers. In this way, incomes will rise and employment opportunities will be created. Training and education become important because a skilled workforce is one of the critical sources of comparative advantage. At the same time, the dislocations inevitably caused by the ongoing structural changes will create demand for labour adjustment programmes and, in some cases, income redistribution.

257

Mobile capital and cost-based competition

The alternative perspective focuses on the interest of 'footloose' capital in finding low-cost and otherwise advantageous locations. This search for a favourable environment can cover a wide range of cost items including taxes, environmental and other regulatory costs, and the cost of capital. Often, though, this perspective tends to focus on labour costs. An important corollary of the cost-competition view is that globalization shifts the balance of power to capital and away from both governments and labour. With its capacity to be mobile, capital, it is argued, can move beyond the reach of domestic laws and collective agreements.

While the conventional trade theory view of economic liberalization fixes the attention of the labour policy-maker on training, adjustment and redistribution programmes, the cost-competition perspective raises another issue – the possibility that the mobility of capital will sharply constrain the range of domestic policy choices. This concern has generated debate about whether policy convergence is inevitable and, if so, whether it will necessarily be convergence downward to the 'lowest common denominator'.

Empirical evidence

The controversy over the implications of globalization is a complex one and there is not much solid, empirical evidence with which to resolve it. However, some insights, albeit limited, can be gained by looking at two different lines of research: studies on the location patterns of production and investment and analysis of the expected impacts of the NAFTA.

Research on the determinants of foreign direct investment attempts to explain the size of FDI inflows into a given country on the basis of national economic and political variables. While labour variables are often included, they are almost always specified either as the average national wage or unit labour cost. Both are obviously loose proxies for the quality and cost-competitiveness of a nation's workforce, something which must be kept in mind in reviewing this literature. Also, much of this analysis has been based on investment data from the 1970s and early 1980s. It reflects corporate behaviour at that point in time and, therefore, it does not capture the emergence of truly global MNC strategies, to the extent these now exist.

The locational literature consistently shows that the size of a country's market (as measured by GDP) is a very important, and often the most important, determinant of FDI. Large, rich countries have received more foreign investment than small, poor ones. Most studies find that a country's cost structure is also an important factor, but not as important in explaining investment location as is market size.[12]

There is mixed evidence regarding the impacts of labour costs. Some researchers have found that high average wages or unit labour costs are indeed a deterrent to foreign investors, while others have found no significant link.[13] Clearly, the role of labour costs differs by industry and product. A recent study by Wheeler and Moody, for example, concluded that low labour costs were positively associated with FDI inflows by US electronics multinationals. However, in other industries characterized by less global integration, they found that labour costs were a far less significant determinant of investment.[14]

The NAFTA, like the Canada–US FTA before it, has been the subject of considerable analysis on employment and income effects. While it should be understood that there are no completely satisfactory techniques for assessing these effects, the modelling exercises and the other approaches suggest three principal implications of the NAFTA for Canadian labour:[15]

- The aggregate employment impacts in terms of numbers of jobs are likely to be relatively insignificant, at least for the foreseeable future.
- Even if the aggregate numbers are not large, however, there will be significant concentrations of employment loss in sectors where low Mexican labour costs do matter.
- Third, the overall effect will likely be to intensify the wage polarization discussed earlier. Canadian workers best situated to benefit will be highly skilled and highly paid 'knowledge' workers.[16] On the other hand, the large, low-wage Mexican workforce will increase the North American supply of unskilled labour, creating downward pressure on the wages of Canadian workers already in the lower part of the earnings distribution.[17]

Summary

What analysis there is suggests that the effects of globalization have been somewhere in between the two polar views set out earlier. The evidence does not show that closer integration has led to a wholesale exodus of jobs from the high-cost to low-cost countries.[18] Low wages have been an advantage in some industries but not others, presumably depending on the skill levels required and the importance of labour costs.

While the data do not indicate that aggregate dislocations from economic liberalization have been huge, employment losses in a country like Canada tend to be concentrated, thereby creating potentially serious adjustment problems. Moreover, there is evidence in support of the proposition that freer trade and investment (particularly between the North and South) are contributing to the growing wage inequality and polarization characterizing the workforces of most developed countries.[19]

Having made these observations, one should be cautious about simply extrapolating from the past into the future. It has already been noted that some MNCs are beginning to structure operations on a truly global basis which allows them to benefit more from comparative advantages such as low costs wherever they exist. And the two biggest obstacles in locating in low-cost LDCs – political uncertainty and technical problems – are becoming less important. Most LDCs are now 'open for business' and they are becoming more able to host technologically sophisticated operations that traditionally have been the exclusive domain of the rich countries. These points suggest that, barring a reversal of trends, the effects of globalization on the industrialized country labour markets will intensify in the future.

GLOBALIZATION AND LABOUR POLICY OPTIONS

As economic integration proceeds, then, decision-makers face a series of questions. Do the labour market impacts of globalization (or regionalization) call for serious rethinking of existing domestic policy approaches? To what extent do our policies have to be in line with those elsewhere? Does closer economic integration require responses in the international policy arena?

In addressing these questions, I consider 'domestic' policy issues first, and then I turn to 'international' policy responses. While this split is useful for organizing the discussion, in reality the domestic–international distinction is becoming blurred. The formulation of traditionally domestic policies increasingly must take into account what is in place in other countries. And international discussions must focus more and more on what historically have been internal concerns.

Domestic policy responses

While there is a great temptation to focus on the international arena when talking about policy responses to globalization, domestic policies may be more important, at least for the moment. Not only are workable international approaches realistically some time away but, also, domestic policy levers can have a significant impact on how Canadian workers fare in the global economy.

Indeed, as economic integration proceeds, domestic labour policies become increasingly critical. There are a number of reasons for this. First, the need for effective adjustment and redistribution strategies increases because of the inevitable structural dislocations and the uneven distributional effects discussed above. At the same time, the development of a skilled and productive workforce is essential for maintaining standards of living in a high-cost country like Canada. As Robert Reich and others have argued, human capital becomes one of the sole sources of national competitive advantage in a global economy where the mobility of other production factors and the constraints of international trade agreements limit the levers available to domestic policy-makers.

On the domestic front, policy-makers have three challenges: first, to create an infrastructure and climate that will enhance the competitiveness of Canadian producers; second, to provide the instruments to support workers in adjusting to the dislocations associated with globalization; and, third, to protect the quality of working life regarding health and safety, protection from discriminatory and unfair treatment, freedom of association, etc.

The only possibility for meeting these challenges in this country is to follow the 'high road' – i.e. a high-wage, high-skill model. In a global economy, a high-cost country must win markets with high-quality and innovative products and services if it hopes to preserve its standard of living.[20] This competitive strategy, in turn, requires a highly educated, trained and productive workforce.

The 'low road' – competing primarily through costs – is not a general option (although it may make sense in certain industries). In the first place, it will not support widespread gains in the standard of living, even if it is successful from a competitive point of view. And that is unlikely: the cost gap between developed countries like Canada and the LDCs is simply too immense (in all but the very long run). Table 11.3 compares compensation costs in manufacturing across a range of geographical areas.[21] The table provides evidence of convergence – witness the index for Japan – but it also suggests that process can take a long time. The Asian NICs' relative cost index has been rising through that region's boom period, but convergence is obviously occurring very slowly. Also, there has been no significant movement in Mexican levels, at least through 1991.

The 'high-road' approach presumes that human resources are now a critical economic input and that investing in people is probably the single best thing that a government can do in a global economy. In emphasizing human resource investments, policy-makers can provide the essential high-skill base, engender a 'learning culture', and offer labour the opportunity to retool as necessary in order to take advantage of and adjust to the inevitable dislocations brought about by globalization.

Table 11.3 Index comparing hourly compensation costs (in US dollars) for manufacturing production workers, Canada and rest of world, 1975–91*

	1975	1980	1985	1988	1991
Canada	100	100	100	100	100
United States	110	118	120	103	89
European Community†	87	118	73	105	102
Germany	110	147	89	135	128
France	78	107	70	96	88
United Kingdom	57	89	57	77	78
Japan	53	67	60	95	83
Asian NICs†	9	14	15	19	24
Mexico	n/a	n/a	15	10	13

Source: US Bureau of Labor Statistics
* Compensation costs include pay for time worked, other direct pay, and employer expenditures for public and private benefit plans
† Trade-weighted average. The Asian NICs include Hong Kong, Korea, Singapore and Taiwan

Unfortunately, many of the elements of this approach to labour and human resource policy are not sufficiently in place in Canada. The weaknesses have now been well documented: a spotty education system generating too many dropouts and people without basic skills; an inadequate framework for labour adjustment; a weak training infrastructure; and industrial relations institutions that do not support workplace innovation.[22]

Making real progress in these areas is proving difficult. The main reason is that a high-road strategy is perceived as a costly strategy. This raises concerns on two counts. The first revolves around the public debt issue, and the difficulties in forging the political will necessary to avoid cutbacks and even increase expenditures at this time. However, while education, training, and strong labour standards are expensive, at least in the short run, there are abundant studies to show that they have impressive long-run returns.[23]

Can we take the 'high road' alone?

Even if a high labour-investment strategy does pay off in the long run, a second concern remains: that the immediate costs involved in financing it will act as a disincentive for investors. Where 'footloose' capital can choose its landing spot, does an individual country realistically have the room to manoeuvre to implement a policy regime that is more costly than those of its neighbours and competitors?[24]

This is a particularly pointed question for Canada, given its proximity to and extensive linkages with the United States. One of the few serious examinations of the issue is Banting's study of the welfare states in Canada and the US.[25] Banting observes that the broad social policy regimes in the two countries have actually diverged since the 1970s, despite the fact that the two economies were becoming more intertwined in this period. He concludes that, up to this point at least, domestic politics seem to have exerted the primary influence on social and labour policies.

Banting does note the real possibility, however, that the pressures for convergence will increase as the full effects of continental economic integration are felt. Certainly, since the FTA, the Canadian business community appears to have become increasingly aware of the relative costs of operating on the two sides of the border. In general, this can be expected to exert downward pressure on the more costly policy regime, unless offsetting benefits are widely recognized (as is the case with the current healthcare debate in the US).

The limitations of the high road

The domestic policies implied by a high-wage, high-skill strategy are essential but they alone will not be enough to ensure a rosy future for Canadian workers in a global economy. Most obviously, there are limits to how much of the required structural adjustment can be handled through investments in human resource development. Indeed, the types of workers most vulnerable to the dislocations arising from globalization – workers without a lot of human capital, often older and in 'old-economy' industries – have not typically benefited much from retraining and other 'active' programmes.[26] This suggests that redistributive programmes will be necessary in some situations.

Furthermore, it is important to recognize that a broader spectrum of the workforce may eventually be vulnerable to dislocations from economic integration. That is, a 'high-skill, *low-wage*' strategy is becoming more of a reality in certain developing countries. Although business still faces serious obstacles in locating high-technology, high-value-added operations in LDCs, this is changing. Examples such as state-of-the-art Indian engineers and world-class Mexican automakers are becoming more frequent. And, while these workers may be highly paid by the standards of their own countries, their compensation is far below that received by similarly productive workers in Canada or any other developed nation.

Economic theory tells us that a high-skill, low-wage country is on its way to becoming a high-wage country. However, this is true in the long run only, as evidenced by the data in Table 11.3. In the meantime, dislocation in the Canadian labour market may be significant.

Policy responses in the international arena

The case for pursuing international co-ordination in the labour area as global integration proceeds rests on three arguments. First, there is a need to ensure that, at a minimum, basic human and democratic rights are protected, particularly in the LDCs where labour exploitation is one way of gaining entry into the global economy. Second, although there has not been over-whelming evidence of a spiral downward to the lowest common denominator in the past, the increasing sophistication of MNCs and the intensified competition for FDI increase the probability of this in the future. Third, national sovereignty simply becomes less workable where markets are global.[27] Globalization makes it increasingly difficult for governments to use domestic policy to protect their citizens and to promote national values.

What should international co-ordination achieve? Options range from the minimalist position of identifying desirable practices and encouraging their diffusion to the most interventionist approach of harmonizing and enforcing national standards. For reasons that should become clear below, the latter option is not realistic, even if it were deemed desirable, while the former is unlikely to have much impact. A more workable proposal would involve identifying and enforcing a set of minimum standards designed to:

- encourage the worldwide diffusion of human rights, democracy, and improvements in labour conditions;

- promote international economic development;
- maintain and further improve the social and economic well-being of workers everywhere; and
- support sustainable global economic growth.

The pessimistic view: experiences in the international arena

It is important to recognize that we are not starting from square one. The International Labour Office, experiences writing labour standards into international trade laws and drafting codes of conduct for multinational corporations, and the construction of the social dimension of the European Union all offer relevant experience. Unfortunately, each of these adds weight to the argument that international co-ordination is not workable.

The ILO has a long history of education and standard-setting in the international labour arena, but its effectiveness is being questioned in many quarters. The convention-and-ratification format that has been the ILO's signature is widely seen as overdone, too complicated and technical and too politicized. Other problems include perceptions of labour domination (despite the tripartite structure) and of too much control in the hands of an inflexible bureaucracy.

The negotiation of the NAFTA side agreements has raised the profile of linking labour standards with trade agreements. This approach is usually intended to achieve one or both of the following goals: to eliminate 'social dumping' and to use market access as a tool for progressive improvements in labour conditions.[28] While there is actually a long history of labour standards being negotiated as a part of trade agreements, it has not been a very successful one.[29] The most serious problem has been the tendency of developed countries to use these clauses to protect their markets from the LDCs, citing substandard labour practices. Largely because of this, the last-minute attempt led by the US and France to get a social clause written into the Uruguay Round of the GATT was unsuccessful.

The concerns about the footloose potential of capital in a global economy lead to the question of whether supranational institutions can be used to ensure that MNCs are responsible to individual countries and their workforces. In fact, OECD and ILO 'codes of conduct' for MNCs have been in place since the 1970s. However, these are only guidelines and, in many respects, they no longer reflect the nature of MNC operations. For nearly two decades, the United Nations has undertaken negotiations for a comprehensive code but these have not yet been successfully completed.

Finally, the European Union has pursued the most comprehensive agenda for political and social, as well as economic, integration. This agenda now has a number of statutory underpinnings, including the Charter on Fundamental Social Rights for Workers and the Social Protocol of the Maastricht Treaty. However, the incorporation of a social dimension into the Union has not met the expectations of its advocates as the original objectives have been compromised considerably. Indeed, the European experience has highlighted the difficulties of tying social and labour issues into economic integration, at least in an interventionist fashion.

A case for optimism?

In the face of these past failures, any optimism for international labour co-ordination rests with two propositions: first, that developing workable forms of international governance in different subject areas is a learning process and, second, that the expansion and intensification of the globalization process will ultimately create the political will to invest in that learning process.

Trade policy in the post-war period has addressed successive generations of issues that have arisen with ongoing global integration. Beginning with tariffs, the international policy regime has moved on to deal with increasingly complex non-tariff barriers. Hart sees this as part of a natural historical process whereby, with globalization, the trade policy agenda progressively widens to handle matters that were traditionally domestic concerns.[30]

Hart argues that the international trade policy regime is once again entering a new stage. Because of ongoing integration, innovations in MNC operations, and changing domestic policy strategies, existing arrangements cannot address some of the most critical challenges now facing the international economy – including the interface between trade and social policy. The optimistic view is that, just as procedures were developed for dealing with earlier issues, workable approaches eventually will emerge to address the labour concerns discussed in this chapter.

Obviously, political will is important. As the history of writing labour standards into trade law suggests, that will has not been there in the past. When proposals have been raised to put labour issues on the agenda, the motivation has been typically protectionist rather than a genuine interest in promoting either the welfare of workers or 'fair' competition.

Workable international co-ordination will not be possible as long as it is disguised protectionism. It must be driven by a long-term vision that labour issues, like others that have been introduced and negotiated in the past, must be incorporated into the 'web of rules' guiding trade and investment into the future. Developed countries, with high wages and standards, will sincerely have to make access to their markets the 'carrot' for LDCs to upgrade their labour regimes. Market access must be the quid pro quo for improved labour and social standards.

There are signs that the political will is building. For example, some observers note that the IMF and the World Bank are becoming more open to social aspects of global economic development than was the case in the past. The NAFTA side agreement is obviously an important step in putting labour standards on the trade negotiation agenda. An important development will be the treatment of this issue in the next multilateral round under the World Trade Organization; it is understood that the feasibility of a social clause will be examined in the preparations for that round. The critical question will be whether innovative norms and methods can be developed which separate genuine social concerns from protectionist tactics.

CONCLUSION

Although economic liberalization historically has brought benefits to workers, the relatively difficult times for labour in Canada, and in other developed countries, have heightened concerns about ongoing globalization. There is little doubt that technological and institutional changes have been eroding the economic borders between countries in new and significant ways.

While the impacts on Canadian workers have not yet been dramatic, there is reason to believe that the pressures stemming from globalization are only now starting to build. In the developed countries, economic integration will hurt lower-skilled workers the most, creating adjustment problems, and exacerbating polarization trends. While highly-skilled workers are more likely to find opportunities in the global economy, the supply of technically sophisticated and still relatively low-paid workers in the LDCs should not be underestimated.

As economic integration proceeds, its impacts can be shaped by effective domestic policies. A high-skill, high-wage strategy emphasizing human resource development and labour adjustment is key. Certainly, much needs to be done on this front in Canada.

However, as markets expand beyond national borders, the reach of domestic policies will not be enough. Co-ordination in the international arena is also important. While history indicates that this will not be easily achievable, future progress will be necessary if globalization is to benefit labour as well as capital.

NOTES

1 This chapter is based largely on research undertaken by the author for the Office of International Affairs, Human Resources Development Canada.
2 To be fair, in each case the strain has been somewhat more moderate here. While Canadian unemployment rates have been at levels observed in much of Europe, job creation has been much healthier here, in contrast to the virtual lack of net employment growth in the European Union countries since the mid-1970s. And, as we will see below, Canadian earnings inequality has increased; however, the expansion of low-wage jobs and the resulting polarization has been much weaker than in the United States. For a cross-country review of earnings distribution trends, see the Organization for Economic Co-operation and Development, *Employment Outlook* (Paris: OECD, 1993).
3 R. Morissette, J. Myles and G. Picot, *What is Happening to Earnings Inequality*

in Canada?, Research Paper No. 60, Analytical Studies Branch, Statistics Canada, Ottawa, 1993.

4   The clearest evidence of this involves the increase in 'involuntary' part-time work. In 1993, 35.5 per cent of part-time workers would have preferred full-time work, the highest share on record. For more details on non-standard employment trends, see Gordon Betcherman *et al.*, *The Canadian Workplace in Transition* (Kingston, Ontario: Queen's University Press, 1994).

5   For a comprehensive analysis of earnings distribution trends in Canada since the 1970s, see Morissette *et al.*, *What is Happening to Earnings Inequality in Canada?*

6   For Canadian evidence, see Betcherman *et al.*, *The Canadian Workplace in Transition.*

7   For a review, see the Organization for Economic Co-operation and Development, *Employment Outlook* (Paris: OECD, 1991).

8   For a review of union trends in Canada and the US, see Pradeep Kumar, *From Uniformity to Divergence: Industrial Relations in Canada and the United States* (Kingston, Ontario: Queen's University Press, 1993).

9   It is important to note that the model of regionalization is very different in each region of the Triad: the differences are most striking between the deep multi-dimensional integration in Europe and the more limited economic integration in North America.

10 United Nations, *1993 World Investment Report* (New York: United Nations, 1993).

11 Research indicates that most MNCs have a strong home-country attachment where the majority of its assets, employees, and decision-makers remain. For an elaboration, see Yao-Su Hu, 'Global or Stateless Corporations Are National Firms With International Operations', *California Management Review* 34, no. 2 (1992): 107–25.

12 Where MNCs are seeking cost-based advantages, they are usually considering less-developed countries. In these situations, political stability tends to have a significant impact on FDI flows. See, for example, Friedrich Schneider and Bruno S. Frey, 'Economic and Political Determinants of Foreign Direct Investment', *World Development* 13, no. 2 (1985): 161–75.

13 For an example of a study showing high labour costs as a deterrent to investment, see Schneider and Frey, 'Economic and Political Determinants of Foreign Direct Investment'. For a study finding no significant impact, see Irving B. Kravis and Robert E. Lipsey, 'The Location of Overseas Production and Production for Export by U.S. Multinational Firms', *Journal of International Economics* 12 (1982): 201–23.

14 David Wheeler and Ashoka Moody, 'International Investment Location Decisions: The Case of U.S. Firms', *Journal of International Economics* 33 (1992): 57–76.

15 A range of methodologies have been used, from *ad hoc* 'trade exposure' studies that focus exclusively on job losses associated with plant closures and mass layoffs, to sophisticated computable general equilibrium (CGE) models that estimate potential impacts on the basis of rigorous analysis of data structured according to a series of theoretical relationships. For a review of the different methodologies and their results, see Morley Gunderson, 'Wage and Employment Impacts Related to the North American Free Trade Agreement', Fraser Institute, Vancouver, 1992.

16 Having said this, the potential of Mexico (and other LDCs) in high-skill, high-technology sectors should not be discounted. In North America, there are a growing number of Mexican establishments, typically of foreign-based MNCs, in

267

high-value-added industries operating at Canadian or American levels of productivity and quality. See *The Globe and Mail*, 18 March 1993: B1.

17 US research has documented this polarization effect of trade on that country's
labour force. See George J. Borjas, Richard B. Freeman and Lawrence F. Katz,
'On the Labor Market Effects of Immigration and Free Trade', NBER Working
Paper No. 3761, Cambridge, Mass., 1991.

18 In a recent book, however, Adrian Wood argues that conventional analyses have
substantially underestimated the job losses in the rich countries due to freer trade.
See Wood, *North–South Trade, Employment and Inequality* (Oxford: Clarendon
Press, 1994).

19 See Wood, *North–South Trade, Employment and Inequality*. Note that some
researchers argue that technological change more than trade is driving the changes
in earnings distributions. See, for example, Robert Lawrence and Mark Slaughter,
'International Trade and American Wages in the 1980s: Giant Sucking Sound or
Small Hiccup?', *Brookings Papers on Economic Activity, Microeconomics* (Washington, DC: Brookings Institution, 1993).

20 This is what Michael Porter calls a 'differentiation' competitive strategy. For a
discussion, see *The Competitive Advantage of Nations* (New York: Free Press,
1990).

21 Note that these comparisons are based on the conversion of national currencies
into US dollars; as a consequence, figures can be affected by short-run exchange
rate fluctuations as well as real earnings.

22 See, for example, the Canadian Labour Market and Productivity Centre, *Canada:
Meeting the Challenge of Change*, A Statement by the Economic Restructuring
Committee of the CLMPC (Ottawa: CLMPC, 1993); Ontario Premier's Council,
People and Skills in the Global Economy (Toronto: Queen's Printer of Ontario,
1990); and the Steering Group on Prosperity, *Inventing Our Future: An Action
Plan for Canada's Prosperity* (Ottawa: Supply and Services, 1992).

23 There is a long and substantial literature in economics indicating high rates of
return to education and training. As well, 'growth-accounting' analyses, that
decompose national economic growth into sources of growth, have consistently
led to the conclusion that improvements in a country's human capital lead to
increases in its rate of economic expansion. Regarding strong standards, it has been
argued by Michael Porter and others that these can force employers and workers
to raise productivity levels and create more competitive industries, particularly at
the high end of the value-added scale.

24 Arguing that there is not much room to manoeuvre, Schott has used a 'beauty
contest' metaphor. 'Countries are now competing in a global beauty contest to
see which have the most desirable economic policies. The judging is being done
by investors – both domestic and foreign – who vote with their capital.' See Jeffrey
J. Schott, 'Comment', in Nora Lustig, Barry P. Bosworth and Robert Z. Lawrence
(eds), *North American Free Trade: Assessing the Impact* (Washington: The
Brookings Institution, 1992), pp. 238–41.

25 See Keith Banting, 'The Social Policy Divide: The Liberal Welfare State in Canada
and the United States', School of Policy Studies, Queen's University, Kingston,
mimeo, 1992.

26 For a summary of the international evidence regarding the effectiveness of active
labour market interventions, see the OECD, *Employment Outlook*, 1993.

27 For an articulation of this argument, see Robert Heilbroner, *Twenty-First Century
Capitalism* (New York: Anansi, 1992).

28 The typical model for linking labour standards with trade agreements is to identify
a set of standards that must be met for trade arrangements to apply; where

standards are not met, some form of trade sanction can be imposed. Note that the NAFTA side agreement, by requiring the application of existing labour laws in each country rather than an agreed-upon set of standards, represents a departure from the usual format.

29 For a review of the problems, see Steve Charnovitz, 'The Influence of International Labour Standards on the World Trading Regime: A Historical Overview', *International Labour Review* 126, no. 5 (1987): 565–84.

30 Michael Hart, 'The End of Trade Policy?', in Christopher J. Maule and Fen Osler Hampson (eds), *Global Jeopardy: Canada Among Nations, 1993–94* (Ottawa: Carleton University Press, 1993), pp. 85–105, and Hart, *What's Next: Canada, the Global Economy and the New Trade Policy* (Ottawa: Centre for Trade Policy and Law, 1994).

12

CORPORATE STRATEGIES
The costs and benefits of going global
Fred Lazar

INTRODUCTION

Corporations increasingly are becoming global institutions. They are adopting strategies which transcend the influence of the small and medium-size industrialized nations of the world. The largest 500 multinational corporations conduct over one-half of world trade.[1] Trade and, more importantly, investment barriers have been lowered dramatically by the NAFTA and the latest GATT agreement, thus strengthening further the bargaining position of highly mobile capital and the clout of global corporations. It is not surprising, therefore, that in this environment, global companies are becoming the principal actors driving the economic and social agendas of all countries. Canada provides a fascinating case study of the potential problems which many countries may shortly face if they fail to develop their national champions and fail to strengthen and broaden their industrial bases, relegating them to a junior role in relation to the global corporations.

Canada's economic prospects continue to be dependent on resources. For example, resource-based products accounted for forty-five of the top fifty Canadian products in terms of world export share at the last economic peak in 1989 (Table 12.1). But natural resources are no longer the staples of the world economy. Instead, the new staples are ideas.[2] Unfortunately, Canada does not appear to be well endowed with the new 'staples'.

Canada appears to lag behind most major industrialized countries in R&D investments and capabilities (Table 12.2). Part of our poor record in this area stems from the industrial structure of the economy; that is, a disproportionately large share of economic activity accounted for by very low R&D-intensive industries (Table 12.3). Part of this results from the high degree of foreign ownership of the industrial sector in Canada. Foreign-owned firms operating in Canada appear to underperform Canadian-owned companies in the high R&D-intensive industries. Canadian-owned companies, on average, allocate a larger proportion of their revenues to R&D expenditures than US companies in the same industries (Table 12.4).

Table 12.1 Top fifty Canadian industries in terms of world export share, 1989

Industry	Share of total world exports	Export value (US$000)
Shingles and shakes	96.0	181,532
Alloy pig iron, etc.	92.9	92,805
Asbestos	92.0	375,570
Granulated slag	86.8	214,727
Maple sugar, maple syrup	85.2	31,389
Linseed	84.0	170,550
Chlorates of sodium	83.5	67,572
Silver ores, concentrates	83.1	4,121
Other precious metal ores, concentrates	81.7	120,003
Mustard seeds	81.1	34,796
Diesel–electric locomotives	76.7	317,312
Unmilled canary seed	76.4	30,247
Potassium chloride	76.2	1,005,257
Semi-chemical wood pulp	70.1	268,261
Crude, unrefined sulphur	70.1	503,903
Other fructose	69.1	53,221
Copper mattes	68.6	40,358
Methanol (methyl alcohol)	65.1	192,931
Nickel mattes	63.4	547,029
Iron ore agglomerates	61.6	591,001
Fish meat, excluding frozen fillets	61.1	161,345
Newsprint, rolls, sheets	60.4	4,793,762
Fish liver, roe, dried, smoked	60.0	140,266
Beaver skins	58.2	5,540
Accounting machines	55.6	27,944
Nobium, tantalum, vanadium	55.1	27,980
Chemical wood pulp, coniferous bleached	54.4	4,375,518
Isobutene-isoprene rubber	53.4	153,249
Gypsum and anhydrite	53.0	44,886
Salmon, whole pieces, prepared, preserved	51.9	129,339
Lentils, dried, shelled	50.2	37,883
Turbo-propeller engines	49.4	507,315
Bran, etc., other cereals	48.3	21,834
Unmilled buckwheat	48.0	6,845
Natural uranium, etc.	45.4	384,872
Sawn conifer wood	45.2	4,547,271
Sulphur dioxide	41.4	7,661
Unmilled oats	40.6	134,983
Rape or colza seeds	40.1	527,207
Copper ores, concentrates	39.7	888,999
Other skins	38.7	28,646
Motor vehicle seats	37.8	185,448
Lucerne (alfalfa)	37.0	62,554
Other public transport vehicles	36.2	168,754
Natural gas, gaseous	36.1	2,493,736
Chlorine	35.9	38,831
Selenium, phosphorus, etc.	35.1	48,342
Ice and roller skates	35.1	25,025
Worked, shaped conifer wood	35.0	156,185
Nickel powders, flakes	34.8	77,189
Total		$25,051,994
Share of total Canadian exports		21.6%

Source: UN SITC Trade Statistics (Revision 3 Preliminary)

Table 12.2 Expenditures on R&D, selected international comparisons, 1989

	GERD/GDP (%)	BERD/GDP (%)	HERD/GDP (%)	GERD (US$ billions)	GERD per capita (US$)
Japan	3.04	2.12	0.55	58.0	4.71
FRG	2.88	2.10	0.41	26.7	4.31
Switzerland	2.86	2.14	0.57	3.4	5.06
US	2.82	1.98	0.43	144.8	5.82
Sweden	2.76	1.83	0.82	3.6	4.29
France	2.32	1.40	0.34	19.0	3.38
The Netherlands	2.26	1.32	0.47	4.3	2.89
UK	2.20	1.37	0.33	17.0	2.98
Canada	1.33	0.74	0.31	6.7	2.56
Italy	1.29	0.74	0.25	10.3	1.80

Source: Industry, Science and Technology Canada, S&T Economic Analysis Division, *Selected Science and Technology Statistics 1991* (Ottawa, 1992)
Notes: GERD = gross expenditure on research and development; BERD = business expenditure on research and development; HERD = higher education research and development; some data are from 1988; FRG data predate unification

It is not surprising therefore, that McMillan warns that 'huge portions of Canadian industry have fallen by the wayside to international competition, management mediocrity, and technological backwardness'.[3] Canada's heavy dependence on foreign investment has not produced the dynamic, innovative economy needed to be successful in today's global village. As corporations become more global in their strategies and operations, the dearth of Canadian multinationals will place our future very much at risk, despite our appearance today as a wealthy country. Canada continues to rely too heavily on the old staples, and lacks the management skills and autonomy (both in the private and public sectors) to compete successfully in the ever-expanding, global economy.

In this chapter, we will address two principal issues: do firms have to pursue an international strategy in order to survive and succeed?; if so, what are the implications of international strategies and the further internationalization of companies and trade for Canada and her future economic prospects?

These issues are important. If Canada is to prosper in the more integrated international economy, it will be crucial for policy-makers to understand the causes and consequences of corporate strategies, new production and contracting relations, investment patterns and the locus of decision-making responsibilities within multinational enterprises as well as the competitive potential of domestic industries. These developments must then be factored into their policy responses and initiatives.

The remainder of the chapter is set out as follows. In the next section we discuss the concepts of globalization and competitiveness and begin to examine the importance of global strategies. We develop the theme of global

Table 12.3 Effect of industrial structure on Canadian R&D, 1987

Industry group	R&D expenses 1987 — as percentage of sales	R&D expenses 1987 — $ million	Sales of firms doing R&D, $ billion	Group sales as percentage of total sales for all four groups
High intensity				
Aircraft and parts	17.1	432	2.5	
Telecommunications equip.	16.9	549	3.2	
Other electronic equip.	12.0	254	2.1	
Engineering and scientific services	11.9	294	2.5	
Computer services	11.7	175	1.5	
		1,704	11.8	
Group average	14.4			4.5
Medium intensity				
Electronic parts and components	5.9	24	0.4	
Business machines	3.7	216	5.8	
Drugs and medicines	3.5	95	2.7	
Machinery	3.2	72	2.3	
Scientific and prof. equipment	2.5	36	1.4	
Other mfg. industries	2.3	29	1.3	
		472	13.9	
Group average	3.4			5.3
Low intensity				
'High end'				
Other electrical products	1.5	58	3.9	
Primary metals, non-ferrous	1.3	96	7.4	
Other chemicals	1.2	151	12.6	
Textiles	1.1	36	3.3	
Metal fabricating	1.1	29	2.6	
Electrical power	1.0	170	17.0	
		540	46.8	
Group average	1.2			17.9
'Low end'				
Other non-mfg. industries	0.9	189	21.0	
Rubber and plastics products	0.7	16	2.3	
Mining	0.6	43	7.2	
Wood	0.6	22	3.7	
Crude petroleum and natural gas	0.5	26	5.2	
Refined petroleum and coal prod.	0.5	105	21.0	
Transp. and other utilities	0.4	111	27.8	
Non-metallic mineral products	0.4	13	3.3	
Pulp and paper	0.3	69	23.0	
Primary metals, ferrous	0.3	26	8.7	
Other transportation equip.	0.3	93	31.0	
Food, beverages and tobacco	0.2	70	35.0	
		783	189.2	
Group average	0.4			72.3
Average for all sectors	1.3			
Total		3,499	261.7	100.0

Source: Statistics Canada, nos. 88–202, Table 13 (1977), Table 15 (1987)

Table 12.4 Impact of foreign ownership on R&D spending, Canada, 1987

| | Canada | | USA |
	Canadian-owned	Foreign-owned	All companies (1986)
Telecommunications equip.	17.0	15.5	11.4
Business machines	12.9	2.9	12.0
Drugs and medicines	10.7	2.6	8.3
Scientific and prof. equipment	11.0	0.9	10.5
Metal fabricating	1.8	0.7	1.4

Source: Statistics Canada and National Science Foundation (US)

strategies as integral for competitive success further in the following two sections on firm-specific competitive advantages. Then we turn our attention to the question of whether Canada needs its own multinationals. In other words, how important is it for a country, such as Canada, to be the home base for a number of multinationals? To emphasize the failings of economic policies in Canada, we present a case study of the machinery industry. The underdevelopment of this industry in Canada jeopardizes our economic well-being and highlights the failure of a policy of relying on the market, especially given the importance of foreign ownership and multinationals. In the last two sections, we set out the challenges facing policy-makers in Canada and outline a course of action for the Canadian government to follow in order to regain some control of our economic destiny.

GLOBALIZATION AND COMPETITIVENESS

Globalization can be defined as the increasing interdependence and interconnectedness of national economies and the resulting erosion in the autonomy of nation-states. Globalization is characterized by an increasing movement of goods, services, capital, ideas and people across national borders; development of regional trading blocs; growth in the number and expansion of global corporations; and a growing number of socioeconomic–environmental problems which require co-operation among several countries.

International integration, which is implicit in the concept of globalization, has both a micro and macroeconomic dimension. Integration at the micro level involves the creation and growth of multinational companies through foreign direct investment, international interfirm agreements, licensing, subcontracting and/or acquisitions. At the macro level, integration results from the lowering of barriers to the movement of goods, services, capital, ideas and people. The factors which produce greater international integration at the macro level, also result in more integration at the micro level. As pointed out in the 1993 World Investment Report, '[m]easures to liberalize trade can boost foreign direct investment by allowing transnational corporations to establish production facilities in low-cost sites from which they can export their output, by allowing transnational corporations to outsource inputs, by enabling the formation of regional networks, and by allowing the integration of production regionally or globally'.[4]

The following data provide a measure of the degree to which the process of globalization has developed. In 1991, world exports of goods and non-factor services totalled approximately $4 trillion (US), one-third of which was intra-firm trade. Exports represented about 19 per cent of world GDP in that year. In addition, there were $34 billion (US) in payments for royalties and other fees. The aggregate stock of foreign direct investment stood at $1.8 trillion (US) and foreign direct investment outflows in 1991 were $180 billion (US). The 170,000 foreign affiliates of some 37,000 parent firms generated approximately $5.5 trillion (US) in worldwide sales in 1991.[5] Moreover, according to the United Nations Center for Transnational Corporations (UNCTC), strategic alliances numbered in the thousands and international sub-contracting agreements were estimated to be in the hundreds of thousands.

NAFTA, Maastricht and the Uruguay Round GATT agreement all will continue the trend towards lower trade and investment barriers, further encourage international integration and possibly accelerate the pace of globalization. The new investment rules will be especially important in this process. They will greatly diminish, over time, the risks faced by foreign direct investments, particularly in developing countries (e.g. exchange controls, expropriation risks, performance requirements) and increasingly circumscribe the ability of any one country to control or regulate inward foreign direct investment. This has obvious implications for Canadian policy-making.[6] But these changes should expand the scope for multinational companies and ensure that they remain the key driving forces behind globalization. In effect, the stage appears to be set for significant, further increases in the number and size of investments by multinational enterprises. Yet despite past trends, the apparent links between trade liberalization and foreign direct investment, and the lessening of restrictions on inward direct foreign investment, there is no assurance that internationalization will be the preferred strategy in the future.

On the one hand, the 'organizational requirements of multinational enterprises involve considerable information flows, relating to reporting, monitoring, appraisal, co-ordination and control',[7] and the resulting costs of internalizing an increasing number of more complex transactions (greater spatial distribution of transactions, increasing dissimilarities of transactions) could rise sharply, thus limiting the advantage of pursuing a global strategy. Streamlining operations, externalizing non-core activities and functions, and serving markets from a smaller number of production and/or distribution platforms may become the more desirable strategy. On the other hand, continued progress in telecommunications, information transmission and data processing technologies together with a reduction in the risks for foreign investment in an increasing number of countries may prevent organization costs from rising.

Handy has commented that organizations need to be both big (to exploit economies of scale, diversify R&D risks, reduce dependence on crucial people, suppliers and markets) and small (for flexibility and innovativeness) at the same time. But the solution to this paradox does not lie in abandoning the global strategy. According to Handy, a federalist organizational structure is required with decentralization of powers and greater interdependence among the various units of the company.[8] Innovations in organizational structures should prevent the costs of internalizing more transactions within the same governance structure from rising.

Porter goes even further and argues that globalization mandates a global strategy and that small and medium-size companies will have to consider international markets and foreign competitors at an earlier stage in their business development cycle. In the past, small companies may have been able to develop and secure their position in their local market and use this base to develop the size and experience necessary to challenge firms in other markets. But Porter claims that this strategy is no longer viable since the domestic market is no longer insulated from foreign competition.[9] Furthermore, a global strategy may be necessary for purely defensive reasons. That is, by having a presence in several markets, a company may be able to prevent being attacked in its home market because it will be able to retaliate against an aggressive competitor in the latter's home market.[10]

Before we conclude that global strategies are necessary and inevitable, we will take a closer look at the evolution of multinational enterprises and global strategies and examine whether an international focus enhances the competitiveness of a firm.

FIRM-SPECIFIC COMPETITIVE ADVANTAGES

The staples model outlined by Harold Innis follows, on one level, the tradition of the classic comparative advantage model of international trade, where trade flows are determined by the relative distribution and availability of factor inputs such as labour, capital and natural resources (including land). According to this theory, Canada's exports should be heavily weighted towards resource-based products. While Innis emphasized that Canada's economic development was based on the exploitation of staples (fish, fur, lumber and minerals), his more important contribution was to point out that Canada's reliance on a staples economy for its growth and prosperity would lead to economic dependency, whereby Canada's economic future increasingly would be influenced by events and decisions outside its borders and beyond the control of the government.

Unlike the classic economic trade model, Innis recognized that cross-border trade does not just materialize between parties located in different countries. One party must initiate the transaction. That is, someone must actively search for an opportunity (resource, product, service, distributor, customer) in another country and structure the arrangement which will result in international trade. This involves risk-taking and the individual and/or company must possess the resources (financial, management) and some form of competitive advantage (based on superior information, lower cost resources, marketing skills, publicly awarded monopoly). The party which initiates the transaction should also be able to acquire the bargaining advantage and dictate the terms of the transaction. The other party, unless it has a superior basis for a competitive advantage (e.g. low-cost supplier of a key resource with no close substitutes), will be relegated to dependency status.

Innis pointed out that since Canadians did not take the initiative in exploiting their staples, Canada became economically dependent on outsiders and so did not maximize the wealth potential provided by the resources. Operating on the periphery of the global economy does not provide the foundation for continuing prosperity for Canada or any other country.

Not only does the traditional international trade model suffer from its inability to explain the process by which trade originates and the competitive and economic repercussions of this process, but it also suffers by being static in structure. That is, by not allowing any role for competitive advantages which result from the selection and successful implementation of various strategies by individuals, the model provides no scope for the interplay between competitive and comparative advantages and thus, for the possibility of continual changes in trade patterns and relationships. But as Innis suggested, international trade cannot occur in the absence of someone creating and exploiting a competitive advantage. Furthermore, as Posner argued in a pioneering article, international trade can be caused by technological change and differences in technology endowments among countries.[11] Differences in the relative endowments of capital, labour and resources alone cannot account for all international trade activities. Posner's argument reinforced the importance of competitive advantages in international trade.

Technical progress, which includes developing new organizational structures, new distribution channels, new markets and suppliers, in addition to developing new products, production processes and services, results from strategic investment decisions made by firms. These decisions depend upon the availability of information, technological and market growth expectations, resource availabilities, competitive pressures, and the history and current competitive positions of firms. More importantly, these decisions are required in order to participate in competitive races/contests to create and/or sustain competitive advantages in order to win the available economic rents and so achieve superior financial performance. These contests and their outcomes determine international trade patterns and the structure of dependency relationships.

International trade requires a foreign market presence (production, distribution, finance) by at least one party and some form of innovation by that party. Hence, a global strategy, admittedly on a limited scale initially, is one of the options available to firms in their pursuit of a competitive advantage. Dunning's 'eclectic' model of international production and multinational enterprises is based on these arguments.[12]

A multinational enterprise is created when a firm adopts a global strategy to leverage its ownership-specific advantage by combining this advantage with country-specific, locational advantages under a common governance structure. The firm- or ownership-specific advantage results from success in a contest to create a competitive advantage. Country-specific advantages include market access, size and growth; availability of relatively low-cost resources; infrastructure; favourable policy environment; and proximity and access to other large markets. There are several options available for benefiting from locational advantage – foreign direct investment, licensing, joint ventures, sub-contracting. The direct investment route (common governance structure) is selected if it minimizes transactions costs, taxes and/or best protects proprietary rights.

While the eclectic theory can explain a multinational strategy for firms in all sectors of the economy, two additional reasons have been suggested for service companies adopting a global strategy. The OECD has stated that '[o]ne of the main motivations of multinational enterprises operating in banking, insurance, advertising and other service sectors to invest in developing countries has been to follow their manufacturing or primary industry multinational clients'.[13] Moreover, for many service functions market presence is necessary.

In evaluating the importance of a global strategy and the implications for Canada, it is necessary to keep in mind that the creation of a firm-specific advantage is not a one-time event. Competitiveness, the successful search for a competitive advantage, is a dynamic process requiring continuous participation in innovation contests. A global strategy which entails capitalizing on the locational advantages in other countries may enable a firm to better defend its competitive advantage or provide the basis for creating a new firm-specific advantage; however, country-specific advantages 'in the home and host countries alike do not constitute an ongoing source of competitive advantage for the company in the international market place'.[14] In other words, a global strategy alone does not assure competitive success.

Porter has emphasized three generic strategies, each one of which can be pursued at one or more locations along the value chain. Consequently, there may be several winners in each contest because firms have many strategic options available. Differences in firm-specific resources, idiosyncratic behaviour of managers, and risk aversion in abandoning successful strategies and experimenting with new ones, also suggest that there will be a diversity of outcomes among firms and that competition will take place among companies with different ownership/competitive advantages.

It is also important to consider the possibility that early success in contests to gain a competitive advantage may give the resulting incumbents an advantage in later contests. Success enables incumbents to benefit from experience; the development of information networks to keep abreast of technological, market and competitive developments; resources (organization, finance); and a wider range of strategic options (incrementalism – marginal changes in existing strategy, radical new strategies, defensive tactics to block entry/imitators). There is no assurance, of course, that incumbents will capitalize on these advantages and solidify their positions and dominance in their markets over time. Furthermore, successful innovations and/or companies may be acquired by others who are better positioned to capitalize and enhance the value of the underlying competitive advantages. Finally, technologies and strategies in later contests may become increasingly more complex and interdependent, so that small firms may not have the capabilities to continue and even large companies may have to collaborate with others to survive and succeed.

While a global strategy offers another option in these continuing contests, and even though all options have some value especially in an increasingly complex and volatile environment, are there more attractive and valuable options available? Bartlett and Ghoshal argue that a global strategy has a very high option value since 'in the future, a company's ability to develop a transnational organizational capability will be the key factor that separates the winners from the mere survivors in the international competitive environment'.[15] They may be right, especially in light of Innis's concerns regarding the economic dependency of a staples-based economy and McMillan's claim that ideas are the new staples.

But even if a global strategy has a low option value, a firm could face a Catch-22 situation. 'In many industries, a firm's competitive position in any one market is dependent on its operations in other markets and the operations of other firms world wide',[16] thus any one company that did not pursue a global strategy might make itself more vulnerable to attack by competitors in its home market. Even though all firms may benefit from abandoning a global strategy, no firm will want to assume the risk and be the first to do so, for fear that its competitors may not follow.

PORTER AND COMPETITIVE ADVANTAGE: IS THERE A NEED FOR A GLOBAL STRATEGY?

Porter has outlined three generic strategies in which a company could choose to participate in the contest to gain a competitive advantage. Of the three, it might appear that only the low-cost strategy could benefit from a global strategy. The differentiation and focus strategies which appear to be more innovation-driven might benefit much less from a global strategy. But since process and organization innovations, for example, can and do play key roles in a low-cost strategy, one cannot argue that selecting a global strategy is determined by whether a company decides to compete on the basis of cost or on the basis of innovation. Indeed, Bartlett and Ghoshal are right in arguing that it is crucial for firms to adopt global strategies to improve their chances of winning the contests to gain a competitive advantage, regardless of the basic strategy selected. A global strategy is not a substitute for the three generic strategies, rather it is a crucial complement to each.

Porter has noted that the dividing lines among the three basic strategies are not precise. Any company pursuing a low-cost strategy must strive to achieve proximity to all of its competitors on the basis of differentiation, otherwise the product may not be viewed by buyers as being comparable in value and so price-cost margins and the resulting economic rents may not be sustainable. A differentiation strategy may be profitable if costs are kept in line with those of all competitors since there is a limit to the value buyers will place on various sources of differentiation. If a focus strategy proves to be a success, more companies may be attracted to that particular niche and cost structures may play an important role in any ensuing shake-out and consolidation in the market niche.

We can better appreciate the importance of a global strategy for both the cost and differentiation strategies by taking a closer look at recent developments in competitive contests. As well, it will become apparent that foreign direct investment is not always the preferred choice for a global strategy.

Rugman and Verbeke, and others, have emphasized the catalytic role played by the convergence of consumer tastes and the technical possibility for standardizing products and processes in the increase in the number and expansion in the size of multinational corporations.[17] As products take on more of the characteristics of basic commodities, cost and price become more important in the competitive contests. As a result, 'as cost considerations have become more important, international competition has increasingly led multinational enterprises to relocate certain activities in lower cost locations'.[18]

Certain location-specific advantages have assumed more important roles in sustaining competitive advantages. But foreign direct investment has not always been the preferred route to exploit country advantages. Firms have externalized non-core functions to increase their flexibility and adaptability to changes in their competitive environment and to decrease costs when outside sources of supply are cheaper and more reliable. Multinational enterprises have been making greater use of the practice of sub-contracting/ outsourcing in order to increase their competitiveness 'through greater flexibility to adjust to global markets, rapid technological change and ever-shorter product life cycles'.[19]

However, there have been several important changes which have lessened the attractiveness of cost-related, location advantages for firms. Innovations in production technologies have significantly lowered the share of labour costs and so have reduced the attractiveness of low-wage countries. Differentiation through customization and quality has become a more and more important competitive strategy as real incomes surpass critical thresholds in more and more countries. Innovations in telecommunications have 'opened up a variety of opportunities for electronic links between suppliers, producers and customers in design, production scheduling, purchasing, shipping'[20] and have led to a logistics revolution.

In just-in-time systems, speed of delivery and quality are critical. Consequently, proximity to the customer becomes a potential competitive advantage. Therefore, presence in the major markets takes on added importance. Despite convergence in tastes and incomes, local differences continue to be important and a physical presence in the regions outside the home base is needed in order to identify and be able to respond quickly to challenges from competitors and to customize the product to serve the needs and tastes of the customers.

In addition, regional strategies have evolved as firms attempt to improve their competitive positions in the markets of the Triad – Europe, North America and Asia–Pacific – by trying to maintain the advantages of economies of scale and achieving the flexibility required by the logistics revolution. The integration of production on a regional basis has been promoted further by the development of regional trade arrangements. Canada should benefit from this trend of the regionalization of global strategies because of its membership in one of the Triad's markets. But we may not benefit unless we are the home base for the regional, product line, or functional headquarters of the multinational enterprises operating in this region. Moreover, Canada may be in the wrong regional grouping.

The apparent acceleration in the pace of technological development and shorter product life cycles create additional pressures on companies to adopt a global strategy and its regional sub-set. To recover the rising costs of R&D, technology-intensive companies must be able to introduce new products in several markets, simultaneously if possible. This requires foreign production, distribution and marketing capabilities. McMillan has remarked that 'it is not the markets which are driving international expansion, it is the soaring costs of production – in technology, capital investment and corporate infrastructure. In short, unless capital costs are spread over large enough markets, unit costs cannot come down far enough and fast enough to provide acceptable levels of return on investment.'[21]

There are alternatives to foreign direct investment as the preferred global strategy to deal with the competitive problems relating to the pace and costs of technological change. Strategic alliances and joint ventures have increased in prominence and number. The key motivations for multinational companies to enter into various types of collaborative arrangements include 'the need to

281

FRED LAZAR

reduce uncertainty regarding which technology will emerge as the future industry standard, the desire to share complementary strengths in R&D (and production) and pool the costs associated with such activit[ies] and the aim to diversify into new lines of business and/or enter new markets'.[22]

Diversification has become another motivating factor for pursuing a global strategy, whatever its form. Kim *et al.* have suggested that diversification might simultaneously increase rates of return and lower risks for companies.[23]

Thus, we must conclude that a global strategy has become essential for competitiveness and success in the contests for achieving a competitive advantage. A global strategy provides more options and greater flexibility than a domestic strategy and so must be more valuable for a firm. Strategic alliances offer scope for risk reduction, facilitate larger aggregate investments in R&D, and can be used as a defensive tactic to co-opt or block competition. As discussed above, a global strategy may be important for defensive reasons alone since this permits companies to establish or maintain blocking positions in other countries. This allows the company to challenge its competitors in their home countries and therefore should minimize the chances of competitors attacking the firm in its own home market. Finally, in certain circumstances, foreign acquisitions may be a lower cost means for entering a foreign market. Acquisitions provide immediate local knowledge and presence, remove a competitor from the next round of contests and may remove excess capacity from the world market.

DO WE NEED CANADIAN MULTINATIONALS?

There is little debate regarding the importance of being the home base for international corporations. But do we need Canadian-controlled multinationals to be competitive and to prosper in the evolving and more interdependent, global economy? Before we consider this question, let us take a brief look at the track record to date in developing Canadian multinationals which have become major players in their industries.

The Fortune 500 largest industrial companies in the world in 1992 provides a good starting point. There were eight Canadian companies on this list. There were no Canadian companies among the top 100; the largest Canadian company, Northern Telecom, ranked 173 on the list. Only Italy, among the other members of the G-7 had fewer companies among the top 500, but Italy had three companies among the fifty largest. On a per capita basis, Canada had a disproportionately small number of major corporations among the top 500 in comparison to the US, Japan, UK, Germany and France. It is also interesting to note that Sweden, Australia and Switzerland had more companies on this list than Canada and that Sweden and Switzerland were both represented among the 100 largest companies (Table 12.5). The UNCTC has noted that despite 'the comparatively small domestic market, a handful of

282

Table 12.5 The 500 largest industrial companies in the world: total numbers in the G-7 and selected other countries, 1992

	1–50	*51–100*	*101–250*	*251–500*	*Total*
Canada	0	0	3	5	8
US	13	19	50	79	161
France	5	3	10	12	30
Germany	7	8	7	10	32
Italy	3	1	2	0	6
UK	1	4	12	23	40
Japan	13	7	40	68	128
Australia	0	0	2	7	9
Switzerland	2	1	2	4	9
Sweden	0	2	3	9	14

Source: *Fortune*, 26 July 1993

Swedish transnational corporations have become global market leaders, and many have done so by well-executed acquisition strategies'.[24]

Even more disappointing is the absence of large Canadian companies in most technology-intensive industries. We have a presence in aerospace, where Bombardier ranks 14 out of 16, and in electronics and electrical equipment, where Northern Telecom ranks 24 out of 46 companies.[25] It is important to note that Bombardier has been strongly supported by both the federal government and the Government of Quebec, and that Northern Telecom's early growth was buttressed by its monopoly supply position to Bell Canada. It is conceivable that in the absence of government support and a monopoly position, neither company would be anywhere near the top 500 companies in the world today. As well, Petro-Canada, another Canadian member of the world's largest industrial companies, is entirely a creation of the federal government.

Admittedly, Canada has many more multinationals, but the largest multinationals play a special role because they can serve as the foundation for creating a cluster of domestic companies which can 'benefit from a shared culture and learning experience, supply capabilities and infrastructure' so that the 'resulting economies give them a competitive edge in both domestic and international markets'.[26]

Reich[27] and Porter[28] appear to agree that ownership does not matter in those cases in which a country becomes the home base for fully integrated operations with decision-making autonomy for serving a regional market in several product lines or the global market in a much narrower range of products. But, as both Porter and Reich point out, if a country does not attract the fully integrated complex, it will receive very limited benefits from foreign direct investment. Porter has indicated that Canada has tended to attract foreign investment to gain access to the Canadian market or acquire resources ('source basic factors'). In both cases, the host country is vulnerable to parent

283

company decisions. According to Porter, '[f]actor sourcing and market access investment . . . tend to be less permanent; they are prone to being reversed as cheaper inputs are located elsewhere or investment in the country is no longer needed to gain market access'.[29] Moreover, these types of foreign investment provide few beneficial spillovers and externalities to other domestic firms and industries.

The centre(s) for strategic decision-making within multinationals (the home base) is(are) critical for Canada since this is where the key decisions are made. The periphery operations/subsidiaries serve as a conduit for information to the centre and for the implementation of the decisions mandated by the centre. The aggressive use by the US of their panoply of trade laws places Canada at a competitive disadvantage in attracting the North American regional headquarters of non-Canadian multinationals, and structural shortcomings in technology-intensive activities diminishes our attractiveness as a home base for many products. Thus, non-Canadian companies are more likely to select the US as the location for their North American regional headquarters and Canada is not likely to rank among the top locations for a product headquarters within a non-Canadian, multinational company. In light of these difficulties and the importance of a home base, Canadian policymakers may have no choice but to concentrate their economic development strategies on promoting the creation of more Canadian multinationals with the goal of increasing the Canadian presence among the largest global, corporate players.

THE MACHINERY INDUSTRY: A CASE STUDY

This industry provides an excellent case study of the serious economic and competitive problems which can arise when policy fails to promote the creation of a significant Canadian presence in a key industrial sector. As Porter has noted, Canada's productivity problems can be traced to several factors 'including a marked tendency to source from abroad . . . In short, with few competitive machinery industries, many Canadian businesses are deprived of the dynamic interactions that foster process innovation and upgrading.'[30]

J. B. De Long has stated that there are several theoretical reasons for believing that machinery and equipment spending is an important transmission mechanism for new technological change. Machinery investments yield large productivity and environmental benefits because they incorporate the latest technologies. Machinery investments also generate indirect benefits since both workers and management must upgrade their skills in order to utilize the new machinery and equipment effectively.[31]

Unfortunately, the machinery sector is one of Canada's weakest industrial performers and is relatively underdeveloped in comparison to its counterparts in other countries. In Canada, the machinery and equipment industry accounts for between 5 and 7 per cent of total manufacturing output, whereas in Germany this industry represents 12 to 15 per cent of manufacturing production. The comparable figures for Japan and the United States are 11 to 13 per cent and 10 to 11 per cent respectively.

Canada's international trade deficit in industrial machinery has risen from $2.3 billion in 1977 to $6.2 billion in 1987. Since 1987, the deficit has fluctuated in the $6 to $8 billion range. In comparison to the industry in the US, the R&D intensity of the Canadian machinery and equipment industry has lagged well behind. In 1984, the R&D to sales ratio in Canada was approximately 40 per cent of the level in the US. Much of this differential can be accounted for by the high degree of foreign ownership of the Canadian industry and the significantly poorer R&D performance of the foreign-controlled companies in Canada. In 1984, the foreign-controlled firms in Canada had an R&D to sales ratio of 0.8 per cent, compared to the 3 per cent ratio for the Canadian-owned companies. In 1989, both foreign-controlled and Canadian-owned firms improved their R&D performance, but the former group still underperformed the latter (R&D to sales ratio of 1.5 per cent for the foreign-controlled companies versus 3.7 per cent for the Canadian-owned ones).

To a large extent, the underdevelopment of this industry in Canada can be attributed to our trade policy for this sector. Neither tariff protection nor free trade has proved to be beneficial. Over the years, Canadian tariff policy for machinery and equipment has attempted to reconcile two competing objectives: the first to encourage the development of a machinery-producing sector, and the second to reduce the cost of capital equipment for Canadian firms. Trade protection resulted in many foreign firms establishing subsidiaries in Canada. Indeed, at present about 80 per cent of Canadian shipments in this industry originate from foreign-controlled subsidiaries.

In 1968, the Machinery Program was introduced which allowed the duty to be remitted in individual cases, when the imported machinery or equipment was not available in Canada. Though this programme was intended to reduce the costs to Canadian users of machinery, this policy has probably contributed further to the underdevelopment of this industry in Canada. The duty remission programme for domestic users did not provide a sufficient incentive to use domestic suppliers. Foreign-controlled companies have pre-empted a large part of the Canadian market in the machinery industry, capitalizing on the advantages provided by economies of scale, the distribution channels of their parents, and the parents' links with customers.

This, in turn, has worked to the long-term disadvantage of Canadian customers, since distance matters in developing production and process technologies and equipment catering to the specific requirements of users and in providing the necessary back-up services. The underdevelopment of an indigenous machinery and equipment industry in Canada has meant that, aside from the largest companies, most other users of production machinery and equipment do not have the information on or access to the newest generations of products and are likely to be inadequately served in terms of technical assistance and training of the workforce in the use of the latest production equipment and technologies.

The economic consequences of an underdeveloped machinery industry and excessive reliance of foreign sources of supply are most visible in the machine tools sub-sector. Machine tools comprise a key component of most machinery manufacturing processes and they are the leading edge of the CAD/ CAM revolution in design and production. The machine tools industry is strategically important in the evolution of the flexible manufacturing system and in supplying the critical frontier technologies to the engineering industries. But Canada has historically had a weak position in machine tools and this has contributed to the limited scale and scope of the domestic machinery manufacturing industry in general. The relatively small domestic market in Canada has required companies to export in order to be competitive. Since the machine tools technology of Canadian companies was not always at the frontier, they failed to be competitive and hence were unable to export sufficiently to remain cost-competitive and generate the cash flows necessary to develop new technologies and invest in training so as to produce the needed skilled workers and engineering talent.

As mentioned above, the reliance on foreign suppliers of machinery and equipment has exacerbated the problem of rapid diffusion of technology in Canada. New technologies, especially for production, are embedded in the latest generation of machines and equipment. A slow rate of diffusion of the latest production technologies may reflect a lack of information on the availability of such products and technologies. Alternatively, it may reflect the inability of management and labour to absorb the new technologies, or the inability of companies to finance the capital. These problems are most pronounced for small and medium-size companies. The suppliers of machinery and equipment play an important role in informing their customers, financing the purchases and in training their workers, and the large, diversified, foreign-controlled companies in this industry favour dealing with large customers.

Close co-operation between suppliers and customers is critical for developing new technologies which are useful. A major customer reduces the development and commercialization risks faced by firms in the machinery industry. At the same time, the new products are developed to meet the specific needs of the main customers and may be less adaptable to the needs of smaller firms. As well, the supplier firms are more likely to provide the necessary support services to the key customers and are less likely to do so for smaller customers located in foreign markets.

The Canadian problem in absorbing new technology is widespread and magnified because so few of the major producers actually have production plants in Canada. 'One of the reasons why German-made computerized machine tools are so difficult to adopt here is that German companies are assuming that workers who will be using their technology have a certain set of skills, industrial and work-place cultures, standards and regulations ... Our training difficulties are magnified because we do not have the producers here.'[32] Since producers in Germany, Japan, Italy and Switzerland have become more dominant, the new long-distance relationship makes it more difficult for Canadian firms to utilize new machinery. It is not surprising, therefore, that Porter attributed Canada's productivity problem, in part, to the underdevelopment of an indigenous machinery and equipment industry.

Unfortunately, the prospects for this important industry in Canada are not promising. Foreign-controlled producers of machinery equipment, in addition to pre-empting key segments of the domestic market, undertake little more than assembly or distribution activities in Canada. Canadian subsidiaries are not the fully integrated complexes praised by Reich for they are not independent product or geographic divisions within the entire organization. Since Canada is not the home base for these companies, the Canadian operations have limited autonomy in the areas of research, product development and marketing. Furthermore, in the case of the major, non-US companies in this industry, the Canadian subsidiaries may have an even more truncated role than in the case of subsidiaries of US companies. Moreover, the organizational structures of the non-US multinational players in the machinery and equipment industry indicate, especially in light of US trade harassment, that Canada will find it extremely difficult to attract new investments by these companies. These companies may nevertheless be scouring the Canadian market for attractive takeover targets to further fill out or enhance their product lines.

Porter also has observed that all of Canada's five main export clusters (transportation equipment, chemicals and chemical products, mining, food and beverages and wood industries) have a high degree of foreign control. Foreign-controlled firms have a tendency to rely on the same suppliers as their parents. Hence, the machinery and equipment requirements in these sectors are likely to be met by suppliers headquartered abroad. Once again, it is not surprising that foreign-controlled companies have pre-empted major segments of this industry in Canada.

As a result, market pressures have driven Canadian companies into niche strategies which are quite risky since customers prefer to deal with one source for all machinery and equipment needs. Furthermore, companies which focus on product niche strategies are less inclined to cater to the needs of large customers for whom continuous interaction is critical for developing the next generation of products. And the small Canadian companies in this industry seem not to be well-positioned to enter into collaborative arrangements with other companies that will be necessary to create the new generations of increasingly sophisticated machinery, particularly relating to flexible machinery systems.

Canada has a major structural defect which jeopardizes the competitiveness of many sectors in the economy because we have failed to develop Canadian multinationals in the machinery industry and we have been unable to become the home base for foreign companies in this sector. Size is critical for success in many segments of this industry. For example, in the construction equipment sector, after-sales service (e.g. the ability to repair equipment and machinery quickly) is very important to customers since the costs of any project delays may far exceed the costs of the equipment. Extensive dealer networks and inventories (to be able to provide replacement equipment when necessary) are critical competitive factors. The largest companies in this industry are typically the low-cost producers (economies of scale, global sourcing), have well-established distribution systems and have widely respected brand names and reputations which comprise their competitive advantages.

Pre-emption of the Canadian market has foreclosed many opportunities for Canadian companies to grow and achieve the critical mass to move beyond the threshold of a peripheral, niche player into the ranks of a global competitor. But not only do Canadian companies have to overcome the market barriers and the subsequent size disadvantage (very significant in R&D, marketing and economies of scale in production), they also face the risk that if they overcome these barriers and succeed, they may be acquired by the larger companies in the industry.[33] While the policy challenge is enormous, it may not be insurmountable. Sweden is the home of five major multinationals in the machinery industry and Finland, an even smaller country, is the home base for two others.

CHALLENGES FACING POLICY-MAKERS

Policy-makers in Canada have to recognize that the variables propelling globalization are largely beyond their control.[34] Thus, they have no choice but to accept globalization and all of its ramifications and strive to reduce the threats posed by globalization and exploit the opportunities which are offered. In addition, government policy-makers will have to encourage Canadian companies increasingly to pursue global strategies. Global strategies offer more options, and in an increasingly uncertain environment the options have greater value. Further, as stated by the UNCTC in its 1992 World Investment Report:[35]

> [G]lobalization means that the boundaries that define an industry are increasingly being drawn across countries rather than within them. The implication of the trend is that, in many instances, strategies to develop independent indigenous industries may no longer be appropriate for developing a dynamic comparative advantage, and that participation in global industries may be a necessary ingredient for the development of a competitive economy.

Consequently, domestic companies will have to be able to access markets, production facilities and resources in the major regions. Collaborative arrangements and foreign acquisitions may become even more attractive global strategies for Canadian companies than direct investment, and government policy should be prepared to promote and facilitate these and other strategies.

The primary objective for policy-makers should be the development and growth of more Canadian multinationals. Foreign investments by small and medium-size enterprises in Canada already are relatively more important than in other OECD countries.[36] However, in addition to the many problems facing small and medium-size enterprises in general, the tendency for such companies to limit their initial investments to nearby countries with close historical, political and commercial ties, even though superior investment opportunities may exist elsewhere, may pose another problem for these companies and Canadian policy-makers. The North American market is the smallest of the Triad in terms of intra-regional trade flows and it may not necessarily be the most rapidly growing and dynamic of the three in the future.

Since the probability of becoming a multinational increases with size, a three-pronged approach should be considered. The least important of the three may be the promotion of new business start-ups. *Ceteris paribus*, an increasing number of start-ups should lead over time to a growing number of threshold firms. But there is no assurance that the probability of survival will remain constant if the annual rate of start-ups increases. There is now a very high failure rate for new companies in Canada and, although this fluctuates with the business cycle, it is possible that there may also be a positive correlation between the failure rate and the rate of new business formation.

While small and medium-size companies generally are perceived to be the engines of job growth, the reality is that the small and medium-size firms which succeed and grow rapidly are the ones which create the new jobs. Hence, the second prong of the government's strategy should focus on increasing survival and growth rates; that is, assist in creating more threshold firms. The third component should concentrate on pushing more of these firms over the threshold into the ranks of major players in the global markets.

One of the major obstacles facing policy-makers in Canada is the pre-emption of both domestic and foreign markets by large, well-financed and diversified foreign multinationals. The problems resulting from market pre-emption stand out in the machinery industry, and they have spilled over to affect other industries adversely. But the pre-emption problems are not specific to that industry.

The 1992 World Competitiveness Report has highlighted other problems for Canadian companies and policy-makers. For example, Canada ranked 21 out of 22 in terms of the degree of seriousness in the erosion of the country's manufacturing base. Canada also ranked twenty-first in terms of the relative time required to launch a new product into the market and nineteenth for time required to develop a new product. The very poor performance of Canadian business in these two areas may reflect the high degree of foreign ownership of Canadian industry and the absence of a home base for these companies in Canada, and the limited presence of Canadian companies in foreign markets. In addition, Canada ranked nineteenth in terms of senior management's experience in international business.

As well, there are the standard problems faced by small and medium-size companies: inadequate financial and managerial resources to identify, plan and implement the strategies needed to best position themselves and to react to various types of changes in both local and international markets; lack of international management and marketing expertise; undeveloped reputations for quality, reliability and performance.

What about solutions then? Many have been offered over the past decade and since there is not likely to be any single set that will adequately tackle the many obstacles, and since what may be an appropriate solution today may not be one tomorrow, policy-makers will have to experiment. They will have to be prepared and willing to admit that some approaches do not work and so change direction accordingly. But, overall, it is imperative that they proactively tackle the threats and opportunities posed by globalization and deal with Canada's serious economic problems, in particular high unemployment and an enormous international debt.[37]

CONCLUSION

The debate on industrial policy in Canada originated at the time of Confederation. But this debate took on a life of its own with the publication of the Report of the Gordon Royal Commission on Canada's Economic Prospects in the mid-1950s. The tilt towards a more activist industrial policy gathered momentum with the publication of the Watkins Report on Foreign Ownership in 1968 and a series of Science Council of Canada pronouncements and studies in the late 1970s. At that time, the Science Council was concerned with the high levels of unemployment, mounting deficits in service transactions and the overall current account balance and the perceived process of de-industrialization of Canadian industry. Not much has changed.

To reverse the tide of de-industrialization and offset the problems stemming from the high degree of foreign ownership, the Science Council advocated an industrial policy built around a technology policy – a 'policy which seeks to influence the selective development and use of technology in the industrial system so that the maximum benefits of economic activity in Canada are realized for Canadians'.[38] The Science Council's approach consisted of a number of initiatives, including the nurturing of Canadian-owned firms in promising high-technology fields.

Supporters of the free trade alternative continually attacked the views of Watkins and the Science Council. Many studies supported the conventional economist's view that free trade would encourage the needed rationalization and specialization of Canadian industry and so increase productivity levels and the competitiveness of Canadian firms. The free trade argument gained its greatest support in the Macdonald Royal Commission in the mid-1980s which led ultimately to the FTA with the US and to NAFTA.

While several proponents of the free trade alternative to a more interventionist industrial policy speculated that more rapid adoption by Canadian industry of best-practice technology, not necessarily developed in Canada, might produce more significant productivity growth than increased levels of indigenous R&D investments, they overlooked the strong link between diffusion of best-practice technology and the existence of a large and technologically advanced, indigenous machinery industry. Indeed, the low rates of adoption of new production technologies by Canadian industries are likely the consequence of the underdevelopment of domestic supply capabilities in this industry.

But despite the implementation of the FTA and other elements of the neoconservative economic agenda, Canada's unemployment experience today is no better than it was when the Science Council was warning about the de-industrialization of this country. In addition, Canada has been unable since the early 1980s to generate a sufficiently large merchandise trade balance to offset the enormous deficit in trade in services, and so we find ourselves in the position where our net international indebtedness increases by about $30 billion annually, a position that is not likely to be sustainable.

The time has long passed to debate whether Canada needs an interventionist economic development strategy. It is time to act; regrettably we are late to start and we have squandered too much time debating the obvious: in an increasingly interdependent world, the Canadian government has to be an active participant in co-operation with Canadian business and labour to make sure that we are not left behind. There is no alternative if we wish to gain some control over our economy and economic destiny. Otherwise, we will be relegated even more to the state of economic dependency which has characterized our history as we have developed as a staples economy.

But we must also recognize that the Government of Canada has very limited autonomy in developing and implementing an interventionist strategy. Economic integration and globalization have constrained the ability of a nation, especially one the size of Canada, to intervene with micro policies. As noted above, the need for companies to adopt a global strategy at a much earlier stage in their development complicates the task for government in trying to promote the creation and growth of Canadian companies. More importantly, international trade agreements and US trade laws circumscribe the ability of the Government of Canada to implement policies which favour domestic companies and attempt to spur their growth.

The FTA, the NAFTA and the GATT do not prevent trade harassment by US companies, nor do they deter the various US government agencies, responsible for administering and enforcing the many trade laws, from producing biased decisions whose objective is to manage trade relations for the benefit of the US. Canadian companies incur significant costs in defending themselves against US actions. The US companies lodging the complaints, on the other hand, are able to free ride on the US government which investigates and rules on the case. The time and uncertainty surrounding the final outcomes deter US customers from dealing with the Canadian companies. The lost sales during this period are not likely to be recovered. Moreover, US companies have the ability to harass their foreign competitors by initiating sequential trade complaints under different US trade remedy laws. Even Americans admit that the US trade remedy laws hinder free trade. Cletus Coughlin, a researcher with the Federal Reserve Bank of St Louis, after reviewing the US trade laws concluded:[39] 'Overall, the evidence is that trade-remedy laws hinder rather than facilitate free trade. U.S. fair trade laws can be more accurately characterized as the bedrock of protectionism.'

Increasing the scope for capital mobility, as is achieved by the NAFTA, will create additional challenges for all governments in regulating capital and economic activity. The setting, monitoring and enforcing of standards for pollution; safety and health; bargaining relations between business and labour; employment contracts; collection, distribution and use of information; and protection of individual rights are critical for mitigating the negative consequences of market failures which may be compounded by the further globalization of companies. By setting and enforcing standards for the direct fiduciary responsibilities of financiers, corporate directors and lawyers, and by establishing the general legal framework within which market transactions take place, government provides the confidence necessary for private markets to function.

But globalization is creating problems for all governments in maintaining their respective systems of fiduciary regulation. Since regulations cannot be applied extraterritorially to providers of services, service companies have an incentive to search for and locate in the country with the most lax standards and so avoid more stringent and costly regulations. There is a tendency for the multinational service companies to shop for the most advantageous regulatory environments. The increasing mobility of capital and innovations in telecommunications and computers are shifting the advantage from governments to transnational corporations who are finding it easier to deal with clients at a distance and thus circumvent government regulations. More foreign service providers may be able to avoid a local presence, yet be 'established' or accessible in the local market and be immune completely or in part from local restrictions or regulations.

In order to prevent a 'race to the bottom' – that is, an erosion in regulatory standards – governments will have to co-operate in either harmonizing their regulations or setting minimum standards (for example the labour and environment codes appended to the NAFTA) or permitting discriminatory treatment of domestic and foreign suppliers. The European Community has long recognized the need for harmonization and co-operation in regulation in order to counterbalance the growing bargaining strength of transnational corporations and now the international financial community and their government overseers have recognized this need too. Canada has found its regulatory sovereignty increasingly constrained and over time will be less capable of unilaterally setting standards and enforcing its regulations.

Co-operation is necessary at the international level in order to control the activities and behaviour of multinational corporations – in essence, to counter the bargaining position of capital. In the absence of international, GATT-type rules and enforcement mechanisms to control competition in international markets and regulate the activities of companies, global corporations will be able to dictate more aggressively the economic and social agendas for even the largest industrialized countries. As for Canada, an interventionist economic strategy will be doomed to failure if it does not satisfy the demands of mobile and unregulated capital.

In an increasing number of areas, government regulation (including competition policy) will have to be conducted by international bodies comparable to the GATT and the new World Trade Organization. Multilateral rules, enforced by the joint actions of the contracting parties to the new international agreements, will be necessary in a world of increasing capital mobility and dramatic disparities in living standards, national regulations and political stability. Moreover, international co-operation will be required to mitigate the natural tendency of competitive markets to become unstable.

Finally, as long as the other members of the G-7 remain committed to reducing their respective deficits, the world economy and the Canadian economy will continue to struggle along. Only a concerted effort by the G-7 to collectively provide stimulus will propel the world economy onto a higher growth path which may begin to make some inroads into the tragically high unemployment levels. Getting the G-7 to act together on the fiscal and monetary policy sides is critical for the health of the world economy and for tackling the unemployment crisis in Canada and elsewhere.

Overall, the Canadian government has some policy-making autonomy left, but unilateral action by the government is unlikely to have any noticeable impact on the serious economic and social problems facing us today.

NOTES

1 A. M. Rugman and A. Verbeke (1988), p. 3.
2 C. J. McMillan (1993), p. 12.
3 Ibid., p. 62.
4 United Nations Center on Transnational Corporations (1993), p. 99.

5 Ibid., p. 15.
6 See F. Lazar (1993).
7 OECD (1985), p. 30.
8 C. Handy (1992).
9 M. Porter (1991).
10 Knickerbocker (1973) popularized the oligopolistic interaction model.
11 M. V. Posner (1961).
12 See J. H. Dunning (1988) and P. J. Buckley and M. Casson (1985).
13 OECD, op. cit., p. 40.
14 A. M. Rugman and A. Verbeke (1990), p. 10.
15 C. A. Bartlett and S. Ghoshal (1989), p. 212.
16 United Nations, Transnational Corporations and Management Division (1992), p. 11.
17 Rugman and Verbeke (1990), p. 10.
18 OECD, op. cit., p. 38.
19 Ibid., p. 23.
20 United Nations Center on Transnational Corporations (1990a), p. 11.
21 McMillan, op. cit., p. 19.
22 United Nations Center on Transnational Corporations (1990a), p. 30.
23 W. C. Kim, P. Hwang and W. P. Burgers (1993), pp. 276–7.
24 United Nations Center on Transnational Corporations (1989), p. 52.
25 The total number of companies in an industrial sector includes only companies on the Fortune 500 list.
26 J. H. Dunning (1992), p. 159.
27 R. Reich (1990).
28 M. Porter, op. cit., p. 73.
29 Ibid., p. 74.
30 Ibid., p. 16.
31 *NBER Reporter*.
32 Canadian Labour Congress (1993).
33 Timberjack, a successful Canadian niche company in the logging equipment sector, was acquired by Rauma Repola, a Finnish-based multinational.
34 The United Nations Center on Transnational Corporations has highlighted the following factors: high and increasing fixed costs of technology-intensive production require worldwide market share to amortize R&D and capital equipment investments; rapid diffusion of new technologies and innovative activities around the world necessitate companies to be present in all major markets in order to avail themselves of state-of-the-art developments; steady advances in telecommunications continuously lower the costs of managing an integrated production and marketing network; and homogenization of product standards and consumer tastes increases the importance of global economies of scale and brand name reputations. United Nations Center on Transnational Corporations (1990b), p. 19.
35 United Nations Center on Transnational Corporations (1992), p. 104.
36 OECD, op. cit., p. 22.
37 At present, our tenuous position is very apparent in our unemployment rate and balance of payments records. The unemployment rate gap between Canada and the US is near record levels (approximately 5 percentage points). It has been almost twenty years since the national unemployment rate in Canada last approached the current level in the US (around 6.5 per cent) and forecasts indicate that we will not get down to this level during the remainder of this century. Our current account deficit, which first surpassed the $10 billion threshold in 1986, has averaged near $30 billion per year in 1991 and 1992. The cumulative current

account deficits between 1986 and 1992 have amounted to almost $150 billion and have accounted for all of the increase in Canada's net international indebtedness during this same period. At the beginning of 1993, Canada's net international indebtedness stood at just over $300 billion (around $11,000 per capita).

38 Science Council of Canada (1979).
39 C. Coughlin (1991), p. 17.

BIBLIOGRAPHY

Bartlett, C.A. and S. Ghoshal. 1989. *Managing Across Borders: The Transnational Solution*. Boston: Harvard Business School Press.

Buckley, P.J. and M. Casson. 1985. *The Economic Theory of the Multinational Enterprise*. London, Macmillan.

Canadian Labour Congress. 1993. *TECHnotes*. Ottowa (February).

Coughlin, C. 1991. 'U.S. Trade Remedy Laws: Do They Facilitate or Hinder Free Trade?' *Federal Reserve Bank of St Louis Review* (July/August).

Dunning, J.H. 1988. *Explaining International Production*. London: Unwin Hyman.

Dunning, J.H. 1992. 'The Competitive Advantage of Countries and the Activities of Transnational Corporations: Review Article.' *Transnational Corporations* 1:1 (February).

Handy, C. 1992. 'Balancing Corporate Power: A New Federalist Paper.' *Harvard Business Review* (November–December).

Kim, W.C., P. Hwang and W. P. Burgers. 1993. 'Multinationals' Diversification and the Risk–Return Trade-off.' *Strategic Management Journal* 14.

Knickerbocker, F.T. 1973. *Oligopolistic Reaction and Multinational Enterprise*. Boston: Harvard Graduate School of Business Administration.

Lazar, F. 1993. 'Investment in the NAFTA – Just Cause for Walking Away.' *Journal of World Trade* (October).

McMillan, C.J. 1993. 'Building Blocks or Trade Blocs: NAFTA, Japan and the New World Order.' Ottawa: Canada–Japan Trade Council.

NBER Reporter Washington, D.C. (Summer 1992).

OECD. 1985. *International Investment and Multinational Enterprises: Structural Adjustment and Multinational Enterprises*. Paris.

Porter, M. 1991. *Canada at the Crossroads: The Reality of a New Competitive Environment*. Ottawa.

Posner, M.V. 1961. 'International Trade and Technical Change.' *Oxford Economic Papers*.

Reich, R. 1990. 'Who is US?' *Harvard Business Review* (January–February).

Rugman, A.M. and A. Verbeke. 1988., 'Canadian Business in a Global Trading Environment.' Ontario Center for International Business, Working Paper Series (No. 1, September).

Rugman, A.M. and A. Verbeke. 1990. 'Is the Transnational Solution a New Theory of Multinational Strategic Management?' Ontario Center for International Business, Working Paper Series (No. 32, June).

Science Council of Canada. 1979. *Forging the Links: A Technology Policy for Canada*. Ottawa.

UNCTC. 1989. 'The Process of Transnationalization and Transnational Mergers.' UNCTC Current Studies, No. 8, Series A. New York: UN.

UNCTC. 1990a. 'New Approaches to Best-Practices Manufacturing: The Role of Transnational Corporations and Implications for Developing Countries.' UNCTC Current Studies, No. 12, Series A. New York: UN.

UNCTC. 1990b. 'Regional Economic Integration and Transnational Corporations in the 1990s: Europe 1992, North America and Developing Countries.' UNCTC Current Studies, No. 15, Series A. New York: UN.

UNCTC. 1992. *World Investment Report 1992: Transnational Corporations as Engines of Growth.* New York: UN.

United Nations Center on Transnational Corporations (UNCTC). 1993. *World Investment Report 1993: Transnational Corporations and Integrated International Production.* New York: UN.

United Nations, Transnational Corporations and Management Division. 1992. *Formulation and Implementation of Foreign Investment Policies.* New York: UN.

Part V

ARE KEYNES AND BEVERIDGE REALLY DEAD? THE STRATEGIC DILEMMA FOR POLICY-MAKERS

13

PUBLIC POWER BEYOND THE NATION-STATE

The case of the European Community

Wolfgang Streeck

If ever there was a region and historical period in which nation-states might have allowed themselves to be replaced with a supranational state, so as to expand the size of political jurisdiction to match that of an expanding market, this was Western Europe after the Second World War. Already Emile Durkheim, in the late nineteenth century, had noticed the development of a common European civil society, based on a growing international division of labour and shared concepts of justice.

Two European civil wars in the twentieth century, each resulting in catastrophic destruction, had discredited the nation-state and given rise to widespread conviction that both nationalism and *laissez-faire* capitalism had had their chance and had been found wanting. There also was the skill and statesmanship of an unusual cast of far-sighted Continental-European leaders, from Schumann to de Gasperi to Adenauer, all of them dedicated to building a lasting, European-wide structure of peace and prosperity, and not least Jean Monnet's grand design of economic unity driving the emergence, ultimately, of a 'United States of Europe'. Given this unique conjuncture of favourable conditions, it would seem plausible that, to the extent that internationalization of the economic functions of the nation-state was *not* achieved in Western Europe in the half-century since the end of the last war, *it is unlikely to be achieved elsewhere*.

In this chapter I will treat the European Union (EU)[1] as the most advanced, and therefore especially instructive, attempt to build *a state-like system of international economic governance for international capitalism*. I argue that the European Union as an institutional system is fundamentally different from the national state that we know, especially with respect to its role and capacity in relation to the economy, and that by all indications it will never become a supranational interventionist state on the model of European nation-states. Rather, I maintain, what is emerging in Western Europe today is a polity of a new kind – an international order, controlled by intergovernmental relations between nation-states, that serves as a domestic order for a trans-national economy, with a unique political economy that is not easily understood and will take a long time to explore. What seems clear beyond doubt, however, is that it is not driven by a logic of 'spill-over' from international economic integration to supranational state-formation, or from market-making to market intervention – and that in particular there is no functionalist dynamic inherent in it that would provide for a supranational replication of the national welfare state, or an internationalization of state-like economic governance.

A POLITICAL ECONOMY PERSPECTIVE ON EUROPEAN INTEGRATION

Political economy analyses the relationship between politics and political institutions on the one hand and the economy, in particular the 'self-regulating market' (Polanyi) of modern capitalism, on the other. In the nineteenth and twentieth centuries European nation-states developed a capacity to govern 'their' economies, applying public power to control economic activities and market outcomes in the 'public interest'. Especially where state interventionism coincided with democracy, or 'social democracy', that public interest was defined to include preservation of social cohesion through prevention of excessive inequality, provision of some degree of social security in the widest sense and generally protection of the citizenry from the worst uncertainties wrought upon them by the 'free play of market forces'.

The *civilization of modern capitalism* under national economic governance was accomplished by mobilization of *public power*, i.e. of a specific capacity of the modern state to create and enforce *status rights and obligations* for participants in economic transactions, in particular rights and obligations of *citizenship*. Citizenship typically and essentially does not arise out of market relations, and can neither be gained nor given away by contract, but is imposed on the market preceding, and defining the conditions of, any voluntary exchange. In fact, political development in modern capitalism can be conceptualized in terms of T. H. Marshall's famous triad of the creation and enforcement by means of public power of, first, *civil rights* to participate in market exchanges and engage in contracts, *political rights* to collective organization and representation, and *social rights* to a basic level of subsistence guaranteed by the public power.[2] Growth of citizenship, according to Marshall, makes capitalist markets possible (through civil rights), and modifies their outcomes (through political and social rights), and in doing the latter makes capitalism as an economic system socially legitimate and sustainable.

The core question of political economy at a time when economic relations systematically outgrow the boundaries of nation-states, then, is whether by undermining the economic governing capacity of the nation-state, internationalization undermines the capacity of society to civilize its economy. In so far as the public power that served in the past to domesticate modern capitalism was vested in the sovereignty of national states, economic inter-nationalization without corresponding internationalization of state sover-eignty results in *an integrated economy governed by fragmented sovereignty*. To the extent that this weakens the hold of politics over markets, the question poses itself whether state-like governance mechanisms can be devised above the nation-state that are capable of mobilizing the same kind of public power *vis-à-vis* the economy as was traditionally mobilized at the national level. Can Polanyi's political 'counter-movement' against the self-regulating market continue in an internationalized economy? Is it possible to develop supra-national political and state capacities strong enough to impose market-correcting rights of citizenship on an international economy? And can what was in the past the principal subject of domestic politics be dealt with as effectively through international relations between nation-states, or do international economic relations have to be transformed into domestic relations in an integrated transnational polity? And what are the prospects for this happening? As pointed out, the European Union represents an ideal research site for exploring these questions.

THE EUROPEAN UNION BETWEEN FREE TRADE AND SUPRANATIONAL WELFARE STATE FORMATION

The history of European integration is one of deep ambiguity and continuous conflict between two alternative political-economic projects, a free-trade and a supranational welfare state-building project. While the former involves common market-making, primarily through negative integration by removal of trade barriers, the latter aims at a positive reconstruction at a supranational level of the national welfare-state regimes made obsolete by economic integration. In a complex variety of ways, the two projects have come to be related, not just to different class interests but also to different national interests as well as to alternative answers to fundamental questions of foreign policy, in particular the position of Western Europe as a unified entity in the world at large.

Historically, those who preferred an integrated Europe to be a negatively integrated customs union, also wanted it to be the European leg of an Atlantic alliance with the United States. By contrast, the state-building version of European integration tended to be associated with a project of European self-assertion against US hegemony. Europe as a customs union was traditionally espoused by the British and by the German 'Atlanticists', especially in the CDU (e.g. Ludwig Erhard), whereas supranational state-building was favoured by the French and, for their own reasons, the German 'Gaullists'. The French position remained ambivalent well into the 1960s and 1970s, when it paradoxically included a strong concern with the preservation of French national sovereignty.[3] But this changed after the failure of the Socialist reflation experiment in the early 1980s, which led to the *relance* of the

Community under French leadership in the middle of the decade. Unions and socialist political parties, to the extent that their positions were not coloured by their respective 'national interests' – which they often were; namely, the United Kingdom – tended to side with European supranationalism. Business, to the contrary, generally abhorred the idea of yet another layer of re-distributive state intervention being added on top of the nation-states, and has mostly favoured the free-trade version of European integration, except for industries hoping to benefit from supranational 'industrial policy'.[4]

Simplifying somewhat and personalizing, as of the 1980s, what may be called 'the two faces of European integration', the supranational welfare state-building project came to be represented by the French-Socialist President of the European Commission, Jacques Delors, with his 'Social Dimension' and his occasional displays of 'Euro-nationalism', especially against the United States. His counterpart was Margaret Thatcher, standing for Europe as a large free-trade zone, politically closely aligned with the United States and inte-grated in NATO under Anglo-American command – with 'socialism' wiped out everywhere on the British model; markets and industries, and especially labour markets, deregulated; the 'sovereignty' of member nation-states strictly preserved; and Britain free to pursue its Atlantic interests without entanglement in a unified European entity dominated by a French–German alliance of *étatisme-cum-Soziale Marktwirtschaft*, or by United Germany alone.

My view is that, today, the battle on the political economy of European Union is over, that Thatcher won and Delors lost, and that this is very likely irreversible. United Europe has not only failed to develop sovereign public power for governing its economy, but has over the years accumulated an institutional legacy – a *de facto* constitution as embodied in the revised treaties and in international custom and practice – that effectively precludes such development for any foreseeable future. As evidenced especially by the outcome of the struggle in the late 1980s over the 'Social Dimension' of the Internal Market, European integration has become locked in a negative, market-making, deregulatory mode, and in an institutional trajectory that almost certainly rules out progress from intergovernmentalism to supra-nationalism, or from national to supranational distributive intervention, and thus perfectly fits the interests behind the 'Thatcherist' *alliance of neo-liberalism and nationalism* that has come to dominate European integration in the 1980s.

THE PERSISTENCE OF THE NATION-STATE

The reasons for this have to do with a deep contradiction in the condition of the nation-state at the end of the twentieth century. While nation-states, especially in Western Europe, have progressively lost the capacity to govern their economies and impose a political will on the free play of market forces on their territories,[5] they have at the same time remained uniquely viable as political organizations and as foci of collective identification. The latter applies even where subnational communities try to break away from existing nation-states; what they aspire to is almost always to set up a nation-state of their own,[6] smaller still than the one that presently governs them, and as a result even less capable of internalizing the external effects that dominate subnational still more than national economies.

Put differently, while nation-states have lost more and more of their *internal sovereignty* (Burnham) over their economies, they have remained in control of international relations, enabling them to protect their *external sovereignty* and thus monopolize an increasingly important political and organizational resource in a rapidly internationalizing world. In this, they continue to draw legitimacy from their historical association with democracy and 'cultural diversity'. Although the market has grown far beyond the scope of democratically organized political and cultural identities, electorates still regard national democratic politics as their principal source of protection, not least from economic dislocations caused by 'market forces', and perceive supranational governance as an undemocratic imposition of external control. The growing gap between the scale of democratic legitimacy and that of the international market as an economic 'community of fate' notwithstanding, defenders of the nation-state find it easy to convince citizens that supranational governance would detract from democracy and replace citizen participation with bureaucratic rule.

The political durability of the nation-state, as demonstrated among other things by the recent emergence of a plethora of new, 'sovereign' states in Eastern Europe, within a rapidly internationalizing world economy, is not entirely surprising. One might remember Karl Marx, who already in the mid-nineteenth century believed that the world market had superseded all national distinctions and had made all national forms of political organization obsolete; or for that matter Emile Durkheim, who wrote of a unified European society with a strong common consciousness well before the formation of the system of European nation-states that was to give rise to the two catastrophic wars of the twentieth century. Indeed, rather than a time-lagged remnant of an economically more localized past, bound at some point to disappear with the progress of economic internationalization, the modern nation-state may be more realistically conceived as a political response to it, *albeit a particularistic and for this reason, if for no other, fundamentally insufficient and potentially regressive one* – that is, as part of Polanyi's 'counter-movement' of human society against the 'self-regulating market'. In this capacity, the nation-state shares all the ambiguities of that counter-movement. In fact, it managed to be compatible with domestic prosperity and international peace only for the short period of welfare-state Keynesianism, invented in reaction to the disasters of the two world wars and the interwar period and dependent for its functioning on being embedded, at an inter-

303

mediate level of economic internationalization, in the unique political and economic order of American hegemony during the Cold War.

Today, as that order has disintegrated, depriving nation-states of their short-lived capacity to deploy their public power for economic objectives like full employment, nation-states are again trying to *compensate for lack of internal sovereignty by jealously watching over their external sovereignty*. The extreme version of this, powerfully described by Polanyi, would of course be aggressive international behaviour in pursuit of particularistic solutions to the domestic difficulties, political and economic, that may result from inter-national economic interdependence. Nothing like this is in evidence in Western Europe as yet. *Instead, nationalism has taken the form of resistance to supranationalism and of deep entrenchment of intergovernmentalism in the quasi-constitution of the European Union.*

Indeed, if there is any consensus at all among the Union's member states, then this is that integrated Europe will not be a supranational 'super-state', and will remain an international arrangement governed, wherever it matters, by unanimous agreement among its 'sovereign' members. From the Luxem-burg compromise to the Union Treaty of Maastricht, member states have successfully defended their position as the masters of their Union, and there is no indication that they may not continue doing so in the future. Rather than nation-states being absorbed into and superseded by new, federal-European institutions, European integration has remained strictly under intergovernmental control. While integration did progress, every step along the way came at the price of further assurances for member states of their supremacy over all other forces within the Union's developing international–domestic polity. Steps that would have undermined this supremacy were mostly not taken, and considerable legal and institutional inventiveness was deployed to enable integration to proceed without damage to national sovereignty, or, indeed, to use integration to fight off challenges to the latter emerging from economic interdependence. In the process the Community's character as an intergovernmental arrangement was continuously reinforced – an arrangement that, rather than replacing national with supranational sovereignty, often served to enable national states to assist one another in protecting as much of their sovereignty as possible, to a large extent turning their Union into a mutual insurance arrangement for nation-states worried about losing their independence.

As a result, there is today even in the uniquely advanced and historically privileged case of Western Europe, no alternative to the nation-state as a source of public power for economic governance, *even though the nation-state has largely lost the capacity to apply that power for market-governing purposes*. Indeed, an important reason why no mechanism of public economic governance is in sight that might replace the nation-state is the nation-state itself, which has been able to retain sufficient political capacity and legitimacy to obstruct the development of supranational governance. In the process

European nation-states have locked themselves and the European international system as a whole in a precarious combination of *nationalism and joint decision-making* – a situation which, as will be seen, has far-reaching consequences for the relationship between political institutions and the economy.

THE ALLIANCE OF NATIONALISM AND NEO-LIBERALISM

Governance of an integrated transnational economy through international relations can do some things better than others. In particular, it is more suited to market-making through negative integration and efficiency-enhancing regulation than to institution-building and redistributive market 'distortion'. This is because removal of barriers to cross-border trade and mobility is less demanding politically than the creation and enforcement of rights and obligations of citizenship, especially the social redefinition of property rights and the institutionalization of social rights to a minimum level of subsistence. International market-making may proceed basically through *deregulation*, which can be achieved by adopting by international treaty relatively simple rules of co-operation between independent national states, supplemented if necessary by narrow commitments to international enforcement. To the extent that this requires institutional innovations, these are precisely about how to ensure cross-national tradeability of goods and services while interfering as little as possible with the sovereignty of the involved nation-states, and in particular about avoiding the need to set up state-like governance at supranational level.

Limiting integration to the removal of trade barriers fits the interests of nation-states and the logic of intergovernmental co-operation, as it can be achieved without investing supranational bodies with sovereignty of their own. Institutionally, the 'elective affinity' between nationalism – with its corresponding mode of joint international decision-making, intergovernmentalism – and a neo-liberal programme of deregulatory market expansion is based in decision-rules of intergovernmental diplomacy that require unanimity in practice even where international treaties may allow for some kind of majority voting. As the example of 'mutual recognition' in the European Community has shown, supranational market integration can in principle be institutionalized as a default option that enters in force unless a unanimous joint decision is made to the contrary. Imposing common standards on markets, by contrast, or regulating their social outcomes by, for example, constructing a floor under them, always requires a positive decision, often one leading to institution-building, which under the rules of intergovernmentalism can be vetoed by just one participating state. The fact that the Council, on behalf of the member states and in the name of national sovereignty, has retained ultimate control over Union legislation thus has fundamental consequences for the European political economy.

Excluding social intervention in markets from common concerns also corresponds to the fact that democracy and citizen participation continue to reside in the member states. Distributive and redistributive politics require democratic legitimation. The way the European Union is designed by its masters, the nation-states, such legitimation remains beyond its reach, and there are no indications that the 'democratic deficit' of integrated Europe will be closed in the foreseeable future.[7] European-wide rules of social protection, for example, rights of workforces to information, consultation and co-determination, thus run into the objection, not just that they impose inefficient 'rigidities' on what is supposed to be a 'flexible' economy, but that they pre-empt the only democratic participation rights on offer, those vested in the sovereignty of nation-states – depriving European-wide redistributive 'inefficiencies' of their only possible justification, that they are the democratic will of the citizens. As a result, while market-opening can be contracted in by member states as an international treaty obligation, common social standards cannot, as they are incompatible with the principle of 'subsidiarity' derived, ultimately, from the impossibility of democratic legitimation at supranational level.

Moreover, while joint market-making does require states to give up control over their economic borders, and in this sense involves a *loss* of sovereignty, it is not difficult today even for the most sovereignty-conscious of nation-states. In the 1950s and 1960s, the formation of the European Economic Community may have advanced the integration of the European economy beyond what it would have been without political intervention. But the relaunch of the European Community in the 1980s was more the ratification of a market-driven, independent process of economic internationalization, not just of trade but, most importantly, of capital markets, technologies and production systems. In this situation, completing the 'Internal Market' is not really something on which European countries have much of a choice. For national economies to prosper at the end of the twentieth century, they must be part of the rapidly expanding global division of labour, and the most elementary assistance their governments can offer them is to remove any 'artificial' barriers to this. Even traditionally neutral countries like Sweden or Austria see no alternative today to joining the European Union if they want their economies to be admitted to an increasingly international system of production, co-ordinated by multinational companies that control the allocation of crucial productive investments and supplier contracts and want to be certain that their choices will not be interfered with by national borders and politics. If participation in the construction through 'negative integration' of this new global economy involves a loss of formal sovereignty for national states, this is a loss that has *de facto* long taken place, and one that must be cut, the earlier the better, for the nation-state to remain politically and economically viable.

It is in this context that, on the surface, the severest curtailment of national sovereignty within the European integration project must be seen, the intended creation under the Maastricht Treaty of a common currency and a European Central Bank, or 'Eurofed'. While it is far from clear whether 'monetary union' will ever come about and in what configuration,[8] it must be kept in mind that most European countries have long effectively lost sovereignty over their monetary policies, as they have for almost two decades now followed the lead of the Deutsche Bundesbank. Moreover, the Bundesbank became the *de facto* European central bank, not just because of the size of the German economy, but because its independence from the German government and its insulation from political pressure made it uniquely capable of behaving in conformity with the pressures of internationalized capital markets. It is on this model that the Eurofed, if at all, will be built.

In agreeing to monetary union, European states will formally give up something that they effectively no longer have. This holds also for Germany which, among other things precisely because of the special status of its central bank, has been aptly characterized by Peter Katzenstein as a 'semi-sovereign state'. Moreover, under monetary union European monetary policy will be handed over to an institution that is carefully crafted, in the image of the Bundesbank, not to require or encourage the growth of a state at a supranational level. Instead, the Eurofed will operate like an independent regulatory agency, reflecting and responding to 'objective market forces' rather than a political will to 'correct' or, for that matter, 'distort' markets; protecting the common currency from being put at the service of political purposes like full employment; and accommodating, not political pressure, but an international capital market that has long outgrown national borders and national control.[9]

Originating in the resistance of national states to supranational sovereignty, the alliance between nationalism and neo-liberalism replicates itself within the politics of individual nation-states. National political systems embedded in a competitive international market and exposed to supranationally un-governed external effects of competing systems are tempted to protect their formal sovereignty by devolving responsibility for the economy to 'the market' – using what has remained of their public powers of intervention to limit, as it were constitutionally, the claims politics can make on the economy, and citizens on the polity.[10] In many countries today, disengagement of politics from the economy is defended with reference to constraints of economic internationalization that would frustrate any other economic strategy. If citizens can be persuaded that economic outcomes are, and better be, the result of 'market forces', and that national governments are, therefore, no longer to be held responsible for the economy, national domestic sovereignty and political legitimacy can be maintained even in conditions of tight economic interdependence: with the nation-state having offloaded its responsibility for its economy to the 'world market', its own insufficiency and obsolescence in relation to the latter ceases to be visible.

Deploying internal sovereignty to liberate and accommodate market forces instead of trying to domesticate them – so as to end once and for all the use of public power for market-correcting purposes – may have become the only national political programme that can still be imposed on internationalized national economies without jeopardizing the integrity of the national state. One may note in this context that domestic deregulation tends to be presented by national governments as the only economically rational political response to internationalization, especially to international competition, and as the only promising way of defending the national interest in economic survival.

NATIONAL POLICY UNDER FRAGMENTED SOVEREIGNTY

Returning the economy to the market does not necessarily mean less state activity and may, in fact, at least for a transition period, require considerable state activism – just as negative integration at the international level is not accomplished without extensive diplomatic and regulatory effort. For national policy-making, this may create an impression of continuity, especially as many state functions remain exempt from international harmonization or regulation, including the provision of social security or the governance of industrial relations. As has been pointed out, citizenship generally remains nationally based, with the welfare state rooted in it. In the European integration rhetoric, the continuity of national-level social intervention is often presented as proof that supranational social protection is not necessary.[11]

But while on the surface national systems may seem to remain intact, market integration and the fragmentation of internal sovereignty to which it, in the absence of a supranational state formation, gives rise – changes the substance of national policy. As nation-states gradually turn into highly interdependent, partial political jurisdictions embedded in a much larger and ever more integrated international economy, their agendas become dominated by three kinds of subjects that tend to crowd out more traditional concerns:

1 *The transformation of formerly national into international markets.* A large and growing share of domestic political activity in European Union countries today is concerned with adjusting national law to the requirements of international market integration, in particular the removal of barriers to the free flow of goods and production factors across national borders. Typically this consists of the translation into national law of directives adopted by the Union (i.e. the collectivity of member states sitting in the Council). Although the aim is often not convergence or harmonization of national regimes, but only their mutual compatibility, the legislative effort

necessary to standardize the interfaces between national systems and make them *gemeinschaftsverträglich* is enormous. For example, beginning with the foundation of the European Economic Community the member states of the Union had to devise complex market-making rather than market-correcting social policies to facilitate the cross-border mobility of workers, among other things by changing national social security statutes to make benefits fully portable and equally accessible to workers from other Union countries. Similarly, joint market-making requires that countries end the subsidization of weak industries and firms, which in the past was sometimes used as a form of social policy but is anti-competitive in an integrated economy.

The joint building of an international market imposes demanding technical and political tasks on national legislatures. Rewriting national law to remove trade and mobility barriers is an exceedingly complex exercise, just as the politics of withdrawing political protection from previously subsidized or supported sectors of the economy or citizenry are risky. This is increasingly noticed and contributes to the discontent among politicians with the Community, in part because the attention and political capital that national legislatures have to devote to what is called the 'completion of the Internal Market' go at the expense of a wide range of other, potentially more rewarding areas of domestic policy-making.

2 *The co-ordination of national economic policy in line with the requirements of integrated markets.* Increasingly, market integration requires that member countries accept responsibility for making their monetary and fiscal policies compatible with those of the other members. Institutionally, this finds expression in the various convergence targets defined by the Maastricht Treaty. To be admitted to European Monetary Union, member countries must not exceed certain inflation rates, and must bring their public debt down to a specified percentage of their gross domestic product. Once monetary union has been achieved, participant countries must observe strict limits on their public borrowing and their budget deficits. Also, joint competition policy *de facto* requires the privatization and deregulation of a wide range of economic activities that in some countries are still conducted in public ownership.

Responsibility for economic 'convergence' lies exclusively with the individual countries, which in many cases will for a considerable time have to commit themselves to rigorous stabilization and austerity measures involving, among other things, cutbacks in domestic welfare state expenditures. While an integrated federal European state could conceivably put monetary and fiscal policy at the service of objectives other than economic stabilization – for example full employment – as long as sovereignty over economic policy remains fragmented, the only economic policy member countries can in the common interest be allowed to adopt is a monetaristic one. *Nota bene* that the Union's convergence criteria and competition rules do not require countries not to exceed a maximum level of unemployment, or to provide for a minimum level of social protection.

3 *The restoration and defence of national competitiveness in an international economy.* In an integrated international market governed by fragmented sovereignty, mobile production factors may easily emigrate from jurisdictions that impose high costs or regulatory burdens on them to others that do not. Pressures for what has been called 'competitive deregulation' result especially from the possibility that firms that are subjected by their home countries to broad social obligations may suffer disadvantages in international markets, and in response move jobs to lower-cost regimes. Short of European-wide harmonization of social obligations at the highest level, this forces national governments to conduct their policies, economic as well as social, in line with imperatives of international 'competitiveness', *as gauged by their attractiveness to mobile investors.* As governments are deprived under fragmented sovereignty of the ability to control market participants, economic intervention thus becomes increasingly limited to provision of support to investors as an incentive to enter or not to exit.

National competitiveness depends not just on costs, although costs are important. Investors may also feel uncomfortable with procedural rules, like those that firms have to obey under co-determination. In any case, the rise of national competitiveness to become the dominant objective of national politics reflects the fact that under fragmented sovereignty governance regimes, rather than containing competition, become themselves exposed to it. One consequence of this in the case of social policy is mounting pressure to shift the financial base of the welfare state from employer contributions to general tax revenues, which for its sheer complexity alone would for a long time displace most other items on national social policy agendas. Also, cost-intensive new legislation, like the German *Pflegeversicherung*, will become increasingly more difficult to pass because of potentially negative effects on competitiveness. Even where re-regulation or outright deregulation of national social policy regimes can be avoided, competitive pressures are likely to result in power shifts inside them in favour of more mobile participants, especially capital, forcing labour and political intervention to be more 'reasonable' and exercise self-restraint in expanding social protection or enforcing existing regulations.

Generally, concerns with national competitiveness in an international economy may give rise to two divergent political responses at the national level, both rather different from the social-democratic welfare-state policies of the post-war past. On the one hand, nation-states embedded in integrated markets may see their principal contribution to competitiveness in handing responsibility for it to the 'market forces'. If carried to the end, as in the case of Thatcher, such a policy would combine large-scale privatization, retrenchment of social protection, market-driven industrial restructuring, restoration of managerial authority, downwardly flexible wages and working conditions, the disablement of organized interests, especially trade unions, and the promotion of a large low-wage, low-skill sector to absorb some of the unemployed.

The alternative response, that what may remain in the 1990s of social democracy, neo-corporatism and social partnership, is the construction at the national level of coalitions to 'modernize' the national economy, with all other political objectives subordinate to that of increasing national competitiveness. Post-social-democratic coalition-building can draw on the institutional and economic nationalism of labour movements prevented from acting at the supranational level by lack of state capacity and employer interlocutors. It may also count on the employers, whose main interest is to forestall supranational state formation and economic intervention; who therefore benefit from labour being contained in national political circuits; and who can be certain that, in the face of external competitive pressures and because of their capacity to exit, they will be the alliance's senior partners. Finally, national governments can hope to increase their support from both business and labour for defending joint national interests in the international arena, thereby defending their own legitimacy as well and further reinforcing the national organization of politics and the intergovernmental character of international economic governance.

Neo-liberal deregulation and competitive coalition-building are not mutually exclusive. Under both, national governments refrain from imposing obligations on market participants, especially business, either because of a general belief in the merits of withdrawal of public power from the market, or because international treaties and factual conditions have already *de facto* limited public intervention to the creation of incentives and the removal of deterrents for mobile investors. Moreover, in both models nationally based democracy is constrained by the need, not only to respond to competitive pressures before responding to citizen demands – or to define the latter in terms of a technically correct response to the former – but also to observe the guidelines on national economic policies imposed by nation-states on themselves through intergovernmental agreement. As both factual and international–legal constraints on national intervention in the economy become more stringent, national governments, ironically in the same way as the supranational regime they have constructed for themselves, become dependent on the *voluntarism of the market-place*, having lost recourse to the 'hard law' that used to be the main tool of state interventionism in the past.

International obligations to open up markets and meet convergence targets, as well as the external effects of an integrated economy dictating neo-liberal or post-social-democratic national policies of competitive adjustment, also affect the character of, still nationally based, democracy. As nation-states factually lose and formally relinquish control over their economies, electorates become liable to fall victim to a 'democracy illusion' comparable to

311

Keynes's 'money illusion': that by exercising their political rights of citizenship they can get purchase on their economic fate. As the gap between formal and effective sovereignty widens and the purchasing power of national citizenship deteriorates, and unless voters can be persuaded that markets must always be given free rein come what may, popular beliefs in the lasting efficacy of national democracy are bound to give rise to distorted expressions of collective preferences, perverse political alliances and self-defeating definitions of interest, opening up extensive opportunities for political opportunism and populist demagoguery.

In democracy under fragmented sovereignty, both voters and politicians are inevitably torn between refusing to recognize the externalities that increasingly govern national polities, and blaming everything on them – at one time calling for national solutions where these are no longer possible, and at another demanding 'European solutions' while in the name of national sovereignty and diversity refusing integrated Europe the means to deliver them, defending national democracy against meddling by 'bureaucrats in Brussels' in its internal affairs. An example of the *twisted populist politics of independence under factual interdependence* is offered by the first Danish referendum on the Maastricht Treaty, when the electorate rejected European Monetary Union to defend the nation's economic self-determination against what was perceived as a German-dominated supranational institution – in a country whose monetary policy had by the time of the referendum for more than a decade been dictated by the Bundesbank in Frankfurt. By voting against Monetary Union, Danish voters thus effectively endorsed a situation in which their elected representatives had no influence at all on their country's monetary policy, and refused to endorse an arrangement under which at least one in twelve governors of the new Eurofed would have been from Denmark. At the same time, of course, is was also true that the way the Eurofed will be organized under the Treaty, all its board members, including the one from Denmark, will be strictly insulated from their countries' democratic politics – and will have to be in order for the common institution to meet the demands of both intergovernmentalism and market conformity.

More of this is likely to come in future years, and not just in Denmark. Nationally confined democracy is increasingly disfigured, not so much by nationalism or 'xenophobia',[12] but by the fact that it is losing the tools to realize the popular will to which it is supposed to give expression, and in particular the capacity to give citizens a modicum of protection from economic uncertainties. As democracy is pre-empted, the space for popular participation becomes available for symbolic and ritual performances of all kinds. Politicians have strong incentives to pretend to their voters that they are in control, or in any case could and should be, and voters have incentives to believe them. As the British example shows, the rhetoric of domestic sovereignty tends to be fiercest where its object is most energetically abandoned to the forces of the market. One day such rhetoric may come home to roost, and democratic politics, having cultivated illusions of political capacity and raised expectations of political protection, may be asked to deliver. Then politicians may find themselves in urgent need of scapegoats on which to blame their impotence, a role for which in Europe the 'bureaucrats in Brussels' and the Germans seem to be the privileged candidates. Political regression has many faces; in coming years national democracy under international interdependence is likely to offer ample opportunity to explore them.

CONCLUSION

After almost half a century of European integration, and with the internationalization of the economy progressing faster than ever, the European nation-state appears obsolete and alive at the same time: obsolete as the wielder of internal sovereignty over 'its' economy, and powerfully alive as the most effective opponent to the recreation of internal sovereignty at the international level. As their governing capacity *vis-à-vis* increasingly integrated markets has withered away, nation-states have successfully defended their control over international relations, which enabled them to protect themselves against international sovereignty succeeding and absorbing them. The result is *fragmentation of public power in a unified economy*, whose domestic governance is dependent for its conduct on international diplomacy.

One way in which European nation-states maintained their internal legitimacy in the face of internationalization was by creating international obligations for themselves to shed domestic economic responsibilities they could no longer fulfil, and by collectively imposing on themselves constraints to use their powers of economic intervention to spin off their economies to the market and set them free from distributive politics. Even in Western Europe, with its unique recent history of political integration, this resulted in the 1980s in international market expansion without corresponding expansion of political constituencies and institutions, combined with gradual transformation of national systems of economic governance towards a growing role of markets and declining economic significance of citizenship.

Today, the European state system is undergoing deep changes in response to economic internationalization, especially with respect to the uses of public power in the economy. The expectation of the 1950s and 1960s that the European nation-states would be gradually superseded by a supranational interventionist state built in their image is now recognized as fallacious. While it is true that the nation-state can no longer perform the functions it was supposed to perform in a Keynesian–Shonfieldian 'mixed economy', it never followed from this that state-like structures will rise at the international level to replace it. Economic internationalization, driven first by political decisions and then by market forces, and political integration controlled by intergovernmental relations have far more changed the nation-state than they have

313

'required', with 'functional necessity', its supranational replacement. Instead of supranational institutions taking over post-war state interventionism, the present condition of the European Union would seem to tell us more about the future condition of the nation-state than the traditional condition of the nation-state prefigures the future condition of the Union.

In the absence of political and cultural resources suitable for constructing international state capacity, national regimes wielding fragmented sovereignty are exposed to competition, especially for the allegiance of mobile production factors. As a consequence, their main tools of economic intervention are becoming rights and incentives rather than obligations and constraints, *reproducing the 'anarchic' voluntarism of the international system at national level*. With national political agendas increasingly set by pressures to open up markets, to meet internationally negotiated, market-conforming 'convergence criteria', and to become and remain internationally competitive, countries are tempted to contract in or out of supranational governance depending on national interests, giving rise to and reinforcing the 'variable geometry' of the international order. Since popular democracy remains vested in national politics, it is at risk of falling victim to 'democracy illusions', among other things making it liable to be used for preventing recovery of economic governance at the supranational level in the name of national interest and identity. Cut off, quasi-constitutionally, from control over the economy, democracy may thus become preoccupied with symbolic politics, or locked into a regressive populism that blames the social dislocations caused by a self-regulating international market on excessive international regulatory intervention in national affairs.

In spite of economic internationalization, the nation-state has not only survived but continues to monopolize sovereignty and public power. This does not mean, however, in the new economic and institutional environment nation-states are facing, that power can still be put to its old uses. While we may now be beginning to grasp the contours of the fragmented international-cum-national order governing, or not governing, the new global economy, the fact that we can describe that order offers no assurance that it may not be fundamentally deficient with respect to the secular task of domesticating and civilizing global capitalism. Nor, indeed, is there assurance that that task will be performed by some alternative structure. It is well possible that the system of international economic governance that is emerging from the defence of the national monopoly on public power will be both: the only one on offer, and far less than what would be needed to make a global economy viable socially as well as, perhaps, economically.

NOTES

1 Since 1993, this is the official name for what before the Treaty of Maastricht was called the European Community (EC) and continues to be called by its earlier

314

names, European Economic Community (EEC) or 'Common Market', especially in Britain.

2 Indeed, there are four steps here, in that between the second and the third step, Marshall locates the emergence of *industrial* rights of citizenship, by which he means rights to collective bargaining and representation in the workplace.

3 The paradox is resolved if one, realistically, assumes that while it was French policy to replicate the French state at the Community level, this was based on the assumption that the future European superstate would be politically controlled by France and, in particular, not by (at the time, West) Germany. In periods in which this premise became doubtful, French policy rediscovered the 'Europe of the Fatherlands'.

4 Unless, of course, 'national' interests in the protection of national home markets took precedence over the desire for market expansion via integration, resulting in typically tacit, but often effective, opposition to European unity. By and large, however, this is not likely to return.

5 So much so that 'politics is nothing if not the distortion of markets'; national politics has become depoliticized.

6 Which is why the Spanish rightly refer to Basque or Catalan regionalism as 'nationalism'.

7 The so-called 'European Parliament' has almost no powers, and the way it is elected consists not of political parties representing social interests in European society as a whole, but of national delegations. As a matter of fact, it is impossible to say who holds the majority in the Parliament, apart from the fact that it makes no difference who does. This, of course, reflects not just the limitations imposed on the role of the Parliament by the member states, but also the absence of a politically articulated 'European society'.

8 Only those member countries will be admitted that meet a set of stringent economic criteria, and some, especially Denmark and the United Kingdom, have explicitly reserved the right not to join.

9 I am not saying that a project like European monetary union is without contradictions, or that the firewalls pulled up between monetary union and supranational state formation will be easy to defend or will hold forever. What is important is, however, that the way monetary union has been designed by the member states perfectly fits the logic of the alliance of nationalism and neo-liberalism, and can certainly not be pointed to as proof of a commitment among member states to supranationalism, to the replacement of national political sovereignty at the supranational level, or to a restoration of state interventionism.

10 Of course, this is the theme of Andrew Gamble's book about Thatcherism, *The Free Economy and the Strong State: The Politics of Thatcherism* (Durham, N.C.: Duke University Press, 1988).

11 In the same way, and at the same time, the large number of rules and regulations emanating from Brussels is used as evidence that integration is advancing, and that integrated Europe will not be a deregulated Europe.

12 This is, of course, the view of the liberal left, which is itself marked by the distortions of national democratic politics in that it also hides its lack of an answer to the problem of externalities and the growing disjunction of political communities and the economic markets behind principled rhetoric. The left's typical rhetorical combination of grass-roots democracy and multicultural internationalism must be less than convincing to citizens experiencing at the same time growing international market pressures and factual disenfranchisement within a formally democratic, and perhaps even 'democratizing', polity.

14

THE WELFARE OF NATIONS

Ramesh Mishra

INTRODUCTION

The neo-conservative assault on the welfare state is very much a political and ideological act. The conflict over social welfare policies continues to be fought squarely on the terrain of domestic and national politics. However, neo-conservative reformers, whether in Britain, the United States or Canada have not dared to go as far as they have wished in dismantling the welfare state because of popular support for universal social programmes and interest group opposition to cutbacks. This has led some analysts like Therborn to conclude that welfare state capitalism 'represents an irreversible development'.[1] In a similar vein Myles observed that Conservative attempts to dismantle the Canadian welfare state had been rebuffed and that the talk of 'crisis' was, therefore, inappropriate.[2] Their assessment has proved somewhat off the mark. Issues relating to globalization such as international competitiveness, capital flight and credit rating of governments by financial institutions have provided new ammunition to call into question many of the fundamental notions underpinning the welfare state. Indeed, among political élites, it is an accepted 'fact of life' that national debt and deficit must be reduced and that this must be done not by raising taxes but by reducing public (read social) expenditures. The principle of universality of social welfare, which seemed so important earlier, has virtually ceased to be a matter of controversy, and for some time now universal social programmes have been dying a death 'by a thousand cuts'.[3] The ideology of neo-conservatism is having a comfortable ride on the back of globalization.

Put differently, globalization has breathed new life into the neo-conservative ideology of social welfare. Whilst governments of the centre and the left are increasingly deterred from following a progressive social policy agenda, rightist governments have a field day in rationalizing the reduction of social expenditure. Coming after the neo-conservative assault, globalization appears as one more giant step towards sharp reductions in social welfare programmes and the delivery of social services. The difference, however, is that globalization provides a far more powerful justification than neo-conservative ideology for retrenching the welfare state. For neo-conservatism at least appears to be a matter of political and ideological choice, albeit one which claims to best promote competitiveness and economic growth. Globalization, on the other hand, appears as an *external* constraint – not a matter of political choice at all, but rather of economic necessity – so that nation-states can do little besides follow the dictates of footloose capital in a downward spiral of deregulation, lower social spending and lower taxes (especially corporate). Indeed, the logic of this approach seems to be to privatize social welfare altogether, reducing the role of the government to that of a provider of last resort (residual welfare). If that trend continues, it would return us to pre-Second World War forms of insecurity and inequality.

Is this the way we are heading? By the early 1990s virtually all countries have had to scale back social programmes, contain if not reduce social expenditure, accept a higher level of unemployment and reduce taxes, especially on corporations and high incomes. The general direction of change is unmistakable. In relative terms, the size and scope of state programmes are being reduced everywhere (see Tables 14.1–14.3).[4]

Table 14.1 Labour force unemployed (%)

Region	1973	1978	1983	1993
EC	2.4	5.3	10.1	11.3
OECD	3.2	5.1	8.5	8.2
OECD Europe	2.8	5.3	9.7	10.7
Sweden	2.0	1.8	2.9	8.2

Source: *OECD Economic Outlook: Historical Statistics 1960–1989*, Paris, 1991; *The OECD Observer* 186 (February/March 1994)

What is new is the sense that this agenda is being driven by forces unleashed by globalization over which nation-states have little control. They have no option but to follow a policy which leads to increasing privatization of services and state withdrawal from its role in public protection. Thus, if there is an alternative it is between drifting haphazardly and piecemeal towards a form of welfare in which the state's role is much reduced or bowing before the inevitable and bidding farewell to the welfare state based on social citizenship. It is a Hobson's choice.

THE NEW FUNCTIONALISM

The idea that a strong system of social welfare is incompatible with the conditions and needs of the global market economy and therefore obsolete is voiced most strongly by business interests and political parties of the right.[5] But it comes increasingly from the left too – especially in some versions of neo-Marxist, feminist and eco-socialist thought.[6] It is argued, for

Table 14.2 Real spending on income transfers per head of target population in the 1970s and 1980s* (average annual percentage change)

Country	Old age, permanent sickness and survivors				Unemployment				Family assistance				Temporary sickness and maternity			
	1970–9		1979–89		1970–9		1979–89		1970–9		1979–89		1970–9		1979–89	
	Real	Relative to per capita GDP	Real	Relative to per capita GDP	Real	Relative to per capita GDP	Real	Relative to per capita GDP	Real	Relative to per capita GDP	Real	Relative to per capita GDP	Real	Relative to per capita GDP	Real	Relative to per capita GDP
United States	3.4	1.0	0.7	-0.5	-1.8	-4.1	-1.5	-2.6	3.2	0.8	0.0	-1.2	2.9	0.6	3.1	1.8
Japan	15.2	12.1	3.7	0.7	0.0	-2.7	-2.9	-5.7	11.0	8.0	1.1	-1.8	3.9	1.1	-2.0	-4.9
France†	5.0‡	2.2	3.3§	1.2	9.6‡	6.7	-0.8§	-2.8	-3.6‡	0.8	3.0§	1.0	2.1‡	-0.6	2.4§	0.3
Italy	4.5	1.1	5.1	2.4	10.6	7.0	-4.3	-6.8	-3.2	-6.4	2.7	0.0	4.3	0.8	-3.7	-6.2
United Kingdom	4.1	1.4	1.8	-0.7	-1.1	-3.7	-1.4	-3.8	10.5	7.7	3.4	0.9	-5.7	-8.2	-0.9	-3.4
Canada	5.9	1.2	3.0	1.5	3.3	-1.3	2.9	1.4	5.1	0.5	-0.5	-2.1	5.9	1.3	4.9	3.3
Austria	4.4	0.6	3.2	1.2	5.3	1.5	2.5	0.5	8.4	4.4	-0.1	-2.1	0.2	-3.4	0.4	-1.6
Denmark	1.8	0.1	1.9	0.4	-1.8	-3.4	-1.1	-2.5	2.2	0.5	5.8	4.2	8.4	6.6	0.0	-1.5
The Netherlands	7.0	4.3	-1.2	-1.9	-5.3	-7.7	-2.3	-3.0	3.1	0.5	-1.6	-2.4	5.5	2.9	-1.6	-2.4
Norway	4.3	0.3	2.0	0.5	1.4	-2.5	8.1	6.5	-2.1	-5.9	8.6	7.0	17.2	12.7	1.9	0.4
Sweden	5.8	3.7	1.3	0.0	7.1	4.9	7.2	5.8	4.7	2.8	0.0	-1.3	8.0	5.8	3.0	1.7
Switzerland	5.6	4.7	1.2	-1.0	1.8‖	0.6‖	-2.0	-4.1	5.9	5.0	5.2	3.0	1.5	0.7	1.5	-0.7
Average	5.6	2.7	2.2	0.3	2.4	-0.4	0.4	-1.4	4.4	1.5	2.3	0.4	4.5	1.7	0.7	-1.1

Sources: OECD Secretariat and Social Expenditure Data File. Also Howard Oxley and John P. Martin, 'Controlling Government Spending and Deficits: Trends in the 1980s and Prospects for the 1990s', *OECD Economic Studies No. 17* (Autumn 1991)
* Deflated by the private consumption deflator
† Break in the series in 1981. After 1981 'welfare' is included in the category 'other' which is not shown
‡ France: 1970–80
§ France: 1981–8
‖ Switzerland 1975–80

Table 14.3 Public health expenditure: annual rate of growth (%) in real per capita spending

County	1970–79	1980–89
Australia	3.0	2.9
Canada	4.6	2.0
France	7.0	3.9
Germany	6.5	0.9
Japan	7.8	3.5
Sweden	3.9	0.7
United Kingdom	5.7	1.1
United States	5.2	1.5
OECD average (20 countries)	5.3	1.9

Source: Howard Oxley and John P. Martin, 'Controlling Government Spending and Deficits: Trends in the 1980s and Prospects for the 1990s', *OECD Economic Studies No. 17* (Autumn 1991)

example, that the post-Second World War capitalist state was based on the strength of its mass production industries, job security in the workplace and social stability, thanks to an extensive network of social policy programmes. The largely male workforce, the power of unions to bargain collectively as well as the pump-priming macroeconomic policies of governments to protect the economy from the business cycle, reflected the needs of this method of production. Markets had to be stabilized and social conflict minimized. With the shift towards lean production and a flexible workplace, many existing programmes are seen as a fetter on capitalist accumulation. Increasingly, they are regarded as being dysfunctional economically and unsustainable politically by élites everywhere. For example, unemployment benefits are seen as hampering worker mobility and the downward adjustment of worker expectations about wages. Universal income-support programs are being seen as unaffordable and wasteful in that they need high levels of taxation yet do not provide adequate benefits to the needy. Current levels of taxation and government expenditure are now considered as a disincentive to enterprise and investment and are unpopular electorally. Governments often talk about reform or the need to reform social policy. In fact, what they really want to do is replace Keynesian welfare-inspired measures with what has been called post-Fordist forms of welfare. Whilst the exact nature of this new form of welfare remains somewhat unclear, something akin to a pro-market and production-oriented approach is suggested. Basically, it means shrinking the state welfare sector in order to lighten the tax burden and lower social benefits; abandoning universality and making benefits and services targeted to a needy population; encouraging privately provided or employer-provided benefits; and introducing more competition in the supply of social welfare through privatization and profit-seeking activity. This reorientation in social policy is seen as driven by economic imperatives.[7]

What is of interest here is the economistic and functionalist nature of this interpretation of the Keynesian or Fordist welfare state and its successor regime. In equating a particular stage in capitalist production with a functionally appropriate form of state modes of economic and social regulation, this approach tends to devalue the role of politics and ideology. As a result, the importance of the political dimension is overlooked and the differences among welfare state regimes in the post-Second World War period played down, notably in respect to full employment, universality and commitment to equality. These differences had to do with politics and ideology as well as historical and cultural factors.[8]

Thus, the United States differed a great deal from countries of Western Europe in respect of policies of full employment and universal social programmes. The United States never accepted the goal of full employment with the result that American unemployment remained at a relatively high level in the 1950s and 1960s.[9] Unlike most Western countries, the United States never instituted a general programme of health insurance, leaving the working population to obtain its own healthcare through employment-related plans or other voluntary auspices. Only the aged (over 65s) were provided with health insurance under the Medicare plan started in 1965. There is a social security programme which includes pensions, survivors' benefits and unemployment insurance but does not provide sick pay or maternity benefits. There is no programme of family allowances. The great post-Second World War era of reform in the United States – the 1960s – did little to expand and institutionalize universal programmes begun in the 1930s. Rather it expanded means-tested benefits, adding two new programmes – namely, medical assistance (Medicaid) and food stamps, and eased on the eligibility of welfare for families with dependent children (AFDC). As a result, the United States has a bifurcated welfare state – one part based on social insurance and entitlement with a strong base of popular support and the other for the low-income population which is far less popular. These programmes targeted at the poor proved far easier to slash than the entitlement programmes during the Reagan presidency. In many respects the United States was and still remains a 'pre-modern' welfare state in that it never embraced the idea of comprehensive social protection based on social solidarity and citizenship.[10]

Japan followed a path rather different from the Western welfare states.[11] The distinctive feature of the Japanese model has been low unemployment sustained through a combination of 'lifetime employment', and a dual labour market with a substantial section of the labour force employed by small firms at low wages and with poor fringe benefits. Full employment has also been helped by low participation rates of women until quite recently. Another feature of Japan's welfare has been its heavy reliance on employment-related welfare schemes, notably in the area of housing and pensions but also medical care, supplementary family allowances and family leave. This, in part, explains

Japan's low level of social expenditure in the 1960s (see Table 14.5). True, later, especially during the 1970s, the state welfare system was expanded and all the basic social security programmes are now in place. But public programmes are still related to employment status (e.g. employees, public officials, farmers and self-employed, the retired). Both health insurance and pensions, for example, are organized in this way and result in unequal benefits.[12] Moreover, there is a yawning gap between small and large firms with respect to fringe benefits.[13] In sum, despite some changes in the 1970s the Japanese system of welfare has remained workplace-centred, segmented and with a weakly developed notion of social citizenship and universality. The state has played a relatively modest role. In Japan, therefore, 'the ethic of collectivist welfare is expressed through the company' rather than through state-provided services.[14]

The Swedish welfare state, on the other hand, developed a unique combination of an active labour market policy, centralized collective bargaining and universal and comprehensive services.[15] It represents the prototypical social-democratic welfare state with a strong commitment to full employment, wage equality and the promotion of gender equality through social policy. Centralized collective bargaining ensured that wage rises were moderate and that inflation – the bane of full employment capitalism – was kept in check. Labour market policy ensured that redundant workers received adequate income support, counselling, retraining and help with relocation. Wage equity policy ensured that through centralized bargaining wage rates for similar skills will be identical across industries and thus prevent the growth of a low-wage sector. Sweden has been the world's highest spender (in terms of the proportion of GNP) on labour market measures.[16] It also has the highest labour market participation rate for women made possible through the growth of part-time employment, generous state provision for parental leave and extensive child care arrangements. Sweden's welfare state, besides being universal and comprehensive, has also been the world's most redistributive (see Table 14.4). Not surprisingly, Sweden also has had the highest level of taxation.[17]

Germany represents another interesting variation on the theme of welfare. It may be described as a Conservative welfare state, i.e. in the tradition of European Conservatism which believed in state responsibility for the economic and social well-being of the nation. Thus, it is worth emphasizing that this – the world's first – welfare state was initiated in 1889, not by socialists but by Conservative statesmen in order to secure economic and social stability and to protect the community from the social consequences of *laissez-faire*. The other remarkable thing about Germany is that after the Second World War it combined full employment and a large welfare state with one of the most competitive and successful economies in the world. Although a big spender and a generous provider of income security, especially pensions, Germany emphasized security and hierarchy rather than equality, linking benefits to occupational status.[18] Unlike Sweden, Germany did not seek to promote income equality or gender equality through social welfare policies. None the less, its welfare system has been large and redistributive enough to ensure that Germany has one of the lowest rates of poverty in the world (see Table 14.4).

Table 14.4 Income redistribution and the welfare state, mid-1980s

Country	Welfare state's redistributive effect (a) (%)	Poverty rate (b) (%): pre- and post-transfer	
Australia	32.7	21.3	10.8
Canada	24.7	21.0	11.0
W. Germany	27.8	24.2	5.8
Sweden	52.8	29.7	5.3
UK	32.8	21.4	7.9
USA	29.6	23.4	18.1

Source: OECD Economic Surveys: Sweden 1993–1994 (Paris, 1994)
(a) Reduction in income inequality in disposable income compared with factor income
(b) Individuals with net income below 50% of median income, adjusted to family size

Thus, social welfare policies of the 1960s show substantial differences among nations with respect to full employment, social expenditure and taxation (see Table 14.5).

Table 14.5 Unemployment, taxation and social expenditure in the 1960s

Country	Unemployment (a) (%)	Tax receipts (b) (% of GDP)	Social expenditure (c) (% of GDP)
Australia	1.9	23	9.5
Canada	4.8	25	11.2
France	1.5	35	14.4
W. Germany	0.8	32	17.1
Japan	1.3	18	7.6
Sweden	1.6	35	15.6
UK	1.5	31	12.4
USA	5.0	26	9.9

(a) 1960–7 (b) 1965 (c) 1960
Source: OECD Economic Outlook: Historical Statistics 1960–1989 (Paris, 1991); M. McKee, 'Paying the Public Sector's Bills', The OECD Observer 149 (December 1987/January 1988); The Future of Social Protection (Paris: OEC, 1988)

At least three more or less distinct models of welfare can be identified. First, the market, or *laissez-faire* model, which sought to restrict the role of the state to providing minimal benefits, preferably for the low income population. The American system of welfare is closer to this type. Second, the social democratic model, which sought to provide universal and comprehensive services based on the notion of social solidarity and citizenship. The British welfare state in the 1950s was a close approximation. Sweden developed a stronger/corporatist version of this model which emphasized equality and linked social welfare to centralized collective bargaining and strong interventionist labour market policies. The third type, represented by Germany, was based on a strong state commitment to social welfare but more from the viewpoint of security and stability than equality. Japan is an interesting hybrid in that it seems to combine features of the first and third of these types along with some features of its own, but in an entirely different cultural context.

Some of these differences among nations in their approach to welfare were mirrored *within* nation-states in terms of their domestic politics. Despite a broad acceptance of state commitment to welfare, political parties differed significantly in their approach to the role of the public sector in providing such things as pensions, education or housing.[19] For example, in 1959 the Conservative government in Britain opted for an occupational (work-related) pension scheme to supplement the inadequate flat-rate state pensions. The Labour Party, on the other hand, was strongly in favour of an expanded and wage-related state pension scheme. Regarding housing policy Conservatives were opposed to rent control and favoured owner-occupation rather than public housing. The Labour Party was in favour of rent control and public housing.[20] In France and Germany, business élites saw the value of social programmes as social stabilizers. By contrast, in Britain and the United States the private sector never fully accepted the rationale for public welfare entitlements and showed a strong preference all along for private solutions for basic needs (e.g. pensions or housing). True, there was a pragmatic acceptance of the mixed economy and the welfare state – largely on account of its electoral popularity – by the political right. However, the main point to be made is that welfare states varied widely and that these variations had to do with the politics and ideology, both past and present, of welfare state regimes. And in so far as the modern welfare state was embedded within the domestic political economy of nations, politics could, and did, matter. But do politics matter in the globalized economy?

Looking at developments since the mid-1970s, a common thread can be discerned. Irrespective of their political complexion most welfare states have abandoned full employment as a national objective, reduced levels of taxation, especially on corporations and high-income earners, trimmed social expenditure and privatized some parts of the welfare state. Universality as a principle of social provision has been compromised. In this sense, welfare states have been constrained to follow a particular direction. None the less, countries have differed and continue to differ a good deal in the nature and extent of such changes. For example, the Thatcher government in Britain followed a policy of deregulation, privatization and upwards income redistribution that had no counterpart in other West European nations. At the other end of the ideological spectrum Sweden followed a path significantly different from neo-conservative regimes. Instead of cutting back on public expenditure and letting unemployment rise, Sweden maintained full employment through a variety of measures, including temporary subsidies to industry, resulting in a steep rise in public expenditure.[21] Swedish social democracy has been distinctive in the way it tried to harmonize economic and social policies, i.e. through the institutions of centralized wage bargaining and labour market policy. Policies for gender equality also have formed an important part of the Swedish approach, at least since the early 1970s. These elements were much less developed in, for example, social democracies of the English-speaking countries. Compared with the new departure in social policy in Britain and the United States under neo-conservatives, continental countries such as Austria, Germany and France show greater stability and continuity in social welfare policy.

No doubt the influence of globalization can be seen at work everywhere. Recent developments in Sweden, for example, show the difficulty of sustaining a strong social democratic welfare state in the context of an increasingly open economy.[22] After maintaining a fairly strict control on foreign capital investment Sweden abandoned it in the 1980s, in line with the trend towards the free movement of capital across countries. The result was a strong capital flight from Sweden after 1986 and a spurt in the growth of Swedish multinationals.[23] Sweden's economy has become internationalized and is much less amenable to national control. Business has demanded and increasingly secured decentralized wage bargaining helped by the fragmentation of worker interests. The level of taxation is being reduced substantially, among other things, in order not to face an investment strike by capital. At the same time the division of interests among workers, e.g. between public and private sectors, blue-collar and white-collar, male and female, has made concerted action difficult. In any case, workers cannot be expected to accept wage restraint and to curb private consumption when profits made by Swedish corporations are not subject to national control and do not result in increased investment in Sweden.[24]

Clearly, globalization of capital gives business a great deal of leverage in vetoing national policies. But the consequences are not necessarily the same everywhere. Historical legacy as well as domestic politics and ideology remain important in shaping national policy regimes. Indeed, continuing national differences in the social policies of EC countries show that despite free trade and the free movement of capital within Europe there has been little convergence in social welfare policy. Thus, down to the mid-1980s, the EC had a 'trade/market outlook which virtually excluded any supranational role in social policy areas'.[25] Attempts at policy harmonization in the 1970s were largely ineffective. More recent endeavours also show meagre results. The Social Charter, meant to complement the creation of a single economic market in 1992, is limited to minimum standards of protection for workers. Indeed,

EC social policy is confined to two main areas: regional development programmes and workers' rights with social welfare policy firmly within the purview of the nation-state.[26] And there is little evidence so far to suggest that the prospect of 'social dumping' – namely that capital and investment will flow to low-wage, low-welfare and low-tax countries – is likely to reduce the welfare states of EC countries to the lowest common denominator.[27]

Japan presents a different picture again. As noted earlier, the Japanese model of welfare has differed in important ways from Western welfare states. Contrary to various theses of convergence of the 1960s, which expected Japan to move closer to the Western economic and industrial model, Japanese social structure has displayed a great deal of persistence and continuity. Lifetime employment and worker identification with the company may be cited as examples. Family life again is very different from the West. For example three-generational ties are strong and a much higher proportion of the elderly live with their grown-up children.[28] No doubt Japan is and will be affected by the changing world economy. And it could be that as Japan loses its protectionist insulation and becomes more exposed to foreign competition its welfare regime will also change. But neither the impact of globalization on Japanese welfare nor its outcome is likely to be the same as in either Europe or North America.[29]

In so far as politics, culture and ideology continue to play a part in the determination of welfare policy, the idea that free trade between nations must reduce all welfare states to the lowest common denominator lacks credibility. Clearly, the argument is partly ideological. Thus, it is hardly a coincidence that it is in the liberal, low-tax and low-welfare region of North America that the threat of globalization is being invoked in the most strident manner in order to justify retrenching social expenditure.[30] A look at the countries of Western Europe and Japan is helpful in appreciating that scaling-down social programmes is a very different policy choice from dismantling the key institutional relationships of the past. This kind of historical and comparative perspective is useful in countering an overly schematic and economistic approach which, eager to write off the post-Second World War welfare state on dysfunctional grounds, risks playing into the hands of neo-conservatism.

THE DECLINE OF LEGITIMATION PROBLEMS

A distinctive feature of the welfare state has been its success in meeting both the accumulation needs and the legitimation deficits of post-Second World War capitalism. What is different about the 1990s and, as far as one can see, beyond is not only the change in the accumulation needs of a globalized, post-national capitalist economy, but also a profound change in its legitimation needs. A major reason why business interests and the political right came to accept the modern system of welfare entitlements was that it helped to legitimize market capitalism. From its earliest beginnings in Bismarck's

Germany, the social welfare state was conceived primarily as a political response to the growing menace of worker discontent and socialism. This particular function of the welfare state has, of course, been closely associated with the rise of the labour movement and the growth of socialist parties. The possibility that a socialist society, superior in economic and social organization to capitalism, might one day supersede the capitalist system has formed the essential context for the development of the welfare state. The post-Depression era made the threat to the capitalist order far more real. The 1930s saw the rise of fascism. The post-Second World War era saw the spread of communism to nearly half of the world. There was a growing acceptance of collectivist and socialist ideas which went hand in hand with the development and consolidation of left parties.[31] The bipartisan acceptance of full employment and the welfare state, it can be argued, had a lot to do with the legitimation problems of *laissez-faire* capitalism seen in the context of worker militancy and the socialist alternative. Politically and ideologically, capitalism was very much on the defensive. The anarchy and waste endemic in a market system, with its booms and slumps, was tragically evident in the 1930s. The economic crisis and its cost in human suffering highlighted the superiority – moral and material – of a system of planned production and distribution integral to socialism. However flawed, Soviet socialism with its full employment, collective consumption and egalitarian orientation represented the translation of this ideal into reality. The Soviet model, followed in broad outlines by the many countries that formed a part of the growing socialist world, was both a challenge and a reproach to unregulated capitalism.

Moreover, there was a strong current of evolutionism and historicism in Western social thought represented most forcefully by Marxism but also by social democracy. These ideologies saw capitalism as a transitory social system destined to be superseded by some form of socialism. This evolutionary perspective also served to delegitimize capitalism in that it appeared not only as a system inefficient economically and unjust socially but also as one that was doomed historically. The post-Second World War welfare state was, in no small measure, capitalism's answer to these legitimation problems.

SOCIAL POLICY IN A POST-COLD WAR WORLD

Today, capitalism no longer faces the challenge of a socialist alternative. The collapse of communism as a social system, after having been hailed as the exemplar of the future society for the best part of this century, has conferred a new legitimacy on capitalism. With no competitor in sight it has acquired a new lease of life, becoming, so to speak, a monopolistic social system! No wonder some see in the situation the 'end of history' itself.[32] The virtual demise of Marxism as a credible social theory and especially as a philosophy of history has also rebounded to the favour of free market capitalism.

Income inequality, a prominent feature of market capitalism, is on the rise everywhere. For example, in the United States the 'growth in the incomes of the richest one percent of Americans has been so large that just the *increase* between 1980 and 1990 in the after-tax income of this group equals the *total* income of the poorest 20 per cent of the population'.[33] Inequality of income and wealth has acquired a new aura of legitimacy. It now appears as a necessary and inevitable, if not also a highly desirable, phenomenon – a small price to pay for the many blessings of capitalism. Lastly, the working class and the trade union movement find themselves much weakened as a result of globalization, the resurgence of a free market economy, and other changes which have fragmented the solidarity of workers' movements. As a result of these developments, the rule of capital has few challengers compared with the past. Not only the socialist alternative but also the social democratic alternative to neo-conservative political economy have both been marginalized.

The decline of the workers' movement, and of the left more generally, as a moral and political force means that one of the major functions of the welfare state – namely legitimation – is no longer a pressing one. Indeed, one might say that democratic consumer capitalism has become self-legitimating. In the absence of a credible alternative to market capitalism the inequality and insecurity inherent in the system is becoming far more acceptable. The absence of a credible alternative and the acceptance of inequality indicate a new situation unprecedented since the birth of industrial capitalism. At the very least it suggests that state welfare programmes and arrangements can expect a period of decline, albeit gradually, given electoral competition, vested interests and democratic procedures. Chronic un-employment – through loss of revenue and payment of benefits – will exert a steady pressure on the state budget. Fiscal constraints plus the need for a 'flexible' labour market will ensure that unemployment benefits are whittled down. Those of working age, whether on welfare or unemployment benefit will be under increasing pressure to get into 'workfare', i.e. they will be obliged to undergo some sort of training or perform some labour in return for their welfare cheque, weakening the notion of entitlement further. Universality of social programmes will be eroded through such devices as the taxback of benefits from high-income earners, the reduction of services (e.g. delisting of medical procedures), and the underfunding of services which make middle- and upper-income earners look for private solutions. These developments, combined with the increasing polarization of work incomes, will inevitably result in greater poverty and inequality. We are likely to see an increasing 'Americanization', or dualization of industrial societies. This would mean a division into a contented majority with regular jobs, work-related benefits and other forms of private protection and a marginalized and impoverished minority in low-paying jobs or lacking regular employment and dependent on state welfare benefits alone.[34]

No doubt countervailing influences are at work too and how far they might be effective in checking the trend towards privatization and dualization remains to be seen. Liberal democracy, with its electoral competition, interest groups and social movements is perhaps the most important of these. Organized labour – despite its waning influence – is another. Indeed, we are faced with something of a paradox here. On the one hand we see an upsurge of the market economy accompanied with deregulation and the downsizing of the public sector. The economy is being freed from public control everywhere. On the other hand we are also witnessing a strengthening of democratic values. Demand for greater political participation, more popular, say, in the decision-making process (e.g. through referenda and calls for greater accountability of politicians to their constituents), is also being heard increasingly. The formation of new interests and social movements continues apace. Women's movement, environmental groups, the aged, gays and lesbians and ethno-cultural groups are among the new or revitalized groups seeking to influence public policy. However, the relationship of these groups to the hegemonic forces of market capitalism remains problematic.

The contradiction between the declining sovereignty of the nation-state over the economy and rising democratic and participatory values will likely intensify, especially if globalization results in substantial dislocation of the economic life of nations. How this contradiction will play itself out in practice remains to be seen. But it is likely that governments will be under twin pressures: from capital to let the social costs of economic change lie where they fall and from labour and other groups to provide social protection, to assist people to adapt to change, and more generally to continue to be responsible for the overall well-being of the nation. Whether and to what extent the pressure for social protection and setting of minimum standards will be deflected upwards and outwards (e.g. to trading blocs and supra-national formations such as the EC, NAFTA and the like) remains to be seen. But thus far, the centre of gravity of social policy remains very much within the nation-state and is likely to remain so in the foreseeable future.

However, there are other imponderables. A serious deterioration of the eco-system could influence the course of events. A sharp decline in the living standards of large sectors of the population could provoke a reaction. Increasing incidence of crime, violence and other forms of deviance could create a strong sense of insecurity among citizens forcing élites to compromise. On the other hand, we have to remember that social systems such as capitalism rely on reform and repression as major instruments of social control. And so long as credible alternatives are lacking, it is unlikely that the system will have any difficulty in dealing with manifestations of protest and unrest, such as increasing crime, violence and urban riots through repressive measures. It is likely that as ameliorative policies are jacked down repressive policies will be jacked up.[35] In any case, given the deficit on the left, it is right-wing populism and extremism that are likely to benefit from economic and social dislocations. Discontent and insecurity may therefore be channelled into racism, economic protectionism and other forms of national chauvinism.

CONCLUSION: FROM SOCIAL CITIZENSHIP TO WELFARE PLURALISM

Given that continuity as well as discontinuity is a feature of welfare states it is likely that in the next decade or so Western industrial countries will move from some version of the social citizenship state towards 'welfare pluralism', i.e. from an institutional, state-centred conception of welfare to one in which the state will play a smaller role in social protection. The non-state sector – commercial, voluntary/non-profit, philanthropic, domestic – will come to play a bigger part in the provision of welfare.

The reasoning behind this 'prediction' is as follows. First, given worldwide political and ideological shifts which have privileged the market economy, individualism and competition, the state sector will be downsized everywhere. Second, the nation-state will remain the basis of the national community and above all the basis of the domestic political order. Citizens will expect and demand government action on vital issues of security and equity. The welfare state cannot therefore be dismantled. But neither can it be sustained on the basis of universality and equality of social provision for reasons noted above. Third, social programmes concerned with income-support, education and child protection – to name but a few – perform important economic, social and political functions for advanced capitalist society. These functional considerations will have a restraining influence on the 'pull' towards the retrenchment of social expenditure. These are some of the main reasons for suggesting that increasingly social welfare will come to be organized in the form of 'welfare pluralism' or the 'mixed economy of welfare' in the post-modern era.

But what exactly is 'welfare pluralism'? What mix of state and non-state welfare does it represent? What are its implications for specific areas of need such as income support or medical care? Welfare pluralism suggests a direction, but in itself does not indicate the precise nature of the 'mix', i.e. the respective roles of the different sectors in the supply of welfare.[36] Several notions of welfare pluralism can be discerned. There is a neo-conservative version which sees the market and the commercial sector as the major players with a vastly reduced level of social entitlement. At the other extreme, there is a somewhat idealized leftist version of a decentralized, democratic and participatory form of social welfare reliant on public resources and under-pinned by a firm commitment to social entitlement.

Typically, however, welfare pluralism represents a middle ground, a centrist position, in the balance between the public and the private, the state and the non-state sectors. It rests on the following premises: (1) that the limitations and limits of state-provided welfare – fiscal and administrative – should be clearly recognized; (2) that the state cannot and should not be the monopoly or near-monopoly provider of social welfare; (3) that non-state providers can and should play a bigger part in the supply, and especially delivery, of services; and (4) that the move from a state-centred welfare towards welfare pluralism could result in greater inequality in the distribution of social benefits but that this is unavoidable. How does it translate into concrete changes in the organization of services? Let us look at income support and medical care. Income support services would be less universal and make more use of targeting by, for example, replacing universal allowances with tax credits or introducing taxback provisions. Employers might deliver some mandated services such as sick pay with perhaps state subsidization. State retirement pensions could be assigned the role of providing a basic income only which must be supplemented by other sources such as occupational pension schemes. A guaranteed annual income might fit into this conception as well, providing that the level of income guarantee remains low, i.e. does not require a high level of taxation and does not create a disincentive to accepting low-wage labour. Investing in labour market measures is certainly compatible with this notion, albeit that welfare pluralism would emphasize the idea of partnership between the state and other sectors, e.g. employers, unions, community groups and other interests involved. With respect to medical care, welfare pluralism implies the co-existence of both private and public sectors. The state should guarantee basic healthcare to all and encourage the supplementation of healthcare through workplace or voluntary insurance. While the state should play a major role in regulating and financing medical care the delivery of services should involve a variety of governmental and non-governmental organizations. Once again it is clear that this will entail inequalities in the distribution of medical care. In sum, welfare pluralism implies greater differentiation, variety and competition but also greater inequality. It is a conception which fits in well with the idea of limiting state responsibility and downsizing the state sector while maintaining a measure of collective responsibility for basic services. It also relates well to the notion of decentralization, competition and greater efficiency in the social services sector. In many ways welfare pluralism represents a form of 'feasible' welfare in the changed circumstances of the 1990s and beyond.[37]

However, if welfare pluralism represents the shape of things to come this change will take place from very different levels of social welfare development, patterns of social programmes and expenditures and in very different national and regional settings. The pace and nature of the change will therefore vary a great deal. If the economic and political conditions of the post-Second World War decades favoured a full employment social citizenship state, the circumstances of the late twentieth century suggest a convergence around welfare pluralism. There will still be a great deal of variation around this central tendency, but it is very likely that the welfare state as we have known it will increasingly give way to a more variegated and pluralist pattern of welfare – extending all the way from service delivery to full social provision.

NOTES

1 Goran Therborn, 'The Prospects of Labour and the Transformation of Advanced Capitalism', *New Left Review* 145 (May/June 1984): 37. See also Goran Therborn and Joop Roebroek, 'The Irreversible Welfare State', *International Journal of Health Services* 16: 4 (1986).

2 John Myles, 'Decline or Impasse? The Current State of the Welfare State', *Studies in Political Economy* 26 (Summer 1988): 73.

3 This is true of many Western, and especially English-speaking, countries. For Canada see, for example, Ken Battle, 'Clawback: The Demise of Universality in the Canadian Welfare State', in Ian Taylor (ed.), *The Social Effects of Free Market Policies* (New York: St Martin's Press, 1990); Grattan Gray, 'Universality is Dead, Long live Universality?', *Canadian Review of Social Policy* 25 (May 1990): 56–8.

4 For changes in public and social expenditure see Howard Oxley and John P. Martin, 'Controlling Government Spending and Deficits: Trends in the 1980s and Prospects for the 1990s', *OECD Economic Studies No. 17* (Autumn 1991): 157–64, 168–73; for changes in taxation see Robert P. Hagemann *et al.*, 'Tax Reform in OECD Countries: Motives, Constraints and Practice', *OECD Economic Studies No. 10* (Spring 1988), and Graham Vickery, 'Tax Reform: What Impact on Industry?', *The OECD Observer* 155 (December 1988/January 1989). It is important to keep in mind that despite cutbacks the share of social expenditure in the GDP may rise as a result of such factors as ageing population, rising relative costs of medical care, and level of unemployment. Between 1985 and 1990 average social expenditure for OECD countries remained stable at around 27 per cent of GDP. See Edwin Bell, 'Social Policy and Economic Reality', *The OECD Observer* 183 (August/September 1993): 15. In 1989 total government share of GDP for OECD countries was still nearly 3 per cent higher than in 1979. See Oxley and Martin, 'Controlling Government Spending and Deficits', p. 173.

5 Mel Hurtig, *The Betrayal of Canada* (Toronto: Stoddart, 1992), pp. 133–6; David Langille, 'The Business Council on National Issues and the Canadian State', *Studies in Political Economy* 24 (Autumn 1987): 56–7.

6 See, for example, Bob Jessop, 'Towards a Schumpeterian Welfare State?', *Studies in Political Economy* 40 (Spring 1993); L. McDowell, 'Gender Divisions in a Post-Fordist Era', in L. McDowell and R. Pringle (eds), *Defining Women: Social Institutions and Gender Divisions* (London: Polity Press, 1991); Claus Offe, 'Democracy Against the Welfare State?', *Political Theory* 15: 4 (November 1987).

7 Jessop, 'Towards a Schumpeterian Welfare State?'

8 Gosta Esping-Andersen, *The Three Worlds of Welfare Capitalism* (Princeton, N.J.: Princeton University Press, 1990).

9 On the United States approach to full employment see Goran Therborn, *Why Some Peoples are More Unemployed than Others* (London: Verso, 1986), pp. 112–13. On rates of unemployment see Tables 14.1 and 14.2 (pp. 317 and 318).

10 On the welfare state in the United States see, for example, Norman Ginsburg, *Divisions of Welfare* (London: Sage, 1992), ch. 4 and 'Statistical Appendix'.

11 Naomi Maruo, 'The Development of the Welfare Mix in Japan', in Richard Rose and Rei Shiratori (eds), *The Welfare State East and West* (New York: Oxford University Press, 1986).

12 See, for example, National Council of Social Welfare, *Social Welfare Services in Japan* (Tokyo, 1986), pp. 121–3; Robert Pinker, 'Social Welfare in Japan and Britain: A Comparative View', in E. Oyen (ed.), *Comparing Welfare States and their Futures* (Aldershot: Gower, 1986), pp. 119–21.

13 National Council of Social Welfare, *Social Welfare Services in Japan*, pp. 121–3.

14 Pinker, 'Social Welfare in Japan', p. 121.
15 On Swedish welfare see Ginsburg, *Divisions of Welfare*, ch. 2; H. Heclo and M. Madsen, *Policy and Politics in Sweden* (Philadelphia: Temple University Press, 1986).
16 Ginsburg, *Divisions of Welfare*, p. 41.
17 In 1990 tax revenue was 56.9 per cent of the GDP compared with the OECD average of 38.8 per cent. *OECD in Figures 1993* (Paris: OECD, 1993), pp. 42–3.
18 See, for example, Wolfgang Zapf, 'Development, Structure and Prospects of the German Social State', in Rose and Shiratori (eds), *The Welfare State East and West*.
19 See for example, Esping-Andersen, *The Three Worlds of Welfare Capitalism*, pp. 81–8; David C. Marsh, *The Future of the Welfare State* (Harmondsworth: Penguin Books, 1964); Timothy Raison, 'The British Debate the Welfare State', in Charles I. Schottland (ed.), *The Welfare State* (New York: Harper & Row, 1967).
20 On Britain see, for example, T. H. Marshall, *Social Policy* (London: Hutchinson, 1965).
21 Ramesh Mishra, *The Welfare State in Capitalist Society* (Toronto: Toronto University Press, 1990), ch. 3; S. Olsson, 'Towards a Transformation of the Swedish Welfare State?', in R. Friedman *et al.* (eds), *Modern Welfare States* (Brighton: Wheatsheaf, 1987).
22 On recent developments in Sweden see Arthur Gould, 'The End of the Middle Way? The Swedish Welfare State in Crisis', in C. Jones (ed.), *New Perspectives on the Welfare State in Europe* (London: Routledge, 1993); Jonas Pontusson, 'At the End of the Third Road: Swedish Social Democracy in Crisis', *Politics & Society* 20: 3 (September 1992).
23 See Pontusson, 'At the End of the Third Road', pp. 322–3.
24 See note 22.
25 George Ross, 'Social Policy in the New Europe', *Studies in Political Economy* 40 (Spring 1993): 63.
26 Ibid., p. 42.
27 Jean-Pierre Jallade, 'Is the Crisis Behind Us?', in Z. Ferge and J. E. Kolberg (eds), *Social Policy in a Changing Europe* (Boulder, Colo.: Westview Press, 1992), pp. 42–4; see also Stephen Leibfried and Paul Pierson, 'Prospects for Social Europe', *Politics & Society* 20: 3 (September 1992).
28 41 per cent of Japanese elders were living with their married sons compared with 0.9 per cent of American elders; 55 per cent of Japanese elders wanted to live with their grown-up children compared with 6 per cent of Americans. See Maruo, 'The Development of the Welfare Mix in Japan', pp. 68–9.
29 Hye Kyung Lee, 'The Japanese Welfare State in Transition', in Robert R. Friedman *et al.* (eds), *Modern Welfare States* (New York: New York University Press, 1987); Maruo, 'The Development of the Welfare Mix in Japan'.
30 James Laxer, *False God: How the Globalization Myth Has Impoverished Canada* (Toronto: Lester Publishing, 1993), p. 10.
31 Therborn, 'The Prospects of Labour and the Transformation of Advanced Capitalism'.
32 Francis Fukuyama, *The End of History and the Last Man* (New York: Free Press, 1992).
33 William W. Goldsmith and Edward J. Blakely, *Separate Societies: Poverty and Inequality in U.S. Cities* (Philadelphia: Temple University Press, 1992), p. 20. The strong economic growth and the fall in unemployment between 1982 and 1990 in the US made only a slight impact on poverty, mainly because of low wages. See Rebecca M. Blank, 'Why were Poverty Rates so High in the 1980s?', in D. B.

Papadimitriou and E. N. Wolff (eds), *Poverty and Prosperity in the USA in the Late Twentieth Century* (New York: St Martin's Press, 1993).

34 In different ways both the United States and Japan, laggards in respect of universal provision, exemplify this tendency. It has of course intensified in the United States since the Reagan presidency. Britain has also been moving in this direction since the Thatcher government came to power in 1979. See Mishra, *The Welfare State in Capitalist Society*, ch. 2; J. K. Galbraith, *The Culture of Contentment* (Boston: Houghton Mifflin, 1992).

35 This is what has happened, for example, in the United States and Britain since the early 1980s.

36 See Norman Johnson, *The Welfare State in Transition* (Brighton: Wheatsheaf, 1987), ch. 4, for a perceptive discussion of pluralism; see also R. Rose, 'Common Goals but Different Roles: The State's Contribution to the Welfare Mix', in Rose and Shiratori (eds), *The Welfare State East and West*.

37 I have tried to formulate the basic tenets of welfare pluralism and some of its policy implications as clearly and as specifically as possible. As mentioned in the text, what I present here is a centrist version of welfare pluralism as I see it. It is presented in a descriptive rather than prescriptive mode. Welfare pluralists may of course disagree with this interpretation.

15

ESCAPE FROM FORDISM

The emergence of alternative forms of state
administration and output

Isabella Bakker and Riel Miller

INTRODUCTION: EMERGING FORMS OF STATE ADMINISTRATION

On the frontier where state workers meet citizens important changes are taking place in what and how the state produces.[1] Like many private sector firms confronting new competitive conditions public organizations are facing pressure to adapt to the new circumstances. As a result, there are significant changes occurring in the state 'production process'. Slowly, and often without explicit directives from the political or bureaucratic command centres, new forms of public administration are emerging. These 'grass-roots' administrative reforms reflect a pragmatic response to both the reduction of public funding for many welfare state activities and the locally specific pressures created by economic, demographic and social need.

In this period of disintegration of the old order, decentralization and flexibility are provoking the development of alternative methods for the provision of collective services as well as new types of public goods.[2] These changes in the nature and means of public sector output are also being accompanied by a new politics of representation. Pushed to adapt to changing circumstances and the breakdown or functional failure of the post-war systems of state provision, groups from across the social and economic spectrum are taking the initiative into their own hands. Communities of interest, geography and history are responding to the fragmentation and privatization of social and economic infrastructure with new collectively determined responses.[3]

The first part of this chapter offers a brief look at two examples of these potentially new forms and functions of the state. The first case examines community economic development (CED), an area of economic policy that is gaining ground over traditional more macro-oriented state programmes like demand-side economic stimulus. The second example considers the field of healthcare where a combination of organizational and technological innovations may transform both the definition of medical services and the distribution of power over the knowledge that contributes to wellness. The examples reviewed in this chapter can only capture the initial contours of emerging methods and types of collective services. It is still too early to provide a full picture of future functional and administrative forms of the state. The case studies do provide a clear sense of both the break with past practice and the potential for positive as well as negative reinventing of the state.[4]

The latter part of the chapter concludes with an examination of two alternative scenarios for the future organization and functioning of the state. One is a 'liberal alternative state'[5] variant that benevolently and paternalistically integrates post-Fordist changes in state administrative processes and products without making the political transition to more direct and effective democracy. With this type of state, generally led by social-democratic-type administrations, the tendency is to seek ways of decentralizing, customizing and improving the efficiency of state services. The political goal is to preserve services through a combination of innovation and centralized supervision. The second alternative is dubbed the 'democratic alternative state' since it not only transforms what and how the public sector produces but also alters the politics of representation towards a much more pervasive and influential democracy. In this scenario the transformation of what and how the state produces moves further away from the traditional practices and hierarchies of the existing state. Power shifts away from the state by virtue of both an explicit abdication of responsibility for collective action and an inability to play a leadership role in establishing new public sector forms and functions. The initiative for collective action emerges, unequally and unevenly, from a wide range of groups with different interests and capabilities.

Clearly, this chapter is prospective. We are aware that often new visions of state forms and functions are not universally applicable nor will they necessarily be of universal benefit. We are also aware that these changes to the state are part of a broader process of transformation in the realms of production, consumption and reproduction. Indeed, the analysis in this chapter starts, at the macro level, from the recognition of the concurrent influences of two powerful forces of change – the polarization of effective state action towards the local and global levels and the transformation of the social and technical relations of production as Fordism decays. These changes are challenging both the functional and administrative foundations of the state. The archetypal Fordist state, with its use of both the homogeneous policy terrain of demand-side Keynesianism and the administrative methods of Taylorist extraction, was fairly well equipped to provide the social and economic infrastructure of the post-war era. These characteristics of the Fordist state have been well documented and will not be the focus here. Instead, in keeping with the forward-looking perspective of this volume, the present chapter concentrates on the possibilities emerging from a transformation of the production conditions of state apparatus – the what and how of public sector operations. The analysis is constructed on the foundation of two related premises. First, that the disintegration of Fordism, with its complex changes in the spatial distribution and organizational attributes of production, is significantly modifying the social and economic relations that characterized the post-war period. Second, there is a related transformation taking place in the 'public sector' production methods that typified the Keynesian Welfare State (KWS) as a producer of infrastructure and the social safety net. The breadth and depth of these changes opens up new functional and administrative options that go beyond the previously stable Fordist state model.

COMMUNITY ECONOMIC DEVELOPMENT: SLOW PROGRESS ON THE PATH TO LOCAL EMPOWERMENT

The trend towards local or community-based economic initiatives represents one area where new state products and processes are emerging. What makes CED (community economic development) particularly interesting in the current conjuncture is the concurrent shift, in both the private and public sectors, away from models of mass-production and mass-consumption (standardized and uniform systems of insurance, schooling, healthcare, etc.). As economies of efficient scale get smaller for both the producer (batch size) and the consumer (product customization) there is a growing viability of supply and demand networks that hinge upon knowledge sharing at a local level.[6]

Governments pursuing CED policies often explicitly argue that they are attempting to adapt for public sector circumstances the creativity and customer satisfaction achieved by private sector reorganization of the firm.[7] One of the stated goals of CED policies is to empower communities, allowing them to create sustainable economic activity through the mobilization of local tangible and intangible assets. Published documents describing the aims and functioning of local employment policies regularly explain how new forms of co-operation and broader-based participation can create a more effective basis for responding to the current economic upheaval. One example of this type of CED policy can be found in Ontario, Canada.

Elected in mid-1990, Ontario's social democratic government has recently attempted to introduce the ideas and principles of local economic development as a way to assist communities to rebuild the economy. To this end, the government brought together a broad range of programmes under one community economic development umbrella called jobsOntario Community Action (jOCA). This new programme consolidated a wide range of existing programmes dispersed across six ministries. Aside from the competitive implications for clients of a common and somewhat reduced pool of funding, it indicates an effort to rethink both the means and ends of local economic policy. As Frances Lankin, the Minister in charge of this programme said in a press release when she introduced it:

> jOCA represents a new way of government doing business with communities – this is a corporate, government-wide approach, involving many different ministries working together as a team. We are changing the way we do business in order to better support communities and their empowerment . . . assistance will be available to help build the capacity of communities to come together and set long term priorities, and to identify ways to turn local plans into actions. In order to ensure that projects are community-owned and community-driven, all partners in the community must be involved in making economic development decisions.[8]

In order to help turn the ambitions into reality jOCA was allocated $300 million over three years and divided into three components: Community Development, Community Financing and Community Capital. These different parts provide fairly comprehensive coverage of the anticipated needs of communities attempting to pursue the new CED path. The Community Development portion is intended to foster the capacity to organize, plan and implement local development. The Community Financing element provides a new legislative avenue for raising bond and share capital within the community. Lastly, Community Capital offers direct assistance for infrastructure investment at the local level.

After six months of operation, at the end of 1993, a team of four people conducted a survey of the status of jOCA implementation and the more general condition of Ontario's community economic development efforts by visiting over twenty locations distributed across every region of Ontario (see Government of Ontario 1994). The team interviewed, participated and listened to well over two hundred people from a wide range of constituencies including: front-line government workers engaged in various aspects of programme administration from some eight different ministries; activists from a number of communities of interest such as aboriginal women, blacks and women farmers; representatives of private sector interests from vice-presidents of particular firms to members of the local trade union council; and many municipal officials, development officers and other local public-service providers.

The results of the survey cover a wide range of issues. Of primary relevance for the discussion here is the extent to which the *Review* exposed both the limits and potential of CED as a new form of state administration. One of the clearest results of the survey is that the existing nexus of Fordist, KWS administrative, institutional and programmatic systems resists movement away from mass-production and consumption norms. The survey of existing practices reveals clearly that the institutions and practices of the Fordist state are deeply entrenched in the everyday conduct of social and economic life.

In turn, this culture plays a major role in inhibiting movement towards new public sector methods and outputs. For the most part the vertical and hierarchical command and control decision-making systems of a Taylorist organization remain largely untouched by the current fiscal and economic turmoil. In fact there is some evidence that the move towards 'leaner and meaner' staffing and funding levels provokes fear and resistance to any type of change at the local level.

Sustained by years of centralized, rule-driven funding schemes, most local development activity no longer addresses either the economic potential or the constraints facing the community. At the moment, so-called community development activities concentrate on traditional forms of infrastructure activity such as roads, schools, government buildings and sports facilities like hockey arenas. For the most part these bricks and mortar investments provide an improved ambience for the community and support the basic needs of the old Fordist industries typical of the post-war manufacturing economy. Recently, with the decline of the Fordist industrial base, communities throughout the OECD have started pursuing scavenger and 'beggar-thy-neighbour' type economic development strategies. As a result, many projects being proposed as 'developmental' are aimed at luring tourism dollars or new business investment away from other regions or towns.[9]

What is perhaps most striking about these efforts at so-called community economic development is the extent to which they side-step the local economic assets embodied by existing firms, skilled labour forces, social infrastructure and natural resources. On the basis of this survey, the Fordist state is at best inadequate and at worst inimical to success in meeting the challenge of facilitating a transition towards an economy that takes advantage of emerging production processes and outputs. Less than a handful of towns considered future market opportunities in a systematic way. However, even these efforts were predominantly tied to the cost-competitiveness issues underlying location competition with little direct analysis or prescription regarding the 'new competition' or post-Fordist challenges to the existing social and technical conditions of production. What little attention there was to these latter, post-Fordist-type issues tended to concentrate on the less contested, more transparent technological attributes of economic change. Here communities turn to the well-trodden path for providing firms with subsidies by establishing sector committees, research coalitions, and training initiatives.

The Fordist state makes little systematic effort to become engaged in the critical tasks of upgrading existing production processes or introducing new ones. Few if any connections are made to knowledge or innovation – the main drivers of economic success in the future. Essentially, jOCA and other CED-type initiatives currently focus on realizing modest to negligible improvements in either local infrastructure such as waterfronts, town halls, arenas or local self-help groups looking to initiate small-scale planning or enterprise/skill-nurturing projects. This does not mean there is a lack of effort. In communities throughout the province people are spending considerable discretionary time and money on local projects. However, the majority of these initiatives are at best tangential to the challenge of economic transformation required to maintain existing economic activity and to introduce new ones. Every community visited by the review team was busy investing in tourism 'strategies' that consist primarily of stand-alone beautification projects. There is generally little assessment of the macro tourism market or the 'beggar-thy-neighbour' implications of one town 'stealing' tourists from another. None of the presentations made to the review team discussed the lower earnings profile associated with most tourism employment when compared to the manufacturing industries that once sustained many of these communities. Nor did the plans assess the demand and supply conditions that determine success or failure in the tourism market.

The reliance on tourism as an economic development strategy is understandable since it provides a way to justify the traditional municipal projects of the past and avoids confronting the radical characteristics of alternative projects sponsored by less traditional constituencies. With few exceptions the same pattern as found in the tourism projects holds for the other sectoral initiatives. Generally, the analysis of the future directions of particular economic sectors avoids the kind of economic critique necessary for arriving at innovative solutions. Where there has been more detailed and critical sector-specific analysis it is often isolated from the practical tasks of mobilizing community resources. Instead, the grander plans pin hope on encouraging existing firms through either some form of subsidy (funding construction or training) or some form of cost reduction (eliminating clean-up costs or using university research). These traditional static approaches miss the dynamic potential of CED as a way to transform the economic and social fabric that underpins innovative investment and quality production. In an era when creativity is more decisive for success than regimentation, CED has the potential to demonstrate that relinquishing authority to direct producers of traded and non-traded output and combining previously distinct activities holds the key to realizing quality and innovation on the supply and demand sides.

In conclusion to this quick overview of one experience with an emerging form of state policy and administration, the evidence demonstrates how difficult it is for the Fordist state to realize the potential contribution of CED to the diffusion of new forms of workplace organization and supplier/ producer clustering. In this case study most CED activity, whether guided by jOCA rules or community initiative, treated the process as an obstacle to be overcome in order to arrive at the funding of a specific project. Where additional effort was made to include new participants or utilize more open decision-making the tendency was to take a mechanistic, getting-past-the-hurdles approach. A head count methodology that mechanistically includes one representative from each distinct community sidesteps the discoveries and incentives that emerge from a more democratic process. Furthermore, without the imagination and commitment that arises from sharing responsibility more fully there is little reason to urge or expect the diffusion of CED methods throughout the administrative and managerial cultures of governments and firms. As a result, one of the main demonstration effects of CED as an alternative form of state administration is lost and the relevance to the emerging knowledge economy diminished.

FROM HEALTHCARE MANAGEMENT TO WELLNESS SELF-ADMINISTRATION?

> Over the next decade, we will see health care become less doctor-centered, and more community- and family-centered. Medicine itself will become less of an art and more fact-based. Yet, at the same time, it will come to feel more humane. The very discoveries and inventions that will continue to transform medical practice will push it to be less about hardware, less about vast and powerful machines watched over by highly trained acolytes, and more about shared information. Health care will shift its center of gravity away from last-minute, traumatic, intensive, expensive, short-term hospital-centered care, and toward early-as-possible, preventive, long-term, intimate, inexpensive application of information in the community and family.
>
> (Flower 1994: 110)

Readers of Marge Piercy's fictional account of the future in *He, She and It* will be familiar with a character referred to as 'House'. This protagonist is essentially the technological 'butler-nursemaid' of the household capable of discussing, monitoring and often meeting a wide range of material and physiological needs. The semiotic drama of the novel turns on the complex relations between animate technology (It) and us humans. This inanimate animation need not be equated with 'intelligence' since pattern recognition, voice interaction and the capacity to filter vast amounts of behavioural and physiological data do not signal the transition to creative or emotive being. Instead, we are confronting a somewhat familiar and more mundane phenomenon – a radical simplification of heretofore complex and inaccessible technology.

A good example of the relevance of radical simplification arising out of more powerful (and relatively less expensive) technology for the post-Fordist state is in the field of healthcare. Before touching on the potential implications, both negative and positive, for the administrative form of the state and the associated power relationships, imagine for a moment the potential capacity of this new technology. Four new and interrelated ways of producing healthcare are emerging from massive improvements in health information (Flower 1994). First, and easiest to relate to, is telemedicine where everything from x-rays to surgery are shared over a network allowing a wider and more timely pooling of expertise. Second, more tentative but gaining momentum, is the pooling of medical data in ways that achieve the objectives of massive clinical benchmarking and accurate, easily accessible personal medical records. Both of these achievements would transform the identification of what works for whom and when. Whether this will occur in ways that are liberating or oppressive is yet to be fully determined.

Shifting out of the healthcare sector *per se* into the home or workplace, the third application of new technology involves the use of telecommunications networks to connect healthcare information with other data such as product toxicity, location of specialized health services and healthier ways of working and living. Finally, and the biggest departure from current practices, is the advent of a personal information leveller that you can query and is capable of 'knowing' your personal history, current and past clinical status, and external biological context in ways that are cross-referenced with the mass of available medical benchmark results. This 'knowbot' (a knowledge robot) could link together a wide range of information from the physical scars of past broken bones and the psychological hurts of job loss or bereavement to the latest medical findings for your gene pattern and the composition of your diet. This information bank would know the chemical status of the broccoli taken from the refrigerator, the heat it was cooked with, the spectral characteristics of the steam vented from the stove; it knows how much water you drink and the most recent results of the toilet's automatic urinalysis. When you ask it a question, as you have been doing since you first started to talk, it can respond with a wealth of information never before available in 'real-time'.

Science fiction? Perhaps, although many facets of this scenario are well on the way to implementation in some OECD countries. What is certain is that change is underway in both the technology and organizational relations of healthcare delivery. As is all too familiar, the cost of healthcare has been rising rapidly and already occupies a large proportion of GDP in many nations. Numerous attempts to address the cost, quality and access tradeoffs in the healthcare field have followed the patterns of the Fordist or competitive state. Given the archaic labour relations and guild-like privileges maintained by doctors in most countries it is not surprising that a more rigorous application of Fordist methods does offer some cost savings for the state. By breaking the special status maintained by physicians and pushing large medical institutions such as hospitals towards more rigorous time-motion efficiency, governments are able to realize considerable cost-savings.

Equally clear is the fact that the outcome of these changes will be strongly influenced by the extent to which equity, empowerment, access and privacy rights are asserted by popular groups. Resistance by healthcare practitioners

341

and community groups to a for-profit mode of medical production can play a decisive role in slowing down the withdrawal of services and forcing a more people- and wellness-oriented reform trajectory. For the most part, the agendas of both the old-line Fordist state and liberal variant of the alternative state are dominated by the imperatives of cost control and profit maximization. Here the priority is put on privatization and the rigorous implementation of private as opposed to social cost/benefit accounting. However, the real gains in wellness – the presumed outcome or product of healthcare – are more likely to be found in a complete redesign and reappropriation of the production process which puts the 'quality' of a person's health in the hands of those who produce it – ourselves. These possibilities have radical implications for the administrative form of the state and the methods whereby public authorities seek to 'produce' a healthy workforce and population.[10]

Realizing such a radical change in the production of wellness takes explicit account of the long-affirmed and recently empirically 'verified' finding that the related conditions of self-esteem and control over one's environment have significant implications for a person's health.[11] Thus, one of the goals for those attempting to reach a more popular or democratic alternative state is to extend the reconfiguration of the social and technical relations of production beyond the medical field to include the more general determinants of wellness. Fully realized, community-driven healthcare extends to the entire sphere of social and economic reproduction. Empowered communities are able to organize and utilize the full range of local assets, inside and outside the monetary economy, to generate sustainable solutions to economic and social well-being.

The liberal alternative state is also probably capable of making many of the changes in production that will improve the quality of healthcare. Even with a less democratic approach, decentralization towards community-based healthcare will improve the capacity of caregivers to address local sources of illness and undertake prevention initiatives. However, the liberal agenda for change stops short of actually transferring power in ways that are not easily reversible. The liberal alternative state may be able to increase quality and efficiency while still guarding against both the risk of extending the meaning of healthcare to include the more general conditions for overall wellness and the operational entrenchment of democratic administration.[12] In short, the prospect of health information systems does open up new horizons for quality of care and personal control over medical data.

LEAVING THE FORDIST STATE BEHIND?

From the vantage point of the falling apart of the Fordist state and the building up of post-Fordist relations of production, it is crucial to reconsider the dividing lines of the past. The 'discourse' that characterizes the traditional

Fordist KWS insists that victory or defeat for popular forces is determined by inclusion or exclusion from the state apparatus. In this framework the meaning of public or collective action is largely coterminous with state institutions. Given this logic, right-wing forces fight to put as much as possible outside the administrative or regulatory reach of the state into the private sphere. Left-wing forces attempt to put as much as possible within the state's administrative reach. Thus the polarity of political gains and losses is defined by inclusion or exclusion from state intervention. What tends to be missed in this ideological equation is the potential for collective action outside of the centralized or administrative apparatus of the state.

In practice, however, changes are taking place. The Taylorist and mass-production/consumption patterns of the state are being disrupted and discarded. Often, these changes are an unintentional outcome of severe fiscal pressures and the delegitimation of existing ineffectual government pro-grammes. In circumstances where programmes lack funding sources or significant popular support the centralized state administration is in a position to reduce its role by delegating and decentralizing responsibility. Such moves are typically rationalized (*ex post*) as a way to enhance local input and participation. At the local level the initial sense of abandonment is being transformed into a recognition that by building up local organizational capacity it may be possible to reduce citizen alienation from collective action and address the deepening inequality currently being generated by economic change. For many constituencies, the combined impact of practical successes at the local level and a general sense of the reduced effectiveness, capacity and willingness of the traditional state apparatus is leading to more explicit challenges to conventional methods of state administration.

Regardless of the source of the challenge, one of the main contentions of this chapter is that the Fordist state's limitations – reviewed in other chapters in this book – are leading to a questioning of the symmetry of left versus right with public versus private. Undoubtedly such shifting of the political dividing lines is difficult given the identification of the public sphere with the KWS expansion of entitlements and improvements in the quality of collective infrastructure. Equally important for those attempting to counter the tremendous economic and political power exercised by corporate inter-ests is the fact that systems of representative democracy do provide some capacity to limit and direct business decisions. As a result, most responses to the redrawing of the functional and administrative boundaries of the state cling to the conventional dividing lines where free-market advocates cham-pion privatization while the supporters of the welfare state defend public subsidies and entitlements. One way of overcoming this impasse, pursued in this chapter, is to examine the ways in which new forms of administration open alternative possibilities for collective action outside the monolithic institutional frameworks of the past.

FORDIST VERSUS ALTERNATIVE STATE ADMINISTRATION: FLIPSIDES OF THE SAME COIN?

How can we begin to explore some of the basic attributes of alternative forms of state administration and output? Initially, there are those features that can be defined simply because they are contrary or distinct from those of the Fordist state. The primary contrast between the typically Fordist and alternative state form is in the nature of the output and the administrative changes involved in the shift from mass-production and consumption patterns to tailored services congruent with the diverse needs of a heterogeneous population. For both the producer and consumer of public services the practical implementation of this transformation requires major changes in how the work is done and consumed. Making these changes in what and how the state produces is also a prerequisite for realizing changes to economic, infrastructure and social insurance policies that are likely to be more congruent with a post-Fordist economy.

The alternative state form alters a number of typical features of the Fordist state by shifting the locus of control from the centralized and hierarchical bureaucracies that are incapable of knowing how to tailor output (see Table 15.1). At this level, the logic of transformation is driven by the dramatic change from a production- to a consumption-determined system. With the consumer of collective services providing the knowledge needed to tailor output – from transportation and healthcare to recreation and culture – the burden is on the supply side to respond. The capacity to understand and tailor supply requires a major change from the deep alienation of conception and execution that currently characterizes state production processes and products.

These alternatives to the bureaucratic state are likely to be better positioned to support the higher demand for information that is a defining characteristic of the knowledge economy. The alternative state re-engineers policies, procedures and outputs to achieve both greater efficiency and responsiveness. The challenge for the alternative state is to redefine what is produced and how the terms and conditions of that collective action are determined. Reshaping institutions needs to be combined with redrawing the boundaries and transparency between the public and private spheres. Consequently, the political challenge involved in the move from a Fordist to an alternative state is much greater than simply flipping the coin from one side to the other.

LIBERAL VERSUS POPULAR STATE ADMINISTRATION: DRAWING DEMOCRATIC BATTLE LINES

The differences between these two variants of the alternative state turn primarily on the ways in which the claims of emancipatory movements for greater equality in decision-making and resource allocation are opera-

Table 15.1 Distinguishing Fordist and alternative state forms

	Fordist state	Alternative state
Economic policy emphasis	Monetary and fiscal macro policies – homogeneous treatment of aggregate demand	Supply-side quality – policies foster labour and product market capacity to customize efficiently
Infrastructure provision	Standardized transportation, education, healthcare services to a uniform population	Tailored transportation, education, healthcare services to a heterogeneous population
Social insurance	Standardized treatment as if the population's needs were uniform	Tailored services aimed at heterogeneous needs of diverse population
Administrative structure	Centralized control and hierarchical decision-making	Decentralized authority and peer-based decision-making
Production method	Mass-production using Taylorist division of conception and execution	Customized production based on the integration of knowledge into both production and consumption
Administrative information and incentive system	Top-down budget control – basically a form of command planning based on targets and strict spending limits	Transparency and choice based on open bidding, rewarding performance and clear user-driven incentives

tionalized by the policies that are internal and external to the state. The similarities between the liberal and popular alternative state stem mainly from the functional need to accommodate the new heterogeneity and uniqueness of social and economic demand and supply. From this perspective the common ground for any variant of the alternative state is in meeting the economic and social challenges posed by the movement away from a system of wealth creation based on mass-production and consumption. The distinctions within this shared functionality are rooted in the political process as a contestatory relationship. Here, politics is treated as a process rather than an abstract set of principles and policy is seen as informed 'by an ongoing and openly contested politics of voice and representation' (Yeatman 1993: 230).

Variations in the possible state administrative forms beyond Fordism as sketched out in Table 15.1 are also distinguished by the political character of the process of contestation. This process of contestation goes beyond demands imposed on the state by various marginalized or interest-based groups. Rather, it is a dual process where '[e]quality exists only within the relationship of political contestation, where those who are excluded by established policy both show its bias and make a claim on a prospectively more inclusive policy' (Yeatman 1993: 235). The politics of the popular state constitute a process within which contestatory relationships flourish. By way of contrast, the liberal state actualizes new administrative methods of collective production and regulation better suited to post-Fordism but reduces the democratic contests that are the defining characteristic of the popular state.

An example of the possible contrast between liberal and popular methods of providing collective services can be seen in the area of unemployment insurance. Recent reforms of unemployment insurance schemes towards self-employment and quasi-workfare in OECD countries are an example of administrative transformation without altering key power relations. Here the liberal state offers greater flexibility and the possibility of using insurance funds as a pool of investment capital for unemployed individuals. However, for most individuals cast out into the 'entrepreneurial' jungle the likely outcome is intense self-exploitation and eventual business failure. An alternative path, not yet explored in depth, is to provide the political basis for collective actions that improve economic sustainability by sharing knowledge, networks and infrastructure. In these circumstances the entrepreneurial option might have the potential to deepen the local economy along sustainable and even non-profit lines.

In an effort to suggest this potential divergence between different forms of state functioning, Table 15.2 offers a series of logical distinctions based on the policies and managerial methods of the state. The aim of Table 15.2 is to distinguish what and how the state produces in the way of services from the related but distinct changes taking place in social and technical relations of production that characterize specific firms, sectors and household arrangements. The different policy areas of state activity are in the policies column of Table 15.2. We can see that economic policy encompasses the range of efforts from macro to micro by the state to influence cyclical conditions. Infrastructure represents the traditional public goods provided for economic purposes, as distinct from the third category that addresses non-economic social reproduction. In order to provide insights regarding the administrative form of the state activity in each of the three preceding categories the top of the matrix distinguishes types of control, production and consumption. The latter three categories cover the basic methods used across the range of state activities. Taken together these six cells display the logical differentiation of state forms according to preponderant managerial and output characteristics.

Table 15.2 is meant to underscore the as yet undefined characteristics of the emerging forms of state administration. In part, this reflects the fact that particularly for innovative systems of non-mass production and consumption the products and production methods are indeterminate until the process actually gets underway. Intangible knowledge-based products and collective goods such as those that are administered by the state are even more subject to non-uniform specification, unanticipated sources of demand and re-configured networks of supply and distribution. Communities attempting to build on local economic assets – both tangible and intangible – are well aware of the importance of learning by doing as a way to define sustainable economic enterprises. In these circumstances the pressure for the state to respond to non-standardized citizen demands reflects, in part, the disruption of past patterns of living and working. Alternative liberal and democratic solutions are only beginning to emerge. Hence, the two upper quadrants of Table 15.2 can only hint at the genesis of decentralized or locally driven approaches to the challenge of meeting heterogeneous needs and combining assets in new ways. On the other hand, the cells in the bottom two quadrants are typified by more traditional mass-production and Taylorist forms of administration and producer/consumer relations. Standardized, universal and bureaucratic social insurance schemes and compulsory education systems are familiar features of the Fordist state.

Looking at the lower two quadrants of Table 15.2, the variations that distinguish the competitive and Keynesian forms of state turn primarily on the degree of universality, the level of benefits and the incentives built into the programme design. Thatcherite versions of the state are generally more ruthless, aimed at reducing the 'disincentives to work' and enhance the role of income-based disincentives to consumption of publicly provided services. The competitive Fordist state uses unemployment, scarcity and selection based on income to reduce the salience of the social wage. Privatized service provision and profit-based allocative mechanisms predominate as ways of forcing market competition into the public realm. Alternatively, the arche-typal welfare state offers stronger supports to aggregate demand, public infrastructure and subsidies to the social as opposed to the economic side of reproduction.

The Liberal variant is based on the prospect that 'enlightened' capitalists and politicians can begin to construct a more effective state apparatus better suited to the demands of the post-Fordist economy. In the same way that private sector enterprises are being transformed the 're-engineering govern-ment' initiatives like those of the Clinton administration are aimed at adapting post-Fordist production methods to public sector service delivery. Using decentralized policies like community health clinics and building upon the successes of private sector efforts to respond more accurately and efficiently to 'clients', the Liberal post-Fordist state of Table 15.2 is able to address more efficiently the heterogeneous needs of flexible and diversified social and

Table 15.2 Distinguishing four types of Fordist and alternative states

Liberal alternative state

Policies	Administrative control	Method of production	Nature of consumption
Economic	Labour market	Networked, non-Taylorist	Transparent, info intensive
Infrastructure	Mixed public and private	Decentralized	Decentralized
Reproduction	Mixed public and private	Decentralized	Decentralized

Democratic alternative state

Policies	Administrative control	Method of production	Nature of consumption
Economic	Socialization of knowledge	Learning	Learning
Infrastructure	Collective	Local/global	Local/global
Reproduction	Collective	Local/global	Local/global

Fordist competitive state

Policies	Administrative control	Method of production	Nature of consumption
Economic	Macro-monetary	Scarcity	Selective
Infrastructure	Private profit	Privatized	Selective
Reproduction	Private profit	Mixed public and private	Incentive driven

Fordist Keynesian welfare state

Policies	Administrative control	Method of production	Nature of consumption
Economic	Macro-expenditure	Mass	Mass
Infrastructure	Mixed public and private	Mass	Mass
Reproduction	Mixed public and private	Mass	Mass

economic reproduction. Still, in the Liberal variant reinventing the state does occur but in a way that is more acutely torn by the contradiction between front-line empowerment and the desire to retain control at the centre. The administrative form changes in so far as there is a decentralization of responsibility to a community health clinic. But the critical capacity to control local resources and pioneer new ways of social and economic participation are blocked by continued administrative and legal barriers.

By way of contrast, the 'popular' post-Fordist state offers significantly greater power to the 'empowered' state worker and citizen.[13] In this scenario, the trajectory for the KWS in the post-Fordist period is towards a more popular democratic or 'developmental' state. The notion of the developmental state refers to a dual shift in *what* and *how* the state fosters economic and social reproduction. A central aspect of this transformation is the redefinition of the operational rules within the state in ways that change the relationships between the state's employees and citizens (Mackintosh 1993: 38). This state form attempts a double balancing act. First, staying on the democratic highwire demands that a balance be found in the tradeoffs between collective (groups, communities, society as a whole) and individual aspirations. Second, a balance must also be found between the centrifugal forces of empowerment and the restraining grasp of capitalist appropriation. What is perhaps at the core of these tensions is the question of how the popular state, with its capacity to diversify its collective actions to meet hetergeneous and locally specific needs, can still ensure basic levels of resources in the face of market and other inequalities. This is a fundamental challenge for empowered democratic systems that inherently respect differences.

Looking at both forms of alternative state it is possible, without extrapolating too much, to identify attributes that are likely to be functionally useful (more efficient) and desirable (more equitable, democratic). In particular, these alternative states are likely to play a critical role in responding to the challenge of the transition from an economy dominated by Fordist manufacturing to one where knowledge production, distribution and consumption predominate. The knowledge economy poses numerous as of yet unresolved problems for both the private and public spheres. For instance, given the inalienable character of human embodied knowledge and the all too alienable character of recorded knowledge, collective participation in the realization of private profit from knowledge will be unavoidable. Already there is a broad range of responses by different states to the pressure of technology and market forces in telecommunications and information technology. Here the contrast between European and North American solutions highlights the fact that the adaptation of state administrative structures and jurisdiction (responsibility for new and old services) depends on too many specific historical factors for detailed speculation here. However, the next section does attempt to provide a few compass points upon which alternative historical paths might be traced.

UNCERTAIN TRAJECTORIES: TRACING THE PATH OF ALTERNATIVE STATE FORMS

One way of imagining new functional and administrative attributes of the state is to project these four types of state onto a plane described by two axes: one axis measures the extent to which the Fordist forms of state production and regulation have been left behind, the other axis measures the degree of democratic power and equity in a society. This is a helpful way to map the various options and directions emerging out of the political and economic disintegration of Fordism. Figure 15.1 sketches a two-dimensional plane where the arrows trace the evolution of various specific states over time. Simply for illustrative purposes arrow 1 shows the case of a state, perhaps like the UK that moves from competitive to KWS back to competitive, but with a slightly less Fordist character. Arrow 2 might be seen as some Scandinavian hybrid. Arrow 3 could show the trend of the Canadian state. And arrow 4 could be seen as tracing the hypothetical trajectory of a decentralized Italian state within a strongly federalist EU. Clearly, this is a heuristic device intended to help imagine possible paths to alternative states.

Tracing these hypothetical trajectories is useful because it invites speculation on the attributes and early signs of emerging alternatives to existing ways of organizing the specifying state activity. This is a logical device for

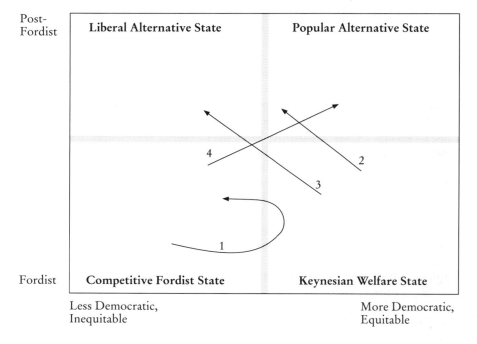

Figure 15.1 Possible state trajectories

350

considering innovative possibilities, not an attempt to describe actual historical paths. The intent of this figure, without going too far down the path of hypothetical historical mapping, is to suggest that certain trajectories are either worth attempting to pursue or to avoid. In this sense, maps are useful for charting both the course you want to follow and the one you want to avoid. A map can also help indicate where you have been and why it is unlikely you will want or be able to retrace your steps.

Without excluding the potential for history to repeat itself (first time as tragedy and second time as farce), it seems unlikely that there will be a general return amongst OECD countries to the state forms that dominate the bottom half of Figure 15.1. As other chapters in this book have pointed out, given the nature of the changes taking place in the spheres of private production and consumption, there are good reasons to question the functional viability of the competitive Fordist state with its privatization and deregulation of state–society relations. Equally dysfunctional is an alternative that depends on a defensive strategy *vis-à-vis* the preservation of public versus private provision of services. Maintaining the status quo does not address the fundamental changes required of the administrative forms of the Fordist state. The centralization of administration, the Taylorist labour process, the emphasis on rules and budgets versus the amount and quality of services (Murray 1991: 22) all reflect the traditional form of a state that fails to meet today's political and economic demands. This failure has, in part, helped public choice theorists to make such inroads in introducing market-driven financial and labour practices to the public sector (see Warskett 1993). In practice, most of these 'competitive state' changes have served to extend and deepen the hold of traditional Fordist administrative and production relations on the state (Murray 1991: 24). As a result, as Murray points out, the 'new commercial Fordism' does not provide a very robust solution to the current challenges of economic and social change.

The weakness of entrenching the Fordist, or competitive Fordist state, are related to service quality, the nature of the labour process, the structure of management and the reliance on contracts as the binding economic and social relationship between producers and consumers. The first issue concerns the control of service quality and the inability of managers to secure improvements through top-down methods. Here, state managers fail to achieve the necessary post-Fordist emphasis on quality through the involvement of front-line workers. As a result, they also fail to make good on the objective of meeting the diverse and often pressing needs of a heterogeneous citizenry and economy.

The second weakness relates to the mismatch between the type of labour training in public administration and the needs of the alternative state. Front-line producers are the key to quality, innovation and production control; however, job security, training and a commitment to work are necessary elements for realizing these goals. This is in contrast to the new commercial or competitive Fordism that relies on de-skilling of front-line workers, contracting out and marketization of the public sector.

Further entrenching Fordist forms of administration introduces a third weakness by keeping hierarchical managerial structures in place. The post-Fordist goal is to 'shift power from officials to elected politicians on the one hand, and to users on the other' (Murray 1993: 54). This means decentralizing managerial control of resources and information and increasing front-line operative autonomy. As Maureen Mackintosh notes, 'This defines a way of working within the state that shifts the location of power, changes the access to information of different social groups, and develops the capacities of the previously less powerful' (1993: 38). Such a shift in the form and location of decision-making can be linked to what Yeatman has referred to as 'the development of the value of equality'. This refers to the willingness of 'the custodians to established policy' to listen to the contestatory voices, 'the act of listening already transforming the established procedures of who gets to participate within the process of governance' (Yeatman 1993: 236). The act of inviting contestatory or marginalized voices to work with the custodians to determine how policy can be more inclusive becomes part of the process of achieving equality.[14]

Finally, the reliance on contracts as the binding factor in relations between suppliers and customers ignores both the incompleteness of contracts and the post-Fordist emphasis on trust or mutual understanding. The state is being called upon to respond in new ways as the economy moves away from the traditional enforcement and binding cultural systems of the self-contained firm. Some important implications follow from this two-pronged evaluation of contracts. What Boyer has termed 'the paradox of trust' is the first aspect of the competitive Fordist state's reliance on contracts. Boyer's discussion (1992) is in the context of comparative private sector industrial relations, but for our purposes can also be applied to the public sector production process where in a similar fashion trust and mutual understanding between suppliers and customers are the cornerstones of innovation and quality service delivery. Here again, the Fordist state and its more conflict-ridden competitive version are unlikely to serve effectively as vehicles for political legitimation or economic transformation. Communities and diverse constituencies must be drawn into the process of defining and delivering collective services otherwise there is little to be gained from reform of state administration.

Another implication of the reliance by the Fordist state on private contracts arises from the fact that the operation of markets, the formation of prices and the organization of production rely intrinsically on social and institutional norms (Bowles 1991: 13). Recognition of the incompleteness of contracts and the non-market relations which surround and structure all markets allows for a reconsideration of the terms upon which people engage in market transactions (Mackintosh 1990). This is significant for a critique of the viability of the commercial, or competitive, Fordist state because it highlights the extent to which private contracts for previously publicly provided goods and services can be inadequate from the perspective of reproduction. By entrenching or exacerbating the relations of dominance and subordination that operate in the realm of private exchange, the competitive Fordist state ignores many of the social and implicit dimensions that are essential for both contracts, in general, and knowledge networks, in particular. The example of pirating of computer software indicates the inadequacy of legal sanctions without cultural norms that make effective enforcement feasible and efficient.

In contrast to the Fordist approach, an alternative state's system of empowered service delivery could take into account the fact that norms and networks are marked by gender, race and other relationships of subordination and domination. This, in turn, has important implications for political cohesion and efficient provision of diverse services to meet heterogeneous needs. The alternative to the Fordist state clearly has a better chance of realizing this type of transformation in public sector production methods and output than the Thatcherite state. And it is equally clear that a variety of forces, both internal and external to the state, and from both the left- and right-wing ends of the political spectrum, will attack the limits of the Fordist state. What is not as clear, within the context of the building up of the alternative state, is what goals, means and outcomes will differentiate future forms of the state. The concluding section offers some thoughts on this difficult question.

CONCLUSION – DISMANTLING THE BOUNDARIES: THE MERGING OF MEANS AND ENDS?

The challenge for the analysis of the disintegration of Fordism is to attempt to identify the causes and characteristics of the new social relations of production in order to gain a clearer sense of how they may re-draw the map of public and private domains. The urgency of this analytical task stems first from the negative pressures exerted by the growing hardship and inequality associated with the demise of the Fordist political compromises and, second, from the need to advance the political debates concerning the means and ends of struggle around the redefinition of the public and private.

An equally pressing question is the extent to which the shift to new social relations of production can occur without the state as pioneer. In previous major social and economic transitions, the state has always played a critical role in establishing and financing new forms of work organization, production technology and social reproduction. As with the state-directed economies of the Second World War, the role of innovation and dissemination occurs both within and outside the public sector proper. This is not to say that the state necessarily invented these new forms. Rather, once the bloody struggle in the workplace and competitive market spawned so-called 'progressive' elements of capital capable of pioneering more productive

353

and efficient methods, the state took on the role of diffusing them more widely – partly by adopting them in the public sphere. This highly functionalist perspective does find some confirmation in current trends towards decentralization and, importantly, is often driven forward by the political struggles of marginalized groups demanding recognition, rights and self-directed forms of organization. This generates a rich dialectic between the development of post-Fordist social relations within the firm and the 'reinventing' of public sector products and production methods.

From the point of view of pursuing greater self-realization in an interdependent society/ecology, the dominant allocation of power within the future alternative state remains uncertain. Still, based on the old Fordist equation, the losses are quite clear and devastating for a large and growing number of marginalized people around the world. This lends logical weight and moral urgency to the defensive struggles aimed at maintaining the purview and operational methods of the Fordist state. However, two important possibilities suggest reconsidering the current approach towards defending the existing welfare state. The first possibility is that the Keynesian welfare state is not very defensible or, if it is, then only at great cost (such as those incurred by social democratic governments that betray their primary constituencies). The second possibility worth considering as part of a reassessment of strategies aimed at influencing the future trajectory of the capitalist state is the potential for seizing new democratic terrain as the reconfiguration of the social/technical relations of production call into question many aspects of the relationship between the state and civil society.

This chapter cannot answer these questions, but the various alternative states and the two case studies do suggest the following observations. On the one hand, defending the existing welfare regime will be exceedingly difficult, not least because its entrenched administrative and organizational traditions fail to address today's economic, social and democratic aspirations. On the other hand, promoting an alternative popular state will entail an imagination befitting a post-modern society and a new type of political engagement that makes the means the ends. This shift from the traditional divisions between conception and execution, methods and goals, calls into question many of the cultural foundations of political action and collective organization. Direct participation in articulating the demand and developing the supply of collective economic and social infrastructure is a long way from the traditions of current political institutions and practices. In the end, however, it is not surprising that the magnitude of this challenge matches the magnitude of what is at stake.

NOTES

1 Note the terms 'administration', 'state production processes', etc. are used throughout this chapter to refer to the means used to organize the largely non-tangible output of the state from income transfers and laws to health advertising and political promotional campaigns. Most of this activity is basically produced

through an administrative production process that involves multiple layers of bureaucracy, parliaments and quasi-governmental organizations of many types. Overall, these production processes are characterized by particular technical/administrative systems in order to generate specific outputs.

2 Without entering into a terminological debate about the open or closed character of the term 'post-Fordist', the goal here is simply to suggest that the hints of post-Fordist production that are starting to crop-up in the private sector may not in fact provide a clear sense of direction for changes in public sector output and methods of production. Also, given the relatively more advanced status of research into the attributes of post-Fordist production in the private sphere it might be useful to consider more neutral or open-ended terms such as 'non-Fordist' to discuss the potential trajectory of state 'production'.

3 We use the term 'community' well aware of the debates around plurality and democracy. We take issue with an undifferentiated (and potentially coercive) view of community that defines certain interests as within its boundaries and others as outside it. At the same time, as Phillips has noted, 'we have to deal in some way with that dangerous sense of being excluded from what ought to be a shared political world' (1993: 136). Opening up the space between established policies and norms and the contestations around these, would be a potential starting point for opening up rather than closing down dialogue (that has previously veered between coercive universalisms and particular interests of sub-groups).

4 This term 'reinventing the state' has been popularized by the Clinton administration picking up on a book with the same title written by Osborne and Gaebler.

5 'Liberal' is used here to refer to the 'benevolent interventionism' of J. S. Mill as opposed to the Thatcherite neo-liberalism that unleashes market forces without any collective or guiding action.

6 A substantial, well-documented and growing literature chronicles and analyses many aspects of CED policy and the economic logic behind it. See references in the bibliography to Murray.

7 Government of Ontario, Ministry of Economic Development and Trade, 1 June 1993.

8 Ibid.

9 Riel Miller, *Investment Knowledge and Knowledge Investment: The Need to Rethink Human Capital and Decision-making Systems* (Paris: OECD, 1995).

10 These information systems also open up the possibility of much greater inequality and Big Brother intrusion into our personal 'databeing', e.g. genetic testing for susceptibility to certain diseases.

11 Premier's Council on Health, Well-Being and Social Justice, Government of Ontario, 1993.

12 The struggle in Ontario around community-based healthcare provides many examples of the contradictions and limits to democratization as championed by a 'benevolent' social democratic government.

13 Decentralization – how to distinguish between off-loading and the building-up of capacity. The outcome is far from certain. But, in the interest of pursuing the progressive potential of transformation, it is important to identify the critical role of practice as it relates to capacity. The capacity to take advantage of greater autonomy and – in a minimalist sense – of empowerment depends in large measure on making the means the ends. Of taking the capacity within a community – defined in geographic or common bond terms – as a starting point for generating economically and socially viable forms of productive/reproductive activity. In this way, capacity building becomes both a means and an end, in a potentially radically democratic way, for establishing new social relations of production/reproduction.

14 Yeatman argues that 'Equality exists only within the relationship of political

contestation, where those who are excluded by established policy both show its bias and make a claim on a prospectively more inclusive policy' (1993: 235).

BIBLIOGRAPHY

Barrett, M. and M. McIntosh. 1980. 'The "Family Wage": Some Problems for Socialists and Feminists.' *Capital and Class* 11.

Bowles, S. 1991. 'What Markets Can and Cannot Do.' *Challenge*, July/August.

Boyer, R. 1992. 'How to Promote Cooperation Within Conflicting and Divided Societies? Some Thoughts About the Transition of Industrial Relations in Europe. Paper presented at conference on 'Convergence and Divergence in Economic Growth and Technical Change: Maastricht Revisited', University of Limburg, 10–12 December.

Community Economic Development Secretariat. 1994. 'Jobs Ontario Community Action: The First Six Months – An Assessment.' Ministry of Economic Development and Trade, Government of Ontario, January.

Elson, D. 1994. 'Micro, Meso, Macro: Gender and Economic Analysis in the Context of Policy Reform', in I. Bakker (ed.), *The Strategic Silence: Gender and Economic Policy*. London: Zed Press.

Fair Tax Commission. 1992. *Working Group Report: Women and Taxation*. Government of Ontario.

Flower, J. 1994. 'The Other Revolution in Health Care.' *Wired* 2.01, January.

Fraser, N. and L. Gordon. 1994. 'A Genealogy of Dependency: Tracing a Keyword of the U.S. Welfare State.' *Signs* 19: 2.

Government of Ontario, CED Secretariat. 1994. *A Review of jobs Ontario Community Action*. Toronto (January).

Jessop, B. 1993. 'Towards a Schumpeterian Workfare State? Preliminary Remarks on Post-Fordist Political Economy.' *Studies in Political Economy* 40, Spring.

Mackintosh, M. 1990. 'Abstract Markets and Real Needs', in *The Food Question: Profits vs. People?* New York: Monthly Review Press.

Mackintosh, M. 1993. 'Creating a Developmental State: Reflections on Policy as Process', in G. Albo *et al.* (eds), *A Different Kind of State?* Toronto: Oxford University Press.

McDowell, L. 1991. 'Life Without Father and Ford: The New Gender Order of Post-Fordism.' *Trans. Inst. British Geography* 16, pp. 400–19.

McDowell, L. 1991. 'Gender Divisions in a Post-Fordist Era: New Contradictions or the Same Old Story?', in L. McDowell and R. Pringle, *Defining Women: Social Institutions and Gender Divisions*. London: Polity Press.

Miller, R. (1995) *Investment Knowledge and Knowledge Investment: the Need to Rethink Human Capital and Decision-making Systems*. Paris: OECD.

Mulgan, G. and R. Murray. 1993. *Reconnecting Taxation*. London: Demos.

Murray, R. 1991. 'The State After Henry.' *Marxism Today*, May.

Murray, R. 1993. 'Transforming the "Fordist" State', in G. Albo *et al.* (eds), D. Langille, (eds), *A Different Kind of State? Popular Power and Democratic Administration*. Toronto: Oxford.

Phillips, Anne. 1993. *Democracy and Difference*. University Park, Pa.: Pennsylvania State University Press.

Spain, D. 1992. *Gendered Spaces*. Chapel Hill: University of North Carolina Press.

Yeatman, A. 1993. 'Voice and Representation in the Politics of Difference', in Sneja Gunew and Anna Yeatman (eds), *Feminism and the Politics of Difference*. Halifax, Nova Scotia: Fernwood Publishing.

Warskett, R. 1993. 'Democratizing the State: Challenges from Public Sector Unions.' *Studies in Political Economy* 42, Autumn.

16

DEBITS, DEFICITS AND FULL EMPLOYMENT*

Harold Chorney

MEASURING THE DEBT: HOW GOOD IS THE DATA?

Public spending and job creation go hand-in-hand. If a country's debt is too high, then governments are reluctant to take on the jobs issue and create employment for all those who want to work. How does one know when debt levels are dangerously high, or whether the deficits are out of control?

One of the biggest problems in debating the debt is the fact that the data is misleading. Usually, the wrong figure is given, or the figure that is cited exaggerates the problem. This happens because of double counting. For example, by not deducting financial assets from the total, or by not taking into consideration inflation, or by representing gross debts rather than net debts, the size the debt burden is exaggerated. Also, too often the measure of debt that is chosen is selected from the public accounts rather than the more accurate figures that are available from the national accounts. The data from the national accounts actually are closest to the net financing costs of government.

While it is very common in the media to discuss the deficit and make it the subject of headlines, in fact it is the net debt in relation to the GDP that is the more accurate statistic of indebtedness. It is rare that the statistic of the net debt to the GDP is given as part of a properly calculated time-series that permits international comparison. Furthermore, the rate of growth in this statistic is equally useful. Generally speaking, if the net outstanding debt is being financed by a real rate of interest that exceeds the growth rate of the economy the net debt to GDP ratio will be rising. If the finance rate is less than the growth rate in the economy the ratio will be falling.

Table 16.1 offers a comparison for the leading G-7 countries of the gross and net debt to GDP ratios for the latest years for which comparable OECD data are available. Note the large discrepancy between gross and net debt for every country except Italy. Whenever the financial community, financial press or government wishes to exaggerate the threat posed by the debt, they rely upon the gross figure. The net figure which deducts some assets and other sources of revenue which are not counted in the public accounts is a much more accurate figure in assessing the burden.

357

HAROLD CHORNEY

Table 16.1 General government debt as a percentage of nominal GDP

	Gross debt/GDP			Net debt/GDP		
	1991(%)	1992(%)	1993(%)	1991(%)	1992(%)	1993(%)
Britain	35.4	40.5	47.3	30.0	35.1	41.9
Canada 71.6*	77.5	83.3	88.3	43.0	49.3	55.0
France†	48.6	51.6	57.1	27.1	30.0	35.6
Germany†	41.8	42.8	46.2	23.1	24.1	27.5
Italy	104.0	108.0	114.0	102.7	106.7	112.6
Japan†	68.2	67.3	68.3	5.9	5.0	6.0
United States	58.9	61.7	63.4	34.0	37.4	39.1

Source: OECD, *Economic Outlook*, Dec. 1993, Tables A29, A30
Notes: All data for 1991, 1992 and 1993 except for Canada which begins in 1990. Data for 1991 except for Canada are actual, all other years are estimates, except for US 1992 which is also actual. Actual figures for 1990 are for Canada *1990; † Financial assets excluding shares and holdings in public corporations are deducted in arriving at net debt

If we take the Canadian case, for example, there is a wide discrepancy between the gross debt to GDP ratio and the net debt to GDP ratio in 1993, 88.3 versus 55 per cent. Furthermore, while the Canadian deficit figure of 42 billion seems like a screaming headline, in reality it is meaningless, particularly because net financing requirements which include non-budgetary transactions in financial assets that belong to the government are some 10 billion dollars lower. While the current debt to GDP ratio of over 65 per cent for 1994 seems high, it is only when it is placed in historical perspective as part of a time-series that runs from 1926 to the present that one can see that at the end of the Second World War the ratio was much higher – in the order of 110 per cent. It is also possible to notice that during the Great Depression of the 1930s and during wartime the debt ratio rose greatly.

The same sort of picture emerges when we study the debt ratios for the US and the UK (Samuelson 1961: 401; Chorney 1989). For example, the debt of the United States in relation to the GDP was about 150 per cent in 1946; in Britain it was 280 per cent at the end of the war. Obviously, in all three countries the burden of the debt was not an obstacle to a strong performance and was reduced following the war. This experience underlines the fact that countries with debt levels of over 100 per cent of the GDP really have no other alternative but to reduce their debt burden by strong economic performance.[1]

CAPITAL VERSUS CURRENT EXPENDITURES

Another major consideration in assessing the debt burden is the treatment of capital versus current expenditures in the budgets of governments. Again, the Canadian case is useful to consider. Here all non-financial assets that belong to the government (for example, land, real estate and structures) are valued nominally at the value of one dollar. This is clearly absurd since an incomplete

358

attempt at a partial evaluation several years ago came up with a figure of 70 billion dollars! At the same time much of the expenditures of the government on education and healthcare are clearly investments in human capital and yield a return that lasts over several decades. Yet, the government of Canada continues to count these expenditures as current expenditures. If they were properly expensed as capital expenditures, the way that a private corporation might treat them, the government's fiscal balance would look very different.

The situation in the other G-7 countries is not much different. In the United States, for example, all the controversy about the size of the US debt has paid virtually no attention to historical trends and commonly has not distinguished between gross and net debt, nor accounted properly for inflation which reduces the real value of debt outstanding, nor for assets held by the federal government. Robert Eisner shows convincingly that because the US Federal government does not keep a separate capital budget the annual deficit is therefore overstated by a very large amount. In 1984, for example, the US deficit of $171 billion would have been largely eliminated simply by accepting the Office of Management and Budget's definition of investment as 'outlays which yield long term benefits' (Eisner 1986: 31). These kinds of practices which tend to exaggerate the deficit and the accumulated debt also apply for the other leading G-7 countries.[2]

So the financial markets, a euphemism for a relatively small number of major speculators, make much of the precise deficit numbers and buy and sell on the basis of these. But one must remember that these financial speculators have an extremely short-term view of what is important. Within a matter of hours, and sometimes even minutes, their focus will have shifted. Furthermore, because of the great increase in the speed of calculation, the growth in financial derivatives and the general growth in speculation their general perspective bears less and less of a real relationship to the actual economy. For example, in early May 1994, the bond markets reacted positively to a major rise in the US Federal Reserve discount rate even though the rise will slow growth in the American economy and increase the risk of a recession.

The perverse logic that lies behind such sentiments may make sense to the speculators, but it is completely illogical from the point of view of the real economy. It would be unwise in the extreme for governments to allow those who operate on such a short-term time horizon and who are obsessed with inflation and care so little about unemployment to set the public policy agenda of their country.

THE INTERGENERATIONAL TRANSFER DILEMMA

Countries that want to ease their debt burden have to look at other alternatives. So long as the bulk of the debt is financed internally by domestic borrowers, the question of intergenerational transfer is easily resolved. Assets are more or less offset by liabilities. The bonds that finance the debt are equally assets to those who purchase them. The future generation may pay taxes to finance the debt, but the future generation also inherits the bonds as well as the debt and whatever new taxes are needed to finance them. But they also inherit the capital infrastructure in health, education, roads, research and development that are financed by present-day levels of indebtedness. Further-more, the reduction in the unemployment rate brought about by a pro-gramme of deficit-financed investment in public works and investment in the skills and education of people produces capital goods and services that would not otherwise exist. When governments do this, it enriches future generations of a society. This is so because a nation's capital stock is renewed by such programmes and the social wealth of society increases at a more rapid rate than the private sector can manage on its own (Domar 1993).

Of course, there are distributional questions for a given policy of debt management. Those who finance the debt receive interest payments that are taxed. In this sense, the higher the rate of interest on the debt the greater the redistribution of wealth from borrowers to creditors. Keynes' dictum about the benefits of a gentle euthanasia of the *rentier* class still holds. That is why it is extremely important to ensure that an appropriate monetary policy that reduces interest charges to a minimum is followed in order to minimize this sort of inequitable transfer of resources from borrowers to *rentier* creditors. As well, an appropriate tax policy that ensures that excessive redistributions if they do take place are ultimately taxed back should be in place.

RICARDIAN EQUIVALENCY?

The question of Ricardian equivalency has loomed large in recent years largely because of the work of Robert Barro on this issue (Barro 1974). The argument which originates with David Ricardo is that today's debts are tomorrow's taxes. But this dictum only holds true if today's debts fail to generate a higher flow of future income. For if they do lead to higher growth rates and lower unemployment than would otherwise have been the case, then the tax burden associated with paying the debt is overshadowed by the additional income and wealth that has been generated.

But Ricardian equivalency means something even beyond this argument about future taxes. It also implies that because of the fear of future taxes, businesses invest less in the present than they would otherwise do. They prefer instead to save their money for the higher taxes they expect to pay in the future on account of the debt. But there is little or no evidence that this in fact takes place.

Paul Samuelson, a leading neo-classical Keynesian economist, discussed this issue in the 1960s in his famous textbook and put the issue in the following way: 'There may well be an irrational fear on the part of the business community that a deficit prone government does not have a firm grip on spending and is running up the debt and this fear may prevent them from investing but as soon as the beneficial effects of aggregate demand stimulation are felt and profit rates rise beyond what business expects, rather than crowding out investment, public sector deficits will crowd it in' (Samuelson 1961).

This kind of response is particularly likely if the deficit-financed expansion takes place at a time of high unemployment, such as now. While it would appear preferable that such a programme specifically targets areas of national investment, research and development, and job training that equip the country to compete effectively in the new global economy, the fact is that additional income raises the level of aggregate demand and thereby restores the animal spirits of private investors and helps launch an investment boom.[3]

IS CUTTING TAX EXPENDITURES THE ANSWER?

Left-wing academics, trade unionists and social activists favour a tax expenditure approach to reduce the deficit. They argue that the rapid growth of the public sector debt lies in the fact that the wealthy do not pay enough taxes and that the corporations have found ways to reduce their contribution to the total revenue base by more than 100 per cent in the last decade. A possible alternative to an increase in taxes on corporate income is the elimination of corporate income tax and a greatly increased tax on distributed dividends, perhaps by treating distributed profits as ordinary income as opposed to preferential rates of taxation. This latter option has been proposed because of the tendency for corporations to either avoid taxes altogether or to pass on tax increases to their customers in the form of higher prices. Further, it is the shareholder who is the real beneficiary and not the legal entity, the corporation (Kierans and Stewart 1989).

It is worthwhile noting that initially the Mitterand government substantially increased taxes on the wealthy as part of its stimulus package. The new taxes, however, brought in less revenue than had been expected, because they also slowed economic growth (Muet and Fontenau 1990: 93–4). There is obviously some substance to the tax expenditure argument. But one of its weaknesses is that it rarely considers whether overall macro performance would have remained the same if the tax loopholes had been closed and the rates of taxation of the wealthy increased. Clearly, there is some scope here for additional revenues to be collected but the total amount is somewhat exaggerated by the failure to take into account the impact on total output and employment by implementing these changes.

THE ROLE OF MONETARY POLICY

The rate of interest plays a critical role in stimulating or depressing purchases made on credit and affects investment decisions made by entrepreneurs. It is an important cost of doing business in terms of carrying inventories through bank loans and helps determine the rate at which outstanding debt grows.[4] One of the major errors made by the generation of Keynesian economists at the height of their power and influence in the late 1950s and 1960s was to overlook the possibility that monetary policy could once again become central to public policy. In those heady days of the Keynesian revolution, the arguments were about how unimportant monetary policy was and how it had to take a back seat to a robust fiscal policy.

The Radcliffe Commission in Great Britain in 1959 argued that monetary policy should largely concern itself with assuring that debt management costs were reasonable and that appropriate liquidity was supplied to the private sector to ensure that fiscal policy could do its work. It came to endorse the position that liquidity itself was a function of the overall animal spirits among investors in the economy, the behaviour of monetary velocity and general aggregate demand. Thus, they believed that monetary policy at best could play a secondary role. Little could they realize that some twenty years later the monetarist counter-revolution would succeed in pushing Keynesian ideas from the centre stage and re-install monetarist orthodoxy in command.

Many of the experts who argue in favour of an industrial strategy are nevertheless very pessimistic about the possibility of doing much about deficient aggregate demand unemployment. They argue that even if governments were able to develop a national industrial strategy that rose to the challenge of global competition they would have their hands tied by the size of their public sector debts.

Very similar arguments were used in the the great depression of the 1930s. Public sector deficits and globalization were the bogey men of that era as well. Even the current fad of blaming the victim by accusing those on unemployment insurance and social welfare of abusing the system is a direct repeat of the 1930s. In those days in Canada, municipal relief was denounced as a 'racket' and citizens were encouraged to secretly denounce their neighbours if they suspected them of fraud (Chorney 1987: 152–3). How has this sorry state of affairs come about? In order to answer this question it is necessary to re-examine briefly the history of the eclipse of Keynesianism by monetarism.

THE ECLIPSE OF KEYNESIANISM

Prior to the OPEC oil crisis of 1974–5 the world of stagflation was largely unknown to the policy-makers and advisers of the G-7 countries. Despite the constant barrage of criticism that Keynesianism had been subjected to from critics like Dennis Robertson, Friedrich Von Hayek and Lionel Robbins in the 1930s, and Milton Friedman, Harry Johnson and Alan Walters in the 1950s and 1960s, Keynesianism displaced classical monetarism in the 1940s and became the orthodoxy in the 1950s and 1960s. Of course, the doctrine of Keynesianism was a very bastardized version of the original doctrine and the conversion to even this watered down and distorted version had not come immediately nor without a major struggle.

Prophetically, it was the British Labour Prime Minister James Callaghan and not Margaret Thatcher who was the first major political leader to pronounce Keynesianism dead. He did so in 1976 when British inflation and unemployment reached 16.5 per cent and 4.1 per cent respectively. While the inflation figure is frightful, by today's standards the then number of un-employed seems innocently low.

But even before Callaghan spoke out publicly about the death of Keynesianism, his Chancellor of the Exchequer, Denis Healey, had been converted to an anti-Keynesian position. Writing in his 1990 political memoir, Healey points out that he lost faith in the Keynesian concept of demand management during the OPEC crisis of 1974–5:

Keynes believed that a government could maintain full employment without creating inflation ... [but] it was ... impossible to know how people would use the money you did inject by cutting taxes or increasing public spending. It might go into higher wages or profits, creating more inflation rather than more jobs. It might be used to buy foreign rather than British goods ... or it might be saved instead of spent.

(Smith 1992: 171)

Healey had decided that Keynes was *passé*. The trouble was that Healey, Callaghan, Thatcher, and many others, got Keynes all wrong. Keynes never suggested that inflation and unemployment were totally unrelated events.[5]

In his chapter on the 'Theory of Prices', Keynes makes it perfectly clear that a realistic model of the economy and the price system must admit that any increase in the quantity of money and the total of aggregate demand will express itself partly in reduced unemployment and partly in a rise in prices. Any other notion has to make a number of unrealistic assumptions that Keynes was unwilling to make.[6] In Keynes's own words:

the increase in effective demand will generally speaking, spend itself partly in increasing the quantity of employment and partly in raising the level of prices. Thus, instead of constant prices in conditions of unemployment, and of prices rising in proportion to the quantity of money in conditions of full employment, we have in fact a condition of prices rising gradually as employment increases.

(Keynes 1936: 296)

Tragically, in discarding this key aspect of Keynesianism, public policy-makers threw away the only viable method for overcoming a deep economic depression in an advanced capitalist economy. The result is that we have suffered the consequences ever since.

In fact a much more realistic model of the inflationary process other than the monetarist black box model exists. In this model we can conceive of the economy as consisting of a range of industries and services. Each industry has its own peculiar circumstances and undergoes price rises or inflation in its own way. In some industries that are dependent on inputs from other more monopolized industries price rises can occur because of bottlenecks in the supply markets. When this happens, inflationary price rises can occur because of the presence of powerful transnational corporations which have the power to dictate prices and restrain supply. Alternatively, if these same sectors have powerful unions which can dictate wage increases that exceed gains from productivity, prices also will rise if the shareholders are unwilling to accept a reduction in their own return. In these same sectors, because of the presence of only a few suppliers and the absence of market substitutes for the goods and the strong attachment of consumers to the goods produced, demand is inelastic and cost increases can be passed on as price increases as soon as capacity utilization passes a relatively low threshold, for example, 60 per cent of total capacity utilization.

These oligopoly sectors are frequently the source of inflationary pressure, and to the extent that they weigh heavily on the overall economy their influence on the inflationary process is greatly magnified.[7]

On the other hand, other sectors of the economy are not dominated by powerful unions nor large firms. They, instead, have many small enterprises and the inflationary pressure does not develop until the capacity utilization point reaches close to 100 per cent. This so-called competitive sector is not the prinicipal source of inflation. Usually when consumer demand is highly elastic, many satisfactory substitutes exist and it requires a general inflationary wave before these sectors display inflationary pressures. If one adds to this mix sociological factors such as keeping up with the Joneses, a much more realistic picture of the inflationary process is possible. In such a model, the quantity of money simply acts as a *means* rather than a *cause* of rising price movements. One can think of it as a wave of water that washes ashore, here lifting boats and flooding land, there only partly filling deep holes and barely leaving its mark. Keynes himself believed that respectable people were required to utter rubbish about the dangers of inflation from deficit-financed public works even at the height of the depression in order to keep their respectability intact (Keynes, Halley lectures, quoted in Chorney 1991). Keynes also believed that if full employment were ever dislodged from the top of the policy agenda it would be extremely difficult to restore it. In both of these matters he was, as usual, very prescient. Any policy of demand stimulation requires the co-operation of the central bank in debt management. The approach can work in one country provided it allows exchange rates to fluctuate. But if it were adopted in each of the G-7 countries simultaneously, it would greatly strengthen the overall impact of the approach. Speculative outflows of the currency in response to demand reflation in one country alone would be eliminated, particularly if the reflation were accompanied by an internationally agreed tax on speculation. To see how this might work, let us begin with an examination of the Canadian case.

THE CASES OF CANADA, FRANCE, THE UNITED KINGDOM, GERMANY, ITALY, THE UNITED STATES AND JAPAN

Canada: privatizing the debt

In the 1950s and 1960s, the central bank in Canada held over 20 per cent of the debt and there was low inflation. Indeed, there is no comparison between the proportion of the total debt held by the central bank in relation to the broadly defined money stock, M2, and the rate of inflation over forty years. There were years when a low rate of inflation went hand-in-hand with a low percentage of monetization in relation to M2 and years when a high rate of monetization went hand in hand with a low rate of inflation (see Table 16.2). It appears that inflation is the consequence of something other than the rate of monetization of the debt in relation to the money stock. Indeed, the lowest rate of inflation, −0.2 per cent in 1953, was accompanied by the third highest rate of monetization, 23.7 per cent. This result has profound consequences for public policy.

Critics of this interpretation of the data suggest that higher rates were possible because of higher reserve ratios (i.e. the proportion of total deposits that the commercial banks were required to leave on deposit with the central bank) in the 1950s. Indeed, recently Canada became one of the very few countries in the world to abolish reserve ratios altogether. It would, therefore, be prudent to reintroduce reserve ratios for the commercial banks when expanding the ratio of government debt held by the central bank.

Today, the central bank, because of its obsessive monetarism, holds less than 7 per cent of the debt. There is clearly room for a much more aggressive programme of demand stimulation without threatening inflation. In the Canadian case, to achieve a ratio of central-bank-held debt to the broadly defined money stock of 20 per cent, an additional 45 billion dollars of debt could be acquired. Obviously, doing this overnight would not be advisable, but given that M1 is about 54 billion, there is definite room for a programme of fiscal stimulation of say 15 billion financed in this way in Canada. Such a programme, if properly targeted in the context of an industrial strategy, would have a major impact upon unemployment and employment expectations. Once inflationary expectations began to increase as the unemployment rate dropped, tripartite discussions could begin on ways of preventing inflation from ruining the recovery.

Obviously, circumstances regarding the proportion of the debt held in this way by the central bank vary from one country to the other. In the US, for example, the federal reserve holds about 10 per cent of the debt in relation to

Table 16.2 Monetized government debt as a percentage of broadly defined money supply and the rate of inflation, Canada, 1989 to 1950

Year	Percentage	Rate of inflation GNE Deflator
1989	7.5	3.6
1988	8.3	4.0
1987	9.1	4.5
1986	8.7	2.9
1985	8.3	3.2
1984	9.6	3.5
1983	9.8	5.4
1982	8.8	10.4
1981	10.1	10.6
1980	10.9	11.4
1979	10.3	10.3
1978	10.6	6.4
1977	10.7	7.0
1976	9.9	9.5
1975	11.1	10.7
1974	11.6	15.3
1973	12.0	9.1
1972	12.7	5.0
1971	13.0	3.2
1970	13.6	4.6
1969	14.3	1.1
1968	14.4	3.3
1967	15.8	4.0
1966	16.4	4.4
1965	17.5	3.3
1964	17.6	2.4
1963	18.6	1.9
1962	19.2	1.4
1961	19.4	0.4
1960	19.7	1.3
1959	20.3	2.0
1958	20.2	1.5
1957	20.6	2.1
1956	21.5	3.7
1955	21.2	0.6
1954	22.0	1.6
1953	23.7	−0.2
1952	23.9	4.4
1951	25.0	11.3
1950	22.9	2.4

Source: Calculated from the *Bank of Canada Monthly Review* and the *Department of Finance Quarterly and Annual Review* (see Chorney 1992)

the broadly defined money stock, M2. All told about 30 per cent of the 4.5 trillion dollar American debt is held by the central bank and government pension funds. The comparable figure for Canada is 22 per cent (*Survey of Current Business* 1994).

The United States: economic recovery or economic illusion

Ever since Ronald Reagan talked about the supply-side miracle while cutting taxes and following a policy of military Keynesianism, American economic performance and its approach to debt management has surprised observers (Weintraub and Goodstein 1983). In May 1994, unemployment fell to 6 per cent, the lowest rate since the recession of 1990–2. During the previous four years, the rate peaked at 7.8 per cent in June of 1992 and has been falling slowly, but steadily, ever since. It has still not regained its pre-recession low of just over 5 per cent, but so long as Alan Greenspan does not raise interest rates too sharply, it should soon. At the same time, as the unemployment rate dropped and economic growth recovered (it hit 7 per cent in the final quarter of 1993, but has now fallen to 3 per cent), the American deficit has faded from the front pages and dropped substantially in both absolute and relative terms. This illustrates the highly ephemeral nature of the debate about deficits and debt. Once economic growth resumes, the shrinkage of the debt in both real and political terms is rapid.

The focus is now on full employment and faster growth, although the bond market and the Fed's fear of inflation are seen as barriers. Despite the Fed's fear, inflation is running at under 3 per cent (see 'Why Are We So Afraid Of Growth', *Business Week*, 16 May 1994).

How has this happened? It would be pleasing to associate the recovery with Keynesian actions by the new Clinton administration. But, in reality, Clinton failed to pass his extremely limited stimulation package through Congress, and his deficit reduction package, while a factor, is much less responsible than the sharp reduction in American interest rates and the willingness of the US Feds to fund considerably more of the debt than the much more monetarist Bank of Canada (Judis 1994). This combination of low interest rates – the Federal funds and the discount rate fell as low as 3 per cent – a significant deficit, higher productivity and a cheapening dollar have been quite stimulative.

Of course, sceptics point out that many of the new jobs are low-paying service positions that do not compare with the manufacturing jobs that have been eliminated by the recession. Furthermore, some market analysts argue that the US balance of payments problems require it to maintain high enough interest rates to draw in sufficient capital to finance its chronic deficit on the current account deficit (Magnus 1994). Of course, this explanation rules out the acceptability of increased productivity and a further devaluation of the US dollar as a solution to the current account problem (Blecker 1992). The European neo-conservatives who shaped the Delors and OECD plan also argue that Reagan and Bush's anti-union measures, and the general move to deregulation, permitted wages to fall far enough for employment to be stimulated. It remains to be seen which explanation will seem more convincing in the future.

So long as Greenspan remains wedded to fearing inflation as unemployment approaches 5 per cent, and committed to interest rate increases, there is still the danger the American recovery will be aborted before it has had sufficient impact on lowering unemployment in the other G-7 countries through the stimulation of export trade (see Alan Greenspan's testimony before the Senate banking committee, *New York Times*, 28 May 1994).

German monetary practice

The Germans, who operate under the terms of the Maastricht European Union Treaty, make it clear in their Bundesbank Monthly Report, March 1994, that the Bank will no longer grant direct credit to any public authorities by acquiring public sector debt. This strict prohibition is in line with the monetarist belief that any monetization of the debt is inflationary despite considerable evidence to the contrary. Prior to 1 January 1994, when this provision came into effect, a limited amount of such monetization occurred to help finance the absorption of East Germany, but the Bundesbank still followed a strict monetarist orientation.[8] The large amount of government debt held by the US Federal reserve reflects the much looser monetary policy that the Americans have followed in the past three years and probably explains partly why American unemployment is much lower than in Canada.

The European Community has been held hostage by the German Bundesbank, the Maastricht Agreement, and its dogmatic doctrine of monetarism. The German refusal to cut rates until recently led to the exit of the British from the Exchange Rate Mechanism and the destruction of the system of narrow bands.

Mitterrand's attempt at reflation

In France, the abandonment by the Mitterrand regime of its extremely brief experiment with reflation in 1981–2 came about because of the strict pressure of the European Monetary System (EMS) and the Bundesbank's pressure on the French government to raise interest rates and cut public expenditures to defend the French franc. Thus, the conventional wisdom is that reflation was tried and failed. The French experiment was quite simply too short in duration and too crippled by the European monetary system to be regarded as the ultimate test of the reflation strategy.

It should be recalled that Mitterrand was elected on 10 May 1981. In the first months of his regime, the government embarked on a programme of reflation and stimulation that included increasing family allowances, the

368

minimum wage, housing benefits for low-paid workers and old-age pensions. It also introduced a programme of reducing the working week from 40 to 39 hours without a comparable reduction in pay. (This measure had only a slight impact upon unemployment, reducing it by no more than 28,000.)

Other measures encouraged early retirement and working time reduction, with state subsidies for new employees. These measures added some 100,000 jobs. As well, the Government hired an additional 140,000 employees (Muet and Fontenau 1990). The government also embarked upon a programme to promote high technology in industry and greater expenditures on research and development. At the local level capital investments were also significantly increased. Finally, the government increased wealth taxes and taxes on windfall profits. The overall programme, despite the criticism it endured, helped keep the French unemployment rate from rising as much as un-employment rose in the US or Germany during the 1981–2 recession. Unemployment rose in France by 4 per cent versus 29 per cent in the US and about the same amount in the UK.

Indeed, despite its short-term duration, its impact upon growth and employment was significant. Overall some 200,000 new jobs could be attributed to the 1981 programme. But despite these modest successes the programme was abandoned when the French franc came under attack because of the failure of export growth to keep pace with import increases. The franc was devalued by 3 per cent in October 1981, by 5.75 per cent in June 1982 and by a further 2.5 per cent in March 1983. All these devaluations took place within the confines of the Exchange Rate Mechanism and with the approval of the Bundesbank. They were also accompanied by upward revaluations of the Deutschmark by about 15 per cent in three stages (Muet and Fontenau 1990: 156).

The balance of payments deteriorated sharply because none of France's trading partners were reflating at the same time. The Mitterrand government came under strong pressure from her trading partners in the EC to abandon the programme. The Germans insisted that the French cut public expend-itures before permitting them to devalue the currency in October 1981, under the terms of the EMS. Although certain additional stimulative measures were introduced after the fall of 1981, the experiment was essentially over within six months because changes were accompanied by austerity measures designed to support the franc. One can make the argument that reflation must be multilateral, but because of its short duration the Mitterrand experiment does not prove the case.

Of course, a general European reflation supported by the Bundesbank and the Bank of England would have made the situation much easier and would have allowed the French to escape from the exchange rate pressures it experienced because its balance of payments would not have suffered export losses. But without the constraints of the EMS France could have devalued a full 10 per cent or even 20 per cent straight away in 1981 and this devaluation might well have provided the necessary protection to pursue its reflationary strategy successfully.[9]

British debt management

The case of British debt management is also very revealing. In Britain, during the Thatcher era, a very strict monetarist experiment was undertaken. During the severe recession of 1981–3, the Thacher government had the Bank of England deliberately overfund the debt in order to drive up interest rates and reduce the proportion of debt held by the central bank. The belief that any underfunding or unfunding of the debt caused inflation was at the core of British monetarism.

The severity of the recession that racked Britain in the early 1980s was a direct consequence of this policy. The Bank of England continued to follow a strict monetarist regime until it was forced to abandon its commitment to the ERM by the speculative pressure of people like Georg Soros. The ERM acted in a similar fashion to the gold standard in the late 1920s by keeping the pound linked at an overvalued exchange rate to the German DM.

Once Britain devalued and cut interest rates somewhat, a small recovery got underway. Within both the British Labour Party and the governing Tories there is now a renewed interest in Keynesian methods of demand reflation, although the ruling groups in both parties are hostile to Keynesian reflation. In the case of the Labour Party, the opposition to adopting a Keynesian reflation within Britain alone is led by Lord Eatwell and Lord Desai, both of whom made their reputations as radical economists at Cambridge and the LSE respectively. Like many people these days they have changed their tune. They now argue that Britain going it alone will simply lead to the kind of balance of payments crisis that the French experienced, because of the underdevelopment of the manufacturing sector in Britain.

Now that Britain is no longer in the EMS there is no constraint on allowing the pound to devalue temporarily to facilitate a recovery. Obviously, a pan-European or, preferably, a G-7-led recovery, would be better, but in the absence of that it is best to try to reflate while protecting one's balance of trade through devaluation (Thirwall 1979).

Italy's debt wars

Of all the G-7 countries, Italy has the largest debt to GDP ratio at 112 per cent, a rate of unemployment of 11.2 per cent and a rate of inflation of 4.2 per cent. It also has the highest prime rate of interest, 9.38 per cent although its real rate of interest, 4.72 per cent, is much lower than that of Canada at 7.74 per cent. In the period 1977–85, the Italian government reduced the portion of its debt that it financed through purchases from the central bank from 30.7 per cent in 1977 to 17.6 per cent in 1985. In 1985, the central bank refused to finance the Italian government's debt until it was forced to do so by a special act of Parliament. Since that time the Italian central bank has attempted to follow a much more orthodox monetarist debt management policy, although not always successfully. Interest rates have risen, the share of debt acquired fallen, and the rate of inflation fallen. The rate of unemployment, however, has not. The debt, as in other countries, has grown with the rise in interest rates and the tightening of monetary policy (Goodman 1992: 175 ff.). Currently, the new Italian government is committed to lowering the unemployment rate. The central bank has already warned the government about the danger of expanding the debt to stimulate economic recovery. The governor of the central bank has insisted that it would raise interest rates if the recovery strategy encouraged 'too rapid' a growth in consumption (Graham 1994).

Japan's monetary and fiscal policy: Keynes in the Orient

The Japanese have pursued an intriguing alternative approach. For a very long time interest rates were kept very low in Japan. Indeed, from the perspective of outside observers it would appear that the Japanese, until quite recently, operated a system of deliberately administered low rates through the central bank and the use of strict window guidance. In fact, it was only under pressure from the Americans and the growing influence of American-trained neo-classical rational expectationist economists that the Japanese relented somewhat (Chorney and Bouska 1992).

Prior to this, economists from all viewpoints had a considerable influence in Japanese economic thought (Morris-Suzuki 1989). During the current downturn, Japan was the only G-7 country to opt for a massive programme of successive stimulations of over 200 billion dollars alongside interest rate cuts. The first stimulus package of $(C) 86 billion was announced on 29 August 1992. It was the largest stimulus package in Japanese post-war history. While critics of such Keynesian-inspired measures suggest that they have not worked, and the actual expenditure of the monies has been delayed due to planning and political problems, the fact is that the recession in Japan has not been as severe in employment terms as that experienced in the more monetarist Western countries.

Experts now agree that the stimulus packages have prevented the recession from being much worse. Once all the expenditures announced actually take place it is quite likely that the recovery will quicken its pace. Finally, it is remarkable that, despite the recession, the Japanese have had to endure a close to 40 per cent upward revaluation of the yen versus the American dollar. That alone would counteract a significant portion of the stimulus package. In fact, the upward valuation of the yen has increased the tendency of Japanese manufacturers to seek foreign sites for plant expansion and production, thereby helping to increase fears of increased unemployment and depressed domestic consumer demand (*Financial Times*, 16 February 1994). Hence, the efficacy of the Japanese stimulus programme has to be judged against the background of this appreciation in the value of the yen.

The current recession in Japan began in January 1991, after the bursting of the bubble economy business boom that had followed the crash of the Japanese stock market in 1987. Since the beginning of the recession, the yen has appreciated considerably against the American dollar. At the beginning of 1990, it was about 140 to the American dollar; currently it is close to par. Japan has come under great pressure from the United States to expand its importation of American products. The Americans argue that Japan, because it imports only 7.6 per cent of its GDP as opposed to the OECD average of 14.6 per cent is running a protectionist trade economy that discriminates against foreign suppliers (Altman 1994; Bhagwati 1994). But Bhagwati shows that despite the claims of the Americans, Japan has significant import penetration in seven of the leading manufacturing sectors, including scientific instruments, aircraft, communication equipment, electrical machinery, computer equipment, pharmaceuticals and chemicals. It continues to run a trade surplus and its official unemployment rate has remained under 3 per cent. In the case of unemployment, this is due to the unique Japanese practice of lifetime employment offered by its corporations to workers up to the age of 55. After this age, unemployment is disguised by compulsory demotion to less well-paid and less responsible positions (Shimada 1985). Nevertheless, despite these features, Japan operates according to its own cultural practices and an overall Confucianist philosophy that makes it rather different from the other G-7 countries (Morishima 1982).

Despite the considerable size of the stimulus packages,[10] the recovery in Japan continues to be slow in the area of private capital and industrial output, but improving in the area of consumer spending (*Financial Times*, 9 April 1994). Unemployment has fallen to 2.8 per cent. As the recession has dragged on, Japanese firms have come under increasing pressure to break with their tradition of lifetime employment, and the business federation, the Keidanren, was the chief backer of the massive stimulus package to relaunch the economy.

The Japanese continue to run a substantial trade surplus with the rest of the world despite the global recession. This situation is a mark of the great strength and dynamism of the Japanese economy. The recession has tended to slow imports rather more than exports, despite the dramatic appreciation of the yen. The most recent budget, a product of the new coalition government that rules the country, included an additional 100-billion-dollar-bond-financed public works programme, a housing loan scheme, cuts in income and other taxes and several other smaller stimulus measures in agriculture and small business. Thus, it is far too soon to assess the Japanese experience as a failure of stimulation, particularly because it has been accompanied by an appreciating yen which would have a dampening effect on export-led growth and because of the slowness with which the actual expenditures have been undertaken because of the Byzantine nature of Japanese politics.

Delors' plan to spend billions on new jobs

Within the European Community, as elsewhere, the current slump has produced an enormous problem of long-term unemployment. Within the OECD the number of unemployed has risen from just over 10 million in 1974 to 35 million in 1994. Seventeen million of the unemployed lie within the European Community where the unemployment rate averages about 11 per cent. More than half of the EC unemployed are long-term unemployed. This has occurred in a series of stages following the recessions of 1974–5, 1980–2, and 1990 to the present. After each recession, unemployment has not fallen back to its pre-recession level.

When one surveys the scene from the perspective of the last twenty years the slump-like nature of the economy becomes clear. It is also revealing that both Japan and the United States have performed much better on the unemployment rate than the EC. Of course, the rate in the US understates the real rate because of a large pool of discouraged workers, and the quality of the jobs created in the low-pay service sector does not match the pre-recession quality of jobs. Nevertheless, the Europeans look with envy at the 6 per cent rate in the US. In the face of this profound policy failure, what has been the response of the leading economic and political international institutions? Regrettably, the response has been most unimpressive.

The Organization for Economic Co-operation and Development prepared a draft study on the problem of unemployment in 1993 (OECD 1993). Their diagnosis of the problem and policy prescriptions is largely drawn from the neo-conservative supply-side, classical-rational expectations perspective. Demand-side considerations hardly enter into their schema of analysis. They have bought completely into the rigid wages argument that suggests that the inability of workers to lower their wage demands and the excessive support to these demands provided by unemployment insurance schemes and related benefit schemes is responsible for much of the unemployment. Employer costs associated with financing the welfare state are also seen as an important factor. About the only useful part of their recommendations pertains to enhancing education and job training, increasing flexibility of working time to permit greater part-time work and job sharing. However, in the absence of any demand stimulus it is unlikely that these measures will reduce unemployment by very much. Clearly, member countries have been relying upon OECD advice in formulating their own policy prescriptions. It is doubtful that the results will yield much beyond greater disillusionment and impoverishment among the unemployed.

This obsession with structural unemployment and enhancing labour market performance is also at the root of the Commission of the European

Communities White Paper, *Growth, Competitiveness, Employment: The Challenges and Ways Forward into the 21st Century*, sponsored by Jacques Delors. Delors, of course, was the leading figure behind the Mitterrand government's austerity programme that replaced the reflationary package in 1982. But this time he and his report, albeit very cautiously, have perhaps begun the process through which Europe can escape from the paralysis of monetarism.

Despite its lofty title and the excessive attention paid to supply-side measures, the report, at least, raises the prospect of demand-side stimulation through investment in transportation, information super highway tele-communications technology, and energy infrastructure financed by union bonds issued by the European Community and convertible bonds issued for long maturities by the private or public company promoting the project, guaranteed by the European Investment Fund. The total value of these investments is 20 billion ECUs or about £16 billion ($(C) 32 billion). Another 6 billion ECUs in loan guarantees is available through the European invest-ment bank. Considering the magnitude of the unemployment problem, this will fall well short of what is necessary, but at least it is a small step in the right direction. It is not surprising that the measure was criticized by the British Major government who remain for the moment strongly wedded to monetarist dogma.[11]

If we add together the EC measures at 32 billion dollars Canadian, the Canadian measures at 6 billion dollars, and the Japanese measures at over 200 billion and remember the failed stimulus package in the United States, it is obvious that the industrial world needs to do much more to spark a recovery. Overall, impact on aggregate demand is undermined by the continued reliance on excessive real rates of interest, the austerity orientation of the public sector budgets in most of the G-7 countries, and the continued support of supply-side measures designed to reduce wage rigidities.

Nevertheless, there is a growing disenchantment with these policies. The possibility for a G-7-led co-operative attack on unemployment through aggregate demand stimulation financed by both bonds and greater central bank purchase of government debt linked to an industrial-strategy-oriented investment programme has never been greater in the past two decades. The intellectual legitimation of the monetarist prescription is increasingly under assault in academic economic theory and it is only a matter of time before the policy-makers and politicians will leap aboard a new bandwagon.[12] But the danger is that the bandwagon will arrive just as it did in the 1930s – too late to spare European and Western civilization the anguish of social anomie. The stakes are high in all the G-7 countries because unemployment has fuelled, just as it did in the 1930s, social disintegration and extremist politics. Coupled with the growing ethnic intolerance the results could be explosive.

It is time once again to rediscover the great truth of the mystery of aggregate demand that Keynes and others uncovered in the 1930s. Capitalism requires regulation, intervention and management if it is to serve the interests of the majority rather than the élite alone. Otherwise its tendency towards depression and prolonged slump threatens the very basis of civil and humane society. Depressions once underway can and do last for very long periods. But real policy alternatives are available if there is the political courage to implement them.

A FINAL WORD

Globalization has enormously complicated the predicament of stabilizing employment and growth in a single country. But it is not, however, an insurmountable barrier, provided a country is willing to allow its exchange rate to float freely. This may have inflationary consequences but, at a high level of unemployment, these may be minimal for a long period. The more serious consequences are the political consequences and the pressure from the financial press and opinion leaders about the wisdom of doing this.

The changing nature of the new information technology and the new international division of labour has disrupted the normal association of growth with jobs. But even here the impact has been exaggerated since the growth rates lag well behind those normally associated with recovery. There is an enormous difference between 3 per cent growth associated with this recovery and 6 per cent growth associated with previous recoveries. The potential output gap remains very high. Over time, it is likely that adjustments will be made that restore the relationship between recovery, higher growth rates and job creation. Once this occurs, the flow of revenues to government will increase enormously and, coupled with the higher growth rate, the debt and deficit problem will fade away.

Nevertheless, a return to a full employment strategy would work much more effectively and have a greater impact if was co-ordinated among the G-7 countries. Such a co-ordination would require a jettisoning of the monetarist strait-jacket and the introduction of a system of taxing international speculation, the so-called Tobin tax, named after the proposal by James Tobin, the Nobel prize-winning Keynesian economist. This tax, plus the introduction of differential higher reserve ratios at the central bank for foreign banking assets held by the commercial banks and greater regulation of the derivatives markets, would act as a disincentive to the worst kind of speculative excesses.

A well co-ordinated multilateral investment programme targeted at infrastructure investment, international super highway information development, research and development, job training and the upgrading of long-neglected educational and social services would help reinforce a multiplier-driven reduction in the rate of long-term unemployment. If such an international effort does not take place, and a given country is unwilling to break loose from the current paralysing consensus, there is little that can be done and very little will, indeed, be accomplished. Even then such a gloomy future will not be tolerated for long. The current unemployment figures are simply too massive. One way or another, they will force themselves to the forefront of the political agenda.

ENDNOTES

* I would like to thank Emily Moody, Natasha Blanchet-Cohen and Annika Martenson for indispensable research assistance in preparing this chapter.

1 Even in the area of capital flow, supposedly the hallmark of the current era where billions of dollars flow about the world on a daily basis through the media of electronics and computerized trading, the actual dimension of the capital flows is smaller in relative terms than that which occurred during the 1930s (see Chapter 9 by Gerry Epstein).

2 Strauss-Kahn, in Cavanna (1988) *Public Sector Deficits in OECD Countries.*

3 Even if the additional income in the first round leaks out in the form of imported goods from one's trading partner, of course the multiplier effect is dampened down prematurely and the overall impact is lessened. But the simple act of spending on imports is not sufficient to reject the demand stimulation model. Once aggregate demand stimulation has begun it can stimulate a secondary boom in exports. See A. Thirwall (1979), for a discussion of the import constraint on demand stimulation for the UK.

4 The precise formula is $e = (E/pQ) = 1 + r/1 + g + p^*(E/Pq^{-1}) + d$

   where $e - e^{-1} = (r - P^* - g)e^{-1} + d$

   $$\text{(change in debt/GDP ratio)} = \frac{\text{(effect of real interest)} + \text{(new borrowing)}}{\text{growth differential on existing debt}}$$

   where e is public borrowing as a ratio of GDP; E is public borrowing; r the nominal rate of interest; p^* the rate of inflation; g the rate of growth of the GDP. When the real rate of interest is lower than the rate of growth the ratio will tend to decline despite new borrowing (see Muet and Fontenau 1990; Chorney 1992).

5 In fact, the aggregate supply curve that Paul Samuelson introduced in the neo-classical world in his article in 1939 in the *Journal of Political Economy*, the so-called Keynesian 45 degree line, was specifically repudiated by Keynes in the *General Theory* in the chapter on prices.

6 Similarly, the ISLM model which grew out of the work of John Hicks, Roy Harrod, David Champernowne and James Meade at a famous conference in Oxford in 1936 (Young 1987) equally bastardized Keynes by neglecting the role of uncertainty and expectations and reintegrating Keynes' work back into the framework of neo-classical orthodoxy and equational general equilibrium. So bastardized Keynesianism was a straw man that incorporated a theoretically weakened model that fell victim to the onslaught of monetarism when the times were ripe.

7 I am indebted to Bill Schrank for introducing me to the work of Charles Schultze for the Joint Economic Committee of the US Congress in 1959 in which some of these ideas are developed; see Charles L. Schultze (1959); also Arthur Okun (1981).

8 From 1989 until February 1994, the Central Bank increased its holdings of public sector debt by 56 per cent. This action has already drawn the criticism of financial sector economists as a risky inflation-prone exercise (Thomas Mayer, *Financial*

Times, 'German M3 boiler builds up steam', 1 June 1994, p. 15). On the whole, however, the Bundesbank has still followed a strict monetarist orientation. In response to the growing view that the Bundesbank has softened its position after the 0.5 percentage point cut in its two key rates, the President, Han Tietmeyer, has reiterated the Central Bank's commitment to controlling inflation and suggested an increase in rates in the 'near future' (*New York Times*, 'A German U Turn on Interest Rates Scares Europe', 29 May 1994).

9 This was precisely the argument of the faction of the French Socialist Party led by Jean Pierre Chevenment at the time. Instead of following the austerity programme proposed by Jacques Delors, the then Finance Minister, Chevenment, Beregovoy and others argued in favour of leaving the European Monetary System, allowing the franc to float free to an appropriate level and introducing trade controls to permit the domestic economic stimulation programme to work. The political defeat of this position meant that the reflation programme was abandoned prematurely (Julliard 1983; Priouret 1983; Machin and Wright 1985; Hall 1986: 192 ff.; Muet and Fontenau 1990).

10 The Canadian equivalent would be 50 billion dollars!

11 See Commission of the European Communities (1993: 271–98, Part C), in which they strongly embrace the structuralist labour market rigidity explanation for unemployment.

12 Perhaps the most significant change is the rejection of the Lucas general equilibrium rational expectations hypothesis and its modifications by the Knight– Keynes uncertainty principle (Mankiw and Romer 1991; Epstein and Wang 1994; Gerrard 1994).

BIBLIOGRAPHY

Altman, Rodger. 1994. 'Why Pressure Tokyo?' *Foreign Affairs*, May/June, 2–7.

Arendt, H.W 1944. *The Economic Lessons of the 1930s*. London: Oxford University Press.

Barro, Robert. 1974. 'Are Government Bonds Net Wealth.' *Journal of Political Economy*, December.

Bhagwati, Jagdish. 1994. 'Samurais No More.' *Foreign Affairs* May/June, 7–12.

Blecker, Robert. 1992. *Beyond the Twin Deficits: A Trade Strategy for the 1990s*. Armonk, NY: M. E. Sharpe.

Cecco, De Marcello and Alberto Giovannini (eds). 1989. *A European Central Bank: Perspectives on Monetary Unification After Ten Years of the EMS*. Cambridge: Cambridge University Press.

Chorney, H. 1987. 'Keynes et le probleme de l'inflation: les racines du retour a une sain gestion financiere', in G. Dostaler, *La theorie generale et le Keynesianisme*. Montreal: ACFAS, GRETSE Politique et Economie no. 6.

Chorney, H. 1989. *The Deficit and Debt Management: An Alternative to Monetarism*. Ottawa: The Canadian Center For Policy Alternatives.

Chorney, H. 1991. 'The Economic and Political Consequences of Canadian Monetarism', Paper presented to the British Association of Canadian Studies annual meeting, Unversity of Nottingham, 12 April.

Chorney, H. 1992. 'Stabilization Policy in Ontario.' Unpublished report for the Ontario Fair Tax Commission, Government of Ontario.

Chorney, H. 1993. 'Rediscovering Full Employment.' Paper presented to the annual meeting of the Society for the Advancement of Socio-Economics, New School for Social Research, New York, March.

Chorney, H. and B. Bouska. 1992. 'Regionalizing Monetary Policy: An Alternative to Monetarism, Learning from the Japanese Example', in A. Calitri and P. Arnopoulos (eds), *Policy Directions*. Concordia University Program in Public Policy, Montreal.

Clarke, Peter. 1988. *The Keynesian Revolution in the Making, 1924–1936*. Oxford: Clarendon Press.

Commission of the European Communities. 1993. *Growth, Competitiveness and Employment: The Challenges and Ways Forward into the 21st Century*. White Paper, Bruxelles.

Domar, E. 1993. 'On Deficits and Debt.' *The American Journal of Economics and Sociology* 52: 4 (October).

Eisner, Robert. 1986. *How Real is the Federal Deficit?* New York: The Free Press.

Epstein, Larry and Tan Wang. 1994. 'Intertemporal Asset Pricing Under Knightian Uncertainty.' *Econometrica* 62: 3 (March), 283–322.

Gerrard, Bill. 1994. 'Beyond Rational Expectations: A Constructive Interpretation of Keynes's Analysis of Behaviour under Uncertainty.' *Economic Journal* 104 (March), 327–37.

Goodman, John. 1992. *Monetary Sovereignty: The Politics of Central Banking in Western Europe* Ithaca: Cornell University Press.

Graham, R. 1994. 'Warming to Berlusconi on Inflation.' *Financial Times*, 1 June.

Hall, Peter. 1986. *Governing the Economy: The Politics of State Intervention in Britain and France*. Cambridge: Polity Press.

Howson, Susan. 1986. 'External Financial Markets, Capital Mobility and Monetary Independence', in Jon Cohen and G. C. Harcourt (eds), *International Monetary Economics and Supply-Side Economics*. London: Macmillan.

Julliard, Jacques. 1983. 'P.S.: les chasseurs d'horizon.' *Le Nouvel Observateur*, 13–19 May.

Judis, John. 1994. 'Clintoneconomics: What's the Deal? The Future of Jobs.' Interview symposium with Laura Tyson, Lester Thurow, John Kenneth Galbraith, Juliet Schor, Atsushi Yamada, Walter Russel Mead, Louis Lampere and Kevin Phillips. *Mother Jones* (April).

Keynes, John Maynard. 1936. *The General Theory of Employment, Interest and Money*. London: Macmillan.

Kierans, E. and W. Stewart, 1989. *The Wrong End of the Rainbow*. Toronto: Collins.

Krehm, William. 1993. *A Power Unto Itself: The Bank of Canada*. Toronto: Stoddart.

Krugman, Paul. 1994. 'The Myth of Globalization.' *Foreign Affairs*, March–April.

Machin, Howard and V. Wright (eds). 1985. *Economic Policy and Policy-making Under the Mitterrand Presidency, 1981–1984*. London: Frances Pinter.

Magnus, George. 1994. 'Too Many Dollars, Not Enough Sense.' *Financial Times*, 26 May.

Mankiw, N. Gregory and David Romer. 1991. *New Keynesian Economics*, Vols 1 and 2. Cambridge, Mass.: MIT Press.

Morishima, Michio. 1982. *Why Has Japan Succeeded?: Western Technology and the Japanese Ethos*. Cambridge: Cambridge University Press.

Morris-Suzuki, T. 1989. *A History of Japanese Economic Thought*. London: Routledge.

Muet, Pierre-Alain and Alain Fonteneau. 1990. *Reflation and Austerity: Economic Policy Under Mitterrand*. New York: Berg.

Priouret, Rodger. 1983. 'Ce que couteraient les pilules de rechange.' *Le Nouvel Observateur*, 27 May–2 June.

OECD. 1993. *Employment/Unemployment*. Study Draft Policy Report. Paris, 6 January.

Okun, Arthur. 1981. *Prices and Quantities: A Macroeconomic Analysis*. Washington, DC: The Brookings Institution.

Radcliffe Committee on the Workings of the Monetary System. 1959. Cmnd. 827. London: HMSO.

Samuelson, Paul. 1939. 'A Synthesis of the Principle of Acceleration and the Multiplier.' *Journal of Political Economy*, pp. 786–97.

Samuelson, Paul. 1961. *Economics*. New York: McGraw-Hill.

Schultze, Charles. 1959. *Recent Inflation in the United States*. Study Paper Number 1, 'Study of Employment, Growth and Price Levels.' Paper prepared for the Joint Economic Committee of the US Congress, Washington.

Shimada, Haruro. 1985. 'The Perception and Reality of Japanese Industrial Relations', in Lester Thurow, *The Management Challenge: Japanese Views*. Cambridge, Mass.: MIT Press.

Smith, David. 1992. *From Boom to Bust*. Harmondsworth: Penguin.

Strauss-Kahn, Dominique. 1988. 'Public Sector Deficits and the Growth of the National Debt', in H. Cavanna (ed.), *Public Sector Deficits in OECD Countries: Causes, Consequences and Remedies*. New York: St Martins Press.

Survey of Current Business. 1994. Washington, DC: US Department of Commerce Bureau of Economic Analysis.

Thirwall, Anthony. 1979. 'The Balance of Payments Constraint as an Explanation of International Growth Rate Differences.' *Banca Nazionale del Lavora Quarterly Review*, March.

Weintraub, S. and M. Goodstein (eds). 1983. *Reaganeconomics in the Stagflation Economy*. Philadelphia, Pa.: University of Pennsylvania Press.

Young, Warren. 1987. *Interpreting Mr Keynes: The IS–LM Enigma*. Cambridge: Polity Press.

Part VI

NEW POLITICS
IN AN
UNCERTAIN WORLD

17

NEW STATE FORMS, NEW POLITICAL SPACES

Janine Brodie

INTRODUCTION

An examination of the politics of social movements during the present era of restructuring may seem somewhat misplaced in a collection celebrating Harold Innis. His influential and substantial research on staples production has been criticized precisely for being dehumanized and deterministic (Berger 1976: 98). This critical assessment of his work, however, is both superficial and misleading. It is true that Innis did not believe that political actors had unrestrained political agency. They were not 'free', in other words, to realize all political outcomes. Instead, Innis conceived of political actors as operating within a historically specific field of constraints imposed by, among other things, international power structures and the force of previous decisions, particularly those relating to economic development strategies. Innis advanced a relational and diachronic vision of the links between staples exploitation, political institutions, cultural forms and political action. He envisioned each phase in a historical series of staples exploitation as a complex web of social relations which cumulatively have 'left their stamp' on Canadian society and politics (Brodie 1990: ch. 3). Innis's conception of these structural and temporal factors, in turn, revealed the margins, 'invariably narrow, in which men [*sic*] were free to make their own history' (Berger 1976: 102).

In many ways, Innis's encompassing vision of the multiple layers and manifestations of staples production is similar to contemporary thinking within regulation theory about the historical fit among capitalist accumulation strategies (the regime of accumulation) and dominant political institutions, behaviours and belief systems (the mode of regulation) (Lipietz 1987). In what follows, I would like to explore tentatively the current era of restructuring from the perspective of the new mode of regulation which appears to be emerging from the crumbling foundations of the old and suggest that these changes in cultural forms have significant implications for the politics of social movements. In particular, I want to suggest that the politics of restructuring revolves around a multi-faceted contraction of the public and the political, as they have been constituted by the Keynesian Welfare State (KWS) in the post-war years, and the simultaneous expansion and re-regulation of the private whether defined as markets or the domestic sphere. The current round of restructuring invites oppositional movements to engage in new strategic thinking about the very meaning of the public.

NEGOTIATING THE PUBLIC–PRIVATE DIVIDE

The liberal democratic state was initially conceived and has been repeatedly restructured thereafter through, what Walzer appropriately terms, 'the art of separation'. The early liberal theorists took the old feudal order, which was grounded in impositional claims about natural hierarchies and the organic whole, and recast it as a 'world of walls'. 'They drew lines, marked off different realms, and created the sociopolitical map' with which, although many times altered, we still live. The Church was divided from the state so the latter could be shaped and governed according to the principles of liberalism and later liberal democracy. The state was separated from the economy so that the market could develop according to the laws of supply and demand, free from political interference. And, finally, a line was drawn between the public and the private so that domestic life remained the preserve of the individual patriarch (Walzer 1984: 315 *passim*).

Classic liberal discourse prescribed and then materialized in the re-organization of metaphorical, economic and political space. It represented a profound shift in cultural forms and the mechanisms through which state and social power were expressed (Harvey 1989: 255). At its heart was a new set of visions and discursive claims about what was natural and universal, what was on and off the political terrain, and the rules and practices which were uniquely applicable to the public world of the state, the private sphere of the economy and the domestic realm of the family. Liberalism pronounced a 'natural' isomorphism or coincidence between sites and practices, institutions and functions (Bowles and Gintis 1986: 100–1).

Although liberal discourse often turns on the distinction between the public and the private – the naming of those things that are or are not naturally and properly subject to state intervention – the private actually had two distinct parts: the capitalist economy and the patriarchal family. Both were immune from public interference but each was governed by different rules, hierarchies and distributive practices (Bowles and Gintis 1986: 98). The market operated under the rules of *laissez-faire* capitalism, creating a pro-foundly unequal and oppressive class system, while the realm of the domestic was subject to the rule of individual men. The family was, in custom and law, sacred ground upon which the state could not tread: a man's home was indeed 'his castle' (Pateman 1988: 192).

Bowles and Gintis appropriately criticize much of contemporary social theory for accepting liberalism's 'world of walls' as real without interrogating how these impositional claims structure and limit politics. Historical experience shows that the public–private partition, the liberal 'sleight of the hand' as they call it, is neither fixed, natural nor obvious (Bowles and Gintis 1986: 66). Feminist theorists, in particular, have been in the forefront in insisting that there are no a priori constraints dictating why some things are intrinsically public and others are not (Fraser 1989). In fact, it is a very public and political act to name something as natural and apolitical. Similarly, objects become 'denaturalized' and drawn into the realm of the public when they are named or identified as being political (Yeatman 1990: 153).

The emergence and consolidation of the Keynesian Welfare State (KWS) in the immediate post-war years is an example of this process. This was another period of restructuring when the boundaries between the economy and the state and the public and the private were altered. The KWS realized the radical expansion of the public through regulation and direct intervention in the economy and by subjecting the family and other aspects of private life to new forms of state scrutiny, regulation and assistance (Andrew 1984: 667). The welfare state rested on a redrawing of the public–private divide and a new 'welfare ideology' which, Ursel argues, 'was an achievement of public consensus equal in significance but substantially different to the Victorian Social Reform Movement' (Ursel 1992: 205).

The question of boundaries – of where to draw the line between the prerogatives of the state and those of the market or of the family – has informed liberal democratic politics, in one form or another, since its beginnings. Oppositional social movements have repeatedly engaged in a tug-of-war with hegemonic forces around the boundary marking the public–private divide. Where this line falls has varied markedly cross-culturally and historically (Phillips 1991: 15). It represents a particular and fragile negotiation which historically constitutes and is repeatedly reinforced by the liberal democratic state through its institutions, policies and regulations (Corrigan and Sayer 1985).

RESTRUCTURING: THE FALLING APART

Canada, similar to all Western liberal democracies, is currently experiencing a pronounced shift in state form and governing practices. It is now widely recognized, by both its friends and foes alike, that the formative pillars of the Keynesian Welfare State (KWS) have not survived the combined forces of prolonged economic crisis, the so-called 'globalization' of production and neo-liberal governing practices. The broad consensus which grounded the KWS and structured the post-war pattern of politics has given way to a very different set of assumptions about the role of government and the rights of citizens. The new orthodoxy suggests that the changing international political economy puts roughly the same demands on all governments: maximize exports; reduce social spending; curtail state economic regulation; and empower capital to reorganize national economies as parts of transnational trading blocs (Friedman 1991: 35). In the process, we have witnessed pronounced changes in the focus of public policy and in governing practices. Governments are abandoning as futile the goals of full employment and an inclusive social safety net in order to achieve the illusive and abstract states of flexibility and efficiency. In effect, governments are acting as the midwives of globalization.

Canada is not the only country that has been submerged into a new politics, disruption, uncertainty and ambiguity. During the past decade, most Western liberal democracies have been forced to re-examine many of their governing assumptions and practices, moving from what the regulation theorists have termed a familiar 'Fordist' past to an unknown 'post-Fordist' future. According to these theorists, the economies and politics of Western democracies after the Second World War were organized around a 'Fordist mode of regulation'. By this they mean that there was a widespread consensus that national governments should take an active role in managing national economies through Keynesian demand management techniques; the labour process was organized around the assembly line and mass production; and redistribution was accomplished through social welfare programmes and collective bargaining (Lipietz 1987). The post-war years brought new shared understandings about state intervention in the economy, an elaboration of bureaucratic institutions and governing instruments and an expansion of the very meaning of citizenship itself. The Keynesian state asserted the primacy of the public over the 'invisible hand' of the market and engendered expectations that the state was responsible for meeting the basic needs of its citizens.

Fordism was a whole package of relations, institutions and arrangements which linked a logic of economic development during a particular historical period (the regime of accumulation) with an equally particular and complementary set of norms, habits, laws, regulations and representations of reality (the mode of regulation) (Harvey 1989: 121–3). Its passing, then, represents much more than a series of strategic responses to a changing international political economy. It signals a paradigm shift in governing practices – a historic alteration in state form which enacts simultaneous changes in cultural assumptions, political identities and the very terrain of political struggle. Restructuring represents a prolonged and conflict-ridden political process during which old assumptions and shared understandings are put under stress and eventually rejected while social forces struggle to achieve a new consensus – a new vision of the future to fill the vacuum created by the erosion of the old. It is a simultaneous 'combination of falling apart and building up again', conveying, as Soja explains, 'the notion of a "brake", if not a break, in secular trends, and a shift toward a significantly different order and configuration of social, economic, and political life' (Soja 1989: 159).

THE BUILDING UP AGAIN

The current process of restructuring in Canada has been guided by what I term 'restructuring discourse'. It is deeply imbued with neo-liberal impositional claims and seeks to renegotiate and recode the public and private by radically shrinking the realm of political negotiation and expanding the autonomy of the market and the family. The central metaphor underlying this new cultural understanding is survival of the fittest: globalization takes no prisoners. There is simply no escaping adjustment, which means reducing fiscal and regulatory burdens on industry and lowering expectations of state responsibility for protecting domestic industries from global pressures or providing a comprehensive social welfare system. In effect, this discourse attempts to decentre and displace the KWS with 'hyper-liberal' impositional claims about self-regulating and competitive market forces and the primacy of the market in generating a new social order (Cox 1991: 342; Drache and Gertler 1991: 7).

This neo-liberal world view was put front and centre on the federal political agenda by the Macdonald Commission (The Royal Commission on the Economic Union and Development Prospects for Canada, 1985) and came to dominate the Mulroney government's front benches, especially after its re-election in 1988 and the implementation of the Canada–US Free Trade Agreement (FTA) in 1989. Throughout the late 1980s, the federal Conservative government had used mounting federal deficits as a rationale for cutting back on the welfare state. By the early 1990s, however, the Conservatives' attack on the welfare state was directly linked to making Canada more 'competitive' – principally by forfeiting the economic terrain to the private sector (Abele 1992: 1). In its 1992 Budget Speech, for example, the Mulroney government announced that its primary legislative priority was to promote greater 'reliance on the private sector and market forces'. Ranked immediately below this were the related goals of deficit reduction, inflation control, free trade and developing a new consensus about the role of government. For the federal Conservatives, a restructured economy required a restructured government that would provide only those public services that were 'affordable' and did not interfere with Canadian competitiveness (McQuaig 1992).

The federal electorate struck a deathblow to the federal Conservative Party in 1993 for betraying their trust, eroding their social safety net, and forcing family members into the growing ranks of the unemployed – all in the name of 'efficiency' and 'competitiveness'. It gave a landslide victory to the federal Liberal Party which promised little more than to be a more honest and compassionate manager of the economic transition. And, since the 1993 federal election, the new federal government has charted essentially the same course as its unapologetic neo-liberal predecessor. Within its first months in office, it had ratified the North American Free Trade Agreement (NAFTA),

prioritized deficit reduction over job creation and infrastructural development and continued to erode the social welfare system that was built-up
piecemeal in the post-war years. Moreover, in its first budget of February
1994, the Liberals made it clear that they had no intention of repairing
Canada's fraying social safety net or returning it to its former presence. The
rookie Finance Minister, Paul Martin, Jr, told Parliament that, 'The days of
government simply nibbling at the edges' of the deficit were over. 'For years',
he continued, 'governments have been promising more than they can deliver,
and delivering more than they can afford. That has to end. We are ending it'
(Canada 1994: 1–2). The Keynesian state, in other words, is no more.

Restructuring discourse attempts to depoliticize the economic by representing market-driven adjustment as self-regulating and inevitable. At the
same time, it recommends and achieves the shrinkage of the public and
political spaces of the KWS through a combination of mechanisms, perhaps
most irreversibly through international trading agreements. These agreements are completely saturated with neo-liberal assumptions and solutions
which effectively act to erode national sovereignty and the state's capacity to
implement politically negotiated solutions. As Stephen Gill has recently
argued, changes in the regulation of international capitalism through the
GATT and regional treaties such as the FTA, NAFTA and the Single
European Act effectively represent a new constitutionalism which defines and
guarantees new rights to transnational capital (Gill 1992). This process is
potentially as significant for the constitution of new political and cultural
forms as was the early *laissez-faire* state's guarantees of the rights of contract
and property (Panitch 1993: 12).

The Canada–US Free Trade Agreement (FTA) specifically limits the terrain
of the political by prohibiting governments from either favouring domestic
producers or subsidizing national industry. The North American Free Trade
Agreement (NAFTA) goes even further by effectively capping the domain of
the Canadian state at both its federal and provincial levels. A profoundly anti-
public document, it refers to the public sector as 'non-conforming', limits the
use of public corporations, and requires that those remaining must operate
according to proper commercial operations and considerations (Cohen
1993b). Moreover, it stipulates that all levels of government must declare
those things which exclusively rest with the public sector within two years
after the implementation of the agreement. Those services not named will be
deemed 'tradable' and thus open to private sector competition and provision.
Meanwhile, explicit exclusions such as healthcare will be reviewed in 1998,
the same year that federal funds for medicare are to be phased out in several
provinces (Woman to Woman 1993). NAFTA, in other words, attempts to
draw a new boundary between the public and private by reducing the public
sector and pre-empting any new growth. Implicit in these restrictions is the
clear message that we have reached, indeed surpassed, the appropriate

boundary between the public and the private and that the new world order demands retreat and attrition.

RECODING THE PUBLIC AND THE PRIVATE

The current era of restructuring involves a complex displacement of the state power and the political terrain once occupied by the welfare state. While the emerging state form maintains all the trappings of sovereignty and executive authority it, none the less, rests on impositional claims which valorize the private over the public (Jessop 1993: 22). Critical governing instruments of the KWS such as public corporations and social welfare programmes are said to be 're-'privatized to the market or the home, thereby creating the illusion that they are being returned to some place they naturally belong. This reprivatization has been enforced through two other 'res' – the 're-commodification' of claims and the 're-constitution' of domestic enclaves. Recommodification rests on the unverifiable assertion that services and assets created in the public sphere are better delivered and maintained through market mechanisms. In the process, they are removed from the realm of political negotiation and subjected to market-oriented rather than political evaluative criteria (Yeatman 1990: 173). In the deceptively simple language of public choice theory, these services and assets are said to be transformed from public goods to private goods.

The reconstitution of the domestic rests on impositional claims about the role and value of the family as a fundamental building block in society. The revalorization of the family is particularly stark in neo-conservative rhetoric, which blames both the welfare state and feminism for the breakdown of the family and the social fabric. More broadly, however, there is a growing consensus that families should look after their own and state policies should make sure that they do (Abbott and Wallace 1992: 2). Increasingly strict enforcement of child support payments, the defunding of battered women's shelters and decreasing public support for day care and elderly care are examples of this trend. More often, however, the state reconstitutes the domestic by fiat instead of explicit regulation. Privatization and the erosion of the welfare state have the effect of forcing healthcare, child care and elderly care back onto traditional family forms and the unpaid work of women.

Reprivatization, however, involves much more than simply removing things from the public basket and placing them on the market or in the domestic sphere. The things moved are themselves transformed into something different – a lesson we ignore only at great peril. As things are shifted from the public to the private they become differently encoded, constructed and regulated. Citizens with a right to healthcare, or just plain sick people, for example, become consumers of alternative medical delivery systems capable of purchasing choice. Meanwhile, healthcare providers and treatments are evaluated in terms of cost-effectiveness, efficiency and market-

389

JANINE BRODIE

ability. Similarly, the realm of family responsibility is magnified but, at the same time, family relations become subject to increasing surveillance ('decentralized social guidance strategies'). Governments become central to 'regulated self-regulation' in the form of anti-smoking campaigns, cash incentives for women to breast-feed their infants (new Quebec initiative), generous tax incentives for retirement savings or new representations of family relations through concepts such as child, wife or elder abuse (Jessop 1993: 10). Whether through market-oriented discourse or some other disciplinary practice, the underside of reprivatization is reregulation.

The reconstitution of the private has been accompanied by a progressive 'hollowing out' of the KWS and, in particular, universal social welfare programmes (Jessop 1993). During the past decade, 'hardly a single federal government social program has not been reduced or altered' (National Forum on Family Security 1993: 8). Governments, however, have been less than forthcoming with the electorate about their repeated attempts to dismantle the welfare state. The Mulroney government, for example, promised that it would guard Canada's social welfare system as a 'sacred trust', and then fundamentally eroded it through a series of budget cuts and regulatory changes. Critics now refer to this process of diminishing the social safety net through budget cuts and seemingly minor adjustments to regulations as 'social policy by stealth' (Cohen 1993a: 267). This politics, which was perfected by the Mulroney Conservatives and subsequently adopted by the federal Liberals and many provincial administrations, enables governments to enact significant changes in social policy without advance notice or public consultation. The federal Conservatives used the politics of stealth to put an end to the principle of universality by 'clawing back' Old Age Security and Family Allowance benefits from all but its most needy recipients. It also wrote new limitations and exclusions into the Unemployment Insurance legislation, a practice repeated by the federal Liberals in their 1994 budget. Most significantly, however, the Mulroney government unilaterally rewrote the terms of the federal government's funding of provincial welfare programmes, healthcare and post-secondary education – again a practice that the federal Liberals have continued. This strategy effectively off-loads the debt crisis onto provincial governments which, faced with increasing need and decreasing resources, have been forced to exact even deeper cuts in social assistance.

The dual forces of reprivatization and reregulation have the additional effect of creating new shared understandings of what it means to be a citizen. Although varying considerably among themselves, post-war welfare states rested on a broad but fragile consensus about the rights of citizenship. The post-war ideal of social citizenship conveyed the idea that poverty was not always an individual's fault and that all citizens had the right to a basic standard of living. The general consensus underlying the creation and maintenance of the KWS was that Canadians did not have to repeat the harsh

390

lessons in public administration dealt out by the Great Depression of the 1930s. The public could enforce limits on the market, individuals were not forced to engage in market activities that denied their dignity and the national community was responsible for the basic well-being of the individual citizen. These are the ideals which are currently contested by the new vision of citizenship. There has been a decided shift away from the ideal of universal publicly provided services. The rights and securities guaranteed to all citizens of the KWS are no longer rights, universal or secure. The new ideal of the common good rests on market-oriented values such as self-reliance, efficiency and competition. The new good citizen is one that recognizes the limits and liabilities of state provision and embraces her obligation to work longer and harder in order to become more self-reliant (Drache 1992: 221).

The disappearance of universal social programmes and the erosion of the social safety net obviously give less substance to the post-war construction of citizenship. More than this, however, it has reintroduced into political discourse concepts such as the 'deserving and undeserving' poor and 'genuine' versus 'non-genuine' poverty (Yeatman 1990: 122). The Mulroney government, for example, established a parliamentary committee, which the opposition parties boycotted, to redefine poverty. More important, the Chrétién government has announced the complete overhauling of Canada's social welfare regime by 1996 – an undertaking that Finance Minister Martin describes as 'the most comprehensive reform of government policy in decades' (Canada, 1994: 8). At the same time, cash-starved provincial governments are desperately seeking new ways to 'reform' welfare programmes and reduce expenditures. This renegotiation of the post-war social welfare regime, as well as anticipated changes to fiscal federalism, represents nothing less than a 'constitu-(tive)-tional' change in cultural understandings.

The details of this new order have yet to be written even though the social security system has been under the microscope of the federal bureaucracy for some time. Many of its contours, none the less, are already discernible. The first change is what the new discourse refers to as a shift from a 'passive' to an 'active' welfare model. It is difficult to ignore the obvious valorization of the new order encoded in these terms. They signal a shift in the philosophy of welfare provision away from the protection of people who are either temporarily or permanently displaced by the wage economy to a new regime where retraining or participation in the job market are conditions for social assistance (Brodie 1994c). The idea here is that all able-bodied people are effectively 'undeserving' of social assistance unless they either retrain to better compete in the job market or take some form of work to supplement their social assistance incomes, and thus reduce the burden they impose on the state. In New Brunswick, for example, an experimental programme now ties social assistance to retraining while, in both British Columbia and Newfoundland, welfare recipients are given bonuses to take low-paying jobs. In the meantime, the new Liberal government has announced its preference for workfare and social assistance plans which act as a 'launching pad in to the job market' (Lloyd Axworthy: *Globe and Mail*, 17 December 1993: A1).

In keeping with the idea that the provinces will implement the new welfare regime, the Liberals made available in their first budget some $800 million for provinces to experiment with 'innovative approaches' that 'will work more effectively in the future' (Canada 1994: 8). The first of these was announced a month after the budget. A joint federal–provincial pilot project, it would provide a guaranteed annual income of $10,000 to older workers in exchange for a fixed amount of work. Essentially a workfare scheme, the participants would be able to retain additional earnings once they met their contractual obligations to the state.

The Liberals also promised in their first budget to honour their campaign promise of creating a job corps for Canada's unemployed youth. The idea that the young are particularly 'undeserving' of social assistance has been increasingly advanced by the right. Judith Maxwell, former head of the Economic Council of Canada, for one has suggested that 'no Canadian under 25 should be eligible for unemployment insurance' because 'it would be a tragedy to let these young people be scarred by long spells of unemployment' (York 1993: A1, A4). What she and others of this school assume but do not articulate is that unemployed youth remain the responsibility of the family until they themselves amass credits in the social welfare system.

More broadly, however, the new thinking about social welfare signals a number of cultural shifts. First, the social welfare system is being redesigned to make it more restrictive, especially for those deemed to be 'employable' and to force them back into the job market even if the only jobs available are 'non-standard' – that is, insecure, part-time and poorly paid (Yeatman 1990: 130). It is no coincidence that these are precisely the kinds of jobs which are being created in Canada's restructured economy. Second, 'active' social welfare programmes serve to rediscipline the workforce both by making the poor dependent on some form of employment and by constructing an image of the 'undeserving' poor as those who do not participate in some form in the job market. Third, all of these factors serve to obscure systemic visions of poverty and unemployment. If people are poor it is because their personal skills do not match the market and not because the restructured political economy is unable to provide employment opportunities to an unacceptable number of Canadians. In the process, the gaze of policy-makers is directed away from macroeconomic solutions to individual self-help therapies.

THE POLITICS OF RESTRUCTURING

The boundary shifting between the public and private, reprivatization discourse, the recommodification of the public, the reconstitution of the domestic, the delegitimization of social citizenship claims, and the individualization of poverty are all symptoms of the breakdown of the post-war compromise. The erosion of the KWS has been protested by a variety of oppositional movements, among them labour, the women's movement and anti-poverty groups. None the less, this political struggle has been a difficult one precisely because restructuring discourse attempts to marginalize and deconstruct oppositional movements. It does so in at least two critical ways. One form of marginalization is to deny the social movements' moral and political significance, depicting them instead as sectoral and self-interested lobby groups. In turn, these so-called interest groups are constructed as threats to democracy and obstacles in the policy-making process. The other form is to constitute particular members of a particular social movement as lying on the outer limits of the norm: they become disadvantaged groups for whom special provision is to be made (Yeatman 1990: 130).

The charge that an oppositional movement is really nothing more than a self-interested and unrepresentative lobby group has been directed at native organizations, anti-poverty groups and, especially, women's organizations such as the National Action Committee on the Status of Women (Phillips 1993). In the dying days of the Mulroney administration, the federal government used this rationale for cutting funding for groups representing the socially disenfranchised in the policy-making process. Later, PC (Progressive Conservative) leadership hopeful, Kim Campbell, vowed to stop giving money to 'advocacy groups' altogether when she became Prime Minister arguing that they should be sponsored by their respective constituencies (*Globe and Mail*, 13 June 1993: A6). This sentiment was revisited in the Liberal government's first budget. Finance Minister Martin reduced group funding by 5 per cent and promised to reconsider whether the federal government should get out of the business of funding 'lobby groups' altogether.

Restructuring discourse's construction of oppositional groups as 'special interest groups' has the effect of casting them outside the community and implies that their demands collide with the collective interests of the community. 'Special interest groups' do not speak for ordinary people but, instead, seek to hijack the political agenda in order to advance their own self-interested ends (Leger and Rebick 1993: 95). In other words, they demand privileges which are unearned and violate the new norms of citizenship. More than this, restructuring discourse attempts to cast social movements which seek to empower the marginalized as threats to democracy itself. It suggests that special interest groups threaten to hijack the political agenda and disrupt the governing process. Barbara McDougall, a former minister in the Mulroney Cabinet, visualized the problem of modern governing as follows. 'So many single or limited interest groups have established their presence on the national political scene that it is virtually impossible for any government to undertake a comprehensive policy platform' (quoted in Phillips 1993: 12).

Restructuring discourse, however, goes further than denying the legitimacy of organized voices in democratic politics. It attempts to deconstruct groups such as, for example, the women's movement into a series of specially

JANINE BRODIE

disadvantaged groups which require 'targeted' social programmes to address their unique needs (Yeatman 1990: 134). The idea of targeting is entirely consistent with the hollowing out of the welfare state. Its overt rationale is that, in an era of fiscal restraint, scarce resources are best targeted at those who need them most. Thus, universal entitlements such as the old age pension or mothers' allowance are transformed into social assistance available only to those defined as the most needy. By concentrating solely on so-called 'special' needs, the targeting strategy accomplishes a number of goals which are consistent with the politics of restructuring. First, it pathologizes those groups deemed to have special needs, casting them outside the community of citizens who presumably are able to meet their own needs without state assistance. Second, the collective claims of oppositional movements are disassembled and diffused, cast into what Yeatman calls 'the ghetto of disadvantaged groups' (Yeatman 1990: 134). As a result, oppositional movements which emerge as historical, moral, collective political actors with a particular vision of political equality are deconstructed and recoded into a series of different and disconnected categories which require some sort of corrective to transform them into self-sufficient individuals. Third, targeting provides a rationale for surveillance and a means to regulate those deemed to be special or different.

Increasingly oppositional movements are contrasted with the favourite son of the emerging order – 'the ordinary Canadian'. The ordinary Canadian has appeared only recently on the Canadian political stage (Brodie 1994b). He was hailed by the Spicer Commission as the source of Canadian values and the holder of the key to Canadian unity; he was invited to the Mulroney government's constitutional forums preceding the referendum on the Charlottetown Accord; and he became a regular on the CBC's 1993 'town hall meetings' election coverage. The 'ordinary Canadian' also figures prominently in the rhetoric of the Reform Party and was cast as the star; indeed, was the only one invited to the federal Liberal's pre-budget consultation meetings.

Although he is increasingly evoked in political rhetoric and folklore, his identity is elusive, defined primarily by the things he is not. The ordinary Canadian is disinterested, seeking neither special status nor treatment from the state. He is not raced, sexed or classed: he transcends difference. But, how do we interpret the ordinary Canadian's rapid ascendancy to the centre of the political stage – a stage which the political élite suggests is congested with selfish special interest groups which threaten to hijack the political agenda and pervert the common good (Leger and Rebick 1993: 95).

Clearly, the 'ordinary Canadian' is a metaphor in the politics of restructuring. None of us is ordinary or, put differently, all of us are special in some way or another. So what does it mean for us to be asked to defer to the voice of the ordinary Canadian? For one thing, this dichotomy between the 'ordinary' and the 'special' sends the clear message that regular people do not require state assistance and protection. As Iris Young suggests, contemporary

394

politics attempts to grant 'political legitimacy to persons on the condition that they do not claim special rights or needs, or call attention to their particular history or culture' (Young 1990: 109). This discursive strategy effectively reinforces privilege by attempting to silence all those deemed to be different.

CONCLUSION

The implication of this analysis of restructuring discourse is that social movements are part of the complex matrix which is transformed during an era of restructuring. Oppositional movements that ignore the shifting discursive terrain, indeed that fail to explore their own discursive construction and reconstruction, necessarily become part of the history to which they cling. If the 1993 federal election demonstrated anything, it was that the terrain of Canadian politics has shifted. The pattern of post-war politics has been pushed aside, revealing in stark relief the uncertain and contested political space we are now occupying.

The passing of the welfare state has displaced many of the sites and objects of political struggle for oppositional movements. At the same time, we perhaps have been too quick to accept the determinism and unrestrained economism of restructuring discourse. We have not sufficiently challenged its impositional claims as 'impositional' – that is, as invested interpretations of reality which are open to political contestation and moral evaluation. We are living through a period of profound adjustment. On this we can all agree. But it is an impositional claim to suggest that this adjustment *must* occur on the terrain of the social and it is an impositional claim to suggest that societies must restructure around market goalposts. Neither of these claims is obvious nor inevitable. Perhaps, more to the point, the emerging mode of regulation rests on very fragile foundations. Neo-liberalism has not produced an economic miracle and, unlike Fordism, it has not succeeded in creating a broad-based consensus around its particular vision of the future. Contrary to the central tenets of restructuring discourse, the present period does not represent the end of politics – the substitution of political negotiation with neo-liberal imperatives. Instead, the profound lack of social consensus, the bypassing of democratic principles to impose new governing forms, the ongoing fiscal crisis of the state and the continuing crisis in unemployment and consumption, all point to the opening of new political spaces and an explosion of alternative visions.

One enduring legacy of Harold Innis's celebrated scholarship was his insistence that we assess the concepts of continuity and change within a country in relation to the international political economy – to think of Canada's economic, institutional and political development as historically linked to each other and to a larger international whole. This is perhaps the most critical lesson that oppositional movements must now embrace. Both the political right and left agree that the new international political economy diminishes the capacity for national governments to exert the same measure of control over a national economy as was afforded by a Fordist mode of regulation. The particular form of displacement of the national state in a post-Fordist period, however, does not mean that political space itself has disappeared or that it has floated upward towards some nebulous and institutional-less international space. The current round of restructuring is shifting the spaces of accumulation and with it the 'real geographies of social action' (Harvey 1989: 335).

The political spaces of restructuring are paradoxical and complex but not necessary or fixed. Restructuring may be closing familiar political spaces but, as surely, it is opening others both absolute and abstract. Some have argued that the new economic order simultaneously moves the political terrain above and below the nation-state, thus calling for new oppositional forms based on international and local struggles. As important, however, the new order also invites renewed struggles over abstract spaces and, in particular, the dividing line between the public and private – the places for the collective and the individual. From this perspective, the most immediate task confronting oppositional movements is not to find the most appropriate place to struggle for the democratic emancipation of the subordinate but, instead, to interrogate restructuring discourse and to understand the new cultural forms and political spaces which are emerging. We must learn how to read the webs of power created by restructuring in order to understand the political potential of new couplings and new coalitions. Most fundamentally, social movements must begin the long process of reclaiming the public. In a sense, they must 're-public-ize' political spaces and build a new social consensus about the boundaries and content of the public and private. As Lipietz has argued, 'even if economic interests and transnational ideological pressures do abolish frontiers, it has to be remembered that the form in which those pressures and interests are integrated is still the state form' (Lipietz 1987: 22). Whether these pressures are integrated in a transformed Canadian state according to neo-liberal dogma or to considerations of the social well-being of Canadians is precisely our political agenda.

BIBLIOGRAPHY

Abbott, Pamela and Claire Wallace. 1992. *The Family and the New Right*. Boulder, Colo.: Pluto Press.

Abele, Francis. 1992. 'The Politics of Competition', in Francis Abele (ed.), *How Ottawa Spends 1992–93*. Ottawa: Carleton University Press.

Andrew, Caroline. 1984. 'Women and the Welfare State.' *Canadian Journal of Political Science*, December.

Bakker, Isabella (ed.). 1994. *Engendering Macroeconomic Policy*. London: Zed Books.

Benhabib, Seyla. 1993. 'Feminist Theory and Hannah Arendt's Concept of Public Space.' *History of Human Sciences* 6: 2.

Berger, Carl. 1976. *The Writing of Canadian History*. Toronto: Oxford University Press.

Bowles, Samuel and Hebert Gintis. 1986. *Democracy and Capitalism*. London: Routledge and Kegan Paul.

Brodie, Janine. 1990. *The Political Economy of Canadian Regionalism*. Toronto: Harcourt, Brace, Jovanovich.

Brodie, Janine. 1994a. 'Shifting Public Spaces: A Reconsideration of Women and the State in the Era of Global Restructuring', in Bakker.

Brodie, Janine. 1994b. 'Politics on the Boundaries: Restructuring and the Canadian Women's Movement.' Eighth Annual Robarts Lecture, Robarts Centre for Canadian Studies, York University, Toronto.

Brodie, Janine. 1994c. 'Social Programs.' *Canada Watch* 2: 6 (March).

Canada. 1994. *The Budget Speech*. Ottawa: Department of Finance, 22 February.

Cohen, Marjorie Griffin. 1993a. 'Social Policy and Social Services', in Pierson *et al.*

Cohen, Marjorie Griffin. 1993b. 'Economic Restructuring Through Trade: Implications for People.' Paper presented at the Shastri Indo-Canadian Seminar on Economic Change and Economic Development. New Delhi, December.

Corrigan, Philip and Derek Sayer. 1985. *The Great Arch: English State Formation as Cultural Revolution*. London: Basil Blackwell.

Cox, Robert. 1991. 'The Global Political Economy and Social Choice', in Daniel Drache and Meric Gertler (eds).

Drache, Daniel. 1992. 'Conclusion', in Daniel Drache (ed.), *Getting on Track: Social Democratic Strategies for Ontario*. Kingston: McGill–Queen's University Press.

Drache, Daniel and Meric Gertler. 1991. 'Introduction', in Drache and Gertler (eds), *The New Era of Global Competition: State Policy and Market Power*. Montreal: McGill–Queen's University Press.

Fraser, Nancy. 1989. *Unruly Practices: Power, Discourse and Gender in Contemporary Social Theory*. Minneapolis: University of Minnesota Press.

Friedman, Harriet. 1991. 'New Wines, New Bottles: The Regulation of Capital on a World Scale.' *Studies in Political Economy* 36 (Autumn).

Gill, Stephen. 1992. 'The Emerging World Order and European Change', in Ralph Miliband and Leo Panitch (eds), *New World Order? Socialist Register 1992*. London: Merlin.

Gotell, Lise and Janine Brodie. 1991. 'Women and Parties: More than an Issue of Numbers', in Hugh Thorburn (ed.), *Party Politics in Canada* (6th edition). Toronto: Prentice-Hall.

Haraway, Donna. 1991. *Simians, Cyborgs and Women: The Reinvention of Nature*. New York: Routledge.

Harvey, David. 1989. *The Condition of Postmodernity*. London: Basil Blackwell.

Jenson, Jane. 1990. 'Representations in Crisis: The Roots of Canada's Permeable Fordism.' *Canadian Journal of Political Science* 23: 4 (December).

Jessop, Bob. 1993. 'Toward a Schumpeterian Workfare State? Preliminary Remarks on Post-Fordist Political Economy.' *Studies in Political Economy* 40 (Spring).

Leger, Nuguette and Judy Rebick. 1993. *The NAC Voters' Guide*. Hull: National Action Committe on the Status of Women.

Lipietz, Alain. 1987. *Mirages and Miracles*. London: Verso Books.

McDowell, Linda and Rosemary Pringle (eds). 1992. *Defining Women: Social Institutions and Gender Divisions*. London: Polity Press.

McQuaig, Linda. 1992. 'The Fraying of Our Social Safety Net.' *Toronto Star* (8 November).

Maroney, Heather Jon and Meg Luxton (eds). 1987. *Feminism and Political Economy: Women's Work, Women's Struggles*. Toronto: Methuen.

National Forum on Family Security. 1993. *Family Security in Insecure Times*. Ottawa: Canadian Council on Social Development Publications.

Nicholson, Linda. 1992. 'Feminist Theory: The Private and the Public', in McDowell and Pringle (eds).

Panitch, Leo. 1993. 'Globalization, States and the Left: Nafta Through the Looking Glass.' Paper presented to 'El Mundo Actual: Situacion y Alternatives'. Mexico City (December).

Pateman, Carol. 1988. *The Sexual Contract*. Stanford: Stanford University Press.

Pateman, Carol. 1992. 'The Patriarchal Welfare State', in McDowell and Pringle (eds).

Phillips, Anne. 1991. *Engendering Democracy*. Pittsburgh: Pennsylvania State University Press.

Phillips, Susan (ed.). 1993. *How Ottawa Spends, 1993–94: A More Democratic Canada*. Ottawa: Carleton University Press.

Pierson, Ruth Roach, Marjorie Griffin Cohen, Paula Bourne and Philinda Masters. 1993. *Canadian Women's Issues, Volume 1: Strong Voices*. Toronto: James Lorimer.

Soja, Edward. 1989. *Postmodern Geographies*. London: Verso Books.

Ursel, Jane. 1992. *Private Lives, Public Policy: 100 Years of State Intervention in the Family*. Toronto: Women's Press.

Walzer, Michael. 1984. 'Liberalism and the Art of Separation.' *Political Theory* 12 (August).

Watson, Sophie (ed.). 1990 *Playing the State: Australian Feminist Interventions*. London: Verso.

Watson, Sophie. (1990). 'The State of Play: An Introduction', in Watson (ed.).

Woman to Woman. 1993. *Changing Economies: Free Trade and the Global Agenda*. Toronto: Global Strategies.

Yeatman, Anna. 1990. *Bureaucrats, Technocrats, Femocrats: Essays on the Contemporary Australian State*. Sydney: Allen and Unwin.

York, Geoffrey. 1993. 'Social Programs Called Outdated.' *Globe and Mail*, 17 November.

Young, Iris Marion. 1989. 'Polity and Group Difference: A Critique of Universal Citizenship.' *Ethics* 99.

Young, Iris Marion. 1990. *Throwing Like A Girl and Other Essays in Feminist Philosophy and Social Theory*. Bloomington: Indiana Press.

18

DEMOCRACY AND THE FUTURE OF NATIONS
Challenges for disadvantaged women and minorities
Marjorie Griffin Cohen

SINGLE MARKET WITH MULTIPLE STATES

The major question of this volume is whether nation-states have a future. There is no doubt that nations will have a future, but the characteristics of nation-states will undoubtedly change. Whether or not these political entities remain states as well as nations will depend on how much each can retain of its own self-determination; some will succeed at this more than others.[1] The imperatives of new international trade agreements provide the impetus for the proliferation of minimalist states whose major function for the international regime will be to control their own people to ensure that they conform to international trade rules. This role for the state coincides with the other functions of the state associated with Reagan and Thatcherite neo-liberal policies, functions which do not go much beyond the administration of justice and, most importantly, the protection of property. Even the traditional justifications for state formation, which in Canada involved moving the mail and national defence, are being gradually abandoned.

The objective of this chapter is to show how the ways in which the free trade agreements Canada has recently entered into will negatively affect equality-seeking groups' democratic options.[2] The situation in Canada is not unique, but it can be instructive for other countries because Canada has experienced the consequences of trade liberalization for a longer time than have most other countries.

Just as women and other disadvantaged groups have begun to understand the ways in which they might be influential in redistributing power, the locus of power has changed and, once again, these people are excluded. So, as women, aboriginals and people from ethnic minorities gain seats in Parliament, are appointed to various courts and are more visible in public forums, these bodies become less and less responsible for the decisions which shape the boundaries for economic and social existence. Just as these groups begin

399

to understand how to manoeuvre and be effective within a nation, the nation itself loses its effectiveness and the target for political action is nebulous.

The equality granting and redistributive aspects of modern 'democracy' have been elusive, but there has, nevertheless, been more power accorded to traditionally disadvantaged groups in recent years. This power has been recognized through public discourse which has had a subtle effect on changing the collective subconscious in thinking about rights. However qualified one must always be in making claims for success, there does seem to be a recognition publicly that women and minorities should not be excluded from democratic organization. While these groups are still denied formal power, they have managed to assert themselves frequently enough to be granted some type of recognition as political actors.[3] And however critical these groups have been of the state and its actions, they none the less understand the significance of collective action for being able to effect redistributive activities through social policy. That is, there is a recognition of the necessity to use political power to bring about a social order which would not occur without state intervention.[4] This activity is guided by objectives and goals which do not coincide with the objectives of profit-maximization on the market. My contention is that these equality seeking groups will have considerably fewer avenues for influencing social policy under the new free trade agreements and that the redistributive features which now exist will contract with the withering of nation-state power and the absence of supranational institutions capable of enacting redistributive social policy.

Two important changes in the relationship between the state and economic activity have occurred with the new trade agreements, and both severely limit the ability of social policy to temper, or modify, the actions of international capital. First, through the FTA and NAFTA, a single market has been created which places corporate behaviour in the advantageous position of being beyond the regulatory control of a single state. As has been frequently noted by free trade critics, these trading agreements grant unprecedented rights to corporations with the main aim being the facilitation of capital mobility. At the international level, there are new institutions of governance, but the scope of these institutions is limited to market-supporting activities: they deal primarily with issues relating to ensuring capital mobility.[5] So unlike the nation-state, which over time has developed institutions (through social policy) to temper the harshest consequences of the 'free market', in the international context of the FTA and NAFTA there is no institutional mechanism through which this can occur. We are then left with a single market without a single state to discipline it.

Second, the institutions to balance or control market power remain at the national level, but ultimately with much less power than they had when the market and the state occupied one space, i.e. within a nation. The limits of nation-state power over market activity in these circumstances are in some way obvious. As nations compete for the favours of capital, the ability to exert any type of discipline over corporate behaviour comes into direct conflict with the increased mobility of capital. Unless all nations, party to an agreement, behave in the same way with regard to corporate discipline, the corporations will not be disciplined at all. Any one nation, by acting on its own, will be disadvantaged by behaving in a stricter way. Since there is no mechanism for the nations to act collectively, individual state action is critically weakened. But this new advantage for capital is not only generated through the market mechanism itself. Equally important are the measures which are explicitly expressed in the trade agreements which place strict limits on the future development of social policy within nations. These are measures which specifically circumscribe state action while at the same time create greater freedom for the private sector.

TRADE AGREEMENT LIMITS ON SOCIAL POLICY

The limits imposed on social policy by the trade agreements undermine the redistributive goals of disadvantaged groups. While the objectives and practices of the welfare state have often been in conflict with the objectives of equality-seeking groups, the very existence of mechanisms to collectively provide services did, in many cases, provide the very tools which were necessary to facilitate the politics of redistribution. It is a mistake to think that because the welfare state retained many of the features of the patriarchal state that it has not been critical to the development of democratic participation for disadvantaged groups. It is also a mistake to hope that the equality-seeking activity it engendered can survive and can be re-adapted to fit other state forms, particularly ones with even more market-oriented structures. As the very strength of national and sub-national governments is eroded through trade agreements, the location for political action for equality-seeking groups evaporates and so, too, does the possibility for democratic participation for disadvantaged groups.

Supremacy of free trade in Canada

The Canada–US Free Trade Agreement was enacted in Canada in a way which set this legislation above all other laws in Canada, including legislation enacted in the past, as well as that which governments may wish to enact in the future. So all Canadian legislation has to conform to the requirements of a trade deal. The US legislation implementing free trade did not elevate this law above all others. For them, it was just another piece of trade legislation which could be constrained by other American laws.

The supremacy of this law has profound implications for Canada as a nation-state. While the media, business and government tend to focus on regulatory aspects of trade in the free trade agreements, these laws are about

401

much more than trade. They are primarily about establishing what constitutes appropriate economic and social activity to support a specific idea about how an economy should function. The implications of this are significant because it establishes one method of economic and social development as supreme, what we commonly know as the 'unfettered market'. This means that the kinds of debates that have occurred in Canada about the function of the economic system, and the concomitant distinctions which have fostered political parties with different goals and methods of achieving them, will be extinguished. No longer will there be much point to arguing, for example, whether the public or private sector would be a superior vehicle for certain types of action or whether supply management is the best way to deal with agricultural problems. All the crucial debates on these issues will be removed from decision-making at the national level and will be argued (if at all) through the supranational agencies set up by the agreements. As ideological issues are removed from national politics, the homogenization of political parties will be secured, the substantive debates about the ideas of how the country should proceed will vanish and more and more elections will be fought over political trivia.

The criticism of free trade in Canada has tended to focus on how the economic regulations will constrain government from acting on behalf of people's economic interests.[6] Many of the ways which Canada has organized its economy are distinct and reflect the ways in which its people have had to deal with unique conditions. The list of Canadian practices which must change to meet new international trade requirements is huge: to accommodate NAFTA alone, twenty-seven major pieces of legislation needed to be amended totalling 4,300 pages of text. All of this occurred without public scrutiny of legislative changes.[7] The problem now is that many of the things which made sense in the context of life in this country are seen as inappropriate ways of behaving and become illegal if trade is to continue.[8] These economic consequences have been explained often and will not be dealt with in this chapter, although they are undoubtedly important in limiting democratic decision-making.

NAFTA and the public sector

NAFTA is distinct from other trade agreements in that it goes much further in securing the rights of capital than does any other trade document and significantly reduces the ability of nation-states to use the public sector for redistributive action. This last feature ultimately may be the most significant in curtailing democratic decision-making within nations. The new requirements for the public sector, while unique in NAFTA and going much further than anything ever attempted in any trade agreement, are an extension of the logic of the ideology of the 'unfettered market' and are likely to be precedent-setting elements for new trade agreements in the future.[9]

NAFTA is an economic document in which the characteristics of the private sector are treated as the norm while public institutions are treated as anomalies. This anomalous position is reflected in the language of the document: anything in the public sector is referred to as a 'non-conforming measure'.[10] The underlying assumption of NAFTA is that the less government, the better, although certain kinds of activities are specifically named as functions which no nation can be prevented from providing, as long as the way in which this is done is consistent with the provisions of the agreement. These include functions such as 'law enforcement, correctional services, income security or insurance, social security or insurance, social welfare, public education, public training, health and child care'.[11] Because public institutions are affected throughout this complex agreement, it will take some time to fully understand all of the implications of providing these services in ways which are 'not inconsistent' with the agreement.[12] Nevertheless, there are certain ways in which the public sector is required to behave which are startling departures from any previous treatment in a trade agreement. The most notable is the requirement that commercial objectives be the principle under which government monopolies perform their functions. The departure from current practice is remarkable because it requires that public programmes be re-shaped to reflect a commercial approach to service provision.

The agreement specifically requires that 'any government monopoly' (this is the term for any state-run programme) must act 'solely in accordance with commercial considerations in its purchase or sale of the monopoly good or service in the relevant market, including with regard to price, quality, availability, marketability, transportation and other terms and conditions of purchase of sale'.[13] 'In accordance with commercial considerations' is defined as behaviour which is 'consistent with normal business practices of privately-held enterprises in the relevant business or industry'.[14] This provision constrains any public corporation, or agency, from acting as an agent of government economic or social policy which is inconsistent with profit-maximizing behaviour, a requirement which ultimately undermines the logic of public institutions themselves, i.e. that they provide goods and services in a way which the private sector cannot or would not.[15]

This NAFTA chapter dealing with state enterprises and monopolies purports to include all competition policy; however, the contrast between the treatment of public and private monopoly action could not be more distinct. The first two paragraphs under the Competition Law dealing with the private sector, talk about the importance of co-operation between the parties to enforce competition law in the free trade area, but this amounts to nothing more than consulting 'from time to time about the effectiveness of measures undertaken by each Party'.[16] While the anti-competitive market activities of the public sector are proscribed, those of the private sector are merely suggested: this section specifically states that NAFTA cannot be used to pursue a dispute with regard to private anti-competition action.[17] The contrast in treatment between the public and private highlights the distinction between the NAFTA institutions which are created to support private market activity and institutions which are absent with regard to its regulation.

The privatization ratchet

NAFTA permits existing public institutions to continue, but it will be extremely difficult, if not impossible, for new public programmes to be established. Technically, instituting new programmes is permissible and the agreement provides exemptions for future 'non-conforming measures' to various programmes which otherwise would be in contravention of national treatment and other types of requirements.[18] However, initiating a new programme would be virtually impossible because of hurdles, unprecedented in international trade agreements which the FTA and NAFTA have established to place the public sector's action under scrutiny. NAFTA includes a series of clauses (replicating those which exist in the FTA) which would place the new programme in a position of being scrutinized by trading partners and if any of the partners' corporate interests are threatened, could be ultimately prohibited from being instituted. Before any new programme begins, the trade agreements require that written notification to trading partners must be given. Then any international business interests that would be affected would have recourse to seek redress through dispute settlement granted in an annex on Nullification and Impairment.[19] As in the FTA, NAFTA requires that any shift in activity from the private to the public sector would require the payment of compensation for all losses to the private sector.[20] This would make the cost of any new programme in Canada prohibitive, considering the extent of US corporate involvement in the Canadian economy. Any government in the future that wanted to establish, for example, a national disabilities scheme or a dental programme, would have to pay out huge sums to international insurance providers. This provision in the FTA has already had the effect of prohibiting the Ontario government under the New Democratic Party from carrying through on its election promise to provide public auto insurance in that province. The auto insurers, who largely represented US corporations, demanded either compensation, which would have made the public programme absurdly expensive, or withdrawal of this action. The Ontario government decided to withdraw its proposal after considerable pressure from the US. This compensation requirement would not share the same impact in the US as it does in Canada because Canadian service providers are virtually non-existent in the US market, while US service providers occupy considerable space in Canada.

The FTA was the first international trade agreement to provide a comprehensive treatment of cross-border trade in services and this has been extended to NAFTA. This gives international service providers the right of establishment and the right of national treatment, something which used to be applied only to trade in goods. The right of establishment gives a corporation the right to operate in the country without having to adhere to specific performance requirements. The right of national treatment does not require that a firm actually be located in the country to bid on service contracts or to conduct any type of business on a 'non-discriminatory' basis. As in the FTA, this feature of NAFTA greatly expands the scope of cross-border trade in services since any service firm need not invest in either a physical presence or local employment in order to be able to sell services in the Canadian market.[21] In the past, the limits of technology restricted service provision to firms located in a specific area, but since space is no longer a barrier to many types of service provision, this right of national treatment in services increases the competition for private sector providers. But even more importantly, it greatly enhances the stakes for international service providers to make incursions into the public sector's provision of services and to challenge any new programmes which could restrict the private market for service delivery.

There is some illusion of protection for existing public services from the cross-border trade in services in that normal activities in the public sector are allowed to continue, but they can do so as long as they are performed 'in a manner which is not inconsistent' with the agreement.[22] But even should the commercial rules which now govern services be met, there are still limits to what can be legitimately part of the public sector. Everything at the federal level which is to be exempt from the agreement's understanding of what will be covered in cross-border trade in services has been specifically listed in an annex to the agreement.[23] Governments at the provincial and state levels have until January 1996 to list all of their regulations or legislation to be exempt from cross-border rules.[24] Anything that is not explicitly named will fall into the 'open for transnational competition' category or it must be amended to conform to NAFTA requirements. As any trade negotiator knows, listing exemptions in this way limits protection: something crucial could be overlooked, or even more importantly a new need may arise in the future. Also, there is the possibility that a local or provincial government may deliberately exclude programmes it wants to privatize. Because of the nature of the trade agreements, most specifically the enormous difficulty of moving anything from the private to the public arena, these programmes could not be re-instituted by another government in the future.

All of these measures, with regard to services, produce what some commentators refer to as a 'ratchet-effect', a mechanism that allows government action to move in one direction (towards privatization) and never to reverse. In other words, an initially protected government service can become more open to transnational bidding, but government is prevented from moving it back to the protected category. It is important to realize that this does not apply only to whole programmes that are privatized, but to any part of public services that are contracted out as well. Once a service has been opened up to tendering and given out, then a decision to bring this service 'in-house' would be subject to the same challenge as a new programme. The practical implications of this are enormous, particularly in times of economic restraint when many aspects of government services are being privatized as ways of dealing with government debt. If this privatization turns out to be less advantageous than expected, there will be no turning back to previous conditions. Privatization involves much more than shifting something from the public to the private sector; rather, it involves a whole transformation of the activity.[25] The shift from collective to individual responsibility for services changes their very character and the nature of their delivery. The result is less a redistributive system than one which 'targets' benefits: only those who can afford help will have access to the private sector and only those who are perceived as the 'deserving poor' can expect benefits from the state.

Democracy and the state in Canada

These new constraints on the actions of the public sector and the restrictions on initiating expansive types of social institutions can be made effective through two different routes. Governments could be forced to comply through direct challenge by way of the trade disputes settlement mechanisms. But matters would likely only get to this stage should a government (most likely a provincial or state government) directly want to challenge the right of the federal government to make laws over its jurisdiction. This would have been possible, for example, in Ontario's dilemma over auto insurance. However, few states or provinces will have the stamina required to proceed with this type of challenge. Rather, self-censorship will be the most likely route for enforcement of the new controls over state action. Because the political élites currently in power essentially concur with the notion that the less state the better, they will have little taste for the effort it would take to stand up to these provisions. As a result, no public exposure will occur to dramatize the ways in which the free trade agreements impinge on the ability of the public sector to meet its obligations to people. Any programme will be simply presented as 'too costly', without proper explanation of why it will cost too much, which is exactly what happened when Ontario withdrew its proposal for public auto insurance. The trade agreements, as originators of restrictions on social policy, recede from view.

The kinds of policies which are in place now were put there through a democratic process, however imperfect. Whenever anyone wanted to change these practices, usually some kind of public debate needed to take place and Parliament was forced to deal with the interests of various people who would be affected by the changes. Now, economic and social policy can be challenged through international trade law. These are laws that are interpreted and enforced by people on a plethora of supranational panels who are not elected and who do not have to respond to people, since individuals within a country have no access to them. The public can neither influence them nor can it determine who will hold these positions. Whenever decisions are made that people cannot influence, democratic rights are in jeopardy. As more and more is occurring in the international arena, where the public have no advocates and no representatives, people's ability to influence their own conditions is diminished.

The shift in relationship between the state and the economic system as a result of the free trade agreements is changing the very concept of citizenship. Citizenship for individuals has been restricted to nations at the same time that world citizenship has been awarded and confined to corporations. With citizenship for individuals limited to nations, corporations then become the only citizens with full rights of mobility, participation and representation. Some attempts are being made by public sector groups to make the various supranational panels established by the FTA and NAFTA more accessible. A US group, Public Citizen, in its brief to the United States Trade Representative on NAFTA's implementing procedures, called for open meetings and open records of decisions for all NAFTA-related committees and working groups.[26] This has not occurred, and the public has no ability to present its position on issues or even to have access to records so that the reasoning behind various positions, or indeed, even how the various cases were argued, can be understood. The secrecy of the supranational decision-making groups violates fundamental democratic rights for citizens.

Women, minorities and the disadvantaged are confronting a very nasty political reality: this is the experience of even less democratic participation than in the past. These groups will not have less formal participation in government bodies because it is probable that this form of representation will increase as it did in the last federal election in Canada, but real decision-making power will continue to elude these groups even if political struggles, which give the illusion that genuine power struggles are occurring, persist. Probably the best example of this is the feminist campaign against the Canadian constitutional changes proposed through the Charlottetown Accord. (This Accord was one in a series of attempts to bring Quebec into the Canadian Constitution.) One of the major reasons women's groups rejected this Accord was because it would destroy the federal system of providing and initiating social programmes and would shift the Canadian social system more towards the US model. Women's groups felt strongly that the ability of the federal government to deal with social issues was crucial for redistributive initiatives nationally. On this issue women, through the National Action Committee on the Status of Women, were critical to the debate. The rational and impassioned arguments which were presented had considerable public influence, especially for the progressive people of this country who had been inclined to go along with the Accord because it had been supported by all the provinces, all three political parties, business and labour. But women could, and did, give thoughtful people reasons to vote against it.

The intent here is not to imply that this action was misguided or ineffectual

– equality-seeking groups must respond whenever their rights are threatened and usually are not in a position to pick their issues. My point, rather, is that activities like this can be overwhelmed by the conditions of the trade deals. There can be an illusion of effectiveness on national issues when in reality the issues themselves are superseded in international forums. In this case, the privatization of social programmes, which was perceived as a likely outcome of the decentralization of powers through the Charlottetown Accord, is propelled forward by the trade deals. When the over-arching legislation, which affects social policy, is the various forms of free trade agreements, efforts to influence legislation at the national level will ultimately require more effort than the results will justify. The future is very likely to generate a state which, surprisingly, considering its past resistance, will be increasingly tolerant of minority rights under formal manifestations of democracy. Even radical departures from past experience, such as self-rule for aboriginal peoples, could emerge in the near future. But this will occur only because these formal rights are not perceived as a real threat to international competition, and the most significant areas of power for any group will be contained by the requirements of formal trade agreements.

THE FUTURE: IS A CHANGE IN THE TRAJECTORY POSSIBLE?

There are possibilities in the future for the role of the state as a protector of different interests of people throughout the world, but states which assume this role will do so only through intense pressure from the people within them. Only through a true democratization of the state itself so that it reflects its people's will can there be any hope for the development of social policy which can exert any discipline on the market at the international level. The likelihood of this happening in Canada appears remote now. This is not because people have acquiesced to the future which has been mapped out by its governments and business leaders. In Canada, the protests against the FTA and NAFTA had the effect of making people acquainted with the problems of free trade, but they were ineffectual in being able either to stop the agreements or change their most damaging aspects even though the majority have been opposed to them. When political rights are whittled away bit by bit, and when the structures of control are so removed from visibility as they have been through these trade agreements, the possibilities for the dramatic kinds of political action which would be necessary to change the trajectory of the global markets evaporate. For many in Canada, it is difficult to see what the options are now and how the might of international corporations could be harnessed. Our most persistent dilemma is that it does not seem to make much sense to continue to argue for national sovereignty when the state itself does not respond to popular sovereignty.

The implementation of NAFTA and the signing of the GATT are not the end of a process. The signing of the agreement was not done with public support and it continues to receive little support. We, in Canada, may be forced to learn to live with free trade, but for a good portion of the world the confrontation is just beginning. Trade liberalization is identified with colonialism, for good reason. Therefore, it is not surprising that poorer countries are experiencing considerable opposition to it. In October 1993, more than half a million farmers staged a day-long rally in Bangalore, India, in what was the largest public display anywhere in the world against the new proposals for the ordering of world production through the General Agreement on Tariffs and Trade. Earlier in the year, 1,000 farmers had broken into the main office of Cargill in Bangalore and made a bonfire of its office documents. In March, 200,000 farmers staged a demonstration in Delhi and in July farmers burned down a Cargill seed plant under construction.[27] On NAFTA's inauguration date, 1 January 1994, peasants in the state of Chiapas, Mexico, seized a city and three towns through armed conflict which resulted in over a hundred people dead. They were protesting against NAFTA, which they characterized as 'the death certificate for the indigenous people of Mexico'.[28] Since then, the collapse of the peso and the dramatic decrease in real incomes have made the trade agreement's threat to the survival of some even more pressing.

The strongest protests against the new trade agreements are about food, for very good reasons: the poorest people on this earth lose everything when they lose their ability to feed themselves.[29] The new trade agreements designed rules to benefit the highly capital- and energy-intensive agricultural industries in countries where its production, at most, involved only single-digit proportions of the labour force. These rules are devastating for countries where huge proportions of the population rely on farming for their subsistence. Intellectual property rights and agricultural subsidies mean very different things for people whose average life span is twenty years less than that in the industrial world and whose incomes are one-twentieth of those of people in industrialized nations. These international trade agreements are immensely long, complicated documents with many intricate details and will take years for those of us who study them to understand the implications of all of their ramifications. But the poor people of this world, many of whom are illiterate, understand what it means when they can no longer rely on the state to protect them from the encroachment of industrialized agriculture and when they will have to pay these huge companies royalties simply to plant the seeds they have saved from previous harvests. For those critics in industrialized countries who have objected to the principles of the new trade agreements, it is a way of life, a standard of living, sovereignty and democratic integrity which is threatened. For the people of countries like India and Mexico it is more fundamental: a report on the GATT prepared by a panel of judges in India described India's acquiescence to the new trade rules as 'an abdication by the State in respect of its obligations to protect the people's right to life'.[30]

The protests of these people may be a political avenue for change and a rallying point for nations which can afford neither to withdraw from the international trade agreements nor to abide by their rules. Certainly, in this round of GATT, the poor countries did not mobilize to see that their interests were protected. But since together they account for about 30 per cent of world trade, any collective move by developing countries could be effective.

The targets for political activity for people in wealthy countries are more nebulous and so far have tended to take two predominant forms. The first focuses on abuses of human rights in other countries and calls on the extension of universal human rights principles through trade pressures.[31] Through this approach, increased trade is presented as a positive force in the humanizing of dictatorial regimes. Even the uprising in Chiapas has been presented as an occurrence which, because of trade, has gained world attention and, as a result, can bring about changes to these injustices. The undemocratic features of poor countries become the target for action rather than the limits on democracy in wealthy ones which are a result of the new trade agreements. Trade and democracy are interrelated, as is often claimed, but not necessarily with the happy consequences that the supporters of trade liberalization assert. It is the traditional élites in poor countries which engage in trade liberalization who are the beneficiaries, not most people.

This is related to, but is distinct from, the second approach, which is the continued pressure from groups within wealthier countries for international standards on labour and the environment. The target here, as well, is conditions in poor countries, only in this case it is corporate behaviour in poor countries which receives attention. The supplemental agreements in NAFTA on these issues in no way can be considered international standards because they merely require the enforcement of existing laws within each country. The agreements on labour and the environment do not represent any type of supranational institution-building in order to standardize the controls on international business. The substance of each country's domestic law is not affected by these supplemental agreements. But even the meagre requirements to enforce each country's own laws have met with resistance from business groups. In the discussion of the proposed procedures for implementing the labour side accord, US trade associations objected to public hearings as being a part of the process because they are 'too confrontational' and, in particular, did not want any companies party to a complaint named in any public record.[32]

The supplemental agreements on labour and the environment in NAFTA are ineffective and the best hope, as expressed by many environmentalists and trade unionists, is to view these supplemental agreements as stepping-stones for more substantial international regulations in the future. The models most often cited for this are the kinds of social policies which have been associated with the European Community's economic unification. There is much about this approach which gives hope to social activists who see an urgent need both for some focus for international popular sector groups in working together and as a logical way to place international markets under political control.

410

But as much as one can have sympathy with these objectives, this route will not bring about the kinds of institutions which are necessary to deal with the major power shift which has occurred with free trade.

First, the likelihood of achieving anything like the European agreement with social issues in North America is remote, primarily because of the extreme disparity between economic and social levels in the countries party to NAFTA. And these disparities are likely to be accentuated as other Latin American, and possibly Asian, countries become part of the agreements. Any kind of code of conduct for transnational corporations would run up against the very logic of capital mobility. There is no doubt that these corporations behave less honourably in poor countries than in wealthy. But it is also true that in many places it is the international corporations which provide better wages and working conditions than do indigenous ones. Any code of conduct, were it to be universally applied to rich and poor countries, would have the effect of eliminating disadvantaged countries from international competition.

Even more significant than the political difficulties associated with a unified social policy among wildly disparate nations is the question about the effectiveness of the goal. Wolfgang Streeck has made the important point that whatever has occurred in the European Community is not a step towards a European welfare state and the political control of markets. He argues that the few changes which have resulted in 'harmonizing up' have been exceptional occurrences which will not continue simply because the institutions have not been established to make market discipline legally binding on all partners. Since the Social Charter is not binding, it has 'no consequences for social policy and industrial relations at the national level' and, therefore, is not a building block for the development of international institutions to provide state-like control over capital.[33] Nation-states, in juxtaposition to international corporations, are slow to develop social institutions to humanize the most brutal aspects of 'restructuring'. This approach, the piece-by-piece building of supranational social policy from extremely modest beginnings, is much too long term to be effective in the immediate face of the FTA, NAFTA and GATT.

This does not mean that nothing can be done, but that the solution has much less to do with proscribing behaviour with regard to labour and the environment than in permitting different economic policies and forms of economic and social organization to exist within nation-states. Since uniformity in these issues is the heart of the free trade agreements, there can be no way in which poor countries can compete internationally if they must both abide by the employment and environmental standards of wealthy countries and maintain the same neo-liberal systems without any ways of circumventing the impossible through collective, public policies. The real task for the future is to find ways to democratize nations so that they, on behalf of people, can insist on tolerance for variation in social and economic policy between nations.

BIBLIOGRAPHY

Brodie, Janine. 1994. 'Politics on the Boundaries: Restructuring and the Canadian Women's Movement.' Eighth Annual Robarts Lecture, York University.

Calvert, John. 1993. *Pandora's Box: Corporate Power, Free Trade and Canadian Education*. Toronto: Our Schools, Our Selves.

Cameron, Duncan (ed.) 1988. *The Free Trade Deal*. Toronto: Lorimer.

Canada, External Affairs. 1987. *The Canada–U.S. Free Trade Agreement*. Ottawa.

Canadian Center for Policy Alternatives. 1992. *Which Way for the Americas: Analysis of NAFTA Proposals and the Impact on Canada*. Ottawa: CCPA.

Marjorie Griffin Cohen. 1987. *Free Trade the Future of Women's Work: Manufacturing and Service Industries*. Toronto: Garamond.

Drache, Daniel and M.S. Gertler, (eds). 1991. *The New Era of Global Competition: State Policy and Market Power*. Montreal and Kingston: McGill-Queen's Press.

Dillon, John. 1993. *Intellectual Property Rights in NAFTA: Implications for Health Care and Industrial Policy in Ontario*. Toronto: ECEJ.

Grinspun, Ricardo and Maxwell A. Cameron, (eds). 1993. *The Political Economy of North American Free Trade*. Montreal and Kingston: McGill-Queen's Press.

Lang, Tim and Colin Hines. 1993. *The New Protectionism: Protecting the Future Against Free Trade*. New York: The New Press.

Laxer, James. 1993 *False God: How the Globalization Myth has Impoverished Canada*. Toronto: Lester.

The North American Free Trade Agreement (Including supplemental agreements) 1994. USA: CCH.

Robinson, Ian. 1993. *North American Trade as if Democracy Mattered: What's Wrong with NAFTA and What are the Alternatives?* Ottawa and Washington: Canadian Center for Policy Alternatives and the International Labor Rights Education and Research Fund.

Sinclair, Scott. 1993. "NAFTA and U.S. Trade Policy: Implications for Canada and Mexico," in Grinspun and Cameron, eds., *The Political Economy of North American Free Trade*.

Stanford, Jim, Christine Elwell, Scott, Sinclair 1993. *Social Dumping Under North American Free Trade*. Ottawa: Canadian Center for Policy Alternatives.

Streeck, Wolfgang. 1993 "From Market-Making to State-Building? Reflections on the Political Economy of European Social Policy," paper presented at the 89th Annual Meeting of the American Sociological Association, August.

Taylor, Charles. 1993. *Reconciling the Solitudes: Essays on Canadian Federalism and Nationalism*. Montreal and Kingston: McGill-Queen's University Press.

NOTES

1 For a discussion of how nations become states, see Charles Taylor, 'Why Do Nations Have to Become States?', in *Reconciling the Solitudes: Essays on Canadian Federalism and Nationalism* (Montreal and Kingston: McGill–Queen's University Press, 1993), pp. 40–58.

2 These are the Canada–US Free Trade Agreement (FTA) which went into effect on 1 January 1989, and the North American Free Trade Agreement (NAFTA) which went into effect 1 January 1994.

3 I am thinking of organizations in Canada like the National Action Committee on the Status of Women and the Assembly of First Nations who have established that they are legitimate advocates for the rights of women and aboriginal peoples and have held crucial roles in constitutional decisions.

4 The very essence of social policy is 'to supersede, supplement or modify operations

of the economic system in order to achieve results which the economic system would not achieve on its own' (T. H. Marshall, as cited by Wolfgang Streeck, 'From Market-Making to State-Building? Reflections on the Political Economy of European Social Policy'. Paper presented at the 89th Annual Meeting of the American Sociological Association, August 1993).

5 The exceptions to this in the NAFTA agreement are the agencies established to deal with the labour and environmental supplemental agreements. But these supplemental agreements merely require the enforcement of existing laws within each nation so do not represent new constraints on market action at the international level.

6 Ian Robinson has written a particularly interesting monograph on the constraints of state regulatory powers under free trade in *North American Trade as if Democracy Mattered: What's Wrong with NAFTA and What are the Alternatives?* (Ottawa and Washington: Canadian Center for Policy Alternatives and the International Labor Rights Education and Research Fund, 1993).

7 In contrast to normal consultative procedures for major pieces of legislative changes, the enabling legislation for NAFTA did not involve hearings outside Ottawa and an exceptionally short time limit was set on the debates in Parliament.

8 So, for example, while it made sense for us to ration our use of resources by requiring that a certain proportion of them be used in this country to make things here, this kind of behaviour is not allowed under GATT, the FTA and NAFTA. We can no longer require that a certain proportion of our fish or minerals actually be processed in Canada. Other things deemed unfair are our wheat pools, the transportation system which takes grain from the prairies to the coast, our supply management agricultural systems and many regional development programmes. The intellectual property provisions in the agreements affect our culture and the ability to provide protection from the monopoly control of life forms by large international corporations.

9 The precedence of the FTA was significant for US negotiations in the Uruguay Round of GATT, particularly with regard to the successful inclusion of services and intellectual property rights. For a further discussion of this, see Marjorie Griffin Cohen, *Free Trade and the Future of Women's Work: Manufacturing and Service Industries* (Toronto: Garamond, 1988), ch. 2.

10 NAFTA, Ch. 11, Article 1108: 1(a).

11 NAFTA, Ch. 11, Article 1101: 4.

12 The provision of public services is affected in various chapters throughout the agreement, including chapters of Investment (11), Competition Policy, Monopolies and State Enterprises (15), Intellectual Property (6), Cross-Border Trade in Services (12), Telecommunications (13), Financial Services (14).

13 NAFTA, Ch. 15, Article 1502: 3(b).

14 NAFTA, Ch. 15, Article 1505.

15 For example, it will affect the use in Canada of having public Crown Corporations achieve non-commercial goals such as the conservation of resources or economic development in specific regions. If equality goals for either individuals or regions counter what is perceived as proper 'commercial considerations', they could be challenged. Likewise, any employment enhancement schemes initiated and financed by government corporations (should any government in the future want to pursue a full-employment policy) would almost certainly be considered beyond 'commercial considerations'. Other types of government initiatives could be challenged such as public investment funds. These now exist in the province of Quebec and are viewed with interest elsewhere because of the impact they have had on stimulating investment in that province. No new fund could have goals which (a) focused on regional development; (b) favoured nationally or provincially based business and (c) promoted local employment as the currently established funds do.

16 NAFTA, Ch. 15, Article 1501.
17 NAFTA, Ch. 15, Article 1501: 3.
18 The reservations for future measures are stated in NAFTA, Annex II.
19 NAFTA, Ch. 20, Article 2004.
20 FTA, Ch. 16, Article 1605; NAFTA, Ch. 11, Article 1110.
21 FTA, Ch. 14, Article 1402: 8; NAFTA, Ch. 12, Article 1205.
22 This repeats the permission for public services that was granted in Ch. 11 on investment. Ch. 12 on Cross-Border Trade in Services (Article 1201: 3(d)) says 'Nothing in this chapter shall be construed to prevent a Party from providing a service or performing a function, such as law enforcement, correctional services, income security or insurance, social security or insurance, social welfare, public education, public training, health and child care, in a manner that is not inconsistent with this chapter.'
23 Ch. 12, Article 1206: 2. For a list of existing practices which Canada has deemed exempt from cross-border trade rules, see NAFTA, Annex I.
24 Financial services were treated differently and each province had to list 'any existing non-conforming measure' at the provincial level by the date NAFTA went into force. This was a haphazard process and few provinces had a clear notion of what the implications of this would be, something which, in fact, turned out to be fairly complex. Often just deciding what to identify as needing exemption was a highly political decision. For example, in British Columbia (BC), the province had to decide whether to try to have health insurance exempted from financial services requirements. If health services were named in this instance, it would mean that BC acknowledged that NAFTA had jurisdiction in this area and it would need to argue for an exemption. On the other hand, it had the option of claiming that exemption was not necessary because this issue was not something appropriate to financial services. Oddly, forty-four US states had an additional year to figure out what non-conforming financial measures they wanted to maintain (NAFTA, Ch. 14, Article 1409: 1).
25 As Janine Brodie says, they 'become differently encoded, constructed and regulated'. *Politics on the Boundaries: Restructuring and the Canadian Women's Movement*, Eighth Annual Robarts Lecture, York University, North York, Ontario, March 1994.
26 'Consumer Advocacy Group Appeals for Democratic NAFTA Procedures', *Inside NAFTA* 1: 2, 26 January 1994, p. 13.
27 Martin Khor, *Third World Network Features*, 1 November 1993.
28 'Death Toll Rises in Mexico Battle', *Toronto Star*, 3 January 1994.
29 The popular sector, even in some wealthy countries, recognizes the dangers of threats to food production. For example, the women's movement in Japan has demonstrated in favour of higher rice prices in order to support farmers' protests against imported cheap rice. Of course, in the Western press this is depicted as a ridiculous political action, but these women understand the relationship between domestic economic security and food production.
30 'Former Judges Warn Against Dunkel Package', *Indian Express*, Kochi, 16 December 1993.
31 See, for example, Edward Broadbent, 'Human Rights Under Siege from Tyranny of World Trade', *Toronto Star*, 26 April 1994.
32 'U.S. NAFTA Labor Rules too Focused on Disputes, Trade Groups Say', *Inside NAFTA* 1: 4, 23 February 1994, p. 6.
33 Streeck, op. cit. Streeck points out that the final version of the Social Charter is weaker than the existing ILO conventions and the European Social Charter passed in 1961 by the Council of Europe.

19

IS A STRONG NATIONAL ECONOMY A UTOPIAN GOAL AT THE END OF THE TWENTIETH CENTURY?

Manfred Bienefeld

INTRODUCTION

Today's received wisdom contends that strong nation-states are happily things of the past; that technological progress and improved human understanding are making it increasingly difficult to maintain barriers between nations; and that these changes will enhance global efficiency and reduce the scope for international conflict. Globalization is treated as beneficial and inevitable, demands for national sovereignty are dismissed as misguided and foolish. From this point of view, strong nation-states cannot even qualify as a Utopian goal since that implies a desirable but unattainable objective. A goal considered both undesirable and unattainable can only appear stupid or perverse, and those pursuing it, ignorant or dishonest. It is thus no easy task to argue for the desirability of sovereign nation-states at the end of the twentieth century.

And yet, the task becomes a little easier as globalization and economic liberalization promote social and economic polarization, political instability, economic insecurity, persistent unemployment and a dangerous erosion of trust in political and economic institutions. After fifteen years of neo-liberal shock treatment, the world economy remains stalled, awaiting the promised benefits while struggling to cope with the 'transitional' costs. In this world, old certainties are dying but, although 'something is clearly amiss', there is, as yet, little consensus regarding possible solutions, or even desirable responses.

At heart, these developments reflect an increasing lack of congruence between the economic, political and social dimensions of reality. The generic nation-state appears as a necessary, and ultimately feasible, response to this imminent crisis because it is defined as a political entity that has the ability to manage its national economy in accordance with a set of socially rooted and politically legitimated values and priorities. Such a generic definition of the nation-state does not restrict the discussion to 'actually existing' states

415

bequeathed to us by history, but allows for the emergence of new states as a result of the division or amalgamation of existing ones. Moreover, although this definition implies that such nation-states would restore a degree of congruence between social, economic and political dimensions of reality, it tells us nothing about the political basis on which that is achieved. The truth is that such congruence is only a necessary, but not a sufficient, condition for the creation of stable, coherent societies able to manage their internal conflicts, their external relations and the natural environment that is both their home and their prison.

This chapter is composed of eight parts. The Introduction is followed by a brief summary of Robert Reich's liberal version of the mainstream's view of globalization, as presented in his book *The Work of Nations*. That summary identifies five critical assumptions on which this argument rests, and each of these is examined in turn in the next five sections. The eighth and final section presents some brief conclusions.

The reader will discover that the choice before us is therefore not one between strong national economies, or a global economy in which national sovereignty is reduced to a minimum, but between a world of nation-states strong enough to combine economic prosperity, liberal democracy, social stability and responsible environmental management, or one of weak and unstable nations, incapable of responding to the demands of their citizens or of managing their exposure to a hostile, volatile and irrational international economy. Ironically, the weakness and instability of these latter states will undermine even their economic efficiency, so that globalization will not even deliver on that promise. That is why the end of history will remain the futile dream of a global élite desperately trying to persuade itself, and others, that its powers and privileges are secure for ever.

If demands for a restoration of national sovereignty continue to be met with utter hostility so long as they take moderate social democratic, or democratic socialist, forms, these demands will eventually reappear in the more strident and intransigent forms of fascism, religious fundamentalism or even revolutionary communism.[1] Unfortunately, the militancy of these responses makes it relatively easy for those committed to globalization to demonize the perpetrators and to persuade the public of the need for massive and even indiscriminate forms of retaliation. In the pursuit of the ridiculous illusion that globalization can be established by means of laser bombs, nuclear threats and cynical subversion, these witless tyrants will usher in a dark, barbaric age. Indeed, a recent, much discussed article in *Atlantic Monthly* has even announced the 'inevitability' of just such a barbaric world.[2] But there is nothing inevitable about this outcome and those who are bringing it about must understand that they will eventually be held accountable.

The generic nation-state is treated in this chapter as an essential mechanism for the management of complex societies. Few debates generate so much heat and so little light as the centuries-old dispute about the merits of nationalism.[3]

Judgements by philosophers and social scientists range from suggestions that it is the root of all evil, to claims that it embodies and gives expression to humanity's finest sentiments and highest social aspirations. This is partly because judgements are derived from widely differing premises, and partly because so much diversity lurks inside the concept of nationalism. In fact, both judgements can be defended, as post-modernists might delight in reminding us, except that they are wrong in thinking that the absence of absolute truth dooms the search for understanding to futility. The equation of knowledge with absolute truth is a tragic, if persistent, delusion. As Bertrand Russell reminded us, education (or, in this case, analysis) is 'a process of becoming confused at a higher level'.[4]

Two interrelated aspects of the nation-state are of central importance to this discussion: the first is its role as an ideologically unifying force which provides individuals with a sense of identity strong enough to lead them to accept the responsibilities and burdens associated with a genuine commitment to the welfare of their fellow citizens; the second is its role as an instrument of social and economic management, required to achieve some ethically and politically defensible balance between the multiple and often conflicting objectives of its citizens. Moreover, these two facets of the nation-state are jointly determined. No proposition regarding either can be evaluated (or understood) in abstraction from the other. Successful economic management both requires, and reinforces, the acceptance of a strong mutuality of interests. And, over an extended period, neither can thrive without the other.

THE ALLEGED INEVITABILITY OF OUR GLOBAL FUTURE

The argument presented in this chapter challenges a widely held position that was succinctly summarized by Robert Reich in his 1992 book *The Work of Nations*.[5] It suggests: that the disintegration of national economies must be accepted by governments and electorates as a fact of life, even though it may condemn the majority of citizens to chronic economic insecurity and gradual immiserization; that globalization provides a secure foundation for the success and prosperity currently enjoyed by a minority of citizens due to their skills or, more often, their ownership or control of capital and knowledge; and that attempts to resist or reverse globalization are politically futile and economically undesirable.

Reich emphasizes the dramatic erosion of national economic sovereignty that has occurred over the past twenty years and declares this transformation to be irreversible. He suggests that these developments have made a mockery of the idea that 'citizens are in the same large boat, called the national economy ... bound together, if not by the threat of a foreign predator, then at least by a common economic fate'.

417

As almost every factor of production – money, technology, factories, and equipment – moves effortlessly across borders, the very idea of an American economy is becoming meaningless, as are the notions of an American corporation, American capital, American products, and American technology.

In such a world national economic policy has become irrelevant, as have concepts like national investment or national competitiveness. The only 'national policies' that still make sense are those designed 'to increase the potential value of what . . . citizens can add to the global economy, by enhancing their skills and capacities and by improving their means of linking those skills and capacities to the world market'. Moreover, such policies have become especially important in the United States because only 'a small portion of America's workers' have been able to ride the global train to prosperity; 'the majority' have been 'losing out in global competition'.

Reich accepts that this process of national disintegration was given a strong boost by the demise of the communist 'threat', which had served to impose a certain distorted sense of common purpose on American (and Western) society. In its absence

America may simply explode into a microcosm of the entire world. It will contain some of the world's richest people and some of the world's poorest, speaking innumerable languages, owing many allegiances, celebrating many different ideals. These individuals will be efficiently connected to the rest of the globe – both economically and culturally – but not necessarily to one another. Our collective identity will fade. There will be no national purpose, and no pretence of one.

Even this extreme scenario is treated as if it was compatible with a business-as-usual world in which growth and prosperity would continue to improve the living standards of the fortunate few. Echoing the timeless line that 'freedom's just another word for nothin' left to lose', Reich suggests that 'this is not an altogether grim picture', since

In contrast to most inhabitants of the planet, who still live in nations that impose on them substantial responsibilities for the well-being of their compatriots, the people who live within the borders of the United states will inhabit a kind of free, universal zone . . . There will be no sense of community. Instead, Americans will secede into smaller enclaves of people with similar incomes, similar values and interests, similar ethnic identities.

Although Reich accepts that 'there is also something terribly sad about this fate', the reason he believes this to be so is that 'it robs America of a moral authority . . . derived from its unique confluence of tolerance and fairness', not because it is a vision of a morally bankrupt, dysfunctional society that would ultimately serve no one's interests. In any case, those familiar with America's labour history, its race relations, its extreme inequality, its deplorable social conditions and its continuing support of brutal and cynical subversion in countries like Nicaragua, Angola and Afghanistan, will find Reich's belief that America still serves as a beacon of 'tolerance and fairness' somewhat strange, and a little pathetic.

Within this context, Reich defines the central challenge facing America as: 'whether there is still enough concern about American society to elicit sacrifices from us all' on a scale sufficient to finance a training effort to 'help the majority regain the ground it has lost and fully participate in the new global economy'. Unfortunately, in the absence of an external threat, he considers it 'far from clear . . . whether it is possible to rediscover our identity, and our mutual responsibility' on the necessary scale. And, despite his repeated appeals to the rich minority's charitable instincts, Reich's analysis will do nothing to change this state of affairs.

In fact, despite his apparent concern for the fate of the declining majority, Reich's argument ultimately provides the privileged minority with a perfect rationale for a unilateral declaration of independence by treating its rejection of the 'burden' of social responsibility as inevitable and rational, in the sense that it would not undermine its own future prospects.[6] And these prospects are depicted in extremely idyllic terms, giving rise to visions of endless rounds of golf with like-minded people after endless, exhilarating hours of commodity futures trading from the communications room in the Malibu mansion. The decline of the majority hardly appears to play a role in this scenario, except as an issue to exercise the comfortable élite's charitable instincts or its vestigial concern for 'America's moral authority'. The thought that the majority might not accept such a 'deal' and might give expression to its opposition through a democratic process hardly enters the discussion, presumably because the destruction of sovereignty has reduced democracy to an empty charade. Given such a vision, it is hardly surprising that Reich doubts the possibility of rebuilding the nation's sense of shared mutual obligation. The lack of outrage or urgency in his delivery of this devastating message to his fellow citizens anticipates the militant complacency this argument could be expected to trigger among the global élite.

Fortunately, the author's epitaph for the old view of the world applies more forcefully to his own. 'This vision's clarity and soothing comprehensibility are its only virtues. The problem with this picture is that it is wrong.'[7] It is wrong in presenting the globalization process as inevitable and irreversible; it is wrong in implying that the successful minority can enjoy real success in a polarizing and unstable world; it is wrong in assuming that a world of five billion disconnected individuals could remain a stable source of markets, profits and royalties; it is wrong in suggesting that 'better training' could rescue the majority from decline; and it is wrong in accepting the mainstream's claim that all attempts to tamper with the liberalization of trade or capital flows would necessarily 'substantially diminish our standard of living'![8] In addition to being wrong, the argument is also normatively unacceptable, because it is incompatible with such basic principles of justice and fairness as equality of opportunity or in the democratic right to determine the shape of one's society.

This is not to deny that formidable obstacles stand in the way of any attempt to reverse the process of globalization, nor that these obstacles are growing by the day. But this process will eventually be overwhelmed by the resulting social, political and economic contradictions. And the longer it is left to run its course, the more disruptive, painful and unpredictable will be the eventual political reactions. And that a reversal will only occur once enough people have understood it is true, long-term implications including the limited success awaiting the fortunate minority and the enormity of the disaster facing the marginalized majority whose future will be firmly tied to the futile hope that flexible wages and working conditions would eventually allow global full employment to arrest the open-ended deterioration of its living standards and its working conditions.

To gain a better understanding of the true promise of globalization, we shall examine each of the five key assumptions on which Reich and the mainstream optimists rest their case. None turns out to be defensible or plausible, let alone likely. But in order for globalization to succeed, all five would have to be true. Alternative policies must therefore be considered, even if they are potentially painful and do not appear immediately implementable. In this way we must free ourselves from the tyranny of the claim that 'there is no alternative'.

IS THE DECLINE OF NATIONAL ECONOMIC SOVEREIGNTY IRREVERSIBLE?

The claim that the nation-state's decline is an irreversible result of exogenous, technological changes is as ubiquitous as it is implausible. In debate it serves as a fail-safe mechanism, to be activated if people cannot be persuaded to espouse globalization out of self-interest. In that case, they are told they must accept it because it is inevitable. This second-best argument is frequently used in discussions of financial deregulation, both because the promised benefits are so difficult to demonstrate and because technological developments have created such significant problems for national regulators. But the argument does not hold water. The emergence of electronic data transfers can no more justify financial deregulation than the invention of the hand gun can justify the legalization of murder, even though both do make law enforcement more difficult.

The primary driving force behind the liberalization of the world's financial markets is political, not technological. The motive force has been the opportunity to amass untold fortunes through the creation of mountains of credit – and debt – as people discovered in the 1970s when this became possible 'in a wonderful country called Offshore . . . where there were no rules at all, because there was no country'.[9] Technology was the excuse used to justify the excesses. How else could one explain that some of the world's most successful economies were slow to liberalize their financial markets and still regulate them extensively and effectively today?[10] Or that the World Bank frequently advises countries to liberalize financial markets gradually to avoid speculative destabilization, thereby implying that the degree of regulation is a matter of policy choice?[11] Or that almost everyone agrees that global financial regulation is both necessary and feasible, even though it assumes that transactions can be monitored at a sub-global (or 'national') level in the first instance?

The implausibility of such a crude technological determinism has led many to argue that the real reason for the irreversibility of financial liberalization is the threat of retaliation, in the form of capital flight or sanctions imposed by trading partners or multilateral institutions. This third-best argument is used even more reluctantly since it highlights the political coercion that lies at the heart of the New World Order. Enforcement costs would surely be far lower if global capitalism could be established as a hegemonic ideology capable of persuading people to accept globalization as a boon or an inevitable, historic challenge.[12]

Focusing on the threat of retaliation as the driving force behind globalization soon leads to the realization that those who so frequently proclaim the inevitability of globalization clearly do not believe it to be so. Otherwise they would not expend so much effort creating mechanisms to sanction those who will not be persuaded. Chief among these has been the conditionality associated with IMF/World Bank policy lending, which has forced beleaguered and distressed developing countries to accept radical economic liberalization programmes by using the leverage conferred on those who control access to credit by the debt crisis.[13] Other recently established reinforcing mechanisms include agreements like the Canada–US Free Trade Agreement and the North American Free Trade Agreement, in which the implicit threat of trade sanctions was used to 'negotiate' highly restrictive agreements with client governments. And, most recently, the successful completion of the GATT's Uruguay Round has transformed that organization into a much more proactive, rule enforcement agency with jurisdiction in new and highly controversial 'trade related areas' like investment, services and intellectual property rights. In the words of one prescient critic, anticipating the possibility of such an agreement:

The powers and position of TNCs would be enhanced, the sovereign space of countries would be reduced and the process of transnationalisation of the world economy (and of the Third World) would be carried forward to an extent where it would not be easily reversible. It will divide the world between the 'knowledge-rich' and 'knowledge-poor', with the latter permanently blocked from acquiring the knowledge and capacity to be rich ... In economic and social terms, Third World countries and their peoples could be said to be on the point of being rolled back to the colonial era.[14]

The unavoidable conclusion must be that globalization is not a technological or historical necessity, but a politically driven process whose apparent irreversibility stems from the fact that its gains have been increasingly institutionalized and protected by new international rules and regulations that threaten deviants with instant, collective retaliation. But the dykes cannot resist the rising tide of discontent. The rules of the Holy Roman Empire also once appeared irreversible. And internationalization was widely declared irreversible by the end of the 1920s. But now, as then, its reversal is actually inevitable because it is socially, politically, economically and environmentally unsustainable.

CAN THE 'FORTUNATE FEW' LOOK FORWARD TO A ROSY FUTURE?

What future awaits the fortunate minority currently riding the global recession to prosperity – or even to fabulous wealth. Will it grow into a majority? How precarious are its gains? Will its material gains be offset by large losses on other fronts? Can it keep the competitive struggle from extending beyond the limits of the law so that corporate competition takes on the trappings now associated with organized crime?

Reich's vision of a 'Malibu forever' future for this group is foolishly naïve. Indeed, a more realistic assessment reveals that, of the associated risks, many members of this group would undoubtedly choose to make do with a somewhat lower personal income in return for the ability to live in diverse, peaceful communities capable of catering to their universal human need for mutuality.[15]

The very existence of communities with the stability and cohesion to fulfil such needs is threatened when the competitive struggle for cost minimization is detached from a social and political framework capable of setting limits to its operation. Such limits may be ethically determined, or they may embody tradeoffs between efficiency (narrowly defined) and other objectives like political stability, social cohesion, full employment, economic security or environmental protection. And sovereign, generic nation-states constitute the political and economic entities within which meaningful political processes can give effective expression to such choices and create the space for the existence of such communities. In their absence the unlimited search for efficiency will preclude such possibilities and condemn even the global élite to a meagre and barren existence.

To understand why this is so, it is necessary to reject the crude but prevalent assumption that increased material wealth necessarily increases happiness by increasing the freedom to choose. Until the social conditions and the working conditions required to achieve any given level of material wealth are specified, no such conclusion can be drawn. As Stephen Marglin has reminded us,

> We torture language when we say our young people 'choose' to join one or another of the authoritarian or destructive cults that abound. Many of them seem to be searching, however desperately, for the community and family that our single-minded attention to GNP has helped to destroy. In short, rather than expanding the domain of choice uniformly, growth expands choice in some dimensions but restricts it in others.[16]

Consideration of this fundamental point reveals that Reich's glowing account of the rosy future awaiting America's members of the global élite neglects many implicit costs of its success. Although he does acknowledge that 'the peace of mind potentially offered by platoons of security guards, state-of-the-art alarm systems, and a multitude of prisons is limited',[17] this is no more than a brief aside which appears to have no bearing on his ultimate judgement that this minority's future is one to be envied.

In fact, even if this élite were to remove itself to some fortified, remote island, it would soon discover that crime and social polarization were not its only problems. It would discover that its own prosperity depends on stable and growing mass markets; that peace of mind is hard to achieve under the shadow of permanent and extreme economic insecurity emanating from a distant, unpredictable global market; and that the poisonous individualism by which it lives would reduce its island retreat into a fractious, unstable collection of isolated individuals enmeshed in endless law suits and seeking solace in alcohol and 'coke'. Given the horrible conditions prevailing 'outside' and the absence of any apparent alternative, people would undoubtedly learn to appreciate their lives within these ghettos; to restrict their travel to approved, 'secure' places; to pretend the chronic poverty and instability outside had nothing to do with them; and to 'love' economic insecurity as proof of their status as 'real entrepreneurs'. But this does not mean they would have chosen this life over one with a lower income, but in stable, peaceful communities of economically secure citizens free to devote time and energy to family and community.

Globalization restricts choice by disempowering the national political processes through which people were able to express such preferences relatively effectively for a quarter century after the Second World War. The resulting loss of control and the dilution of citizenship is deeply felt and much deplored even by members of the global élite, but their concerns remain muted so long as they continue to believe that a 'recovery' is just around the corner, or that the return of some modest growth and profitability can be termed a 'recovery' even when it creates no jobs and is made possible only by reductions in the social wage and a neglect of infrastructure. Only when they realize that a 'jobless recovery' is no recovery at all, will the limits of political possibility once again begin to expand. The new political possibilities that will emerge in this context will all appear nationalist in some sense because their common denominator will be the demand for a greater degree of sovereign control over the destructive processes now shaping people's lives.

The proliferation of such demands is an inevitable outcome of globalization. And the political form in which these demands will ultimately succeed will largely depend on the kind of resistance they meet. The stronger and more intransigent that resistance, the more likely will be the emergence of intolerant, militaristic, fascist states because the extreme cohesion needed to survive in such a world can only be forged in the hellish furnaces of ethnic revanchism, religious fundamentalism or Stalinist communism. That is what will emerge if market extremists are allowed to continue to implement ideological policies that punish and ostracize all efforts to rebuild moderate, sovereign economies capable of responding to the needs and demands of their citizens. Examples abound, but Russia may turn out to be the most eloquent reminder of the dangers of ideological extremism because

> by demanding draconian economic changes, by giving full unconditional support to the Yeltsin team and by ostracizing the previous Parliament – thereby contributing to the collapse of the political centre – the Clinton Administration (along with the international financial institutions) has contributed to the Zhirinovsky phenomenon ... Ironically, what the West predicted would happen without Yeltsin – that is, the rise of a nationalist-Communist movement – has happened because of him ... The boosters of shock therapy should be chastened by what they have wrought. In the future they must pay more attention to the virtues of stability and consensus.[18]

Of course, the market extremists will not see it that way. They will press on, blaming some local factor (maybe an alleged lack of entrepreneurship) for the failure of their policies, but this merely confirms the ideological nature of their policy prescriptions. Policy has to be judged by its results in the real world, not by its conformity with textbook models.[19]

Both the threatening proliferation of extremisms around the world, and the apparent inability of the hegemonic powers to deal with them, is increasing the unease felt by many members of the global élite. One must hope that this will lead to the abandonment of neo-liberal extremism and of the policy prescriptions that are creating the conditions giving rise to these desperate political reactions. One must pray – and struggle – to ensure that a further hardening of the brain cells does not lead the hegemonic powers to respond to these developments simply by escalating repression and reinforcing their demands for economic liberalization, thereby combining 'smart bombs' with stupid and self-defeating policies.

Apart from these ominous political threats there are also purely economic reasons why the global élite cannot simply project its good fortune into a blissful future. The markets to which its fortunes are tied will become increasingly unstable, oligopolistic and lost in a legal limbo of conflicting jurisdictions. In such a world, the value of its skills (and assets) will be constantly threatened, not merely by rapid technical change but also by the fact that more and more income will be earned as rent deriving from the contested ownership and control of physical and financial assets, market access, information or intellectual property rights. The resulting claims and counterclaims will become more opaque and uncertain as law enforcement is undermined by the blurring of jurisdictional boundaries, a loss of moral authority and the paralysis of law enforcement agencies caught between the millstones of increasing lawlessness and declining resources. Here too, Eastern Europe may turn out to be the model of our future.

In a globalizing world, the future will come to resemble the distant past, as law and contract enforcement are privatized either by design or by default.[20] While almost all economists may agree that contract enforcement is a fundamental responsibility of the state, many do not seem to realize that this is possible (at reasonable cost) only in societies in which the state has enough moral authority, resources and political legitimacy to ensure that its citizens have enough respect for the law to stay within its prescribed limits most of the time and that those who do not are very likely to be prosecuted and punished. But these conditions will not be met in a world in which citizenship is treated as an irrelevance. And global regulation is not an answer to this problem since global regulators would face the same constraints in an even more acute form. Indeed, international regulation is only conceivable in a world in which secure and cohesive nation-states could co-ordinate their regulatory activities, confident of their ability to ensure compliance within their own borders. Just as such nation-states must rely on communities, municipal governments and the organizations of civil society to bridge the enormous distance between the citizen and the modern state.

WILL THE GLOBAL ECONOMY KEEP PAYING (THE) RENT?

The third assumption underpinning Reich's version of the mainstream argument is that globalization will continue to generate the markets, profits and rents that are the basis of the fortunate minority's prosperity. Indeed, mainstream economists never tire of repeating that more economic liberalization will always add further to the global cornucopia. But such universal predictions are derived from ideology dressed up as theory, not from history, evidence or science.

In fact, excessively unregulated markets tend to be unstable and to overshoot targets. The resulting fluctuations misallocate resources and can give rise to protracted and dangerous crises as past errors have to be rectified or reversed.[21] The optimists contend that such fluctuations will tend to be mild and self-correcting, but history confirms the real possibility of major disruptions leading to protracted periods of economic stagnation in which the contradictions generated in one period stifle growth and investment in the next, imposing massive economic costs on society as a result of un-employment, idle capacity and the destruction of past investments through bankruptcies and failures. This was the tragedy of the 1930s and it is the main reason why the global economy cannot return to stable, full employment growth in the 1990s.[22]

Sovereign states are necessary, though not sufficient, mechanisms for managing and containing the dangerous centrifugal tendencies of markets by curbing the speculative tendencies of credit-based economies, by allocating the subsequent costs in a fair and ultimately efficient manner between various actors and by ensuring that the severe competitive pressures associated with the ensuing economic crises do not lead economic actors to transgress certain socially and ethically defined limits. Since these functions are inherently political and since they have to deal with disequilibrium situations in which markets are totally unreliable, they must be performed by sovereign states that have both the legitimacy and the power to act in the public interest.

This judgement is shared by leading neo-classical theorists and occasionally even by the international financial institutions. Thus, Frank Hahn of Cambridge University, writing in the early stages of the Thatcher revolution, warned that neo-liberal 'advocates say much more than even pure theory allows them to say, and infinitely more than the applicability of that theory permits'.[23] Even neo-classical theory clearly shows that markets cannot achieve rational or defensible outcomes if they are not supplemented by social and political mechanisms capable of performing certain critical functions.

> If the invisible hand is to operate there must be sufficient opportunities for . . . contingent intertemporal trade . . . The lack of contingent markets means that the market economy is associated with more uncertainty than pure theory allows. The lack of intertemporal markets means that great weight must rest on market expectations. The Rational Expectations hypothesis substitutes an internal and psychic hand for the market. Each individual somehow has learned how the invisible [hand] would have performed if it had been given markets within which to perform. If it is agreed that this is not of high descriptive merit, there is, in fact, no obvious mechanism by which intertemporal decisions can be co-ordinated. This was Keynes's view. I have yet to see it refuted. The French drew the conclusion that they at least required indicative planning. The Japanese have for a long time employed non-market

426

institutions to supplement private investment decisions. In Germany, the banks seem to act as market substitutes. In Britain, where politicians now follow gurus rather than arguments we are all set to rely on the invisible hand doing a job which, in practice, it will not and cannot do.[24]

That is also why there can be no single, unified global economy. Mechanisms to 'co-ordinate intertemporal decisions' at the global level would be unworkable both because of the scale of the problem and because they would lack the necessary political legitimacy in the absence of a meaningful global political process. And that, in turn, is why

it was not simply 'capitalist production' which historically demonstrated its relative superiority in the competitive struggle. It was 'capitalism, as organised in an effective, modern nation-state', which must claim this distinction. The qualification is most important.[25]

More recently, Professor Krugman has reinforced the message that markets need a significant degree of regulation to function efficiently. After assessing the empirical evidence pertaining to the performance of deregulated international currency and asset markets, his conclusions contrast sharply with the endless claims that market liberalization will yield substantial benefits at little risk. In fact, the evidence shows that

at this point, belief in the efficiency of the foreign exchange market is a matter of pure faith; there is not a shred of positive evidence that the market is efficient, and . . . similar results obtain for other asset markets . . . that is, both the bond and the stock market . . . The bottom line is that there is no positive evidence in favour of efficient markets, and if anything a presumption from the data that [these] markets are not efficient . . . The important conclusion . . . is that we are freed from Friedman's . . . argument . . . that an efficient market could not exhibit destabilizing speculation . . . Now we know that in fact no evidence supports this hypothesis – that it is one maintained purely on faith.[26]

This is a devastating conclusion for those who have placed such blind faith in globalization, especially since there is no way of dealing with these global risks without first restoring the effectiveness of national financial regulation. The World Bank indirectly confirmed Krugman's judgement in its 1989 *World Development Report* where it suggested that the international lending spree of the 1970s, which triggered the debt crisis of the 1980s, constitutes evidence 'that competitive financial markets . . . can still make mistakes'.[27] Unfortunately, this breathtaking admission came ten years too late and did not induce the Bank to explain why the costs of those mistakes had been so one-sidedly imposed on the poor developing countries who were forced to repay these debts in full despite the often devastating social and economic impact of this demand. It is hard to imagine a better example of the potential inequity of a situation in which those allocating the costs of such mistakes are not subject to the discipline of a political process that represents all the parties involved in the rectification of such errors.

Concern over the impact of global financial deregulation on the real global economy continues to grow. Even the World Bank has warned that 'market-based financial systems can be unstable and susceptible to fraud';[28] the IMF has noted that financial liberalization 'may ... result in destabilizing and inefficient capital market speculation';[29] *The Economist* has reminded us that 'even under floating exchange rates, great volatility in capital flows – and hence in exchange rates – does harm';[30] and the chairman of a large Canadian insurance company greeted a government proposal 'to globalize the financial services sector' with a warning that this 'could weaken Canada's financial sector' and a reminder that 'the problem with a very liberal regulatory regime is that it is an invitation to get yourself into trouble'.[31]

As these problems are more widely acknowledged, things held to be impossible yesterday are deemed possible today. This need not yet make them likely, but it should remind us that the limits of the politically possible change over time. Presently, concern about the nationality of capital appears to be creeping back onto the agenda. Thus, in late 1992, *The Economist* concluded that the turmoil of the international financial markets had reached such a level that 'increasingly, the case for a return to (explicit or implicit) restrictions on capital flows is likely to be put, on both sides of the Atlantic'.[32]

Even the possibility of a major disruption of the world economy on the scale of the 1930s depression is no longer ruled out. A World Economy Survey published by *The Economist* in 1992 began by suggesting that the 1980s had witnessed a 'decisive change' in the world economy as 'many of the boundaries between national financial markets dissolved'. The resulting 'trend towards financial integration ... makes exchange rates ever more volatile, harder to control, more disruptive of economic policy-making and ever more of a nuisance to companies that trade and invest across borders'. By 1992 'financial dread' was said to be 'the mood of the moment', and this extended even to the possibility of a full-fledged depression. Thus,

> The changes in international finance of recent years have not made ... a crisis any less likely. In some ways, quite the reverse ... Just as the new international dimension of finance has added to some risks that may help to start a crisis – greater instability in currencies, faster transmission of economic disturbances across borders, new opportunities for leverage, increased susceptibility to the illusion of liquidity and so on – so it has also weakened (or anyway complicated) the traditional remedies of economic policy. In the new world of finance, the seas are rougher and the life-rafts flimsier.[33]

The glib assumption that globalization will increase overall prosperity and growth is therefore untenable. In fact, it is far more likely to yield to instability, conflict and polarization ultimately leading to stagnation and decline. Even the global élite will find its privileges threatened in this process, which may be why some issues long declared dead or irrelevant are suddenly back under discussion.

THE TRAINING MYTH: CARGO CULT OR SMOKESCREEN?

The fourth assumption to be examined is that the fortunes of the declining majority could be restored through massive training schemes financed by the privileged minority. Four features make this claim very popular even in circles where government intervention is shunned like the plague. It blames the victims by implying that their difficulties are basically due to their personal deficiencies; it obscures the fact that competitiveness and efficiency are primarily socially, not individually, based, so that an efficient plant moved with all of its staff to a remote part of Liberia would soon cease to be competitive; it assumes that the dilution of sovereignty has so undermined the democratic power that could be wielded by the majority to make the latter dependent on the charity of the fortunate few; and, because the claim is effectively untestable, it is also irrefutable. After all, both success and failure in the global economy are purely relative, so that any given type or level of education can lead to either outcome at any time.

So can training rescue the floundering majority? As a generalized solution to the deteriorating conditions facing working people around the world, it is totally implausible. So long as labour remains globally surplus to effective demand, globalization will continue to undermine the wages, the living conditions and the working conditions of most working people.[34] Indeed, increased training will probably even reduce the size of the 'fortunate minority' and increase the size of the 'declining majority' by eliminating the relative scarcity that allows some skills still to command a relatively high wage. That is why the threat of economic insecurity and of wage and salary cuts is moving inexorably up the occupational hierarchy and into the ranks of skilled and managerial workers in many countries.

Theoretically, if the demand for labour rose fast enough (or if one simply assumed full employment!) this downward pressure on wages and working conditions would cease. But this is not very likely since globalization is not even likely to be associated with strong or stable growth in output, let alone in employment. In fact, the employment problem has recently become especially severe because the debt crisis is both inhibiting investment and forcing capital to restore (short-term) profitability by cutting employment, wages and benefits and intensifying labour across a broad front. But indebted and unemployed workers are not good customers, which is why the capital being accumulated has such difficulty finding productive investment opportunities and tends to seek refuge in speculative areas where returns are generated through asset price inflation. Far from solving the problem, this merely distorts the economy further.

Under such circumstances training cannot restore the prospects of working people in general. However, it could rescue the fortunes of specific groups of workers – such as Reich's American majority – by allowing them to capture a larger share of the world's high-wage jobs. Unfortunately, those who pin their hopes to this solution must remember that dozens of countries are presently rushing to increase their share of a limited number of relatively stagnant high-wage labour markets. The net effect is very likely to remind everyone of the experience of those producing primary commodities and simple manufactures who have faced ever lower prices as oversupply has taken its toll of rents and profits.

In any case, training must not be treated as a 'cargo cult'.[35] One cannot assume that 'if we train them, the jobs will come'. Training must be complemented by active investment in relevant infrastructure, industry and technology. Thus, a recent comprehensive review of the literature concluded that a high pay-off has been achieved only when 'investment in vocational education [has occurred] ... in those skills relevant to rapidly growing industries, and, more generally, in industrially dynamic economies'.[36] And the ability of education to reduce poverty was similarly shown to be dependent on complementary policies: 'to reduce poverty, the public sector has to invest in education, to plan balanced growth, and to manage an incomes policy that "lifts all boats"'.[37] Simply focusing on education and training is therefore unlikely to succeed.

In any case, the training mystique is rapidly losing its allure as armies of retrained or highly educated people wait in vain for the promised 'good jobs'. In Canada, where the government has strongly encouraged students to study science and engineering, a recent survey has suggested that

> corporate demand for R&D personnel in Canada will remain weak for some time to come ... because of the slow economy, cost reductions and corporate efforts to improve productivity, *there will be little or no growth in R&D employment over the next five years* ... [since] the current aim of the corporation is to achieve higher productivity with the same or already diminished number of employees (emphasis added).[38]

Faced with such evidence, one must recall that the training argument was used to overcome opposition to high-risk policies that have contributed to the destruction of the compromise on which the economic security and prosperity of the declining majority depended. Their opposition was 'bought off', in part, by the claim that their interests *could and would* be protected through increased education and training. But this turned out to be an empty promise.

The training effort never materialized because, in a world weighed down by unmanageable mountains of private and public debt, financial constraints were bound to get in the way of good intentions; because the fortunate few were never going to fund a huge national training effort out of some sense of social obligation or charity when they were so busy organizing tax revolts and diversifying their portfolios to hedge against the risk of Canadian economic decline; and because, in a world of large-scale graduate unemployment, the passion for more training was always going to wane once people realized that no one actually knew what kind of training was needed.

Worse yet, even if a big training effort had materialized it would have failed because global employment growth was so much more sluggish than expected in the shadow of the debt; because the global supply of highly skilled people is rising so fast; and because training in the absence of complementary infrastructural investment and the presence of industrial and infrastructural decline never had much of a chance. Hence, many of the Canadians who were trained for high-skill occupations in recent years have been unable even to catch a glimpse of a well-paying, permanent job that might provide the foundation for a fulfilled life as a socially engaged and responsible citizen.

IS PROTECTIONISM A UNIVERSAL BAD?

The fifth and last question concerns the claim that government intervention, especially if it takes the form of protectionism, would necessarily reduce the general standard of living. This forms the basis of the 'globalization is good for you' argument and may be the issue on which mainstream economists agree most unanimously. It rests on an almost mystical belief in free trade.

Sweeping claims on behalf of free trade are nothing more than ideological assertions reflecting the a priori assumptions of neo-classical theory. They are sometimes given the appearance of empirical evidence when models built on those same assumptions are used to generate such assertions in a quantitative form. As such, they are sometimes confused with empirical evidence when, in fact, they merely give numerical expression to the axiomatic assumptions built into those models, usually including the assumption that economic liberalization increases efficiency and growth; and that optimal outcomes as 'those outcomes produced by perfectly competitive markets'. This explains why the true believers in the economics profession seem to advocate the same solution to every problem, namely 'market liberalization'.

The moment economists step outside of this tautological world and take the real world seriously, the blanket condemnation of protection or intervention has to be abandoned. Under real-world conditions economic liberalization is not necessarily beneficial, and protection, or intervention, is not necessarily detrimental, especially if one is dealing with the long-run effects of complex policy packages. In fact, many such claims appear not even to realize that neo-classical 'trade theory provides little guidance as to the role

431

of trade policy and trade strategy in promoting growth'.[39] It only promises a one-time increase in allocative efficiency from trade liberalization.

Many empirical studies have drawn attention to the ambiguous impact of economic liberalization in the real world, especially when introduced in the presence of significant imbalances in goods, labour and financial markets. Indeed, the evidence that liberalization can increase economic instability,[40] is so strong that a technical IMF paper on the theoretical foundations of adjustment ends by warning that its standard adjustment package cannot be recommended in the presence of 'a large external debt' because this would make their impact quite unpredictable and could trigger a destabilizing vicious cycle.[41] Ironically, most of the countries forced to seek such assistance carried heavy burdens of debt when they did so.

Many other mainstream studies have reached similar conclusions, pointing out that 'liberalization may force de-industrialization',[42] or that 'when the first-best policies are either unavailable or damaging on other dimensions, a proindustry trade regime has a second-best role to play'.[43]

More generally the 'new trade theory' had shown that once oligopoly, imperfect information flows, externalities and learning effects were fully integrated into the analysis, it could be shown that significant dynamic benefits could result from apparently inefficient trade and industrial policies.[44] The rediscovery of this old truth soon showed why it had so long been ignored or relegated to a brief *caveat* in the early pages of most mainstream studies. Recognition of these possibilities opened a Pandora's Box of possibilities that reminded everyone how little economists had to say about policy choices in an imperfect, disequilibrium world such as the real world.

Many economists must, therefore, have been relieved when most new trade theorists quickly slammed the lid shut by 'discovering' that once the possibility of retaliation was integrated into the analysis the old truths about free trade could be broadly reaffirmed. With some notable exceptions,[45] they reached the conclusion that retaliation would generally negate the potential benefits of intervention. The case for free trade now appeared even stronger because it appeared to have been established not just in pure theory but in relation to the real world, with all its imperfections.

However, this only follows if one takes the international trade regime as given, since it is that regime which determines the likelihood and the extent of the retaliation to be expected in response to the use of a given policy instrument. While this is justified when a single, small nation is making short-term policy choices, it is not if one is discussing the structure of the global trade regime itself. In such a context, the new trade theory radically challenges the current consensus in favour of enforcing global economic liberalization.

In so far as the new trade theory has demonstrated that a range of interventionist policy instruments have the capacity to generate important dynamic efficiency gains, it follows that an optimal trade regime should allow and encourage economies, especially weak economies, to make maximum but co-ordinated use of such policies. And it should provide for collective sanctions against countries choosing to retaliate against their use. In sharp contrast, the current trade regime is actively eliminating the use of an ever wider range of national policy instruments by threatening users with collective retaliation. Thus, in the words of one Third World spokesman, the new GATT agreement 'will prevent the developing countries from . . . guard[ing] and serv[ing] their development interests by protecting their economies against domination by the stronger economies',[46] as well as preventing them from using many critically important policy instruments that were once used to great effect by the industrial countries in the course of their earlier development.

The weakness of the theoretical and the empirical basis of the claims made on behalf of trade liberalization is surpassed by the weakness of the broad historical claims sometimes made to support the converse claim that protectionism must be avoided at almost any cost. The two most common generalizations are: that the 1930s depression illustrates the disastrous impact of nationalism and protectionism; and that the spectacular success of the early post-war period demonstrates the enormous benefits that follow from trade liberalization. Although these crude assertions are frequently encountered, neither is tenable.

As regards the lessons of the 1930s, Karl Polanyi has provided a very different and far more persuasive interpretation in which the depression appears as the dangerous and painful, but ultimately inevitable, consequence of the 1920s, when excessive economic liberalization had generated unbearable social and political tensions in societies around the world.[47] This account does not deny or minimize the dangers or the difficulties inherent in the adjustments eventually forced upon people in the 1930s, but it leads to diametrically opposite policy conclusions. Economic liberalization appears not as a solution of the depression, but as a primary cause.

In constructing his argument, Polanyi brilliantly describes the single-minded fanaticism with which the world, under the leadership of the League of Nations, sought for many years to resolve the growing crisis by ever more radical forms of market liberalization. But these efforts, just like those of the neo-liberal crusaders of today, only increased the destructive gyrations of a rudderless global economy. They were ultimately abandoned when the resulting problems had become so overwhelming that they triggered political explosions around the world.

The lesson of the 1930s is therefore the lesson of the 1920s – namely, that the longer markets are left to function without adequate social and political management, the greater will be the eventual contradictions and the more painful and dangerous their eventual resolution. By the end of the 1920s those contradictions included a level of debt that stifled investment and led to economic stagnation and mass unemployment; a degree of economic instability that misallocated resources, heightened economic insecurity that destroyed many fundamentally sound businesses through excessive short-term fluctuations in prices, exchange rates and interest rates; and an explosion of inequality that undermined the system's moral legitimacy because rewards were delinked from effort and ever more people were threatened with destitution. The similarity of these problems to those prevailing at the end of the 1980s is no accident.

The other broad generalization claims that the great boom of the early post-war period can be ascribed primarily to economic liberalization. This is even less well founded, especially now that the deplorable results of twenty years of neo-liberalism are there for all to see. A much more plausible assessment of this period, which echoed Polanyi's interpretation of the 1930s, appeared in the *Financial Times* (London) in the wake of the 1987 stock market crash. It suggested that:

> The post-war economic system was designed by people who had endured the chaos of the 1930s. They may have erred too far on the side of controls and constraints on markets – *although it is at least arguable that the 'golden era' of trade expansion was possible only because the regime governing capital flows was so illiberal* (emphasis added).
>
> It now seems increasingly clear, however, that the reaction against government intervention and managed markets in the 1970s and early 1980s went too far. There was a pervasive retreat from responsibility.[48]

Now that this retreat from responsibility has gone so much further, this appeal is even more powerful, but a reversal will also be much more difficult to achieve. The trajectory of change continues firmly in the wrong direction, driven by the short-term financial flows that now define the limits of national economic and social policy and intimidate even those policy-makers who understand the disastrous implications of these trends but who lack the courage or the political base to act on this insight.

CONCLUSIONS

This chapter has argued that a return to stronger nation-states is not Utopian, but inevitable. The only question is what form these states will take and whether the restoration of national sovereignty can be achieved before globalization drags the world into a dark age of chaotic instability and conflict. Globalization is essentially a negative phenomenon, destroying the sovereignty and cohesion of nation-states, and thereby depriving markets of the social and political guidance without which they cannot function effectively. Since those vital management and intermediation functions cannot be performed at a global level, it will prove impossible to contain the centrifugal forces generated by unconstrained competitive markets. Such markets will not serve social or political objectives because it will prove impossible to prevent the competitive struggle for survival from transgressing all social, ethical and legal limits. The result will be socially divisive, politically destructive, ethically abhorrent and even economically inefficient. The pressure to return to some version of the generic nation-state will therefore become ever more explosive. Eventually these demands will become overwhelming, although this may take a long time and much suffering. In any event, the longer it takes, the higher the eventual costs.

The mainstream's belief that globalization will lead to desirable social, political and economic outcomes rests on five assumptions articulated by Robert Reich which have been examined and rejected. Globalization is not inevitable or irreversible; the global élite cannot look forward to steady improvements in its quality of life; a globalized economy will not remain stable or dynamic; training will not rescue the marginalized majorities from decline; and the restoration of national controls would not inevitably lead to disaster, even though, by now, substantial adjustment costs will have to be borne. Just how large these will be depends on whether those who dominate today's policy process respond to such efforts with the massive retaliation they have threatened for so long now.

But if the sovereign, secular and democratic state is worth preserving – or restoring – it is not easy to identify the forces that could provide the political impetus to lead us in this struggle back to the future. The negative, centrifugal forces are clear enough; as is the widespread revulsion from politics and from politicians; the increasing popularity of single issue movements; and the proliferation of disasters like Yugoslavia, Somalia, Haiti, Afghanistan, the Soviet Union, Liberia. Not so clear are the positive forces that could restore enough social cohesion to support a tolerant, stable world; a world in which individualism and diversity are valued, but in which individuals define themselves as responsible and caring members of society, and in which that implies their willingness to make personal sacrifices in order to contribute to the creation of a humane and caring society whose success was measured by its ability to enrich its citizens spiritually and culturally, its ability to promote harmony and well-being among its citizens, and its ability to live in harmony with other societies and the natural environment.

There is no doubt that this would be possible, given today's technologies. But much conspires against such an outcome in the world as it is now constructed. Volatile and destructive short-term economic and political pressures are powerful and hard to resist. Conflicts breed conflict and sow the seeds of enduring enmity. The current globalization and monopolization of communications poses new and difficult challenges. But, all is not lost. As contradictions deepen, new political possibilities will continue to emerge as people seek to regain some control over their lives. This provides new foundations for collective political action that must, first, define a future worth struggling for; second, restore the sovereign powers needed to build such a future; and third, develop social and political practices, build local economic networks and define value systems that will allow the forces of globalization to be managed and contained.

The fact that the limits of political possibility are shifting is increasingly evident. Who would have thought that in 1992 a long time correspondent of the *Financial Times* (London) would call for the nationalization of Britain's banks! In his own words:

> The latest analysis from the invaluable Professor Tim Congdon ... which examines the current state of British banks, savings institutions and insurance companies ... describes a catastrophe waiting to happen ... This crisis of the financial intermediaries rules out any domestic recovery for years, even assuming that it can be contained. Congdon puts the earliest date at the late 1990s. That could be optimistic. The private sector's boot-straps are broken ... There is one tried and proved remedy: bank nationalisation.[49]

No doubt the prescriptions contained in this chapter will sound general and vague to some, but this is inevitable in such turbulent times. There is no ready-made map to lead us out of the wilderness, but it is well to remember that people have met similar challenges under seemingly equally hopeless circumstances in the past; and that the events we are witnessing are neither incomprehensible, nor random. There is method in the madness. But, although the logic of the global market determines the direction of present trends, it is human agency that has created a world in which that logic is allowed to wield such excessive influence. And it will have to be human agency that rebuilds the generic nation-states that will, once again, allow competitive markets to be embedded in social and political structures capable of forcing them to function in the service of society and people.

And so, as the earth begins to move, it behoves us to have some idea of where to turn for refuge. Globalization is no destination. It is merely a scene in a drama for whose outcome we will all bear some small degree of responsibility. In responding to it, it is of the greatest importance that we should distinguish short-term expedients from long-term objectives. And that we should not throw out the baby, in the form of the generic nation-state, with the putrid bath water, in the form of the ethnic, religious or neo-liberal nationalism.

NOTES

1 This danger was nicely captured by Frank Hahn of Cambridge University, a leading neo-classical growth theorist, who warned his fundamentalist colleagues early in Mrs Thatcher's reign that the claims which they had allegedly derived from neo-classical theory went far beyond anything that theory would actually allow them to say, especially in relation to the real world. In this context, he warned that when it became evident that markets 'would not and could not' perform the functions being entrusted to them by these ideologues, the reaction

might be so fierce and angry 'that the [invisible] hand was chopped off once and for all, to all our cost'. (F. Hahn 'Reflections on the Invisible Hand', *Lloyd's Bank Review*, April 1982.)

2 Robert Kaplan (1994) 'The Coming Anarchy', *Atlantic Monthly*, February, pp. 44–76. Although the article's hard-nosed realism is chillingly persuasive within its own terms, it is also an almost grotesque example of the moral bankruptcy of those willing to accept, or advocate, 'globalization' at any cost. If these are the costs of globalization then any degree of political extremism is justified in opposing it. Those who are sagely nodding at Mr Kaplan's 'insight' and 'wisdom' had better understand this implication. And they had better also understand that under such circumstances crimes of omission will eventually come to weigh heavily in the scales of justice. To understand the world as Kaplan does and to fail to attempt to avert such an outcome is a crime by even the most diluted standards of justice.

3 The term 'nationalism' is said to have been coined only in the late 1790s, some twenty years after Adam Smith's *The Wealth of Nations* had mounted its frontal attack on mercantilism's protectionist proclivities. This will come as something of a surprise to those who regard mercantilism, protectionism and nationalism as three sides of the same coin. In fact, mercantilism was a system designed to defend the interests of monarchical states, while nationalism had a more populist meaning that tended to equate 'nation' with 'people'. The concept emerged as the old monarchical and feudal certainties retreated before the onslaught of rationalism and commerce, leaving people to redefine the basis and content of the link between the individual and society. Thus, 'it was the 1750s ... that saw new intellectual distinctions being made between the monarchical state [the government] and the nation. In 1755 an obscure [French] cleric named G. F. Coyer, condemning his more sophisticated contemporaries, began to preach that no love was so pure as that felt for the nation, and that this embraced both the state and all orders of society. Amidst the growth of French cultural nationalism ... a new political attitude, a "new patriotism", ... was coming into existence, pairing together king and the whole French people as the proper objects of patriotic feeling.' These inchoate beginnings appear to have culminated in the concept of 'nationalism' only after the French Revolution had brought these beliefs to power – and to grief – in a major nation. (G. Newman, *The Rise of English Nationalism*, London: St Martin's Press, 1987, pp. 162–3.)

4 Russell actually said: 'Education is a process of becoming confused at a higher level.' Some post-modernists might claim that this is a meaningless phrase because no absolute meaning can be given to the concept of a 'higher level'. However, such a response would merely indicate that the remark had not been understood.

5 The rather familiar arguments presented in Reich's book attracted special attention because the author was a leading liberal democrat, who has since become Secretary of Labour in the Clinton administration. It is worth noting that Clinton garnered much electoral support by voicing 'grave, but unspecified' reservations about NAFTA, and then proceeded to make its passage an overriding policy priority, achieving Congressional victory in which a Republican majority voted with a Democratic minority. (R. B. Reich, *The Work of Nations*, New York: Vintage Books, 1992.) The quotations which do not have page references are from pages 3–8, or 321–3.

6 In the terminology of an earlier age one might say that Reich envisages the emergence of a 'comprador élite' in the metropolitan centre. In so doing, Reich refocuses attention on (global) class divisions and away from national (core–periphery) conflicts. This is both important and defensible when it is viewed as a

shift in emphasis. It is not defensible if it is used to suggest that the nation is now irrelevant.

7   R. Reich, op. cit., p. 5.

8   The incredulous reader discovers this warning in the penultimate paragraph of the book. The book that began by announcing that the citizens of the world's nations were 'not in the same boat' and did not have their economic fortunes linked to national economic policies, concludes by repeating the ubiquitous warning that tampering with the liberalization of trade or markets would 'substantially diminish our standard of living, and theirs'. But who is we? (R. Reich, op. cit., p. 323.)

9   A. Smith, *The Roaring Eighties* (Toronto: Summit Books, 1988), p. 19.

10 This has been especially true of Japan and South Korea. Thus a special report on 'offshore banking in Asia', in the *Far Eastern Economic Review*, described the rapid expansion of this phenomenon in each of seven Asian countries, but concluded with a report on Japan which declared that in Japan such capital flows were still closely controlled by the government. Typically, the *Review* then denounced the 'anachronistic bureaucratic culture' that was impeding progress in Japan. It did so despite the fact that the section had begun by announcing that the entire offshore phenomenon was primarily driven by the desire to avoid taxation! *Far Eastern Economic Review*, 'Investing Offshore', 5 March 1992, pp. 29–46.

11 Obviously if one can deregulate slowly, then the degree of regulation is a matter of policy choice, not a technological given. These issues are more extensively discussed in M. A. Bienefeld, 'Financial Deregulation: Disarming the Nation State', *Studies in Political Economy*, No. 37, Spring 1992.

12 This reticence is not apparent in discussion of trade policy choices confronting particular economies, where the threat of retaliation is, quite rightly, emphasized as an important fact of life. The issue is more fully discussed in a later section dealing with the question of protectionism.

13 That this was primarily the result of coercion, and not persuasion, can be inferred from the fact that these policies were implemented most forcefully in the weaker less-developed countries. Indeed, a 1989 IMF study reminded us that 'the structural reforms now being considered in the industrial countries are relatively minor compared to [the] comprehensive stabilization-cum-liberalization programs' implemented in large parts of the developing world. (R. A. Feldman *et al.*, 'The Role of Structural Policies in Industrial Countries', *IMF Staff Studies for the World Economic Outlook*, IMF: Washington, DC, August 1989, p. 1.) For an extended discussion of the weakness of the theoretical, empirical and historical under-pinnings of the structural adjustment policies imposed on the developing world under policy lending see M. A. Bienefeld, 'The Significance of the Newly Industrialising Countries for the Development Debate', *Studies in Political Economy*, No. 25, Spring 1988, pp. 7–39; and M. A. Bienefeld, 'Structural Adjustment: Debt Collection Device or Development Policy?', *ADMP Series No. 5*, Sophia University – Institute of Comparative Culture: Tokyo, 1993.

14 C. Raghavan, *Recolonization: GATT, the Uruguay Round and the Third World* (London: Zed Books, 1990), p. 45.

15 A. Etzioni, *An Immodest Agenda: Rebuilding America Before the 21st Century* (Toronto: McGraw-Hill, 1983), p. 33.

16 S. Marglin, 'The Wealth of Nations', in *The New York Review* XXXI: 12, 19 July 1984, pp. 41–4. (A review of I. M. D. Little, *Economic Development: Theory, Policy, and International Relations*, New York: Basic Books, 1984.)

17 R. Reich, op. cit., p. 302.

18 Editorial, *The Nation*, 3/10 January, 1994, pp. 3–4.

19 The World Bank has actually described the policies that it imposed on its clients during the first decade of policy lending, as 'textbook' policies, because they took inadequate account of local social and economic realities. (World Bank, *Adjustment Lending: An Evaluation of Ten Years of Experience*, Washington, DC: World Bank, 1988, p. 66.)

20 One middle-sized town in the United States has recently announced the complete abolition of its police department as part of its budget cuts. What law enforcement remains will have to be provided by private security agents, hired by businesses, individuals or groups of residents. *The New York Times* article reporting this news noted that the decision raises the risk of endless litigation since these private law enforcement agencies have, as yet, no legal right to use force in the performance of their duties. (M. Geyelin, 'Hired Guards Assume More Police Duties as Privatization of Public Safety Spreads', *The New York Times*, 1 June 1993, p. B1.)

21 An excellent discussion of capitalist crisis is to be found in D. Harvey, *The Limits to Capital* (Oxford: Basil Blackwell, 1982). My own attempt to establish some stronger links between the Marxian concept of crisis, and the business cycle literature, can be found in M. A. Bienefeld, 'The International Context for National Development Strategies: Constraints and Opportunities in a Changing World', in M. A. Bienefeld and M. Godfrey (eds), *The Struggle for Development* (Toronto: Wiley, 1982), pp. 40–3.

22 Recently the IMF has accepted the view that the current recession was largely due to the imbalances created in the course of the 1980s and not yet 'digested'. What it did not mention was the fact that similar, or even larger imbalances, continue to be created by a global financial market whose volatility and tendency to excess has not diminished one iota since that time. Only the nature of the speculative bubbles has changed, shifting from junk bonds and real estate, to mutual funds, the stock market and the 'emerging markets', recently renamed the 'submerging markets' by some of the financial press. See IMF, *International Capital Markets II. Systemic Issues in International Finance*, World Economic Survey, August 1993, pp. 2–3.

23 F. Hahn, 'Reflections on the Invisible Hand', *Lloyd's Bank Review*, No. 142, April 1982, p. 20.

24 Ibid., p. 12.

25 M. A. Bienefeld, 'The International Context for National Development Strategies: Constraints and Opportunities in a Changing World', in M. A. Bienefeld and M. Godfrey (eds), *The Struggle for Development* (Toronto: Wiley, 1982), p. 31.

26 P. Krugman, 'The Case for Stabilizing Exchange Rates', *The Oxford Review of Economic Policy* 15: 3, Autumn 1989, pp. 65–6.

27 World Bank, *World Development Report 1989* (Washington, DC: World Bank, 1989), p. 4.

28 Ibid.

29 IMF, *Staff Studies for the World Economic Outlook* (Washington, DC: IMF, August 1989), pp. 8–9.

30 'Economics Focus: The Way We Were', *The Economist*, 3 October 1992, p. 70.

31 K. Dougherty, 'Open war feared in finance reform', *The Financial Post*, Toronto 13 November 1990.

32 'Economics Focus: The Way We Were', *The Economist*, 3 October 1992, p. 70.

33 'Peaceful Co-existence', in 'World Economy: Survey' section, *The Economist*, 19 September 1992, p. 46.

34 For a fuller discussion of this issue see M. A. Bienefeld, 'Basic Needs in the Competitive Economy', *IDS Bulletin*, Sussex (England): Institute of Development Studies (University of Sussex) 9: 4, June 1978; and M. A. Bienefeld, 'The

International Context for National Development Strategies: Constraints and Opportunities in a Changing World', in M. A. Bienefeld and M. Godfrey (eds), *The Struggle for Development* (Toronto: Wiley, 1982).

35 The term stems from several documented instances in which residents of some remote Pacific islands responded to the cessation of air traffic at the end of the Second World War by clearing 'runways' in the bush, hoping that this would bring back the planes on which they had come to depend for many things.

36 W. H. Haddad *et al.*, 'Education and Development: Evidence for New Priorities', *World Bank Discussion Paper No. 95*, Washington, DC: World Bank, 1990, p. 49.

37 Ibid., p. 15.

38 P. Hadekel, 'Future Bleak for R&D Students', *The Ottawa Citizen*, 24 December 1993, p. F1. The article summarizes the findings of a survey of the research and development spending plans of 160 companies, undertaken by the Conference Board of Canada.

39 A. O. Krueger, 'Trade Policy as an Input to Development', *American Economic Review* 70: 2, May 1980, p. 288.

40 D. Rodrik, 'How Should Adjustment Programs be Designed?', *World Development* 18: 7, July 1990.

41 IMF, 'Theoretical Aspects of the Design of Fund-Supported Adjustment Programs', *IMF: Occasional Paper No. 55*, Washington, DC: IMF, 1987, p. 55.

42 L. Taylor, *Varieties of Stabilization Experience: Towards Sensible Macroeconomics in the Third World*, WIDER Studies in Development Economics (Oxford: Clarendon Press, 1988), p. 153.

43 D. Rodrik, 'Conceptual Issues in the Design of Trade Policy for Industrialization', *World Development* 20: 3, 1992, p. 312.

44 P. Krugman, 'Scale Economies, Product Differentiation, and the Pattern of Trade', *American Economic Review*, Vol. 70, 1980, pp. 950–9.

45 Some neo-classical economists did not share this view and concluded that, even after accepting the risks of retaliation, there was still a case to be made for 'targeted, firm specific intervention' designed to strengthen specific, high-value-added parts of the manufacturing sector. In Canada this view was eloquently presented by Professor Richard Harris in a study written for the Royal Commission on the Economic Union and Development Prospects ('the McDonald Commission'). However, the Commissioners, in their wisdom, summarily dismissed this argument without refuting any of its central propositions. See R. G. Harris, *Trade, Industrial Policy and International Competition* (Toronto: University of Toronto Press, 1985).

46 J. K. Nyerere, 'Foreword' in C. Raghavan, op. cit., p. 24.

47 For a fuller discussion of this argument and of its relevance to the current crisis, see M. A. Bienefeld, 'The Lessons of History and the Developing World', *Monthly Review*, 41: 3, July–August 1989.

48 M. Prowse, 'The Message of the Markets', *Financial Times* (London), 24 October 1987, p. Weekend FT 1.

49 A. Harris, 'Time to Nationalise Private Sector Debt', *Financial Times* (London), 19 October 1992, p. 23.

INDEX

acquisitions 282, 289
Aglietta, M. 69, 85, 87
America: *see* US
American Institutionalist School 99
Asia (East): ASEAN 160; currency
162–5; inter-/intra-regional trade
158; Japanese FDI 159–60; Japanese
transplants 137–42; NICs 160, 165,
167; trade bloc 166
assembly-type manufacturing 16–17
AT&T 65
Austria 94

Bank for International Settlements 204
banking 118, 202, 307, 368
Banting, K. 262
Barro, R. 360
Bartlett, C. A. 279, 280
Basle–Nyborg Agreement 199, 200, 205
Berger, C. 383
Bhagwati, J. 49, 372
Boyer, R. 42, 85, 87, 95, 352
Braudel, F. 63, 98
Bretton Woods system 91, 164
Britain: *see* UK
Bundesbank 307, 368

CAMI (GM-Suzuki) 233–9
Canada 385–6, 394–5, 401–2, 406–8;
community economic development
336–40; company size 282–4; debt
358–9, 365–6; employment 21, 46–7,
251–6; exports 270, 276–7; FDI
283–4; foreign ownership 270, 274,
290; free trade agreements 21, 290–2,
388, 399–404; government spending
48–9; high-technology 262–3;
Japanese car transplants 227–43;

Macdonald Commission 387;
machinery industry 284–8;
multinational corporations 282–4,
289; National Forum 58 (n7); niche
strategies 287–8; public institutions
403–4; R&D 270, 272, 273, 274;
resources 270, 276, 412 (n8), 413
(n15); restructuring 387; Science
Council 290–1; stock market
investment 213; unemployment
251–2, 253, 294–5 (n37), 392; US
trade laws 284, 292; wages 46, 253–4,
255; welfare state 316–17, 390;
workers 260–2
capital flows 155; flight capital 195, 220,
421; global capitalism 68–71;
inflation 363–5; international 69–70,
82 (n16), 183–4; investment 68–71,
117, 181–4; nation-states 219;
regional blocs 158–61
capital mobility 196, 211–21, 258
capital–labour accord 33, 36, 45–7, 87
capitalism 67, 106, 328, 374–5, 427;
financial 117; global 68–71, 82 (n13);
international 299–300, 388; market
325–7; modern 300; national 68;
welfare state 316
car industry: American/Japanese
overseas production plants 140–2;
CAMI 233–9; globalization 71–2;
Honda Canada 230–5, 242–3, 246
(n4), 247 (n16); Toyota Canada
230–1, 234, 235, 239–40
Chicago Schools 98–9
citizenship: alienated 343; and
consumption 389–90, 391; in
democracy 306; globalization 423–4,
425; industrial 246 (n4); norms

441

Hart, M. 265
Hayek, F. von 108
Healey, D. 363
healthcare management 334–5, 340–2
Honda Canada 230–1, 234, 235, 242–3, 246 (n4), 247 (n16)
Horioka, C. 213–14
human resource management 149, 150, 235, 261

IMF 265, 421, 428, 439 (n22)
income support 319
incomes 18, 90–1, 322, 327; see also wage levels
India, GATT protests 409–10
industrial relations 143, 229–32; see also trade unions
inflation 363–5
information technology 130–1, 375
infrastructure 75, 346
Innis, Harold 8, 10–12, 276–7, 383, 395–6
innovation 4, 14–15, 89–90, 105–6, 130
institutions 12, 16–17, 21–2, 87–91, 270, 403–4
integration, economic 53–5, 66, 274
intellectual property rights 129
interdependency 53–4
interest rates 47–8, 214
intergovernmentalism 304–5
international credit regime 218–19
International Labour Office 264
international political economy 193
internationalization 14–15, 19–21, 63
investment 180–9; capital flows 68–71, 117, 181–4; data problems 181–2; developing countries 70–1; domestic 213–14, 215; international diversification 213; NAFTA 220; portfolio 69, 188; and production 49–51; for training 430; and unemployment 375–6
investment havens 57
Italy 20, 370–1

Japan: capital flows 69–70, 183; cultural practices 151–2, 372; development assistance 161–2; domestic investment 213; exports 176, 177–8, 179–80; FDI 159–60, 185; import securing 161; industry associations 125–6; managerial skills 132, 152; monetary and fiscal policy 134,

371–3; multinationals 64; production models 136–7, 142–3, 227–8; productivity 178; protectionism 372; R&D 120, 124–5; resource-poor 125; science organization 123–6; service sector 123; state intervention 4; technology 118–21, 123–6, 127–32; unemployment 52; welfare programmes 320–1, 323, 325; yen 155, 159, 162–5, 371–2; see also Japanese transplants
Japanese Multinational Enterprise Study Group 137
Japanese transplants 14–15, 137–42; Canada 227–43; hybridization 142–9, 150; job classification 146–9; job rotation 146; Korea/Taiwan 143–5; local content purchasing 146; union representation 146–9; US and Korea/Taiwan compared 142–9, 150
job creation 21, 74, 252–3, 357–8
job quality, Canada 252–3
jobsOntario Community Action (jOCA) 336–40
just-in-time systems 281

K-Mart state 36, 45, 53–5
kaizen 233, 241, 242, 245
Katzenstein, Peter 307
Keynes, John Maynard 8–9, 18, 33, 36, 95, 110, 363, 364
Keynesian welfare state 336, 343, 347, 348, 350, 362–5, 384, 385, 386, 393
Kim, W. C. 282
knowledge economy 349
Krugman, P. 427
Kuttner, R. 35

labour 6, 10, 328; and capital 33, 36, 45–7, 87; exploitation 263; flexibility 89; industrial relations 143; investment 260–6; job-centred/personal-skills centred 150; overtime 241–2; service quality 351; skills and training 257, 268 (n23); social contracts 45–6, 227; standardized conditions 263–4, 265–6
labour costs 7, 258–9
labour division 105, 375
labour market 17, 45, 107, 109
lean production 227–9; Canadian problems 244–5; employment norms

poverty, deserving/undeserving 391
pricing 51–2, 87–8, 97–8, 173, 364
private sector, state support 75
privatization 59 (n9), 365–6, 389–91,
    403–5
production: international 278; and
    investment 49–51; Japanese models
    136–7, 142–3, 227–8; Japanese
    transplants 143–5, 150; mass 344;
    new social relations 353–4; public
    sector 336, 354; technologies 75–6;
    see also lean production
profit-sharing schemes 89
protectionism 35, 52, 64, 372, 431–4
pseudo-markets 101
public choice theory 389
public power, fragmented 313
public spending 48–9, 316, 319, 357–8
public/private domains 353, 384–5,
    387–92

R&D 120, 124–5, 127, 130, 281–2
recession 181
reflation 364–5
regionalization 155, 167, 267 (n9)
Régulation School of Political
    Economy 5–6
Reich, R. 283, 417–20, 422–3, 435,
    437–8 (n6)
rentier class 360
repression 328
reprivatization 389–91
restructuring, politics of 37, 383–4,
    385–9, 392–5
Ricardian equivalence 360–1
Ricardo, David 360
rights, civil/political/social 300, 305,
    308, 315 (n2), 407
risk-reduction 57
Royal Commission on Market Rights
    and Tolls, UK 97
Rugman, A. 280
Ruigrok, W. 38
Russia 424

Samuelson, P. 360–1, 376 (n5)
savings 95, 213–14
Schumpeter, J. 95
security 104
self-regulation 93, 303–4, 390
semiconductors 119, 142
service sector: exports of 174, 176, 275;
    growth areas 122–3; Japan 123; job

numbers 17; privatization 59 (n9);
    quality 351
single issue movements 435
Smith, Adam 86, 97, 100, 105 *Wealth of
    Nations* 94, 105
social assistance, redefined 330, 390,
    391–2
social conditions 423
social democracy 92
social inequalities 109
social movements 20, 21–2, 328, 383, 393
social policy 34; Beveridge 33, 36, 43; post-
    cold war 326–8; Thatcher 35–6, 43–5;
    trade agreements 401–8
social standards 265, 309–11
social unrest 374
socialism 326
sovereignty 417, 420–2; Canada 408; in
    European Union 301, 302;
    fragmented 301, 308–13;
    internal/external 303, 304, 308; loss
    of 306
special interest groups 393–4
specialization, comparative advantage 36
speculation 195, 199, 359, 429–30
stagflation 362
state: administration 334–6, 344–9;
    alternative forms 344, 345, 347, 348,
    350–3; deregulation 90–1; global
    strategies 50–1; and market 1, 7–8,
    56–7, 109–10; new structure/new
    market forces 32, 34; policy
    instruments 4–7; regulatory policy
    34; spending cuts 5; support for
    private sector 75; supranational
    301–2; worker protection 256; *see
    also* nation-state; welfare state
state intervention 33; capitalism 374–5;
    education, healthcare and innovation
    86; elites 406; European 33, 36; and
    free trade 19–20; Japan 4; and market
    forces 7, 109–10; protectionism 431
Strange, S. 195
strategic alliances 72–3, 77–8, 281
Streeck, W. 411
sub-contracting 280
subsidiarity 306
Sweden 20, 92, 321, 324

tariff barriers 42–3, 156, 265
Tavlas, G. 164
taxation 48, 49, 75, 361; *see also*
    transaction tax

women, and disadvantaged groups
  399–400, 407–8
workers 256, 326, 429–30; *see also*
  labour
workfare 44–5, 327, 346
working conditions 423
workplace, lean production 230–1,
  235–6, 244

World Bank 265, 421, 427–8
World Investment Report 274–5, 288
World Trade Organization 266

Yeatman, A. 346, 352, 385, 389, 393, 394
yen 155, 159, 162–5, 371–2

Zevin, Robert 211, 214